Strategy in the Contemporary World

# New to this edition

Significantly updated, the fifth edition features several new chapters including:

- 'Geopolitics and Grand Strategy', which looks at the modern concept of geopolitics and its significance.
- 'History of the Practice of Strategy', by Professor Beatrice Heuser, which takes you from the wars of Ancient Greece to Napoleon.
- 'Strategy and Defence Planning', which considers the relationship between strategy and operational issues
- 'Theory and Practice of Continental Warfare', which uses four case studies to explore the theory-practice relationship.

# Strategy in the Contemporary World

## An Introduction to Strategic Studies

FIFTH EDITION

Edited by

John Baylis,

James J. Wirtz,

Colin S. Gray

OXFORD
UNIVERSITY PRESS

# OXFORD

UNIVERSITY PRESS

Great Clarendon Street, Oxford, OX2 6DP,
United Kingdom

Oxford University Press is a department of the University of Oxford.
It furthers the University's objective of excellence in research, scholarship,
and education by publishing worldwide. Oxford is a registered trade mark of
Oxford University Press in the UK and in certain other countries

Second edition 2007
Third edition 2010
Fourth edition 2013

Impression: 2

Published in the United States of America by Oxford University Press
198 Madison Avenue, New York, NY 10016, United States of America

British Library Cataloguing in Publication Data
Data available

Library of Congress Control Number: 2015941376

ISBN 978-0-19-870891-9

Printed in the UK by Bell & Bain Ltd, Glasgow

*This book is dedicated to the memory of Professor John C. Garnett*

# Brief Contents

## PART I:  Enduring Issues of Strategy

# Detailed Contents

# Acknowledgements

We would like to thank Sarah Iles, Eleanor Chatburn, and Martha Bailes of Oxford University Press for their advice and support with the fifth edition of our text. In particular, their very efficient analysis of a wide range of reviewers' comments on the previous edition of the book has been invaluable in improving the text and adding new chapters. We would also like to thank Wendy Leutert of Cornell University for all her efficiency, expertise, support, and hard work during the production of the book. Her valuable assistance has helped considerably to lessen the burden on the shoulders of the editors. Finally, we are grateful to Dr Kristan Stoddart for sharing his expertise on issues relating to cyber warfare.

John Baylis, James J. Wirtz, and Colin S. Gray

# List of Contributors

**John Baylis** is Emeritus Professor of Politics and International Relations and a former Pro-Vice Chancellor at Swansea University. Prior to that he had been Professor of International Politics and Dean of Social Sciences at Aberystwyth University. He has published more than twenty books and over a hundred chapters and articles. His books include *Anglo-American Defence Relations 1939–1984* (Macmillan, 1984); *Anglo-American Relations since 1939: The Enduring Alliance* (Manchester University Press, 1997); *Alternative Nuclear Futures: The Role of Nuclear Weapons in the Post-Cold War World*, with Robert O'Neill (Oxford University Press, 2000); *The Makers of Nuclear Strategy*, with John Garnett (Pinter, 1991), *The Globalization of World Politics*, with Steve Smith and Patricia Owens (6th edn, Oxford University Press, 2014); *An Introduction to Global Politics*, with Steven Lamy, Steve Smith, and Patricia Owens (Oxford University Press, 2010); and *The British Nuclear Experience: The Role of Beliefs, Culture and Identity*, with Kristan Stoddart (Oxford University Press, 2015). He has a BA, MSc (Econ), PhD, and DLitt, from Swansea and Aberystwyth Universities.

**Stephen Biddle** is Professor of Political Science and International Affairs at George Washington University and Adjunct Senior Fellow for Defense Policy at the Council on Foreign Relations. He is the author of *Military Power: Explaining Victory and Defeat in Modern Battle* (2004). Before joining the George Washington University faculty in 2012, he was the Roger Hertog Senior Fellow at the Council on Foreign Relations, and has held teaching and research positions at Columbia University, the US Army War College Strategic Studies Institute, the University of North Carolina at Chapel Hill, the Institute for Defense Analyses, and Harvard's Belfer Center for Science and International Affairs.

**Eliot A. Cohen** is Robert E. Osgood Professor of Strategic Studies at Johns Hopkins University's School of Advanced International Studies. His books include *Supreme Command: Soldiers, Statesmen, and Leadership in Wartime* (2002) and, most recently, *Conquered into Liberty: Two Centuries of Battles Along the Great Warpath that Made the American Way of War* (2011). From 2007 to 2009 he served as Counselor of the Department of State.

**John Ferris** is Professor of History at the University of Calgary; Honorary Professor at the Department of International Politics, the University of Wales, Aberystwyth; and Adjunct Professor at the Department of War Studies, the Royal Military College of Canada. He publishes widely in military, international, strategic, and intelligence history, and strategic studies.

**Sir Lawrence Freedman** is Emeritus Professor of War Studies at King's College London, where he has taught since 1982, and served as Vice-Principal since 2003. Elected a Fellow of the British Academy in 1995 and awarded the CBE in 1996, he was appointed Official Historian of the Falklands Campaign in 1997. He was awarded the KCMG in 2003. In June 2009 he was appointed to serve as a member of the official inquiry into Britain and the 2003 Iraq War. Professor Freedman has written extensively on nuclear strategy and the cold war, as well as commentating regularly on contemporary security issues. His book, *A Choice of Enemies: America Confronts the Middle East*, won the 2009 Lionel Gelber Prize and Duke of Westminster Medal for Military Literature.

**The late John Garnett** was Woodrow Wilson Professor of International Politics at the University of Wales, Aberystwyth, and, until his retirement, Chairman of the Centre for Defence Studies at King's College London. He was educated at the London School of Economics where he received a first-class honours degree and master's in International Relations. He was the author of numerous books on International Relations and Strategic Studies, including *Contemporary Strategy*

(Croom Helm, 1975) with John Baylis, Ken Booth, and Phil Williams; and *Makers of Nuclear Strategy* (Pinter, 1991) with John Baylis.

**Roger Z. George** is Professor of National Security Practice at Occidental College and formerly taught strategy at the National War College. He was a career CIA intelligence analyst who served at the State and Defense departments and has been the National Intelligence Officer for Europe. He is co-editor (with James B. Bruce) of *Analyzing Intelligence: Origins, Obstacles, and Innovations*, 2nd edn. (2014) and co-editor (with Harvey Rishikof) of *The National Security Enterprise: Navigating The Labyrinth* (2011).

**Colin S. Gray** is Emeritus Professor of Strategic Studies at the University of Reading. He has advised the American and British Governments for many years. Among his books are a trilogy on strategy with Oxford University Press: *The Strategy Bridge: Theory for Practice* 2010); *Perspectives on Strategy* (2013); and *Strategy and Defence Planning: Meeting the Challenge of Uncertainty* (2014).

**Sheena Chestnut Greitens** is Assistant Professor of Political Science at the University of Missouri and a Nonresident Senior Fellow at the Brookings Institution in Washington, DC. Her work focuses on the domestic and international politics of security, particularly in East Asia and in non-democratic regimes. Her book *Dictators & Their Secret Police: Coercive Institutions and State Violence*, is forthcoming in 2016 from Cambridge University Press.

**Beatrice Heuser** is Chair in International Relations at the University of Reading. She holds degrees from the Universities of London (BA, MA) and Oxford (DPhil), and a Habilitation from the University of Marburg. She has taught at the Department of War Studies, King's College London, at four French universities/higher education institutions, and at two German universities, and has briefly worked at NATO headquarters. Her publications include *The Evolution of Strategy* (2010); *Reading Clausewitz* (2002); and many works on nuclear strategy, NATO, and transatlantic relations.

**Darryl Howlett** teaches at Southampton University. He obtained his master's degree from Lancaster University and his PhD from Southampton University. His most recent publications include 'The Emergence of Stability: Deterrence-in-Motion and Deterrence Reconstructed', in Ian R. Kenyon and John Simpson (eds), *Deterrence and the Changing Security Environment* (Routledge, 2006).

**Jeannie L. Johnson** is Assistant Professor at the Political Science Department at Utah State University. Dr Johnson co-edited the volume *Strategic Culture and Weapons of Mass Destruction: Culturally Based Insights into Comparative National Security Policymaking* (Macmillan, 2009) and is completing a second book examining the internal culture of the United States Marine Corps and its impact on USMC-led counterinsurgency operations. Dr Johnson worked in the CIA's Directorate of Intelligence as a member of the Balkan Task Force from 1998–1999. The cultural research methodology she pioneered with co-author Matt Berrett was featured in the CIA's June 2011 edition of *Studies in Intelligence*. Dr Johnson received her doctorate from the University of Reading in 2013.

**James D. Kiras** is an Associate Professor and Director of International Programs at the School of Advanced Air and Space Studies, Air University, Maxwell Air Force Base, Alabama, where he has directed the course on irregular warfare for the past decade and also teaches on the subjects of military theory and defence policy. He received his PhD from the University of Reading (UK), is an Associate Fellow of the Joint Special Operations University, United States Special Operations Command, Tampa, Florida, and consults and lectures frequently on the subjects of special operations and terrorism. Dr Kiras co-authored *Understanding Modern Warfare* (Cambridge University Press, 2008) and his first book was *Special Operations and Strategy: From World War II to the War on Terrorism* (Routledge, 2006).

**Jeffrey S. Lantis** is Chair of the Department of Political Science and Professor of Political Science/International Relations at the College of Wooster. He earned a PhD in Political Science from Ohio State University. A former Fulbright Senior Scholar in Australia, he is an expert on strategic culture, international security, and nuclear non-proliferation. Among his many books and academic journal articles, Lantis is author of *Arms and Influence: U.S. Technology Innovations and the Evolution of International Security Norms* (Stanford University Press, forthcoming 2015) and editor of *Strategic Cultures and Security Policies in the Asia-Pacific* (Routledge, forthcoming 2015).

**Thomas G. Mahnken** is currently Jerome E. Levy Chair of Economic Geography and National Security at the US Naval War College and a Visiting Scholar at the Philip Merrill Center for Strategic Studies at The Johns Hopkins University's Paul H. Nitze School of Advanced International Studies (SAIS). His books include *Competitive Strategies for the 21st Century* (Stanford University Press, 2012); *Technology and the American Way of War Since 1945* (Columbia University Press, 2008); and *Uncovering Ways of War: US Intelligence and Foreign Military Innovation, 1918–1941* (Cornell University Press, 2002). He is editor of *The Journal of Strategic Studies*.

**Justin Morris** is Senior Lecturer in the School of Politics, Philosophy and International Studies at the University of Hull, UK. He was Head of the (then Department) from 2007 to 2013. His primary research interests include international organizations, particularly the United Nations Security Council, humanitarian intervention, the relationship between power and responsibility, and the role of international law in international politics. He is co-author (with the late Professor Hilaire McCoubrey) of *Regional Peacekeeping in the Post-Cold War Era* (Kluwer, 2000) and co-editor (with Dr Richard Burchill and Professor Nigel White) of *International Conflict and Security Law: Essays in Memory of Hilaire McCoubrey* (Cambridge University Press, 2005). He is currently working on a project on great powers and international hierarchy.

**Stefanie Ortmann** is a lecturer in international relations at the University of Sussex. Her research interests include Russia as a great power in the post-cold war world and the effects of the narrative of rising powers on world affairs. She convenes the MA in Geopolitics and Grand Strategy at Sussex.

**Columba Peoples** is Senior Lecturer in International Relations in the School of Sociology, Politics and International Studies at the University of Bristol, UK. He received his PhD from the University of Wales, Aberystwyth in 2007, and is the author of *Justifying Ballistic Missile Defence: Technology, Security and Culture* (Cambridge University Press, 2010).

**Michael Sheehan** is Professor of International Relations at Swansea University. He is a graduate of Aberystwyth University (BSc in International Politics 1976, PhD 1985). He was formerly Director of the Scottish Centre for International Security at Aberdeen University. He is the author of 11 books on security, the most recent being *International Security: An Analytical Survey* (Lynne Rienner, 2005); *The International Politics of Space* (Routledge, 2007); and *Securing Outer Space* (Routledge, 2009, co-edited with Natalie Bormann). He is currently researching security issues facing the Arctic Sami people, with the Arctic Centre at Lapland University, and is writing a book about John F. Kennedy and the Second World War.

**John B. Sheldon** is the Executive Director of the George C. Marshall Institute, Washington, DC; the founder of the Torridon Group LLC, a space and cyberspace consulting company; and a Senior Fellow in Global Security Studies at the Munk School of Global Affairs at the University of Toronto in Canada. A former British diplomat, John holds Bachelor and Master's degrees from the University of Hull, UK, and a Ph.D. in politics and international relations from the University of Reading, UK.

**C. Dale Walton** is an Assistant Professor in International Relations and Strategic Studies Lindenwood University, St Louis. His previous career experience includes serving on the faculty of

Defense and Strategic Studies Department at Missouri State University and as a Senior Analyst with the National Institute for Public Policy. His works include *Grand Strategy and the Presidency: Foreign Policy, War, and the American Role in the World*; *Geopolitics and the Great Powers in the Twenty-first Century: Multipolarity and Revolution in Strategic Perspective*; and *The Myth of Inevitable U.S. Defeat in Vietnam*. He is also a co-author of *Understanding Modern Warfare*.

**Nick Whittaker** is a PhD student in the Department of International Relations at Sussex University and holds a MA in Geopolitics and Grand Strategy. He works on Britain's identity as an island state and its effect on British foreign policy.

**James J. Wirtz** is the Dean of the School of International Graduate Studies, Naval Postgraduate School, Monterey, California. He is the co-editor of *Over The Horizon Proliferation Threats* (Stanford University Press, 2012).

# Guided Tour of Textbook Features

**This book is enriched with a range of learning tools to help you navigate the text and reinforce your knowledge of Strategic Studies. This guided tour shows you how to get the most out of your textbook package and do better in your studies.**

### Reader's Guide

This chapter looks at the way that the theory and p
the past two hundred years. It examines how the de
changed the way that wars are fought, and it look
Revolution on the planning for and conduct of wa
of some of the key thinkers on war during the pa
practice, and the conduct of war is influenced by g

## Reader's Guides

Reader's Guides at the beginning of every chapter set the scene for upcoming themes and issues to be discussed, and indicate the scope of coverage within each chapter topic.

### Critical Thinking   Debating … Doe
disrupt the military balance?

For

● **Successful organizations cannot move away from o**
technologies have such strong constituencies that turr
For example, a navy like that of the United States will

## Critical Thinking

By debating a key topic from each chapter, these boxes encourage you to critically evaluate core questions—presenting both sides of the argument so that a reasoned and well-informed conclusion can be constructed.

### BOX  11.5   Arms Control Treaties an

History seems to indicate that arms control treaties, by th
danger level in the international environment. If they did
World War, because the period after the First World War
itself essentially being banned by the 1928 Kellogg–Brian
possessed by Russia and the United States decreased radi

## Boxes

Throughout the book, boxes provide you with extra information on particular topics that complement your understanding of the main chapter text.

### Key Points

● The post-cold war period saw a flurry of arms control
● Despite the lessening of hostility between the United
and intermittent.
● Increasingly the utility of arms control was perceived
environment which emerged after 9/11

## Key Points

Each chapter's main sections end with a set of key points that summarize the most important arguments developed within each chapter topic.

**Questions**

1. Why was humanitarian intervention rare durin
2. How did peacekeeping change in the 1990s? W
3. Is regionalization of peace operations a good i
4. Is impartiality possible during peacekeeping? W
5. Are you an intervention optimist or pessimist?

## Questions

A set of carefully devised questions has been provided to help you assess your comprehension of core themes, and may also be used as the basis of discussion and coursework.

 **Further Reading**

J. Agnew, *Geopolitics: Re-visioning World Politics*, 2 investigates the way that modern world politics i imagination associated with the rise of the great

H. Brands, *What Good Is Grand Strategy? Power a S. Truman to George W. Bush* (Ithaca, NY: Corne

## Further Reading

To take your learning further, reading lists have been provided as a guide to find out more about the issues raised within each chapter topic and to help you locate the key academic literature in the field.

 **Web Links**

International Security Network, University of Zurich relevant information, including articles on geopo

Exploring Geopolitics **http://www.exploringgeopo** updated as of 2014, this remains a rich resource

*Foreign Policy* magazine **http://foreignpolicy.com** a

## Web Links

At the end of every chapter you will find an annotated summary of useful websites that are central to Strategic Studies and that will be instrumental in further research.

# Guided Tour of the Online Resource Centre

The Online Resource Centre that accompanies this book provides students and instructors with ready-to-use teaching and learning materials. These resources are free of charge and designed to maximize the learning experience.

www.oxfordtextbooks.co.uk/orc/baylis_strategy5e/

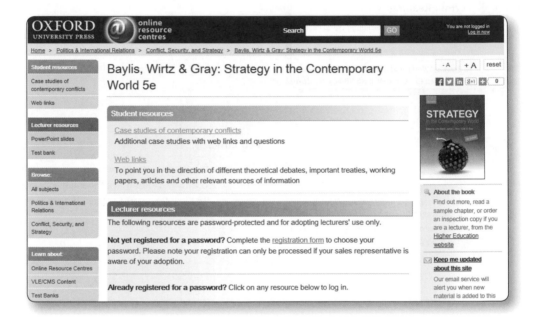

## For students:

### Case Studies

Six additional case studies with web links and questions on the following conflicts:

1. Afghanistan

2. The South Ossetian war

3. The US–Coalition invasion and occupation of Iraq

4. The conflict in the Congo

5. The Russian war in Chechnya

6. The Iran–Iraq War

**The First Congo War**

The complex background of the First Congo War violence in other African countries, particularly Rw 1994, a very great number—perhaps even more ethnic group were massacred by Hutus, the majo

### Web Links

Web links have been provided to point you in the direction of different theoretical debates, important treaties, working papers, articles, and other relevant sources of information.

## For adopting instructors:

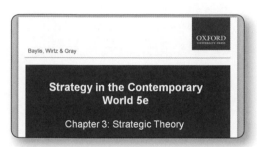

### PowerPoint Slides

These complement each chapter of the book and are a useful resource for preparing lectures and handouts. They allow you to guide students through the key concepts and can be fully customized to meet the needs of the course.

### Test Bank

This ready-made electronic testing resource can be customized to meet your teaching needs, offering a range of questions to use in lectures and seminars, or set as tasks to help consolidate learning.

# Introduction: Strategy in the Contemporary World: Strategy after 9/11

JOHN BAYLIS AND JAMES J. WIRTZ

## Chapter Contents

## Introduction

Books often reflect a specific historical context, shaped by the hopes, fears, and problems that preoccupy authors and policymakers alike. This is especially true of books on strategy, security studies, and public policy because contemporary issues are of paramount importance to authors in these fields. Our efforts also reflect contemporary threats and opportunities. When we gathered in September 2000 to present chapters for the first edition of this volume, we wanted to create a textbook that demonstrated the continued relevance of strategy and strategic studies to interpret contemporary issues using insights gained from the classic works on strategy. At that time, some observers suggested that strategy was an obsolete vestige of a dark past, something that would be forgotten in a brighter future. Little did we know that one year later, the 'New World Order' would be shattered by the al-Qaeda attacks on the Pentagon and the World Trade Center. The wars in Afghanistan and Iraq, the terrorist bombings in Madrid in 2004 and London in 2005, and the proliferation of nuclear weapons to North Korea, erased any lingering doubts about the relevance of strategy when it came time to produce the second and third editions of this volume. By the time we gathered again in September 2011 to discuss the 4th edition of our project, the 'al-Qaeda' decade appeared to have come to an end. But as we scanned the strategic horizon, we began to consider the possibility of a renewal of balance of power politics along the Pacific Rim, a showdown between the West and Iran over its nuclear weapons programme, and the potential threat posed by cyberwar. The list of challenges and issues confronting us continued to grow as we worked to assemble our 5th edition. The death of Osama bin Laden did not bring an end to transnational terrorism, especially in the form of ISIS, new forms and weapons of warfare are becoming commonplace, and a return of Great Power rivalry not only in Asia, but also in Europe, is more than a possibility.

It is clear that interest in strategic studies is cyclical and reflects the times. Strategic studies emerged during the early years of the cold war when political leaders, government officials, and academics interested in security issues wrestled with the problems of how to survive and prosper in the nuclear age, when Armageddon might be just minutes away. Given the experiences of the 1930s, when appeasement and 'utopian' ideas of collective security had largely failed to ensure peace, the prevailing mindset during the cold war was one of 'realism'. It was believed that in a world characterized by anarchy and unending competition, states inevitably exercised power to secure their national interests. For nuclear age realists, however, power had to be exercised in a way that promoted the interests of the state, while at the same time avoiding conflict which would lead to the destruction not only of the states involved but of civilization as a whole. This predicament gave rise to theories of deterrence, limited war, and arms control that dominated the literature of strategic studies (and indeed international relations) during the period from the 1950s to the 1980s. Writings by Herman Kahn, Bernard Brodie, Henry Kissinger, Albert Wohlstetter, and Thomas Schelling became classics in the field.

Did the key assumptions inherent in the strategic studies literature lead to the adoption of particular security policies or did policy itself drive the writing on the subject? The answer to these questions remains a matter of debate. Some believed that the literature reflected existing realities, others believed that the writings themselves helped to generate a particular way of looking at the world and legitimized the use of military power. An iterative process was probably at work, however, as theory and practice modified and reinforced each other.

The great strength of the literature on strategic studies was that it reflected the harsh realities of a world in which military power was (regardless of utopian ideals) an instrument of state policy. One of its weaknesses, however, was the inherent conservatism in realist thinking that implied that the contemporary world was the best of all possible worlds. For good theoretical and practical reasons, realists hoped that the cold war, with its magisterial confrontation between the United States and the Soviet Union, would continue into the indefinite future. Significant change, because it raised the spectre of nuclear Armageddon, was a prospect that was nearly too horrific to contemplate and too risky to act upon.

With the relatively peaceful collapse of the Soviet Union, realism came under suspicion and the ideas and policies of disarmament advocates and utopian thinkers began to hold greater sway in policy circles. The 1990s was the decade of the 'peace dividend' and 'dot. com' mania as the information revolution entered consumer and business culture. The preoccupation of strategists with the state, and its use of military power, was viewed by a new generation of 'utopian' scholars as part of the problem of international security itself. Strategists were often seen as 'dinosaurs'. Preoccupied with 'old thinking', they appeared unwilling to come to terms with the fact that force was apparently fading as a factor in world politics. The traditional emphasis on the military aspects of security was challenged by scholars who believed that the concept should be broadened and deepened. According to this view, there were political, economic, societal, and environmental aspects of security that had been ignored. Some scholars asserted that 'security' as a concept had been used by elites to push issues to the top of the political agenda or to secure additional resources for particular policies and government organizations and military programmes. In the view of some critics, official policy was pushed along by armies of military contractors and manufacturers, government workers, and members of the military who had a vested interest in keeping war alive to preserve their careers and livelihoods.

By the mid-1990s, these criticisms of traditional realist thinking were transformed into mainstream scholarship. Security studies emerged as an area of intellectual enquiry that increasingly eclipsed strategic studies. Researchers came to focus on the nature of security itself and how greater security might be achieved at the individual, societal, and even global levels, compared with the cold war preoccupation with state security, defined only in military terms. Although security studies reflected a wider range of theoretical positions than had characterized strategic studies in the past, there was a strong normative (realists would say utopian) dimension to much of the writing, especially from those of a post-positivist persuasion. The end of the cold war fundamentally challenged the conservative tendency in realism (and the strategic studies literature). Peaceful change was now a reality and military power was no longer seen by many as the predominant prerequisite for security. The balance of terror between East and West had not simply been mitigated (in line with the theories proposed in the strategic studies literature) but had now been transcended, opening up the prospects for a new more peaceful world.

Although the post-cold war euphoria and the literature that followed in its wake were very much a product of their time, there were warning signs in the years leading up to the millennium that the emergence of peace, or as Francis Fukuyama put it 'an end of history' (meaning an end of major conflicts), might have been premature. The first Gulf War, the conflicts associated with the disintegration of Yugoslavia, and civil wars in Africa demonstrated all too clearly that military force remained a ubiquitous feature of the contemporary world. It was at this point, just as the attacks on the Twin Towers and the Pentagon took place in September 2001, that the first edition of this book was published. The book reflected a growing feeling that perhaps too much emphasis in security studies literature had been given to non-military security. The argument contained in the book was that, useful as this new literature was, there was still room for writing and scholarship that focused on the sad, but continuing, reality that military power remained a significant feature of world politics

Although the first edition had much to say about those present circumstances, the second, third, fourth, and now our fifth editions contain a more mature set of reflections on the role of military power in the contemporary world and the changes that have occurred over the last decade. While our fifth volume includes analyses of the conflicts in Afghanistan, Iraq, Libya Georgia, Lebanon, and Gaza, our contributors have also broadened the coverage of key facets of strategy. We also explore the debates about whether there has been a revolution in military affairs and the future of warfare, given the phenomenal pace of innovation in electronics and computer systems, which is often referred to as cyberwar. Attention is also given to the strategic implications of the changing structure of global politics and the role of American military power in a world in transition. At a broader conceptual level, this edition also explores the continuing relevance of various theories of peace and security in a world that is vastly different from the cold war era when these concepts were central to most thinking about strategic studies. Looking back from the perspective of this fifth edition, it is illustrative to note that issues that barely received mention at the turn of the last century—cyber warfare, transnational terrorism, and 'hybrid warfare'—now seem to be enduring issues for consideration by strategists. Great power competition, which then seemed to be a vestige of the past, now appears to be a more prominent phenomenon in our future.

To set the scene for the chapters that follow, this introduction answers three questions: (1) What is strategic studies? (2) What criticisms are made of strategic studies? and (3) What is the relationship of strategic studies to security studies?

# What is Strategic Studies?

The definitions of 'strategy' contained in Box 0.1 display some common features but also significant differences. The definitions by Carl von Clausewitz, Field Marshal Count H. Von Moltke, B. H. Liddell Hart, and André Beaufre all focus on a fairly narrow definition, which relates military force to the objectives of war. This reflects the origins of the word strategy, which is derived from the ancient Greek term for 'generalship'. The definitions from Gregory Foster and Robert Osgood, however, draw attention to the broader focus on 'power', while Williamson Murray and Mark Grimslay highlight the dynamic quality of 'process' inherent in the formulation of strategy. Recently, writers have emphasized that strategy (particularly in the nuclear age) has a peacetime as well as a wartime application. Strategy embodies more than just the study of wars and military campaigns. Strategy is the application of military power to

---

 **BOX 0.1   Definitions of Strategy**

Strategy (is) the use of engagements for the object of war.

Carl von Clausewitz

Strategy is the practical adaptation of the means placed at a general's disposal to the attainment of the object in War.

Von Moltke

Strategy is the art of distributing and applying military means to fulfill the ends of policy.

Liddell Hart

Strategy is . . . the art of the dialectic of force or, more precisely, the art of the dialectic of two opposing wills using force to resolve their dispute.

André Beaufre

Strategy is ultimately about effectively exercising power.

Gregory D. Foster

Strategy is a plan of action designed in order to achieve some end; a purpose together with a system of measures for its accomplishment.

J. C. Wylie

Strategy is a process, a constant adaptation to the shifting conditions and circumstances in a world where chance, uncertainty, and ambiguity dominate.

W. Murray and M. Grimslay

Strategy must now be understood as nothing less than the overall plan for utilizing the capacity for armed coercion—in conjunction with economic, diplomatic, and psychological instruments of power—to support foreign policy most effectively by overt, covert, and tacit means.

Robert Osgood

The realm of strategy is one of bargaining and persuasion as well as threats and pressure, psychological as well as physical effects, and words as well as deeds. This is why strategy is the central political art. It is about getting more out of a situation than the starting balance of power would suggest. It is the art of creating power.

Lawrence Freedman

achieve political objectives, or more specifically 'the theory and practice of the use, and threat of use, of organized force for political purposes' (Gray 1999a). Broader still is the concept of Grand Strategy, which involves the coordination and direction of 'all the resources of a nation, a band of nations, towards the attainment of the political objectives' sought (Hart 1967).

Because strategy provides the bridge between military means and political goals, students of strategy require knowledge of both politics and military operations. Strategy deals with the difficult problems of national policy, the areas where political, economic, psychological, and military factors overlap. There is no such thing as purely military advice when it comes to issues of strategy. This point has also been made in a different way by Henry Kissinger, who stated that:

> the separation of strategy and policy can only be achieved to the detriment of both. It causes military power to become identified with the most absolute application of power and it tempts diplomacy into an over-concern with finesse.
>
> Kissinger (1957)

Strategy is best studied from an interdisciplinary perspective. To understand the dimensions of strategy, it is necessary to know something about politics, economics, psychology, sociology, and geography, as well as technology, force structure, and tactics.

Strategy is also essentially a pragmatic and practical activity. This is summed up in Bernard Brodie's comment that '[s]trategic theory is a theory of action'. It is a 'how to do it' study, a guide to accomplishing objectives and attaining them efficiently. As in many other branches of politics, the question that matters in strategy is: will the idea work? As such, in some ways strategic studies is 'policy relevant'. It can be an intellectual aid to official performance. At the same time, however, it can also be pursued as 'an idle academic pursuit for its own sake' (Brodie 1973).

Strategic studies, however, cannot be regarded as a discipline in its own right. It is a subject with a sharp focus—the role of military power—but no clear parameters, and it relies upon arts, sciences, and social science subjects for ideas and concepts. Scholars who have contributed to the literature on the subject have come from very different fields. Herman Kahn was a physicist, Thomas Schelling was an economist, Albert Wohlstetter was a mathematician, Henry Kissinger was a historian, and Bernard Brodie was a political scientist.

Given the different academic backgrounds of strategic thinkers, it is not surprising that strategic studies has witnessed an ongoing debate about methodology (i.e. how to study the subject). Bernard Brodie, who more than anyone else helped to establish strategic studies as a subject in the aftermath of the Second World War, initially argued that strategy should be studied 'scientifically'. He was concerned that strategy was 'not receiving the scientific treatment it deserves either in the armed services or, certainly, outside them'. In his 1949 article entitled 'Strategy as Science', Brodie called for a methodological approach to the study of strategy similar to the one adopted by economics. Strategy, he argued, should be seen as 'an instrumental science for solving practical problems'. What he wanted was a more rigorous, systematic form of analysis of strategic issues compared with the rather narrow approach to security problems adopted by the military, who were preoccupied with tactics and technology.

As Brodie himself was later to recognize, however, the enthusiasm for science, which he had helped to promote, meant that strategic studies in the 1950s 'developed a scientistic strain and overreached itself'. By the 1960s, Brodie was calling for a 'mid-course correction'. The conceptualization of strategy using economic models and theories had been taken further than he had expected. Brodie was concerned about the 'astonishing lack of political sense' and the 'ignorance of diplomatic and military history' that seemed to be evident among those writing about strategy. Brodie's worries were heeded. From the 1970s onwards, more comparative historical analysis was introduced into strategic studies (see Chapter 9).

The academic approach to the study of strategy also raised concerns about the neglect of operational military issues. For Brodie (echoing Clemenceau) strategy was too serious a business to be left to the generals. As strategic studies developed in the late 1940s, civilian analysts came to dominate the field. By the 1980s, however, there was a growing feeling that many of the civilian strategists in university departments and academic think tanks were ignoring the capabilities and limitations of military units and operations in their analyses and theorizing. For a new breed of strategists, the reality of operational issues had to be brought back into their studies. Military science had become the 'missing discipline'. Writing in 1997, Richard K. Betts suggested that 'if strategy is to integrate policy and operations, it must be devised not just by politically sensitive soldiers but by military sensitive civilians'. Just as Brodie had been concerned about the overly narrow approach of the military in 1949, so Betts was concerned that the pendulum had swung too far in the opposite direction. As Stephen Biddle has demonstrated in his volume entitled *Military Power*, in the end it was left to civilian strategists to make headway in understanding the changes unfolding on the modern battlefield (Biddle 2004).

This concern with operational issues helped to revive an interest among strategists about the different 'elements' or 'dimensions' of strategy. In his study *On War*, Clausewitz argued that 'everything in strategy is very simple, but that does not mean that everything is very easy'. Reflecting this sentiment, Clausewitz pointed out that strategy consisted of moral, physical, mathematical, geographical, and statistical elements. Michael Howard, in a similar vein, refers to the social, logistical, operational, and technological dimensions of strategy. This notion of strategy consisting of a broad, complex, pervasive, and interpenetrating set of dimensions is also explored in Colin Gray's study, entitled *Modern Strategy*. Gray identifies three main categories ('People and politics'; 'Preparation for war'; and 'War proper') and 17 dimensions of strategy. Under the 'People and politics' heading he focuses on people, society, culture, politics, and ethics. 'Preparation for war' includes economics and logistics, organization, military administration, information and intelligence, strategic theory and doctrine, and technology. The dimensions of 'War proper' consist of military operations, command, geography, friction, the adversary, and time. Echoing Clausewitz, Gray argues that the study of strategy is incomplete if it is considered in the absence of any one of these (interrelated) dimensions.

## Strategic Studies and the Classical Realist Tradition

What are the traditional philosophical underpinnings or assumptions of the scholars, soldiers, and policymakers who have written about strategy? Most contemporary strategists in the Western world belong to the same intellectual tradition. They share a set of assumptions about the nature of international political life, and the kind of reasoning that can best handle political–military problems. This set of assumptions is often referred to by the term 'realism'.

Although there are differences among 'realists', there are certain views and assumptions that most would agree upon. These can be best illustrated under the headings of human nature; anarchy and power; and international law, morality, and institutions.

## Human Nature

Most traditional realists are pessimistic about human nature. Reflecting the views of philosophers like Thomas Hobbes, people are seen as 'inherently destructive, selfish, competitive, and aggressive'. Hobbes accepted that human beings are capable of generosity, kindness, and cooperation, but the pride and egoism inherent in human nature mean that mankind is also prone to conflict, violence, and great evil. For realist writers, one of the great tragedies of the human condition is that these destructive traits can never be eradicated. Reflecting this view, Herbert Butterfield argued that 'behind the great conflicts of mankind is a terrible human predicament which lies at the heart of the story' (in Butterfield and Wight 1966). Thus, realism is not a normative theory in the sense that it purports to offer a way to eliminate violence from the world. Instead, it offers a way to cope with the ever-present threat of conflict by the use of strategy to minimize the likelihood and severity of international violence. Realists tend to stress what they see as the harsh realities of world politics and are somewhat contemptuous of Kantian approaches that highlight the possibility of 'permanent peace'. As Gordon Harland has argued:

> Realism is a clear recognition of the limits of reason in politics: the acceptance of the fact that political realities are power realities and that power must be countered with power; that self-interest is the primary datum in the action of all groups and nations.
>
> Herzog (1963)

In an anarchical system, power is the only currency of value when security is threatened.

## Anarchy and Power

Given this rather dark view of the human condition, realists tend to view international relations in similarly pessimistic terms. Conflict and war are seen as endemic in world politics and the future is likely to be much like the past. States (upon which realists focus their attention) are engaged in a relentless competitive struggle. In contrast to the way in which conflicts are dealt with in domestic society, however, the clash between states is more difficult to resolve because there is no authoritative government to create justice and the rule of law. In the absence of world government, realists note that states have adopted a 'self-help' approach to their interests and especially their security. In other words, they reserve the right to use lethal force to achieve their objectives, a right that individuals living in civil society have given up to the state. Who wins in international relations does not depend on who is right according to some moral or legal ruling. As Thucydides demonstrated in his account of the Peloponnesian wars, power determines who gets their way. In international relations, *might* makes *right*.

## International Law, Morality, and Institutions

Realists see a limited role for 'reason', law, morality, and institutions in world politics. In a domestic context, law can be an effective way for societies to deal with competing selfish interests. In an international system without a supranational government, states will agree to laws when it suits them, but will disregard them when their interests are threatened. When states want to break the rules, there is very little to stop them from doing it apart from countervailing force.

Similarly, realists do not believe that moral considerations can significantly constrain the behaviour of states. Some realists believe that very little attention should be given to moralizing about the state of world politics. They point to the absence of a universal moral code and to the disregard of constraining moral principles by policymakers, especially when they believe their vital interests are threatened. This is not to argue that realists are wholly insensitive to moral questions. Great realist thinkers, including Rheinhold Niebuhr and Hans Morgenthau, agonized about the human condition. Most realist writers, however, attempt to explain the way the world is, rather than how it ought to be. Realists view international institutions (e.g. the United Nations or the Nuclear Nonproliferation Treaty) in much the same light as they view law and morality. Just as law and morality are unable to constrain state behaviour significantly when important state interests are threatened, international institutions can also only play a limited role in preventing conflict. Realists do not dismiss the opportunities created by institutions for greater cooperation. They see these institutions, however, not as truly independent actors but as agents set up by states to serve their national interests. As long as institutions do this, the member states will support them, but when support for the institution threatens national interests, nations tend to abandon or ignore them. Realists point to the inability of the League of Nations in the interwar period to stop aggression, or the way the United Nations became a hostage to the cold war, as evidence of the limited utility of these organizations. When it really mattered, international institutions could not act against the interests of their member states.

## What Criticisms are Made of Strategic Studies?

Although the shared philosophical underpinnings of strategists have helped to give the subject intellectual coherence, many realist assumptions have been subjected to fierce criticism. This critique has been discussed in detail elsewhere (Gray 1982 and Chapter 18), but our purpose here is to give a flavour of the concern expressed by critics of strategic studies. Strategists are said to be:

- obsessed with conflict and force,
- insufficiently concerned with ethical issues,
- not scholarly in their approach,
- part of the problem, not the solution,
- state-centric,
- liable to adopt a narrow theoretical approach.

Many critics argue that because strategists focus on the role of military power, they tend to be preoccupied by violence and war. Because their view of the world is conflict-oriented, they tend to ignore the more cooperative, peaceful aspects of world politics. This leads critics to claim that strategists have a distorted, rather than realistic, view of the world. Some critics have gone so far as to suggest that strategists are fascinated by violence, and even take grim satisfaction in describing the darker side of the human condition.

For their part, strategists accept that they are interested in violence and conflict. In their own defence, however, they point out that just as a doctor of heart disease does not claim to deal with all aspects of health, so they do not claim to be studying every aspect of international relations. They reject the view that they have a distorted view of the world, and that they are fascinated in an unhealthy sense by violence.

The claim to moral neutrality, sometimes made by strategists, is another shortcoming identified by critics. Strategists are depicted as clinical, cool, and unemotional in the way they approach the study of war, despite the fact that, in the nuclear age, millions of lives are at risk in the calculations that take place about strategic policies. Emphasizing the moral outrage felt by some, J. R. Newman described Herman Kahn's book, *On Thermonuclear War*, as 'a moral tract on mass murder, how to commit it, how to get away with it, how to justify it'. Philip Green, in his study entitled *Deadly Logic* (1966), also accused strategists who wrote about nuclear deterrence as being 'egregiously guilty of avoiding the moral issue altogether, or misrepresenting it'.

Although many strategists have justified the moral neutrality of their approach in terms of scholarly detachment, some have been sensitive to this criticism. As a result, a number of studies of ethical issues have been written. These include Joseph Nye's book *Nuclear Ethics*, Michael Walzer's *Just and Unjust Wars*, and Steven P. Lee's study *Morality, Prudence and Nuclear Weapons*. These books (together with the more critical studies by writers like Green) now form an important part of the literature on strategic studies.

Another important criticism levelled against strategic studies is that it represents 'a fundamental challenge to the values of liberal, humane scholarship that define a university'. The implication is that strategy is not a scholarly subject and should not be taught at a university. This criticism has a number of related parts. First, according to Philip Green, strategy is pseudo-scientific, using apparent scientific method to give it a spurious air of legitimacy. Second, because strategists often advise governments on a paid basis, they are operating 'in a manner incompatible with the integrity of scholarship'. E. P. Thornton described the cosy relationship between strategists and government officials as 'suspect, corrupt and at enmity with the universal principles of humane scholarship'. Third, critics charge that strategists not only provide advice to governments, but they are also involved in policy advocacy—which is not part of scholarship. Critics claim that strategists are a vestige of government and spend their time either providing advice on how to achieve or justify dubious international objectives.

With a qualification on the issue of policy advocacy, strategists reject the view that their subject should not be found in a university (see Box 0.2). They would argue that war cannot

---

 **BOX** 0.2   Strategic Studies in the Academy

The study of strategy in universities may be defended on several different, yet complementary, grounds. In strictly academic terms, the subject poses sufficient intellectual challenge as to merit inclusion in, or even as, a course of study fully adequate to stretch mental resources. In, and of itself, that argument is sufficient to justify the inclusion of strategic studies in university curricula, but one can, and should, proceed to argue that the study of strategy is socially useful . . . Many views are defensible concerning the proper and appropriate duties of a university. This author chooses a liberal, permissive perspective. He sees value in a field of study that seeks truth and may have relevance to contemporary policy and, as a consequence, may contribute to the general wellbeing.

C. S. Gray

In strategic studies the ability to argue logically and to follow a piece of strategic reasoning is very important, but even more important is the elusive, almost indefinable quality of political judgement which enables a man to evaluate a piece of analysis and locate it in a wider political framework.

J. C. Garnett

be made to disappear simply by ignoring it (Leon Trotsky, a leading figure in the Bolshevik revolution, put it best: 'You might not have an interest in war, but war has an interest in you'). They argue that the study of war and peace are issues of profound importance that can, and should, be studied in a scholarly way. There have been attempts at developing a scientific approach to strategy (and as Brodie recognized, some writers might have taken this too far) but the debate about methodology is not confined to strategic studies. The nature of science in a social science context remains a lively, ongoing debate.

In general, strategists recognize the dangers of developing too cosy a relationship with officials when they advise governments on a paid basis. Like many other experts (e.g. economists), however, they see no necessary inconsistency between scholarship and advice. Because it is a practical subject, there are some benefits from analysing strategic issues at close hand, providing that a detached approach is adopted. Policy advocacy, however, is a different matter. Some strategists do drift into the realm of advocating specific policies, but when they do so they slowly but surely lose their credibility. People who make a career out of arguing for the adoption of specific policies or weapons systems gain a reputation for knowing the 'answer' regardless of the question that is posed.

Another forceful criticism of strategic studies is that it is part of the problem, not the solution. What opponents mean by this is that the Clausewitzian perspective of strategists, which sees military power as a legitimate instrument of policy, helps to perpetuate a particular mindset among national leaders and the public that encourages the use of force. It is this realist thinking, critics argue, which lies behind the development of theories of deterrence, limited war, and crisis management that were especially dangerous during the cold war. Anatol Rapoport is one writer who charges strategists with a direct responsibility for promoting a framework of thinking about security which is largely hostile to what he regards as the proper solution to global conflict, namely disarmament. In a stinging attack he argues that:

> the most formidable obstacles to disarmament are created by the strategists who place their strategic considerations above the needs of humanity as a whole, and who create or help maintain an intellectual climate in which disarmament appears to be unrealistic.
>
> Rapoport (1965)

Instead of spending their time thinking about how better to justify and conduct mass murder, critics suggest that strategists should spend their time devising disarmament strategies, cooperative security arrangements, and global campaigns to denounce violence.

Linked to this criticism is the view that because strategists are so pessimistic about human nature and the chances of significant improvements in the conduct of international politics, they *ignore the opportunities that exist for peaceful change*. It is suggested that to see the past as a history of constant conflict and to suggest that the future will be the same is to help create a fatalistic impression that plans for human progress will always fail. By emphasizing mistrust, self-help, and the importance of military power in an anarchic international system, their advice becomes self-fulfilling. In other words, if policymakers take strategists' advice to heart, deterrent threats and defence preparations would lead to a spiral of hostility and mistrust as leaders respond to the defence policies of their competitors. Given this 'socially constructed' view of the world, it is not surprising that states will constantly find themselves in conflict with each other.

Once again, strategists vigorously contest these criticisms. They argue that their ideas reflect (rather than create) the 'reality' of world politics. The fact that most policymakers and elected officials tend to share their realist assumptions is not due to an intellectual climate 'socially constructed' by academic strategists, but by the challenges and threats presented to them by international relations. The notion that strategic studies as a subject is 'a monstrous crime committed by self-interested strategists against the general public' is seen as absurd. Of course, throughout history, various observers have championed war as a preferred instrument of statecraft. Often they depict war in romantic or heroic terms; today's romantic image of war found in movies and video games is simply a technologically embellished version of this traditional imagery. Enthusiasts see war as a relatively bloodless contest in which technically adept professionals use their superior skills and equipment to paralyse the opponent's military command, leading to quick and humane victories. Strategic studies, however, stands as a major impediment to those who claim to have found a quick and easy path to guaranteed victory. Because they recognize the true nature of war, most strategists consider armed conflict to be a tragedy, an activity unfit for human beings that must be limited to the greatest extent possible.

On the question of peaceful change, strategists do not dismiss the fact that there are opportunities for periods of peaceful coexistence. They are, however, very sceptical about the prospects for 'perpetual peace' based on a radical transformation of world politics. They believe that conflict can be mitigated through effective strategy, but it is highly unlikely that it can be transcended completely. In such a context, it is impossible to abolish the need for strategic studies.

The fact that strategists focus on the task of creating effective national strategies or international initiatives creates the basis for another criticism of the enterprise. Strategic studies incorporates a state-centric approach to world politics. According to this critique, strategists are so preoccupied by threats to the interests of states that they ignore security issues within the state or new phenomena such as transnational terrorist networks. Many observers argue that the state is not the most appropriate referent for studying security. Rather, attention should be focused on the individual whose security is often threatened, rather than protected by the state. Other writers, who perceive the growing erosion of the state, prefer to focus on 'societal security' or even 'global security' issues.

Strategists would argue that while they have stressed the role of the state, they have not neglected intra-state conflict. Clausewitz himself dealt with people's war and a considerable part of the strategic studies literature addresses revolutionary and irregular warfare. As wars of national disintegration (Bosnia, Kosovo, Chechnya) and even creation (the Islamic State in Iraq and Syria) have become more prevalent, more attention has been given in the literature to the problem of ethnic and identity conflict. The emergence of al-Qaeda has led to an explosion of research and writing on the origins, objectives, strategies, and tactics of violent non-state actors, with an eye towards destroying international terrorist networks and other criminal organizations. Despite the prevalence of intra-state violence or the rise of important non-state actors, strategists continue to argue that, even with all the contemporary challenges to the modern state, it continues to be the major actor in world politics. In fact the importance of the state, with its access to a myriad of resources and instruments of control and surveillance, has only been highlighted by the emergence of 'super-empowered individuals' and transnational terrorism. Strategists offer no apologies for their continuing interest in issues of state security.

Another criticism often levelled against strategic studies is that the traditional dominant realist approach is theoretically too narrow, closing off insights that can be gained from other theories of peace and security. In the study of *Strategic Studies and World Order*, written in 1994, Bradley S. Klein argued that it 'was important to take seriously the realist tradition's emphasis upon power in world affairs, and there can be no escaping a sustained engage-ment with the primary texts that demarcate that tradition'. Nevertheless, he argues that it was important 'to see that tradition not as some fixed map of the yellow brick road to modern realism or its "neo" variants for contemporary articulations of the genre have tended to sever the tradition from its roots in political theory'. In their *Evolution of International Security Stud-ies*, Buzan and Hansen highlight the limitations of realist thinking which gave rise to a range of new theoretical approaches to the study of security in the 1990s, including Constructivism, Critical Security Studies, Feminism, and Poststructuralism (2009).

These are criticisms that have some merit. Bradley S. Klein's own study and Peter J. Katzen-stein's study *The Culture of National Security Studies*, to name but two, have attempted to broaden the theoretical basis of Strategic Studies. We have also included two chapters in this book (Chapters 5 and 18), which reflect alternative perspectives on strategic studies. This said, realism remains the dominant approach to the subject, which is one factor that distinguishes the study of strategy from the broader field of Security Studies (see Chapter 19).

## What is the Relationship between Strategic Studies and Security Studies?

One of the main challenges to strategic studies since the end of the cold war has come from those who argue that attention should be shifted away from the study of strategy to the study of security. According to this view, security, defined in terms of 'freedom from threats to core values', is a more appropriate concept for analysis. The problem with strategy, it is argued, is that it is too narrow and increasingly less relevant at a time when major wars are declining and threats to political, economic, social, and environmental security interests are increasing. This is often referred to as 'the widening and deepening' debate (see Buzan and Hansen 2009: 187–211). Because it is defined more broadly, security is depicted as more valuable than strategy as an organizing framework for understanding the complex, multidimensional risks of today.

However, as Richard Betts noted in his 1997 article 'Should strategic studies survive?', those who champion new definitions of security run two risks. First, Betts noted that even though it is appropriate to distinguish between 'strategy' and 'security' studies, security policy requires careful attention to war and strategy. In other words, military power remains a crucial part of security and those who ignore war to concentrate on non-military threats to security do so at their peril. Second, he argued that 'expansive definitions of security quickly become syn-onymous with "interest" and "wellbeing", do not exclude anything in international relations or foreign policy, and this becomes indistinguishable from those fields or other subfields'. In other words, by including potentially everything that might negatively affect human affairs, security studies creates the risk of being too broad to be of any practical value.

The contributors to this book recognize the importance of security studies and at the same time share these concerns about the coherence of the field. Strategy remains a distinctive and valuable area of academic study. Strategy is part of security studies, just as security studies is part of international relations, which itself is part of political science. This relationship is expressed in Figure 0.1 (see Chapter 19).

Despite all of the changes that have occurred in world politics since the late 1980s, there is in many respects an underlying continuity with earlier eras. The euphoria produced by the hope that a fundamental transformation of international relations was under way has proved

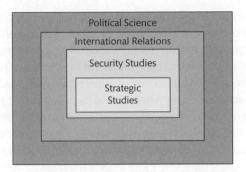

**Figure 0.1** The relationship between strategy, security studies, international relations, and political science

to be ill-founded. As we have seen from the Gulf Wars I and II, the Iraqi insurgency, Bosnia, Kosovo, Chechnya, Libya, Syria, terrorist attacks launched by al-Qaeda and ISIS, and the forceful annexation of the Crimea, force and military power continue to be an important currency in the contemporary international system. Particularly worrying at the time of writing is the emergence of what has been described as 'hybrid warfare' in Eastern Ukraine. This term refers to a wide range of hostile actions, including the use of military force, which are part of a wider flexible strategy with long-term aims. Certainly important geopolitical changes are taking place in contemporary world politics, associated with the twin forces of globalization and fragmentation. Wars between the great powers may have slipped into the background, but 'great power' competition between the United States, Russia, and China is no longer a remote possibility. The sad fact remains that the utilization of military power as an instrument of political purpose, and therefore strategic studies, remains just as relevant today as it has been in the past.

Our exploration of strategy in the contemporary world is divided into three sections. In Part I, our contributors describe the enduring issues that animate the study of strategy and provide a historical and theoretical overview of the topic for our readers. Our study opens with a new essay on the history of strategic thinking from Antiquity to the First World War to provide context for what follows. Next are chapters focusing on the evolution of warfare since the Napoleonic Age and key strategic thinkers. After this is a chapter on the causes of war, a complex issue that ultimately shapes approaches to mitigate inter-state violence. The issues of culture, morality, and war are also addressed in the first section, reflecting some of the changes in methodology that have taken place in strategic studies. Despite popular imagery of military armaments, cultural, legal, and moral considerations play a role in shaping both the recourse to and the conduct of war. These chapters are important because they illustrate the normative basis for strategy: to help mitigate both the occurrence and the death and destruction produced by war. Three further chapters focus on the so-called 'revolution in military affairs' which continues to shape the evolution of warfare; the critical issue of intelligence in modern conflicts; and the relationship between strategy and defence planning.

In Part II, our contributors explore issues that appear in today's headlines and that animate strategic debate today. The section opens with a chapter on terrorism and irregular warfare, which, with the emergence of Islamic State, continues to be a central problem of international security. The next chapter examines the role of nuclear weapons in the contemporary world which, after a period of marginalization, are once again beginning to preoccupy strategic thinkers. Attention is also given to arms control issues and fears about North Korean and Iranian nuclear programmes, together with the possibility that terrorists might acquire and use weapons of mass destruction. All this suggests that it is time for a reappraisal of the threat posed by nuclear, radiological, chemical, and biological weapons. This section also explores emerging issues that are likely to animate debate not only about weapons of mass destruction but also about conventional military power, including the role of land warfare. This is followed by a chapter focusing on peacekeeping and humanitarian intervention, which continues to pose unique problems for military forces—especially when treated by policymakers as an afterthought in the global war on terrorism or to encourage greater democracy in areas like the Middle East. Part II concludes with an examination of emerging issues related to cyber warfare, which is increasingly seen as a dangerous feature of the contemporary world, and geopolitics involving the changing nature of power relationships, especially those among the great powers.

Part III offers a conclusion to our overview of contemporary strategy not by summarizing the findings of each of our contributors, but by considering new approaches to the study of security that have emerged in recent years and by charting a new way forward for strategic studies. In this section the chapter entitled 'Strategic Studies and Its Critics' surveys and assesses the literature on the subject, highlighting some of the more critical approaches to the subject.

 **Further Reading**

A. Beaufre, *An Introduction to Strategy* (London: Faber & Faber, 1965) and *Deterrence and Strategy* (London: Faber & Faber 1965) both provide an alternative and distinctly French approach to strategic studies during the cold war.

B. Brodie, *War and Politics* (London: Cassell, 1973) is a key text by one of the leading American strategic thinkers during the 'golden age' of strategic studies.

L. Freedman, *Strategy: A History* (Oxford: Oxford University Press, 2013) is one of the best histories of strategy.

J. C. Garnett, 'Strategic Studies and its Assumptions' in J. Baylis, K. Booth, J. Garnett, and P. Williams, *Contemporary Strategy: Theories and Policies* (London: Croom Helm, 1975) is a very good analysis of the philosophy behind classical realism and the early strategic studies texts.

Colin S. Gray, *The Future of Strategy* (Cambridge, UK: Polity, 2015) is an excellent contemporary analysis of the enduring principles of strategy.

B. Heuser, *The Evolution of Strategy* (Cambridge, UK: Cambridge University Press, 2010) is also an excellent history of strategy.

M. Howard, *War In European History* (Oxford: Oxford University Press, 1976) provides an important historical analysis of war in modern European history by a leading British historian and strategic analyst.

H. Kahn, *On Thermonuclear War* (Princeton, NJ: Princeton University Press, 1960) was written by one of the most important and controversial American strategic theorists of his day and provides a cold and unemotional view of how a nuclear war might be fought.

P. J. Katzenstein (ed.) *The Culture of National Security: Norms and Identity in World Politics* (New York: Columbia University Press, 1996) challenges realist and neo-realist approaches to strategic studies and argues for an alternative 'social constructivist' approach.

W. Murray, M. Knox, and A. Bernstein (eds), *The Making of Strategy: Rulers, States, and War* (Cambridge: Cambridge University Press, 1994) is a very good analysis of the strategic and operational side of nuclear strategy.

R. Niebuhr, *Moral Man and Immoral Society* (London: Charles Scribner's Sons, 1932) deals with the ethical issues of strategic studies written from a sophisticated realist thinker's viewpoint.

# Part I

## Enduring Issues of Strategy

# 1

# The History of the Practice of Strategy from Antiquity to Napoleon

BEATRICE HEUSER

## Chapter Contents

 Reader's Guide

This chapter outlines the history of the *practice* of strategy, predating the introduction of the term. It homes in on episodes of European history since Antiquity for which historians claim to have found evidence of the practice of strategy, defined by Kimberly Kagan as 'the setting of a state's objectives and of priorities among those objectives' in order to allocate resources and choose the best means (Kagan 2006: 333–5). While focusing only on Europe, this chapter covers case studies over nearly 2,500 years, ranging from the wars of Ancient Greece, of the Romans to medieval warfare (here with a focus on English history), the warfare of Philip II of Spain, Louis XIV of France, Frederick II of Prussia, the French Revolutionaries, and Napoleon.

## Definitions of Strategy

The word 'strategy' is derived from the Ancient Greek '*strategía*' or '*strategike*'. It was used inconsistently, sometimes meaning ruse, sometimes 'the art of generalship', especially in the definition of the East Romans (Byzantines). West European languages owe the term to late eighteenth-century translations of a work attributed to East Roman Emperor Leo VI, which explores the skills a general has to master in planning and executing a military campaign, including: 'tactics'; constructing fortifications; siegecraft; and the knowledge of geography, climate, the human body (medicine), but also politics (Leo VI *c.*900/2010).

Since then, many authors have tried to better Leo's idea of 'strategy'. The summary of their views might be taken to be that '[s]trategy is a comprehensive way to try to pursue political ends, including the threat or actual use of force, in a dialectic of wills' (Heuser 2010: 27f). The term has since been applied to many other spheres of life, most notably the business world (Freedman 2013). Kimberly Kagan's definition can serve as a useful tool to explore the question as to whether strategy was practised before we had a word for it in the West: at the highest level, where it overlaps with political aims in the grandest sense (sometimes referred to as 'grand strategy'), strategy 'involves the setting of a state's objectives and of priorities among those objectives'—assuming resources are not unlimited—in order to allocate 'resources among them', and choose the best instruments, military and non-military, to pursue them (Kagan 2006: 348). According to this definition, we can say that where we can find evidence, or infer, that state leaders have defined large-scale objectives (such as the construction of defences to guard one frontier against invasion while seeking to defeat an aggressive incursion on another in battle) and allocate resources (such as to raise new taxes to pay more soldiers or build ships), we are dealing with strategy.

The term 'grand strategy' that came into wide use at the beginning of the early twentieth century was influentially defined by the British strategist Basil Liddell Hart as follows: 'The role of grand strategy—higher strategy—is to coordinate and direct all the resources of a nation, or band of nations, towards the attainment of the political object of the war—the goal defined by fundamental policy' (Liddell Hart 1929: 150f). We will also examine where and when this term could be applied.

 **Key Points**

- Strategy can be defined as 'the setting of a state's objectives' and of 'defining priorities among those objectives' (Kagan).
- If resources are limited, strategy involves decisions about their allocation in the pursuit of its objectives.
- Where multiple means exist, strategy involves the choice of the best means in pursuit of its objectives.

## Greece, Rome, and Constantinople

The sources of Antiquity speak much of warfare, and some of these are so well written up by classical historians that they have greatly shaped later generations' understanding of warfare and its underlying strategies. The Persian Wars (499–449 BCE) initially presented a simple scenario, as the expansionist Persian Empire sought to absorb Greek states. Persia, however, had Greek allies, so this was not entirely a clash of civilizations, but also a conflict within the Hellenic world. Athens took the lead in opposing Persia, and after a prolonged struggle (in which the Persians got as far as burning the Acropolis) forced the Persians to withdraw back into Asia. Persian expansionism would periodically renew such wars for the next thousand years.

The Peloponnesian War (431–404 BCE) that followed the fifth-century Persian Wars, essentially between Sparta (and its associates) and Athens (and its associates), presented an even more complex picture, with the Persians hovering in the background as potential allies for either side, and other Greek states changing sides, sometimes more than once. One of the most frequently quoted lines from Thucydides' history suggests that Sparta resorted to war against Athens, alarmed by Athens' growth of power as the outcome of the previous war against Persia, which the Spartans perceived as a threat (Thucydides I.1.23).

The ensuing war between Sparta and Athens has been called a war between dog and fish: Sparta was a land power relying almost exclusively on its army, while Athens' strength lay in its navy. This strategic asymmetry contributed to the long duration of the war, as both sides could elude the confrontation with the other on the latter's terms. Thus both sides resorted to a strategy of attrition: unsuccessfully, Sparta tried to devastate Attica to starve Athens into submission, while Athens continued to get supplies from the sea through the port of Piraeus, now linked with Athens by long land walls. Athenian naval expeditions raided the Peloponnese, but could not reach enough of Sparta's main agricultural land to strangle Sparta. Eventually Sparta decided on an indirect approach (see Box 1.1), still aiming for attrition: to cut off Athens from its grain supplies from areas beyond the Black Sea, through the Bosporus and Dardanelles, but launching an attack, commanded by Brasidas, on Athens' allied lands along the littoral of Thrace. This finally persuaded Athens to accept a compromise peace in 421 BCE, ending the 'Archidamian' phase of the war (Brunt 1965a). However, the peace broke down and was followed by another long period of attritional conflict in which Athens sought to defend a Sicilian ally against the Sicilian city state of Syracuse and to establish itself on the island (421 or 415–412 BCE), an expedition which ended in disaster for Athens. Finally, there was the Decelian or Ionian war (412–404 BCE), eventually won by Sparta and its allies at great cost.

In the following century, Sparta stood aside when an outsider, Macedonia, assumed the leadership of the Hellenic world under young Alexander III ('the Great'). To avenge its previous attacks on Greek states and to free the Greek city states under its dominance, he went to war against the Achaemenid Persian Empire. But with success came ever greater appetite. Alexander thought of himself as a second Achilles, and presenting himself as the adopted son of Zeus (or the Egyptian version, Ammon), he wanted to surpass Zeus' most famous offspring, superhero Hercules, by conquering all the places where Hercules had been. Thus taking over the Persian Empire was not enough: Alexander pushed on to India, and would in all likelihood have set out to conquer the Mediterranean littoral had early death not struck him down (Brunt 1965b). In pursuit of these strategic aims, Alexander rallied first the youths of Macedonia and surrounding populations, then most of the Hellenic city states to the cause of moving against Persia. After military victories against Persian armies, and subsequent massacres

 **BOX** 1.1   Binary Options in Strategy

On the most basic level, strategy offers the choice defensive vs. offensive, yet one might be strategically defensive while launching a tactical offensive. But there are more options, again, often both on a strategic and a tactical level. In the Punic Wars, Hannibal surprised the Romans by attacking them in Sicily only to invade the Italian peninsula coming over the Alps, but also by enveloping their forces and coming at them from a surprising side, which he practised especially at the battle of Cannae. Ever since, surprise, envelopment, and other forms of indirect approaches have formed part of tactics and strategy. Hans Delbrück (1848–1929) contrasted strategies of attrition with strategies seeking to crush the enemy in a shorter campaign. Basil Henry Liddell Hart (1895–1970) perceived a similar pair of opposites in the form of the 'direct' and the 'indirect approach'.

and enslavement of defeated populations, Alexander in a third strategic phase aimed at consolidating his conquest by trying to integrate Greeks and Persians through marriages and attempts to fuse the cultures in his new-won realm. The miracle of his stunning conquests, made when he was between 22 and 31 years old, is generally attributed to the appeal of his two earliest proclaimed war aims above; to his personal charisma, especially his appeal to other young men and loyalty to his companions or *hetairoi* (a circle he widened to admit new allies); and to his tactics and consequent battlefield victories.

Meanwhile, in the West, another city state was beginning to dominate the Mediterranean: Rome. It conquered its neighbours one by one, having been attacked and threatened by several of them, so that Roman conquests could largely be portrayed as defensive countermeasures, aimed to eliminate perpetual sources of danger and the more remote places of refuge for defeated enemy leaders. Polities ever further afield were thus conquered by Rome, lest aid would come from them to Rome's more immediate adversaries. Rome did suffer at the hands of invaders, especially the Celts or Gauls (providing the reason for the conquest and pacification of lands inhabited by them in northern Italy and today's France and Britain).

Rome also clashed repeatedly in the third and second centuries BCE with the Punics (Phoenicians), whose network of cities extended around the Mediterranean, with its main centre in Carthage. In particular, their leader, Hannibal Barca, would present the Romans with a great strategic challenge. At the time of the second Punic War (218–201 BCE), the southern part of the Iberian peninsula was under Punic domination, bordering on Roman domains, both now contested by each side. The most famous campaign of Hannibal would give posterity the great model for a 'strategy of indirect approach' and for strategic surprise. In 219 BCE, Hannibal first launched an attack against the Roman ally Saguntum (near modern Valencia on the Iberian peninsula's western coast), drawing Roman armies away from the Italian peninsula for its defence, while Hannibal and his main army, coming up from the Iberian peninsula and moving across coastal Gaul crossed the Alps in 218 to invade Italy from the north, his forces famously including war elephants. With the bulk of the Roman army dispatched to the south and to Iberia, Hannibal defeated remaining Roman contingents in three successive battles in northern Italy.

In turn it was a Roman general, Quintus Fabius Maximus, who would give his name to the 'Fabian' counterstrategy: avoiding a pitched battle while harassing enemy forces with small units adopting hit-and-run tactics. Fabius' procrastinating approach (he was nicknamed the *cunctator* or hesitator) did not drive the Punics out of Italy, however. Eventually Rome gave battle at Cannae (216 BCE), another brilliant victory for Hannibal who once again through an indirect approach and tactical surprise outmanoeuvred the Roman army, with the Punic cavalry enveloping the Roman army to attack from its opposite flank. Cannae would resonate as a model throughout history and become the inspiration for the German operations against France in the early stages of both the First and the Second World Wars.

As Hannibal established himself and turned clients of Rome into allies, his war aims seem to have stopped short of the conquest of Rome itself. The Romans were horrified at having him 'at their doors'. Nor were they going to accept this massive reduction of their sphere of influence. The conflict spread across the Mediterranean, with several polities changing sides more than once. Despite Hannibal's brilliant strategic successes, he was ultimately driven out of Italy and Sicily. A Third Punic War in the following century would persuade the Romans to adopt a true strategy of annihilation: after decisively defeating the Punics, they utterly destroyed Carthage and carried its remaining population away into slavery (Goldsworthy

2001). The killing of all men and the enslavement of women and children was a staple, geno-cidal tool of strategy in Antiquity.

It has been debated for decades now whether the Romans, who famously did not have a word for 'strategy', developed strategies and applied them. Edward Luttwak (1976) and Giusto Traina (2014) claim they did. Traina argues that Caesar had embarked on the conquest of the known world not only with his subjection of the Celts and his union with Egypt, but also with planning for wars against the Parthians and Persian Empire, which were cut short by his assas-sination. Mark Antony and Octavian/Augustus tried to follow through with his plans, both unsuccessfully, until in later life Augustus adopted a strategy of consolidation. Further to this period of expansion (which for Luttwak ended only with Augustus' immediate successors up to Nero who died in 68 CE), Luttwak identified a strategy of consolidation and liminal defence (including the construction of *castra* and other static fortifications) marking the period up to the death of Emperor Septimius Severus (68–211). In the subsequent strategy of the Third Century, the Roman Empire switched to defence in depth, with a reduced force guarding Rome's borders and a mobile army that could be deployed to any border area.

Critics argued over Augustus' overall strategy (was it continuity or did it contain a rup-ture), over his interpretation of border fortifications, and over his interpretation of the Third Century Crisis. Nevertheless, applying Kagan's definition, there is plentiful evidence that Roman emperors took strategic decisions—withdrawing legions in one province to deploy them against a perceived greater threat elsewhere, dealing with steady small incursions of nomadic horsemen by recruiting them into the Roman army, and pacifying conquered peo-ples by granting their leaders citizenship and sharing with them the benefits of Roman civi-lization. The organization of the transport of grain from one end of the empire to the other to feed Rome's legions, the recruitment and rotation of forces throughout the empire, and the building and maintenance of Rome's two navies cannot be seen as *ad hoc* measures but presuppose strategic planning of sorts—even if, in the absence of evidence that underpinning concepts for these measures were articulated, some experts would rather call them 'small strategy' than 'grand strategy' (Le Bohec 2014).

It was again Luttwak (2009) who drew attention to the sophisticated handling of all tools of statecraft in what can only be called 'strategy' by Rome's Constantinopolitan (Byzantine) successors. Justinian I (emperor 527–565) and Heraclius (emperor 610–645) clearly had a great strategic aim: the liberation of the former possessions of the Roman Empire in the West, now in the hands of Germanic tribes. Both had amazing, but not lasting, success, while almost incessantly fighting on two fronts: in the West and also in the East with the ever-expansionist Persian Sassanids.

No sooner were the Persians finally and definitively defeated by Heraclius' host than a new threat arose: the explosion of Islamic fervour in the great Arab conquest of the Middle East and the southern and western shores of the Mediterranean under the green banner of their prophet. Four centuries later, the Arabs in turn were vanquished by nomadic Turkish tribes, who, once converted to Islam, also embarked on conquest, pouring in waves from Central Asia into the Middle East. Within a century, they seized most of Asia Minor, Persia, and the Middle East, then savagely hacked chunk after chunk out of what remained of the (East) Roman Empire, until its fall in 1453.

Until then, Rome lived on in the East, for an astonishing further millennium after the fall of the eternal city on the Tiber. With a shrinking landmass and population, the East Roman

Empire was soon outnumbered by its assailants, and had to devise new ways of fending them off. Given the imperial overstretch of Constantinople's armies, one was the constitution of small raiding parties to intercept Turkish incursions when the invaders were on their way back to their own territories with their booty (Nikephoros Phokas *c*.950), but this was a tactic rather than a strategy. The Byzantines used the lure of their own culture in the form of soft diplomacy, bought off enemies (who unfortunately developed a taste for these bribes and kept coming back for more), and spread Christianity to acculturate barbarian neighbours, thus complementing their military strategy in many ways (Luttwak 2009).

---

 **Key Points**

- The writings of Herodotus and Thucydides furnish evidence of complex reasoning in warfare that satisfies Kagan's definition of strategy.
- The Hellenes fighting the Persians and among the Hellenes, the Spartans fighting the Athenians, clashed in a variety of asymmetric ways.
- Roman expansion and then defence constituted different phases that can be seen as strategies.
- The East Romans/Byzantines defined the term 'strategy' as making use of all tools of statecraft in addition to military means.

---

## The West European Middle Ages

In the West there are parallels to such chequebook diplomacy in the form of the '*Danegeld*', which the English paid Danish invaders in the late tenth and eleventh centuries. Beyond that, with little literacy among political leaders (let alone treatises on anything resembling strategy), we hardly find strategy in Kagan's sense. Great migrations which swept over Europe from the third century onwards, mainly from East to West or from North-East to West and South (ending with the Norman conquest of England in 1066), reduced warfare to a matter of invasion/attack and defence. There were some big constructions such as Offa's Dyke and the Danevirke or the Götavirke, for which labour force had to be marshalled and fed, but this degree of organization within the community can be traced back far into prehistory and hardly requires any strategic concept. Moreover, subsistence levels were so low and economies so basic that we have hardly any stone castles before 1000 CE, a large step down in sophistication from the Roman Empire.

Things changed from about 1000 to the end of the Middle Ages, when entities emerged that were ruled by dynasties laying claim to scattered territories which had to be defended, sometimes against several adversaries. Automatically, this meant that armies had to be moved around to meet contingencies in several places, arrangements had to be made to recruit them (as local militias for local defence were not sufficient for such tasks), to feed, equip, and ultimately pay them, if they were required beyond the month or so of military service which vassals owed their lords in the seigneurial system. The dynasty ruling England, moreover, had to make arrangements to transport their soldiers across the Channel, and in that process, protect them against naval attacks. In short, they needed a navy. Given the number of principalities in Europe, each had several neighbours with whom potentially to quarrel over territory; alliance politics of a form unknown to imperial Rome—which at best had had client states—but well known to Ancient Greece, came to the fore again, and with it, a diplomatic game of counter-balancing an adversary's power and influence. A new element was that of dynastic marriages to complement warfare or tribute payments. It was an instrument developed by the Byzantines but it really came into its own in the Occident, where it determined many an alliance and caused many wars over inheritance claims. The delineation of state boundaries became progressively more fixed or else fought over; the lords over marches—disputed border area or areas difficult to control because of their geographic features—often grew in power to pose threats to their royal overlords, perhaps throwing in their lots with neighbouring powers, or claiming kingship for themselves. At the very least they wanted to be consulted on military measures taken by their liege as the construction and upkeep of castles in such border areas usually fell to them, leading to wrangling about who was to pay what, and who was to furnish, feed, and pay the garrisons. This resulted in contests for power both within countries and beyond their borders. It also led to the struggle over resources, their allocation, and the taxation required to meet the costs of defensive measures and other warfare, which took place between the monarch and his or her main retainers, and soon also in formal 'parliaments'. This would force monarchs and their advisors to articulate reasons for why they wanted, say, to invest scarce resources into repairing castles in one place instead of building ships or hiring mercenaries.

An example of medieval strategy making is arguably that of Edward III, king of England and contender for the French crown which he claimed through his mother, who also sought to gain overlordship of Scotland. By the fourteenth century, the kings of Scotland and France appreciated that they had better chances of holding their own against bellicose Edward by co-ordinating their military operations against his lands. Edward in turn learnt from the devastating border raids effected by the Scots on his territories and in turn successfully applied the same practice to France (Rogers 2000). These basic patterns of counterbalancing alliances, often with a dynastic element, and of internal disputes about the financing of wars survived into modern times.

Arguably medieval princes' strategies differed from later strategies on account of the different mindset and culture dominating their times. They were generally reluctant to give battle, as opposed to denying it by adopting a purely defensive stance, or besieging an enemy's cities or fortifications, or employing the *chevauchée* (a destructive raid of the enemy's lands). Philippe Contamine argued that medieval strategy was dominated by two principles: the avoidance of pitched battles and the 'obsidional reflex', the tendency to seek refuge in fortifications (Contamine 1986: 365). Battles were indeed rare in the high and late Middle Ages. One explanation, underscored by Jan Willem Honig (2012), is that they were seen in large part as divine ordeal, and that specific cultural norms prevailed over patterns of warfare that are found across the centuries. By contrast, John Gillingham (1992) is more inclined to identify non-cultural circumstantial factors—that made battle more risky and less likely to bring about the desired end, leading medieval leaders to be reluctant to give battle. Clifford Rogers (2000, 2002) argues, however, that victories in battle were needed by princes whose claim to the throne was contested in some way; but as the other side had more to lose, the coincidence of both sides' wish to give battle was lower than in later times. Edward III's strategy in the Hundred Years' War was to use the *chevauchée* time and again to try to force the French monarch to give battle. Economic and social parameters taken into account, Francisco García

Fitz (1998) shows convincingly that medieval monarchs did seek to impose their will on their adversaries (to use Clausewitz's definition of the aims of any war) drawing on a selection of tools, military as well as political and economic; he concludes that medieval man was no less 'strategic' than his forebears or descendants.

 **Key Points**

- Evidence for complex decision-making involving multiple tools—strategy—increased as the Middle Ages went by.
- Some historians argue that medieval warfare was conditioned by different cultural premises.
- Others argue that it was the function of more primitive reasoning than in previous or later periods, framed by more primitive means available.

## Early Modern Europe

Two sets of incremental changes ultimately led to the transformation of warfare and of strategy. One was the growth, centralization, and diversification of the structure of states in Europe, partially caused by wars—and in turn partly the cause of them, as Charles Tilly (1975) argued. A state apparatus with a growing number of professional civil servants—not merely clerics or local magistrates doubling in that role—meant more efficient records of populations; more efficient collection of taxes; more money to make war; and a move from armies made up of peasants (obliged to perform military service for a certain number of days per year for their lord) to standing armies of professional soldiers (who could be drilled to use new arms requiring training and discipline). The other was technological innovation, which had begun in the thirteenth century but came to revolve increasingly around what could be done with gunpowder, and how to defend against it. The result after two to three centuries of experiments was the use of cannon—first in sieges, then aboard ships and in battles, and finally transformed into hand-held firearms—resulting both in a gradual transformation of the battlefield and in the architecture of fortifications which became several times larger (to allow for defence in depth, avoiding right angles of impact of cannon balls), more complex, and consequently more expensive (Roberts 1956; Parker 1988).

Meanwhile, the invention of the compass and other strident advances in navigation and improvements in shipping heralded ventures onto the high seas and global navigation. As fleets became capable of missions beyond the carrying of troops and the protection of short-range commerce, and with a mindset increasingly open to new ideas and discovery, more complex strategic thinking emerged. By the late sixteenth century we find what could be called the first comprehensive strategic concept covering more or less the ground of modern national security strategies, and articulating strategic options for England's security that were actually implemented (Sutcliffe 1593). Thinkers and practitioners explicitly weighed different strategic options—should England defend against Spain by continuing to send soldiers in support of the Dutch rebels fighting against Spain on the other side of the Channel? Or was it preferable to concentrate resources on ships to blockade the Spanish navy in its home ports? Or to attempt to intercept the flow of silver from the Caribbean to Spain, the main source of

Spain's wealth and ability to fund her wars (Heuser 2012)? In late Elizabethan England, we have all necessary evidence of 'grand strategy' existing in theory and applied practice.

Strategies were made not only on the basis of calculations of likely success or failure, resources available and resources required, geography, alliances, and dynastic links. They were also, as in the Middle Ages before, influenced by the highly ideological element of religion. While dissent among Christians had already troubled the late Roman Principate, and while quarrels over Christian dogma played into the hands of Islamic conquerors, leading to the loss of Constantinople's North African and Middle Eastern provinces, religious wars in early modern Western Europe cut across state boundaries, creating two opposing camps repeatedly locked into war with one another. While the two camps—the Catholic and the Protestant—were not without their own internal tensions, Nicholas Rodger has aptly called one the world-wide 'Catholic International', with the Roman Papacy as its dogma-formulating centre and its tentacles spreading from Portuguese and Spanish possessions in Latin America to the Philippines in the Far East. At least, he emphasized, it was perceived as such by its Protestant adversaries. Consequently, strategy assumed global dimensions for the European great powers of the time.

Thus Geoffrey Parker (1998) could identify a 'grand strategy' in the ambitions of Philip II of Spain. The empire he inherited was the first in which the sun did not set. His grand strategy was to preserve his inheritance, threatened especially by the insurgence of the protestant Dutch in quest of independence. Secondly, he tried to keep what he had acquired in his own lifetime: the English crown through his marriage with Mary Tudor, lost again once she predeceased him without issue, and that of Portugal. Thirdly, he was encouraged to be the champion of Catholicism—by now world-wide—with the ultimate aspiration of re-establishing a universal monarchy. While his resources—local taxation in his united kingdoms covering the Iberian peninsula and also revenue from his overseas' empire—were several times larger than those of Elizabethan England, there were still limits, not merely financial but also technological, to what he could do. Despite the ambitious ideas about how to use sea power entertained by some Englishmen, ships in the age of sail were still helpless in adverse winds. Two further fleets launched by Philip against England after the famous Armada of 1588 were both driven back by gales, a problem that would not disappear until the age of steam. Ultimately, Philip was so preoccupied by pursuing his two conservative goals that he could not act much on the third. Parker concluded that, like governments until this day, Philip was unable to follow all his ambitions or to apply a grand strategy coherently, as he was exceedingly preoccupied with the minutiae of running his vast empire, making him predominantly reactive in his decision-making.

The greatest conflagration of this period was the Thirty Years' War, again waged in part over the implicit bid for a universal monarchy, in part over the vertical distribution of power (here mainly within the Holy Roman Empire), and in part over religious allegiance. It was contemporaneous with the Wars of the Three Kingdoms on the British Isles, which also shared the latter two components. While the latter wars are seen mainly as civil wars, the great war that engulfed continental Europe from France to Poland and from Sweden to the shores of the Mediterranean dragged on because its fragile alliances as an element of *state* interest, *raison d'Etat*, began to counterbalance religious allegiances, and because a multitude of strategic experiments often cancelled out previous ones. While this was a period of great intellectual productivity in other areas (to mention only Hobbes and Grotius), oddly enough there was little originality in writing about war in the seventeenth century.

In his subsequent wars, Louis XIV's France and Frederick II's Prussia had state apparatuses to match their strategic aims (Cénat 2010). Louis XIV of France was able to espouse a clear overall strategy: in a first phase (1661–1675), he sought glory in pushing the country's borders outward up to geographic obstacles. In a second phase (1676–1697), designed to consolidate his victories, he sought to straighten French borders through further small acts of aggression (such as the seizure of Strasbourg and Luxembourg), devastating contested areas with scorched earth tactics that complemented the direct battles with his adversaries (chief among them, Habsburg Spain and, as ever, the Empire). Meanwhile, with the help of his architect and minister Vauban, Louis fortified the frontier regions. At the heart of the third and last phase of Louis' wars (1697–1714) was the War of the Spanish Succession, which secured the Spanish crown for his grandson and his descendants. Designed to be defensive, the latter two phases of Louis' wars deeply frightened his neighbours and deepened Habsburg and Dutch suspicions about France's hegemonic ambitions, increasing the cost of these wars in terms of blood and treasure (Lynn 1999: 17–46). Louis' wars wrought great suffering on the areas where he waged them, especially Flanders (the Spanish Netherlands which he coveted) and the Palatinate and what today is Southern Hesse, where villages and cities were burned and scorched earth tactics led to mass starvation. It was fairly clear, however, that his territorial ambitions were limited to areas that he could claim for dynastic reasons or that had long been disputed between France and the Empire.

From 1754/1756 until 1763, the Seven Years' War (known in the United States as the French and Indian War) involved complex alliance strategies among multiple powers in theatres of war around the globe. The main players were Britain, France, Prussia, and the Holy Roman Empire, with various allies and colonies thrown into the bargain. It involved global logistic planning, with soldiers recruited by the United Kingdom, for example, from small German states against payment and shipped to North America to fight. While the co-ordination of the war efforts of the parties involved was at times sub-optimal, this was clearly 'grand strategy' in the Liddell Hartian definition put into practice. Frederick II in his successive testaments presented his very sophisticated and complex views of inter-state relations in his times, prescribing for his heir how to handle different countries and what factors—from geopolitics to economics, finance, and demography—to take into account in his strategy making. While we find here little abstraction made (Frederick was not interested in speculations about powers A and B and C, but was in concrete terms preoccupied with the Empire, France, and other European states), he spelled out what he regarded as the underlying strategic imperative: 'The first preoccupation of a prince must be to protect what he has (*de se soutenir*), the second his aggrandisement' (quoted in Heuser 2010: 63). And indeed, especially the latter strategic aim characterizes his aim in the wars in which he tried to enlarge his own realm at the expense of neighbouring states.

How did Louis XIV and Frederick II manage to prevail, even if they had all of Europe against them at times, when after them, Napoleon ultimately did not? One answer is that they did not seek 'regime change'. They were upsetting the balance of power in Europe and beyond, and this made the other states gang up on them. But in turn, their adversaries' war aims were limited. For even if both Louis and Frederick did all within their power to enlarge their respective dynasties' possessions at the expense of all their neighbouring powers, they never sought to change the social structure of the conquered areas (except for imposing Catholicism, on the part of Louis, or granting religious freedom, on the part of Frederick). They did not introduce revolutionary reform agendas that could prove contagious and incite populations in countries further afield to rise up and overthrow their governments to replace them with regimes in the image of Louis' or Frederick's. Neither monarch challenged the order of society and of the worldview on which societies were constructed. In that sense, despite the terrible woes that especially Louis inflicted on Flanders and the Palatinate, their wars were limited.

The wars of Frederick II of Prussia in particular were to provide data and arguments for the growing output of literature on the art or science of war. The most influential author writing on war and the state in the Age of Reason was French Count Guibert, whose writings presaged the *levée en masse* and the ideal of the citizen-soldier of the French Revolution. While previously treatments of the subject had mostly been couched in terms of Christian values and divine retribution in case of malpractice, Guibert provided a new, secular rationale for just war in self-defence, a moral imperative that had been omnipresent in European writings about war in previous centuries, even though in practice many princes merely paid lip service to it (Guibert 1772). Guibert contributed to the creation of the myth that the wars of the Anciens Régimes—the monarchies of France, Prussia, and Austria—were limited, which they were in so far as they had only very 'limited' effects on the subjects of the monarchs who waged them, especially relative to the effects of wars in later periods. In absolute terms, however, the wars had devastating effects also on the civilian populations in the theatres of war, and not just on the non-combatants. But in the absence of universal conscription, of a devastation of the homelands of the monarchs, and of revolutionary or territorially unlimited war aims, and compared with the subsequent wars of Napoleon, they could be seen as 'limited' in scope (see Box 1.3).

---

 **Key Points**

- Complex strategy making was still handicapped by the limitations of the state apparatus well into the seventeenth century.

- Thereafter, Louis XIV's France and Frederick II's Prussia had state apparatuses matching their strategic ambitions.

- The wars of the Anciens Régimes were seen as limited in aims and in effects on the citizens of their own countries, even if populations in foreign theatres of war suffered greatly. From this arose the partial myth of the limited scope of the eighteenth-century wars.

---

## From the American War of Independence to the Napoleonic Wars

The humanistic conceptual framework was thus in place for the French Revolutionary Wars, which were initially fought mainly in reaction to the assaults on France by the Empire and other monarchs, horrified by the Revolution's implications for their world. The American War of Independence or American Revolutionary War (1775–1783) presented the crucial precedent in several ways. On the American side it was, to paraphrase, a war of the people, for the people, waged by the people. Alongside the clash of regular (professional) armies, it saw, on the American side, the extensive use of militia and irregular fighting.

This asymmetry heralded the configuration of the French Revolutionary Wars. Julius von Voß wrote in 1809 that the French Revolutionary Wars were like small wars fought on a large scale (quoted in Rink 1999: 197); this was a reflection of the revolutionary change in tactics. And the issues over which the American War of Independence and the French Revolutionary Wars were fought were, of course, almost the same: people's self-determination vs. monarchy. Both were largely defensive: they were not wars of conquest, and even the French Revolutionaries' steps to liberate oppressed peoples beyond France's borders were sparked off by the campaign against Revolutionary France of the monarchs of Europe who intended to restore the French monarchy (Belissa and Leclerq 2001).

That there was also resistance against change must not be denied. The anti-revolutionary uprising in the Vendée, which burst into full flame in 1793 and was not entirely extinguished even ten years later, had much in common with previous religious wars in France and elsewhere, and indeed with the Spanish resistance to Napoleon that would become known as 'La Guerrilla', the small war. The Vendéeans and the Spaniards after them were just as motivated as the French Revolutionaries; passions were aroused not only on one side. This also applied to other areas of Europe that would be occupied by Napoleon's *Grande Armée* or those of his allies, which, living off the land, by and by made themselves thoroughly hated. Henceforth the term 'small war', which had previously referred to the special operations of special units or detachments, would acquire the connotation of 'people's war', insurgency, a war of opposition against a regime or occupying power fought by the aroused masses. Defined in this way, paradoxically, the French Revolutionaries could be said to have fought just such a people's war against their regime, while provoking others to fight a people's war against them.

The French Revolutionary and then the Napoleonic Wars unleashed French passions in a way predicted by Guibert. It was not technological innovations but a change in society and war aims that underlay the revolutionary nature of the wars of the 1790s with an appeal to the French masses (and indeed to the populations of neighbouring areas) unknown since the wars of religion well beyond living memory. Napoleon, in turn, the captain-turned-emperor, with his charismatic appeal to the French soldiers, was a quintessential case of Caesarism, creating for himself armies that would blindly follow him to Moscow and to Egypt.

The contrast between the French Revolutionary Wars and the wars of Napoleon could hardly have been greater where strategic aims are concerned. The French say that appetite comes with eating, and as Charles Esdaile has argued, Napoleon's grew with every success (Esdaile 2008). While in his tactics he built on the innovations of the Revolutionary Wars, both the scope and aims of his campaigns, and his strategic ambitions, were dramatically different. From securing France's territory and thus the Revolutionary *acquis*, he turned to the conquest of all neighbouring countries (only the invasion of Britain did he not follow through with), and indeed took his forces as far as Egypt and Russia. The strategy he pursued was to deal with the other states of Europe one at a time, and to sign bilateral peace agreements which he would ignore when the situation allowed, while turning on the next victim of his aggression. The admixture of benevolent measures to secure the support of liberal elements in the population—the imposition of liberal legislation including, for example, the emancipation of Jews—for several years undermined the resistance against his invasions, until the experience of long-term occupation by large armies living off the land sapped initial liberal enthusiasm throughout Europe. The coalitions that formed against Napoleon were thus of his own making, as the other states of Europe began to realize that neutrality was not an option, and that

**BOX** 1.2 The Napoleonic Paradigm

The Napoleonic Paradigm of warfare is based on the interpretation of the Napoleonic Wars by Henri Baron de Jomini and Carl von Clausewitz. Ignoring entirely that Napoleon ultimately failed to secure his conquests and to establish a lasting empire, they focused narrowly on his short-term successes and his military victories. Until the First World War and beyond, this short-sighted preoccupation with military victory, eclipsing the question of how to achieve a lasting peace after the end of hostilities, dominated in writing on and the practice of strategy. Both before and after this period, there was and has been greater awareness that military victory cannot be the ultimate aim in warfare, but it must be a lasting, bearable peace.

Napoleon could not be stopped unless all of Europe ganged up on him. The Battle of Leipzig of 1813, hailed as the 'battle of nations', was thus above all a counterbalancing act by powers joining up to put a stop to Napoleon's otherwise unstoppable expansionism. Waterloo was only an *encore*.

Curiously, Napoleon's ultimate strategic failure, his inability to turn his conquests into a lasting empire, barely marked the two strategists to whom we owe chiefly the interpretation of Napoleon's way of war and its transmission to posterity: Antoine Baron de Jomini and Carl von Clausewitz. Focusing excessively, perhaps, on Napoleon's victories, both failed to comment on his singular lack of success in bringing about what had previously been seen in Europe as the only acceptable aim of warfare, a lasting peace. Their writing ushered in the era dominated by the Napoleonic Paradigm (see Box 1.2), where strategy making was dominated, not by the quest for a lasting (and thus peaceful) settlement of the issues over which a war had been fought, but by the quest for military victory (Heuser 2010).

 **Key Points**

- As Guibert had predicted, with the American War of Independence and the French Revolution, war became the business of the people and was greatly transformed.

- Napoleon's '*système*' was one of ruthless opportunism, breaking all the rules of peaceful cohabitation, with the result that all of Europe united against him. His strategy ultimately foundered on the opposition he had created with his unlimited expansionism.

- With the French Revolutionary and Napoleonic Wars, the term '*guerrilla*' (small war) acquired the meaning of people's war or insurgency.

 **Conclusion**

History did not start with Napoleon, even though he transformed Europe, mainly in unintended ways. Over time the practice of strategy took many forms, and there were many variables influencing it. Apart from obvious ones like size and geographic position, the technology available, the resources (human and physical) of the entity (city state, kingdom, state) waging war, it also included the world views, ambitions, and thus strategic aims of the political leaders, the degree of engagement of the populations, and the capacity of the former to harness the latter to their project.

The practice of strategy was for long stretches of European history bounded by rules such as not killing non-combatants, or not destroying church property. Such limitations were not always

**BOX** 1.3  'Absolute War' is NOT 'Total War'

Clausewitz differentiated in ideal terms between wars limited by political and other factors, as opposed to wars that might in theory consist of unconstrained violence, violence *absolved* from all bounds. This latter ideal concept was later referred to as 'absolute war', as opposed to *limited* wars. For Clausewitz, absolute war was an abstract, but the wars of Napoleon had come close to this abstract: 'one could doubt that our idea of the absolute nature [of war] has any reality,' he wrote in *On War*, 'had we not precisely in our own time seen real war appear in its absolute perfection. After a short introduction by the French Revolution, the reckless Bonaparte has brought it to that point [of perfection]' (*On War* VIIIB).

'Total war' is not at all the same thing as 'absolute war'. The term 'total war' was coined only in the twentieth century. In 1918 French politician Léon Daudet defined it as the total mobilization of one's own population, while in 1935 German general Erich Ludendorff added to that the genocidal dimension of treating every member of the enemy nation as a target to be killed. The latter definition matched the German National Socialist idea that Slavs and Jews had to be killed or at least turned into a serf-people to be exploited by the Aryan 'master race'. This connotation was absent before the development of racist ideas in the nineteenth century, especially in Clausewitz's idea of 'absolute war'. Admittedly, cruel strategies of annihilation and enslavement that could be termed 'total war' *in practice* can be traced back to Antiquity. However, they took place on a smaller scale than the genocides of the twentieth century, not least because overall populations were smaller then.

observed and indeed generally discarded when the adversaries were seen as illegitimate (that is, as rebels or heretics), or themselves acted with such disrespect for limitations (as, for example, the Huns or the Ottoman Turks tended to do). There was an assumption until Napoleon came along that a legitimate excuse for expansionist ambitions must be found. This assumption gave way to the Napoleonic Paradigm which still haunts many cultures: the assumption that might is right, and that 'national interest', what had previously been called *raison d'Etat*, could justify anything. And yet it is the period dominated by the Napoleonic Paradigm which is the exception in the history of Europe, not the norm. The need for a just cause to warrant any military action and determine the aims of strategy has gained new prominence since 1918, and especially since the end of the cold war, at least in Europe. Curiously, insistence on limiting one's conduct in warfare (and thus again, on what strategy one can espouse) by rules did not disappear even in the nineteenth century, but led to the adoption of various conventions agreed multilaterally. During the period dealt with in this chapter, by contrast Europeans saw themselves as bound by rules of conduct dictated by Christianity, and adopted self-denying ordinances when encountering enemies they saw as legitimate. Again, Western powers find themselves closer to pre-Napoleonic practice in this respect than to the excesses of the Total Wars of the early twentieth century. The practice of strategy by all ages and cultures yields many lessons for the present, not just the practice of the most recent past.

 **Critical Thinking**    Debating … Was strategy practised from Antiquity to the Napoleonic period?

For

- *Recent use of the term.* The word 'strategy' in a modern sense only came into usage in Western Europe in the late eighteenth century. It was then first introduced into Western languages from the Byzantine Greek text of Emperor Leo VI, written around 900.

**Critical Thinking** *(continued)*

- *No 'strategy' in Roman times.* There is no Latin word for strategy, so the Romans could not have thought in those terms and categories.
- *The modern state and link between strategy and resources.* Prior to the creation of the modern state with its tax system and central revenues, European powers could not afford a standing army. Thus the means needed to underpin strategy did not exist.
- *Clausewitz as a key strategic thinker.* Before Clausewitz there was little writing amounting to general reflection on ends, means, and ways.

## Against

- *Wars have been perennial.* Throughout history, choices have been made by key decision-makers conducting wars about allocating resources for its conduct.
- *War planners have always had to link means to ends.* They made choices between different tools (means) available, e.g. between spending more money on building ships, or raising more troops, employing mercenaries, or introducing conscriptions, raising more taxes, forming alliances with outside powers.
- *Historically 'strategy' has been a reality, if not an articulated concept.* While prior to the sixteenth century, few decision-makers articulated abstract reasons, decisions about ends, means, and ways can be documented since Antiquity.
- *'Strategic' thinking has a long history.* There are a good number of authors before Clausewitz, from Christine de Pizan and Machiavelli to Matthew Sutcliffe, Santa Cruz de Marcenado, and Count Guibert, who analysed war. Clausewitz borrowed ideas from several of them.

 **Questions**

1. By what criteria can one tell that a 'strategy' was being practised?
2. Can contemporary strategists learn lessons from the wars of former times?
3. Was it Ancient Greece, Ancient Rome, or the East Roman Empire (Byzantium) which made a greater contribution to our understanding of strategy?
4. Is it useful to reduce strategy to binary options?
5. Can one argue that strategy was practised in the Middle Ages?
6. How did the practice of strategy in the sixteenth century differ from that of Ancient Greece?
7. How did recruitment patterns of armies influence strategy making through the ages?
8. Which was a greater driver of wars, religion or nationalism?
9. How does a strategy of attrition differ from a strategy of indirect approach?
10. Compare and contrast the strategic aims of Louis XIV of France, Frederick II of Prussia, and Napoleon.

 **Further Reading**

**L. Freedman, *Strategy: A History* (Oxford: Oxford University Press, 2013)** discusses strategy in all areas from military to business.

A. Hartmann and B. Heuser (eds), *War, Peace and World Orders from Antiquity until the 20th Century* (London: Routledge, 2001) has expert chapters covering different periods.

B. Heuser, *The Evolution of Strategy: Thinking War from Antiquity to the Present* (Cambridge: Cambridge University Press, 2010a) discusses the history of strategic thought (as opposed to practice).

B. Heuser, *The Strategy-Makers: Thoughts on War and Society from Machiavelli to Clausewitz* (Santa Barbara, CA: ABC-Clio, 2010b) contains excerpts in English translation or modernization of texts dating from the sixteenth to early nineteenth centuries.

*Small Wars and Insurgencies* (2014) Special Issue: *The Origins and Diversity of Small Wars* 25(4) explains what was originally meant by 'small wars' when the term became generally used in the seventeenth century and how this developed into ideologically motivated insurgency.

R.F. Weigley, *The American Way of War: A History of United States Military Strategy and Policy* (New York: Macmillan, 1976) is a widely cited point of reference.

 ## Web Links

*War and History* **http://wih.sagepub.com** is the most important journal dealing with strategic studies that also carries an historical dimension.

*Journal of Strategic Studies* **http://www.tandfonline.com/toc/fjss20/current** is a valuable reference in strategic studies.

*Small Wars and Insurgencies* **http://www.tandfonline.com/toc/fswi20/current** concentrates especially on insurgencies and counterinsurgency; one will find the main debates here.

*RUSI Journal* **https://www.rusi.org/publications/journal** is published by the Royal United Services Institute, and gives current debates on the theory and practice of strategy. For the US Army see the *Military Review* **http://usacac.army.mil/cac2/militaryreview/index.asp** and for the US interservice debate, see *Joint Force Quarterly*. **http://www.dtic.mil/doctrine/jfq/jfq.htm** published by the US National Defense University.

*British Journal for Military History* **http://bjmh.org.uk/index.php/bjmh** is a fairly new and ambitious journal devoting a section to the practice of strategy.

# The Evolution of Modern Warfare

MICHAEL SHEEHAN

## Chapter Contents

 **Reader's Guide**

This chapter looks at the way that the theory and practice of war has changed over the past two hundred years. It examines how the development of modern states has changed the way that wars are fought, and it looks at the impact of the Industrial Revolution on the planning for and conduct of war. It also examines the influence of some of the key thinkers on war during the past two centuries. War is a social practice, and the conduct of war is influenced by changes in military theory, in the development of new technologies, and crucially, by the evolution of society itself.

## Introduction

War has been a perennial feature of human history. It is condemned as an evil activity in which human beings show the darker side of their nature by using violence and killing to achieve their ends. Yet at the same time war is a peculiarly *social* activity, demanding high levels of organization and depending upon bonds of loyalty, obedience, and solidarity for its effective prosecution.

In the modern period, war between developed states assumed a particular form, characterized by a symbiotic relationship between increasingly well-organized states, the industrialization of warfare, and a growing totality in the manner in which it was conducted. By the end of the twentieth century, however, there was some evidence that this era of 'modern' industrial warfare might be ending and a new one beginning.

What do we mean by 'modern' warfare? It is the forms of warfare shaped by and reflecting the 'modern' era of human history; however, modernity and modern war mean much more than simply technological progress and wars fought with increasingly sophisticated and mass-produced weaponry. The nineteenth-century military theorist Carl von Clausewitz argued that the prevailing form of war always reflects the era in which it occurs, and this is certainly the case with modern warfare. However, it should be noted that in any era there is more than just one characteristic *form* of war.

Modern warfare developed in terms of a number of broad themes that were increasingly characteristic of society as a whole, such as the growing power of the state through processes of centralization, bureaucratization, and, to some extent, democratization. It was influenced by the rise of powerful ideologies, such as nationalism. Other important developments were rapid technological progress and industrialization driven by the scientific method, an associated swift rise in national populations, and a growing insistence that the citizen owed a duty to defend the state.

These forces took form during the course of the nineteenth and early twentieth centuries in a military revolution focused on mass conscript armies of ideologically motivated citizens, armed with mass-produced, long-range weapons of incredible killing power, and logistically sustained by industrialized economies that could maintain armies on distant fronts almost indefinitely. This produced a form of war where the absolute defeat of the enemy was the objective, and the entire population of the opposing state became potential targets.

## The Napoleonic Legacy

The second half of the eighteenth century in Europe was characterized by comparatively 'limited' warfare. The spread of the rationalist values of the Enlightenment, and the lingering memory of the horrors of the religious wars of the seventeenth century were influential in moderating the conduct of warfare. Socio-economic factors were also important. The dynastic states of the period had limited tax and recruiting bases.

All states faced major difficulties both in recruiting and retaining soldiers. Military service was not popular and most armies relied upon a combination of long-serving professionals and foreign mercenaries. Such professionals were expensive to recruit and train, and governments encouraged their generals not to risk such expensive assets in pitched battles.

Military factors also tended towards limited war. The linear warfare of the age required soldiers to have great training and discipline, and such trained troops were too valuable to be lightly thrown away. Fighting in line or square meant that infantry could only move very slowly, making it difficult to take opposing armies by surprise or to pursue them to the point of destruction. The ferocious discipline of armies encouraged desertion, making generals reluctant to order their troops to an unrelenting pursuit that might turn a limited battlefield success into absolute victory.

The horrors of the wars of the previous century also meant that commanders were reluctant to allow their soldiers to pillage. This meant that armies had to carry all their supplies with them, or else amass huge stockpiles of supplies at depots in advance, to which they were subsequently tied. Supply limitations and poorly developed road networks also restricted the size of the armies that states could put into the field.

The basis for change occurred in 1792, with the creation of the French Republic. To defend itself against its many enemies, the revolutionary regime embraced a radical new approach to the conduct of war, including the creation of a citizen army raised by conscription, the beginnings of economic regimentation and large-scale war production, as well as ideological warfare and indoctrination.

Unlike the limited war of the eighteenth century, the purpose of ideological war became the complete overthrow of the enemy. Rather than minor territorial gains, the objective of war became massive gains or even outright annexation. In the Revolutionary and Napoleonic period the French army deliberately sought out battle, and the army's ability to manoeuvre quickly compelled the enemy to fight or retreat.

The French Revolution allowed France to raise mass armies, and these proved decisive in the early years of Napoleon's empire. Only the difficulties of supplying such huge numbers in the age before railways and mass production had previously limited army size. But by 1812, Napoleon was able to invade Russia with an army of nearly 600,000.

These huge armies raised new issues for generals and strategists. They were too large to be easily moved along a single road, but to spread them along several parallel roads left them vulnerable to being defeated in detail. The creation of the corps system overcame this danger, since each corps was essentially a small army of up to 50,000 men, with its own infantry, cavalry, and artillery, powerful enough to defend against the enemy army until the rest of the French army could be concentrated, yet small enough to advance rapidly.

These new massive armies posed another problem: they were difficult to feed and supply. The traditional supply depots used by eighteenth-century armies were soon left behind by the rapidly moving corps, yet the supplies required were so great that they would dramatically slow the army if it had to transport them. The solution was a reversion to pre-eighteenth century practice. This was for the army to 'live off the land', to forage ruthlessly in the territories through which it marched.

This in turn meant that war necessarily had to be offensive war. Such foraging could not be practised in one's own country without producing economic and political disaster, so it must be carried out abroad where the war could be made to pay for itself. However, this encouraged an attitude of callous indifference towards the sufferings of those in the lands so pillaged, and as a result triggered guerrilla war against the French.

With huge numbers of soldiers at their disposal, generals such as Napoleon Bonaparte felt able to squander their lives on a lavish scale in pursuit of military and political ambition. As revolutionary fervour faded and casualty lists grew, the huge French armies increasingly had to be maintained through the use of the totalitarian powers that the new modern state possessed, which were far greater than those of the old monarchical regime. The French successes with huge armies in the Napoleonic period encouraged the erroneous assumption that *only* numbers were decisive (see Box 2.1).

Unlike his eighteenth-century predecessors, Napoleon commanded armies that could move rapidly enough to *force* their opponents to give battle. He exploited this capacity to the full, deliberately seeking battle in order to defeat the enemy's army, and then destroy them with an unrelenting pursuit. Destroying a country's army in this way would then allow him to occupy and control the enemy's resources and leave them helpless to resist any political demands that France chose to make (Jones 1987: 350). A classic example of such warfare was the 1806 campaign against Prussia. The Prussian army was shattered at the twin battles of Jena-Auerstädt and then destroyed by a vigorous and continuous pursuit.

**BOX** 2.1   Napoleonic Warfare

At its apogee, the Napoleonic way of war threw armies of unprecedented size on country-smashing campaigns of conquest through decisive manoeuvre and, usually, battle. The forces employed to accomplish such heroic tasks were an assemblage of professional soldiers, fairly patriotic French conscripts, and sundry (but increasingly reluctant) foreign mercenaries. The soldiery was articulated into an autonomous *corps d'armée* and led with a variable operational artistry by the Zeus of modern war, the Corsican mastermind himself, variously aided and frequently abetted by his Imperial Headquarters (*very* approximate general staff) and, after 1804, his Marshalate. In its prime, which is to say in 1805–07, the Napoleonic style at least appeared to restore the power of swift decision as an instrument of foreign policy.

Gray (2003: 140)

## Clausewitz

Carl von Clausewitz (1780–1831) was a Prussian career soldier, with extensive experience in the conduct of war at all levels. His thought was influenced by the German nationalism of Schiller and Goethe and by numerous military writers, such as Berenhorst, who had argued that 'war is a natural social phenomenon, susceptible to analysis' (Nofi 1982: 16).

Clausewitz saw war as a political instrument, guided by rational decision-making, he emphasized that it depended on the willingness to inflict violence and to suffer casualties. The purpose of war was to seek battle and to impose one's will on the opponent through violence.

Clausewitz emphasized that victory would come when the opponent's centre of gravity, or the focal point of power, was captured or destroyed. The destruction of the adversary's armed forces was the key to political victory, but this destruction was moral, not *necessarily* physical. It was the destruction of the opponent's capacity to resist, though for Clausewitz decisive battle was the surest way to achieve this outcome, and the heart of the enemy army was normally the decisive centre of gravity. Though tactics and strategies could be pursued that were designed to create a decisive advantage on the battlefield, for Clausewitz, numbers were ultimately decisive if all other things were equal. For many, this logic would be decisively demonstrated in the Prussian victories over Austria in 1866 and France in 1870.

In time Clausewitz's ideas would become decisively influential, though many of his disciples failed to note the caveats in some of his arguments, and they underplayed his emphasis on the power of the defensive in war. Although reflecting the lessons of Napoleonic warfare, Clausewitz's thinking was subtle and imaginative enough to remain of relevance throughout the period of industrialized mass warfare, and into the age of nuclear weapons and limited war (see Box 2.2).

 **BOX** 2.2   Clausewitz's Key Ideas

- War is a normal part of politics, differing only in its means.
- War is an act of violence designed to achieve otherwise unattainable goals.
- Each age creates its own form of war.
- Since war involves people, it is inherently unpredictable.
- Victory is of no value unless it is a means to achieve a political objective.
- Other things being equal, numbers are ultimately decisive.

**Key Points**

- The Napoleonic period saw the emergence of mass armies produced by conscription.
- Napoleonic warfare focused on seeking decisive battle in order to destroy the opponent's army and capacity to resist.
- Ideology and nationalism helped to produce a more ruthless form of warfare and generated resistance by guerrilla war in many countries.

## The Industrialization of War

During the nineteenth century, warfare became industrialized in two important senses. Modern technology was applied to the production of more sophisticated weaponry, but in addition a wide variety of developments in essentially civilian technologies proved immensely important for the future conduct of war. Weaponry, ammunition, and all the other material of war could now be mass produced. Armies of much greater size could therefore be sustained on campaign. Small developments such as the ability to store tinned food made it easier to provide food supplies for campaigning, even in harsher winter months. Supplies could be moved quickly to the front in great quantities using the new railways. The first rail journey was made in 1825; by 1846 Prussia was able to move an army corps, with all its equipment, 250 miles in two days, rather than the two weeks a march would have required (Preston and Wise 1970: 244).

The use of railways meant not only that soldiers could be moved quickly, but that they remained relatively fit and unexhausted at the end of their journey, an important consideration with armies largely composed of reservists. Railways could be used to move wounded troops to rear-area hospitals, thereby improving their chances of survival. They could also bring replacements and reinforcements on a more regular basis. In 1870, Prussia invaded France with an army twice the size of the historically massive one Napoleon had led into Russia 60 years earlier. The much smaller French army, which had not been able to mobilize quickly enough, was simply overwhelmed. By 1914, the forces employed had doubled again.

The strategic value of railways was quickly realized. France moved 120,000 men to Italy during its 1859 war with Austria. Two years later the utility of railways for strategic advantage was clearly demonstrated in the opening campaign of the American Civil War. In July 1861, the movement of Johnson's Valley Army to Manassas enabled the Confederacy to achieve numerical parity and to win the Battle of First Manassas, when a defeat might have led to an almost immediate end to the Civil War. The United States subsequently organized a Military Railway Department, which played an important role in the ultimate Union victory in the war. However, this was not before the Confederacy had used the railway system to achieve important strategic advantages in the Kentucky campaign of 1862 and Chickamauga campaign of 1863. The Union countered the Chickamauga setback with a massive rail movement of reinforcements to relieve besieged Chattanooga. During the Franco–Prussian War of 1870, the superior Prussian use of railways enabled it to heavily outnumber the opposing French armies and overwhelm them.

Another civilian technology of immediate military importance was the telegraph, which allowed political leaderships and theatre commanders to maintain communications with army leaders over distances that would previously have meant delays of days or weeks in communicating orders.

During the course of the nineteenth century, a series of crucial developments in weapons technology transformed both strategy and tactics. Infantry weapons were revolutionized by the introduction of rifled gun barrels, smokeless cartridges, breech-loading, and eventually magazine weapons. Rifled weapons were far more accurate, and infantry could now hit their targets at ranges of several hundred yards, without necessarily exposing themselves to counter-fire. Rifled weapons rapidly proved their superiority in the early stages of the American Civil War, and breech-loaders became standard in European armies after the Prussian success with using them in the 1866 Austro–Prussian War. By 1884, however, the development of the Maxim machine gun produced an effective weapon which would revolutionize tactics.

During the 1860s rifled artillery also became the norm, and even muzzle-loading examples had ranges of two miles. By 1870, Prussia had produced efficient breech-loading rifled artillery, which outranged those of their French opponents, giving them a huge tactical advantage. In the 1890s, quick-firing technology increased the effectiveness of artillery still further.

The experience of the American Civil War (1861–1865) and Franco–Prussian War (1870–1871) demonstrated that these new weapons made it extremely difficult for infantry to close successfully with their enemy and that they suffered very heavy casualties if circumstances forced them to carry out such attacks. Battles such as Malvern Hill, Fredericksburg and Gettysburg in the American Civil War, and Gravelotte in the Franco–Prussian War, were characterized by infantry suffering very heavy casualties against prepared defenders. When manoeuvrability was lost and the enemy entrenched, the difficulties for the attacker became even greater, as the final months of the Civil War in the east demonstrated. The search for decisive victory encouraged a greater willingness to target civilians (see Box 2.3).

On the evidence of the Prussian wars of 1866 and 1870, European strategists became convinced that mass armies, rapidly transported to the military theatre by train, and manoeuvring swiftly thereafter, would guarantee quick victory to the side prepared to take the offensive. Overlooked was the danger posed if the defender also mobilized rapidly and used railways as efficiently to mass defenders in the attacking army's path (Quester 1977: 80). The wars of the mid-nineteenth century had provided mixed lessons. The Crimean War and Franco–Austrian War had seen the early use of rifled weapons and railways, but in many ways had been characteristically

 **BOX** 2.3   Colonial Warfare

Although histories of war tend to focus on the collisions between the major powers in the nineteenth century, for many states—notably Britain, France, and Spain—colonial and imperial campaigns against non-European enemies absorbed much of their military energies and attention. Such conflicts were often characterized by extreme brutality. Decisive victories for the European powers were rare and were invariably followed by years of indecisive guerrilla warfare. Colonial commanders frequently resorted to massacres and the deliberate destruction of the local population's homes and food supplies in order to undermine their opponents' guerrilla campaigns. The contemporary military writer C. E. Callwell argued that 'in small wars, one is sometimes forced into committing havoc that the laws of regular warfare do not sanction' (Porch 2001). It was a form of war from which European generals derived few lessons for European war, yet it was a precursor of the total war of the first half of the twentieth century, and a style of war that in some ways would be echoed in the so-called 'New Wars' that followed the end of the cold war.

Napoleonic conflicts. The Austro–Prussian War of 1866 had seen the use of mass armies and the importance of technological superiority, but had otherwise demonstrated none of the elements of total war. This was not the case with the Franco–Prussian War, which saw not only the effective use of staff work, railways, and the telegraph, but also heavy casualties produced by new long-range rifled weaponry. Ominously the French defeat had also triggered political revolution and regime change in France, guerrilla warfare against the Prussians, and often savage reprisals by the occupying German forces.

European observers also failed to take regard of the warnings from outside Europe. Colonial warfare was often notably savage but indecisive. In addition, a number of the large-scale wars fought outside Europe in the second half of the nineteenth century demonstrated many of the features of twentieth-century total war. The American Civil War was an ideological struggle to the death between two incompatible nationalisms, involving the use of mass conscription and a wide range of novel technologies, including rifled weapons, steam-ships, landmines, barbed wire, and observation balloons. Over 20 per cent of the Southern population fought in the war, and the Confederacy enlisted nearly 90 per cent of its available military manpower. Casualties were extremely heavy on both sides and Union forces deliberately targeted the southern civilian population in the Atlanta and Shenandoah campaigns of 1864, with General Sherman declaring: 'we are not only fighting hostile armies, but a hostile people and must make old and young, rich and poor, feel the hard hand of war' (Janda 1995:15). However, for the most part it was property rather than the lives of civilians that was targeted (O'Connell 1989: 201). Even more savage was the Great Paraguayan War between Brazil, Argentina, and Paraguay, which resulted in the death of over half of Paraguay's male population. These lessons were repeated in the Russo–Japanese War, characterized by massive armies, horrendous casualties, battlefronts of enormous length, and battles that went on day and night, for weeks on end.

 **Key Points**

- In the nineteenth century, the Industrial Revolution dramatically altered the conduct of war.
- Civilian technologies such as railways, steamships, the telegraph, and mass production made it possible to raise, equip, and control huge armies.
- New weapons such as rifled and breech-loading weapons, machine guns, armoured warships, mines, and submarines appeared.
- Governments sought to mobilize their populations to support the war effort.
- Because tactics were slow to change, heavy casualties were typical.

## Naval Warfare

Naval warfare went through an equally dramatic revolution during the nineteenth century. During the Napoleonic Wars, warships were made of wood and powered by the wind. As the century progressed, they were increasingly armoured in metal, equipped with long-range rifled weapons, and, most importantly, given engines that enabled them to operate independently of the wind. In 1822, General Paixans published *Nouvelle force maritime*, in which he argued that ships armed with explosive shells and protected with armour plate would be able to annihilate the existing wooden, cannon-armed warships (McNeil 1982: 226). The European navies began adopting such naval artillery in the 1830s and steam engines were introduced in the 1840s. The application of armour plate soon followed.

It was France that led the way in naval design in the mid-nineteenth century, with Britain being reluctant to encourage developments that might challenge her supremacy at sea. For decades warships had combined sail and steam propulsion, but as guns became more powerful, they needed to be based in revolving turrets, for which masts and sails were an obstacle. Britain launched the first battleship without any sails in 1873.

Although warship design was undergoing rapid evolution, strategic thinking about naval warfare was slow to evolve. Only towards the end of the century did significant developments take place. In 1890, Alfred Mahan published *The Influence of Seapower on History, 1660–1783*. Mahan argued that naval power had always been crucial in history, that the purpose of a great power's navy was to attain command of the sea, and that the way to achieve this was to concentrate naval capabilities in a powerful battle fleet and to seek out and destroy the major battle fleet or fleets of the enemy.

New schools of naval thought were emerging, which were unsettling to traditional naval commanders. For example the *Jeune École* in France argued that new systems such as torpedo boats would make commerce raiding the primary form of naval warfare in the future. Proponents of the new technologies argued that the massive battle fleets of countries like Britain would be made obsolete.

These ideas alarmed proponents of traditional naval power in Britain, Germany, and Japan. Navalists, such as Colomb in Britain, Von Maltzen in Germany, and Saneyuki in Japan, argued that sea power would continue to dominate the world, because of its inherent advantages of mobility and flexibility. Admiral Columb's *Naval Warfare: Its Ruling Principles and Practices Historically Treated* appeared at the same time as Mahan's book and argued that naval supremacy was critical for effective power projection, like Mahan insisting that battle fleets would dominate the sea and thereby the world.

Mahan's ideas contrasted with those contained in the geopolitics of Sir Halford Mackinder, who argued that world domination would go to the land power that controlled the Eurasian land mass in the era of railways. His theory downplayed the importance of naval power in the contemporary world. The proponents of naval power envisaged war at sea in terms strongly reminiscent of key features of Napoleonic land warfare. Once the main enemy battle fleet had been located and destroyed, command of the sea could then be exploited by the protection of trade, the destruction of the enemy's trade, and the projection of military power ashore.

A different view was offered by the British naval theorist, Sir Julian Corbett. Corbett argued that sea power was no more than a means to a political end. It was therefore important for a state to have a maritime strategy that was in tune with its political aspirations. However, Corbett was well aware that sea power on its own could not overwhelm a strong and resolute land power. Sea power had its limits, and a major naval power like Britain had historically always needed continental allies with land power at their disposal. He also argued that there was far more to maritime strategy than simply the pursuit of decisive battles, emphasizing the crucial importance of trade protection, commerce raiding, amphibious warfare, and transport of armies by sea.

In practice, armoured fleet action did not prove historically decisive. Only in the 1905 Japanese victory over Russia at Tsushima did such a victory occur. During the First World War, most of the new technologies failed to be decisive and simply made the fleet commanders more cautious. Britain imposed a naval blockade on Germany, which ultimately made a major contribution to the Allied victory. Britain also sought to bring the main German fleet to battle, but the encounters at Dogger Bank in 1915 and Jutland in 1916 were not immediately decisive. Jutland was a tactical victory for the German fleet, but ultimately a strategic victory for the British, since the German fleet never again challenged the British and was therefore unable to counter the Allied blockade. In fact, Jutland would turn out to be the last fleet action between battleships in history.

Germany turned instead to submarine warfare, and submarine campaigns would be vital in both world wars. By late 1917, British merchant shipping losses were becoming almost unsustainable, but as would happen in the Second World War, the introduction of the convoy system, along with better tactics and equipment, allowed the allies to defeat the German submarine challenge. In the end, neither the *navalists* nor the *Jeune École* were vindicated by the outcome of the war at sea, which saw the battle fleets prove largely impotent. The torpedo proved a crucial, but not a war-winning weapon.

Nevertheless sea power, understood in Corbett's terms, was important to the outcome of the First World War. Allied naval superiority allowed them to seize Germany's overseas colonies, and to impose the ultimately devastating blockade. It also allowed the Allies to transport enormous quantities of men and material from outside Europe to the war zone, including one million French soldiers and two million American troops.

---

 **Key Points**

- Naval technology was revolutionized during the nineteenth century.
- Steam power gave navies even greater flexibility and manoeuvrability.
- Heavy guns in revolving turrets, plus armoured warships produced a new generation of all-gun ironclad battleships.
- Mahan argued that fleets of such warships would dominate the seas, while the *Jeune École* insisted that submarines and torpedo boats would be decisive.

---

## Total War

By the beginning of the twentieth century, the major powers had come to accept the Clausewitzian idea that the threat and use of war were appropriate instruments of political purpose in the industrial era. The experience of the European wars of 1864, 1866, and 1870 encouraged the great powers to believe that any future war between the major powers would be both short and decisive.

By 1914, the political, economic, social, technological, and doctrinal trends of the nineteenth century had coalesced into a recipe for catastrophe. Doctrinally, armies were convinced of the virtues of Napoleonic warfare—mass armies, seeking out the army of the adversary, enveloping it, destroying it, and then pursuing the remnants of enemy forces until ability to resist any political demands had been crushed. Conscription and nationalism would provide the mass armies, which would be transported and supplied using the railway networks and the industrialized economies of mass production. Rapid movement, combined with the killing power of advanced weaponry, would deliver swift victory to the army that could mobilize and manoeuvre most efficiently.

The reality was that by 1914 the battlefield had grown in size enormously in comparison to the Napoleonic era, and so had the armies that occupied it. By the winter of 1914, the trench line on the western front stretched from Switzerland to the English Channel. There were no flanks to go round, and no way of 'enveloping' the enemy army, which by this period consisted of over three million men on each side. Nor could the armies move as rapidly as the era of railways and aeroplanes might suggest. In 1914, warfare was still not fully mechanized. The German army advanced into Belgium and France in 1914 with fewer than 7,000 motor vehicles, but with 726,000 horses and 150,000 wagons (Addington 1994: 104).

Armed with powerful defensive weapons such as machine guns and long-range artillery, protected by trenches and barbed wire, and supplied with all the resources that the railways could deliver from a mobilized industrial economy, defending armies could not be swiftly shattered and dispersed in the Napoleonic fashion. The defending forces enjoyed an unprecedented ratio of force to space, making the stalemate which followed virtually inevitable. Once this stalemate had been created, it became a war not of rapid military offensives, but of 'economic and human endurance' (Quester 1977: 114).

Instead the enemy had to be worn down by brutal frontal assaults that produced enormous casualty figures, while technological advances were sought which might break the battlefield stalemate. Germany attacked with poison gas at Ypres in 1915, while the British used the first tanks in the closing stage of the Battle of the Somme in 1916.

The conflict also saw war moving into a new dimension as air power became increasingly important. Aircraft were used for reconnaissance from the beginning of the war, and fighters evolved to destroy the reconnaissance aircraft. As the war continued, aircraft were increasingly used for tactical fire and bombing support to ground forces, and eventually for long-range strategic bombing. In their reconnaissance and raiding roles, the aircraft of the First World War essentially took on the role played by light cavalry in the Napoleonic period, just as tanks took on the role previously played by heavy cavalry.

Increasingly too, warfare became more total in its scope and application. Because it was so difficult to break through in the main theatre of war, the geographical scope of war expanded, as the combatants sought to place additional pressure on the opponent by opening new theatres of operations, such as Italy, the Balkans, and the Middle East.

The expansion of the geographical scope of war was accompanied by a greater willingness to deliberately target non-combatants. In the First World War this was seen in the use of unrestricted submarine warfare, with merchant ships being sunk without the crews being given a chance to take to the lifeboats, as Germany attempted to prevent France and Britain from being supplied by sea. It was seen also in the blockade of Germany, which made a critical contribution to Germany's military collapse in the autumn of 1918 but also caused enormous civilian suffering and death. Both Germany and Britain inaugurated the long-range bombing of cities by aircraft.

Major war increasingly came to involve much of the manpower, and material and moral resources of the state. Any object whose destruction promised to weaken the war effort of the enemy came to be seen as a legitimate target. Warfare was increasingly directed as much against the civilians and industries that produced the weapons of war, as against the soldiers who actually used them. The idea of illegitimate objectives or targets, of criteria of justness and proportionality, increasingly came to be seen as irrelevant to the conduct of modern war, moving the major powers closer to total war.

Totality in warfare can be assessed by a number of elements, including: the type of weaponry employed; the strategy and tactics used; the proportion of a state's resources that are committed; the degree to which every human and material resource of the opponent is seen as a legitimate target; and the extent to which social and cultural pressures towards unrestricted warfare exist.

The elements of totality in warfare that had become prominent in the First World War came into full flower in the Second. Once again the combatants mobilized their military, economic, and human resources to the maximum extent possible. Conscription was now extended beyond the men called up in the First World War, to embrace also the female population. Women took the place of men in agriculture and industry, and they also served in huge numbers in the armed forces in non-combatant roles. In some cases, such as the Soviet Air Force, they also served as combatants. Industry and the merchant navies were taken under government control and subordinated to the war effort. Rationing was introduced to conserve supplies of vital commodities such as food and oil. Germany not only drew on its own population but, by the use of conscript and slave labour, on that of its enemies as well. The social totality of war increased still further with the systematic use of censorship and propaganda; the promotion of nationalism and demonization of the enemy; and the restriction or imprisonment of groups deemed to have suspect loyalties, such as conscientious objectors or citizens of foreign descent (see Box 2.4).

At the strategic and tactical level, the Second World War saw the implementation of military doctrines designed to restore the manoeuvre and offensive capacity that had been so conspicuously absent for most of the First. Germany scored dramatic successes with its blitzkrieg tactics from 1939–1941, in which combined arms tactics involving tanks, infantry, and dive-bombers sought to bypass and disrupt enemy resistance, rather than to destroy it through frontal battles of attrition (see Box 2.5).

The effectiveness of blitzkrieg owed much to the inferior doctrine of the opposing British and French armies. The allies outnumbered the Germans in tanks in the campaign of 1940 and their tanks were superior in quality. However, the French viewed the tank as an infantry support weapon, as they had in 1918, while the Germans concentrated them in armoured divisions, with a view to rapid mechanized offensives. Germany also integrated its air power to support its ground offensives. The Luftwaffe was designed for tactical support of the army, a feature that would disadvantage it in the strategic bombing campaign against Britain in 1940–1941, but which made it highly effective in the blitzkrieg land campaigns of 1939–1941.

As with the First World War, technological advances prior to and during the war were crucial in a way that had not been typical in earlier wars. Radar helped the RAF win the Battle of Britain in 1940, while the use of the Anti-Submarine Detection technology ASDIC (sonar) and aircraft carriers were crucial in the anti-submarine detection war in the Battle of the Atlantic. Nuclear weapons played a key role in bringing about the unconditional surrender of Japan. German technological breakthroughs, such as the ME262 jet fighter, V-1 cruise missile, and V-2 ballistic missile, became operational too late in the war to affect its outcome. In the European

**BOX** 2.4   Total War

In the long history of warfare, it is natural that some wars will be less limited than others. The causes, the objectives of the belligerents, their cultures and the history of their previous interactions, the beliefs and values of the era, the prospects for victory, the possibility of outside intervention—these and many other factors influence the manner and means of waging war.

Totality in war is a relative rather than an absolute concept. Total war in the absolute sense would mean fighting without any restrictions. After the experience of Germany's defeat in the First World War, Erich Ludendorff, former Chief of Staff of the German armies on the western front, remained unconvinced by those in the interwar period who argued that a particular technology such as tanks, aircraft, or poison gas would bring swift victory in a future war. Nor did he believe that a tactical or strategic doctrine such as blitzkrieg would be able to do so.

For Ludendorff, the key to victory in war between industrialized nations was to follow to its brutally logical conclusion. War should therefore be characterized by total mobilization of all the military, economic, and human resources of the state. The enemy's civilian population should be deliberately targeted, and one's own civilians would suffer similar assault. Mobilization of the population should therefore embrace ideological features to sustain the war effort, and a political dictatorship to focus all the state's energy on winning the war.

In total war, governments are as demanding of their own citizens as they are ruthless towards their enemies. States draw on every natural resource that they can successfully mobilize, and treat virtually every element of the adversaries' society as a legitimate target, using all the weapons that are available to them. The citizens of the state are obliged to serve in the armed forces or participate in the production of war material; civil and political rights are constrained; the economy is subordinated to the war effort; every weapon, no matter how indiscriminate or terrible, is utilized; and the armed forces, industrial capacity, and the unarmed citizens of the opponent are deemed legitimate targets, because they all contribute to the enemy war effort in either tangible or psychological ways. This logic reached its height with the systematic area bombing of civilians in the Second World War, and in the cold war plans to inflict genocidal 'assured destruction' in a retaliatory nuclear strike.

In practice, wars invariably fall short of totality in one or more dimensions, such as: geographical scope; weaponry employed; mobilization of national resources and population; attitude towards neutrals; targeting strategies, and so on.

 **BOX** 2.5   Blitzkrieg

Blitzkrieg, or 'lightning war', was the term used to describe the successful German tactics for armoured offensives in the opening phase of the Second World War. It was an attempt to overcome the defensive dominance and static warfare characteristic of most of the First World War. Like Napoleonic warfare, it was a triumph based on superior doctrine rather than technological advantage. The theory was propounded by Basil Liddell Hart, Charles de Gaulle, and Heinz Guderian during the interwar years.

Available tanks were concentrated in a limited number of Panzer (armour) divisions, along with antitank and anti-aircraft guns, armoured cars for reconnaissance, and infantry support. The emphasis was on rapid advances designed to dislocate the enemy by breaking into the rear and throwing them off-balance. The objective was deep penetration on a narrow front. Certain supporting technologies were important, for example radios in tanks for communication and co-ordination. Because the speed of the advance made it difficult for heavy artillery support to keep up, tactical airpower was used as a form of artillery to help the breakthrough. The Ju-87 Stuka dive-bomber attacked defenders' positions and also attacked rear-area command and supply positions, reinforcements, and even refugee columns in order to create confusion and panic ahead of the advancing Panzer divisions. A crucial requirement for successful blitzkrieg is that the attacker must achieve air superiority over the battlefield.

war it was once again mass and industrial power that proved ultimately decisive, along with Germany's strategic problem of fighting a two-front war against the American and Soviet superpowers.

Whereas in the First World War the bombing of civilians had been a secondary tactic in support of the conventional ground war, in the Second, it became one of the primary war-fighting strategies. The opponent's cities and populations were deliberately targeted in an attempt to break the will to resist. By destroying the enemy's productive capacity, such attacks sought to undermine the ability of its armed forces to operate effectively. This logic reached its peak with the nuclear attacks on Japan in August 1945, when civilian targets were deliberately annihilated in order to compel the Japanese government to end further resistance in the Pacific theatre.

For much of the war, strategic bombing failed to produce the dramatic results that prewar advocates such as Douhet had predicted. Losses among the attacking aircrew were extremely heavy, forcing both the Germans and British to carry out their attacks at night, making precision bombing virtually impossible. In the closing months of the European war, as German air defences became increasingly suppressed, the allies shifted their attacks to key production 'bottlenecks', such as oil refineries. Such attacks proved far more effective in undermining Germany's war-fighting capacity than the earlier assaults on its overall economic capability had been.

The Second World War was global in scope, and naval power was more crucial to the outcome than it had been in the First World War. As island nations, both Britain and Japan depended on resources imported by sea. In the Battle of the Atlantic, Germany sought to strangle the Anglo-American war effort by destroying the merchant shipping bringing supplies, weapons, and soldiers across the Atlantic to Britain and into the Mediterranean. Although ultimately unsuccessful, the German U-boat campaign came close to success. In the Pacific, a similar American submarine campaign had brought the Japanese war effort to its knees by the summer of 1945.

Germany succeeded in the early part of the war because land-based air power compensated for its naval weakness. British naval losses to German air attack in the Crete campaign were equivalent to a major fleet action. However, once Allied fleets had acquired effective anti-aircraft weapons and carrier-based fighter protection, navies were able to resume their offensive role once more. The early phases of the Second World War demonstrated that both on land and at sea, obtaining air superiority, or at the very least, denying it to the enemy, had become an essential prerequisite to successful military operations. Air power on its own could not guarantee victory, but its absence guaranteed defeat. By the end of the war, all major states had come to recognize that 'combined arms' or 'joint' warfare was the key to success in modern industrial war.

Amphibious operations were a minor feature of the First World War, and the largest such operation, the landings at Gallipoli in 1915, was a tactical and strategic failure. In the Second World War in contrast, amphibious operations were crucial to the final outcome in both the European and Pacific theatres. The invasions of North Africa, Sicily, Italy, and France saw major amphibious landings allow the Allies to seize the strategic initiative, while the American 'island-hopping' campaign in the Pacific outflanked and overcame Japanese power in the region, while ultimately moving American forces close enough to Japan to launch devastating conventional and nuclear attacks on the Japanese home islands.

In both the antisubmarine and amphibious offensive campaigns, the role of the aircraft carrier was of decisive importance. The aircraft carrier had replaced the battleship as the primary naval weapons platform, and the Second World War saw five major aircraft carrier battles in the Pacific war, as well as 22 other major naval engagements. In the European war, sea power was a crucial, but not a sufficient cause of the Allied victory, the Soviet land offensives being decisive. In the Pacific, however, sea power was decisive in the ultimate Allied victory.

The Second World War also saw large-scale parachute offensives. These operations were crucial in the German capture of Crete in 1941 and the Allied invasion of Normandy in 1944, as well as the Rhine crossings in 1945. The failure of the Arnhem operation in 1944, however, was a demonstration of the limitations of such forces. Unless reached by substantial heavy reinforcements quickly, parachute forces were too lightly armed to hold out against armoured forces, and large-scale parachute operations did not become a feature of the post-1945 environment, though they were employed in the 1956 Anglo–French Suez war against Egypt.

---

 **Key Points**

- The First World War was a conflict between mass armies, which technology made difficult to defeat decisively.

- New technologies such as chemical weapons and tanks were used in an attempt to regain manoeuvre and decision.

- All of a state's economic and human resources increasingly came to be seen as legitimate targets.

- By the Second World War, airpower had become crucial in support of forces on the battlefield and as the means to launch strategic attacks against the opposing homeland. Aircraft carriers emerged as the decisive naval weapon.

- Technology, amphibious landings, and parachute operations sought to avoid the deadlock characteristic of the First World War.

---

## Nuclear Weapons and Revolutionary Warfare

Total war reached a peak with the Second World War. The ultimate example was the destruction of the Japanese cities of Hiroshima and Nagasaki in 1945. Yet paradoxically, the unleashing of the nuclear weapon ushered in an era of limited warfare. During the 1950s, as the United States and Soviet Union acquired larger and larger stockpiles of increasingly accurate and destructive nuclear weapons, it became clear that a full-scale war between the two countries would be mutually suicidal.

As a result, both states saw it as essential to avoid a full-scale war at all costs. Therefore, they sought to exercise restraint in their relations with each other and to avoid taking military actions that risked escalating to a full-scale conflict which might go nuclear. For the same reason, they sought to restrain the policies and war strategies of their allies and other states over which they had influence, in order to avoid being dragged into conflicts originating elsewhere.

A full-scale nuclear war would involve mutual assured destruction—a simultaneous genocide that bore no relation to the idea of war as a political act in the terms in which Clausewitz and his successors understood it.

However, while it was understood that strategic nuclear weapons could not perform a meaningful war-fighting role, their possession in large numbers was seen as necessary in order to deny a unilateral military and political advantage to the other side. They became central to the strategic doctrine of deterrence.

Tactical, and to some extent theatre nuclear weapons, however, were seen as retaining a function in war. With more limited nuclear yields, and assuming they were not employed in overwhelming numbers, it was believed that they could play a role in great power war, as long as a final escalation to a full-scale strategic nuclear exchange could be avoided. The dangers involved in such an ambiguous strategy were obvious, and the evidence from war games manoeuvres conducted throughout the cold war suggested that once the nuclear threshold was crossed, escalation to full-scale strategic conflict would be virtually impossible to prevent.

Conflicts during the cold war were therefore characterized by restraint shown by the nuclear superpowers in terms of the kinds of wars they fought. In Korea and Vietnam, for example, the United States limited its war effort in terms of the weaponry used, the geographical scope of the war, and the objectives pursued; all restraints characteristic of limited rather than total war. During the 1973 Arab–Israeli War, the United States and Soviet Union pressured their allies to end the fighting, because they were concerned that it might escalate and draw them into the conflict on opposing sides.

The reluctance of the most powerful states to employ the techniques of total war created an opportunity for their opponents to employ asymmetric tactics and strategies against them successfully. In the Korean War, comparative American restraint meant that the vastly less well-equipped Chinese forces were able to achieve a military stalemate and preserve the independence of communist North Korea. In the Vietnam War, despite an even more dramatic disparity in military resources between North Vietnam and the United States, the North was able to deny the US victory. Once it had forced the US to withdraw from South Vietnam, it achieved its objective of the unification of Vietnam under a communist government. The Soviet Union encountered similar problems in its war in Afghanistan.

The cold war period was therefore characterized by smaller-scale conventional wars and by campaigns of insurgency and counterinsurgency. Conventional wars tended to be limited in their outcomes and duration, and profoundly influenced by the geopolitical context of the cold war environment. The wars between Israel and its neighbours, as well as those between India and Pakistan, and Ethiopia and Somalia were typical of this pattern. However, these wars were unusual in one respect—they were inter-state conflicts. More typical was the prevalence of civil, rather than international war. Most wars in the second half of the twentieth century were civil wars and insurgencies, most notably in Africa and South East Asia.

 **Key Points**

- Nuclear weapons ended the era of total war.
- Major powers subsequently engaged only in limited war.
- Insurgency and counterinsurgency were more typical forms of war during the second half of the twentieth century.

**Critical Thinking**    Debating . . . Has war between the major powers become obsolete?

**For**

- *Costs of war.* The costs of war have risen dramatically and the potential gains have fallen. Weapons of mass destruction mean that the potential casualties and destruction a state would suffer outweigh any conceivable policy goal.

- *Other mechanisms available.* States have a variety of other diplomatic tools available to influence rivals, including sanctions and the UN.

- *Absence of decisive victory.* In recent decades great powers have found it increasingly difficult to achieve decisive military victories. In Vietnam, Afghanistan, and Iraq victory against far weaker opponents proved elusive.

**Against**

- *War creating issues still exist.* War between great powers may be less likely, but it is still possible. Such wars tend to be struggles for dominance of the international order. Great powers cannot opt out of such conflicts. Nuclear weapons certainly induce greater caution, but this would shape the form the war took, rather than its likelihood.

- *Irrational decisions.* War is not always a result of rational policy decision. War decisions are influenced by emotion and irrational factors. War has a metaphysical not just an instrumental dimension.

- *Historical precedent.* This is not the first time in history that the end of war has been predicted. For example, early-twentieth-century writers argued that technology and democracy had changed the situation. They were proved wrong.

 ## Conclusion: Postmodern War

The end of the cold war also ended the classic period of nuclear deterrence and was followed by a number of wars in Eastern Europe and Africa characterized by the employment of relatively low-tech weaponry, but with very heavy death tolls. Some of these conflicts were also marked by great savagery, leading some commentators to suggest that they were a novel form of war and that such wars would be characteristic of the post-cold war, postmodern world: that the era of industrialized great power war had passed.

It can be argued that global society is in the midst of a transition from modernity to postmodernity. The architecture of world order is changing as part of a long-term process and with it will change the associated institution of war, as happened in the earlier transition to modernity in the seventeenth century. The distinctively 'modern' state is evolving in the face of globalization, and shedding many of its responsibilities, including military responsibilities, to private actors.

This transition to postmodernity can be expected to influence war as a politico-cultural institution. 'Modern' war was conducted by the state. The postmodern era has seen a dispersal of control over organized violence to many forms of non-state actors. Modern wars were fought by formally organized, hierarchically structured, specialized armed forces of the state. Postmodern wars are fought by a disparate array of fighting forces, many of which are informal or private (i.e. non-state). These include guerrilla armies, criminal gangs, foreign mercenaries, kin/clan-based irregular

**BOX** 2.6   Revolution in Military Affairs

The nature and frequency of such revolutions is a matter of dispute. Andrew Marshall defines them in relation to technology, doctrine, and force structure, declaring that a Revolution in Military Affairs (RMA), is a major change in the nature of warfare brought about by the innovative application of new technologies which, combined with dramatic changes in military doctrine and operational and organizational concepts, fundamentally alters the character and conduct of military operations

Robertson (2000: 64)

Kapil Dek sees the second and third elements as the key, arguing that the 'historical record appears to suggest that technological change represents a relatively small part of the equation, the crucial element in most RMAs being conceptual in nature'.

Broader in concept than an RMA is the idea of a *military revolution*. Whereas many RMAs can be identified in history, true military revolutions are rare. Military revolutions are dynamically interactive social processes which, according to Williamson Murray, 'recast the nature of society and the state as well as of military organizations'.

Murray (1997: 71)

forces, paramilitary groups raised by local warlords, international peacekeepers, national armies, and de-territorialized terrorist networks. Some of these groups do not seek decisive battle in the Clausewitzian sense; in contrast, they avoid it in favour of protracted asymmetric conflict. The war objectives of such groups are usually as political as are those of states themselves, so that war has not lost its 'Clausewitzian' character. Indeed, where no such political rationale exists, it is arguable whether we can even speak of such conflicts as 'war' (see Box 2.6).

At the same time as the shift downwards towards more low-tech wars, the so-called 'revolution in military affairs' has seen the United States at the leading edge of a technology-based enhancement of conventional military capability (see Box 2.6).

The purposes and objectives of armed conflict are also changing. Modern wars originated in the pursuit of perceived national interests. Wars tended to be driven by geopolitical assumptions, such as those fought in defence of the balance of power. Postmodern wars are often focused on 'identity politics'. These wars may break out in an effort to pursue ethnic cleansing, or religiously inspired holy war. Such conflicts are often particularly ferocious, and may not have clearly defined beginnings and endings, but they are no less political. They are conducted with strategic objectives, such as the acquisition of control over valuable resources or of the determination of state policy.

The political economy of war-making is also being transformed. During the modern era, military forces were maintained by state-based production and financing systems, preferably organized on a national basis. Postmodern non-state institutions of violence tend to draw material sustenance not from such formal and centralized national economies and defence industries, but from private production and finance networks organized either locally or on a global scale. Such sources may include: plunder and theft; hostage-taking for ransom; extortion; drug trafficking; arms trafficking; money laundering; remittances and material support from relevant diaspora communities; foreign assistance; and the diversion of humanitarian aid. For many of the combatants, such wars are an end in themselves: they are 'military entrepreneurs' exploiting a new form of 'war economy'.

Postmodernity is perhaps continuing to loosen the grip that 'modern' war has had for the past two centuries. The emergence of nuclear weapons had already initiated this process by neutralizing the most powerful weapons possessed by the leading military powers, and encouraging a particular security policy restraint. Postmodernity may be reinforcing this process. Just as feudalism and modernity each produced their own distinctive forms of war, so the transition to postmodernity is producing its own unique politico-cultural form of organized violence, even while the *nature* of war remains constant.

War remains a purposeful instrument of political violence in many parts of the world, although decisive victory has become more elusive. In all ages, older forms of war and violence do not entirely disappear even as new forms gradually supplant them.

 ## Questions

1. How valid is it to argue that the French Revolution unleashed an era of unlimited warfare?
2. Evaluate the thesis that Clausewitz still has something worthwhile to teach students of war in the contemporary world.
3. In what ways was warfare in the nineteenth century significantly affected by advances in technology?
4. Is war a catalyst for significant social and political change, or a reflection of it?
5. What do you understand by the phrase 'total war'? Does modern history provide examples of such a conflict?
6. How would you define 'limited war'? Is limited nuclear war a contradiction in terms?
7. What do you understand by the concept of *either* 'sea power' or 'air power'?
8. To what extent have the objectives of war changed in the post-cold war world?
9. How useful is the distinction between 'revolutions in military affairs' and 'military revolutions' in understanding the evolution of modern war?
10. In what ways do the so-called 'new wars' of the post-cold war period differ from earlier forms of war?

 ## Further Reading

G. Best, *War and Society in Revolutionary Europe, 1770–1870* (**London: Fontana, 1982**) effectively captures the inter-relationships between politics, technology, and warfare during this turbulent and formative period.

J. Black, *War* (**London: Continuum, 2001**) gives an interesting and provocative exploration of the nature of war in the contemporary age and its likely evolution in the next few decades.

A. Gat, *Clausewitz and the Enlightenment: The Origins of Modern Military Thought* (**Oxford: Oxford University Press, 1993**) explores the intellectual origins of the revolutionary military thinking of the nineteenth century.

A. Jones, *The Art of War in the Western World* (**Chicago, IL: University of Illinois Press, 1987**) is an impressive and very readable single volume treatment of the development and evolution of the military art over the centuries.

C. Messenger, *The Art of Blitzkrieg* (**London: Ian Allan Ltd, 1976**) presents a lively analysis of the effectiveness of superior doctrine over numbers and technology, and a useful case study of the impact of military evolution.

H. Munkler, *The New Wars* (**Cambridge: Polity Press, 2005**) provides an insightful and thought-provoking analysis of postmodern warfare, with a historical depth lacking in most studies of this subject.

D. Porch, *Wars of Empire* (**London: Cassell, 2001**) is a very accessible and readable study of the 'little wars' of the nineteenth century, written by an acknowledged expert on colonial warfare and the French military experience in particular.

M. Waltzer, *Just and Unjust Wars* (London: Allen Lane, 1978) is a study in ethics, but is extremely useful in understanding traditional and contemporary approaches to the question of morality and warfare.

G. Wright, *The Ordeal of Total War 1939–1945* (New York: Harper & Row, 1968) brings out the scope and totality of the Second World War and the impact that it had on civilians as well as the military.

## Web Links

The Clausewitz Homepage **http://www.clausewitz.com/index.htm** is a comprehensive site for Clausewitz studies.

The US Army Centre for Military History **http://www.history.army.mil** is a very good source on American military history.

Naval Warfare Blog **http://navalwarfare.blogspot.co.uk** has excellent links to a wide range of naval warfare sources.

# 3

# Strategic Theory

THOMAS G. MAHNKEN

## Chapter Contents

 **Reader's Guide**

This chapter discusses strategic theory, which provides a conceptual understanding of the nature of war. It argues that the logic of war is universal. Although strategy is an art, it is one that can be studied systematically. The chapter begins by exploring the logic of strategy. It then discusses some of the most valuable concepts in strategic theory as contained in Carl von Clausewitz's *On War*. It briefly compares and contrasts these with the concepts contained in Sun Tzu's *Art of War* and the military writings of Mao Tse-Tung and jihadist writers, before considering and rebutting the main arguments about the obsolescence of classical strategic theory.

## Introduction

The logic of war and strategy is universal; it is valid at all times and in all places. This is primarily because war is a human activity, and human nature has remained unchanged in the face of material progress. The same passions that motivated those who lived millennia ago continue to drive us today. Although such strategic theorists as the nineteenth-century Prussian officer and philosopher Carl von Clausewitz and the ancient Chinese author Sun Tzu wrote from very different historical and cultural experiences and thus viewed strategy from unique perspectives, the phenomenon they described—war—is the same. It is the character and conduct of war—how it is waged, by whom, and for what ends—that has changed over time.

Strategic theory provides the conceptual foundation of an understanding of war. It offers a toolkit that can be used to analyse problems of war and peace. An understanding of theory equips the student with a set of concepts and questions to guide further study. As Clausewitz wrote, the purpose of theory is not to uncover fixed laws or principles, but rather to educate the mind:

> [Theory] is an analytical investigation leading to a close *acquaintance* with the subject; applied to experience—in our case, to military history—it leads to a thorough *familiarity* with

it . . . Theory will have fulfilled its main task when it is used to analyse the constituent elements of war, to distinguish precisely what at first sight seems fused, to explain in full the properties of the means employed and to show their probable effects, to define clearly the nature of the ends in view, and to illuminate all phases of warfare in a thorough critical inquiry. Theory then becomes a guide to anyone who wants to learn about war from books; it will light his way, ease his progress, train his judgment, and help him to avoid pitfalls . . . It is meant to educate the mind of the future commander, or, more accurately, to guide him in his self-education, not to accompany him to the battlefield; just as a wise teacher guides and stimulates a young man's intellectual development, but is careful not to lead him by the hand for the rest of his life.

Clausewitz (1989: 141)

In other words, Clausewitz suggests, we study strategic theory in order to learn how to think strategically.

Because the stakes in war are so high, strategy is a supremely practical endeavour. The most elegant theory is useless if it is inapplicable to real problems. Strategic theory succeeds or fails in direct proportion to its ability to help decision-makers understand problems of war and peace and formulate sound strategy. As the twentieth-century American strategist Bernard Brodie put it, 'Strategy is a field where truth is sought in the pursuit of viable solutions' (1973: 452–3).

## The Logic of Strategy

Strategy is ultimately about how to win wars. Any discussion of strategy must therefore begin with an understanding of war. As Clausewitz famously defined it, 'War is thus an act of force to compel our enemy to do our will' (1989: 75). Two aspects of this definition are notable. First, the fact that war involves force separates it from other types of political, economic, and military competition. Second, the fact that war is not senseless slaughter, but rather an instrument that is used to achieve a political purpose, differentiates it from other types of violence, such as criminality. Distinguishing war from non-war is important because it determines whether strategic theory can provide insight into the problem at hand.

It is the political context of war, and not the identity of those who wage it, that is its key characteristic (see Box 3.1). Empires, city-states, subnational groups, and transnational movements have all used force to preserve or aggrandize themselves. The fact that United Nations forces in Somalia in 1993 fought Mohammed Farah Aideed's Habr Gidr clan rather than a recognized state matters less than the fact that both sides were strategic actors possessing political objectives and that each sought to use force to compel the other. Similarly, the struggle against violent Islamic extremist groups such as al-Qaeda and its affiliates as well as the Islamic State of Iraq and Syria (ISIS) fits the classical definition of a war, in that both sides have political aims and are using military means to achieve them. It is, to be sure, a strange war, one waged by irregular forces with unconventional means. However, the fact that it is a violent clash of wills means that it is amenable to strategic analysis. Conversely, the use of force to curb criminal behaviour such as piracy is not war, because pirates seek material gains rather than political aims.

Strategy is about making force useable for political purposes. If tactics is about employing troops in battle and operational art is concerned with conducting campaigns, then strategy

**BOX** 3.1 War as a Political Instrument

War is a matter of vital importance to the State.

Sun Tzu (1963: 63)

It is clear, consequently, that war is not a mere act of policy, but a true political instrument, a continuation of political activity by other means.

Clausewitz (1989: 87)

War is only a branch of political activity; it is in no sense autonomous.

Clausewitz (1989: 606)

No major proposal required for war can be worked out of ignorance of political factors; and when people talk, as they often do, about harmful political influence on the management of war, they are not really saying what they mean. Their quarrel should be with policy itself not with its influence.

Clausewitz (1989: 608)

The object of war is a better state of peace.

Liddell Hart (1967: 351)

[Irregular warfare is] a violent struggle among state and non-state actors for legitimacy and influence over the relevant population(s).

Department of Defense Directive 3000.07 (2008: 1)

deals with using military means to fulfil the ends of policy. It is the essential link between political objectives and military force, between ends and means. As Germany demonstrated in two world wars, mastery of tactics and operations counts for little without a coherent or feasible strategy.

The logic of strategy applies not only in wartime, but also in peace. Edward Mead Earle, writing during the Second World War, argued that strategy was 'an inherent element of state-craft at all times' (Earle 1943: viii). Throughout history, states have formulated and implemented strategies for competing with their rivals in peacetime, including: Athens and Sparta in the third century BC; France and Great Britain from the eighteenth to the nineteenth centuries; Germany and Great Britain in the nineteenth and twentieth centuries; the United States and Great Britain in the nineteenth and early twentieth century; the United States and Japan during the first half of the twentieth century; and the United States and the Soviet Union during the second half of the twentieth century. Some, such as the Anglo–American rivalry, ended peacefully and amicably. Others, such as the Anglo–German competition, led to war. Still others, such as the US–Soviet competition, yielded conflicts on the periphery and an armed and sometimes uneasy peace between the central actors.

Strategy is, or rather should be, a rational process. As Clausewitz wrote, 'No one starts a war—or rather, no one in his senses ought to do so—without first being clear in his mind what he intends to achieve by that war and how he intends to conduct it' (1989: 579). In other words, successful strategy is based upon clearly identifying political goals, assessing one's comparative advantage relative to the enemy, calculating costs and benefits carefully, and examining the risks and rewards of alternative strategies.

Clausewitz's formulation acknowledges, however, that states sometimes go to war without clear or feasible aims or a strategy to achieve them. Statesmen have embarked on war for ill-defined aims. At other times, statesmen and soldiers have failed to develop a strategy that will readily translate into achieving political aims. In the absence of a coherent policy, strategy can become ineffective because it lacks direction.

Sound strategy is formulated by individuals, but all strategies are implemented by bureaucracies. As a result, even a rational strategy can fail in execution. It is often difficult to determine, even in retrospect, whether failure was the result of the poor execution of a sound strategy or a strategy that was fundamentally unsound. Historians will, for example, long debate whether the decision to disband the Iraqi army and ban the Ba'ath Party after the 2003 invasion of Iraq were mistakes in implementing an otherwise sound strategy, or whether the insurgency that followed the overthrow of Saddam Hussein was inevitable.

Strategy is more an art than a science. It is the realm of the probable rather than the certain. Sound strategy improves the chances of strategic success; it does not guarantee victory. Moreover, the range of strategic choice is inevitably constrained by material and political reality. The reciprocal action of the belligerents introduces further complications. In addition, war is rife with passion, inaccurate information, misperception, and chance:

> Efforts were . . . made to equip the conduct of war with principles, rules, or even systems. This did present a positive goal, but people failed to take adequate account of the endless complexities involved. As we have seen, the conduct of war branches out in almost all directions and has no definite limits; while any system, any model, has the finite nature of a synthesis. An irreconcilable conflict exists between this type of theory and actual practice.
>
> Clausewitz (1989: 134)

Or, as Sun Tzu put it more succinctly, 'In the art of war there are no fixed rules' (Sun Tzu 1963: 93). As a result, a military problem may have many—or no—potentially correct solutions rather than one optimal one.

The fact that strategy is more an art than a science doesn't mean that it cannot be studied systematically. Rather, the theory of strategy consists of concepts and considerations instead of fixed laws.

Military success by itself is insufficient to achieve victory. History contains numerous examples of armies that won all the battles and yet lost the war due to a flawed strategy. In the Vietnam War, for example, the US military defeated the Vietcong and North Vietnamese Army in every major engagement they fought. The United States nonetheless lost the war because civilian and military leaders never understood the complex nature of the war they were waging. Conversely, the United States achieved its independence from Britain despite the fact that the Continental Army won only a handful of battles.

It is axiomatic that policy drives strategy. Policymakers and senior officers nonetheless frequently misunderstand the relationship. During the 1999 Kosovo War, for example, US Secretary of State Madeleine Albright was wrong in arguing that '[u]p until the start of the conflict, the military served to back up our diplomacy. Now, our diplomacy serves to back up our military' (Isaacson 1999: 27). Similarly, Lieutenant General Charles A. Horner, at the time the commander of US Air Force units in Saudi Arabia, was wrong when he said that war 'should not be dragged out in an effort to achieve some political objective' (Gordon 1990: 1).

It is worth emphasizing that the primacy of politics applies not only to states, but also to other strategic actors. As Ayman al-Zawahiri, al-Qaeda's leader and chief theoretician, wrote in his book *Knights Under the Prophet's Banner*:

> If the successful operations against Islam's enemies and the severe damage inflicted on them do not serve the ultimate goal of establishing the Muslim nation in the heart of the Islamic world, they will be nothing more than disturbing acts, regardless of their magnitude, that could be absorbed and endured, even if after some time and with some losses.

Clausewitz would doubtless approve of Zawahiri's understanding of strategy, if not his goals.

The political context of warfare can in some cases extend to tactical actions, particularly when they hold the potential to change the character of a war. During the North Atlantic Treaty Organization (NATO) war over Kosovo in 1999, for example, a US B-2 bomber accidentally dropped three precision-guided munitions on the Chinese embassy in Belgrade, killing four. The incident was a mistake that the Chinese government interpreted as a deliberate act. Moreover, it was a tactical error with strategic consequences, triggering a diplomatic crisis between Washington and Beijing, disrupting moves to negotiate an end to the war, and prompting a halt to the bombing of targets in Belgrade for the next two weeks. Similarly, the abuse of Iraqi prisoners by a group of poorly trained and led guards at the Abu Ghraib prison in Iraq represented a strategic setback to American efforts to build legitimacy among the Iraqi population.

Although policy drives strategy, the capabilities and limitations of the military instrument also shape policy. As Clausewitz wrote, the political aim 'must adapt itself to its chosen means, a process which can radically change it' (1989: 87). To choose a ridiculous example to illustrate the point, it was one thing for Russia to invade Georgia in 2008; it would have been quite another for Georgia's tiny army to try to occupy Russia.

Just as it would be wrong to view war as nothing more than slaughter, it would be misleading to believe that force can be used in highly calibrated increments to achieve finely tuned effects. War has its own dynamics that makes it an unwieldy instrument, more a bludgeon than a rapier. The pages of history are full of wars in which soldiers and statesmen sought quick, decisive victories over their foes; militaries have actually achieved such results only rarely, however.

Interaction with the adversary can make it difficult to achieve even the simplest objective. As Clausewitz reminds us, 'War is not the act of a living force upon a lifeless mass but always the collision of two living forces' (1989: 4). In other words, just as we seek to use force to compel our adversary to do our will, so too will he attempt to use force to coerce us. Effectiveness in war thus depends not only on what we do, but also on what an opponent does. This interaction limits significantly the ability to control the use of military force.

---

 **Key Points**

- War is an act of force to compel your enemy to do your will.
- Strategy is about how to win wars. It is the essential link between political objectives and military force, between ends and means.
- Strategy is—or should be—a rational process.
- Strategy is more an art than a science.
- Interaction with the adversary makes it difficult to achieve even the simplest objective.

# Clausewitz's *On War*

Carl von Clausewitz's unfinished masterpiece, *On War*, should form the cornerstone of any understanding of strategic theory. Unfortunately, the book is all too often misunderstood. *On War* was left incomplete by the author's death from cholera in 1831. Book 1, Chapter 1 was the only part of the volume that Clausewitz considered complete. Like the Bible, *On War* is more frequently quoted than read, and more frequently perused than comprehended. It is not a book that can be understood fully after a single reading, but rather demands careful study and reflection, raising as many questions as it answers and forcing serious readers to grapple with the author's concepts.

Clausewitz's methodology, which distinguishes between 'war in theory' or 'absolute war' and war in reality, has led many mistakenly to identify him as an apostle of total war. In fact, he uses the approach of defining war in its ideal or pure form as a way of identifying the many considerations that shape war in reality. It is akin to a physicist examining mechanics in a frictionless environment or an economist describing an ideal market. In each case the observer is portraying the theoretical, not the real. In fact, Clausewitz argues that war can be fought for limited or unlimited aims with partial or total means.

As Hugh Smith has written, Clausewitz views war in four different contexts (Smith 2005: chapters 7–10). First and foremost, in his view war is ultimately about killing and dying. He is dismissive of the notion that war can be waged without bloodshed:

> Kind-hearted people might of course think that there was some ingenious way to disarm or defeat an enemy without too much bloodshed, and might imagine that this is the true goal of the art of war. Pleasant as it sounds, it is a fallacy that must be exposed: war is such a dangerous business that the mistakes which come from kindness are the very worst.
>
> Clausewitz (1989: 75)

Second, war is a contest between armies, generals, and states. Clausewitz invokes the metaphor of wrestling to describe war as a physical and mental competition, with each side trying to pin the other while simultaneously trying to avoid being pinned.

Third, war is an instrument of policy. It is not to be pursued for its own sake, but rather to serve the ends of the state.

Finally, he argues that war is a social activity. As someone who had lived through the French Revolution and fought in the Napoleonic Wars, he was acutely aware of the fact that social conditions mould the character and conduct of war.

A number of the concepts that Clausewitz introduces in *On War* are central to the study of strategy. These include the trinity, the need to understand the nature of a war, the difference between limited and unlimited wars, the rational calculus of war, and friction.

## The Trinity

Clausewitz's description of war is one of his most enduring legacies. He views war as a 'paradoxical trinity—composed of violence, hatred, and enmity . . . the play of chance and probability . . . and of its element of subordination'. He wrote that each of these three tendencies generally (but not always) corresponds to one of three groups in society: the people, the military, and the government (1989: 89). Passion is most often associated with the people, whose animosities move states to fight. Probability and chance are the realm of the military. Indeed, soldiers most constantly deal with uncertainty and friction. Reason is generally a characteristic of the government, which determines the aims of war and the means for waging it.

Clausewitz argued that the relative intensity of and relationships among these tendencies change according to the circumstances of the war:

> Three different codes of law, deep-rooted in their subject and yet variable in their relationship to one another. A theory that ignores any one of them or seeks to fix an arbitrary relationship between them would conflict with reality to such an extent that for this reason alone it would be totally useless. Our task therefore is to develop a theory that maintains a balance between these three tendencies, like an object suspended between three magnets.
>
> Clausewitz (1989: 89)

The interaction of these three tendencies thus determines the character of a war.

## Understanding the Nature of a War

Clausewitz argues that understanding the nature of a war is a necessary precondition to developing an effective strategy:

> The first, the supreme, the most far-reaching act of judgment that the statesman and commander have to make is to establish by that test the kind of war on which they are embarking, neither mistaking it for, nor trying to turn it into, something that is alien to its nature. This is the first of all strategic questions and the most comprehensive.
>
> Clausewitz (1989: 88–9)

In Clausewitz's view, the nature of a war is the result of the interaction of the objectives of the two sides; the people, government, and militaries of the belligerents; and the attitudes of allies and neutrals. He goes on to write:

> To assess these things in all their ramifications and diversity is plainly a colossal task. Rapid and correct appraisal of them clearly calls for the intuition of a genius; to master all this complex mass by sheer methodological examination is obviously impossible.
>
> Clausewitz (1989: 585–6)

This is yet another example of the fact that strategy is more an art than a science.

Because the nature of a war is the product of the interaction of the belligerents, every war is unique. The nature of a war is also dynamic because a change in any of its elements can change the nature of the conflict. A change in the aims of one or more of the participants, for example, can change the nature of a war. So too can the entry of new participants. China's entry into the Korean War, for example, markedly changed its complexion.

Understanding the nature of a war is both necessary and difficult. Both participants at the time and historians subsequently debated whether the Vietnam War was an international communist war against South Vietnam, a civil war between North and South Vietnam, an insurgency in the south supported by the north, or all of these. Similarly, American statesmen and soldiers largely failed to comprehend that the swift defeat of Saddam Hussein's regime in the Iraq War would lead to a sustained insurgency. Even as the insurgency began to grow, it proved difficult for leaders at all levels to recognize it. As Linda Robinson notes:

> One of the enduring mysteries of the war, and a testament to its shape-shifting complexity, was that so many intelligent officers of all ranks made superhuman efforts to grapple with the task of analysis and prescription to relatively little effect. The long hours and press of battle and the proximity to the daily minutiae made it hard for many to see the forest for the trees.
>
> Robinson (2008: 13)

Inherent in understanding the nature of a war is gaining an appreciation of one's comparative advantage. This, in turn, forms the basis of sound strategy. The key to doing so, in Clausewitz's view, is understanding the enemy's centre of gravity:

> One must keep the dominant characteristics of both belligerents in mind. Out of these characteristics a certain center of gravity develops, the hub of all power and movement, on which everything depends. That is the point against which all our energies should be directed.
>
> Clausewitz (1989: 595–6)

In Clausewitz's view, a state achieves victory by seeking out and attacking the enemy's centre of gravity. He wrote that the centre of gravity was most likely the enemy's army, capital city, principal ally, leader, and public opinion, in descending order. In practice, however, it can often be difficult to determine the adversary's centre of gravity. In the 1991 Gulf War, for example, US decision-makers viewed Iraq's military—particularly its Republican Guard—as the centre of gravity, when in fact the 'hub of all power' was Saddam Hussein's government.

## Limited versus Unlimited Wars

Wars can be fought for a wide range of objectives, from a quest for land and resources to the utter destruction of the enemy. In a note for the revision of *On War*, however, Clausewitz drew a distinction between wars fought for limited aims and those fought for unlimited aims:

> War can be of two kinds, in the sense that either the objective is to *overthrow the enemy*—to render him politically helpless or militarily impotent, thus forcing him to sign whatever peace we please; or *merely to occupy some of his frontier districts* so that we can annex them or use them for bargaining at the peace negotiations. Transitions from one type to the other will of course recur in my treatment; but the fact that the aims of the two types are quite different must be clear at all times, and their points of irreconcilability brought out.
>
> Clausewitz (1989: 69)

This distinction affects the way that wars are fought and how they end. In wars for limited aims, soldiers and statesmen must translate battlefield success into political leverage over the adversary. As a result, they must continually reassess how far to go militarily and what to demand politically. Such wars end through formal or tacit negotiation and agreement between the warring parties. Wars for unlimited aims are fought to overthrow the adversary's regime or achieve unconditional surrender. They end in a peace settlement that is imposed rather than negotiated.

The 1991 Gulf War and 2003 Iraq War illustrate the difference between the two types of wars. In 1991, the US-led coalition fought to liberate Kuwait from Iraqi occupation, restore Kuwait's government to power, ensure the safety of US citizens in the region, and ensure the security and stability of the Gulf region. In 2003, the United States and its allies fought to overthrow Saddam Hussein's Ba'athist regime.

The end of limited wars can lead to dissatisfaction on the part of one or more of the parties as well as a prolonged military commitment. A strong case can be made, for example, that the US-led coalition ended the 1991 Gulf War prematurely, before Saddam Hussein had been forced to admit defeat. As a result, the United States acquired a prolonged commitment to the Gulf region, one that led to the stationing of US forces in Saudi Arabia and fostered resentment among Muslims in the region and across the globe. The aftermath of a war for unlimited aims leads to a protracted commitment of another sort, as the victors must install or support a new government. In the wake of the overthrow of Saddam Hussein's regime in 2003, the United States and its partners faced the daunting task of nation-building under fire: creating new political, economic, and military institutions in order to build political legitimacy and provide security for the Iraqi people while combating a widespread insurgency.

## The Rational Calculus of War

Another concept that flows from Clausewitz's work is the notion that there should be a correlation between the value a state attaches to its ends and the means it uses to achieve them:

> Since war is not an act of senseless passion but is controlled by its political object, the value of this object must determine the sacrifices to be made for it in *magnitude* and also in *duration*. Once the expenditure of effort exceeds the value of the political object, the object must be renounced and peace must follow.
>
> Clausewitz (1989: 92)

States should thus be willing to fight longer and harder to secure or defend vital interests than peripheral ones. It helps explain, for example, why the US government chose to withdraw from Somalia after the death of 18 soldiers but remained in Korea despite suffering 33,000 deaths.

The notion of a rational calculus of war would appear to be one area in which strategy most resembles a science. However, although the notion makes sense in theory, it is far more problematic to apply in practice. It is often difficult, for example, for decision-makers to determine the costs and benefits of military action beforehand. Furthermore, estimates of the political, social, and economic costs change as war unfolds. As Clausewitz notes, 'The original political objects can change greatly later during the course of the war and many finally change entirely since they are influenced by events and their probable consequence' (1989: 92). States may continue fighting beyond the 'rational' point of surrender when their leaders' prestige becomes invested in the war or the passions of the people become aroused. Alternatively, heavy losses may lead to escalation of a conflict, changing its character. During the 1990s, for example, al-Qaeda's attacks on Western targets led to a series of limited responses, such as the 1998 cruise missile strikes on Sudan and Afghanistan in retaliation against the bombings of the US embassies in Nairobi and Dar es Salaam. However, its attack on the United States on 11 September 2001, which killed nearly three thousand innocents, raised the stakes of the conflict considerably, triggering the invasion of Afghanistan, the overthrow of al-Qaeda's Taliban hosts, and a protracted series of campaigns to counter the terrorist movement world-wide.

## Friction

Another concept with enduring value is that of friction, which Clausewitz defined as 'the only concept that more or less corresponds to the factors that distinguish real war from war on paper' (1989: 119). Clausewitz derived the name and the concept from physics. As he wrote in *The Principles of War*, 'The conduct of war resembles the workings of an intricate machine with enormous friction, so that combinations which are easily planned on paper can be executed only with great effort' (quoted in Smith 2005: 77). The sources of friction include the danger posed by the enemy, the effort required of one's own forces, the difficulties presented by the physical environment, and the problem of knowing what is occurring.

Examples of friction abound in recent wars. For example, the largest Iraqi counterattack of the 2003 Iraq War, which occurred early on 3 April near a key bridge over the Euphrates south-west of Baghdad, surprised US forces. US sensors failed to detect the approach of three Iraqi brigades composed of 8,000 soldiers backed by 70 tanks and armoured personnel carriers.

 **Key Points**

- Clausewitz viewed war as a paradoxical trinity composed of passion, probability, and reason. These tendencies generally correspond to the people, the military, and the government.
- Understanding the nature of a war is a necessary but difficult precondition to developing an effective strategy.
- In war it is important to identify and attack the enemy's centre of gravity. In Clausewitz's view, this was most likely the enemy's army, capital, ally, leader, or public opinion.
- Clausewitz distinguished between wars fought for limited and unlimited aims. The former are fought over territory; the latter are fought to overthrow the enemy's regime or achieve unconditional surrender.
- Clausewitz argued that there should be a correlation between the value a state attaches to its ends and the means it uses to achieve them. In practice, however, this is often difficult to determine.

# Sun Tzu, Mao, and the Jihadists

There is a seemingly wide gulf between Clausewitz and Sun Tzu. The former wrote from the perspective of early nineteenth-century Europe, the latter from the perspective of ancient China. The books they wrote are also strikingly different. Whereas *On War* is often a thicket of prose, much of *The Art of War* is made up of deceptively simple aphorisms. *On War* is close to 600 pages, *The Art of War* totals fewer than 40 pages in English and 6,600 characters in

Chinese. Yet as the British strategist Basil Liddell Hart observed, Clausewitz's *On War* does not differ as much from Sun Tzu's *Art of War* as it would appear on the surface (Handel 2001: 20).

Sun Tzu does, however, provide contrasting perspectives on several aspects of strategy. For example, the two authors exhibit different strategic preferences and offer contrasting views of intelligence and deception. Sun Tzu's approach has inspired subsequent generations of strategic theorists as diverse as Mao Tse-Tung and a number of contemporary Islamist theoreticians.

## Strategic Preferences

Sun Tzu's strategic preferences are significantly different from those of Clausewitz. Sun Tzu extols victory without bloodshed as the ideal, writing that 'to subdue the enemy without fighting is the acme of skill' (Sun Tzu 1963: 77). Clausewitz, by contrast, is sceptical of such an approach to combat, arguing that a reluctance to shed blood may play into an opponent's hands.

Sun Tzu sees war as a search for comparative advantage. He believes that success in war is less a matter of destroying the adversary's army than shattering his will to fight. In his view, the most successful strategies are those that emphasize psychology and deception.

To Sun Tzu, information represents a key to success in war. As he puts it, 'Know the enemy and know yourself; in a hundred battles you will never be in peril' (Sun Tzu 1963: 84). Typically, however, such pithy injunctions conceal the many challenges that make it difficult to understand oneself and one's adversary, including imperfect information, ethnocentrism, and mirror-imaging.

Whereas Clausewitz writes that destroying the enemy's army is most often the key to victory in war, Sun Tzu recommends that the best alternative is to attack the enemy's strategy. The next best alternative is to attack the opponent's alliances. Destroying the enemy's army ranks third on his list of preferred strategies.

## Intelligence

Another contrast involves the two authors' views of intelligence. Sun Tzu is an intelligence optimist, claiming that the outcome of a war can be known in advance if the leader makes a complete estimate of the situation:

> To gauge the outcome of war we must compare the two sides by assessing their relative strengths. This is to ask the following questions: Which ruler has the way? Which commander has the greater ability? Which side has the advantage of climate and terrain? Which army follows regulations and obeys orders more strictly? Which army has superior strength? Which officers and men are better trained? Which side is more strict and impartial in meting out rewards and punishments? On the basis of this comparison I know who will win and who will lose.
>
> Sun Tzu (1993: 103–4)

Two aspects of this passage are noteworthy. First, he emphasizes 'relative strengths', not absolute capabilities. In other words, one's capabilities only matter when considered in relation to those of the adversary. Second, most of the factors that he identifies as being important are qualitative, not quantitative.

Clausewitz, by contrast, is an intelligence sceptic:

Many intelligence reports in war are contradictory; even more are false, and most are uncertain . . . One report tallies with another, confirms it, magnifies it, lends it color, till he has to make a quick decision—which is soon recognized to be mistaken, just as the reports turn out to be lies, exaggerations, and so on. In short, most intelligence is false, and the effect of fear is to multiply lies and inaccuracies.

Clausewitz (1989: 117)

The failure of the US intelligence community—indeed, of all major intelligence services—to determine that Iraq did not possess nuclear, biological, or chemical weapons prior to the 2003 Iraq War is evidence of the fact that despite the development of highly sophisticated means of collecting information, intelligence continues to be an uncertain business.

Sun Tzu is also a proponent of deception. He repeatedly discusses how the successful general can surprise and deceive an opponent and how he should gather good intelligence and weaken the morale of the enemy. Yet he seldom alludes to the fact that an enemy may be able to do the same.

Sun Tzu's imprint can be seen in the writings of Mao Tse-Tung. Mao never summarized his theory of warfare in a single work. Rather, his theoretical contributions are scattered throughout several different writings. Taken as a whole, they offer a blueprint for the defeat of a stronger power by a much weaker force through a sophisticated politico-military strategy involving the incremental establishment of political control over the countryside, near total mobilization of the peasantry, and deliberate protraction of a conflict. He emphasizes that social, political, and economic developments have a decisive impact on the outcome of such a conflict. The concrete manifestation of his philosophy is a three-phase approach to war that begins with the revolutionary movement on the strategic defensive, builds to a strategic stalemate characterized by intensified guerrilla warfare, and culminates in a strategic counteroffensive that witnesses the defeat of the adversary in a decisive conventional battle (Mao Tse-Tung 1967).

Although Chinese in origin, Mao's writings have served as the template for revolutionary movements throughout the developing world. They have, in turn, influenced jihadist strategic thinkers who see in Mao's writings a model for how to overthrow a local government through a protracted insurgency.

 **Key Points**

- Sun Tzu argues that success in war comes from shattering the adversary's will to fight rather than destroying his army.
- Sun Tzu recommends that the best alternative is to attack the enemy's strategy.
- Sun Tzu claims that the outcome of a war can be known in advance if the leader makes a complete estimate of the situation.
- Mao Tse-Tung offers a blueprint for insurgents to defeat a strong power through a protracted revolutionary war.

**Critical Thinking**    Debating . . . Is classical strategic theory obsolete?

### For

- *Information-age warfare*. The advent of the information age has invalidated traditional theories of warfare. Technology either has or will soon overcome much of the friction that has historically characterized combat. Some even argue that it demands a new body of strategic theory, one drawing its inspiration from business theory, economics, or the so-called new physical sciences.

- *Non-state actors*. The utility of classical strategic theory is limited to wars between armies and states, whereas war today more often involves trans- or subnational groups. In John Keegan's characterization, Clausewitzian thought makes 'no allowances for . . . war without beginning or end, the endemic warfare of non-state, even pre-state peoples' (Keegan 1993: 5). Implicit in this critique is the assumption that such conflicts obey logic distinct from those involving states.

- *Strategy is an illusion*. In this view, strategic concepts are misleading, even harmful. As the military historian Russell Weigley put it:

War . . . is no longer the extension of politics by other means. It is doubtful whether the aphorism affirming that war is such an extension of politics was ever true enough to warrant the frequency with which it has been repeated.

Weigley (1988: 341)

### Against

- *The enduring nature of war*. First, although the growth and spread of stealth, precision, and information technology has had a dramatic influence on recent conflicts and portends even greater changes, there is as yet no evidence that it has altered the fundamental nature of war. The increasing complexity of modern wars in Kosovo, Afghanistan, and Iraq has demonstrated both the multiplying sources and enduring value of such concepts as friction. In fact, strategic theory and concepts such as war for limited and unlimited aims and the rational calculus of war enable assessment of new ways of war such as cyberwarfare.

- *Non-state actors are strategic actors*. It is unclear that war involving non-state actors is any different from that between states. The strategic questions most relevant to the struggle against Islamic terrorist networks differ little from those in previous inter-state wars. Although al-Qaeda looks and operates very differently than a conventional state adversary, it is nonetheless a strategic actor. Islamist authors such as Hasan al-Banna, Abu Bakr Naji, Abu' Ubayd al-Quarashi, and Abu Musab al-Suri have all penned works on strategy, including some that invoke the ideas of Clausewitz, Sun Tzu, and Mao (Stout et al. 2008: 123–32).

- *Strategy is difficult, but vital*. Those who argue that strategy is an illusion confuse the difficulty of executing strategy with the existence of an underlying strategic logic. Some strategic concepts may indeed be of limited utility in practice. For example, leaders may be unable to estimate the value of an objective before the fact. However, ignoring these concepts and guidelines will only diminish the prospects of success.

 ### Conclusion

Strategic theory reminds us that despite significant changes to the character and conduct of war brought by the development of new technology, the nature of war is constant. War remains the use of force to achieve political aims, regardless of whether the group seeking those aims is a state or terrorist network. Similarly, interaction with the adversary remains one of the key dynamics that prevents strategy from becoming a science.

Concepts found in Clausewitz's *On War* and Sun Tzu's *The Art of War* have similarly enduring value. Clausewitz's discussion of the remarkable trinity, the need to understand the nature of a war, the differences between limited and unlimited wars, the rational calculus of war, and friction are all useful precepts. Sun Tzu, for his part, reminds us that victory does not always require the physical destruction of an adversary. He also highlights the importance of intelligence. Together, these concepts can help us better understand contemporary conflicts.

 ## Questions

1. Why is it important to study strategic theory?
2. In what ways is strategy an art? A science?
3. What are the main differences between Clausewitz and Sun Tzu's views of strategy?
4. What considerations should decision-makers keep in mind as they contemplate using force?
5. What limits the utility of strategic theory as a guide to action?
6. What differentiates war from other forms of violence?
7. What are the main contributions of Clausewitz to strategic theory?
8. What are the main contributions of Sun Tzu to strategic theory?
9. Does Clausewitz or Sun Tzu have a more realistic view of intelligence?
10. Which elements of strategic theory are most relevant to the world of the early twenty-first century? Which are least relevant?

 ## Further Reading

C. von Clausewitz, *On War*, edited and translated by M. Howard and P. Paret (Princeton, NJ: Princeton University Press, 1989) deserves to be read in its entirety.

J. F. C. Fuller, *Armament and History* (New York: Scribner's, 1945) offers the most articulate consideration of the role of technology in warfare.

C. S. Gray, *Modern Strategy* (Oxford: Oxford University Press, 1999) similarly argues for the unity of all strategic experience because nothing vital to the nature of warfare changes. He also makes a persuasive case that Clausewitz stands head and shoulders above other strategic theorists.

M. I. Handel, *Masters of War*, 3rd edn (London: Frank Cass, 2001) convincingly argues that Clausewitz, Sun Tzu, Mao Tse-Tung, and other theorists employ a common strategic logic. What at first glance appear to be divergences and contradictions are often upon closer examination differences of methodology, definition, or perspective.

B. H. Liddell Hart, *Strategy* (New York: Praeger, 1967) argues that decisive victories usually involve prior psychological dislocation of an adversary. Rather than concentrating one's troops, the commander should force his enemy to disperse his forces. Despite the author's overly narrow interpretation of Clausewitz and selective use of history, this is nonetheless an important work.

E. Luttwak, *Strategy: The Logic of War and Peace*, revised and enlarged edition (Cambridge, MA: Belknap Press, 2001) explores the paradoxical nature of strategy. It is a classic treatment of paradox in strategy.

T.G. Mahnken, *Competitive Strategies for the 21st Century: Theory, History and Practice* **(Palo Alto: Stanford University Press, 2012)** discusses the theory and practice of developing and implementing strategy in peacetime.

T. G. Mahnken and J. A. Maiolo, *Strategic Studies: A Reader, Second Edition* **(Abingdon: Routledge, 2014)** provides a useful compilation of many of the most valuable readings in strategic studies.

P. Paret (ed.), *Makers of Modern Strategy: From Machiavelli to the Nuclear Age* **(Princeton, NJ: Princeton University Press, 1986)** offers an intellectual history of strategic thought from Machiavelli to modern times. It includes chapters on Machiavelli, Clausewitz, Jomini, and Mahan, and essays on the practice of strategy.

**Sun Tzu,** *The Art of War.* The serious student should read several translations. The best are the translations by **Samuel B. Griffith (Oxford: Oxford University Press, 1963)** and **Roger Ames (New York: Ballantine Books, 1993).**

J. C. Wylie, *Military Strategy: A General Theory of Power Control* **(Annapolis, MD: Naval Institute Press, 1989)** is also a valuable work on strategy.

##  Web Links

The Clausewitz homepage at **http://www.clausewitz.com/index.htm** contains a variety of useful research resources, including indices and bibliographies.

The Sun Tzu Art of War site **http://www.sonshi.com** contains a translation of *The Art of War*, reviews of the other major translations, and other works of strategy online.

The US Military Academy's Combating Terrorism Center **http://www.ctc.usma.edu/** contains the center's reports, which include some insightful analyses of jihadist strategic theory and practice.

Military History Online **http://www.militaryhistoryonline.com/18thcentury/articles/thesuccessofnapoleon.aspx** discusses many useful issues relevant to strategic theory along with a large number of case examples.

*The Journal of Strategic Studies* **http://www.tandfonline.com/loi/fjss20** is the premier journal of strategic studies and frequently publishes articles on strategic theory.

# 4 The Causes of War and the Conditions of Peace

JOHN GARNETT AND JOHN BAYLIS

## Chapter Contents

 **Reader's Guide**

Scholarship dealing with the causes of war is voluminous and multidisciplinary. This chapter describes and explains theories that have been advanced by biologists, philosophers, political scientists, and sociologists about why wars occur. It groups their ideas into categories and shows how different explanations of war give rise to different requirements or conditions for peace. It is argued that it is useful to make distinctions between immediate and underlying causes of war. The chapter pays particular attention to explanations of war based on human nature and instinct, but it also considers those psychological theories that emphasize misperception and frustration as causes of aggression. The ideas of those who find the causes of war in human collectives—states, tribes, and ethnic groups—and those who favour 'systemic' rather than 'unit' explanations are also described. The chapter also looks at the debate between 'greed' and 'grievance' as a cause of civil wars.

## Introduction

Though 'strategy' these days is as much concerned with the promotion of peace as with the conduct of war, the phenomenon of war remains a central concern. Previous generations might have seen virtues in war, for example, as an instrument of change or as a vehicle for encouraging heroic virtues, but these ideas have been rendered obsolete by the destructiveness of modern warfare. In the twentieth century, abolishing war became a top priority. The first step in ending war, however, is to identify its causes.

Historians sometimes argue that since wars are unique events, the causes of war are as numerous as the number of wars and nothing in general can be said about them. This chapter takes a different view. It identifies similarities and patterns between the causes of wars so that we can group causes under such headings as human nature, misperception, the nature of states, and the structure of the international system. Its aim is twofold. First, to relate contemporary scholarship across a range of disciplines—biology, political science, philosophy, and history—to the problem of war causation, and second, to elaborate a number of distinctions which help us to identify different kinds of 'causes' (e.g. underlying and immediate causes). Throughout the chapter these distinctions are used to identify the various causes of war and to discriminate between them.

Since there is little scholarly agreement on what causes war, this chapter is directed towards explaining the debate rather than to answering the question in a decisive way. The arguments are more than academic because, if the cure for war is related to its causes, then different causes will lead to different policy recommendations. If, on the one hand, wars are caused by arms races, then policies of disarmament and arms control are appropriate solutions to the problem of war. On the other hand, if wars are instigated by despotic or authoritarian states, then the way to peace lies in the spread of democracy. If the basic cause of war is deemed to be the 'international anarchy' which characterizes the current system of states, then attempts to rid the world of war will be geared towards promoting system change—perhaps in the direction of strengthened international law or a system of collective security or world government. Some explanations for war offer less hope for finding a way to end armed conflict than others. For example, those that locate war in a fundamentally flawed human nature suggest a bleaker future for the human race than those that locate the causes of war in learned behaviour. If war is learned rather than instinctive, then there is a possibility that it can be eliminated through social engineering.

Three conclusions emerge from this analysis. First, the search for a single cause appropriate to all wars is futile. Second, because war comes in a variety of forms and has a multiplicity of causes, its elimination will almost certainly require simultaneous domestic and international political action. Third, a world-wide 'just' peace is unattainable.

## The Study of War

In the field of international relations, no question has attracted more attention than 'Why war?' The reason for this interest is that war is almost universally regarded as a human disaster, a source of misery on a catastrophic scale, and, in the nuclear age, a threat to the entire human race. But war has not always been viewed so negatively. In the nineteenth century, for example, numerous writers identified virtues in war (see the Introduction). The philosopher G. W. F. Hegel believed that war preserved the ethical health of nations, and in a similar vein H. von Treitschke regarded war as 'the only remedy for ailing nations' (Gowans 1914: 23). For Treitschke, war was one of the conditions for progress, the cut of the whip that prevents a country from going to sleep, forcing satisfied mediocrity to leave its apathy. This kind of thinking alerts us to the idea that war can be thought of as a purposive, functional thing. E. H. Carr regarded it as 'the midwife of change' (1942: 3): 'Wars . . . break up and sweep away the half-rotted structures of an old social and political order.' These authors suggested that wars herald rapid technological progress, territorial change, strengthen group consciousness, and economic development. The idea of war as a purposive, functional thing, however, sits uneasily in an age that typically interprets war as an abnormal, pathological condition that threatens us all.

Idle curiosity or an aimless spirit of enquiry has not motivated most investigations into the causes of war. Theorists have studied war to abolish it. They have believed that the first step towards eliminating war is to identify its causes because, in much the same way that the cures for disease are related to the causes of disease, so the cures for war are to be found in its causes. As long as students of war do not allow their enthusiasm for prescription to affect their diagnostic skills, no harm is done. However, there is a danger that researchers may be tempted to gloss over the more intractable causes of war in favour of those which suggest the possibility that solutions to human conflict can be readily found.

Many social scientists recoil from the idea that though particular wars may be avoided, war is endemic in the human condition. The idea that war is inevitable is pretty difficult to swallow, psychologically speaking, and that may explain why pessimistic interpretations of the causes of war meet with resistance. Take, for example, the view that the root cause of war is to be found in human nature, i.e. that aggression and violence are genetically built into humans and that we do what we do because of what we are. Despite some scientific evidence in support of this idea, there is enormous resistance to it. Why? Because, if human nature is fixed in our genes, we are helpless in the face of ourselves. For many observers, the conclusion that war is built into us is an intolerable counsel of despair, even though it is a useful reminder that just because the elimination of war is desirable does not mean that it is therefore possible.

A gloomy interpretation of human nature and an admission of its intractability, however, do not automatically lead to despair of ever being able to rid the world of war. Some would argue that wars are not caused by human *nature*; they are caused by human *behaviour*, and while it may not be possible to change human nature, it is certainly possible to modify human behaviour—by offering rewards, by making threats, by education programmes, or by propaganda.

Civilized societies spend a great deal of energy on making people behave themselves despite their natures. The law, the police, schools, and churches all play a part in modifying human behaviour in the domestic environment. The possibility of modifying state behaviour is also widely recognized. Diplomacy, force, trade, aid, and propaganda are all instruments used by leaders to affect the behaviour of the states they are dealing with. Deterrent strategists, for example, argue that even if human nature is fatally flawed (and most of them think it is), states can still be deterred from aggression by the threat of unacceptable punishment in much the same way that many potential criminals can be deterred from robbing banks by the threat of imprisonment (see Chapter 11).

Unlike those who believe that peace can best be promoted by removing the causes of war, nuclear deterrent strategists hardly care at all about why wars occur. Their policy is simply to make the *consequences* of war so bad that nobody will dare fight even if they want to. In other words, the strategy of nuclear deterrence is unique in that its effectiveness does not depend either on particular interpretations of why wars occur or on treating the underlying pathologies that cause people or states to fight. The only assumption that deterrent theorists make about human beings is the fairly uncontroversial one that on the whole people prefer to be alive rather than dead and hence are likely to be deterred from aggression by the threat of annihilation.

## Difficulties in Studying War

No clear authoritative answer has emerged, and perhaps one never will, to the question 'Why war?' One of the reasons for this is that the word 'war' is a blanket term used to describe diverse activities. There are total wars and limited wars, regional wars and world wars, conventional wars and nuclear wars, high-technology wars and low-technology wars, inter-state wars and civil wars, insurgency wars and ethnic wars. In recent years, wars have also been fought by coalitions on behalf of the international community. It would be very surprising if these widely different activities—linked only by the fact that they involve organized military violence—could be explained in the same way.

Another reason for the absence of an authoritative answer is that the question 'What are the causes of war?' is a complicated, 'cluster' question. Under its umbrella, as Hidemi Suganami has pointed out, we may be asking a number of different questions. We may, for example, be asking 'What are the conditions that must be present for wars to occur?' or we may be asking 'Under what circumstances have wars occurred most frequently?' or we may be asking about how a particular war came about (1996: 4). Lumping these questions together inevitably leads to complicated and unsatisfactory answers.

An additional reason for complex answers to the question of war causation is that the concept of causation itself is fraught with philosophical difficulties. One may note that X is often a prelude to Y, but that is not at all the same as proving that X caused Y. Various writers, for example, noting that wars are often preceded by arms races between the belligerents, have claimed that arms races *cause* wars. Arms races sometimes cause war, but an *automatic* connection has not been conclusively demonstrated. Arguably, human beings do not fight because they have weapons; they acquire weapons because they already wish to fight. Further, it is worth pointing out that not all arms races have led to war. Anglo–French naval competition in the nineteenth century led to the *entente cordiale*, while the cold war arms race between the United States and the Soviet Union led to a deterrent stalemate and one of the most prolonged periods of peace in European history.

Given the difficulties inherent in the problem of causation, some writers (particularly historians) have preferred to talk about the 'origins' of wars rather than 'causes'. They believe that the best way of explaining why wars occur is to describe how they come about in terms of the social context and events from which they spring. Thus, if we are investigating the causes of the Second World War, we need to look at the Treaty of Versailles, the world depression, the rise of Hitler, German rearmament, the foreign policies of Britain and France, etc. When we have done this, we are well on the way to understanding the circumstances that led to the Second World War. Those who emphasize the origins of wars hold the view that telling the story of how they come about is as close as we can get to understanding why they come about.

Historians who favour this very specific 'case-study' approach to the identification of the causes of war tend to believe that since every war is a unique event with unique causes, the causes of war are as numerous as the number of wars. Hence, providing an authoritative answer to the question 'What are the causes of war?' would involve a detailed examination of every war that has ever occurred: the uniqueness of every war means that there is nothing in general to be said about them. For investigations concerned with the causes of individual wars this is a fair point. Nevertheless, while acknowledging the uniqueness of individual wars, most political scientists see merit in shifting the level of analysis from the particular to the general so that we can see patterns and similarities between the causes of one war and another. At this more general level of analysis we may identify some causes which are common to many, if not all, wars.

## Immediate and Underlying Causes

One of the most useful distinctions to be drawn between the various causes of war is between 'immediate', proximate causes and 'underlying', more fundamental causes. Immediate causes, the events that trigger wars, may be trivial, even accidental. For example, the spark that ignited the First World War was the assassination of the Austrian Archduke Franz Ferdinand while he was visiting Sarajevo and being driven in an open car. The death of the Archduke was a tragedy, but it was essentially a trivial event, and no one seriously believes that its occurrence provides an adequate explanation for the momentous events that followed. What is more, it was an accident that might easily not have happened. If the duke's chauffeur had not deviated from the planned route and then stopped the car to rectify his error, the assassin would not have had an opportunity to shoot the Archduke and his wife. The assassination was undoubtedly the immediate cause of the First World War, and it is true to say that if it had not happened the war which broke out in 1914 would not have happened. However, there is plenty of evidence to suggest that a war would have occurred sooner or later. In 1914 war was in the air: Europe was divided by hostile alliance systems; tensions were rising; mobilization timetables were pressuring decision-makers; and an arms race was under way. In short, the background circumstances were highly inflammable, and if the assassination of Franz Ferdinand had not set the powder keg alight, sooner or later something else would probably have provided the spark. Most commentators believe that a useful examination of the causes of the First World War should pay more attention to those underlying causes than to the immediate triggering events.

Emphasis on underlying causes is a structural interpretation in the sense that it emphasizes the importance of international circumstances rather than deliberate state policies in causing wars. It suggests that statesmen are not always in control of events; they sometimes find themselves caught up in a process that, despite their best intentions, pushes them to war. Of course, background conditions are not always a reliable barometer of the danger that war will break out. In some situations the setting seems relatively benign and responsibility for war is more easily allocated to the particular policies followed by the governments involved. Wars often come about as a result of aggressive, reckless, thoughtless, and deliberate acts by statesmen. It would be impossible to discuss the causes of the Second World War, for instance, without drawing attention to the persistently aggressive behaviour of Hitler and the weak, appeasing policies of Chamberlain. Similarly, the actions of Nasser in seizing the Suez Canal in 1956, and Eden in responding to that with military action were critically important causes of the Suez War.

 **Key Points**

- The idea that war is endemic in the human condition is psychologically unpalatable, but it may nevertheless be true. Even if human nature cannot be changed, it may be possible to modify human behaviour so that wars are less frequent.

- Since there are many different kinds of war, it is not surprising that no single cause of war can be identified.

- It is often useful to distinguish between underlying causes of war and the events that trigger them.

## Human Nature Explanations of War

There is widespread agreement that one of the things that distinguishes human beings from animals is that most of their behaviour is learned rather than instinctive. No one knows what the relative percentages are and there is an ongoing debate about the relative importance of 'nature' versus 'nurture' (heredity versus environment) as a determinant of human behaviour. Inevitably this debate has raised the question of whether war is an example of innate or learned behaviour. If it is *innate* then we must accept it, since in any reasonable timescale biological evolution is too slow to modify it. If it is *learned*, however, then it can be unlearned and there is hope for us all. Liberal thinkers prefer to emphasize the importance of nurture and are naturally attracted to the idea that aggression and war can be tamed. Conservative thinkers tend to throw their weight behind nature and are therefore sceptical about the possibilities of ridding the world of war.

Though they are disposed to minimize its significance, even committed liberals admit that there is a genetic, instinctive element in human behaviour. We do not start with clean slates on which life's experiences are written to make us what we are. We come with genetic baggage, biologically programmed, with built-in drives and instincts, one of which, it is argued, is a predilection for aggression and violence. In a celebrated exchange of letters in 1932, both Albert Einstein and Sigmund Freud agreed that the roots of war were to be found in an elemental instinct for aggression and destruction. Einstein thought that 'man has in him an active instinct for hatred and destruction', and Freud believed he had identified a 'death instinct' which manifested itself in homicide and suicide (Freud 1932). In the 1960s, ethological and socio-biological research brought new life to 'instinct' theories of aggression. Konrad Lorenz argued, largely on the basis of his observations of the behaviour of birds and fish, that an aggressive instinct is embedded in the genetic make-up of all animals (including man), and that this instinct has been a prerequisite for survival (1976). Robert Ardrey, in *The Territorial Imperative*, reached a similar conclusion and suggested a 'territorial' instinct to run alongside Lorenz's four instincts—hunger, fear, sex, and aggression (Ardrey 1966). Edward O. Wilson in *On Human Nature* noted that human beings are disposed to react with unreasoning hatred to perceived threats to their safety and possessions, and he argued that 'we tend to fear deeply the actions of strangers and to solve conflict by aggression' (Wilson 1978: 119).

Although Richard Dawkins in his book *The Selfish Gene* has shifted the level of analysis from the individual to the genes that help make him what he is, he too is under no illusions about human nature. His argument is that

> a predominant quality to be expected in a successful gene is ruthless selfishness. This gene selfishness will usually give rise to selfishness in individual behaviour . . . Much as we might wish to believe otherwise, universal love and welfare of the species as a whole are concepts which simply do not make evolutionary sense.
>
> Dawkins (1976: 2–3)

This analysis leads Dawkins to the bleak conclusion that 'if you wish . . . to build a society in which individuals cooperate generously and unselfishly towards a common good, you can expect little help from biological nature' (1976: 3) (see Box 4.1).

**BOX** 4.1 The Causes of War

One may seek in political philosophy answers to the question: 'Where are the major causes of war to be found?' The answers are bewildering in their variety and in their contradictory qualities. To make this variety manageable, the answers can be ordered under the following three headings: within man, within the structure of separate states, within the state system.

There is deceit and cunning and from these wars arise.

Waltz, *Man, the State, and War*

Whatever can be said in favour of a balance of power can be said only because we are wicked.

Confucius

It is quite true that it would be much better for all men to remain always at peace. But so long as there is no security for this, everyone having no guarantee that he can avoid war, is anxious to begin it at the moment which suits his own interest and so forestall a neighbour, who would not fail to forestall the attack in his turn at any moment favourable to himself.

Woodrow Wilson

Force is a means of achieving the external ends of states because there exists no consistent, reliable process of reconciling the conflicts of interest that inevitably arise among similar units in a condition of anarchy.

Rousseau

The human nature explanation of war is a persuasive one, but at least two qualifications need to be made about it. First, we need to ask whether the evidence produced by the study of animals is really relevant to the behaviour of human beings. The animal behaviourists say it is, because man is simply a higher animal, connected to the rest of the animal kingdom by evolution. To deny that human beings have instincts in the same way that animals do is to deny the almost universally accepted principle of evolution, which links all life on the planet. Even so, we cannot help wondering whether the kind of cross-species generalization engaged in by biologists is valid. After all, human beings are very different from animals. They are more intelligent. They have a moral sense. They reflect about what they do; they plan ahead. Some would claim that these differences are so important that for all intents and purposes they lift man out of the animal world and reduce his instincts to no more than vestigial significance. Waltz notes in his book *Man, the State, and War* that arguing that human nature causes war is not very helpful since if human nature causes war then, logically, it also causes everything else that human beings do. In his words, 'human nature may in some sense have been the cause of war in 1914, but by the same token it was the cause of peace in 1910' (1959: 28). In other words, human nature is a constant and cannot explain the wide variety of activities that humans exhibit.

## Frustration Explanations of War

Social psychologists, while still locating war in 'man', offer explanations for its occurrence that rely less on instinct and more on socially programmed human behaviour. Typically, they argue that aggression is a result of frustration. When individuals find themselves thwarted in the achievement of their desires, goals, and objectives, they experience frustration which causes pent-up resentment that needs to find an outlet. This frequently takes the form of aggressive behaviour which, in turn, has a cathartic effect of releasing tension and making those who engage in it feel better. Usually aggression is levelled at those who cause the frustration, but sometimes it is vented against innocents who become scapegoats. This psychological process of transferring aggression to a secondary group is called 'displacement'. Sometimes individuals project their frustrated desires and ambitions onto the group or collective, be it tribe or state, to which they belong. In the words of Reinhold Niebuhr, 'the man in the street, with his lust for power and prestige thwarted by his own limitations and the necessities of social life, projects his ego upon his nation and indulges his anarchic lusts vicariously' (1932: 93).

There is a sense in which the 'frustration/aggression' hypothesis, which emphasizes the connection between violence and the failure of human beings to achieve their objectives, is somewhat more optimistic than instinct theories of aggression. Although frustration in life is unavoidable, it may be possible either to channel aggression into harmless activities like sport (psychologists call this sublimation), or to organize society in ways that minimize frustrations (sociologists call this social engineering).

## Misperception Explanations of War

Accepting that wars cannot occur unless statesmen decide to wage them, many believe that decisions to go to war are often the result of misperception, misunderstanding, miscalculation, and errors of judgement. Essentially, those who think in this way regard wars as *mistakes*, the tragic consequences of failing to appreciate things as they are. This being the case, they are caused more by human frailty or fallibility than malice. Robert Jervis (1976), building on the ideas of Kenneth Boulding (1956), has contributed enormously to our understanding of these psychological causes of war. He makes the point that in order to make sense of the world around us, all of us develop images of reality through which we filter the welter of information that bombards our senses. These 'images' of reality are more important than reality itself when it comes to determining our behaviour; they act as a distorting lens which inhibits our ability to see reality as it is and predisposes us to judge the world in ways that confirm our pre-existing concepts.

Critically important misperceptions likely to lead to war include mistaken estimates of both enemy intentions and capabilities, inaccurate assessments of the military balance between adversaries, and failures to judge the risks and consequences of war properly. Quite frequently these kinds of misperceptions are made by both sides involved in a conflict. For example, Greg Cashman has argued that in the Gulf War, Saddam Hussein may have perceived a threat from Kuwait's reluctance to allow Iraq to cancel its debts and its unwillingness to pump less oil. He may even have perceived a joint American-Israeli-British conspiracy to deny Iraq sophisticated weaponry. On the other hand, leaders in virtually all of the Middle East capitals underestimated the degree of threat posed by Iraq and were taken by surprise when Kuwait was invaded. Thus, while Iraqi leaders overestimated the degree of threat to their interests, their opponents underestimated the hostility of Iraq (Cashman 1993: 63). But perhaps the most critical misperception of all was Saddam Hussein's failure to anticipate Western resolve and the creation of a powerful military coalition against him. There were at least as many misperceptions surrounding the 2003 Iraq War. Despite the unambiguous warnings he had received, Saddam was convinced that the United States and Britain would not invade. For their part the Americans and the British believed that Saddam possessed weapons of mass destruction and was well on the way to acquiring nuclear capability. They also believed that invasion would be universally welcomed, that Iraq was a haven for terrorists, and that democracy could be created with relative ease. None of these beliefs were true, but for the participants they formed the psychological reality against which they made their decisions.

Before the Second World War, Hitler mistakenly believed that Britain would not fight and Chamberlain mistakenly believed that Germany could be appeased by concessions. Other delusions and misconceptions that contributed to the outbreak of war in 1939 have been identified by A. J. P. Taylor. Mussolini was deluded about the strength of Italy; the French believed that France was impregnable. Churchill believed that Britain could remain a great power despite the war, and Hitler 'supposed that Germany would contend with Soviet Russia and the United States for mastery of the world' (Nelson and Olin 1979: 153–4). In Britain hardly anyone expected that German *blitzkrieg* tactics would bring France down in a matter of weeks, and throughout Europe people grossly overestimated the power of strategic bombing. Given this plethora of misunderstandings, misjudgements, and misperceptions, it is easy to argue that statesman stumbled into the Second World War because they were out of touch with reality.

Much the same point can be made about the Falklands War in 1981. Misperceptions abounded. Britain seriously misinterpreted Argentine intentions with respect to invasion, and Argentina badly misjudged Britain's determination to resist. For years the two governments had been involved in intermittent negotiations about a possible transfer of sovereignty, and, though little progress had been made, the Conservative government could not believe that the Argentine junta would seize South Georgia before the possibilities of negotiation had been exhausted. What the British government failed to appreciate was the significance of the Malvinas in the Argentine psyche and the domestic pressures to act that this put on President Galtieri and Dr Costa Mendez. For its part, the government of Argentina could not believe that at the end of the twentieth century a Eurocentric, post-colonial Britain was prepared to spill blood for the sake of a barren relic of empire 10,000 miles away.

There is a sense in which the misconceptions prevalent both in Germany before the Second World War and in Argentina before the Falklands War are understandable. The signals transmitted by the policy of appeasement may have suggested to Hitler that since he had got away with swallowing the Rhineland in 1936, and Austria and the Sudetenland in 1938, he could probably get away with aggression against Poland in 1939. In the case of the Falklands, the casual pace of British diplomacy and the absence of any serious military capability in the area may have suggested to the Argentines that Britain was not much interested in the fate of the Falkland Islands and was unlikely to defend them. Perhaps, in both of these cases, it was not so much that signals were *misread* but that *the wrong signals were sent*. Either way, Britain's enemies made serious miscalculations of her intentions and war resulted.

If wars are caused by misperceptions and misunderstandings created by cognitive biases, then conditions of peace include more clear thinking, better communications among countries, and education. This thought lies behind the United Nations Educational, Scientific, and Cultural Organization (UNESCO) motto 'Peace Through Understanding', various 'education for peace' proposals, and the attempts that are frequently made to get potential adversaries around the conference table so that they can better understand each other. The basic idea is that if enemies can be brought to appreciate each other's perspectives, then the disputes that divide them will dissolve because they will be seen to be either illusory or not sufficiently serious to justify war. Perhaps we can detect in this approach relics of the idea of a natural 'harmony of interests', which would prevail if only misunderstandings were cleared up.

Before we are persuaded by this idea that wars can be prevented by removing misperceptions and misunderstandings, a word of warning is appropriate. It may not be possible to eradicate misperception from human affairs given the inherent cognitive weaknesses of the human mind. The need to simplify, the inability to empathize, the tendency to ethnocentrism, the reluctance to relinquish or recognize prejudices—all familiar human weaknesses—may make some degree of misperception inevitable. Herbert Butterfield recognized this point when he identified an 'irreducible dilemma' lying in the very geometry of human conflict. Butterfield imagined a situation in which two potential enemies, both armed, face each other. Neither harbours any hostile intent but neither can be sure of the intentions of the other.

> You cannot enter into the other man's counterfear [and] it is never possible for you to realize or remember properly that since he cannot see the inside of your mind, he can never have the same assurance of your intentions that you have.
>
> Butterfield (1952: 21)

Butterfield makes the point that the greatest war in history could be caused by statesmen who desperately want peace but whose cognitive limitations lead them to misinterpret each other's intentions (Butterfield 1952: 19). (Discerning students will realize that Butterfield's 'ultimate predicament' has, in recent years, surfaced in the literature of strategic studies as 'the security dilemma'.)

Additionally, not all wars are caused by misperceptions and misunderstandings, even though they may be surrounded by them. Some wars—perhaps most—are rooted in genuine disagreement and conflicting interests, and in these cases discussions between enemies simply promote a better understanding of the disputes that divide them. Indeed, in some situations improved understanding may actually exacerbate the divisions between adversaries. When it was suggested to him that international hatred and suspicion could be reduced by getting nations to understand one another better, Sir Evelyn Baring, British governor in Egypt between 1883 and 1907, replied that 'the more they understand one another the more they will hate one another' (Waltz 1959: 50). Perhaps it can be argued that for most of the 1930s Britain was at peace with Germany precisely because the British did not understand Hitler. When, in September 1939, the penny finally dropped, Britain declared war on Germany.

## Group Explanations of War

Though embarked upon by individual human beings, war, by definition, is a group activity. It is waged by human collectives—factions, tribes, nations, states, and even perhaps by 'civilizations'. This has led some to shift the responsibility for war from human beings to the group within which they live and to which they owe varying degrees of allegiance. Those who argue in this way believe that there is nothing much wrong with human beings per se, but they are corrupted by the social structures in which they live. In the words of Friedrich Nietzsche, 'Madness is the exception in individuals but the rule in groups' (Nietzsche 1966:

15). Essentially, the argument is that there is something about human collectives that encourages violence.

Perhaps the trouble starts with the sense of difference that we all feel between 'us' and 'them'. Whenever people can make a distinction between those who belong to their own collective grouping—be it tribe, state, or nation—and other groups with which they cannot identify easily, they have laid the foundation for conflict. It is all too easy for a group to slide from recognizing that it is different from other groups to believing that it is superior to them. Hence, this sense of differentiation readily leads to group selfishness, inter-group conflict, and ultimately war. As Niebuhr once observed, 'altruistic passion is sluiced into the reservoirs of nationalism with great ease, and made to flow beyond them with great difficulty' (Niebuhr 1932: 91).

G. Le Bon was one of the earliest social psychologists to notice that the behaviour of social groups is different from—and usually worse than—the behaviour of the individuals comprising them. He developed the idea of crowd psychology, that in a crowd a new entity or collective mind comes into being. He believed that while in groups, individuals lose their normal restraints, become more suggestible, more emotional, and less rational. What is more, groups have reduced feelings of responsibility, because the more responsibility is diffused in crowds, the less heavily it weighs on each individual. Since responsibility is everywhere (and therefore nowhere), blame cannot be allocated specifically, and this frees human collectives from normal moral restraints (Le Bon 1897: 41). This thought was neatly captured in the title of Niebuhr's classic *Moral Man and Immoral Society*. Eric Hoffer, in discussing the appeal of mass movements, makes the same point very graphically: 'When we lose our individual independence in the corporateness of a mass movement, we find a new freedom—freedom to hate, bully, lie, torture, murder and betray without shame or remorse' (Hoffer 1952: 118).

Human beings have always lived in differentiated groups and it is unlikely that this will change in the foreseeable future. The interesting question is whether some groups are more war prone than others. In the context of inter-state wars, for example, are capitalist states more warlike than socialist states or vice versa? There is no clear answer to that question. Can we argue that democratic states are more peace-loving than authoritarian states? Again there is no clear answer. Although some evidence suggests that democracies do not fight *each other* very often, other historical evidence suggests that democracies fight as often as do other types of states. As the wars in Iraq and Afghanistan (as well as the struggle against ISIS) have shown, democratic states have also demonstrated some enthusiasm for wars of intervention in support of human rights. This current fashion for waging wars in support of liberal values does not augur well for a peaceful world.

Various observers have noted, however, that democracies seldom, if ever, *fight each other*. Michael Doyle, for example, has argued that liberal states are more peacefully inclined towards each other because their governments are more constrained by democratic institutions, and because they share the same democratic values. Commercial interdependence between liberal states also gives them a vested interest in peace (Doyle 1983, 1986). If Doyle and those who share his views are right, one of the conditions of peace is the spread of democracy—a trend that has gathered pace particularly since the end of the cold war. For the first time ever, almost half of the world's governments are now democratic. The thesis that the spread of democracy will promote peace is no more than plausible, however, and it would be unwise to accept it uncritically.

**Key Points**

- Some believe that human beings are genetically programmed towards violence, but there is an ongoing debate about whether war is an example of innate or learned behaviour.

- Social psychologists have argued that aggression is the result of frustration. Some believe feelings of aggression can be channelled into harmless activities like sport.

- Wars that result from misperceptions, misunderstandings, and miscalculations by statesmen might be prevented by better communications and more accurate information.

- Some believe that there is something about human collectives that encourages violence.

- There is some evidence, however, that though democratic states fight as frequently as other states, they do not fight each other.

## Wars 'Within' and 'Beyond' States

Perhaps because of the spread of democracy, it is often argued that *inter-state* violence is now less of a problem than it was just a few years ago. Indeed, it has been calculated that since 1970 fewer than 10 per cent of armed conflicts have been inter-state wars fought for traditional objectives. Sometimes, of course, wars straddle both the 'internal' and 'inter-state' categories. The Indo-China war, for example is a case in point. What started as a colonial war developed into a civil war and became an inter-state war with the intervention of the United States and its allies in Vietnam. In Libya in 2011 resistance to Colonel Gaddafi, triggered by 'the Arab Spring', also led to Western intervention in support of the rebels. The subsequent overthrow of Gaddafi meant that the distinction between civil conflict and inter-state conflict was blurred.

One reason why it is argued that inter-state wars may be going out of fashion is that in a globalized world the expected value of conquest has diminished and its costs, both economic and political, have escalated. States bent on improving their standards of living are better advised to spend their money on education, research, and technology than on conquering other countries and trying to hold down hostile populations. The contemporary moral climate makes aggressive wars difficult to justify, and the media revolution makes it difficult to avoid the opprobrium attached to waging them.

General Sir Rupert Smith is one of the most recent in a long line of commentators who echo this fashionable perception that old-fashioned wars are old hat. Violence exists, he says, but 'wars in the future will not be waged between states. Instead we will fight among the people' (Smith 2006: 1). The general may be right, but a little reflection suggests that both he and those who think like him may be premature in their judgement. The conflicts between Israel and Hizbullah in Lebanon in 2006, Russia and Georgia in 2008, and Israel and Hamas in Gaza in 2008 and 2014, and Russia and Ukraine over the Crimea in 2014, all took place across neighbouring borders. Levy and Thompson have argued that inter-state wars are normally much more significant in their consequences than intra-state conflicts (Levy and Thompson 2010). It is also possible to envisage a scenario, perhaps not far into the future, when there is a desperate scramble for scarce resources by capitalist countries that find it increasingly difficult to sustain their profligate lifestyles as vital minerals, particularly fossil fuels, start to run out.

If that should happen, advanced industrial countries might face the stark choice between going under or waging inter-state war to secure supplies of essential materials. Take oil for example. To deny a modern industrial state oil is to deny it the means of survival. Since no state has ever committed suicide, who can doubt that, faced with the destruction of their way of life, states will do whatever is necessary to secure adequate supplies of oil—including waging inter-state war. In short, inter-state war is not yet off the agenda, even for civilized states that pride themselves on their peaceful intentions.

Even if it is accepted that there has been a decline in inter-state wars, this does not explain the rising incidence of internal war. There are a number of reasons why civil wars have become common, but perhaps the most basic is that in many parts of the world sovereign states—which are usually defined in terms of the monopoly of military power that they wield within their territory—have lost that monopoly to a variety of bodies, be they tribes, ethnic groups, terrorists, warlords, splinter groups, or armed gangs. As the conflict in Syria demonstrates, when governments lose their monopoly of military force they can no longer control their territory or their people. The domestic environment begins to resemble the ungoverned international system which, as we saw earlier in this chapter, is a structural, 'permissive' cause of war. In Hobbesian anarchy, ancient tensions and hatreds that were previously contained burst to the surface. We have also seen the consequences of this in Bosnia, Kosovo, Chechnya, Afghanistan, Sierra Leone, Somalia, East Timor, and Haiti.

What is particularly horrifying about ethnic wars is that people are brutalized and killed not because of anything they have done, not even because of their politics, but simply because of who they are. That is what is so terrible about the persecution of the Tutsis in Rwanda, the Tamils in Sri Lanka, the Kurds in Iraq, the Muslims in Bosnia, and the Albanians in Kosovo. Ethnic wars are quite different from Clausewitzian politically motivated conflicts where the belligerents disagree about something and seek to resolve their disagreement by inter-state war—an activity conducted according to moral and legal rules. It may be going too far to describe run-of-the-mill inter-state wars as rational and civilized, but there is a grain of sense in the thought. Ethnic wars are quite different. They are not about the pursuit of interests as normally understood. They are about malevolence and they are unrestrained by any legal or moral rules. As the rise of Islamic State in Iraq and Syria (ISIS) in 2014 demonstrates, 'religious' or 'ethnic cleansing', like 'the final solution', is surely one of the most sinister phrases to enter the political vocabulary of the twentieth century.

It is ironic that authoritarian governments, so frequently blamed for inter-state wars, were instrumental in preventing civil wars in countries like Yugoslavia and the Soviet Union. Hobbes's *Leviathan* may have its attractions if the alternative is genocidal violence. If the thousands of ethnic groups that exist in the world can no longer be contained within nation states, then we face the break-up of international society into a myriad of micro-groups. The consequences of 'Balkanization' on this scale are unlikely to lead to a more peaceful world. But is it possible to generalize about the origins of civil conflicts?

There is a significant and interesting literature about the causes of civil wars. One of the liveliest areas of scholarship is 'the greed versus grievance debate'. Paul Collier and Anke Hoeffler wrote an important piece in 2000 which argued that 'greed' was much more important than 'grievance' in understanding why civil wars began and why they often lasted for considerable periods of time. Focusing on an economic explanation of causes, they argued that those involved in armed conflicts were largely motivated by a desire to improve their own financial situation (ie 'greed'), rather than by 'grievances' related to issues of identity, such as ethnicity, religion, or social class. Civil wars, they argued, were more likely to occur where there were lootable natural resources such as diamonds, drugs, or timber. The examples often cited to justify this theory include the role of diamonds in the conflict in Sierra Leone, Angola, and the Democratic Republic of Congo, timber in Cambodia, and the poppy trade controlled by the insurgents in the conflict in Afghanistan. According to this view, rebels often have an incentive to keep civil wars going to improve their own or the group's financial position.

Those who reject the 'greed thesis' do so either because they believe that 'grievances' relating to such things as oppression, inequality or discrimination are at the root of civil wars or because they believe that civil conflicts are much more complex than the 'greed versus grievance theory' suggests. 'Greed' and 'grievance' may be interrelated or other factors may be involved. David Keen, in his study of 'Complex Emergencies', argues that it is important to look at the 'specifics' of particular conflicts. Different types of conflicts have different causes and this requires a mix of multiple theories to understand their causes. (See Critical Thinking.)

---

 **Critical Thinking**    Debating ... Is 'Greed' more important than 'Grievance' as a cause of civil wars?

### For

- **The importance of economic forces.** 'Ethnic tensions and ancient political feuds are not starting civil wars around the world—economic forces such as entrenched poverty and the trade in natural resources are the true culprits.' (Collier, 2004)

- **The key role of lootable resources.** 'Greed' in terms of lootable diamonds, timber, and drugs were the critical factors in the conflicts in Angola, Nigeria, Democratic Republic of Congo, Cambodia, Liberia, and Sierra Leone.

- **The importance of the 'Resource Curse'.** At the heart of civil conflicts is the 'Resource Curse'—i.e. the richer a country is in natural resources the more likely it is to suffer civil violence.

- **Greed is the key.** 'Grievance discourse is merely window dressing.'

### Against

- **The roles of poverty and justice**. While greed may be present, relative deprivation and the search for social justice are more often at the heart of civil wars.

- **Libya as a case study.** Libya, with the fall of Gaddafi, does not conform to the idea of a greed-based rebellion. Several grievances such as vertical inequalities, involving economic grievances and a lack of political rights, as well as horizontal inequalities, involving regional and tribal differences, were the main motivation for the conflict.

- **The role of corruption and ethnicity**. Ukraine provides a good example of the role that grievances relating to corruption and ethnicity play in civil conflicts.

- **Religion as a cause.** Grievances associated with religion are often a fundamental cause of civil conflict. Iraq provides a compelling evidence of this.

**Key Points**

- As inter-state war has waned, intra-state conflict has become more frequent.
- Ethnic conflicts do not easily fit the Clausewitzian model. They are particularly violent and people are often killed because of who they are rather than because of their behaviour and politics.
- There is a major debate between those who believe that 'greed' and 'grievance' are the main causes of civil wars.

 ## Conclusion

There is no shortage of 'cures' for the 'disease' of war. Some are bizarre. For example, Linus Pauling once suggested that wars are caused by a vitamin deficiency and that we could eat our way out of aggression by swallowing the appropriate tablets. Others—like calls to change human nature, to reconstruct the state system, to redistribute equitably the world's wealth, to abolish armaments, or to 're-educate' mankind—follow with faultless logic from the various causes of war which scholars have identified. But since there is no prospect of implementing them in the foreseeable future, in a sense they are not solutions at all. Henry IV's reputed comment on an equally impractical proposal for peace is still appropriate, 'It is perfect,' the king said, 'Perfect. I see no single flaw in it save one, namely, that no earthly prince would ever agree to it'. Hedley Bull has rightly condemned such solutions as 'a corruption of thinking about international relations and a distraction from its proper concerns' (Bull 1961: 26–7).

We have to begin by recognizing the limits of what is possible. Maybe we can then edge our way forward by improving our techniques of diplomacy, communication, crisis avoidance, and crisis management; by developing a concept of enlightened self-interest which is sensitive to the interests of others; by extending the scope of international law and building on existing moral constraints; by learning how to manage military power through responsible civil–military relations and sophisticated measures of arms control; and by strengthening cooperation through international organizations and world trade. These are not spectacular, radical, or foolproof solutions to the problem of war. That is why practical foreign policymaking is more akin to weeding than landscape gardening. However, they are practical steps that offer the possibility at least of reducing its frequency, and perhaps also of limiting its destructiveness. Even if war could be abolished, we need to remember that peace is not a panacea in which all human antagonisms are resolved. Peace is simply the absence of war, not the absence of conflict. As the cold war demonstrated, it is just as possible to wage peace as it is to wage war. Though 'peace' and 'war' are usually regarded as opposites, there is a sense in which both are aspects of the conflict that is endemic in all social life. War is simply a special kind of conflict that differs from peace only by its violent nature. The fact that peace is not a panacea explains why, when confronted with the stark choice of peace or war, leaders sometimes choose war. Some kinds of peace—under dictatorships, for example—may be worse than some kinds of war. In other words, although almost everyone wants peace, almost no one (apart from strict pacifists) wants only peace or peace at any price. If it were otherwise, the problem of war would disappear since as a last resort states can always avoid war by surrendering. Capitulation might bring peace, but it would almost certainly entail the loss of some of those other things that states want—like independence, justice, prosperity, and freedom. When it comes to the crunch, leaders may think that some fundamental values or goals are worth fighting for.

Ideally, of course, what people want is a world-wide just peace. Unfortunately, this is an unattainable dream. It would require agreement on whose justice is to prevail. It would require a redistribution of the world's wealth from the haves to the have-nots. Just peace would require religious and political movements—Muslims, Christians, Jews, Hindus, communists, capitalists—to tolerate each other. It would also require an end to cultural imperialism and an agreement that differing cultural values are equally valid. It would probably require the disappearance of borders and differentiated societies with their 'them' and 'us' mentalities. In short, it would require human beings to behave in ways in which they have never behaved. Since justice and peace do not go together, statesmen will have to continue choosing between them. The pursuit of justice may require them to wage war, and the pursuit of peace may require them to put up with injustice. During the cold war years, Western politicians, by abandoning Eastern Europe to its fate under Communism, thought, probably rightly, that peace was more important than justice. Since the end of the cold war, they have tended to put justice before peace—witness the upsurge of violence caused by wars of intervention in support of human rights and democratic values. The critical question now is whether, in juggling the priorities of peace and justice, we have got the balance right, or whether our current enthusiasm for Western values and human rights implies an ever so slightly casual attitude to the problem of war. Perhaps, in the interests of peace, there is something to be said for the realist policy of fighting necessary rather than just wars.

 ## Questions

1.  Are the causes of war unique in each case or is it possible to find similarities and patterns in the causes of war in general?
2.  Do you think the spread of democracy will solve the problem of war?
3.  To which would you allocate priority: the pursuit of peace or the pursuit of justice?
4.  Is aggressive behaviour instinctive or learned?
5.  How convincing is the argument that wars are a result of misjudgement and misperceptions?
6.  Is war inevitable?
7.  Is war an instrument of policy or an outburst of irrationality?
8.  Are inter-state wars going out of fashion?
9.  If international order rests on the principle of 'non-intervention', using Libya or Syria as an example, how can military intervention in the internal affairs of sovereign states be justified?
10. Can the problem of war be solved through education?

 ## Further Reading

J. S. Levy and W. R. Thompson, *The Causes of War* (Chichester: Wiley-Blackwell, 2010) provides a comprehensive analysis of the leading theories on both inter-state and civil wars.

R. Niebuhr, *Moral Man and Immoral Society: A Study in Ethics and Politics* (New York and London: Charles Scribner's Sons, 1932) is one of the best studies of ethics and conflict.

E. Nietzsche, *The Philosophy of Nietzsche* (New York: New American Library, 1966) is a useful source of Nietzsche's views.

S. P. Rosen, *War and Human Nature* (Princeton, NJ: Princeton University Press, 2005) gives an analysis of the contribution that neuroscientific and biological research can make to the study of war.

S. Van Evera, *The Causes of War* (Cornell: Cornell University Press, 2009) provides an up-to-date analysis of the causes of war.

K. Waltz, *Man, the State, and War* (New York: Columbia University Press, 1959) is one of the best studies of the causes of war.

## Web Links

See **https://ideas.repec.org/p/wbk/wbrwps/2355.html** for an analysis of Paul Collier's views on 'greed' versus 'grievance' as a cause of civil war see: **http://www.delmar.edu/socsci/rlong/intro/perspect.htm** provides an interesting sociological analysis of the causes of war.

Robert A. Hinde, *The Psychological Basis of War* **http://www.unc.edu/depts/diplomat/AD_Issues/amdipl_7/hinde.html** is another useful source on the psychological causes of war.

David Keen looks at the links between 'greed' and 'grievance' in **eprints.lse.ac.uk/44901/**

# Strategic Culture

JEFFREY S. LANTIS AND DARRYL HOWLETT

## Chapter Contents

 **Reader's Guide**

This chapter considers ways that strategic culture can aid academic understanding as well as analysis of security policies of many actors in the international realm. This approach is especially salient because of the many conflicts around the world that seem to exhibit cultural dimensions. The chapter is divided into three sections. First, it presents an overview of approaches exploring the relationship between culture and nuclear strategy during the cold war. This section also includes a synopsis of the various sources of strategic culture identified in the literature. Second, the chapter discusses theoretical issues related to strategic culture, including: the contribution of constructivist approaches to security studies; the question of 'ownership' of strategic culture; and whether non-state, state, and multi-state actors can possess distinctive strategic cultures. The final section of the chapter provides an overview of recent work that explores the relationship between strategic culture and the acquisition of and threats to use weapons of mass destruction.

## Introduction

This chapter provides an overview of the scholarly and policymaking relevance of strategic culture in the contemporary world. Strategic culture may challenge and enrich prevailing neo-realist assumptions regarding strategy and security. It provides a bridge between material and ideational explanations of state behaviour, adding valuable perspectives to understand different countries' contemporary security policy choices.

Many consider that culture has a profound impact on strategic decision-making, and in recent years there has been renewed academic and policy interest in exploring its role in international security (Johnson, Kartchner, and Larsen 2009; FIU-SOUTHCOM

2010; Lantis 2014). Scholars and practitioners have begun to study issues like the United States' relations with countries such as China, Russia, and Iran, European security cooperation, conflicts in the Middle East, counterterrorism policies, and weapons of mass destruction (WMD) proliferation through the lens of strategic culture. The challenges of terrorism and insurgencies in Iraq, Syria, and Afghanistan also have underscored the importance of cultural considerations at political and strategic levels.

Recognizing the impact of diverse strategic cultures seems especially pertinent in the twenty-first-century security arena. This requires accepting, and attempting to overcome, a measure of ethnocentrism in the enterprise (Booth 1981). Jeannie Johnson, Kerry Kartchner, and Jeffrey Larsen write:

> All cultures condition their members to think certain ways, while at the same time providing pre-set responses to given situations. Thus culture bounds our perceptions and the range of options we have for responding to events. However, when a society experiences a severe shock or major disaster, it forces that culture to become more open-minded, as it becomes momentarily susceptible to new explanations, new paradigms, new ways of thinking, all in search of understanding and mitigating the shock that has befallen them. The events of 9/11 did that to America.
>
> Johnson, Kartchner, and Larsen (2009: 5–6)

Thus, comprehensive understanding of security dilemmas requires stepping outside one's own cultural perspective in order to embrace the possibility that non-Western cultures may exhibit different ways of thinking and acting. Engagement in this enterprise could help reduce the criticism that strategic studies has traditionally been too Western-centric, and it could also aid contextual understanding of the study of postcolonial societies and the issues associated with nation-building. This deviates from interpretations of security policy behaviour purely as a function of material opportunities and constraints in the external environment, and offers instead a route to recognize ways that 'cultural, ideational, and normative influences' impact the motivations of states and leaders (Glenn 2009: 523).

## Thinking about Culture and Strategy

There are three main approaches to the study of culture and strategy. The first views culture as a value-added explanation of strategic behaviour. Culture is used to fill in the gaps of explanation by supplementing theories centered on national interest and the distribution of power. Culture is considered a variable that may influence behaviour but is characterized as secondary to international systemic pressures. The second approach views culture as a conceptual vehicle that can explain some, if not all, strategic behaviour. This approach draws on other areas of knowledge such as political psychology in order to create a theory of strategic culture that is falsifiable, and it also contributes to a cumulative research programme. Strategic culture in this sense is an independent variable that explains decision-making in international security as well or better than neorealism or neo-liberal institutionalism. The third scholarly approach argues that aspects of human conduct can be understood only by becoming immersed within a given strategic culture. Consequently, the search for falsifiable theories is unachievable. Some anthropologists and sociologists consider that the relationship between

**Box** 5.1   Differing Perspectives on Culture

Culture is comprised of 'interpretive codes' including language, values, and even substantive beliefs like support for democracy or the futility of war.

Parsons (1951)

Culture is 'an historically transmitted pattern of meanings embodied in symbols, a system of inherited conceptions expressed in symbolic form by means of which men communicate, perpetuate, and develop their knowledge about and attitudes towards life'.

Geertz (1973)

Political culture is 'that subset of beliefs and values of a society that relate to the political system'.

Almond and Verba (1965)

culture and strategy is inordinately complex because it consists of a combination of discursive (what is said) and non-discursive (what is unsaid) expressions. Hence, they argue, it is impossible to measure the influence of culture on strategy (see Box 5.1).

## Political Culture

The idea that culture could influence strategic outcomes was first captured in classic works, including the writings of Thucydides and Sun Tzu. In the nineteenth century, Prussian military strategist Carl von Clausewitz identified war and war-fighting strategy as 'a test of moral and physical forces' (Howard 1991c: A23). The goal of strategy, he argued, was more than defeat of the enemy on the battlefield—it was the elimination of the enemy's morale.

The Second World War prompted a new wave of research on the distinctive 'national character' of countries, which were rooted in language, religion, customs, and the interpretation of common memories. Scholars became curious about how a country's national character could lead them to fight wars differently. Some sought to understand how Japanese culture, for example, fomented a spirit of self-sacrifice, such as in the kamikaze attacks against US warships and battles to the death over remote South Pacific islands (Benedict 1946). While this work was criticized for reifying culture and promoting stereotypes, anthropologists including Margaret Mead and Claude Lévi-Strauss continued to refine these studies. In the 1980s, sociologist Ann Swidler defined culture quite broadly as consisting of 'symbolic vehicles of meaning, including beliefs, ritual practices, art forms, and ceremonies, as well as informal cultural practices such as language, gossip, stories, and rituals of daily life' (Swidler 1986: 273). Building on the arguments of Max Weber and Talcott Parsons, she contended that interest-driven, cultural 'strategies of action' were important mediating conditions on state behaviour.

Meanwhile, political scientists Gabriel Almond and Sidney Verba generated interest in the comparative study of political culture, which they defined as the 'subset of beliefs and values of a society that relate to the political system' (Almond and Verba 1965: 11). Political culture included a commitment to values like democratic principles and institutions, ideas about morality and the use of force, the rights of individuals or collectives, and predispositions toward the role of a country in the world. This political culture, Almond and Verba argued, was manifest on at least three levels: 'the cognitive, which includes empirical and causal beliefs; the evaluative, consisting of values, norms, and moral judgments; and the expressive or affective, which encompasses emotional attachments, patterns of identity and loyalty, and feelings of affinity, aversion, or indifference' (quoted in Duffield 1999: 23).

However, even though sociological models of culture became increasingly complex, subsequent studies of political culture yielded little theoretical refinement. Critics argued that the approach was subjective and that the explanatory power of political culture was more limited than its proponents claimed. This was also a period when the behavioural revolution was making an impact in the social sciences, contributing to a loss of interest in cultural interpretive analyses in mainstream international relations scholarship.

## Strategic Culture and Nuclear Deterrence

In 1977, Jack Snyder introduced culture into modern security studies by developing a theory of strategic culture to interpret Soviet nuclear doctrine. The predominant approach to nuclear strategy up to this juncture had been shaped by econometric treatments of rational utility. The United States and the Soviet Union were characterized as rational actors responding to each others' moves in a calculated way in the strategic nuclear realm.

Snyder's alternative approach to analysing US–Soviet nuclear interaction focused on what he viewed as the distinctive strategic cultural differences between the two states. Snyder's work was influenced greatly by prior studies of military affairs that highlighted cultural distinctions, including Basil Liddell Hart's classic, *The British Way in Warfare* (1932), and Russell F. Weigley's *The American Way of War* (1973). Snyder suggested that elites articulate a unique strategic culture related to security–military affairs that is a wider manifestation of public opinion, socialized into a distinctive mode of strategic thinking. He contended: 'a set of general beliefs, attitudes, and behaviour patterns with regard to nuclear strategy has achieved a state of semi-permanence that places them on the level of "cultural" rather than mere policy' (Snyder 1977: 8). Snyder concluded that the Soviet military exhibited a preference for the preemptive, offensive use of force and that the origins for this could be found in Russia's history of insecurity and authoritarian control (see Box 5.2).

---

 **BOX 5.2**  Definitions of Strategic Culture

Strategic culture is 'a set of general beliefs, attitudes, and behavior patterns with regard to nuclear strategy that has achieved a state of semi-permanence that places them on the level of "cultural" rather than mere policy'.

Snyder (1977)

Strategic culture is the 'ideational milieu that limits behavioral choices', from which 'one could derive specific predictions about strategic choice'.

Johnston (1995)

Strategic culture is 'a distinctive and lasting set of beliefs, values and habits regarding the threat and use of force, which have their roots in such fundamental influences as geopolitical setting, history and political culture'.

Booth and Trood (1999)

Subsequent studies of strategic culture continued to explore the ideational foundations of nuclear strategy and US–Soviet relations. Colin Gray suggested that distinctive national styles, with 'deep roots within a particular stream of historical experience', characterized strategic development in great powers. Strategic culture thus 'provides the milieu within which strategy is debated' and serves as an independent determinant of strategic policy patterns. Like Snyder, Gray considered that strategic culture would be a semi-permanent influence on security policy (Gray 1981: 35–7). At the same time, Ken Booth was concerned about the impact that ethnocentrism could have as a source of errors in both the theory and practice of strategy. For Booth, ethnocentrism meant that strategists might be culture-bound, unable to escape 'one's own cultural attitudes and imaginatively recreate the world from the perspective of those belonging to a different group' (Booth 1981: 15).

While these path-breaking works represented a call for new attention to ideational factors, few strategic cultural theorists viewed this as an 'either–or' debate with rationalism. Nevertheless, sceptics perceived the growth of cultural theory as a challenge to traditional strategic thought and argued that the theory was too subjective, reliant on narrow contextual historiography. Based on questions regarding the difficulty of operationalizing culture in any meaningful sense, critics claimed that early proponents had overstated the analytic and policymaking relevance of strategic culture.

 **Key Points**

- Early studies linking culture and strategic action focused on 'national character' as a product of language, religion, customs, socialization, and the interpretation of common historical experiences.

- Almond and Verba integrated cultural approaches into political science by identifying the features of what they called 'political culture', including values like democratic principles and institutions, ideas about morality and the use of force, and predispositions towards the role of a country in the world.

- Jack Snyder coined the phrase 'strategic culture' to focus on the relationship between culture and nuclear strategy. This led to significant applications of strategic culture to the study of deterrence.

## Sources of Strategic Culture

Several sources of strategic culture, encompassing both material and ideational factors, are identified in the literature. First, geography, climate, and resources have been key elements in strategic thinking throughout the millennia and remain important sources of strategic culture today. Geographical circumstance may be one key to understanding why some countries adopt particular strategic policies rather than others. For example, proximity to great powers has been viewed as an important factor. In the cases of Norway and Finland, for example, both countries had to tread carefully and remain neutral on some matters because their immediate neighbour during the cold war was the Soviet Union (Graeger and Leira 2005; Heikka 2005). Relative isolation for countries like Australia enabled a focus on continental defence in the past. Additionally, while most territorial borders are settled by negotiation, others have been forged through conflict and remain contested. Some states have multiple borders and may be confronted by multiple security dilemmas. Such factors appear to have shaped the strategic orientations of countries like Israel and South Korea (the Republic of Korea). South Korea experiences insecurity as a function of its geographical proximity to its adversary, North Korea (the Democratic People's Republic of Korea), as well as its regional rivals Japan and China (Kim 2014). Ensuring access to vital resources is also deemed critical to strategy, and this and other factors seem especially significant in changing global territorial and resource landscapes today.

History and experience are important considerations in the evolution of strategic culture. International relations theory has identified several ways to categorize states, ranging from weak to strong, colonial to postcolonial, and pre-modern, modern, and postmodern. This raises the prospect that different kinds of states may confront different strategic problems, and with varying material and ideational resources, apply unique responses. For newly formed states, the difficulties of nation-building can compound insecurities and thereby help shape strategic cultural identities. Conversely, for states of ancient standing, the longevity of their existence may prompt consideration of factors that contribute to the rise and fall of great powers or civilizations and shape their policies to suit.

Some scholars argue that generational change and technology, particularly information and communications technology, can have important ramifications for issues of empowerment and strategic reach. While information technology has transformed societies, it has also allowed individuals or groups to communicate in novel ways and cause disruption at a distance. This and other technologies may empower individual and group identities in ways unlike ever before in history.

Another source of strategic culture is the nature of a country's political structure and defence organizations. Some countries adopt a broadly Western liberal democratic style of government, while others do not. Some are considered mature democracies while others are undergoing democratic transformations. Where the latter are concerned there may be cultural variables such as tribal, religious, or ethnic allegiances that operate within and across territorial boundaries, which determine the pace and depth of consolidation. Similarly, many regard defence organizations as being critical to strategic cultures but differ over the precise impact these organizations have (Scobell 2014; de Castro 2014). Military doctrines, civil–military relations, and procurement practices may also affect strategic culture (Adamsky 2010).

Myths and symbols are considered to be part of all cultural groupings and both can act as a stabilizing or destabilizing factor in the evolution of strategic cultural identities. The notion of myth can have meaning different from the traditional understanding 'as something unfounded or false'. John Calvert writes that this can refer to a 'body of beliefs that express the fundamental, largely unconscious or assumed political values of a society—in short, as a dramatic expression of ideology' Calvert (2004: 31). At the same time, historical narratives also impact conceptions of state roles. According to Marijke Breuning, roles are an extension of cultural 'axiomatic beliefs' regarding the state's relation to the international environment (actor versus subject orientation); the nature of the international environment (universalistic versus particularistic worldview); and understandings of rules of behaviour (intent-based versus results-oriented) (1997: 113). These roles then manifest themselves in different foreign and security policy behaviours.

Related studies of symbols also suggest that these act as 'socially recognized objects of more or less common understanding' and 'provide a cultural community with stable points of reference for strategic thought and action' (Elder and Cobb, quoted in Poore 2004: 63). Political unrest and cyber-attacks in Estonia in the late 2000s show just how powerful symbols may be. This turmoil was sparked by Estonia's decision to move a Soviet war memorial from the centre of the capital, Tallinn, to a military cemetery. For Russia and the ethnic Russian population in Estonia, the statue had symbolic value related to historic sacrifice in the Second World War; for Estonia, in contrast, it represented a symbol of past occupation. The resulting protests and cyber-attacks launched from Russia drove a deep wedge between the populations of the country.

Traditional analyses of peace and conflict have long pointed to the influence of key texts as formative throughout history and in different cultural settings. These may follow an historical trajectory—from Sun Tzu's *Art of War*, considered to have been written during the time of the warring states in ancient China, through the writings of Kautilya in ancient India—and into Western understandings of peace and conflict as a result of Thucydides' commentary on the Peloponnesian War and Clausewitz's writings on the nature of war stemming from his observations of the Napoleonic period. At the same time, there may be competition between texts for influence on society. In a study of Greek strategic culture, for example, the oscillating influence of two distinct strategic traditions has been identified. 'Traditionalists' derive their intellectual sustenance from the exploits of Achilles, hero of the *Iliad*, and tend to view the world as an anarchic arena where power is the ultimate guarantee of security, while 'modernists', followers of Odysseus, the hero of the *Odyssey*, consider that Greece's best strategy is to adopt a multilateral cooperative approach to peace and security (Ladis 2003). This dualism in strategic culture reflects the influence of long-held myths and legends, which continue to find resonance in narratives of the modern era.

Finally, the relationship between transnational norms, generational change, and technology and strategic culture may be a two-way street. Norms are understood as 'intersubjective beliefs about the social and natural world that define actors, their situations, and the possibilities of action' (Wendt 1995: 73). Theo Farrell and Terry Terriff consider that norms can define 'the purpose and possibilities of military change' and 'provide guidance concerning the use of force' (2001: 7) (see Box 5.3). At the same time, Amitav Acharya (2004) contends the effects of international norms on state behaviour may be mediated through a cultural lens, suggesting a process of 'norm localization'. This and related research on culture and norm diffusion represents a rich, contemporary area of scholarly investigation.

---

**◉ BOX 5.3   Potential Sources of Strategic Culture**

| Physical | Political | Social/Cultural |
|---|---|---|
| Geography | Historical Experience | Myths and Symbols |
| Climate | Political System | Defining Texts |
| Natural Resources | Elite Beliefs | |
| Generational Change | Military Organizations | |
| Technology | | |

◄──────── **(Transnational Forces/Normative Pressures)** ────────►

**Key Points**

● Snyder brought the political cultural argument into the realm of modern security studies by developing a theory of strategic culture to interpret Soviet nuclear doctrine.

● Scholars have argued that national styles, with 'deep roots within a particular stream of historical experience', characterized nuclear strategy-making in the United States and the Soviet Union during the cold war.

● The sources of strategic culture are considered to be: geography, climate and resources, history and experience, political structure, the nature of organizations involved in defence, myths and symbols, key texts that inform actors of appropriate strategic action, transnational norms, generational change, and the role of technology.

● Contemporary scholarship has begun to investigate the complex relationship between international norms and strategic culture.

## Constructivism and Strategic Culture

In the 1990s, the influence of constructivism prompted renewed interest in strategic culture. While constructivism encompasses many theoretical positions, some scholars became interested in how ideas, norms, and cultural factors might be as influential as material factors in international security. One of the early writers in this tradition, Alexander Wendt, consequently argued that state identities and interests were 'socially constructed by knowledgeable practice' (1992: 392). For Valerie Hudson, constructivism embraced the study of culture 'as an evolving system of shared meaning that governs perceptions, communications, and actions' (1997: 28–9).

Notable studies bridging constructivism and strategic culture soon emerged. Alastair Iain Johnston's *Cultural Realism: Strategic Culture and Grand Strategy in Chinese History* (1995) is a quintessential work on strategic culture influenced by constructivism. The study set out to investigate the existence and character of Chinese strategic culture, and its potential causal links to the use of military force against external threats. Johnston characterized strategic culture as an 'ideational milieu that limits behavioral choices', from which 'one could derive specific predictions about strategic choice'. Focusing on the Ming dynasty in China (1368–1644), he concluded China 'has exhibited a tendency for the controlled, politically driven defensive and minimalist use of force that is deeply rooted in the statecraft of ancient strategists and a worldview of relatively complacent superiority' which had a 'nontrivial effect on strategy' (Johnston 1995: 1). New theoretical attention to the concept of the strategic culture also helped foster broader comparative studies (see Box 5.4).

Another strand of this scholarship focuses on military and/or organizational cultures. Elizabeth Kier described the significance of organizational culture in the development of French military doctrine (1995). Steven Rosen provided an account of the ways that the military and organizational cultures in India have shaped strategy over time. Jeffrey Legro's work on military restraint during the Second World War, and Roland Ebel, Raymond Taras, and James Cochrane's (1991) work on the cultures of Latin America all concluded that culture

**BOX** 5.4    Case Studies of Strategic Culture

### People's Republic of China

Culture plays a strong role in shaping strategic behaviour in China. Scholars have identified two dominant strands of Chinese strategic culture today—the *parabellum* focused on *realpolitik* and the *Confucian–Mencian* strand, a philosophical orientation used mainly for idealized discourse. Scobell contends that these two strands sometimes intertwine to shape a 'Chinese cult of defense'. Chinese civilian and military leaders repeatedly stress China's commitment to the Confucian saying 'peace is precious' (*he wei gui*), and they assert that China has never been an aggressive or expansionist state (2014). A study by Huiyun Feng suggests that China displays a more defensive posture in relation to the use of force and that the Confucian elements of its strategic culture have been 'underrepresented' (2009: 172). But not all are agreed on this, as Scobell concludes that Chinese leaders assume that any war they fight is just and any military action defensive, 'even when it is offensive in nature' (2002: 11). In 2013, China's President Xi Jinping underscored these themes, stating 'China will stick to the road of peaceful development but never give up our legitimate rights and never sacrifice our national core interests . . . No country should presume that we will engage in trade involving our core interests or that we will swallow the bitter fruit of harming our sovereignty, security or development interests' (quoted in Anderlini 2013).

### United States of America

Scholars argue that several core principles have defined US strategic culture over time. Thomas Mahnken suggests: 'American strategic culture was shaped by free security and imbued with exceptionalism . . . American military culture, the so-called American way of war, emphasizes direct strategies, an industrial approach to war, and firepower—and technologically intensive approaches to combat' (Mahnken 2009: 69–70). Many writers also point to the impact of the 9/11 terrorist attacks on US strategic culture. This resulted in the George W. Bush administration's declaration of a war on terror and the initiation of new strategic cultural orientations. These included a positive reaffirmation of US dominance in international security affairs, with priority to homeland security, a new doctrine of pre-emption that includes a willingness to use military force to achieve security objectives, and a preference for unilateral actions internationally. At the same time, the new strategic cultural orientations were packaged rhetorically as a demonstration of continuity in US support for democracy and freedom (Lantis 2005; Harris 2014).

### Japan

Throughout the cold war, Japan fostered an 'antimilitarist political–military culture' that was characterized by pacifism and dependence on its security alliance with the United States. The Yoshida Doctrine stressed that Japan focus on its own economic and technological development while establishing military security through its alliance with the United States. For Thomas Berger, Japan's antimilitarist sentiments became deeply institutionalized through a long historical process that included legitimated compromises. However, in wake of the 9/11 attacks and North Korean nuclear weapon tests, Japan has undertaken a fundamental re-assessment of its security (Oros 2014). The government has provided logistical support to US and multinational coalition forces fighting in Afghanistan and Iraq, and it began pursuing significant defence modernization in 2013 under Prime Minister Shinzo Abe's leadership. Japanese leaders are also reconsidering restrictions on military activity embedded in Article 9 of the Peace Constitution, and the country has bolstered its contribution to United Nations peacekeeping operations around the world (Berger 1998; Hughes 2004).

**BOX** 5.4 *(continued)*

## The Nordic Region

The strategic cultures of Denmark, Finland, Norway, and Sweden have been shaped by their proximity to great powers during the cold war (and in previous eras). Analyses of Sweden and Denmark have revealed two forms of strategic culture. In the case of Sweden, the first form emphasizes professional and technologically advanced military forces, while the second revolves around notions of a people's army based on conscription and the democratic involvement of citizens. Where Denmark is concerned, the two forms have been labelled cosmopolitanism and defencism. Cosmopolitanism stresses neutrality, alternative non-military means of conflict resolution, and the importance of international institutions such as the former League of Nations and the United Nations. In contrast, defencism emphasizes the importance of military preparedness encapsulated in the dictum 'if you want peace, you must prepare for war' and the importance of regional military organizations, such as the North Atlantic Treaty Organization (NATO), in defence and deterrence (Graeger and Leira 2005; Heikka 2005).

## Russia

Experts on Russia highlight the importance of strong leadership, geography, history, and ideology in the context of its strategic culture (Glenn 2004). Factors such as political stabilization within Russia's vast landmass, concerns about future military encirclement, and fears of attack on its territory stemming from past historical experience are deemed instrumental in the development of a distinct Russian strategic culture. The Russian takeover of Crimea in 2013 and support for separatists in eastern Ukraine may be seen as an extension of historical and cultural interests. Fritz Ermarth (2009) considers that Russian strategic culture has also traditionally been among the most militarized of any state. In recent years, the world has witnessed a new assertiveness linked to the strong leadership of Vladimir Putin and a strategic culture centring on nationalism as the ideological foundation and fuelled by Russia's oil and gas revenues (Ermath 2009: 93).

makes a difference. More recently, a comparative strategic cultures project jointly sponsored by Florida International University and the US Southern Command found a significant role for military organizational cultures in shaping security policy behaviour in South America (FIU-SOUTHCOM 2010). Together, these studies suggest that organizational culture can be a powerful factor influencing strategic choice.

 **Key Points**

- The rise of constructivism in international relations theory helped fuel a revival of interest in strategic culture.
- Strategic cultural studies have proliferated in recent years, including works that compare strategic cultures of countries in key regions such as Europe, Latin America, and Southeast Asia.
- Another strand of this scholarship focuses on how military/organizational cultures can shape security policies.

## Continuing Issues: Change or Continuity?

The focus of most studies of strategic culture is on continuity or at least semi-permanence in state behaviour. Harry Eckstein (1998) suggested that the socialization of values and beliefs occurs over time. According to this view, past learning coalesces in the collective consciousness and is relatively resilient to change. Lessons of the past serve as a filter for any future learning that might occur. The process of transformation consequently is often slow and involves generational change. If historical memory, political institutions, and multilateral commitments shape strategic culture, then it would seem plausible to accept that strategic cultures around the world are undergoing 'enduring transformations'. Conversely, other scholars argue that strategic cultures can change more dramatically.

Research suggests that at least two conditions can cause strategic cultural dilemmas and produce changes in security policy. First, external shocks may fundamentally challenge existing beliefs and undermine past historical narratives. This appears to be illustrated in the case of Japan over the past decade, as elites revisit questions of security in a changing threat environment. For German leaders in the 1990s, the scale of the humanitarian tragedies in the Balkans served as a catalyst for consideration of policy options outside the traditional bounds of German strategic culture (Lantis 2002). When North Korea detonated its first atomic bomb in 2006, Japanese and other Asian strategic cultures were prompted to adapt; when China asserted its sovereign control of contested territory and resources in the South China Sea, its neighbours seemed to shift course in military-security policy.

Second, foreign policy behaviour may break the traditional bounds of strategic cultural orientations when primary tenets of strategic thought come into direct conflict with one another. Ann Swidler recognizes the potential for dynamism 'in unsettled cultural periods . . . when explicit ideologies govern action [and] structural opportunities for action determine which among competing ideologies survive in the long run' (1986: 274). For example, a country with interpretive codes of support for democracy and an aversion to the use of military force faces a strategic cultural dilemma when confronted by a challenge to democracy that necessitates a military response. Thus, strategic cultural dilemmas define new directions for foreign policy and demand the reconstruction of historical narratives. Changes, including abrupt and fairly dramatic reorientations of security policy, are possible, and strategic cultural analysis must be more reflective of the conditions that lead to such changes.

### Who are the Keepers of Strategic Culture?

One theme of contemporary strategic cultural studies has been the effort to identify the 'keepers' of strategic culture. These studies also allude to the subtleties associated with determining whether individuals or elite and non-elite groupings have the most influence in strategic cultural outcomes.

While past work tended to describe political and strategic cultures as properties of states only, reflecting the ideas of 'collectives rather than simply of the individuals that constitute them' (Wilson 2000: 12), elites (high level policymakers) may represent the primary keepers of strategic culture or purveyors of a common historical narrative. While strategic culture can have deep roots in society, newer works on policy discourse suggest that strategic culture is best characterized as a 'negotiated reality' among elites (Swidler 1986). For example, Jacques

Hymans contends that identity is as much *subjective* as intersubjective and that leaders often adopt their own specific conceptions of national identity from among a competitive market-place of ideas (2006). Sociologist Consuelo Cruz contends that elites have more latitude than scholars generally allow. They may 'recast a particular agenda as most appropriate to a given collective reality' or 'redefine the limits of the possible, both descriptively and prescriptively' (2000: 278). Post-structural constructivists also look at how elites may be both keepers and strategic users of culture, manipulating cultural frames as a way to take exception to intersub-jective structural limits (Milliken 1999; Miskimmon 2004; Mattern 2005).

The organizational culture literature suggests that state behaviour is a function of specific institutional orientations or prevailing cultures. Studies of Japan's and Germany's foreign policy decisions in the 1990s, for example, identified enduring institutional manifestations of strategic culture, but the keepers of the culture are not necessarily *military* bureaucracies. In Germany, the Foreign Ministry has control over foreign and security policy. In Japan, political institutions from the Diet to the Liberal Democratic Party to the Japan Self-Defense Forces share commit-ments to a foreign policy of restraint (Eden 2004). Finally, there may be an important public dimension to strategic culture. Charles Kupchan has argued that the foundations of strategic culture are *societal*. 'Based on images and symbols,' he says, strategic culture 'refers to images that shape how the nation as a collective entity defines its well-being and conceives of its security' (Kupchan 1994: 21). Broad support for a prevailing historical narrative may condition security policy responses as well as the potential for strategic cultural change.

 **Key Points**

- Many studies of strategic culture have focused on continuity, but new scholarship suggests potential scope conditions of change including external shocks and internal cognitive dissonance.
- Strategic cultural dilemmas may define new directions for foreign policy and foster the reconstruction of historical narratives.
- While traditional studies suggest that strategic culture is the property of collectives, new work explores the potential for agency in cultural framing.
- Keepers of strategic culture may include elites, bureaucratic organizations, and society at large.

 **Critical Thinking:** Debating ... Will states in regions like Europe and the Asia-Pacific ever 'get over' cultural differences and create true regional security identities?

**For**

- *States do cooperate in regional organizations.* States recognize that the benefits of cooperation outweigh the costs. The record shows that states have gradually overcome challenges to cooperation, including a reluctance to cede sovereignty, and coordinated their policies through common markets, fiscal and monetary policy, and justice issues. For example, the Asia-Pacific has seen the creation of the Asia-Pacific Economic Cooperation (APEC) forum and the emergence of a new Trans-Pacific Partnership.

(*continued ...*)

**Critical Thinking:**   *(continued)*

- *The European Union has established a strong regional defence identity.* The European Union clearly illustrates that countries can cooperate in functional economic and political areas as well as military-security affairs. In December 2003, the common European Security Strategy (ESS) was formalized, marking the emergence of a common European strategic culture (Cornish and Edwards 2001; Meyer 2007). Europe has taken fairly cohesive stands on reconstruction and stabilization in Iraq and Afghanistan, responses to Russian aggression, and human rights issues. This suggests that efforts to align strategic cultures can help diffuse dangerous crises.

- *Regional cooperation is aided by the engagement of a hegemon.* Countries may be better able to cooperate in military-security affairs with the support of a 'benevolent hegemon'. The United States after the Second World War helped promote functional integration in Europe, and its leadership of the North Atlantic Treaty Organization (NATO) aided the melding of European countries' strategic cultures and security policies. The United States was directly engaged in the transformation of Germany's strategic culture and the promotion of antimilitarism and pacifism in Japan's post-war Constitution. In 2013 President Obama announced a US 'pivot' to the Asia-Pacific region that was expressly designed to help boost cooperation.

### Against

- *States don't cooperate well in regional organizations.* Despite the optimism of some policymakers and experts, strategic cultural differences often inhibit integration. The European Union has existed for decades, yet it has been slow to establish and implement a common European Security Strategy (ESS). It still has no European Constitution, after decades of efforts. Countries in the Asia-Pacific seem more hesitant to join any form of security policy cooperation.

- *Governments are reluctant to coordinate security policies through regional organizations.* Countries around the world must consider national interests first—and national interests are often a manifestation of strategic cultural identities forged out of historical experiences, geography, the views of multiple actors and institutions, and transnational forces. Governments are often hesitant to build beyond existing bilateral and regional relationships to construct a stronger alignment of military organizational cultures (Williams 2007).

- *Hegemons interfere with regional cooperation.* The presence of significant power imbalances, especially involving a hegemon, represents a serious challenge to regional cooperation. In Europe, Germany is seen as an economic engine for the region, but also as a powerful political actor with its own distinct interests that may undermine regional prosperity. In the Asia-Pacific, countries face an emerging hegemonic rivalry between the United States and China (Schweller and Pu 2011). Many ponder American commitments to the region and 'whether the United States intends to use its power to help or hurt China' (Nathan and Scobell 2012: 4).

## Delineating Non-state, State, and Multi-state Strategic Cultures

An exciting new area of research focuses on the degree to which non-state and multi-state actors may be said to possess strategic cultures. This approach has important implications for the study of a number of contemporary themes in international politics, from counterinsurgency to European integration (see Box 5.5). In December 2003, the European Union (EU) formalized a common European Security Strategy (ESS) for the first time in its history. That document called for the development of a 'strategic culture, which fosters early, rapid, and when necessary, robust intervention' (European Union 2003: 11). This initiative suggested that European countries might be able to foster common European responses to regional and global challenges such as terrorism, humanitarian crises, and proliferation of weapons of mass destruction (Schmitt, Howlett, Müller, Simpson, and Tertrais 2005; Vasconcelos 2009). The 2009 Lisbon Treaty promised even greater cooperation on multilateral responses through a Common Defence and Security Policy architecture.

However, scholars continue to debate whether we are witnessing the emergence of a truly new EU strategic culture. Optimists such as Paul Cornish and Geoffrey Edwards believe 'there are signs that a European strategic culture is already developing through a socialization process'. They define EU strategic culture as 'the institutional confidence and processes to manage and deploy military force as part of the accepted range of legitimate and effective policy instruments' (Cornish and Edwards 2001: 587). For Christoph Meyer, establishment of the ESS in 2003 provided a necessary 'strategic concept' upon which to focus attention and resources (Meyer

---

 **BOX** 5.5  Culture and Counterinsurgency?

Can knowledge of cultural dynamics in countries like Iraq and Afghanistan bolster counterinsurgency and stability operations? This question has generated significant debate in the last decade. Some strategists have embraced the idea that cultural understanding matters for counterinsurgency operations. At the same time, social scientists have debated whether it is ever ethical to provide assistance for military operations.

In 2005, the US Army established an experimental counterinsurgency programme called the Human Terrain System (HTS). Human terrain was defined as the 'social, ethnographic, cultural, economic, and political elements among whom a force is operating . . . characterized by sociocultural, anthropologic, and ethnographic data' (Kipp et al. 2006: 9). Five-person human terrain teams made up of regional studies experts, linguists, and social scientists would be assigned to brigades or combat headquarters to provide 'cultural knowledge' for more effective military planning. These groups were deployed in Iraq and Afghanistan in daily civil operations, including engagement with populations in areas of insurgency, to promote more effective cooperation. By focusing on civil society as the 'centre of gravity' in counterinsurgency operations, the military hoped to make stronger links between occupation forces and local civilians.

The system was self-consciously 'designed to address cultural awareness shortcomings at the operational and tactical levels' (Kipp et al. 2006: 8). However, since the establishment of HTS, the military has provided few public statements regarding its effectiveness; the programme has been plagued by recruitment and operational problems; and other sectors of the government have raised questions about its value. Acting on these concerns, in 2010 the House Armed Services Committee limited funding for the programme until an independent assessment was completed.

The question of assistance for military operations also fostered a bitter debate within the social sciences. While optimists saw this as a modified version of ethnographic research—and a tacit endorsement of the importance of learning about foreign languages and cultures—critics charged that these teams were collecting intelligence on local tribes for more effective targeting by the military. In other words, the work of the teams was more directed to *controlling* populations, to 'combat support', rather than civil reconstruction. In 2007, the Executive Board of the American Anthropological Association formally denounced the programme and argued that the operations might have the effect of harming societies more than helping them (Weinberger 2008).

2004). Conversely, Julian Lindley-French considered that Europe lacks both the capabilities and will to establish a common foreign and security policy in the foreseeable future. He characterized the Europe of today as 'not so much an architecture as a decaying arcade of stately structures of varying designs reflective of a bygone era' (2002: 789). Given the disagreements over threat perception and inconsistent policies in response to challenges such as the war on terrorism and the Arab Spring in the Middle East and North Africa, the EU may be unlikely 'to develop a coherent and strong strategic culture' any time soon (Rynning 2003: 479).

Another issue concerns whether the strategic culture frame applies to terrorist groups or groups operating across territorial boundaries where identities may be formed in the realms of both physical and cyberspace. Mark Long contends that al-Qaeda and other transnational terrorist organizations can have identifiable strategic cultures. He suggests that the study of strategic culture of some non-state actors, especially organized terrorist groups or liberation movements, may actually be *easier* than the study of state strategic cultures (Long 2009). The cyber revolution also deepens the complexity of the non-state actor threat assessment (Rattray 2002; Goldman 2003). Victor Cha argues: '[T]he most far-reaching security effect of globalization is its complication of the basic concept of "threat" in international relations' (2000: 392).

Additionally, while acknowledging that the technologies associated with globalization have enabled terrorist groups to conduct operations that 'are deadlier, more distributed, and more difficult to combat than those of their predecessors', James Kiras argues that these same technologies 'can be harnessed to defeat terrorism by those governments with the will and resources to combat it' (2005: 479). Cha concludes that technology enhances 'the salience of substate extremist groups or fundamentalist groups because their ability to organize transnationally, meet virtually, and utilize terrorist tactics has been substantially enhanced by the globalization of technology and information' (2000: 392).

---

 **Key Points**

- One of the more complex questions that carries across generations relates to what types of actors are most likely to have defined strategic cultures: states, regional organizations, civilizations, and even non-state groups such as terrorist networks?

- The HTS programme represents a foray into bridging the gap between academic study and policymaking, but this counterterrorism initiative has generated significant controversy.

- Globalization and revolutions in information technology suggest that future threats will be more diffuse, more dispersed, and more multidimensional.

---

## Strategic Culture and Weapons of Mass Destruction

What can strategic culture tell us about WMD proliferation and emerging deterrent situations? Recent studies have highlighted the role that strategic culture plays in decisions to acquire and potentially threaten to use WMD (Johnson, Kartchner, and Larsen 2009). In some ways, this work hearkens back to the foundations of strategic cultural studies, but it also reflects a globalizing world characterized by more actors and rapid technological innovation.

Among the questions being revisited are: Whether deterrence is an accepted universal norm that predetermines behaviour, or are attitudes toward nuclear strategy largely indigenous constructs that emerge from within the cultural context of particular actors? Early scholarship on this question is mixed. For example, Keith Payne considers that past 'deterrence concepts, buzzwords, and terms of art have essentially lost their meaning because the conditions of current power and political relationships have become so different from cold war conditions' (2007: 2). Jeffrey Knopf identifies a new fourth wave of deterrence literature as distinct given its asymmetric focus on deterrence relationships between the United States and rogue states or violent non-state actors (VNSAs), and the relaxation of traditional standards of deterrence (Knopf 2010).

In related work, Ian Kenyon and John Simpson contend there is significance in the 'ongoing debate between universal rationality and particular strategic cultures in relation to the mechanisms and effectiveness of deterrence' (Kenyon and Simpson 2006: 202). This has implications for threats of weapons of mass destruction attacks by non-state actors and perceived 'rogue states'. Contemporary scholarship also tends to recognize the importance of contextualizing relationships when it comes to specific settings, or scope conditions within which cultural factors may play a larger role in strategic decisions. For example, Sten Rynning posits that 'a strong strategic culture' may make a state more willing to use military force and better able to triumph in zero-sum conflicts, while states with a 'weak strategic culture' might seek more diplomatic means of conflict resolution (Rynning 2003: 484).

Kartchner has hypothesized that specific conditions can enable strategic culture to play a more dominant role in WMD policy. These include: when there is a strong sense of threat to a group's existence, identity, or resources, or when the group believes that it is at a critical disadvantage to other groups; when there is a pre-existing strong cultural basis for group identity; when the leadership frequently resorts to cultural symbols in support of its national group security aspirations and programmes; when there is a high degree of homogeneity within the group's strategic culture; and when historical experiences strongly predispose the group to perceive threats (2009).

New studies of 'tailored deterrence' stand squarely at the intersection of traditional and cultural approaches. Traditional deterrence theory is rife with discussions of *persuasion* of the adversary. For instance, Thomas Schelling defines deterrence as 'influencing the choices that another party will make, and doing it by influencing his expectations of how we will behave' (1963: 13). In other words, theorists of deterrence also implicitly recognize the significance of the target of their policies. Any thoughtful attempt to reflect on coercion dynamics and persuasion generates consideration of value hierarchies and vested national interests, which, in turn, can be the product of elite strategic calculations embedded within a larger cultural context.

---

 **Key Points**

- Strategic culture has implications for state policies regarding weapons of mass destruction.

- Though not emphasized in early theoretical work on deterrence, cultural dynamics can impact perception of threats and opportunities and help mediate attempts at persuasion. They may augment understandings of bounded rationality, for example.

- Strategic cultural understanding is directly related to the concept of tailored deterrence, recognizing the importance of targeting and contextualizing deterrence messages carefully to potential adversaries.

- Identity and strategic choice may sometimes be a function of culture.

Conclusion

Recent events have renewed scholarly and policymaking interest in strategic culture. As Western leaders attempt to respond to Russian aggression in Ukraine, NATO leaders adapt their strategic concept for a changing world, and Asia-Pacific states reassess commitments to regional security, research on strategic culture can offer important insights to improve knowledge as well as enrich policy recommendations. Culturally interpretive models are gaining increased attention in academia and policymaking circles, and all signs point to further development of this worthwhile endeavour.

Comparative analysis represents one of the more fertile areas for advancement of cultural understandings in policymaking and academic research. Studies of strategic culture often apply the theory to a single case or make general comparisons with other like-minded countries. This tradition has produced rich and compelling works, such as Andrew Oros' study of the changing security identity of Japan (2014), Ade Adefuye's fascinating study of the culture and foreign policy of Nigeria (1992), or Marcin Zaborowski's study of the evolution of Polish strategic culture (2004). Yet more rigorous cross-national comparison can promote cumulative knowledge in the field. Academics, strategists, and defence planners should more openly recognize variation in instruments and incentive structures associated with deterrence of specific threats, while at the same time searching for identifiable patterns among nations. As one senior State Department official, Kerry Kartchner, argued, '[s]trategic culture offers the promise of providing insight into motivations and intentions that are not readily explained by other frameworks, and that may help make sense of forces we might otherwise overlook, misunderstand, or misinterpret' (2009: 56). In this context, there appears to be an important convergence of interest in deterrence and strategic cultural studies around the theme of contextualizing strategic choice and identifying scope conditions for more reflective models of deterrence and dissuasion for the twenty-first century.

Finally, culturalists remind us of important caveats in these pursuits, including that, in seeking to identify causal relations, there is a risk of oversimplifying the social world and, consequently, categories from one case may be applied inappropriately to others. An inadequate knowledge of a given strategic culture may lead to misinterpretation of attributes such as pride, honour, duty, and also security and stability. Even long-time proponents of cultural interpretations warn of the potential pitfalls that accompany an over-reliance by policymakers on the insights that this area of knowledge can give.

 Questions

1. What are the different definitions of culture and what implications do these differences have for the study of security policy?

2. What are some specific examples of strategic cultures (or historical narratives) in countries around the world?

3. What are the sources of these strategic cultures? In your opinion, which are the most important and why?

4. What should be the historical starting point for research on strategic culture?

5. What conditions might cause strategic cultural change?

6. Identify the primary themes that define a country's strategic culture. Can you imagine scenarios in which these themes might come into conflict with one another?

7. Can a strategic cultural framework be applied to a non-state or multi-state actor?

8. What are the implications of globalization for our understanding of strategic culture?

9. Why is it important to study the linkages between strategic culture and WMD proliferation?

10. What are the benefits and pitfalls of incorporating strategic culture from a policymaking perspective?

## Further Reading

J. Glenn, D. A. Howlett, and S. Poore (eds), *Neorealism Versus Strategic Culture* (Aldershot, UK: Ashgate, 2004) is a recent classic that addresses head-on the theoretical debate over the explanatory power of cultural and ideational models versus more parsimonious neo-realism.

J. L. Johnson, K. M. Kartchner, and J. A. Larsen (eds), *Strategic Culture and Weapons of Mass Destruction: Culturally Based Insights into Comparative National Security Policymaking* (London: Palgrave Macmillan, 2009) presents theoretical foundations for the study of strategic culture and a number of rich comparative case studies.

J. S. Lantis (ed.), **Strategic Cultures and Security Policies in the Asia-Pacific: Special Issue of** *Contemporary Security Policy,* **35(2) (2014)** is a collection of original essays by country specialists examining the value of strategic cultural models to explain rising tensions in Asia-Pacific security.

E. Lock, 'Refining Strategic Culture: Return of the Second Generation', *Review of International Studies*, 36(1) (2010): 685–708 gives an interesting survey of the evolution of strategic culture scholarship, with particular emphasis on insights that were 'missed' from second-generation works.

C. O. Meyer, *The Quest for a European Strategic Culture: Changing Norms on Security* and *Defence in the European Union* (London: Palgrave-Macmillan, 2007) provides a rich and engaging exploration of debates about strategic culture and security norms in Europe.

P. Schmidt and B. Zyla (eds), *European Security Policy and Strategic Culture* (London: Routledge, 2013) critically examines European efforts to develop a common security policy identity using a strategic cultural lens; it also features a rich set of case essays.

 ## Web Links

The Florida International University-US Southern Command Comparative Strategic Cultures Project **http://strategicculture.fiu.edu/Studies.aspx** adopts a framework to examine fascinating historical traditions, keepers of culture, and the importance of military and organizational cultures across the Latin American region.

The Stockholm International Peace Research Institute (SIPRI) **http://www.sipri.org/** monitors trends in military expenditures and policies throughout the world.

European Union **http://europa.eu/pol/cfsp/index_en.htm** is the main website of the EU, which includes valuable archival materials as well as descriptions of contemporary EU foreign and security policy institutions and initiatives.

Washington Institute for Near East Policy **https://www.washingtoninstitute.org/uploads/Documents/pubs/PolicyFocus72FinalWeb.pdf** features a compelling work linking strategic culture and contemporary deterrence challenges, entitled *Deterring the Ayatollahs: Complications in Applying Cold War Strategies to Iran* (Patrick Clawson and Michael Eisenstadt (eds), July 2007).

*Strategic Insights* **http://www.ccc.nps.navy.mil/si/2005/Oct/khan2Oct05.asp** contains the October 2005 special issue of the online journal, *Strategic Insights*, examining the theme of comparative strategic culture. The journal is sponsored by the Center for Contemporary Conflict at the Naval Postgraduate School in Monterey, California.

## Acknowledgement

The authors gratefully acknowledge the research assistance of Rachel Wilson.

# Law, Politics, and the Use of Force

## JUSTIN MORRIS

## Chapter Contents

 **Reader's Guide**

This chapter discusses the role of international law in international politics, focusing specifically upon the efficacy of legal constraint of the use of force by states. It is not intended that the chapter will provide a detailed examination of the substantive legal provisions relating to the use of force, though the basic pro-scriptions will be outlined and commented upon. Rather, the intention is to focus upon the manner in which legal regulation influences the behaviour of states and in particular the political and strategic decisions that they take. It will be argued that international law exerts a significant, though by no means always decisive, influence on such behaviour, and that this is the case even when states are dealing with issues which are perceived to be of great national interest and where the use of force is at issue.

## Introduction: The Efficacy of International Law

There is a commonly held view that international law has little effect upon the behaviour of states. According to this view, international law is simply a tool in the diplomatic kitbag that can be utilized to justify politically motivated actions. Ken Matthews captures this sentiment:

> The common view seems to be that international law is honoured more in its breach than in its observance and that since it seems to be broken so much it can hardly be said to exist at all. Moreover . . . there is little evidence that international law restrains states from pursuing their interests in the international system.
>
> Matthews (1996: 26)

**BOX** 6.1  Symptoms of the Perception–Reality Gap

| Perception | Reality |
| --- | --- |
| International law is regularly flouted | International law is usually obeyed |
| Military conflict is the norm | Military conflict is the exception |
| International law regulates the use of force | International law regulates almost all aspects of inter-state activity |
| Law is prohibitive | Law is facilitative |

This assessment of international law is reflected in the dominant approach to international politics known as Realism. Realists portray the world as being dominated by states that act only in pursuit of their national interests. These states interact in a world that is anarchic, in the sense that sovereign states recognize no higher authority. In such a world, interaction is regulated through the exercise of power (and ultimately through the utilization of military power). For realists there is little scope for effective international legal regulation.

This view of the world and international law's role within it is challenged by scholars such as Louis Henkin. Henkin observed that 'it is probably the case that almost all nations observe almost all principles of international law and almost all of their obligations almost all of the time' (1968: 47). So why does the common perception of international law not reflect this? The answer lies in what one might call a 'perception–reality gap' (see Box 6.1).

## The Perception–Reality Gap

The perception–reality gap operates at a number of levels. The low regard in which international law is commonly held is partially a consequence of inappropriate parallels drawn between domestic and international law, often leading to the unwarranted conclusion that international law lacks the status of true 'law'. Even among those immersed in international law such doubts sometimes appear: as Sir Hersch Lauterpacht famously commented, 'international law is the vanishing point of law' (Lauterpacht 1952: 381). The common assumption is that at the international level the norm in response to legal edicts is breach, whereas domestically the norm is compliance. In reality the norm in both cases is compliance, though this may be less so at the international level than at the domestic.

The common failure to recognize this is the consequence of another misleading idea, namely that to operate effectively it is essential that a system of law possesses the 'legal trinity' of a legislature, an effective and centralized police force, and a judiciary. At the international level, this trinity is all but absent and the conclusion commonly drawn from this is that international law is unable to influence the behaviour of states effectively. The argument is misleading because it is predicated on the erroneous notion that domestic law is synonymous with criminal law, resulting in a misguided preoccupation with issues of apprehension and enforcement, and hence the legal trinity. As Hilaire McCoubrey noted, 'Enforcement—specifically processes of criminal enforcement—tends to be emphasised in external observation of the operation of law and legal systems . . . but it can be argued that this is a seriously misplaced emphasis' (McCoubrey 1998: 271).

It is, of course, true that domestic criminal law is obligatory, policed by the state, and enforced through the imposition of judicially passed sanctions—it possesses the legal trinity—yet this does not result in the effective control of *all* members of society. Conversely, other forms of legal regulation function effectively without such characteristics. Contract law, for example, impinges only upon the lives of those who choose to enter into contracts, its enforcement is dependent upon the parties resorting to self-help, and in many systems it does not provide a punitive response to breaches. Despite these 'deficiencies', contract law effectively regulates an important aspect of domestic behaviour; in a similar vein the fact that international law does not conform to the familiar model of criminal law does not necessarily deprive it of its efficacy.

Another reason for the perception–reality gap is the manner in which international politics is portrayed, be it in academic or journalistic writing. The former tends to concentrate on conflict rather than cooperation, portraying a world in which international law, depicted as synonymous with the regulation of the use of force, is invariably disregarded by states. But inter-state military conflict is really the exception, and—the focus of this chapter notwithstanding—for the most part international law provides for orderly and predictable intercourse between states at a mundane, 'everyday' level that has nothing to do with military conflict. The media's coverage of world events shares academia's preoccupation with conflict, and while in the commercial world of journalism the need to generate attention-grabbing headlines and stories is readily understandable, the size of the audience makes its impact all the more deleterious.

## Why States Obey the Law

The observation that states generally obey the law should come as no great surprise. International law, and indeed law more generally, is designed not to prohibit those actions which states (or individuals in the domestic setting) would normally choose to undertake, but rather to codify accepted modes of behaviour; good law is facilitative, not prohibitive. Law reflects and strengthens social order and values, it does not seek to impose them. Were this not the case it would be both ineffective and short-lived. The law should not be viewed as an end in itself, but rather as a means to an end. It is a mechanism through which societies seek to achieve political objectives, though once these objectives have become enshrined in law, the law in turn serves to define modes of acceptable political activity (Reus-Smit 2004).

This observation raises a further difficult question: *which* social values and objectives are to be legally codified? For realists, it will always be those that secure and perpetuate the privileged position of the satisfied powers, but this is an oversimplification of the complexities involved in the development of normative frameworks (Morris 2005). Not even the most powerful are free to dictate an order purely on their terms, but rather must establish one premised upon the codification of behavioural norms in which a sufficiently large proportion of states believe themselves to have an interest. As Henkin observes, 'even the rich and the mighty . . . cannot commonly obtain what they want by force and dictation and must be prepared to pay the price of reciprocal or compensating obligation' (Henkin 1968: 31). The exact nature of what such a compromise requires is likely to be a source of perpetual debate, but the basic point remains: for the international order to be stable, a sufficiently

**BOX** 6.2 Why Do States Obey International Law?

- Coercion: involves an asymmetric power relationship in which one actor is, through exercise of power, forced to comply with a rule.
- Self-interest: involves an *ad hoc* calculation of whether compliance with a rule will result in a beneficial or detrimental outcome.
- Legitimacy: compliance results from the belief that a rule is of value. Rule compliance is an integral part of an actor's identity.

high proportion of states must perceive it to be just and conducive to their own interests (see Box 6.2).

## Coercion, Self-Interest, and Legitimacy

The suggestion that states are more likely to obey the law because they deem it to be in their interests is not to reaffirm the realist position that law is simply a diplomatic tool to be employed to justify politically motivated actions. Ian Hurd's work provides a particularly lucid explanation of this point (Hurd 1999). Hurd explains how states are induced to accept rules through coercion, calculations of self-interest, and/or legitimization. Coercion involves an asymmetric power relationship in which one actor is, through the exercise of power, forced to comply with a rule. Where compliance results from calculations of self-interest, it is self-restraint motivated by the likelihood of a beneficial outcome that induces compliance. In both cases, compliance results from prudential calculation. In neither is the content of the rule or its associated institution(s) valued or relevant. What distinguishes the two scenarios is that in cases of coercion, states obey the law to avoid punishment but find themselves, in contrast to cases of self-interest, ultimately disadvantaged by doing so.

Systems that depend on coercion in order to ensure compliance are difficult to sustain because forcibly policing them is highly resource-intensive. Systems that depend on self-interest to ensure observance are less costly, but they tend to be unpredictable and unstable because of their reliance on *ad hoc* cost–benefit calculations. For these reasons it can be concluded that legal systems that depend primarily on coercion and/or self-interest for their observance are likely to be ineffective and relatively short-lived. Sustainable and effective legal regulation depends, therefore, on a widespread shared perception of legitimacy. In such cases, compliance is motivated neither by fear of punitive sanction nor by self-interest (as we have defined) but rather by the belief that the law is, in some sense, of intrinsic value. In such circumstances its observance and general standing form a constituent element of states' interests and identities. Interest is defined in relation to the law itself rather than by consideration of the beneficial or detrimental consequences of compliance. While states are 'interested' in the sense that they pursue goals, they do so within behavioural parameters that are internally driven and hence non-compliance is the exception to the rule.

Whether in any particular case it is fear of coercion, calculations of self-interest, or perceptions of legitimacy that lead to observance of the law is likely to be unclear and any claims on the matter non-falsifiable. In keeping with the generally low esteem in which international law is held, there tends to be an assumption that prudential calculations are the primary motivating factor. However, as Hurd notes:

> [It] is unreasonable to use the difficulty of proving any one motivation to justify the retreat to the default position that privileges another, without requiring similar proof . . . We have no better reason to assume coercion [or self-interest] than to assume legitimacy.

> Hurd (1999: 392)

In fact, given its nature, in the case of international law coercion is unlikely to be the most significant motivation. Considerations of self-interest and legitimacy provide more plausible explanations, though determining the relative importance of these motivational factors is a complex process. Consider, for example, the reputational benefits that states derive from observance of legal obligations. States seek to avoid the stigma of being branded a 'law-breaker'—or in current parlance a 'rogue state'. They expect that having a trustworthy reputation will be advantageous because others will reciprocate in future dealings with them, not simply with regard to the specific rule or agreement in question, but with regard to legal commitments more generally. This could, therefore, be said to be a prudential calculation, i.e. observation is motivated by self-interest. Against this, however, there is ample evidence that policy leaders, and particularly those who operate within systems long immersed in liberal-democratic traditions, do not want to be branded as law-breakers because they attach significant value to the notion of the rule of law. They consider rule observance to be of value in itself.

A second reason for abiding by the law is the perception that it is of substantive value, in other words the modes of behaviour enshrined within particular rules warrant respect. Legal rules are a means by which societies pursue collective goals. The greater the extent to which states share these aspirations, and that a specific rule assists in their attainment, the more likely it is that the rule will be accepted and obeyed by states (Franck 1990). A third reason why state officials observe international legal obligations is that they perceive international law to be of functional value. While the importance of a particular law may be questioned, leaders recognize the contribution that legal regulation as a whole makes to the orderly functioning of international society. Since the authority of the law will be undermined if states pick and choose the rules by which they abide, all rules must be followed.

A final factor that gives rise to the general acceptance of legal regulation and conformity to the law is inertia: states become habituated into formulating and adopting policies that accord with legal rules. This may be because under monist constitutional arrangements international legal obligations become incorporated into the body of domestic law (Brownlie 1990: 32). Where this occurs, government policies that violate international legal obligations may give rise to action in the domestic courts. There is, however, a less tangible way in which states become habituated into following the law: individuals who comprise governing elites and bureaucracies become socialized into behaving in certain prescribed ways. Moreover, where democratically elected policymakers are subject to public, media, and legislative scrutiny, policies that violate legal obligations may be perceived as electorally non-viable.

## Understanding Breaches of the Law

Although states generally act in accordance with the law, they do not of course *always* obey it. What do breaches of international law tell us about its role and status in international politics? While perhaps counterintuitive, law-breaking often serves to demonstrate the strength of the law, at least insofar as it remains the exception (see Box 6.3). Because states normally obey the law, any breach is likely to occur against a background of general conformity to both the body of international law in general and to the specific rule in question. Where the breaking of a rule attracts widespread international censure, this demonstrates the efficacy, rather than inefficacy, of the rule. Iraq's 1990 invasion of Kuwait was, for example, such a clear breach of international law and was so overwhelmingly criticized that its effect was to bolster, rather than undermine, the legal prohibition of the use of force in international relations. In less clear-cut cases where there exists legal ambiguity, 'breach' may result from a genuine disagreement over the legality of an act and may, therefore, in fact embody some element of conformity. The general prohibition of the use of force, for instance, is subject to numerous alternative interpretations regarding the extent of the prohibition and the permissibility of exceptions to it (e.g. pre-emptive strike and humanitarian intervention). Finally in this regard it should be noted that violations of the law are invariably accompanied by an assertion that, while the rule in question is perceived by the offending state to be ordinarily valid and applicable, exceptional circumstances or the existence of a competing principle necessitate breach. Particularly in the latter case, a degree of caution is necessary for history is replete with disingenuous claims of this sort, but it is nevertheless clear and notable that from invulnerable superpowers to the most delinquent of rogues, when states opt to break the law, they seek to justify their actions in terms of it.

---

 **BOX** 6.3   Understanding Breaches of the Law

- The fact that a state breaches a rule of international law does not in itself demonstrate the inefficacy of the rule or of international law more generally.
- Breaches of the law invariably occur against a background of general conformity to both the specific rule and the law in general.
- Widespread censure following a breach reinforces the rule.
- Breach is invariably accompanied by an explanation based on recourse to legal argument.

---

 **Key Points**

- States are motivated to obey the law by a complex combination of factors (fear of coercion, self-interest, and perceptions of legitimacy).
- Breaches of the law often serve to demonstrate its strength and not its weakness.
- Where states break the law they very rarely seek to repudiate the validity of international law completely and invariably attempt to justify their actions in terms of the law.

# International Law and the Use of Force

The two broad functions of the laws of armed conflict are performed respectively by the *jus ad bellum* and the *jus in bello* (see Box 6.4). The *jus ad bellum* (literally the law towards war) governs and seeks to avert or limit resort to armed force in the conduct of international relations. The *jus in bello* (literally the law in war) governs and seeks to moderate the actual conduct of hostilities. It should be made clear from the outset that these sectors are distinct in both purpose and implication. The applicability of the *jus in bello* is not affected by the legitimacy or otherwise of the initial resort to armed force by either of the belligerents; where armed conflict breaks out, the *jus in bello* becomes operative and equally applicable irrespective of which party initially transgressed the law.

The idea of legal constraint upon the waging of war, though ancient in origin, seems profoundly paradoxical. Two distinct lines of argument underpin this apparent paradox, each corresponding to the two areas into which the laws of armed conflict are divided. In striving to control the circumstances in which states use force in their international relations, the *jus ad bellum* seeks to operate when the logic of 'power politics' appears most intense and hence factors mitigating in favour of legal observance are likely to be most compromised. Hence, to quote him more fully, Lauterpacht asserted not only that 'international law is . . . the vanishing point of law' but also that 'the law of war is even more conspicuously the vanishing point of international law' (Lauterpacht 1952: 381). Evidence for such a claim might, at first sight, appear to lie in the German Chancellor Theobald von Bethmann-Hollweg's infamous Reichstag speech at the outset of the First World War where he declared:

> We are now in a state of necessity, and necessity knows no law . . . He who is menaced as we are, and is fighting for his highest possession, can only consider how he is to hack his way through.
>
> As quoted in Wilson (1928: 305)

Yet the Chancellor's statement actually suggests something quite different: whilst necessity might demand that the law be broken, nevertheless the decision to which he was referring (namely to invade two neutral states) was taken not in *disregard* of the law, but rather in *conscious* breach of it. The lawfulness of the action being contemplated was clearly a pertinent issue in the decision-making process.

This is not to suggest that legal questions are necessarily at the forefront of policymakers' minds when they contemplate the use of force. The uppermost questions will be ones relating

---

 **BOX** 6.4   The Laws of Armed Conflict

### Jus ad bellum (the law towards war)

Governs and seeks to limit resort to armed force in the conduct of international relations.

Major source: Articles 2(4) and Chapter VII of the UN Charter.

### Jus in bello (the law in war)

Governs and seeks to moderate the actual conduct of hostilities.

Major source: the four Geneva Conventions of 1949 and the Hague Conventions of 1899 and 1907.

to whether policy objectives can be achieved through the use of force at a reasonable cost and this, in turn, will depend on the perceived importance of the objective in question. In a fight for ultimate survival almost any cost may appear reasonable, whereas in one fought for political aggrandizement or to secure the welfare of non-nationals, the threshold of acceptability may be much lower. We may conceive of the notion of 'cost' in several ways. There are the direct costs of conflict, of lives and assets, both military and civilian, lost in the fray. Given the destructive power of modern weaponry these may be almost without limit; in such situations legal niceties may seem at best a tangential consideration. There are political costs: what will be the response, both domestically and internationally, to a policy involving the use of force? Much may here depend upon the outcome of the conflict, but even victory cannot guarantee acclaim. If the action is perceived to be in violation of the accepted norms of international behaviour enshrined within international law, even political allies may disapprove. Despite the improbability of effective direct sanction, legal considerations are paramount here, for international law provides the medium of diplomatic and political exchange on the basis of which states will formulate, articulate, and justify their responses.

Normative costs also must be considered. How might a breach of the cardinal rule prohibiting the use of force affect international order in the longer term? Repeated violations can only undermine an order in which both the powerful and the weak have a vested interest. For the former, the incentive in preserving the existing order and its rules is readily apparent, though the rules themselves may militate against great powers adopting policies that are blatantly self-interested. For the weaker members of international society, the legal framework's prohibition of the use of force is also beneficial. Many states are militarily incapable of defending themselves, and their survival is therefore dependent upon the general observance of these rules. As Robert Jackson observes: 'Ramshackle states today are not open invitations for unsolicited external intervention . . . They cannot be deprived of sovereignty as a result of war, conquest, partition, or colonialism such as frequently happened in the past' (Jackson 1993: 23–4). This may have as much to do with the utility of territorial possession in contemporary international politics as with more enlightened post-1945 political outlooks, but nevertheless, for a significant number of the world's states, sovereign independence is primarily legally enshrined rather than militarily ensured.

Whatever contribution international law plays to the preservation of international order, conflicts do still occur. What role can international law play *once hostilities have commenced*? Is war, as the ultimate collapse of 'normal' international relations, not a situation in which the most ruthless use of force must prevail and in which the acceptance of legal constraint can serve only as a potentially fatal self-inflicted impediment to effective action? In war is not the paradox of legal constraint thus most apparent? If it was indeed the purpose of legal norms to obstruct and diminish the combat efficacy of fighting forces, such strictures would be fully justified and norms so conceived could not long endure. That, however, is neither their purpose nor their effect. The real foundation of legal constraint upon warfare can be found clearly stated in a much misrepresented passage in Carl von Clausewitz's classic work *On War*. The great Prussian strategist wrote:

> He who uses force unsparingly, without reference to the bloodshed involved, must obtain a superiority if his adversary uses less vigour in its application . . . From the social condition both of States in themselves and in their relations to each other . . . War arises, and by it War is . . . controlled and modified. But these things do not belong to War itself, they are only

given conditions; and to introduce into the philosophy of War itself a principle of moderation would be an absurdity.

Clausewitz (1982: 102)

If war is analysed as a phenomenon in isolation, a logic of illimitable force might indeed seem to be suggested. However, as Clausewitz indicates, wars and armed conflicts do not arise in isolation, but occur in the real context of international relations, which imports expectations that not only condition reactions to armed conflict but themselves have real political and military effect.

In the first place, needless barbarity renders both the conduct and the ultimate resolution of conflict more difficult than it otherwise might be. As Colonel Klaus Kuhn commented, 'the quickest way of achieving and maintaining a lasting peace is to conduct hostilities humanely . . . It is evident that humanitarian considerations cannot be dissociated from the strategic concept of military leaders' (Kuhn 1987: 1). The proscription of unnecessary barbarity is counselled not only by ethical and humanitarian considerations but also by reference to the response of other states to a belligerent power and the likelihood that conflict will be prolonged when fear of probable mistreatment renders a cornered enemy desperate. The idea is not new: it was asserted in the fifth century BC by the Chinese philosopher Sun Tzu in advising, 'Do not press a desperate foe too hard'. There is ample historical evidence to support the contention. In 1945 the forces of the Third Reich sought to resist the advancing Soviet army, whose fury was at least in part occasioned by prior German conduct, long after it was clear that all hope of success was gone and even as vast numbers hastened to surrender to the Allies in the west. All wars must eventually end, if only through the economic exhaustion of the belligerents. Peaceful relations must be resumed. This process is, *ex hypothesi*, never easy and the more brutal the conflict the more difficult post-war reconstruction will be.

A second criticism levelled at the *jus in bello* is that, to the extent that it humanizes war, it also encourages it. This argument, however, has a major flaw: the inherent cruelty of war does not prevent its occurrence. If the argument were correct, it is difficult to imagine how war could have been contemplated after the carnage of Verdun, the Somme, and Passchendaele. That war continues to occur is a reflection of the fact that its instigators rarely have to fight or otherwise become its victims. To deny humanitarian mitigation to those who do find themselves engaged in combat would be the cruellest of logics.

There are powerful ethical and practical arguments for norms of constraint in armed conflict. However, norms governing the conduct of war, in distinction from those governing resort to armed force, are by their nature no more than mitigatory in effect. If it were to be pretended that either ethics or law could render war humane, the 'absurdity' to which Clausewitz referred would rapidly become all too evident.

---

 **Key Points**

- Even in the most extreme of circumstances, such as those involving contemplation of the use of force, legal factors continue to influence decision-makers.
- War is a social phenomenon and hence the notion of legal regulation of warfare remains pertinent.
- Norms governing the conduct of war are no more than mitigatory in effect.

## Jus ad Bellum

The *jus ad bellum* is now founded primarily upon Article 2(3)–(4) and Chapter VII (Articles 39–51) of the UN Charter. Article 2(3)–(4) of the UN Charter provides that:

3.  All Members shall settle their international disputes by peaceful means in such a manner that international peace and security, and justice, are not endangered.

4.  All Members shall refrain in their international relations from the threat or use of force against the territorial integrity or political independence of any State, or in any other manner inconsistent with the Purposes of the United Nations.

The basic proscription set out by Article 2(4) is recognized as having the character of *jus cogens* and as such is, under Article 53 of the Vienna Convention on the Law of Treaties 1969: 'a peremptory norm of general international law . . . accepted and recognised by the international community of States as a whole as a norm from which no derogation is permitted'.

The Article 2(4) prohibition is qualified by two essential exceptions: (1) the inherent right of individual and collective self-defence in the face of armed attack, preserved by Article 51; and (2) action for the maintenance or restoration of international peace and security authorized by the UN Security Council under Article 42. Article 51 of the UN Charter states:

> Nothing in the present Charter shall impair the inherent right of individual or collective self-defence if an armed attack occurs against a Member of the United Nations, until the Security Council has taken the measures necessary to maintain international peace and security.
>
> United Nations (1945)

Taken in conjunction with the wording of Article 2(4), Article 51 raises a number of issues. In the case of Article 2(4) what, for example, constitutes 'the threat or use of force' and is such a threat or use which is not 'against the territorial integrity or political independence' of a state permissible? What, under the terms of Article 51, constitutes the 'inherent right of individual or collective self-defence' and at what point can the Security Council be deemed to have 'taken the measures necessary to maintain international peace and security'?

Such questions are central to debates regarding the legality of practices such as anticipatory self-defence, military intervention to protect nationals abroad, and humanitarian intervention. The terrorist attacks of 11 September 2001 and the subsequent pursuit of the so-called 'war on terror' (WoT) brought such matters into even sharper focus. Those who argued in favour of a relaxation of the rules prohibiting the use of force maintained that the presence of global terrorist networks which reject all aspects of international regulation, combined with their potential use of nuclear, chemical, and biological weapons, necessitated a reinterpretation of the law so that states could legally undertake *preventive* military action against such networks and the states which harbour or otherwise assist them. More radical than the assertion that the Charter allows for proportionate pre-emptive strike in certain narrowly prescribed circumstances (Arend and Beck 1993: 71–9), advocates of preventive strike sought to reformulate the rules on anticipatory self-defence by discarding the requirement that the threat of attack posed must be imminent (Gray 2008). Security strategies issued by both the United States (United States White House 2002: 15) and the European Union (2003: 7) alluded to such a right and it was a key issue in the debates over the legality of the 2003 Iraq War. Yet many EU Member States, despite their 2003 declaration, remained deeply uneasy about the notion of preventive strike, as did the majority of other UN member states. Much of the debate over the legality of the 2003 Iraq conflict bore testament to the reluctance of states to countenance any loosening of the bonds of legal control which serve to limit conflict. Any such amendments run counter to the ultimate goals of international society. Accordingly, exceptions to the prohibition of the use of force should be interpreted in a highly restrictive manner.

One more issue regarding the *jus ad bellum* requires consideration, namely the relationship between the prohibition of the use of force enshrined in Article 2(4) and the collective security provisions of the United Nations (UN) Charter. The drafters of the UN Charter envisaged not only the establishment of a legal structure that would prohibit the use of force (other than in the case of self-defence) but also the creation of a collective security mechanism that would operate to ensure the security of states. In accordance with Article 39 of the Charter:

> The Security Council shall determine the existence of any threat to the peace, breach of the peace, or act of aggression and shall make recommendations, or decide what measures shall be taken in accordance with Articles 41 and 42, to maintain or restore international peace and security.

> United Nations (1945)

Where necessary, the Security Council may impose non-military (primarily economic) sanctions under Article 41 or military measures under Article 42. These articles are not mandatorily sequential. It is entirely lawful in appropriate cases to proceed straight from Article 39 to Article 42, as is made clear by the provision of Article 42 that it may be applied if the Council considers that non-military sanctions 'would prove inadequate'. Moreover, the oft-cited rationale for arguing that non-military sanctions must be exhausted prior to the employment of military ones, namely the assumption that economic measures are more humane, is increasingly questionable given that economic sanctions fall disproportionately on innocent populations rather than culpable leaderships. To the extent that technology allows ever more precise military targeting, economic sanctions may come to be seen as the indiscriminate option, especially when leaders of target states are less interested in the welfare of their citizens than in the political capital which can be generated by images of suffering appearing in the world's media. The prospect of increasingly 'clean' military conflicts with minimal 'collateral damage' that modern technology appears to offer is to be welcomed, but to the extent that 'acceptable'—and ultimately legal—war comes to be equated with 'clean' war, it has very significant political implications. 'Smart' weaponry is currently the preserve of the powerful few and is likely to remain so for many years. If the use of force becomes the exclusive legal preserve of these states then the implications for the *jus ad bellum* are considerable.

The Chapter VII mechanism gives rise to a number of grey areas, not least of which is what constitutes a 'threat to the peace, breach of the peace, or act of aggression'. The Charter provides no guidance on this and it is clear from the *travaux préparatoires* that those responsible for the Charter intended that the Security Council should have a wide discretion in reaching such a determination (Goodrich and Hambro 1949: 262–72). Proposals to include a definition of aggression were rejected because states were reluctant to impede with legal definitions the deliberations or actions of a Council that was intended to act as a political rather than a judicial body. Nevertheless, some limitations were placed on the Council. It was initially limited to dealing with matters that were *international*, i.e. inter-state, but this restriction has been massively eroded over time (Bellamy 2009). Another major—and prevailing—curtailment of the Chapter VII mechanism is that it cannot be applied to the activities of the Security Council's five permanent members (the 'P5'—China, France, UK, USA, and USSR) since these states are, as a result of the veto power granted to them under Article 27(3), exempt from UN sanction. The veto was intended to assist in the maintenance of P5 unanimity and was the price to be paid for ensuring crucial great power participation in the UN (Russell 1958). But it was also widely welcomed by the organization's broader membership; on balance the prospect of veto-induced stalemate seemed preferable to that of being dragged by treaty obligation into an intra-P5 dispute which might ultimately end in large-scale conflict (Claude 1962: 161).

The vulnerability of the UN's security mechanisms to veto-induced paralysis—a condition to which the organization largely succumbed for the first 45 years of its existence—raises one final question: should Article 2(4) be viewed as being *contingent* upon the effective operation of Chapter VII? The logic of such a proposition is not without merit, but neither the provisions of the Charter nor state practice lend it much support. Despite the absence of an effective collective security mechanism, for almost 60 years no state directly refuted the validity of Article 2(4) on these grounds, but as the twenty-first century began this central facet of the UN system was subjected to two challenges. The first of these was grounded in the earlier discussed arguments in favour of a more expansive right of self-defence. The second came in the assertion that where the Security Council fails to authorize, through the passing of a resolution, action to maintain or restore international peace and security, states may themselves act in order to do so. In claiming that they were acting to enforce legally binding obligations previously imposed by the Security Council in 1991, the US and its allies made this argument the central legal point of their justification for action against Iraq in 2003 (Kritsiotis 2004). This represented a fundamental departure from previous state practice, but the largely critical international response to the initiation of the war suggests that few states were willing to endorse this challenge to the prohibitory norm.

With post-Iraq changes of government in the US and UK, the appetite for taking military action without a UN mandate appears to have dissipated and domestic legislatures appear increasingly reluctant to allow their executives the scope to embark on military ventures of questionable international legality (Strong 2014; Dunne and Vaughn 2014). The US and UK, along with France, members of the Arab League, and other allies, were careful to secure Security Council authority before military action aimed at protecting civilians through the establishment of a no-fly zone was undertaken in Libya in March 2011. Conversely, failure to gain Security Council backing for measures against the Syrian government as a consequence of Russian and Chinese vetoes was a major impediment to international action. Within the context of the debate about the legal use of force the import of the Syrian case should not be overstated since, dissuaded primarily by prudential geo-strategic calculations, none of the resolutions tabled and subsequently vetoed involved proposals for military action. Nevertheless, in their tone and content, the Security Council debates over Syria—and, indeed, over Libya—serve to reinforce the proposition that the Council remains the primary source of international legitimacy (Morris 2013).

**Key Points**

- The *jus ad bellum* governs and seeks to limit resort to armed force in the conduct of international relations.

- Recourse to force is prohibited other than in cases of individual or collective self-defence or where action is taken to restore international peace and security as mandated by the UN Security Council.

- Exceptions to the prohibition of the use of force should be interpreted restrictively.

- The prohibition of the use of force is not viewed by most states as being contingent upon the successful operation of the UN collective security mechanism. The 2003 Iraq conflict challenged this, but elicited little support.

- No state has openly repudiated the general prohibition of the use of force.

## Jus in Bello

The *jus in bello* has two principal subdivisions, which have conventionally been categorized as 'Geneva' and 'Hague' law in recognition of the principal treaty series upon which each is founded. Modern 'Geneva' law is specifically concerned with the protection of the victims of armed conflict. 'Hague' law is concerned with methods and means of warfare, including controls on weapons type and usage, and on tactics and the general conduct of hostilities. It should be noted that the Geneva–Hague distinction is today artificial; both are premised upon a humanitarian concern for the moderation and mitigation of warfare and for this reason there is a considerable degree of overlap between them. In modern usage the term 'international humanitarian law' (IHL)—historically used to refer specifically to Geneva law—is taken to comprise the whole *jus in bello* in both its Geneva and Hague dimensions.

Both sets of norms rest ultimately upon a fundamental principle of proscription concerning the infliction of militarily 'unnecessary suffering'. This principle was stated expressly in the 1868 Declaration of St Petersburg:

> The only legitimate objective which States should endeavour to accomplish during war is to weaken the military forces of the enemy . . . this objective would be exceeded by the employment of arms which uselessly aggravate the suffering of disabled men . . . [and] the employment of such arms would therefore be contrary to the laws of humanity.
>
> McCoubrey (1998: 212)

The modern foundations of the 'Hague' sector are primarily to be found in the Hague Conventions of 1899 and 1907 and the 1977 Additional Protocol I to the Geneva Conventions, which makes provision for methods and means of warfare and discrimination in bombardment. Modern Geneva law is based on the four 1949 Geneva Conventions, dealing respectively with: (I) wounded and sick on land; (II) wounded, sick and shipwrecked at sea; (III) prisoners of war; and (IV) civilians. On the basis of this treaty and customary provision the basic rules of IHL are well settled, but it must be conceded that all too often its application remains inconsistent and problematic (see Box 6.5).

**BOX** 6.5  *Jus in bello*

| **'Geneva' Law** | **'Hague' Law** |
|---|---|
| • Concerned with protection of victims of warfare. | • Based primarily on the four 1949 Geneva Conventions. |
| • Concerned with methods and means of armed conflict. | • Based primarily on the 1899 and 1907 Hague Conventions. |

The causes of this inconsistency are to be found in significant part in our apparently innate ability to inflict horrendous suffering on our fellow human beings, especially those deemed to be enemies or threats, and most particularly during times of great stress and conflict. However, to some—no doubt more limited—extent the failure to observe IHL stems from disputes about its applicability, and in particular the degree to which it is based upon reciprocal obligation. As a starting point it is worth noting that IHL is closely related to the general law of human rights, and this creates a powerful argument that the obligations created by it are essentially unilateral and non-reciprocal in nature (McCoubrey 1998: 187). Such a view is certainly taken by the International Committee of the Red Cross (ICRC), which has commented that a state should not observe IHL simply in the hope that this will be reflected in the treatment by others of its own nationals; it should do so 'out of respect for the human person as such' (Meron 2006: 11). The Nuremberg Tribunals provide strong supporting evidence for this position (Meron 2006: 10) as do the Geneva Conventions, Common Article 1 of which provides that 'The High Contracting Parties undertake to respect and ensure respect for the present Convention *in all circumstances*' [emphasis added] (ICRC 1949).

At least with regard to armed conflicts between states, the applicability of IHL on a non-reciprocal basis has become increasingly embedded. There has also been significant progress toward regulating internal conflict which had, despite its tendency to involve the cruellest acts of violence, traditionally lain outside the ambit of IHL (Moir 2002). Yet despite these legal developments, in practice intra-state/inter-ethnic conflicts all too often continue to testify to the horrific barbarity that accompanies fighting between irregular combatants who routinely fail to conform to the—perhaps idealized—traditional expectations of regular military forces. Another area with which the law is still struggling to get to grips is international terrorism (Sassòli 2004; Barnes 2005). The manner in which the Bush Administrations chose to prosecute the WoT illustrates the point in the starkest manner, most particularly in the claim that individuals detained pursuant to the WoT and held at the US's Cuban Guantanamo Bay military facility enjoyed neither protection under IHL nor the right of recourse to US domestic courts. Both of these arguments were ultimately rejected by the US Supreme Court, but this rectification of the legal position came too late to repair the self-inflicted diplomatic and reputational damage which arose from the impression of American ambivalence to its obligations under IHL and, indeed, international law more generally (Forsythe 2008; Carvin 2008). The ongoing failure of the Obama Administrations to deliver on the 2009 promise to close the Cuban detention camp serves only to prolong this inauspicious episode in US history (Yin 2011).

It will be apparent from the preceding discussion that IHL's applicability in theory and its application in practice are far from being the same, and to the extent that variation exists the victims of conflict suffer all the more. The 'theoretical' position does, however, remain highly significant, since the behaviour of those who violate IHL is increasingly viewed in the light of its legal demands and the ethical principles that underpin them. As such, the political implications of perceived violation are considerable, manifesting themselves in highly practical and strategically important ways. The willingness of others to become or remain allies and so to share the costs arising from conflict is among the most important of these consequences, since even the most powerful benefit from being able to socialize the costs of their actions (Reus-Smit 2007). Nor is this a purely international phenomenon. A growing public awareness resulting from 24-hour real-time TV coverage, advances in global communications, and the campaigning work of non-governmental organizations (NGOs) such as Amnesty International and Human Rights Watch are also important. The high profile now enjoyed by humanitarian issues can place considerable domestic political pressure on governments and can have significant electoral implications. Moreover, non-state actors, be they NGOs or less formalized grass-roots movements, can play a significant role in shaping the very legal framework against which the behaviour of states comes to be judged, as, for example, the adoption of the Convention on the Prohibition of Anti-Personnel Landmines shows.

Another major advance in IHL that may yet see a closing of the gap between theory and practice was the establishment in 2002 of the International Criminal Court (ICC). The court is competent to prosecute cases of genocide, crimes against humanity, war crimes, and potentially at some future date the crime of aggression. Its jurisdiction extends over nationals of state parties and crimes committed on their territory where such states are either unable or unwilling to prosecute themselves (Schabas 2004). The court is not without its detractors, not least amongst them the United States (Ralph 2007), but its very existence is a development that few could realistically have even dreamt of only a generation ago. It is early days for the court, but already there are fears that some conflicts may have been prolonged by the prospect that the parties to them, especially the vanquished, may face prosecution once hostilities cease. This has long been the crux of the argument in favour of granting immunity to belligerents and though the establishment of the ICC does not provide a definitive resolution to the debate over whether we should prioritize 'peace' or 'justice' in such situations, it does appear to be a significant step in favour of the latter.

Of course the extent to which IHL (including the ICC) is able to realize the objectives which it enshrines is contingent upon the degree to which belligerents actually eschew proscribed modes of behaviour in practice. As noted earlier, excessive concern with punishment, in this case of war crimes, misses the point that the primary function of IHL is not to punish those who violate its edicts but rather to protect the victims of armed conflict by preventing war crimes in the first place. Indeed, before any question of punishing war crimes or other enforcement action can arise, failure in this primary endeavour must be presupposed. In this sense, issues of enforcement must be viewed as secondary to the imperatives of effective dissemination and training. That in many states the latter is now a foundational element of military training bodes well, though such practice is far from ubiquitous and deficiencies in this regard are often exacerbated through shortcomings in discipline and command and control (Robinson, de Lee, and Carrick 2008).

**Key Points**

- The *jus in bello*, often split into the subdivisions of Geneva and Hague law, and commonly known now as IHL, governs and seeks to moderate the actual conduct of hostilities.

- 'Geneva' law is concerned with the protection of victims of armed conflict. 'Hague' law is concerned with methods and means of warfare.

- Much of Geneva and Hague law has the status of *jus cogens*.

- The primary function of IHL is to protect the victims of armed conflict through preventing war crimes. Such objectives are best pursued primarily through education and training rather than through post-violation prosecution.

 **Critical Thinking**   Debating … Renowned jurist Sir Hersch Lauterpacht asserted that 'if international law is … the vanishing point of law, the law of war is even more conspicuously the vanishing point of international law'. Is it naive and unrealistic to expect the laws of war to influence the behaviour of either states or combatants when conflicts arise?

**For**

- *International law is a mere cloak for power.* In the anarchic international environment, international law is little more than a diplomatic tool, developed by the powerful to maintain an order from which they have the most to gain. When it suits the interests of the powerful they act to ensure that weaker states abide by the law. But if their interests require it the powerful break the law with impunity. In the absence of a centralized, impartial enforcement mechanism this problem is inescapable.

- *Necessity will always trump the* **jus ad bellum**. When states are compelled to contemplate the use of force they often do so in the direst of circumstances where crucial national interests are at stake. In such situations the obligation to abide by the strictures of a largely unenforced law will inevitably be outweighed by the fear and uncertainty which characterizes inter-state relations and the political and strategic demands of *realpolitik*.

- *In battle legal regulation is ineffective and self-defeating.* Individuals engaged in combat justifiably harbour existential fears. The logic of 'kill or be killed' must prevail and where this is so then aberrant legal considerations can only serve to reduce operational effectiveness and hence increase the likelihood of defeat and possible death. Consequently, combatants will always do whatever is necessary to win, irrespective of what the law says.

- *Acts committed in battle cannot reasonably be subjected to subsequent legal adjudication.* Often combatants must make split second decisions based on limited and uncertain knowledge and whilst experiencing immense stress and fear. To review such decisions and the acts/omissions which follow from them in the safety and detached calm of a courtroom is inappropriate since those who sit in judgement have not experienced such circumstances and cannot, therefore, realistically place themselves in the shoes of those they seek to judge.

*(continued . . . )*

**Critical Thinking**   (*continued*)

## Against

- *Preoccupation with enforcement distorts our view of the law.* Coercion is only one means by which legal compliance can be secured, and its role is often significantly over-stated. Self-interest, and even more significantly perceptions of legitimacy are crucial to ensuring legal observance. Consequently, whilst the powerful may be the most significant writers of the law, it must nevertheless be accepted as legitimate by a sufficiently large proportion of society if it is to prevail and work effectively.

- *International law acts as a benchmark.* International law may not be able to stop states, especially powerful ones, resorting to force in breach of its edicts, but it is the basis against which such actions are judged. Where states are deemed to have acted illegally it becomes more difficult to socialise the costs of action and this in turn compels states to seriously consider legal issues when deciding whether or not to resort to force in pursuit of their international objectives.

- *State practice increasingly demonstrates the efficacy of the laws of war.* Particularly following the Iraq conflict of 2003, national legislatures are increasingly inclined to try to ensure that their executives act in accordance with the *jus ad bellum*. Where this occurs leaders have no option but to factor in the legalities of the situations with which they are dealing. Meanwhile, domestic legal systems are increasingly adept and inclined to address alleged breaches of the *jus in bello*. Whilst the significance of enforcement should not be exaggerated, these developments are nevertheless significant.

- *Failure to (at least) attempt to limit the excesses of war is morally indefensible.* The aim of the *jus in bello* is to reduce the infliction of militarily unnecessary suffering. Its application and observation may be imperfect, but the very statement of the parameters of acceptable behaviour is in itself valuable, and it serves as the foundation upon which education and training can be based.

 ## Conclusion

The low regard in which international law is customarily held is the consequence of several factors. It is a result of our perception of the world of international politics and the extent to which we tend to see this as an environment characterized by conflict rather than cooperation and thus ill-suited to legal regulation. But this perception is profoundly misleading. Rather than wringing our hands over the frequency of military conflict in the world we might, without forgetting the devastation and suffering inherent in conflicts when they do arise, marvel at the degree to which an increasing number of states manage to coexist in a cooperative and often mutually beneficial manner. It would be folly to suggest that this is the consequence of some great legalistic enterprise, but equally it would be foolhardy to suggest that international law has no role to play in influencing the manner in which states behave. To borrow a phrase from Robert Keohane, international law 'prescribes behavioural roles, constrains activity, and shapes expectations' (1989: 3).

At times, of course, international law, like all law, is broken. This, however, is the exception rather than the rule. Moreover, in cases where international law is broken one would be hard pressed to find a transgressor who does not at least attempt to provide a legally couched justification for their behaviour, and the more prominent and significant the breach, the greater these efforts become. Nowhere are breaches of international law more significant or prominent than with regard to the laws of armed conflict. Nowhere are the stakes higher or the pressures greater. It is, therefore, all the more noteworthy that even here, for the most part, the law prevails.

Questions

1. Why is international law held in such low regard? Is this a deserved reputation?

2. Does international law really influence the behaviour of states? If so, how, and why?

3. How does the relative power of states affect the ability of international law to influence their behaviour?

4. Can you cite examples involving the use of force in which states have breached international law and not attempted to justify their actions in terms of the law?

5. Are exceptions to the prohibition of the use of force—such as anticipatory self-defence, action to protect nationals abroad, action to punish state-sponsored terrorism, and humanitarian intervention—justifiable?

6. Should the prohibition of the use of force be contingent upon the existence of an effective mechanism by means of which the security of states can be assured?

7. Are limitations upon the means by which war is waged practicable?

8. Should international humanitarian law only be applied on a reciprocal basis?

9. Is the establishment of the International Criminal Court more likely to lead to more just post-conflict settlements or to prolong conflicts?

10. What effect did the 'war on terror' have on international humanitarian law?

 Further Reading

I. Brownlie, *International Law and the Use of Force by States* (Oxford: Clarendon Press, 1963) gives a detailed discussion of key issues in the development of the *jus ad bellum*.

H. Bull, *The Anarchical Society: A Study of Order in World Politics* (London: Macmillan, 1977) provides the seminal discussion of the idea that states form an international society.

M. Byers (ed.), *The Role of Law in International Politics: Essays in International Relations and International Law* (Oxford: Oxford University Press, 2000) comprises a collection of essays that consider the role which international law plays in international politics.

H. Duffy, *The 'War on Terror' and the Framework of International Law* (Cambridge: Cambridge University Press, 2005) offers an analysis of international humanitarian law in the context of the 'War on Terror'.

D. Fleck (ed.), *The Handbook of International Humanitarian Law 3rd edn* (Oxford: Oxford University Press, 2013) provides a comprehensive discussion of the *jus in bello*.

W. A. Schabas, *An Introduction to the International Criminal Court* (Cambridge: Cambridge University Press, 2007) presents discussions on the history and operation of the International Criminal Court.

M. Weller, *Iraq and the Use of Force in International Law* (Oxford: Oxford University Press, 2010) analyses legal key questions raised by the 2003 Iraq conflict.

 Web Links

United Nations **http://www.un.org** provides a huge array of UN-related resources, including UN resolutions and minutes of meetings.

International Court of Justice **http://www.icj-cij.org** gives details of how the Court is structured, how it works, and details and materials relating to past and present cases.

International Criminal Court **http://www.icc-cpi.int/en_menus/icc/Pages/default.aspx** provides details of how the Court is structured, how it works, and details and materials relating to past and present cases.

International Committee of the Red Cross **http://www.icrc.org/eng/index.jsp** explains what the ICRC is and provides details of the work it does. It has a particularly good section on 'War and Law'.

Human Rights Watch **http://www.hrw.org** provides details of the work of Human Rights Watch, highlighting specific human rights concerns around the world.

International Campaign to Ban Landmines **http://www.icbl.org/en-gb/home.aspx** looks at the specific issue of landmines, their use, the movement to have them banned, and the work that continues in addressing matters arising from their use.

# 7

# Technology and Warfare

ELIOT A. COHEN

## Chapter Contents

 **Reader's Guide**

Debate exists about the relative importance of technology when compared to other factors, such as training or morale, in achieving victory in battle. Scholars also offer competing explanations about how and why certain technologies are integrated into military organizations while others are ignored. The pace of technological change is not uniform: some technology and procedures become fixtures in militaries while others become obsolete quickly and are discarded. To complicate matters further, some observers today believe that the world is witnessing a revolution in military affairs, a relatively rare event when technologies are combined to produce a fundamental transformation in the way war is fought. This chapter explores these issues and offers some observations about the emerging technological trends that are likely to transform future warfare.

## Introduction: Technophiles and Technophobes

Military historians—and sometimes soldiers themselves—cannot make up their minds about how to view military technology. Much contemporary policy debate centres on technical decisions—how many aircraft to buy, what type, over what period of time, and so on. The general public tends to ascribe remarkable—sometimes even magical—properties to modern military technology.

By contrast, many military historians and soldiers deprecate the importance of technology. They believe that skill and organizational effectiveness, not pieces of hardware, determine the outcome of battle. Although technical enthusiasts and sceptics sometimes clash in their assessment of a particular contest, rarely does the debate occur at a conceptual level. Only one major figure in the last century—Major General J. F. C. Fuller, a British war planner, pioneer of armoured warfare, and prolific military historian—attempted to write theoretically about the role of technology in strategic studies (Fuller 1926, 1932, 1942, 1945). This chapter therefore introduces some concepts about military technology, and then discusses the key technological issues and trends of our time.

## Some Ways of Thinking about Military Technology

Consider as a point of departure the question: 'Where does military technology come from?' We often think of technology as something predetermined, the product of technologies from the civilian sector that are readily available to military organizations. Most historians of technology and engineering reject this view, believing that the final forms of technology are far from being predetermined (MacKenzie 1990). Some contend that 'form follows function': military technology evolves to meet particular military needs. There are, however, other possibilities. One author, Henry Petroski, talks about 'form following failure', a concept first applied to his study of the history of bridge building, but applicable to military technology as well (Petroski 1982). In this view, new technology emerges as a response to some perceived failure or fault in existing technology. Other theories of technological invention include the suggestion that technologies emerge from aesthetic or other non-rational considerations, such as custom or organizational convenience (Creveld 1989). These different theories offer varying explanations of how innovation occurs or fails to occur. Why, for example, did it take more than 30 years for the United States, which successfully deployed unmanned aerial vehicles (UAVs) in the Vietnam War, to introduce them into the armed forces? The technology may have been immature (the fruits of civilian industry theory); there may have been no mission crying out for UAVs (form follows function); there may have been no visible failure in the existing technology (form follows failure); or, finally, the technology may have been thwarted by pilots hostile to the notion of aircraft without pilots (non-rational explanations).

No one of these theories is completely satisfying. Their very range, however, should prompt us to look more closely at how and why military technologies come into existence. There are distinctive national styles, for example, in military technology: the Israeli Merkava tank differs subtly from American M1 Abrams (M1A2). These changes reflect differences in design philosophy stemming from where the two countries believe they will fight (the slow Israeli tank is designed for the rocky Golan Heights; the much faster Abrams tank can best exploit its high speed in desert warfare). The Israelis have given exceptionally high value to crew safety. They accepted mechanical inefficiency by placing the engine in front of the crew space rather than (as is normal) behind it. In armoured warfare, most hits occur on the frontal armour of the tank, and the engine can thus absorb the impact of a hit. The Americans, by employing a fuel-hungry high-powered turbine engine, assumed that they could readily resupply their tanks with fuel in vast quantities on the battlefield (see Box 7.1).

National styles in technology may reflect political assumptions about war at the time that a design is frozen. By 2012, for example, the United States was poised to buy large numbers of the F-35 Joint Strike Fighter (JSF), a short-ranged fighter bomber. This decision reflected a political assumption, namely, that the United States would fight its wars within a few hundred miles of its opponents, and, presumably, with extensive access to secure fixed bases.[1] This assumption may well prove incorrect.

**BOX** 7.1 The American M1A2 vs the Israeli Merkava

|  | M1A2 | Merkava (Mk3) |
| --- | --- | --- |
| Weight (fully armed) (tons) | 69.54 | 62.9 |
| Length (gun forward) (metres) | 9.8 | 8.8 |
| Height (metres) | 2.9 | 2.8 |
| Width | 3.7 | 3.7 |
| Range (miles) | 265 | 311 |
| Crew | 4 | 4 |
| Road speed (km/hour) | 90 | 55 |
| Main armament | 120mm | 120mm |
| Engine | Gas turbine | Diesel |

Although similar in some respects, the Merkava is very different from the M1 in others. It is much slower (perhaps half as fast): the Israelis value absolute speed much less than the ability to manoeuvre under fire, particularly over the lava-strewn Golan Heights. They also lack the super-fast infantry fighting vehicles to keep up with the tanks. There is a rear hatch on the Merkava that allows the evacuation of wounded or resupply of ammunition without exposing the crew—again, requirements derived from the peculiar problems of keeping a firing line on the Golan Heights. Finally, the Israeli engine is at the front of the tank, where it can absorb an incoming round—a sacrifice of mechanical efficiency for crew protection. The M1 gets a similar effect by unusually good (and expensive) armour.

*Sources:* http://www.army-technology.com/projects/merkava/
http://www.army-technology.com/projects/abrams/

*Note:* The stated speed for the M1A2 is considerably slower than its actual speed.

One way to penetrate the essence of national design style is to ask what kind of trade-offs designers accepted. A tank, for example, has three fundamental characteristics: protection, firepower, and mobility. Increase the amount of armour and one sacrifices the tank's ability to move quickly; put a small-bore, low-recoil cannon on it and one gains a great deal of mobility for a penalty in firepower; increase horsepower and pay a penalty in terms of the size of the tank (and hence protection) or how far it can go (and hence mobility).

Military technology also reflects processes of interaction. Tanks did not grow to be today's 60-ton monsters because of the growth of their power plants or guns. Developments in armour were to blame, as tank hulls have come to consist of materials as exotic as depleted uranium. These changes reflect the development of ever more powerful antitank weapons—depleted uranium rods and so-called shaped charges (explosives configured to create a jet of hot metal that burns its way through armour). Even in peacetime, measure and counter-measure rule the choices designers make. These interactions create a kind of evolutionary process, by which a weapon system settles into its own 'ecological' niche. Birds and lizards evolve an amazing variety of counters to their predators, who in turn come up with a range of adaptations that enable them to find and devour their prey. So too with weapon systems. As in nature, interaction may yield odd outcomes, where one kind of highly sophisticated adaptation to a particular environment makes a platform utterly unsuited to a different battlefield. The first two generations of stealth aircraft, for example, evolved to avoid detection through the use of adroitly shaped surfaces that would disperse or absorb radar energy: they were difficult (not impossible) to detect using the radar technology of the time. Their odd shaping, however, made them slower and less manoeuvrable than other aircraft; they therefore became night-time-only systems that were vulnerable to optical detection during the day.

In assessing military technology one should look at invisible technology as well. What gave the German tanks an edge over their French counterparts in the Second World War, for example, was not superior armour, guns, or engines, so much as a piece of technology barely noticed by outside observers—the radio (Stolfi 1970). Often, the most important elements of a military system are not the ones most evident to the casual observer, yet mastery of such technologies may weigh most in battle. American forces in the south-west Pacific in the Second World War struggled not only with the Japanese, but also with disease. The insecticide DDT, as much as any bomber or battleship, won the fight for New Guinea.

One should consider the role of systems technology and not just its parts. A novelist described a Second World War warship this way:

> One way of thinking of the ship was as of some huge marine animal. Here on the bridge was the animal's brain, and radiating from it ran the nerves—the telephones and voice tubes—which carried the brain's decisions to the parts which were to execute them. The engine-room formed the muscles which actuated the tail—the propellers; and the guns were the teeth and claws of the animal. Up in the crow's nest above, and all round the bridge where the lookouts sat raking sea and sky with their binoculars, were the animal's eyes, seeking everywhere for enemies or prey, while the signal flags and wireless transmitter were the animal's voice, with which it could cry a warning to its fellows or scream for help.

> Forester (1943: 22–3)

As the war progressed, the brain of the ship vanished into its bowels, so to speak—becoming the combat information centre of modern vessels. But Forester's point was that the effectiveness of the ship rested not simply on the working of all the different technologies individually, but rather on their effectiveness as a whole. The very use of the term weapon *system* implies that the art of putting technologies together is more important than their individual excellence. In war, more than in most other activities, the whole can be far greater than the sum of its parts.

Our last concept is that of the technological edge. It is not always decisive, but it is almost always important. J. F. C. Fuller once suggested that Napoleon himself would have succumbed to the semi-competent British general in the Crimea, Lord Raglan, simply because the latter's army had rifles, while the former had smoothbore muskets (Fuller 1945: 18). It is only recently that the advanced powers have assumed that they would go to war with a decided technological edge over their opponents, and that this advantage would prove decisive. Technological superiority does not necessarily extend across the board. In the Persian Gulf War of 1991, for example, some Iraqi artillery pieces (e.g. their South African made G-5 howitzers) outranged Western counterparts such as the American Paladin system, by 6 kilometres or more (30 vs 24 kilometres, to be precise)—much as Russian-made 130mm guns outranged their American 155mm counterparts in the Vietnam War.[2] The poorer, smaller, or weaker side may have some niche competencies that will surprise a richer and more powerful opponent. The technological edge may be dramatic (the quintessential case being the Dervish armies of the Khalifa crumpling under the fire of Lord Kitchener's Anglo-Egyptian infantry using the Henry-Martini rifle), or quite subtle—a matter of a few seconds' difference in the flight time of an air-to-air missile, or a few hundred yards in the effective range of a tank gun. The technological edge may have a psychological dimension that vanishes over time, as with Second World War-era German dive bombers with their unearthly wailing sirens, or American heliborne infantry in Vietnam appearing from the skies in remote jungles; or it may reflect fleeting disparities in commercial technology (e.g. commercial global positioning system navigation receivers purchased by Americans, but not Iraqis, in the Gulf War).

 **Key Points**

- There are a range of divergent and contradictory theories about how military technology develops.
- Military technologies often reflect different national styles.
- Different national styles are determined by a variety of considerations, such as political assumptions, trade-offs between various features of hardware, processes of interaction, invisible technologies, systems technology, and the search for technological edge.

## Mapping Military Technology

Since the middle of the nineteenth century, change in military technology has become a constant, through what Martin van Creveld has called 'the invention of invention'. The traditional picture of soldiers suspiciously rejecting new technology in favour of old standbys was always overdone: before the First World War, for example, the armies of Europe embraced the machine gun and the aeroplane. Their difficulty lay, and lies today, in recognizing what broader changes new technology may entail. For powerful institutional reasons, military organizations tend to fit new technologies into old intellectual and operational frameworks.

One question to ask in assessing technological change is whether what one is witnessing is a change in *quantity* or a change in *quality*. It is a more complicated question than it might appear. Marginal increases in speed, protection, mobility, or payload, to take just a few design parameters, are quantitative: they may have cumulative effects, but in and of themselves should not bring about radical changes in war. Sometimes, however, a seemingly incremental improvement augurs, in fact, qualitative change. Early firearms, for example, delivered rather less effective lethality than a good longbow; oil-fired ship engines offered moderate increases in speed over their coal-powered counterparts; and the first generation air-to-air missiles provided only marginal improvements over a well-aimed burst of cannon fire. All of these changes, however, foreshadowed tremendous upheavals in the conduct of war. Mastery of the longbow could take a lifetime. Mastery of the musket took a few months of drill, and its incidental qualities—the noise, smoke, and flash, none of which had direct effects on the enemy—made it a more fearful, that is, psychologically effective, weapon. Oil propulsion reduced the size of crews, increased the speed of ships, and, perhaps most importantly, made the world's oilfields prime strategic real estate. Air-to-air missiles improved far beyond the capability of mature aircraft cannon, to the point of engaging targets well beyond visual range.

Contemporary observers will often get it wrong. Military organizations (the US navy in particular) had experimented with satellite-based navigation systems since the early 1960s

(Friedman 2000). It took the experience of the Gulf War in 1991, however, to make average sailors, pilots, and soldiers realize that the global positioning system could transform all aspects of navigation from art to science, or rather to mere technique. By contrast, the advent of nuclear weapons in the late 1940s and 1950s convinced some professionals that all military organizations would have to be radically restructured to accommodate the new weapons. As it turned out, however, only selected military organizations needed to adapt their tactics and structures to the new devices (Bacevich 1986). Military organizations and platforms do not change at a uniform rate. Some aspects of military technology change very little over the decades. Visit an aircraft carrier's deck, and one is struck by how little many procedures have changed in well over half a century. Steam catapults—themselves solid pieces of mid-twentieth-century engineering—loft jet aircraft off angled decks devised shortly after the Second World War. The crews, in multicoloured jerseys, each of which identifies their function, work pretty much as their grand fathers did during the Korean War. Inside, the Air Boss and his (or her) staff track the movement of aircraft using model aeroplanes on a large flat table; below decks illuminated glass grids show the status of all aircraft. There are important changes—more accurate and powerful bombs, far better intelligence flowing in, better aircraft—but the overall structure is remarkably durable.

Some military processes change to a considerably greater extent. A large desert armoured battle, for example, bears some resemblance to the clashes of the Second World War: masses of ponderous armoured beasts manoeuvring over open ground, generating vast clouds of smoke and dust, swirling in a mêlée where the advantage goes to the quicker shot and calmer head. But much has changed, too. Today's armoured battle might take place at night, using thermal imaging devices that are in many ways better than optical sights even on a clear day. A well-calibrated gun, with even a moderately competent crew (aided by laser range finders and ballistic computers) can score a first-round hit at a distance of several kilometres—which, combined with the rise of night vision, yields a significant change in the way tank battles are fought.

Some changes are larger. The first night of an air operation, for example, is now completely different from what occurred during the Second World War, Korean War, and Vietnam War. In one or two nights a competent air force can shut down an enemy's air defence system. It is not the case that air power can do more efficiently that which it did in the past—it can do things that it never could have done before. Thus, for example, with adequate intelligence and planning, a well-conducted air strike can cripple a nation's telecommunications system, in part by attacking targets (relay towers or switching centres) that previously were not susceptible to mass attack, or target particular individuals.

---

 **Key Points**

- One of the problems of understanding the role of military technologies is the constant process of change that takes place.
- One difficult issue concerns the relationship between qualitative and quantitative change.
- Another difficulty is that some technology is slow to have an effect, while some is much more immediate and radical in its impact.

# The Revolution in Military Affairs Debate

When a set of changes comes together, the result (some soldiers and historians would argue) is a revolution. Normally, military technology merely evolves, at greater or lesser speeds, and unevenly. Occasionally, however, several developments will come together and yield a broader transformation.

Since the late 1970s, a number of observers have suggested that a revolution in military affairs is under way. Senior Soviet military officers, including the then Chief of the Soviet General Staff, Nikolai Ogarkov, suggested that modern conventional weapons would soon have the effectiveness of tactical nuclear weapons. Long-range sensors, including powerful radars mounted on aircraft, combined with precision weapons, would allow the detection and destruction of armoured units long before they ever approached the battlefield. Soviet military leaders believed that the United States, with its superior technological base, would drive these developments, and that their consequence would fall very much to the disadvantage of the Soviet Union, reliant as it was on waves of armoured forces that could move into Europe from their mobilization areas in the western USSR.

In the West, a number of technologists had similar, if less well-articulated, aspirations for weapons systems that would combine accuracy, range, and above all 'intelligence'—the ability to home in on, or even select, their own targets. It took the 1991 Gulf War to convince a broad spectrum of officers that very large changes in the conduct of war had occurred. The lopsidedness of that war, the undeniable effectiveness of precision weapons, and the emergence of a host of supporting military technologies (stealth, for example, which is actually a cluster of technologies) convinced many observers that warfare had changed fundamentally. The developments first noted in the Gulf War continued in a decade of smaller-scale military engagements thereafter, including repeated American and British strikes against Iraqi targets, and North Atlantic Treaty Organization (NATO) operations against Yugoslavia as a result of the wars in Bosnia in 1995 (Operation Deliberate Force) and in Kosovo in 1999 (Operation Allied Force). Similarly, the combination of special operations forces, UAVs, and aircraft delivering precision weapons (and unguided ones for that matter) had a devastating effect on admittedly ragtag Taliban troops in Afghanistan in 2001. These and American regular ground and air forces occupied Iraq and crushed the regime of Saddam Hussein, and its admittedly fragile and obsolescent military, in less than three weeks in 2003.

An adequate conceptual description of these changes, however, remained elusive. The Vice-Chairman of the American Joint Chiefs of Staff, Admiral William Owens, described what he termed 'the system of systems' as the ultimate potential of the new technologies, if not their actual achievement (Owens and Offley 2000). By integrating long-range, precision weapons with extensive intelligence, surveillance, and reconnaissance, and vastly improved capabilities for processing information and distributing it, he believed the United States could hope to detect and destroy any enemy target over swathes of the earth's surface as large as 200 by 200 miles. Some in the military scoffed at this as a technologist's fantasy, pointing to the persistence of what Carl von Clausewitz termed 'the fog of war' even in seemingly immaculate military operations against feeble opponents—the limited success of NATO aircraft in knocking out Serb tanks in 1999 being a case in point. Owens himself declared that enormous bureaucratic impediments—the persistence of individual service cultures, in particular—stood in the way of his dream being achieved.

In truth, the revolution in military affairs debate remains unsatisfying. The military tests that have occurred thus far involved the wildly disproportionate forces of the United States and its allies against far smaller opponents. In 1999, for example, Yugoslavia's gross national product was barely a fifteenth the size of the American defence budget. The outcome of such ill-matched encounters could serve as indicators, perhaps, but not proof of a large change. More important was a series of wars in the Middle East—in 2006, 2008, 2011, and 2014— between Israel and quasi-regular opponents that seemed to augur a shift in war, incorporating as it did new technologies of precision (both missiles and antimissiles); updated old technologies (sophisticated tunnelling); information management (the synthesis of surveillance and databases); and new means of communication (social media, in particular). At the same time, the rise of China and its heavy investment in advanced technologies, to include long-range highly accurate missiles and torpedoes, as well as cyberwarfare, seemed to suggest that a fundamental change in war was indeed under way. To begin sorting this out, one can examine at least three broad features of the new technological era in warfare: the rise of quality over quantity, the speciation of military hardware, and the centrality of commercial military technology.

## The Rise of Quality Over Quantity

Historians will describe the period extending from the French Revolution to at least the middle of the twentieth century as the era of mass warfare (e.g. Howard 1976a: 75ff). During this time, those countries that could mobilize men and military production most effectively could generate the most military power—and this was true of the largest powers (like the Soviet Union) and the smallest (like Israel). Broadly speaking, the bigger the force the better—a far cry from the days of the eighteenth century when military authorities believed that armies could not operate beyond a certain optimal size, and when the way of war and contemporary economics dictated the protection of civil society from widespread compulsory military service.

The age of the mass army is over (see Moskos, Williams, and Segal 2000). The near annihilation in 1991 of the Iraqi army, the world's fourth largest, marked the emergence of a world in which modestly obsolescent technology had become merely targets for more sophisticated weapons. Around the world, states abandoned compulsory military service and shrank the size of their armed forces, even in those countries (China and Turkey, for example) where they actually increased their defence expenditures substantially. Several converging developments produced these changes: the growing incompatibility between civil and military culture, the increased expense of military training and technology, and the vulnerabilities created by large forces. But nothing mattered more than the emerging importance of the technological edge in combat.

To a degree far greater than, say, during the Second World War, quality now trumps quantity. That quality, moreover, lies in the combination of manpower and technology. Superbly trained troops in mediocre tanks and aircraft might do well against mediocre troops in correspondingly magnificent weapon systems, but in the real world such match-ups rarely occur. The old systems of estimating military power no longer apply, be they the crude tabular comparisons of forces that appear in newspapers or weekly news magazines, or the seemingly scientific calculations of attrition-driven Pentagon models.

## The Speciation of Weapons

In the nineteenth century, and for most of the twentieth, the armed forces of the world shared similar weaponry. There have always been minor differences: even an early twentieth-century Mauser differed from a Lee Enfield or Lebel rifle. More important differences began to emerge in the First World War when, for example, the Allied states invested heavily in tanks, where the Germans did not; and certainly by the Second World War, when the United States and Great Britain developed heavy bombers that were imitated by neither their enemies nor their chief ally, the Soviet Union. The British concentrated on aircraft optimized for night bombing, with heavy payloads and sophisticated night navigation, but little defensive ability, where the Americans concentrated on daylight bombing of industrial targets. Still, during the Second World War, and even during much of the cold war, basic weapons systems were similar. By the end of the twentieth century, however, weapons had evolved much like a sophisticated ecological system.

An example of the first development is the 1980s British runway-attack munition JP233. This system was capable of discharging 30 penetrating rockets and over 200 scattered mines from a low-flying Tornado fighter bomber. The RAF developed tactics and practised skills suited to its capabilities; however, when put to the test in the Gulf War, it proved nearly useless and indeed dangerous for pilots who had to fly low and straight over Iraqi runways. JP233, an extremely expensive munition, was in truth, designed for a single scenario, that is, conventional conflict in Europe. Designed for a single flyover of cramped East European airfields, it turned out to be both ineffective and dangerous for the pilots using it in Iraq.

Some weapons are now out of reach of any but the wealthiest and most developed economies. Only one country, the United States, can afford a large, stealthy, long-range bomber like the B2. Relatively few countries can afford large sophisticated surface warships. By contrast, most countries can afford highly accurate surface-to-surface ballistic and cruise missiles, UAVs, and the latest (and most lethal) antitank missiles. This does not guarantee success to one side or the other, but it means that to the extent they still occur, arms races are more likely to be asymmetric. Thus Syria, which once hoped to achieve conventional parity with Israel in the late 1970s and early 1980s, during the 1990s stopped trying to match the Israeli Air Force in the air. It built, instead, a sophisticated Russian-made air defence and created an arsenal of thousands of surface-to-surface missiles and rockets of varying types and quality.

A third form of military evolution has to do with the development not of weapons systems per se, but of meta-systems of extraordinary complexity. Networked sensors and command and control, such as the air operations centres that managed Allied air forces in the Gulf and Yugoslav Wars, are one example. The US Navy's Cooperative Engagement Capability, which allows all the ships in a task force to share a common picture based on the sum of all data in the system was an early example of technologies that are now commonplace in the civilian sector. Increasingly, these systems reflect less a traditional system of military command and control—in which information flows up and decisions down—than a far less hierarchical sharing of information and with it a certain dilution of authority. Engineers use the term 'systems integration' to describe the art of putting together a complex of technologies to achieve a purpose, and not all countries excel at it. Conventional military power rests, increasingly, on the ability of states to put together combinations of sensors and weapons and to make them function together in a fluid environment. Other forms of military power (terror or low-intensity warfare at one level, weapons of mass destruction at the other) do not demand these qualities.

## The Rise of Commercial Technology

Some percentage of military technology has always derived from the civilian sector. The famous Higgins boat of the Second World War, for example, which landed hundreds of thousands of Allied soldiers on beaches around the world, was a modification of a small craft originally designed for work in the Everglades swamps of Florida. Following the Second World War, however, to an unprecedented degree the armed forces of the developed world created vast research establishments operating on the cutting-edge of technology; military inventions tended to spill over into the civilian realm more than the other way around. The transistor and modern jet engines, to take two radically different-sized technologies, emerged from military research and development.

The information age is fundamentally different in this respect. Civilian technology, particularly in the area of software, leads military applications. Civilian encryption systems, and the fibre optic cables that carry secret information, have put secure communications within the reach even of non-state actors. Even when civilian technology does not yet lead military technology (in space-based sensing, for example) it is not very far behind: civilian satellites today can achieve resolutions (one metre or less) barely imaginable for their military counterparts only a decade or two ago.

These three trends—the rise of quality, the speciation of weapons, and the increased role of commercial technology—generally work to the benefit of developed open societies. They require a sophisticated industrial base for their manufacture, a skilled workforce for their maintenance, and, above all, flexible organizations for their intelligent use. These are qualities most likely to be found in democracies. As recently as a few decades ago, many thoughtful observers believed that democratic states stood at a near-ineradicable disadvantage vis-à-vis authoritarian or totalitarian counterparts, and indeed many of those weaknesses persist: the potential for indecision and volatility, indiscipline, and more recently, a pervasive sensitivity to casualties. Outweighing these and other weaknesses, however, are liberal democracies' strengths: their wealth (which makes military hardware affordable), their citizens' relative comfort with technological change, and fluid, egalitarian social relationships that breed a willingness to share rather than hoard information. However, not all technologies play to liberal democracies' strength—the proliferation of both information technologies and unmanned vehicles useful for the targeting of individuals in open societies most notably.

 **Key Points**

- There are three main features of the new era in warfare: the importance of quality over quantity; the speciation of military hardware; and the increased role of the commercial technologies.

- On occasions in history several developments have come together to create a revolution in military affairs (RMA).

- Following the Gulf War in 1991, changes in accuracy, range, and intelligence led many to believe a new RMA was taking place.

- Recent conflicts between unequal adversaries make it difficult to discern if a real RMA has occurred.

## Asymmetric Challenges

There is an apparent strategic paradox in the increasing technological edge of advanced, conventional powers who find themselves baffled or even defeated by irregular opponents. Israel's unsuccessful decade-long war with Hizbullah guerrillas in southern Lebanon (from 1991 to 2000, although preceded by skirmishes beforehand), is a dismaying example of how a vastly superior force, armed with high-tech weapons, can find itself defeated by an adroit opponent who knows how to play on the sensitivity of a democracy to its own casualties, and on world concern for civilians caught in a crossfire. American forces in Iraq following the over-throw of the Saddam Hussein regime in 2003 were bedevilled by a robust insurgency that, through the use of improvised explosive devices (IEDs), suffered far heavier casualties than during the swift, violent, and overwhelming march to Baghdad. These experiences, like those of Russia in Chechnya in the preceding decade, have caused some to suggest that guerrilla or irregular warfare can reduce or eliminate the importance of technological advantage on the modern battlefield.

This is not quite true. Modern guerrillas and terrorists make use of cell phones, electronic triggering devices, and extremely sophisticated explosives for their bombs; those countering them use even more sophisticated forms of electronic sweeping and neutralization, UAVs looking for those who plant IEDs, and precision-guided missiles to destroy specific vehicles or rooms in a building. In the hard urban fight for Falluja in November 2004, US Army and Marine forces took casualties in the scores, not the hundreds that would have been character-istic of city fighting even during the Vietnam War. The Israelis experienced similarly low losses in their operations in the urban environment of the West Bank and Gaza in the years preced-ing. Technology remains critical even in low-intensity conflict, and technological competi-tions—between bomb-maker and bomb-seeker, between guerrilla in ambush and convoy ready to fight its way through, between those protecting voting places and those seeking to prevent elections—persist. And technology in the form of commercial encryption and social media is vital for the communications and propaganda of insurgent groups.

The same might be said of another asymmetric strategy for technologically inferior powers—the resort to missile forces equipped with weapons of mass destruction, which offer non-democratic states the possibility of counterbalancing some, if not all, of the conventional predominance of their richer and more sophisticated opponents. Even the best missile defenc-es cannot guarantee a state's safety against such threats. Yet on the other hand, in the competi-tion between advanced and less developed states, a real nuclear edge, if such a thing exists, will go to the more developed state. In the ensuing stand-off, low-intensity conflict will flourish.

Thus far it turns out that advanced liberal states can use modern technology—from biomet-rics to robotics—to fight irregular opponents, and succeed. Israel's success in containing the second Palestinian intifada, reducing its own casualties, and inflicting crippling losses on the middle and senior levels of leadership of extremist organizations, speaks to the effectiveness of high technology, and the concerted will that can be evoked in the face of what society agrees is a serious threat. Similarly, the United States public displayed remarkable persistence in a counterinsurgency operation in Iraq that has inflicted substantial casualties (some 4,500 deaths as of 2012, and nearly seven times as many wounded), and that was, arguably, badly mismanaged in its early phases. In both cases, high technology played a role in limiting losses and achieving some successes.

>  **Key Points**
>
> - Superior conventional technology can be counterbalanced, to some extent, by asymmetric responses, such as irregular warfare and the threat of weapons of mass destruction.
> - High technology, however, continues to play a role in conflicts fought out in this sphere.
> - A critical question, in both cases, concerns societal willingness to persist in such conflicts.

## Challenges of the New Technology

Industrial age militaries could compete fairly easily with private enterprise because, at some level, they resembled it. A caste system resting on soldiers, non-commissioned officers, and officers mirrored a civilian stratification of workers, foremen, and managers. Compensation and deference structures were similar, although room could be made in the military, as in the civilian world, for more highly paid technical experts.

In the information age, the similarities between military and civilian organizations have broken down. Military organizations remain more hierarchical than many of their civilian counterparts, but more importantly, they find it difficult to obtain the human resources they need. A software engineer in the civilian sector is a highly paid, fairly autonomous employee, working with relatively little supervision. It has become acutely difficult for armed forces to recruit (and more importantly, retain) skilled men and women in these fields. Similarly, talented young officers are far more aware than ever before of the possibilities open to them outside the military. Retaining their services in an age of economic opportunity is difficult not merely because of compensation inequities—those have always existed—but because the civilian sector can often offer far more opportunity for change, autonomy, and unfettered responsibility.

The information technologies have other, perhaps more subtle effects on the conduct of war. As a general rule, the greater the flow of information, the more possibility for centralized control. During the Second World War, for example, the Royal Navy and then the United States centralized antisubmarine warfare in shore-based organizations that exploited reliable long-range radio communications and critically important advances in intelligence gathering. Such a development was very much the exception, however. Today, videoconferencing and the electronic transmission of data mean that generals in national capitals can exercise close supervision over their subordinates. The challenge for mid-level and senior leaders has become one of controlling the instinctive desire to take charge of a junior officer's problems. That impulse has become all the greater the more politically visible military action has become: when the result of a botched operation shows up immediately on CNN and a hundred websites, the inclination of higher authority to exercise the control that technology makes possible becomes all the greater.

Warfare often now occurs under the watchful eyes of the video camera and satellite uplink. Today insurgents put pictures of their attacks online within hours, and sometimes minutes, of their taking place. There are exceptions: the Russians excluded the press from much of the second Chechen war, and the Rwanda massacres occurred before journalists could cover them adequately. The Arab–Israeli conflict, however, may prove to be more the norm: rock throwing and shooting watched by (indeed, often staged for) journalists. Propaganda, always an adjunct of war, became a central element in the Arab–Israeli struggle, and both sides have found themselves structuring military action with reference not only to the traditional considerations of geography and tactics, but also to publicity. Adults manoeuvred Palestinian stone-throwing children into positions for optimal camera shots of 14-year-olds with rocks up against 19-year-olds with rifles. Meanwhile, after some abysmal failures, the Israelis reverted to sniper work and night-time kidnappings and assassinations precisely to avoid teams of journalists. Both sides created their own websites, and wrecked their opponents', as the conflict extended into cyberspace. The real and virtual battlefields have become a complex and inextricable whole. This development persisted in the Iraq War, which took a much grislier turn. Insurgent strategy included kidnappings and gruesome beheadings, which were the stuff not only of broadcasts on Arab-language television, but of film clips on jihadi websites, seeking to intimidate opponents, discourage foreign development aid, and enlist new supporters. To some extent, it worked.

 **Key Points**

- The civilian sector poses a major challenge to retaining military expertise.
- Information technology may lead to greater centralization of military control.
- Media coverage of conflicts poses challenges for military and political leaders.

 **Critical Thinking**   Debating … Does advanced military technology disrupt the military balance?

**For**

- **Successful organizations cannot move away from old technologies.** In war as in business, old technologies have such strong constituencies that turning one's back on them is nearly impossible. For example, a navy like that of the United States will find it almost impossible to forgo aircraft carriers even if they become increasingly vulnerable to the kinds of long-range precision strike that the Chinese military seems to be developing.

- **Weakness is the mother of innovation.** Hizbullah and Hamas could not hope to match the Israel Defense Forces tank for tank, battalion for battalion, brigade for brigade. Instead, they chose to create hybrid forces of guerrillas and commandos, armed with the latest antitank weapons, linked with fibre optic cables, and hidden in elaborate and well-concealed tunnel systems. For all the sophistication of Israel's Iron Dome anti-missile system, the Israelis could not prevent rockets from hitting its major cities during the several conflicts it has had with both enemies since 2006.

- **Modern technology intrinsically benefits the weaker side.** Hundreds of thousands of unmanned aerial vehicles or UAVs are commercially available. One even landed on the White House lawn in January 2015, much to the chagrin of the Secret Service. The electronics that enable such systems to fly and be remotely controlled far exceed anything in the superpower arsenals only 30 years ago. As cheap, unmanned commercial vehicles—drones, robotic vehicles, and even watercraft—proliferate, the balance of power will change. Far more numerous and, of course, without fear because they have no human beings inside, the drone swarm will put at risk not only large, clunky military technologies, but the vulnerable civilian infrastructure on which it depends.

*(continued . . .)*

**Critical Thinking** *(continued)*

## Against

- **Technological advantages are not magical.** They arise from the societies and organizations in which they are embedded. Moreover, if there is one constant in military history it is that for every measure there is a countermeasure, and for every countermeasure a counter-countermeasure, and so on without end. If swarms of drones become a threat, one can anticipate that there will evolve a variety of systems—weaponized lasers, in particular—to knock them out. Similarly, if groups or countries attempt to develop tunnel warfare, technologies that can see through rock or successfully attack underground forces will also emerge.

- **Successful militaries emerge from technologically advanced societies.** Israel is again the most interesting example, as it is the modern democratic state most often engaged in war. There is a connection between the inventiveness of a software industry that has created Waze, the iPhone app that allows one to navigate through databases and crowdsourcing, and the development of a system that can do something once thought impossible—detect short-range rockets, calculate whether they are going to hit inhabited space, and shoot them down with one or at most two shots.

- **Systems integration is the key.** Even if weak states or non-state actors can use advanced technology—such as drones or precision guided antitank missiles—a great deal of modern military power stems from the ability to put it all together. The ability to build organizations that can tap multiple sources of intelligence, communicate large amounts of information quickly, and bring many different types of weaponry to bear rests with developed societies and economies. Therefore, countries like the United States will keep the decisive edge.

 ## Conclusion: The Future of Military Technology

Military technology has contributed to a far more complicated environment for war than that of previous centuries. To the extent one can generalize about its effects, one would have to say that where the dominant forms of war in the past were few, today they are many. The challenges for armed forces are correspondingly immense.

Nor have the changes wrought by the new technologies come to an end. The increasingly easy access by countries to space, and their reliance on space for routine communications, navigation, and information gathering, seems almost certain to propel war into the heavens. For the moment, no country seems to have placed, or at least used, weapons in space that can disable or destroy either other satellites or targets on earth, but that is changing. Similarly, countries have experimented with, but not yet used, technologies on earth capable of affecting space-based systems. However, technology clearly permits this, in the form of lasers that can blind satellites, or mere lumps of metal that can hurtle from space to earth delivering enormous amounts of kinetic energy against their targets hundreds of miles below. The opening of space to full-fledged warfare would be as large a change as the opening of the air was during the First World War. New organizations, new operational conditions, new incentives to strike first, and new ways of war will blossom overnight.

Warfare also appears to be moving to cyberspace. Thus far, despite persistent stories about mischievous teenagers, clever criminals, or nefarious agents creating havoc with computer systems, there is little evidence of large-scale, lethal damage done by cyber-attack. It remains a theoretical possibility, however, and the unleashing of a potent virus (STUXNET) on the Iranian nuclear programme in 2009 is reported to have had considerable success in retarding, though not stopping, that enterprise. (See Chapter 16 for a strong case that cyberpower may transform conflict.)

A third sort of change already under way consists of advances in manufacturing, particularly in what are known as the nanotechnologies, robotics, and artificial intelligence. While it is highly unlikely that human beings will ever leave the battlefield (if only because the battlefield will surely come to them), more of the dangerous work may devolve upon small autonomous, intelligent machines that creep or fly, or merely sit and wait, classifying and attacking opponents. Animated, intelligent minefields transposed on land might make movement or manoeuvre by conventional forces extremely difficult. More importantly, the creation of such machines will mean that humans have gradually begun to cede much of their decision-making ability to silicon chips. It is a process already well under way in some areas. For example, modern aircraft are so intrinsically unstable that an automatic system, rather than a human being, must adjust their trim.

In all these cases, the most interesting and important consequences of technological change will probably flow from its effect on how human beings think about and conduct war, specifically: how they conceive of military action, how they assign responsibility, how they calculate military effects, and how they attempt to harmonize means and ends. But a fourth set of changes, perhaps the most profound of all, looms larger still. The biological sciences increasingly make it possible to change the nature of human beings themselves (Fukuyama 1999). The intriguing theoretical pondering of Greek philosophers has become, in our age, the challenge of scientific researchers. One can scarcely doubt that an Adolf Hitler would have availed himself of the resources of bio-technology to breed new kinds of human beings—such as super-soldiers, insensitive to fear and truly loyal to the death—who could serve his purposes. Our common understanding of war rests on some of its deeply human features, which have not changed since the days of Homer or Thucydides. This is so, however, only because the same species, *homo sapiens*, has continued to wage it. If—when?—humans are replaced by a variety of creatures, some subhuman, and others, in some respects, superhuman, war itself will have become an activity as different from traditional human conflict as the murderous struggles between competing anthills or the stalking of deer by packs of wolves.

 ## Questions

1. Take a representative military technology such as the tank. Using several examples, how would you characterize the national style embedded in its design?

2. What is stealth technology? Does the concept of interaction apply to it?

3. In what cases does military technology require high levels of technical expertise and education, and in what cases does it actually reduce or even eliminate such a requirement?

4. What are some of the military technologies that only the United States has available to it? Other great powers? Smaller states? Non-state actors?

5. What are some examples of 'the technological edge'? How fragile are such leads by one state or another?

6. Is cyberwarfare really 'warfare'?

7. What implications are there if warfare extends to space? Will it impact more on commercial or military technology?

8. What are some of the technologies most useful to the conduct of irregular warfare, including guerrilla and terror operations?

9. Are democracies or authoritarian/totalitarian regimes better placed to adapt to the changing nature and problems of technological warfare?

10. What would be the strategic and moral implications of advances in biological science that would allow governments to enhance soldier performance far beyond current norms?

## Further Reading

J. D. Bergen, *Military Communications: A Test for Technology* (Washington, DC: Center of Military History, 1986), chapters 16–17, pp. 367–408 describes a competition in communication technology and electronic warfare between an extremely sophisticated state (the US) and a more backward one (North Vietnam), in which the more developed society did not necessarily do well.

A. Beyerchen, 'From Radio to Radar: Interwar Military Adaptation to Technological Change in Germany, the United Kingdom, and the United States'. In W. Murray and A. R. Millett (eds), *Military Innovation in the Interwar Period* (Cambridge: Cambridge University Press, 1996) is a good example of how national style appears even in the electronic realm.

W. Churchill, *The World Crisis, 1911–1914* (New York: Charles Scribner's Sons, 1926), chapter 6, 'The Romance of Design', pp. 125–149 brilliantly describes military design challenges from a decision-maker's point of view.

A. C. Clarke, 'Superiority', in *Expedition to Earth* (New York: Harcourt, Brace and World, 1970) is a science fiction story with a whimsical but wise warning on the dangers of becoming too sophisticated.

M. van Creveld, *Technology and War from 2000 B.C. to the Present* (New York: Free Press, 1989) is considerably more up to date than Fuller 1945.

J. F. C. Fuller, *Armament and History; A Study of the Influence of Armament on History from the Dawn of Classical Warfare to the Second World War* (New York: Charles Scribner's Sons, 1945) remains an excellent short treatment of the relationship between technology, tactics, organization, and strategy.

W. Hughes, *Fleet Tactics: Theory and Practice* (Annapolis, MD: Naval Institute Press, 1986) gives a thoughtful treatment of the role of technology in warfare.

H. Petroski, *To Engineer is Human: The Role of Failure in Successful Design* (New York: Random House, 1982) argues that 'form follows failure', that is, engineering advances occur only as a result of the failure of current materials or designs.

G. Raudzens, 'War-Winning Weapons: The Measurement of Technological Determinism in Military History', *Journal of Military History*, 54 (October 1990): 403–33 is a sceptical view of technology's importance and the impact of technology on war.

P. W. Singer, *Wired for War: The Robotics Revolution and Conflict in the 21st Century* (New York: Penguin, 2009) gives a first comprehensive look at the impact of unmanned technologies on the conduct of war—surely an augur of things to come.

 ## Web Links

Jane's Information Group **http://www.janes.com** has many reputable articles on the links between technology and warfare.

Aviation Week **http://www.aviationweek.com/aw** is another reputable website.

Global Security **http://www.globalsecurity.org/military/systems/index.html** also hosts articles on a range of technology issues, including valuable primers on the subject.

Military Technology **http://www.monch.com** has regular updates on recent developments in military technology.

Wired Danger Room **http://www.wired.com/dangerroom** has excellent reporting, particularly on cyber-related issues.

8

# Intelligence and Strategy

ROGER Z. GEORGE

## Chapter Contents

 ## Reader's Guide

This chapter examines how intelligence enables but does not guarantee successful strategy. It opens by discussing what intelligence is and how strategists have talked about its utility. It then traces the development of US intelligence in its early efforts to support cold war strategies of containment and deterrence and in its more recent support to US strategies for counterterrorism and counter-insurgency. The chapter briefly examines the challenges and causes of 'strategic surprise', bringing to bear key historical cases of Pearl Harbor in 1941, the 1962 Cuban Missile Crisis, the 1973 Yom Kippur War, and the 11 September 2001 attacks. While suggesting some possible correctives, it concludes that there are no complete solutions to inevitable intelligence failures. It also identifies some of the new challenges intelligence faces after a decade of war in Iraq and Afghanistan as well as in dealing with the new 'big data' problem.

# Introduction

Good strategy is dependent on understanding the nature of war, key aspects of the international system, and an adversary's intentions and capabilities.[1] Inherently, then, strategy must be based on good intelligence. Yet, while strategic theorists have acknowledged the importance of intelligence, many also express their discomfort with its quality and reliability. Theorists can be categorized as either optimists or pessimists regarding the role of intelligence. Sun Tzu, the optimist, advised the warrior to 'know the enemy and know yourself and in a hundred battles you will never be in peril'. Carl von Clausewitz, the pessimist, barely acknowledges the value of intelligence in his writing, concluding that 'many intelligence reports are contradictory, even more are false, and most are uncertain'. Nevertheless, both recognize that no strategy can be formulated or implemented without assessing the challenges and opportunities that it might encounter. Today, decision-makers are no different. As one senior US official described policymakers from several past administrations: 'The ones that were sceptical when they came in [to government] became increasingly dependent or, at least reliant on it' (Center for the Study of Intelligence 2004).

Throughout history, intelligence has played a role in the development and execution of national strategies. Moses sent his spies into Canaan. In Napoleon's time, diplomats often assumed the roles of spies while serving as representatives of their monarchs and prime ministers. Some would say Paul Revere provided the first 'warning' of war to the colonists that the British were coming. General George Washington was, in effect, the first head of American intelligence, as he doled out funds for agents who worked against the British. In 1941, decoding of Japanese military communications provided American negotiators with a tip-off that Tokyo was breaking off negotiations and contemplating war. Although this warning was not understood well enough to avert the Pearl Harbor attack, this code-breaking ultimately helped to destroy the Japanese fleet at the 1942 Battle of Midway. In 1944, General Dwight Eisenhower constructed one of the most daring strategic deception campaigns to mislead Hitler's Germany regarding the Normandy invasion; a deception campaign that was based on an accurate reading of Nazi preconceptions of Allied intentions. Indeed, Eisenhower and British Prime Minister Winston Churchill stand out as decision-makers with a keen sense of how to use Allied intelligence for wartime purposes.

Intelligence was a major element of strategies aimed at supporting America's containment and deterrence policies during the cold war. Today, it is central to the challenge of defeating terrorism and the spread of weapons of mass destruction (WMD). As intelligence activities have grown and become more complicated, there is increasing concern that they need to be effectively guided to support national security strategies. Far from becoming irrelevant in the post-cold war world, as some thought in the 1990s, the 2009 US National Security Strategy highlighted its principal missions to be combating violent extremism, proliferation, and cyber threats in addition to providing strategic warning and supporting ongoing military operations (National Security Strategy 2010). The latest 2014 National Intelligence Strategy singles out cyber threats, counterterrorism, and counterproliferation as key missions as well as conducting broad strategic intelligence analysis of enduring security issues and anticipating emerging threats (National Intelligence Strategy 2014).

## What is Intelligence?

The term intelligence is commonly used to describe only that information provided to policy officials by government organizations, in order to distinguish it from a much broader body of information available to those inside and outside the US government. Intelligence is often secret information, which is collected through clandestine means or technical systems (e.g. satellites in earth-orbit, monitoring communications or electronic signatures). The sources and methods used to collect this information are risky, expensive, and often fragile, so their unauthorized exposure to adversaries would weaken US national security. Part of the intelligence mission, then, is to protect this information (called counterintelligence) as well as to penetrate the intelligence services of adversaries (counterespionage). Intelligence information also is 'tailored' to respond specifically to the requirements and needs of government officials. Generally speaking, intelligence is focused on the policies, intentions, and capabilities of foreign governments and increasingly on the plans and activities of non-state actors that threaten the United States and its allies. Intelligence can also be understood as the programmes and processes used by the 16 separate agencies currently comprising the US intelligence community to collect, analyse, and disseminate secret information throughout the US government. The production of finished intelligence reflects this 'intelligence cycle': decision-makers' needs are translated into information requirements for collection, which lead to analysis and the writing of finished intelligence reports, which are then disseminated back to the original requestors of that information.

These intelligence programmes and processes require the coordination of hundreds of separate programmes and thousands of individuals across the US government. In 2010, such activities constituted as many as 100,000 people and as much as US$53 billion dollars per year (Director of National Intelligence, 2010). US intelligence budgets have more recently been falling, in line with a general decline in US military defence budgets and the trend seems likely to continue (Benson 2012). On a daily basis, individuals and organizations must collect huge volumes of raw (unevaluated) information; sift through it to separate fact from rumour, propaganda, and fiction; search for the most valuable insights; interpret facts to form important analytic judgements about their meaning and significance to US policy interest; and communicate it to senior civilian and military policymakers in the United States or to allied and friendly governments.

## Intelligence Collection

The collection of raw intelligence information takes the lion's share of American intelligence resources (roughly 80 per cent). Most collection efforts are located inside in the Department of Defense. Its National Security Agency operates major signals intelligence (SIGINT) programmes, while the National Reconnaissance Office builds and operates major satellite reconnaissance programmes and the National Geo-spatial Intelligence Agency exploits and analyses the imagery produced by the satellite collection systems. These agencies are considered so vital to the conduct of US military operations that they are designated 'combat support' elements of the US intelligence community, and the Secretary of Defense takes special care to ensure that they are properly funded, staffed, and managed. The Central Intelligence Agency (CIA) runs the other major intelligence programme focused on collecting clandestine HUMINT or human intelligence. The classic job of recruiting secret agents who can penetrate the internal workings of foreign adversaries and terrorist groups falls to the CIA's National Clandestine Service. Its case officers are deployed all over the world to identify important intelligence targets and learn the plans and intentions of America's enemies, which cannot be so easily gleaned from overhead satellites or intercepted electronic messages.

Although not new, global collection of so-called 'open source' information has taken on greater prominence. There has always been an interest in reading foreign publications or listening to and watching radio and TV broadcasts. The advent of the Internet, however, has caused a dramatic explosion in the volume and scope of foreign open source information, leading to the development of the intelligence community's Open Source Center. The Center monitors thousands of publications, broadcasts, and websites, and it produces media reports for intelligence analysts and decision-makers alike. Moreover, in the battle against violent

**BOX** 8.1   Intelligence Collection: Sources and Methods

Finished all-source intelligence rests on the collection and careful weighing and evaluation of multiple pieces of clandestinely or openly gathered information. This information comes from a variety of sources.

- *Human intelligence (HUMINT)* is gained overtly by diplomats and military attachés or secretly from foreign agents who have access to the plans, intentions, and capabilities of foreign adversaries.

- *Signals intelligence (SIGINT)* is the technical interception and exploitation of an adversary's communication and other electronic systems.

- *Imagery intelligence (IMINT)* is collected from ground, overhead, and space-based imaging systems (often satellites) using visual photography, electro-optics, radar, or infra-red sensors.

- *Open source (OPINT)* intelligence is the collection, translation, and analysis of foreign broadcasts, news media, and increasingly Internet websites.

extremism, information warfare now involves monitoring and disrupting jihadist websites often used for recruitment and communications (see Box 8.1).

## Intelligence Analysis

The least expensive part of the intelligence enterprise is analysis. Country and functional analysts must make sense out of the millions of clandestine reports, electronic intercepts, or digital imagery that are gathered by their collection partners. These analysts are to be found in the Central Intelligence Agency, the Defense Intelligence Agency, the Department of State's Bureau of Intelligence and Research, as well as in sizeable units in the Federal Bureau of Investigation (FBI), the Department of Homeland Security, and other national security agencies. They have the responsibility of giving US policymakers the knowledge needed to fashion and implement effective national security strategies. They provide this analysis to a wide array of government officials throughout the Executive Branch and the Congress in written, oral, and electronic formats. From the most sensitive and limited production of the President's Daily Brief (PDB) to the posting of numerous intelligence assessments on the Intelligence Community's classified website (called INTELINK), these assessments are tailored to suit a variety of decision-makers, from the President down to diplomats and field commanders. The purpose of these reports is both to inform as well as to enable decision-makers to construct and implement policies that advance US strategies, identify threats, and evaluate the actions and intentions of foreign adversaries. Seldom, however, do intelligence analysts provide sufficient factual details or highly confident forecasts that completely satisfy policymakers.

The task for intelligence analysts, then, is to distinguish carefully between what they know and do not know and then to present what they believe might happen and explain why it is significant. It is up to the decision-maker to decide how to fashion strategies and policies that take note of these intelligence judgements. Intelligence analysis, however, faces increasing competition from other sources of information. Decision-makers often consider themselves analysts, who are also utilizing the Internet, have their own networks of experts and have more direct contact with foreign government officials than analysts working at the CIA or other intelligence agencies. Hence, analysts must work hard to develop special insight and expertise based on their access to a wider range of sources of intelligence. In some cases, analysts' credibility can rest as much on their academic credentials, foreign area travels, and language skills as on their access to highly classified information. Such experts also have the advantage of focusing their entire workday on a single issue or country and the ability to task intelligence collectors to provide new information of use to decision-makers. By quickly preparing new assessments directed at the specific interests or needs of a decision-maker, they can provide actionable (useful in taking decisions) information.

## Special Intelligence Missions

While collection and analysis form the core of the intelligence mission, these missions rest on effective counterintelligence and counterespionage. Information provided to key decision-makers must be protected from falling into the hands of enemies. Strategic deception can occur—a situation when an adversary understands how an opponent perceives a threat and succeeds in undermining or distorting accurate threat perceptions. The 'Wikileaks' disclosures and the ongoing 'Snowden' controversies—that is, the unauthorized disclosure of hundreds of thousands of classified US diplomatic and military reports in the former and the massive exposure of sensitive NSA technical collection programs—continues to complicate US foreign relations with many close allies and partners. Key allies, including Germany, have strongly criticized alleged NSA operations against its citizens and leaders and allegedly punished US intelligence by expelling senior US intelligence officials operating in Germany (Miller 2014). Such disclosures by 'cleared' employees and contractors have also generated calls for better 'vetting' of the nearly 2 million people who handle sensitive information.

To ensure that intelligence agencies are not penetrated, it is necessary to conduct counterespionage operations; these activities are aimed at recruiting agents inside hostile intelligence services, in order to determine if they have recruited agents inside one's own government or intelligence services. This competition often prompts Hollywood to develop fantastic versions of what is often called the 'spy-versus-spy' game. In real life, counterespionage is far less romantic but no less vital to protecting information which intelligence provides to the most senior decision-makers in a government.

Another distinct and apparently expanding mission for intelligence is conducting covert action. While most intelligence merely enables the use of military, economic, informational, and diplomatic power, covert action is in fact the *covert* use of these instruments. Sometimes known as 'special activities', covert action is run in the United States by the CIA at the specific request of the President. These actions are kept secret in order to achieve important strategic objectives, without directly associating them with the US government. First established by the National Security Council in the late 1940s, special activities have become a tool of US foreign policy, used by virtually every President in some fashion. Both the Bush and Obama administrations authorized such special activities in order to disrupt terrorist plans and proliferation networks. However, these activities can have a 'blow back' effect, if they become known and complicate relations with other governments or if they become so large and overt as to negate the benefits of using these tools covertly. So, a strategist will need to weigh the risks and benefits of covert actions knowing that sooner or later they will become known to an adversary, the US public, or the international community.

The intelligence community's role in covert activities has steadily grown during the decade of wars in Afghanistan and Iraq. US strategists have increasingly relied upon non-conventional approaches to combating terrorism and overcoming internal conflicts in Iraq and Afghanistan. Presidential Findings have been issued for the CIA to conduct extensive covert activities to disrupt, defeat, and destroy terrorist cells around the world. The most significant aspect of these special operations was the location and elimination of Osama bin Laden in Pakistan in 2011. This event highlighted both the utility but also the controversial nature of using combined intelligence and military assets to eliminate a major terrorist figure operating in a safe haven. In addition, the US military and intelligence agencies have operated unmanned airborne vehicles (UAVs or 'drones') to identify and kill key al-Qaeda leaders. The extent to which the US will be able to rely on such methods in the future remains to be seen, as they are not only highly effective, but also fiercely criticized by countries, where reportedly the US has used them without their explicit approval. The debate over the pros and cons of drone warfare is addressed later in this chapter.

---

 **Key Points**

- Strategy rests on accurate perceptions of an adversary's plans, intentions, and capabilities, and intelligence enables decision-makers to develop and implement good strategy.

- Intelligence is more than just information. It is focused on the special needs of decision-makers and usually requires secret collection methods to uncover the true plans and intentions of a foreign actor.

- Producing actionable (useful in decision-making) intelligence requires careful collection, exploitation, analysis, and dissemination of intelligence. This is called the 'intelligence cycle'.

- Good intelligence requires good counterintelligence aimed at understanding an adversary's efforts to penetrate one's own intelligence apparatus.

- US intelligence also has the responsibility for carrying out special activities designed to hide the US role in using military, political, or economic measures against an adversary. This is commonly known as covert action.

- Covert activities have grown significantly as the US counterterrorism and counterinsurgency strategies have demanded more sensitive, small-scale paramilitary operations to complement and reinforce major military operations.

---

## Intelligence as Enabler of US Strategy

When the cold war began, the United States was in search of both a national security strategy as well as a concept of intelligence. Neither was well defined until important seminal thinking had occurred within the US government and in the major research centres of the time. George Kennan coined the containment strategy in 1946–1947 and further developed the concept while at the State Department's Policy Planning Staff. A deterrence strategy also emerged from the strategic thought of Bernard Brodie and Herman Kahn among others, who were working at the Rand Corporation in the early 1950s. In the meantime, Sherman Kent—a Yale historian and colleague of both Kennan and Brodie at the National War College—developed the concept of strategic intelligence. In his groundbreaking 1949 book, *Strategic Intelligence for an American World Policy*, Kent laid out the basic principles that should drive intelligence. In its simplest sense, intelligence should 'raise the level of discussion' around the policymaking tables. In Kent's view, intelligence should not advocate a specific policy position; instead, it should inform policy. Intelligence analysts should be cognizant of, but detached from, any specific policy agenda. Kent knew that lively debates among strong-willed policymakers would make intelligence prone to manipulation and that intelligence analysts had to maintain their objectivity and integrity in presenting unbiased intelligence. Stating this objective, however, was not to say it would be easy to achieve in practice. Nor were intelligence assessments uncontroversial when matters of war or peace were to be based partly on their findings. Throughout the cold war, time and again US intelligence was faulted for being wrong, biased, or both. It also became embroiled in debates over strategy and was sometimes accused, rightly or wrongly, of becoming 'politicized' (distorted by political agendas).

## The Soviet Legacy for US Intelligence

As the cold war developed in the 1940s, the principal function of American intelligence became penetrating the veil of secrecy that surrounded the Soviet Union. The highest collection priorities were aimed at understanding Moscow's communist ideology and internal policy processes as well as its strategic objectives and military–industrial complex that presented the key military threat to US and allied security interests. Early intelligence failures drove changes in the operation of US intelligence. New procedures to produce national intelligence estimates became a centrepiece of intelligence support to Presidents and the National Security Council in shaping national security policies vis-à-vis the Soviet Union, the Warsaw Pact, and its communist allies in Asia and the Third World. An elaborate schedule of national estimates was designed to monitor and forecast the growth of Soviet strategic and conventional forces, so that Washington's defence planners could build and size US forces appropriately. Other estimates were aimed at comprehending Moscow's global political strategy to spread its influence beyond its East European sphere of influence and into the developing world; still others were produced to assess how resilient were parts of the free world and the so-called non-aligned countries, where the East–West contest was fought through proxies and wars of liberation.

Whenever debates over US cold war strategies began to arise, there was a good possibility that US intelligence estimates would be dragged into these disputes as well. The Vietnam War also occasioned major intelligence arguments. Senior US military and civilian leaders challenged and sometimes overruled pessimistic CIA estimates, so they did not undermine the conduct of the war itself. The 1970s American détente and arms control policies designed by President Nixon and Henry Kissinger were periodically bedevilled by intelligence debates over the nature of the Soviet military threat, Moscow's willingness to fight a nuclear war, and the adequacy of the US–Soviet strategic balance. At the heart of those debates were the strategic intelligence assessments made by the CIA and the Defense Intelligence Agency. During the 1980–1988 tenure of President Ronald Reagan, US intelligence was often viewed as having taken too benign a view of the Soviet military threat and having allowed itself to become 'politicized' by adopting the 'détentist' tendencies that would support Henry Kissinger's arms control agenda.

With the fall of the Berlin Wall, the Warsaw Pact, and the Soviet Union, CIA's intelligence was faulted for not having predicted the end of the cold war. Intelligence professionals and outside scholars have since defended the CIA's record, noting that even the Russians had not anticipated the end of the Soviet Union, so how could CIA have predicted it. Along with this criticism, there were calls to dismantle the CIA as being no longer needed, once the Soviet threat had disappeared. Needless to say, the rise of Russian belligerence toward the West and President Putin's decision to seize the Crimea in Ukraine have increased strategists' need for intelligence on Moscow's intentions and capabilities.

During President Truman's time, the CIA also began a daily intelligence update, culled from a variety of diplomatic, intelligence, and military intelligence sources, featuring key overnight developments that he might wish to see. This daily intelligence support continued for every president thereafter and became more formalized as the CIA and IC became more sophisticated in the analysis of world events. One of the many legacies of the Soviet era was, thus, the practice of preparing both the National Intelligence Estimate (NIE) and the PDB as crucial vehicles for conveying long-term as well as current intelligence assessments to key US policymakers (see Box 8.2).

## Evolution of the Intelligence Community

Over the past half century, the profession of intelligence has continued to evolve. With each decade, there were problems to be addressed, organizational changes to be made, and new

 **Box** 8.2   The National Intelligence Estimate and the President's Daily Brief

National Intelligence Estimates (NIEs) are prepared for the President, his Cabinet, the National Security Council, and other senior civilian and military decision-makers. NIEs focus on strategic issues of mid- or long-term importance to US national security policies. They represent the combined views of all 16 intelligence agencies that comprise the US intelligence community. The NIE process has evolved over time, since first being established in the 1950s by the Board of National Estimates. As practised today, they are produced by the National Intelligence Council, reviewed by all heads of the US intelligence community, and approved by the Director of National Intelligence. These estimates are provided not only to the Executive Branch officials but also to members of congressional intelligence oversight committees. As in the past, NIEs are often a source of major controversy with the President, the Congress and the US public. The most infamous of the post-9/11 era is the 2002 Iraq WMD estimate, which asserted that Saddam Hussein retained substantial weapons of mass destruction and might be on the verge of having a nuclear weapons capability. The 2007 Iran NIE on its nuclear programme also became controversial after the released Key Judgments seemed to suggest Iran might be halting aspects of its nuclear weapons programme, a judgement that was viewed by some as undermining the Bush administration's efforts to keep pressure on Iran.

The PDB also has become a better known and highly prized daily intelligence report. Written explicitly for the President and his principal White House and Cabinet-level advisors, it constitutes what the IC believes are the most important current intelligence developments and most sensitive information. Delivered by senior intelligence briefers, these reports can often lead to new policy decisions and actions. PDBs are largely prepared by the CIA; however, analysts in the Defense Intelligence Agency and State Department's Bureau of Intelligence and Research (INR) also submit items for inclusion on occasion. The Director of National Intelligence now manages the PDB process, ensuring that all analytic agencies' views are reflected in the product, not just the CIA. The PDB has become a key driver for CIA analysis, superseding in many respects the production of NIEs and other longer-term assessments. Unlike NIEs, PDBs are not shared with the US Congress, and they are highly tailored to each president's policy agenda and personal style. Of late, the PDB has gone 'electronic' and it has been provided in a classified notebook form to President Obama.

substantive issues to be followed. By the end of the cold war, the intelligence community amounted to over a dozen large and small agencies, most of which were contained within the Departments of Defense, State, Justice, and now Homeland Security. This growing 'intelligence community' drove the need for better organization of intelligence activities, highlighting the need for a far stronger role than the Director of Central Intelligence (DCI) could provide. The DCI, who also had to lead the CIA, could not effectively coordinate the far-flung activities of a dozen or more intelligence agencies.

As intelligence became a more acknowledged function of government, there was more appreciation and criticism for its role in shaping strategy and policy. Since its very beginning, the CIA and other intelligence agencies inspired controversy. The very role of intelligence in a democratic society caused law-makers to be anxious about having sufficient controls over its methods, targets and uses. The revelations during the Bush and Obama presidencies regarding counterterrorist intercept programmes and the interrogation methods employed by the US intelligence community has sparked congressional criticism and investigations. The post-9/11 era silenced the calls for eliminating the CIA that were often heard after the end of the cold war, but they were soon replaced by demands for overhauling the way the United States runs the intelligence community. Major organizational changes were instituted to enable better information sharing and coordination of 16 major foreign and domestic intelligence agencies (including the creation of a Department of Homeland Security). Reforms included the establishment of a new position of Director of National Intelligence, separate from the Director of the CIA, as head of the US intelligence community. The new philosophy appears to be that the Director of National Intelligence will be the leading presidential advisor on and organizer of all intelligence activities, while the CIA Director will oversee the collection of HUMINT, production of all-source intelligence analysis, and planning of presidentially approved covert action. This new organizational division of labour has been in place for a decade now and seems likely to continue, although further adjustments could occur as intelligence needs and international conditions change. More importantly, each president will shape the intelligence community's leadership, missions, and operations to suit his or her preferences. Not surprisingly, this factor—including a president's comfort level and familiarity with national security problems—is likely to shape the intelligence-policy relationship even more than any changing international conditions.

---

 **Key Points**

- US intelligence was created initially to deal with the Soviet threat, but continues to evolve in order to assess new global and transnational threats.

- The intelligence community provides both long-term estimative analysis (such as NIEs) as well as current intelligence products (e.g. PDBs).

- The intelligence record is often the focus of controversy, reflecting as much a debate over strategy as over the quality of intelligence.

- The CIA was joined by more than a dozen other intelligence agencies during the cold war to form what is now commonly called the 'intelligence community'.

- Intelligence must adjust to a president's personal priorities and style as well as address intelligence needs driven by different strategic approaches and international conditions.

# Strategic Surprise: Causes and Correctives

The US intelligence community was created after the 1941 Pearl Harbor attack in an effort to prevent another strategic surprise. The notion of strategic surprise, highlighted in Roberta Wohlstetter's seminal work on Pearl Harbor, continues to drive the development of US intelligence capabilities and the standard by which the CIA and other intelligence agencies are often judged. A working definition of strategic surprise has at least three key elements:

1. It is a development having significant negative impact on national interests;
2. Alternative strategies might have been chosen to avert the consequences; but
3. Accurate and timely intelligence information was lacking, not transmitted, or not correctly understood by senior officials.

This definition makes a distinction between a strategic surprise and an intelligence failure; the former is often the result of ineffective interaction between strategists and intelligence professionals in identifying and responding to major threats. An intelligence 'failure' generally places the blame for some disaster on the intelligence community and constitutes only one element of the broader notion of strategic surprise. In fact, some intelligence failures may not jeopardize overall US strategy, because their consequences are not so grave or because the strategy itself is not so dependent on specific intelligence judgements.

## Causes of Surprise

There are many causes of strategic surprise and intelligence failures. A strategic surprise can occur when decision-makers fail to absorb and use information and analysis provided by intelligence professionals. Cases of this include not only Pearl Harbor, where information was available, but also the Soviet placement of nuclear-armed missiles into Cuba in 1962, the 1973 Yom Kippur War, and most recently the 9/11 attacks on New York City and the Pentagon. In each case, there was some warning of a possible threat, but the information was scanty or not properly interpreted. Moreover, policymakers as well as most intelligence analysts dismissed the possibility of such bold actions being plausible and therefore took no steps to avert those actions or mitigate their effects. In virtually all these cases, both decision-makers and intelligence professionals share the blame. In the Pearl Harbor case, there was information indicating Japan planned attacks against US interests in the Pacific; however, it was not disseminated quickly to senior commanders, nor did commanders imagine the attack might be as far forward as Pearl Harbor, so they took minimal and mostly ineffective preventive or defensive actions. In the Cuban Missile Crisis, US intelligence was observing Soviet military transfers to Cuba, but analysts as well as President Kennedy's advisors dismissed the possibility that Moscow would place nuclear weapons on an island 90 miles from American shores. In the 1973 Yom Kippur War, both US and Israeli intelligence had good information that Arab states were planning an attack, but they misinterpreted available information as evidence of military exercises rather than preparation for war. Ironically, US and Israeli decision-makers discounted such moves believing that Egypt and Syria would not contemplate attacking Israel after their decisive defeat in the 1967 Middle East War (often called the Six-Day War because of the rapidity with which Israel dispatched both combatants).

The September 2001 attacks by al-Qaeda are a classic case of an intelligence failure that led to decision-makers' inattention to a strategic warning that then contributed to a major strategic surprise. The 9/11 Commission Report documents the fact that terrorism analysts at the CIA's Counterterrorism Center were well aware of the growing danger that al-Qaeda posed to American interests. Counterterrorism analysts believed an attack was likely to occur in the autumn of 2001 but they could not provide details of how, when, or where such an attack might occur. As summer 2001 ended, senior intelligence officials provided 'strategic warning' by telling the George W. Bush administration that something big was planned and that counterterrorism analysts were monitoring a huge increase in activity ('chatter'). On 6 August 2001, the President was briefed on terrorist plots against the American homeland, but American intelligence had no specific, tactical intelligence on when or where attacks might occur. Sadly, as the Commission recounts, there was information held by the FBI and other agencies, which was not effectively combined with what the CIA knew about al-Qaeda in time to realize that the plotters were already in the United States and making their final preparations for the attacks. Moreover, the 6 August briefing did not lead decision-makers in other parts of the government to highlight the threat or take any actions that might have tightened airport or airline security. Unheeded strategic warning and the lack of more specific tactical intelligence reporting, according to some intelligence practitioners, encouraged policy inaction, setting up the conditions necessary for a major strategic surprise (Pillar 2011).

## Key Factors: Seven Deadly Sins

No single factor is the cause of a major surprise or intelligence failure. Indeed, seven factors are often present in some combination. First, there is usually a collection failure. As Clausewitz warned, information is often lacking or contradictory, or both. Second, analysts can often misinterpret the available information because of an outmoded or inadequate understanding of an adversary's objectives, plans, or capabilities; this is often termed the 'mindset' problem. Even the best experts can develop a benign or 'stylized' view of the adversary that clouds their ability to see how an enemy might take great risks or attempt an unconventional attack. Third, deception employed by an adversary can often feed analysts' inaccurate mindsets and cause them to misread tell-tale signs of danger. Fourth, an adversary can deny—through excellent operational security—to intelligence analysts sufficient information to form an accurate picture of the threat. Fifth, information available to intelligence collectors or analysts might not be rapidly or effectively shared among themselves. Compartmentation (security rules limiting the sharing of information through a 'need to know' principle) can inhibit intelligence organizations from passing what they know to other agencies that can compare it with their own information. Sixth, there can be a failure to communicate threat information effectively to decision-makers, so leaders do not appreciate the dangers in time to take appropriate action. And finally, decision-makers may suffer from their own outmoded mindsets regarding the adversary's intentions and capabilities, and therefore dismiss intelligence warnings or take no countermeasures.

At the core of the problem of strategic surprise and intelligence failures is the presumption that decision-makers and intelligence analysts correctly and completely understand the intentions and capabilities of an adversary. In fact, most strategic surprises result from an inaccurate assessment of how an enemy sees his own situation and how that opponent assesses the benefits and risks of war. Stalin dismissed intelligence that Germany would launch an eastern offensive in the spring of 1941. Hitler suffered the same fate of believing he correctly understood how an Allied invasion would begin in 1944, which Eisenhower reinforced with the Allied deception plans. Israelis underestimated the risk-taking of Arabs in 1973 after their drubbing in 1967, which Egyptian President Anwar Sadat exploited by launching a surprise attack under the cover of military exercises. US analysts and decision-makers likewise underestimated the risk-taking calculations of Soviet leaders in the 1962 Cuba case and again in the 1979 Soviet invasion of Afghanistan. All of these examples highlight the role of human perceptual frailties, to which all analysts as well as strategists are prone. Such cognitive biases, as many psychologists would recognize, are hard to identify and even harder to eliminate.

## Correctives, Not Cures

Correctives to future strategic surprises or intelligence failures are difficult if not impossible to guarantee. As intelligence scholar Richard Betts has put it, 'intelligence failures are almost inevitable', because there is almost no way to guarantee sufficient information and correct analysis of all threats in order for policymakers to pre-empt them (Betts 2007). Nonetheless, there are three correctives that can be employed to reduce the chances of strategic surprise and intelligence failures. First, improved collection, of course, is always to be hoped for; however, few analysts can depend on perfect intelligence information to guide their analysis. Analysts can assess the gaps in their information and accordingly qualify their judgements to alert decision-makers to the 'unknowns' present in any decisions they make. Second, analysts can assess an adversary's motives and capabilities for conducting major deception and denial campaigns. Typically, the weaker the adversary, the more it might rely on surprise—using deception and denial—to compensate for an opponent's stronger military forces. Third, analysts can develop a greater awareness of their own mindsets and other cognitive biases, which can distort their interpretation of available information. There is a growing social science literature on structured analytic techniques, which analysts can use to make their work more rigorous. These techniques—such as devil's advocacy, team A/ team B, analysis of competing hypotheses, or scenario analysis—can help analysts to challenge analytical assumptions, make analytic arguments more transparent to peers as well as decision-makers, guide intelligence collectors to filling significant information gaps, and ultimately caution intelligence users on the limitations of available information to their decision-making processes (see Box 8.3).[2]

Strategists must appreciate that all intelligence is imperfect and not likely to be sufficient to make all decisions with high confidence. Whether it is the case of the 1962 Cuban Missile Crisis or the more recent example of the 2002 Iraq WMD National Intelligence Estimate, intelligence is not entirely right or wrong but rather has both strengths and weaknesses. In 1962, Sherman Kent's estimators misread Soviet intentions and its risk calculations when they judged that the Russians were unlikely to place nuclear-armed missiles in Cuba. Despite this flawed estimate, it was intelligence—via U-2 flights over Cuba—along with SIGINT and some HUMINT that gave the Kennedy administration sufficient insight into subsequent Soviet moves to then face down Moscow and eventually negotiate the missiles' removal. For those 12 days in October 1962, the Kennedy administration had good enough intelligence

**BOX** 8.3   Warning Problems: The Inevitability of Intelligence Failures

Major insights into intelligence failure have emerged from strategic surprises, such as Pearl Harbor and the German invasion of the USSR in 1941, the North Korean attack and Chinese intervention of 1950, the Middle East wars of 1967 and 1973, the Tet offensive and the Soviet invasion of Czechoslovakia in 1968, the Soviet invasion of Afghanistan in 1979, the Argentinean invasion of the Falkland/Malvinas islands in 1982, the Iraqi attack on Kuwait in 1990 and other cases. All involve two common problems. First, evidence of impending attack was available but did not flow efficiently up the chain of command. Second, fragmentary alarms that did reach decision-makers were dismissed because they contradicted strategic estimates or assumptions.

Richard Betts (2007: 22)

supporting the secret EXCOM meetings (Kennedy's high-level policy team), where options were debated and actions were planned and executed.

In like fashion, the 2002–2003 Iraq intelligence story is not entirely negative. To be sure, the October 2002 National Intelligence Estimate on Iraq's WMD capabilities was deeply flawed. The intelligence community misinterpreted outdated, limited, and in some cases fabricated information, thereby basing its judgements too heavily on outmoded mindsets and on Saddam Hussein's earlier success at deception and denial (Iraqi WMD Commission 2005). However, while these estimates of Saddam's WMD capabilities were wildly off the mark, two other important estimates were largely correct regarding how Saddam would conduct the war and what conditions the United States would face in a post-conflict Iraq (Kerr 2005). As is often the case, some intelligence judgements are always closer to the truth, while others are not. In the Iraq case, what is most remarkable is how little attention was actually paid to intelligence, regardless of whether it was right or wrong (Pillar 2006).

 **Key Points**

- Strategic surprise can result when decision-makers fail to act upon intelligence warnings, or when those warnings are ineffectual or not provided at all.

- Intelligence failures result from inadequate collection, effective deception and denial operations, flawed analysis, poor information sharing, and poor communication of warning.

- Analysts can suffer from cognitive biases that create inaccurate perceptions of an adversary's intentions and capabilities, often termed a 'mindset'.

- Decision-makers also run the risk of dismissing intelligence warnings if they harbour strong mindsets of an adversary's intentions and capabilities that do not conform to reality.

- An adversary can employ deception and denial to reinforce flawed mindsets to mislead decision-makers as to a possible attack.

- Averting surprise requires better collection and greater attention to possible deception efforts as well as analysts' cognitive biases and mindsets.

- Strategic surprises and intelligence failures are impossible to eliminate, but taking steps to improve collection and analysis can reduce the odds of them occurring.

# The Post-9/11 World of Intelligence

The 9/11 attacks dramatically altered how US strategists think about the role of intelligence. Not only has the threat changed but also the strategic paradigm—both the ends and means of strategy—has shifted. The George W. Bush administration developed explicit strategies for counterterrorism and counterproliferation. Part of this review of US strategy necessarily involved rethinking intelligence priorities and programmes. The 2004 Intelligence Reform and Terrorism Prevention Act (IRTPA) is the most dramatic reorganization and revitalization of the US intelligence community in nearly six decades. It expanded the scope and missions of the intelligence community to make it a far more powerful set of institutions and agencies. First, the legislation created a new national chief of intelligence in the form of a Director of National Intelligence, aimed at giving this official more authority than previous Directors of Central Intelligence possessed. Next, it created new institutions like the National Counter-terrorism Center and the National Non-proliferation Center aimed at better integrating the different activities and skills of the 16 agencies. Finally, it took note of the creation of a new Department of Homeland Security, one element of which had intelligence functions and would, in conjunction with the FBI, constitute a more prominent domestic intelligence arm of the US government. Large increases in funding and personnel followed, which have also been employed in providing intelligence to support the ongoing conflicts in Iraq and Afghanistan. The Obama administration has worked within the intelligence reforms made in 2004, but has made adjustments that reflected altered presidential priorities, including the ending of the wars in Afghanistan and Iraq and greater emphasis on counterterrorism than counterinsurgency strategies.

## Intelligence during a Decade of War

The Iraq and Afghan wars have challenged the US intelligence community to develop new missions, procedures, and capabilities. Since the 2001 and 2003 operations in Afghanistan and Iraq began, the intelligence community has grown and adapted to a state of almost seemingly permanent conflict. This has meant deploying large numbers of intelligence collectors and analysts into theatres of operations, developing new surveillance and reconnaissance capabilities, and focusing much more on sub-national or tribal-based targets. This has been a huge challenge in terms of resources and expertise. Numerous studies have suggested that the US went to war in Iraq and Afghanistan with little understanding of the social-cultural environments, the key actors and their motivations and capabilities, or the consequences of US actions on a whole range of issues. At the heart of these critiques is a question of whether US intelligence was adequately prepared or agile enough to adjust to the realities of war in the Middle East and South Asia. The Department of Defense has issued lengthy studies regarding lessons learned from the so-called 'decade of war', which include the observation that US strategists did not understand the environment at the beginning of the conflict and had to adjust its operations from more conventional warfare to counter-insurgency and hybrid warfare (Joint Staff 2012). A major cause of this surprise was the inadequacy of intelligence. Major General Michael Flynn, the US military intelligence chief in Afghanistan until 2011, has emphasized that information gathered for a counterinsurgency differs fundamentally from the way intelligence is collected for conventional war;

instead of information flowing from national systems such as satellites and other techni-cal collectors down through higher headquarters to the tactical level, counterinsurgency intelligence must flow from the soldier and analyst in the field up to higher headquarters. This was not being done effectively at the beginning of the wars in Afghanistan and Iraq (Flynn 2010).

Some of the new missions, procedures, and capabilities used during this decade of war have generated considerable controversy and debate. Four of the most prominent controver-sies have been the use of UAVs or drones, the expansive presidential authorities provided to the intelligence community to conduct counterterrorism operations, the practice of detain-ing and interrogating terrorists captured in overseas operations, and the use of highly intru-sive technical collection methods impacting both US citizens and allied populations. This has thrust the US intelligence community into the middle of vigorous debates over the suitability of such methods, when they might have major domestic and foreign policy consequences that some believe undermine the overall strategy for defeating terrorism. First, the use of armed drones has been widely debated, and many believe more clarity and transparency is required for the US to harness this new technology in a way that serves both a near-term bat-tlefield requirement as well as longer-term US interests (see the Critical Thinking box regard-ing debate on this issue). As the Obama administration increased the use of armed drones and the issue became more public, the President announced he would review US policy, establish more transparent rules, and be more judicious in the use of armed drones. At the same time, CIA Director Brennan announced in 2013 that he hoped to 'rebalance' the CIA's focus away from war-fighting and more toward intelligence gathering and analysis. At this date, there still appear to be active armed drone programmes, conducted jointly by the mili-tary and intelligence services (Mazetti 2013).

Second, many constitutional experts question whether the 2001 Authorization for Use of Military Force (AUMF) can still be used to justify counterterrorism operations against a wide range of terrorist organizations and individuals who may have only tenuous ties to the al-Qaeda network, which the AUMF was designed to combat. Legal authorities continue to debate whether the Obama administration has expanded its CT operations beyond the scope of this congressional authorization and many believe a new AUMF is now in order. Some experts also criticize the Obama administration for using this statute to conduct attacks on US citizens, based on secret legal opinions and without any judicial review. Third, US deten-tion and interrogation methods also brought criticism upon the US military and the CIA for alleged violations of anti-torture statutes and basic civil liberties. Senior CIA officials have been accused of authorizing torture and destroying evidence that would implicate them. While the Justice Department has ruled that the techniques were legal at the time, then CIA Director Hayden eliminated those infamous methods such as 'waterboarding' to prevent fur-ther damage to CIA and US opinion abroad. Finally, the publicized and now admitted collec-tion of so-called 'meta-data' of international Internet and phone calls by the United States has produced public, congressional, and international criticism of the excessive collection methods used by the National Security Agency in the pursuit of legitimate terrorism targets. A Presidential Commission has reviewed the NSA programmes and has recommended major changes to reassure the American public that its privacy is being protected even while intel-ligence agencies continue to conduct authorized collection of suspected terrorists' commu-nications both abroad and in the United States (President's Review Group 2014).

**Critical Thinking:**    Debating … Should the US use armed Unmanned Aerial Vehicles (UAVs)?

## For

- *Military utility.* Using armed drones provides precise targeting of high value counterterrorism targets at the least risk to the civilian population and US military forces. They are far less intrusive than putting US forces into a sovereign country and pose less risk to US personnel. The UAV's ability to 'loiter' over a target to confirm a target's identity results in fewer casualties than dropping imprecise 'dumb' bombs. Being able to observe CT targets in a stealthy fashion also makes them more effective than other forms of reconnaissance. According to the White House, more than 3,000 al-Qaeda and other jihadists have been eliminated since President Obama took office.

- *Minimal casualties.* Non-combatant casualties using armed UAVs have been minimal. Proponents dispute sensationalist reporting that estimate thousands of civilian casualties. There are some think-tank studies that estimate the numbers of between 100 and 500 since 2010; however, there are no reliable figures. The key point is that these casualties are far lower than those caused by other forms of attack.

- *Politically acceptable.* This form of military operations against terrorists is less intrusive and objectionable than all the others. Putting US boots on the ground in Pakistan, Yemen, or other terrorist safe havens would be too risky and politically explosive. In fact, there are many times when a host government desires US drone attacks to eliminate threats to its own regime, and foreign officials are largely posturing against the attacks in order to lower the domestic political clamouring against them. Privately, governments mostly support these measures, since they are not prepared to see the US initiate ground operations or large-scale bombing inside their countries.

## Against

- *Casualties are too high.* The US government is playing down the actual non-combatant numbers and there are many eye-witnesses who claim there have been large numbers of women and children killed or maimed by US drone attacks. The fact that UAVs pose almost no risk to US personnel, in fact, encourages a more cavalier use of drones and has accelerated the American government's reliance on them. The US has long ago abandoned a more selective use against so-called high value targets and is using UAVs more indiscriminately to go after any target that might be judged a possible jihadist, thereby increasing the chances that attacks will target unwitting non-combatants.

- *Blow-back effect.* Heavy use of drones actually produces more jihadists than it kills. When the US unleashes a drone attack on terrorists in a village and kills heads of households or tribal leaders, it will turn the entire village against the US and the host government. According to the *New York Times*, host governments like Pakistan have demanded that the US stop its drone attacks as a violation of their national sovereignty (Masood 2012). Such attacks, if they appear to be causing large civilian casualties, will reduce a government's willingness to cooperate with the US in other counterterrorism measures. Many US allies and their publics are also overwhelmingly critical of US drone policies and this has resulted in stronger opposition to US policies in the Middle East and South Asia.

- *Setting a harmful precedent.* The US should be wary of setting the precedent for using armed drones for targeted killings. The fact is that drone technology is entering the military arsenals of many other governments, including those hostile to the US and its allies. If the US can use armed UAV attacks to eliminate terrorists in a foreign territory, then other governments could claim the same right and employ drones in the same fashion. The prospect that Iran, China, Russia, and other potential adversaries might launch drone attacks on groups or individuals they judge to be threats could prove impossible to control.

## The Information Glut and 'Big Data'

The twenty-first-century intelligence world is not solely the result of the 11 September attacks. Indeed, many new challenges would have existed regardless of the emergence of al-Qaeda or the global war on terror. Among the most pressing are the information technology revolution and a more global and multifaceted definition of national security threats. Along with rising terrorism and proliferation threats, these global developments require different strategies for coping with the world. As in the past, different national security strategies will often redefine national intelligence strategies and policies.

Information technology is changing the world and the workplace. As it does, it puts more information in the hands of decision-makers and makes it available at increasingly faster rates. Nanotechnology and miniaturization of communications and computing systems makes information flow around the world virtually instantaneously. Not only is time for analysis and action reduced, but also the amount of information that must be absorbed to reach judgements and decisions is far greater. In 2006, then Director of National Intelligence John Negroponte noted that 'the National Security Agency estimated that the Internet will carry 647 petabytes of data each day . . . By way of comparison, the holdings of the Library of Congress represent only 0.02 petabytes' (Negroponte 2006). The advent of the computer era has also magnified the targets of intelligence value, for example, capture and analysis of the so-called 'Sinjar'. The take-down of Osama bin Laden also resulted in the capture of valuable computer disks and other media that yielded invaluable information on the al-Qaeda organization's future plans and organization (Busmiller 2011). But this data often requires detailed scrutiny, translation, and interpretation. Technology can partly solve the problem it has created, but the point has been reached where no single analyst or policymaker can possibly be an expert on all aspects of an international problem. As a former senior intelligence official has noted, future intelligence will be more team-based to take advantage of the special knowledge that political, economic, military, and science and technology (S&T) analysts collectively bring to a problem (Medina 2008). In her view, such multidisciplinary analysis will increasingly become routine, as most global problems are not easily dissected into exclusively political, or military, or economic issues.

The information explosion has led to the promise as well as the problem of analyzing 'big data'. The term has come to mean the massive and often unstructured data sets that are difficult to process using traditional software. The mere capture and storage of such data is challenging, even for the US intelligence community; however, the intelligence community is developing new 'search engines' or sorting techniques to exploit these sources. For example, the National Security Agency has taken the lead in developing an accessible and secure cloud computing environment, which is aimed at giving the IC the necessary analytic tools required to exploit such information (Seffers 2013). As already mentioned, the Snowden revelations highlighted some of the techniques which the NSA has employed to shift through huge amounts of so-called 'meta-data' in search of information related to terrorism operations (Konkel 2014). This has raised privacy concerns but also has posed challenges to the intelligence community in terms of developing techniques that can analyse volumes of unstructured, fragmented data. At some point, the intelligence community must decide 'how much is enough' given the difficulty of storing, searching, and analysing the haystack in an effort to find the needle, especially when it produces such public and foreign criticism.

Providing intelligence assessments has already become a 24/7 operation and different users will pull their products off as fast as the electrons allow. The danger lies in making intelligence operate faster than the analyst can think or even verify the quality and reliability of the information being passed on to policymakers. Processing raw information is one thing, but making sense of information is still a human factor that cannot be accomplished without time to weigh evidence, identify key strategic dangers, and map their likely consequences. Information technology can assist the analyst in processing large volumes of information by providing analytic tools to help filter and find patterns in the data, but the human mind is still required to see the significance of such patterns to the policymaker. Both the producers and the users will have to work harder to preserve the quality of intelligence as it becomes more ubiquitous and timely.

 **Key Points**

- The 11 September terrorist attacks have put new emphasis on strategies of prevention and pre-emption, which will demand even better intelligence than the strategies of containment and deterrence.
- Relying on preventive and pre-emptive strategies requires solid information to justify taking military action even before an enemy has acted.
- Globalization has been accompanied by a global information revolution, speeding up the rate and volume of information which the intelligence community must monitor and understand.
- The rise of 'big data' offers the intelligence community new ways to detect threats but also poses new challenges in terms of processing this information as well as raising major privacy concerns.

 **Conclusion**

Intelligence remains a vital ingredient to the development of effective national security strategies. It will have to adapt constantly to keep pace with changing conceptions of national security interests and the associated strategies that emerge. As in earlier times, no intelligence system will ever produce entirely perfect insight or prescient forecasts. The world is simply too complex and the decision-making styles of foreign adversaries too unpredictable to know how they will choose to challenge the interests of the United States and its friends and allies. What we can say, however, is that decision-makers will require intelligence to reduce the uncertainty surrounding the future actions of strategic rivals as much as possible.

As in the past, strategic surprises and intelligence failures cannot be ruled out. Steps have been taken, however, to improve collection, analysis, and the intelligence–policy relationship to reduce the likelihood, severity, and consequences of surprise and intelligence failure. Moreover, the need for decision-makers and intelligence professionals to work together makes it clearer than ever that strategy depends on a good understanding of what intelligence can and cannot do. Although centuries old, Sun Tzu's advice to 'know oneself' as well as the enemy is as relevant today as it was then.

 **Questions**

1. Is intelligence a necessary ingredient to good strategy?
2. How does a strategist use intelligence to improve on strategy?

3. What roles can intelligence play in improving strategy?

4. What are the key limitations of intelligence that a strategist should be aware of?

5. What lessons can be learned from past intelligence failures? What is a working definition of failure?

6. How successful have efforts been to reform intelligence activities to help inform decision-makers? What have been the problems?

7. What is the role of covert action in assisting the strategist?

8. How useful do you think the role of analytic bias or 'mindsets' are in explaining intelligence failures?

9. What can be done to improve intelligence analysis? Is failure inevitable as some writers suggest?

10. How does intelligence need to adjust to the post-11 September realities? In particular, what problem is posed by the challenge of 'big data'?

 ## Further Reading

R. Betts, *Enemies of Intelligence: Knowledge and Power in American National Security* (New York: Columbia University Press, 2007) offers a recapitulation of the author's many excellent articles on intelligence that takes a balanced view between many critics and the few apologists for US intelligence.

T. Fingar, *Reducing Uncertainty: Intelligence and National Security* (Stanford, CA: Stanford University Press, 2011) gives an insider's view of the challenges of post-9/11 intelligence, with special attention to the intelligence–policy relationship and how intelligence weathered the controversies surrounding the 2002 Iraq WMD NIE.

R. George and J. Bruce (eds), *Analyzing Intelligence: National Security Practitioners' Perspectives,* 2nd edn. (Washington, DC: Georgetown University Press, 2013) a recently revised collection of articles focused on improving the profession of intelligence analysis written by leading practitioners and scholars.

Robert Jervis, *Why Intelligence Fails: Lessons from the Iranian Revolution and the Iraq War* (Ithaca New York: Cornell University Press, 2010) an excellent post-mortem by a recognized intelligence scholar on the sources of cognitive and bureaucratic bias in intelligence analysis.

L. Johnson and J. Wirtz, *Intelligence: The Secret World of Spies: An Anthology* (Oxford: Oxford University Press, 2014) an excellent collection of articles that surveys key intelligence topics, including the analysis, collection, covert action, politicization, and the ethics of intelligence.

M. Lowenthal, *Intelligence: From Secrets to Policy,* 5th edn. (Washington, DC: CQ Press, 2011) the best and most well-known introduction to the role of US intelligence.

P. R. Pillar, *Intelligence and US Foreign Policy: Iraq, 9/11, and Misguided Reform* (New York: Columbia University Press, 2011) the best well-argued, if provocative defence of the intelligence community's performance and scathing critique of 2004 intelligence reforms by a senior retired intelligence official.

 ## Web Links

Federation of American Scientists **http://www.fas.org** contains a treasure trove of intelligence assessments and studies useful to students interested in seeing actual intelligence products.

CIA **http://www.cia.gov** includes the Center for the Study of Intelligence, where CIA's official 'Studies' journal is available, along with many other descriptions of the intelligence process and products.

The Office of the Director of National Intelligence **http://www.odni.gov** houses official press releases, statements, and directives; it also contains unclassified national intelligence estimates and other community products like the Global Trends series.

Defense Intelligence Agency **http://www.dia.mil** explains the roles and missions of defence intelligence organizations and offers an unclassified history of the agency.

National Security Agency **http://www.nsa.gov** provides some glimpses into the US government's most secret agency and its new responsibilities regarding cyber defense.

Central Intelligence Agency factbook **https://www.cia.gov/library/publications/the-world-factbook** houses the voluminous CIA factbook that catalogues the key facts regarding nearly 300 countries including their demographics, economy, history, political structure, and other pertinent characteristics.

# 9 Strategy and Defence Planning

COLIN S. GRAY

## Chapter Contents

 **Reader's Guide**

All states have to conduct defence planning because of their official, indeed also their moral, duty, but because the future never happens how can planning be done prudently? This chapter examines the implications of the defence planner's ignorance of the future, and looks critically, though empathetically, at ways in which understanding might be improved. It is argued here that science and social science cannot be of much assistance to the planner, given the enduring certain fact that we are unable to access data about the future from the future. There is found to be no alternative approach to defence planning superior to the careful use of historical understanding, controversial though that often is.

## Introduction

Because security is non-negotiably a very high, if not the highest, human priority, defence planning effectively is both a universal and an eternal activity. All human communities necessarily must also be political communities for their common security. In order to provide security, humans need to organize for collective governance, and that requires a political process. Defence planning can sound like, and may even appear to be, a cool and deliberate function of government, one performed prudently by notably expert functionaries, both professional military and civilian. More often than not, however, defence planning gives a substantial appearance of being conducted in a hurry by officials who are not truly expert in matters that would appear to warrant most careful consideration of a strategic kind. In practice, regardless of the character of a polity's governance, defence planning is ruled by political, not technically expert military, choice. Defence planning bears upon the future and therefore concerns crucially a temporal zone about which little of vital importance is known reliably. While defence planning must depend for its relevance and suitability upon strategic guidance, what—one must ask—is the source of that guidance?

## Strategy, Politics, and Defence Planning

Much of the subject matter of strategic studies is more or less technical, and is appropriately understandable by technical experts. For example, logistical questions, issues concerning the supply and movement of troops, their necessary equipment, and everything now deemed essential to their tolerably competent functioning, typically lend themselves to calculable treatment. There are reliably discoverable right answers to logistical questions, even if in practice quite often a military system will settle knowingly for quantities and qualities believed, or hoped, to be good enough to serve the needs of the moment. The defence planner needs to know, at least know how to discover, what is required in order for his polity's military forces to function both tactically and operationally. The acquisition of this knowledge is not a task for the amateur. However, the relatively happy condition of the generally calculable tasks of the tactician and the operational artist come rudely to an abrupt halt when the challenge to comprehension shifts on to, or across, the strategy bridge (Gray 2010). It is not possible to determine the suitability and relevance of one's defence establishment, its character and size, unless first one has secured good enough understanding of its purposes, functions, and adversaries abroad. Appreciation of this abiding reality leads unavoidably to recognition of the critically important role of politics in defence planning.

Strategy is and has to be political. Strangely, perhaps, although all strategy is political in meaning, nonetheless it is not simply politics in disguise. Although strategy inexorably has political consequences, it is nonetheless distinctive from them. Much as the conduct of warfare may or may not serve to advance the political interests on behalf of which a war is waged, so defence planning may or may not provide support of high utility for a polity's policy objectives. For the purpose of this chapter, *defence planning is defined as referring to preparations for the defence of a polity in the future (near-, medium-, and far-term)* (Gray 2014: 4). Such planning is conducted both in peacetime and wartime, though the focus of this chapter primarily is upon the former.

To understand the challenge of defence planning it is essential to follow the logical and authoritative audit trail both to and then across the strategy bridge (see Box 9.1). How should a polity decide upon the quality and quantity of its national defence provision? How much is,

---

 **BOX** 9.1   Strategy Bridge

The metaphorical concept of a strategy bridge is employed for the purpose of explaining the functions strategy performs. Strategy can be considered in functional terms as a bridge that should connect the distinctive realms of politics and their policymaking on the one side, with military operations and tactics on the other. Since strategy is defined as the use made by policy of its military servant's efforts as threat and in combat, the bridging concept is an appropriate view to take of strategy's function (see Gray 2010).

or ought to be, enough (and enough of what)? Because there is much visible and tangible evidence of computation and calculation about the products of defence planning, it is only too understandable why confidence that is by no means well merited may be felt in the results of the official activity. The apparent orderliness of administration and the veritable blizzard of statistics on many issues in defence, not unusually serves to conceal what not infrequently truly are deep uncertainties that have to be managed in a process of defence planning characterized by the necessity for heroic choice.

The problem most central to the defence planner's efforts is that of an irreducible ignorance about the detail of the future (Gray 2014). Defence planning in all polities potentially is intensely political for two abiding reasons. First, the function of national security almost inevitably is a relatively heavy burden on society, given that there will always be alternative possible uses for scarce resources. Second, the permanent fact that the future is neither reliably known nor knowable means that typically there is scope for political argument over what the country needs in order to be sufficiently secure. It is important that we back-track to examine closely and critically just how the national defence planning function is supposed to work. This examination reveals that much of what may appear to be founded solidly and prudently, in point of fact is better described as guesswork. Close examination of the major working part of a national strategic function reveals that defence planning cannot help but be more art than science. With rigorous attention to the proper and consistent meaning needed for key concepts, it is no triumph of scholarship to discover that the requirements of strategy are far beyond the reach of science. Since science refers to reliable knowledge, acquired and testable by empirical method, it is obvious that the defence planner is fundamentally limited by an inability to know with certainty just what his polity will need to acquire and how it should behave, in order to be secure in the future.

In order to aid comprehension of the defence planning function and the scale of analytical challenge to the planner, it is helpful to appreciate the basic structure and nominal working of the relations among four key concepts: ends, ways, means, and assumptions (Yarger 2008). In theory, at least, policy ends provide essential purpose to guide the selection of strategic ways in which military means can be threatened or exercised in the national interest, and the whole process is informed (or misinformed) by the prevalent assumptions. These four basic ideas understood as a process, admittedly constitute a greatly simplified model of the reality of defence planning, but not one that misrepresents what usually is untidy in practice. What looks logically robust when presented in PowerPoint form, however, is likely to mislead. It is no great achievement to recognize some basic difficulties in the bald structure of strategy making just outlined. Indeed, every element in the strategy-making model for defence planning is likely to prove challengeable.

The policy ends needed to animate all else typically are anything but stable. The reason is because policy is rarely regarded as being a final product of careful official consideration and analysis. Instead, policy is almost an organic product that will have a shifting shape and intensity, depending upon the evolution of circumstance. Policymaking usually is somewhat open ended, providing some possibility for change if events do not occur as previously anticipated. In short, more often than not the defence planner will find that his policy directives and guidance have a discomforting quality of flexibility about them. Just as defence planning is a continuous activity, so also is policymaking. This fact is best appreciated by recognition that defence planning thoroughly and continuously is a political activity. Key political decisions tend not to be made and subsequently regarded as definitively settled. Because they must function in the great stream of time, defence planners know that the requirement for policy is permanent and that its content always is made by and in a political process (Neustadt and May 1986). The content of policy demand for defence preparation inevitably varies with official and general public mood. How secure do we feel? How, if at all, has this necessarily subjective sentiment altered recently? Of particular moment is the question concerning anticipation of future menace.

Even if a particular government's preferred approach to defence planning can be summarized as a willingness to spend what is needed for national security, the substantial problem remains of knowing what that apparently prudent approach requires. In order to behave prudently over defence planning, first it is important to be able to know what it is that prudence requires (Aron 1966: 285).

 **Key Points**

- The defence planner needs to know what the country will require in order to be sufficiently secure in the future.

- What the defence planner needs to know is not knowable, so what he has to do is to plan for what policymakers can guess about the future.

- Defence planning decisions regarding the future are the product of a political process of negotiation; this is inevitable and unavoidable.

## Problems with the Future

Defence planning may choose to ignore the fact of irreducible ignorance about the future, but that unavoidable absence of reliable understanding is likely to prove of commanding relative importance. The most critical of questions that the defence planner needs answering include the following: what to buy (acquire), how much to buy, and by what date(s) to buy it. Because defence planning must involve decisions about the quality and quantity of human and mechanical (and electronic) military capability, it is not sufficiently enlightening to policymaking for prudent ideas to lurk simply as interesting and possibly valid speculative propositions. Defence planning requires some certainty over types of forces and their numbers.

The process of defence planning may well proceed more by apparent inertia for years, than in an agile manner responding to shifts discerned in a polity's security environment. There is no doubt that abrupt, or even substantial though cumulative, changes in defence posture will be profoundly disruptive. Mobilization for war and subsequent demobilization, even if the polity is victorious, are periods of especially deep uncertainty, as a relatively settled and stable quality and quantity of military capability changes radically. Several propositions that comprise the core of my argument will be, or at least appear to be, seriously controversial; they are summarized in Box 9.2.

It might be tempting to reason that because the future is and must remain foreign to us, we are incapable of conducting purposeful defence planning prudently. After all, if we do not know and cannot discover what our security context will be in the future, how can we plan

**BOX** 9.2 Core of the Argument

1. The future is both unknown and unknowable in detail.
2. Policy ends that should rule the whole process of defence planning concern matters for political choice.
3. All strategy requires the presence or at least the plausible prospect of an adversary (or two, or more).
4. The performance of a defence establishment in war is not akin to that of some programmable machine. Forces for defence have the potential to vary significantly in the strategic value of their military product.
5. All wars have much of great importance in common, but also each crisis and war assuredly will be quite individual in some detail.

our nation's future defence? There is a responsible answer to this significant empirical objection, but first it is necessary to underline the temporal reality that the future never comes, together with the apparent paradox that, nonetheless, we are obliged to plan for, or rather against, our security needs of the future.

Politicians, and even some scholars who should know better, persist in keeping alive the substantially fallacious concept of a foreseeable future. It is possible, indeed it is necessary, to ignore our ignorance of the future in detail, and act as if we know well enough what the situation of our future security will require of our defence establishment. However, notable guesswork must be the hallmark of our decisions and behaviour. Notwithstanding substantial and sometimes methodologically ingenious efforts, endeavours to discover reliable major facts that will have important consequences for our defence planning inevitably disappoint. Surprise happens! Moreover it happens time after time in its capacity to deliver us into substantially unanticipated security terrain (Taleb 2010: xxii–xxiv). It is necessary to conclude, on the unmistakeable evidence of past failed efforts to foresee the strategic future, that defence planning should not be geared to predictions that are unavoidably vulnerable to potentially lethal error (US Joint Forces Command 2008: 7).

The unforeseeability of the future should command a quality and quantity in defence plans recognizing the necessity for some agility, even flexibility, in our policy. The mantra of 'ends, ways, and means', governed by prevailing assumptions, obliges us to examine critically both the reliability and the prospective longevity of contemporary policy. Probably above all else we need to be willing to locate and acknowledge the origins and nature of our policy ends. It is important to appreciate that all defence planning must be done at distinctive points in what has been characterized as a stream of time. The posing of significant questions about the future of national defence will elicit different answers at different dates. Answers that seem to be right enough as of today, may well appear in retrospect tomorrow to have been more or less imprudent.

Although the force of inertia can in the main be authoritative, ultimately the local political process will rule as well as reign. International strategic relations are also political relations. Objectively right answers cannot be provided to the strategic questions that defence planners have to address, because there are too many variables in the relevant equations for statecraft. Admittedly, there is scope for some highly pertinent calculation of variables in strategic studies, but even in those cases thoroughly reliable certainly should not be assumed (O'Hanlon 2009). The stability of strategic nuclear deterrence between super and great powers understandably has attracted a vast amount of analytical attention of a metric kind. Drawdown curves allegedly showing levels of strategic forces' survivability in face of surprise attack have long been a focus of official superpower attention. Always there has been an incalculable risk of policy error leading to nuclear war as a malign result of imprudent human behaviour. Some dysfunctional performance by complex organizations, unanticipated and therefore possibly shocking behaviour on the part an adversary, and the ill consequences that could follow untimely accidents and sheer bad luck, also could result in catastrophe. A political context may be strategically robust in favour of stability, but rogue behaviour by individuals, organizations, and third parties, is possible. A certainty of national security on tolerable terms is strictly unattainable. There will always be room for some political argument between competing interests and beliefs bearing upon national defence.

The second point registered in Box 9.2 asserts a claim with which many people may be uncomfortable. The choices that serve as the policy 'ends' for strategy are nearly always political—even if they did not appear initially to be political, nonetheless they soon become such. Particular tactical military behaviour is selected for strategic effect that is hoped will advance the security of our interests. It is obligatory to notice that although this chapter is focused primarily upon the challenge in preparing purposefully for defence against foreign dangers, defence policy everywhere is made at home. In practice, and possibly even in theory, it is not possible to conduct a process of policymaking and its enabling strategic planning, in any manner other than one dominated by politics. In good part because defence planning is about national security in the future, there are not and can never be answers to the classic question, 'how much is enough?' that are demonstrably empirically correct. Defence planners everywhere must try to provide good enough answers to these key questions:

- How much defence do we need to buy?
- What kind(s) of defence do we need to buy?
- By what date(s) do we need to acquire the products of our defence planning?

Particularly if there is little palpable sense of immediate dire national peril, the answers to the above trio of questions are unlikely to be unchallengeably obvious. Metaphorically expressed, a strategy bridge exists functionally in order to enable the complementary, yet distinctive, realms of policy and (military) strategy to conduct an unequal dialogue (Cohen 2002: ch. 7). The politician cannot simply challenge defence planners to devise plans that are unmistakeably correct in their prospective efficiency for the alleviation of national peril. Opinions on dangers and possible responses to them will differ, and the differences will reflect the distinctive interests as well as genuinely divergent beliefs of the institutions and some of the individuals who are active participants in the making of policy and strategy. Moreover, much of the concern of high relevance to defence planning will derive potently from largely domestic circumstances that can have a logic almost entirely indifferent to a country's external context.

Although politicians are inclined strongly to talk about 'what the country can afford,' in reality the authoritative issue is one of choice. Defence planning always and everywhere is a political exercise. Planners cannot know what the country needs in order to be secure, and in practice security is very much a sentiment, a feeling, not a quality expressible metrically. Defence budgets are the negotiated outcome of more or less intense argument—with some purportedly supportive quantitative analysis—among key stakeholders. The defence planner is not engaged in producing and refining plans that assuredly are the correct ones in order to keep the polity safe, though that is a general sincere intention. Rather it is the practical challenge of the need to devise plans that provide for national security likely to prove 'good enough', in circumstances riven by deep uncertainty (Gray 2010b). Recall that tomorrow never comes!

Of emphasis here is both the inalienably political nature of the guidance that policy provides to defence planning, and the fact that the content that is fuel for political debate and dispute may well contain little of strategic merit. People and their institutional interests differ over policy and about menaces from abroad, actual or only potential. Menace spotting often is employed more as support for argument with implications for decisions about the allocation of scarce resources, than as evidence of threat and danger that requires expensive answers.

All strategy, with defence planning as an enabling executive agent, is and has to be adversarial. Such planning is not analogous to a game of solitaire. An adversary is required for strategy to be needed or work. In theory a defence planning process could all but demobilize itself and simply go through the motions of pretending to provide for the common defence against any or all comers, but the practice of politics could not be friendly to such behaviour. The General Theory of Strategy is not at all confused or confusing on the fundamental need of strategy makers for actual and typically plausible threats. They comprise the fuel of menace that can be assumed to be normal to the nature of world politics. It remains a dominant fact that in the world politics of the twenty-first century all large and even modest-sized polities conduct defence planning. Enemies worthy of such a prejudiced categorical assignment may not be too obvious or even plausible. However, if we adopt firmly the modern (i.e. twentieth-century) understanding of the meaning of strategy, we are able to appreciate that few polities can or could be truly indifferent to the subject of defence planning. The strategy that the defence planning process typically seeks to implement and advance is not one geared for military success 'in the field'. Instead, the purpose of defence planning is to enable strategic advantage, and hopefully deny disadvantage, to attend the choice and pursuit of chosen policy. The subject here is defence planning, not war planning.

Because defence planning by definition must relate to the future, and because that future cannot be known confidently, let alone reliably, it has to be recognized that defence planning must be likened to a journey of indeterminate duration into terrain that on the one hand is known for certain to be dangerous, but on the other is known not to be predictable as to the actual menaces that will be more or less active.

It is necessary both for defence planners who are military professionals, and the politicians (and civil servants) they serve, to acknowledge the uncertainties that must attend all possible military behaviour in the future. Because war is systemically adversarial, it is important to be able to plan to acquire military forces that would be relatively effective in future combat. Furthermore, it is reasonable to aspire to own military forces that have fairly reliable merit as threat. It is and remains a fact, however, that every war is more or less unique in some of its vital detail. If one plans to be ready enough for whatever demands the political-policy bank of the stretch of water supposedly bridged by strategy chooses to make, what does one purchase? Do we acquire military forces wide in the range of their competence, but as a consequence distinctly thin in their ability to sustain costly action? Or, do we elect to invest heavily in capabilities greatly limited in their relevance, regarded politically, geostrategically, or even fundamentally, against better armed foes? The political context postulated here could provide fuel for conflict that politician policymakers may discover they wish to conduct, or at least to contribute with capabilities deemed useful by a larger ally. In principle at least, the following non-trivial causes of uncertainty are inalienable from peacetime defence planning.

1. The political context. Since all war, though not all warfare, is political, what will the world be like that produces circumstances in which we may wish, or even need, to perform militarily for strategic effect?

2. What do we think we know about the character of war and its warfare in the future? And, how far into the future is relevant to our planning today?

3. How well will our military forces fight tactically, and how useful will that prove to be, when regarded operationally, strategically, and ultimately politically?

Whatever else can be written about defence planning, the beginning of wisdom must be registration of understanding that necessarily it is an exercise conducted in a condition of true ignorance. *Defence planning is and can only be based on guesswork.* Obvious though this fact ought to be, it is nonetheless resisted by many social and other scientists, and it is rejected as unacceptable by many politicians. It is only sensible to be sympathetic to the plight of politicians, civil servants, and professional soldiers who have no practical choice other than to do their best to cope adequately with a strategic future that simply is not and will never be knowable in advance.

---

 **Key Points**

- All defence planning is conducted in what essentially is a political process.
- Defence planning has proved historically nearly always to be marked by substantial error.
- Objectively and checkably correct answers to the basic question, 'what should we buy for our future security?'—are simply not obtainable.
- Because there is never any information available *from the future about the future*, it is not possible to prove that some defence acquisition scheme is wrong (or right!).
- Defence planning is a necessity for all countries.

---

## Approaches to Defence Planning

Not infrequently is it anticipated that an impressive combination of analytical sophistication and rigorous method will yield understandably what is needed for a polity to have confidence in its defence planning. However, common sense soon reveals the continuing sovereign authority of an all too enduring golden rule: specifically, it is impossible to know the

**BOX** 9.3 Rumsfeld Amended

Former US Secretary of Defense Donald Rumsfeld amused and intrigued us with his 'known and unknown' shortlist. He told us that: (1) there are things we know we know; (2) there are things we know we do not know; and also (3) there are unknown unknowns. Two additional items merit addition to Rumsfeld's list: (4) things that we believe we know, but in fact we do not; and (5) things it is impossible to know (e.g. about the future). (Rumsfeld 2011: xiii)

unknowable (see Box 9.3). The practical challenge cannot sensibly be the continuing devotion of scarce analytical talent to an impossible quest. Despite the obvious merit in this negative judgement on much futurology, governments persist in the endeavour to achieve the impossible and peer into the future in a forlorn quest for reliable knowledge. Inconvenient though it is and must remain, there is little, indeed possibly even nothing, about science that is of value to the more demanding of the defence planner's tasks (Grygiel 2013). For two reasons, hard science and its junior social science relative(s)—e.g. economics and sociology—cannot be mobilized in the quest for reliable truth. First, we are unable to predict reliably the whole context that will be relevant to decisions in the future—both our own and that of our possible adversaries. Second, we cannot be certain as to how the character of the game of nations (and tribes and factions) will alter in the great stream of future time. Many elements that could shape the strategic future are both unknown and unknowable in possibly important detail, and cannot be modelled in a productive quest for reliable knowledge. The necessary concerns of the defence planner do not lend themselves to scientific enquiry legitimately worth of the name. Certainty of strategic knowledge about the future is unobtainable by any analytical method, no matter how robust.

If we define science as we should, it should refer strictly to reliable and certain knowledge. Quite obviously, the mission of defence planning is a light year or two from being likely to discover what will certainly be the right answer(s) to the challenge of defence in the future. Although science and social science can be of some limited assistance to defence planning, that help cannot be provided with respect to the temporal uncertainties that must dominate the subject of this enquiry. Since science cannot assist in understanding what is unknowable, we are obliged to look for help elsewhere.

Historians are right to warn us that their subject is not an agent of advice, because it comprises the entire confused and often confusing narratives of human strategic experience (Howard 1991a: ch. 1). The abundance of motive and action in the strategic past is the heart of the analytical problem. Everything of strategic concern today and for tomorrow has some provenance. The challenge to defence planners posed by the sheer quantity of variably accessible detail is not easily met. That conceded, the dominant fact remains to the effect that although defence planning must always be a venture into the unknowable, nonetheless generically it is one in which the human race is very experienced. After all, the essential challenge to those charged with the vital task of defence planning has not altered through the entire course of strategic history. The rich variety of historical experience means that each strategic episode is different from all others in some measure, great or small, and in quantity, quality, or both. But, approached with regard to its functional working, defence planning can be considered with common reference to all periods and material and cultural contexts. While science and social science have little to tell us about defence planning, the creative arts, history in particular, are a source for empirically impressive advice (Gaddis 2002).

Although defence planning is always novel, given that the 'future' is ever moving and is strictly a notional destination that can never be reached, nonetheless it is a behaviour that has been necessary from the beginning of time. Groups of people always have had to organize themselves for security, an enduring necessity that resulted in the creation of political units known to us today as states. These political communities had to function strategically competently or otherwise.

Science and social science cannot be of much assistance to the defence planner because the subject requires judgement educated by familiarity with past as well as contemporary experience. The defence planner cannot usefully seek theory that explains from the ranks of scientists and social scientists, because their specialist knowledge does not encompass the variety in strategic history, its continuity in nature, and changing character in detail over time. Also, the adversarial nature of strategic historical experience requires a mature perspective and hopefully some understanding only through appreciation of a whole historical context; this need is met and somewhat tamed by the grand concept of the great stream of time. The relatively high value of historical understanding to defence planning is best appreciated if one considers the rather barren alternatives. If one rejects or scarcely employs historical knowledge, what remains in the shot locker? Since the future has not occurred it is unable to provide data, reliable or other, while the present is too recent to be a source of knowledge upon which one could place high confidence.

Only the humanities can aspire to achieve useful understanding of international and national security contexts in the future, however far over the temporal horizon we choose to strive to peer. The historian alone might achieve understanding in the width, depth, and context necessary for competent treatment of security troubles in the future (Howard 1983: 215–16). The claim here is not for some high putative value of specific historical analogy. This chapter is not endorsing the absurdly dangerous idea that tomorrow's challenges and crises should be considered in the presumptive light cast by some selected particular past event or events. History is far too richly variable to be safely usable as a source of analogy for concerns about the future. Since we cannot know exactly, or with confidence even approximately, what will happen in the future, we cannot analogize historically in a quest for anticipatory understanding (Fischer 1970: 257). Instead of the necessarily and inevitably flawed historical analogy, defence planners should be content with historical parallels.

It is an unfortunately persisting fact that many scholars, especially those raised as social scientists, are wont to dismiss past strategic historical experience as irrelevant to the strategic future. This widespread anti–historical attitude reflects a shallow view of relevant strategic education. An appropriate comment on the issue of continuity, change, and enduring relevance, has been made by Robert Gilpin of Princeton University. He speculates thus:

> But, in honesty, one must inquire whether or not twentieth-century students of international relations know anything that Thucydides and his fifth-century BC compatriots did not know about the behavior of states. What advice could today's students give that would have enabled the Greeks to have prevented the great war that destroyed their civilization?
>
> (Gilpin 1981: 227)

The contemporary scholar-soldier Robert Johnson has sought to address directly the question of the possible practical utility of historical education. He advises that:

> ... the true value of history is not to invoke direct analogies, nor does the answer lie in trying to extract selections to suit a particular agenda, as so often occurs. The value of history is rather in encouraging critical reflection, to ask questions, and to challenge the positivist assumptions that crowd our field of view. We are subject to the flux of history, and we cannot entirely escape our present, but we should seek to break free of unreasoned supposition about the future through critical thinking.

(Johnson 2014: 66)

Defence planners should not seek detailed solutions to particular current or anticipated future problems in beliefs and actions lifted from the past. However, they will find that history typically is stocked abundantly with yesterday's challenges that may be understood reasonably as having been common in kind to many of those today. Issues of crisis management, manipulation of threat, alliance, and of all aspects of war and peace, have been substantially continuous and common through all strategic history. The historical experience of international relations over the rise and demise of great and lesser states is as extensive as it is depressingly repetitive. History offers a treasure trove of examples of behaviour relevant to our contemporary case. Provided one never forgets that a parallel discovered between then and now must be regarded only as being situational, such appreciation of possible utility in relevance should only be positive. Historical education cannot provide training for the conduct of defence planning. But it can provide education that fits people so that they are better able to cope with today's challenges.

---

 **Key Points**

- Science and scientific method cannot penetrate the future to reveal for certain what the content of defence plans should be.
- 'History', per se, cannot offer advice, it has to be interpreted by expert historians.
- Only the historian is able to offer the understanding of the width, depth, and context of the past that might be of assistance to the defence planner.
- The course of history can be examined in order to locate plausibly parallel episodes to those of concern to us today.
- Historical analogy cannot be employed to help make sense of an unknown and unknowable future.

---

## Guidance for Defence Planning

Because defence planning relates to activities that must provide answers to uncertain questions, this must always be a subject in which there will be no reliably correct answers. The defence planner is committed to a profoundly unscientific exercise. The challenge is to identify and develop answers for the character of national defence good enough to neutralize menaces that cannot be defined with certainty today. These are the principal uncertainties:

1. Our own political variability of possible policy demands.
2. Choices by adversaries.
3. Most relevant geographical contexts for conflicts.
4. Quality of combat performance of our 'home team', adversaries, and our (and his) allies.
5. The course and dynamics of particular wars.

The defence planner should know a great deal about war and its warfare. History, and even possibly personal experience, can prepare the planner to cope with his subject. But there is a non-trivial difficulty in that although all wars share key qualities, identified by Clausewitz as comprising 'the climate of war: danger, exertion, uncertainty and chance', in non-trivial addition, every war is uniquely different (Clausewitz 1976: 104). We know a great deal about the eternal phenomenon we understand as war, but we know little, if indeed anything, reliably certain about the particular wars we may decide we will need to wage in the future. In drafting principles of guidance for defence planning, the salience of the distinction drawn starkly between war in general, and particular wars in the future, is of fundamental importance. All countries do decide, in effect, that they would, and if need be will, fight in the future only in wars of particular kinds. Such, at least, would be the political intention, though frequently the course of events leaves little practical choice other than to attempt what seems to be needed. The historical record shows quite clearly that states often do fight the wars that happen, rather than the one or ones for which they were particularly well prepared.

Historical reality reveals wartime contexts wherein belligerents have been obliged to fight as they had prepared, even though skills and equipment were not well matched to the demands of the day. It is a fundamental challenge to defence planning either to avoid the 'wrong war' problem, or at least to make some provision for alleviation of that difficulty should it arise. Although wars and their warfare happen in good part whether or not belligerents' defence planning staffs guessed correctly about future combat, one should not simply assume that warfare must be a near autonomous independent actor following its own adversarial logic (Porter 2009: 170). War and warfare should be approached as competitive exercises wherein victors are the belligerents who succeed strategically in imposing their preferred style of combat upon the enemy.

What follows is a short-list of principles selected for reasons both of their inherent merit and also their general relevance to most countries.

1. *Prudent policy goals (ends)*

    Given that strategy always is about politics, it is scarcely surprising to advise that a prudent choice of policy (political) ambition is by far the most significant element bearing upon the whole process of defence planning. No matter who else is important in the process, if politicians insist upon achievement of impossible or impracticably difficult goals, defence planning must fail to serve a polity well. For example, in the 1960s under US Secretary of Defense Robert McNamara, the Pentagon brought quantified defence analysis to an historically unparalleled pitch of expertise, with an Office of Systems

Analysis that was the envy of many defence departments around the world (Enthoven and Smith 2005). Unfortunately, the newly numerate and rational management of the American defence establishment was, in large part, applied in the service of imprudent US political choices as policy for Vietnam. Even if one performs militarily with competence, it is a general rule that executing the strategically imprudent well will not offset far enough unwise political guidance sufficiently. Prudent defence planning refers to a process mindful of the possible consequences of decisions and actions. Policy options do not appear on policymakers' desks marked helpfully with stickers indicating their certain prudence or imprudence.

2. *Prioritize*

A defence planning process may be unable to anticipate what particular politicians will want to do, but it should be capable of understanding what is more, and what is less, important for a state's national security. Since resources always are limited it is essential for government to address in some rank order the problem areas about security likely to cause the most damage to national well-being. It is necessary to ensure that the most damaging menaces to the country are covered, indeed preferably are neutralized, as well as can be achieved at socially bearable cost—which is a matter of domestic politics. One can seek to insist that the bigger threats are treated with the serious commitment for their alleviation or eradication that they merit. For reasonably enduring reasons of geopolitics and geostrategy, many—probably most— polities have persisting understanding of the strategic geography exceptionally pertinent to their particular national security context.

3. *Tolerance of error*

Errors are certain to be made in defence planning. Indeed, error is entirely normal, which has to mean that adequacy in plans requires the ability to correct for past mistakes. Inevitably there is a need to be able to find usable compensation for past error and its consequences. In desperate times a truly strategic competence may well be required to identify ways to accomplish tasks for which past planning has left one thoroughly unprepared. Far more often than not, error in defence planning will only be revealed beyond room for argument by the rapid unanticipated failures in severely adverse events.

4. *Adaptability and flexibility*

It is important that a defence establishment should be committed to the qualities conveyed by the concepts of adaptability and flexibility. The preservation of good order in defence programmes often discourages willingness to change current goals and habits. As military historian, Williamson Murray, has explained: '... one of the foremost attributes of military effectiveness must lie in the ability of armies, navies, or air forces to recognize and adapt to the actual conditions of combat, as well as to the new tactical, operational, and strategic, not to mention political, challenges that war inevitably throws up' (Murray 2011: 1). It is commonplace for military forces to discover that their largely unilateral, almost autistic, preparation for warfare needs sharp adjustment and adaptation when an enemy is met in combat. This is a usual situation, it is not the exception.

**Key Points**

- With scientifically correct decisions unobtainable, the defence planner has to attempt to provide good enough solutions to future defence problems.
- Uncertainty rules over the world of the defence planner.
- Prudent political choices of policy are critically important. No analytical expertise in defence planning can correct for serious errors in policy.
- Defence planners must be clear about their priorities. They cannot plan to defend everywhere and in all ways.
- Because errors will certainly be made in defence planning, the process must be capable of tolerating some error.
- In order to tolerate past error it is essential for the defence establishment to be adaptable and flexible.

 **Conclusion**

Three principles conclude this explanation of defence planning. They may be summarized as: (1) the 'good enough' rule; (2) recognition of the principle that it is legitimate and sensible to accommodate change in continuity and continuity in change; and (3) acceptance of the necessary reality that all defence planning is about politics, indeed is political in meaning, and yet strategy and its defence planning is not just politics by another name (Milevski 2014).

Because of the interactive quality to strategic performance, the rich variety of its human dimension, and the sheer complexity of strategy, it is never feasible to calculate scientifically for a certainty in answers to the challenges that defence planners are obliged to try to meet. However, the essential incalculability of problems for national security do not absolve would-be defence planners from the task of settling upon answers to problems. Key to approaching the dilemmas of defence planning is the golden rule of the 'good enough'. Although we cannot know for certain whether particular numbers of military assets will be sufficient for the necessary tasks of the future day, we should be capable of estimating by means of our education from experience what ought to prove good enough. Trial and error may well be required as well. It is necessary for a defence planning process to understand that it should be capable of choosing to invest in forces approximately suitable, or at least in the zone, to meet future threats.

The second general principle pertains to the relationship between continuity and change. Only rarely does a national defence establishment not have to handle a substantial material and ideational legacy from the past that is leaning into the present and potentially out into the uncertain future. Defence planning always must involve management of some controversial relations between past and present. Armed services are by their nature usually highly conservative organizations, understandably strongly committed to ideas and habits of relevance to willpower and morale. Understandably, also, the dangers of military duty are likely to encourage soldiers to be cautious in the acceptance of novelty.

Finally, no matter how technically wondrous or humanly poignant a defence issue may be, the defence planner should never forget that his professional subject is all about politics, meaning relative influence over others, preferably foreigners (Lasswell 1936). So absorbing and dangerous a commitment is the conduct of warfare that often there is some likelihood that the legitimate relationship between political purpose and military enablement unfortunately is reversed. The result can be that in effect politics serves war rather than vice versa. War and its warfare should always be subject to the discipline of politics.

**Critical Thinking** Debating … Can history be helpful to defence planners?

### For

- *History is the data!* History can provide the only source of real data on human experience: the future never arrives (by definition), while the present is too immediate to have been understood regarding its consequences.

- *Continuities in history.* The most significant continuities in history include: (1) human nature; (2) the necessity for governance—which requires political process; and (3) the logic of strategy.

- *Great stream of time.* Although there have been enormous changes of detail, human history should be regarded as a great stream of time, with no beginning and (hopefully) no end.

- *Prudence is key.* The most valuable lesson we should draw from history is the supreme importance of the necessity for prudence.

### Against

- *No learning from history.* We should learn from history that we do not learn and have never learnt from history.

- *Lack of authority in history.* Our defence challenges tomorrow must flow from today, so the key to their anticipatory treatment is deep understanding of where we are and what it means. Past experience (history) is ill digested, controversial, and must lack authority.

- *False assumptions.* The past and our memories of and from it are more likely to hinder than to help us. It is apt to fuel us with false assumptions.

- *Invention by historians.* Because history is invented by historians, 'it' cannot be trusted to convey prudent advice.

 **Questions**

1. Since the future never happens, how can we go about trying to prepare for it?

2. How useful is the past in providing some guidance for the future?

3. Can the future be studied scientifically? What do we mean by science?

4. Why is historical analogy invalid as an approach to understanding the future?

5. What are the problems in seeking to use understanding of the past and the present as assistance in preparing for the future?

6. What are the pros and cons of the concept of the great stream of time?

7. How competent have defence planners been over the course of the past 100 years?

8. Why do you believe it has been so commonplace for large-scale errors to be made in defence planning?

9. How vulnerable is a defence planning process of government to misdirection by imprudent political choice?

10. What are the better, as contrasted with the worse, ways to conduct defence planning? Are there any good ways?

**Further Reading**

A. C. Enthoven and K. W. Smith, *How Much is Enough? Shaping the Defense Program, 1961–1969* (1971; Santa Monica, CA: RAND, 2005) is a classic memoir on defence analysis, McNamara-style.

S. Frühling, *Defence Planning and Uncertainty: Preparing for the Next Asia–Pacific War* (Abingdon: Routledge, 2014) is a valuable innovative venture.

J. L. Gaddis, *The Landscape of History: How Historians Map the Past* (Oxford: Oxford University Press, 2002) offers a brilliant long view of the meaning of history.

R. M. Gates, *Duty: Memoirs of a Secretary at War* (London: W. H. Allen, 2014) gives an incredibly detailed account of one of the world's toughest jobs—US Secretary of Defense.

C. S. Gray, *Strategy and Defence Planning: Meeting the Challenge of Uncertainty* (Oxford: Oxford University Press, 2014) seeks to explain the difficulties in planning for an unknowable future.

C. S. Gray, *The Future of Strategy* (Cambridge: Polity Press, 2015) presents the reasons why strategy has a healthy future, fortunately.

M. Howard, *The Lessons of History* (New Haven, CT: Yale University Press, 1991), chapter 1, 6–20 is an exceedingly wise brief treatment of a vital subject.

K. Knorr, ed., *Historical Dimensions of National Security Problems* (Lawrence, KS: University Press of Kansas, 1976), 78–119 is by far the best analysis available on the nature of threat.

E. S. Quade and W. I. Boucher (eds), *Systems Analysis and Policy Planning: Applications in Defense* (New York: American Elsevier, 1968) offers a valuable explanation of defence analytical methods.

H. R. Yarger, *Strategy and the National Security Professional: Strategic Thinking and Strategy Formulation in the 21st Century* (Westport, CT: Praeger Security International, 2008) is an important book that covers the basics well.

 **Web Links**

RAND Corporation **http://www.rand.org/nsrd.html** is a treasure trove on most defence-related subjects.

Strategic Studies Institute **http://www.strategicstudiesinstitute.army.mil** belongs to the US Army and offers a wide range of free material, most of it of high quality.

War on the Rocks **http://warontherocks.com** offers mainly blogs by many well-known strategic commentators.

War Council **http://www.warcouncil.org** offers short essays and blog-type contributions, many of which are quite intelligent.

Centre for Strategic & International Studies (CSIS) **http://csis.org/category/topics/defense-and-security** presents analysis on a valuable wide range of defence subjects.

# Part II

# Contemporary Problems

# Irregular Warfare: Terrorism and Insurgency

JAMES D. KIRAS

## Chapter Contents

 **Reader's Guide**

Western democracies have had some difficulty adjusting to the 'new reality' of global violent extremist terrorism and revolutionary violence. These difficulties are reflected in two themes that run through the long history of irregular warfare. The first is that all types of irregular warfare, including terrorism and insurgency, are appealing to those who are seeking to change the status quo. But what role can politics possibly play for those who are willing to kill themselves and others for rewards in the afterlife? Global violent extremists and modern revolutionaries, including anarchists, share much in common with their historical antecedents. The second theme is that conducting irregular warfare to achieve change successfully is a very challenging undertaking. Historically the balance sheet favours those who fight against terrorist and insurgent groups. For dissatisfied groups and individuals, however, irregular warfare will continue to be used as it offers the promise of change to right perceived injustices and wrongs.

## Introduction

At the height of the period in irregular warfare known as the 'wars of national liberation' (1962–1965), journalist Robert Taber, who had spent time in Cuba during the revolution there, stated that 'the guerrilla fighter's war is political and social, his means are at least as political as they are military, his purpose almost entirely so. Thus we may paraphrase Clausewitz: *Guerrilla war is the extension of politics by means of armed conflict*' (emphasis in original; Taber 1970: 26). More recent critiques suggest that identity or culture explain substate violence; conflict today is, as General Rupert Smith suggests, 'war amongst the people' instead. In addition, the technologies associated with globalization, including the Internet, are reshaping politics and violence.

The aim of this chapter is to demonstrate that the spirit of Clausewitz is still very much relevant to current and future irregular campaigns. Historical experience cannot be summarily dismissed. Religious, social, cultural, and economic factors provide the context which shapes the conduct of irregular conflicts. Terrorists and insurgents, however, ultimately seek to achieve a *political* result from their use of force. These political results in turn serve goals defined by states fighting insurgencies or those aspiring to change the system through armed conflict.

Such motives are discernable even in the cases of al-Qaeda, the Taliban in Afghanistan and Pakistan, and the Islamic State of Iraq and Syria (ISIS). The very nature of the extremist interpretation of Islam impedes Western understanding of the violence. As Johannes Jansen points out: 'Islamic fundamentalism is both fully politics and fully religion' (Jansen 1997: 1). For Westerners, the affairs of the church and those of the state are separable, while within the militant Salafist strain of Islam they are not. Indeed, adherence to religious tenets becomes a form of governance. While religion justifies killing and suggests spiritual rewards, leaders such as Ayman al-Zawahiri stress political power and control: 'victory of Islam will never take place until a Muslim state is established in the manner of the Prophet in the heart of the Islamic world, specifically in the Levant, Egypt, and the neighbouring states of the Peninsula and Iraq' (al-Zawahiri 2005: 2). More recently, the leadership of ISIS declared a de facto religious state, or caliphate, in Iraq and Syria with Abu Bakr al-Baghdadi as its head. From this established political base, the revolution can continue to spread.

## Definitions

The first problem associated with the study of terrorism and irregular warfare relates to the relative and subjective lenses that one applies to the subject. One cannot simply compare accidental death figures, such as those from traffic fatalities, with purposeful violence intended to spread fear among the populace. Much of the confusion associated with terrorism and irregular warfare stems from the use of either value-laden or emotive language. The term 'freedom fighter' suggests heroism while 'terrorist' conveys cowardice. The term 'guerrilla' still evokes the romance and adventure of rebellion embodied by the iconic Ernesto 'Che' Guevara. There is also little agreement on what to call these types of violence: political violence, terrorism, irregular warfare, military operations other than war (MOOTW), low intensity conflict (LIC), people's war, revolutionary warfare, guerrilla warfare, and hybrid warfare, among others. Terrorism and insurgency are still viewed at best as a nuisance by many military professionals, or a form of 'dirty war' at worst. The line between combatants and non-combatants is unclear, objectives unspecified, and timeline for victory unknown. In addition, military forces must conduct policing functions in this environment, with all of the dangers but little glory.

Irregular warfare, which is different in form but warfare nonetheless, describes types of violence conducted by sub-state actors including terrorism and insurgency. Terrorism is easily the most contentious and elusive type of violence to define. For the purposes of this chapter, terrorism is defined as *the sustained use of violence against symbolic or civilian targets by small groups for political purposes, such as inspiring fear, drawing widespread attention to a political grievance, and/or provoking a draconian or unsustainable response.*

Terrorism cannot result in change on its own. By provoking a response, terrorists hope that their opponent will overreact and reveal their true nature. Some debate exists over whether *terrorism is a tactic* within a broader strategy of insurgency or whether groups can conduct a *strategy of terrorism* (O'Neill 1990: 24). What separates terrorism from other forms of violence is that the acts committed are legitimized to a degree by their political nature. Hijacking, remote bombing, and assassination are criminal acts, but the legal status of those who conduct them can change if the violence is carried out for a recognized political cause. Two examples illustrate the point. The bombings conducted by anarchists against monarchs in the late nineteenth and early twentieth century are considered acts of terrorism given their stated objective of changing the political environment. Any one of the number of hijackings of ships off the coast of Somalia and in the Indian Ocean, in contrast, are criminal acts because the motivation behind them is financial gain. Problems exist in determining *who* recognizes the cause, beyond the terrorists themselves, as well as shifts in motive over time. Terrorists seek attention to generate domestic and international empathy and support for the cause that 'drove' them to arms.

Defining insurgency is equally problematic. Insurgency is perhaps best understood by first considering what it is not. Insurgency is not conventional war or terrorism, for example, but it shares with them the use of force to achieve a political end. The crucial difference is the scope and scale of the violence. Terrorism rarely results in political change on its own, while insurgency attempts to bring about change through force of arms. The principal difference between irregular and conventional war is relatively simple: the latter involves adversaries more or less symmetric in equipment, training, and approaches to fighting. In an insurgency, the adversaries are asymmetric and the weaker, and almost always a sub-state, group attempts to bring about political change by administering and fighting more effectively than its state-based foe through the use of *guerrilla tactics*. These tactics are characterized by hit-and-run raids and ambushes against local security forces. Confusion often results from insurgent movements using terrorist tactics to achieve local results. Insurgency, unlike terrorism, is characterized by the support and mobilization of a significant proportion of the population. Individual insurgencies differ widely in terms of character (social, cultural, and economic aspects) and type (revolutionary, partisan, guerrilla, liberation, or civil war), but obtaining power and political control is the desired outcome. Finally, external physical and moral support for an insurgent cause is a prerequisite for success.

Definitions are not the final word on a subject but merely act as gateways. Capricious categorizations can lead to a misleading and seemingly irreconcilable divide between forms of irregular conflict. Terrorism and other forms of irregular warfare are plainly not the same activity. But how does one then classify the so-called '*urban guerrilla*' phenomenon and its ideological impact on terrorist groups during the 1960s? In addition, some terrorist groups adopt parallel efforts that are more commonly associated with insurgencies—have they now become insurgents, do they remain terrorists, or have they become something else? The Lebanese organization known as Hizbullah has used terrorist tactics (kidnappings and suicide bombings) and it fought both long and short guerrilla campaigns against Israeli forces (1983–2001 and 2006), but it also has provided social welfare to local communities and, more recently, elected members of parliament. Ultimately, some arbitrary distinctions must be made in order to grasp the business at hand, without losing perspective on the numerous 'grey areas' endemic to this and other areas of strategic studies.

# Subverting the System: The Theory and Practice of Irregular Warfare

Those undertaking insurgency and terrorism are trying to find a way to use their strengths such as mobility, organization, and relative anonymity or stealth, against the weaknesses of their more powerful adversary. Bernard Fall reduced this equation even further when he suggested that '[w]hen a country is being subverted, it is being out-administered, not out-fought' (Fall 1998: 55). But subversion is a time-consuming and resource-intensive activity that does not guarantee success. In almost every case, the length of terrorist and irregular warfare campaigns is measured in *decades* not years. They achieve success by gaining an advantage over their adversaries in terms of time, space, legitimacy, and/or support.

These dimensions of conflict are not mutually exclusive and excellence in one dimension will not compensate for drastic shortcomings in the others. Regardless of the space and time available, for example, a terrorist or insurgent campaign will almost always fail if it cannot attract substantial internal or international support. As in all forms of strategy, insurgencies or terrorist campaigns are *dialectical struggles* between competing adversaries; outcomes are determined by the interaction between opponents (Gray 1999: 23–5). The goal for the irregular leader is to pit the organization's strengths against enemy weaknesses. The value ascribed by different writers to and perceived relationships among time, space, legitimacy, and support create substantial variations in the theories of irregular warfare. These theories often reflect the circumstances that are unique to specific conflicts, a fact that has contributed to failed government efforts to stop insurgents or terrorists. The unconsidered application of a theory based on a specific context to another conflict can lead to disaster.

## Time

Time is the most important element required for the successful conclusion of an insurgent and terrorist campaign as it is a commodity that can be exchanged to make up for other weakness. With sufficient time, an insurgent group can organize, sap the resolve of its adversary, and build a conventional force capable of seizing control of the state. Mao organized time in his writings into three interrelated phases: the strategic defensive, the stalemate, and the strategic offensive (see Box 10.1).

---

 **BOX** 10.1    Mao's Three Stages of Insurgency

**Stage I, Strategic Defensive**: This phase is characterized by avoidance at all costs of pitched, set-piece battles. Tactical offensives, with local numerical superiority, are carried out to further stretch enemy resources.

**Stage II, Stalemate**: This phase begins the prolonged battle to attrite the enemy's physical and moral strength. Government control, in the form of local officials, is targeted and its representatives killed or forced to leave.

**Stage III, Strategic Offensive**: The end game of the conflict, in which popular and main forces conduct the battle of manoeuvre and use overwhelming force to destroy decimated enemy forces in their defensive positions.

Tse-Tung, Mao (1966), *Selected Military Writings of Mao Tse-Tung* (Peking: Foreign Languages Press), 210–19

---

Each phase, carefully conducted, would lead one step closer to victory no matter how long it eventually takes. For example, Mao once stated in 1963 that his forces had 'retreated in space but advanced in time'. He understood that the sequence of phases leading to victory was not necessarily linear; unforeseen circumstances could lead to setbacks and perhaps regression to a previous phase of the insurgency. Endless struggle without an obvious victory would eventually lead to the exhaustion, collapse, or withdrawal of the enemy. The dimension of space works with time, providing insurgents with the leeway to manoeuvre and demonstrates their superior legitimacy to the population. Perceived legitimacy in turn will generate internal and external support for the insurgents. With popular support, insurgents will be able to raise a superior army, launch bolder attacks, and achieve victory.

Many irregular campaigns result in deadlock after a period of time with neither side able to decisively conclude the conflict. The Liberation Tamil Tigers of Eelam (LTTE) waged insurgency within Sri Lanka for more than four decades; the *Fuerzas Armadas Revolucionarias de Colombia—Ejército del Pueblo* (FARC) has conducted insurgent and terrorist campaigns within Columbia for almost a half-century. Only very rarely does guerrilla struggle end quickly. The most famous quick insurgent success is the Cuban revolution (1957–1959). Led by Fidel Castro, this irregular war was concluded in just three years. A number of factors contributed to the rapid collapse of the government forces in Cuba. While few states are as corrupt, inept, and fragile as the Batista regime in the late 1960s, the government of Nouri al-Malaki in Iraq provides a recent example and explanation for the explosive growth of ISIS.

Such brittle adversaries are rare but local circumstances can convince insurgents or terrorists that time works against them. Carlos Marighella believed that circumstances in Brazil in the 1960s demanded a response other than organizing and waiting for the right revolutionary conditions. Marighella favoured immediate action as he believed the state grew stronger every month while the Brazilian Communist Party did little but talk. By taking action, Marighella believed that the 'urban guerrillas' would build a critical mass for the guerrilla organization, catch the Brazilian state authorities off-guard, and provoke an extreme response. In other words, he believed that the state of affairs within Brazil called for reversing the typical relationship between the guerrilla and time.

## Space

Space allows irregulars to decide where and when to fight. If their adversary appears in overwhelming numbers, irregulars can make use of space to withdraw and fight when the odds are in their favour. Defenders against sedition cannot be everywhere at once without spreading their forces too thinly and inviting attack from locally superior guerrilla forces. This becomes particularly problematic for those fighting irregulars when they cross state borders or operate across different geographic domains such as air, land, and sea.

The exploitation of formidable terrain that limits the manoeuvre of government forces is a potent way in which lightly armed and mobile terrorists or insurgents offset their relative weaknesses in technology, organization, and numbers. Insurgents have often used difficult terrain for tactical advantage, often against foes ill-equipped to deal with the challenges presented by mountains, jungle, swamps, and even deserts. For example, Afghan guerrillas have used mountainous terrain to their advantage against the NATO-led coalition (2003–2014), Soviet forces (1980–1988), as well as the British (during the nineteenth century). Triple-canopy jungle limited US and South Vietnamese attempts to apply overwhelming manoeuvre and firepower against the Viet Cong and North Vietnamese forces. Urban terrain can also be an arduous obstacle as the Russians found in 1994. Chechen guerrillas used buildings and narrow roads to offset their weakness and isolate and destroy Soviet formations during the battle for Grozny; Iraqi insurgents tried to do the same in Fallujah a decade later. Terrain difficult for government forces, including sanctuaries across state borders, provides insurgent forces with the opportunity to establish safe areas or bases from which to expand the struggle.

Force-to-space ratios also influence the course and duration of insurgencies. If much territory needs to be defended by a government, terrorists or insurgents can compensate for their operational or strategic inferiority by massing forces locally to achieve tactical superiority. Government forces often attempt to defend territory or resources that have political, economic, social, and/or military value. For example, governments under siege often abandon the countryside in favour of more defensible cities and military bases. More often than not, states have the resources to protect many, but not every local target as their resources are stretched. Col. T. E. Lawrence, for instance, used the Arab force-to-space ratio advantage against the Turks to good effect during the Arab Revolt (1916–1918). Given the amount of terrain to be covered, Lawrence calculated that the Turks would need 600,000 troops to prevent 'sedition putting up her head' across the entirety of the Transjordan, a figure six times larger than the forces available to the Turks (Lawrence 1920: 60). One of the most persistent criticisms against US and coalition leaders in defeating insurgency in Afghanistan and Iraq was the lack of enough forces, including competent and motivated Iraqi and Afghan ones, for the space of each country.

Force-to-space ratio superiority does not require irregulars to operate over huge geographic areas in order to be successful. In the case of the guerrilla campaign conducted against the British in Cyprus, the nationalist group EOKA was limited to a space little more than three per cent of that roamed by Lawrence's forces. EOKA's leader, George Grivas-Dighenis, based his strategy on the assumption that substantial numbers of British troops would attempt to put down the insurgency. EOKA members operated in small groups and conducted ambushes, bombings, and assassinations. These actions convinced the British that the benefits of remaining in Cyprus were not worth the political and military price to be paid.

## Support

Few insurgencies or terrorist campaigns succeed without some form of support. In addition to munitions, insurgents must look after casualties and continually replenish their supplies, including food and water. They must also constantly update their intelligence on the whereabouts and activities of government forces as well as train new recruits. Support, however, is interlinked with and inseparable from the legitimacy of the organization. Violence conducted without a comprehensible political purpose will generate little popular support. Without support, insurgents and terrorists will eventually succumb to the efforts of the state or a hostile population. Clausewitz suggested that support, in the form of public opinion, was one of the centres of gravity in a popular uprising (Clausewitz 1993: 720).

Insurgents and terrorists can look for support from both domestic (internal) and international (external) sympathizers. Almost all theorists agree that substantial popular support is required to compensate for the resources available to the state. Even Carlos Marighella, who believed initially that urban guerrillas could find and seize the necessary resources in major towns and cities to sustain the struggle, eventually relented and recognized the need to cultivate rural popular support. Domestic support can be forced from the population, using terror and intimidation, but long revolutionary struggles should not rely exclusively on such measures.

Although it is now a cliché, Mao's analogy describing the relationship between the guerrilla and the people is still evocative. The guerrillas were likened to 'fish' that swim in a 'sea' of popular support. Without the sea, the fish will die. A dramatic example of the consequences of failing to have domestic support is the fate of Che Guevara. Guevara believed that conditions in Bolivia in 1967 were ripe for a guerrilla insurrection led by his 'foco'. He overestimated, however, the amount of support he could receive from local Communists and farmers in Bolivia. The Bolivian Communists were hostile to advice on how to run their revolution from outsiders. More importantly, the local peasants were indifferent to the message preached by Guevara given government sponsored land reform initiatives that addressed some of their grievances. Guevara and his *foco* lacked popular support; the insurgents were either killed or captured within seven months of the first shots being fired (see Box 10.2).

Support is also contingent on the circumstances within a specific country. A danger exists in trying to reproduce success elsewhere using a previously effective revolutionary formula without first identifying the specific base of potential popular support. The uprising of the urban proletariat was considered a necessity in Marxist-Leninist revolutionary theory but failed dismally when attempted in China (1930) and Vietnam (1968). The agrarian character of China and Vietnam doomed urban revolts to failure; in both states most of the rural population were peasants. As a result, Mao Zedong and Vietnamese General Vo Nguyen Giap respectively modified their strategies and eventually succeeded.

External support for irregulars largely depends on both the geography of the country and the political relations maintained by the insurgents or terrorists. Such support can be material, in the form of resources or cross-border sanctuaries, or moral, in the case of political recognition and lobbying. Many Marxist terrorist groups during the 1970s, such as the German *Rote Armee Faktion*, received physical support from Soviet Union or its client states. Tangible support included money, advanced weapons, and training. Insurgent and terrorist leaders in countries ranging from the Dutch East Indies (1950, later becoming Indonesia) and British Palestine (1948, later becoming Israel) received external support, as part of a backlash against colonialism, that tipped the balance in their favour. States harbour or support terrorist or insurgent groups for reasons of political expediency and to suit their own policy objectives rather than genuine sympathy for the cause such groups espouse. The ruling authorities in Jordan and Afghanistan made decisions regarding the relative political cost of providing

 **BOX** 10.2   Ernesto 'Che' Guevara and the Theory of the *Foco*

Ernesto 'Che' Guevara de la Serna Rosario (1928–1967) developed (and Régis Debray expanded on) the idea of *foco* or the centre of gravity of the guerrilla movement. Practically, the *foco* refers to the initial critical mass of the guerrillas, the vanguard of the revolution, from which all else is derived. Philosophically, the *foco* represents the political and military 'heart' of the insurgency, and from it Guevara and Debray believe that *the guerrilla movement itself* can generate the conditions for a revolutionary victory.

sanctuary for their respective 'guests': the Palestinians in Jordan (1970) and Osama bin Laden and al-Qaeda under Taliban protection in Afghanistan (2001). In addition, irregulars can serve to fight proxy wars against their patron's rivals. For example, Iran and Iraq sponsored rival terrorist groups designed to conduct attacks against one another below the threshold of conventional war.

## Legitimacy

Insurgents and terrorists fighting irregular wars require internal or external support to sustain their struggle. Terrorists and insurgent leaders need to convey the reason for their actions or else lose sympathy for its cause. They often seek to legitimize their use of violence and translate this into meaningful support for their cause by demonstrating moral superiority over those who represent the state; supplanting the functions of the state at the local level; and spreading a persuasive message.

The moral superiority of the guerrillas is a cornerstone of all irregular and terrorist theory, especially those fuelled by religious zeal. Insurgents derive support from the people and they often cultivate their relationship with them. Mao went so far as to outline a 'code of conduct' for the guerrillas, known as 'The Three Rules and Eight Remarks', as a way to demonstrate their moral superiority. The most important job of the guerrilla is to demonstrate this moral superiority in routine contact so that people differentiate the guerrillas from bandits or 'counter-revolutionaries'. Che Guevara insisted that the peasants understand that the guerrillas were as much social reformers as they were protectors of the people.

Peasants who cooperate with the insurgents often face harsh retaliation from the government but frequently this only further legitimizes the revolutionary cause. Government brutality also allows insurgents to act as the avengers of the people, helping to cement the ties between them. Carlos Marighella, for example, hoped that the actions of the Brazilian authorities would demonstrate conclusively that the 'government is unjust, incapable of solving problems, and that it resorts simply to the physical liquidation of its opponents. The political situation in the country is transformed into a military situation in which the "gorillas" appear more and more to be the ones responsible for violence, while the lives of the people grow worse' (Marighella 1969).

Of course, the admonitions to behave better than government troops often are applied only to those who actively assist insurgents in their struggle. In a number of irregular conflicts, guerrillas and government forces alike regarded an unwillingness to help as aiding and abetting the enemy. Absolute popular support can never be guaranteed. Populations invariably split into willing assistants, staunch foes, and the undecided majority. To help make up the minds of those undecided, insurgents can demonstrate legitimacy by becoming the de facto government in areas under their control. This can include taking 'positive measures' such as the establishment of schools and clinics or 'negative measures' such as tax collection. In Afghanistan, for example, the Taliban used a system of mobile judges as a positive measure to provide swift and impartial justice, as well as negative measures including the imposition of taxes, public beheadings, and threats of violence through 'night letters' to cement their control over the population. The use of terror as a negative measure to intimidate the population is a matter of debate by irregular warfare practitioners to this day. For Che Guevara, terror tactics were unjustified because they invariably delegitimize the guerrilla's message. Both Mao and Marighella disagree, noting that acts of terror may be necessary to convince the population of the occupational hazards of working for the government, or to provoke a repressive response. Negative measures backed by proselytizing can be an effective way of legitimizing the insurgent cause by showing conclusively that the government can no longer protect them. Intercepted communications between al-Qaeda leaders suggest that negative measures remain a concern for contemporary insurgents and terrorists in that short-term gains may upset long-term goals. The rationale for the executions and harsh punishment meted out for the forces of ISIS may be a severe form of governance or local vendettas gone out of control; the reasons remain unclear at this point.

The most powerful method of legitimizing a struggle is to link military operations with a justifiable political end. Causes vary, but self-determination has been the most pervasive and successful rallying cry. Given the fundamental rights outlined in the Atlantic Charter (1941) and the United Nations Charter (1945), it was difficult for nations such as Great Britain, France, the Netherlands, and Portugal to maintain possession of overseas colonies in the face of native insurgencies claiming the right of self-governance. Other successful causes blend social, cultural, and economic issues into a powerful political message that the government or an international audience finds difficult to counter or resist.

 **Key Points**

- Terrorism and insurgencies can be examined in terms of time, space, legitimacy, or support, reflecting specific local contexts rather than predetermined goals attributed to a general theory.

- Time is an important element in the success of insurgencies, involving a non-linear progression that includes the space to manoeuvre and to gain legitimacy and/or support, all of which are necessary for eventual victory.

- Support is dependent on legitimacy and moral justification provides the cornerstone to sustain the struggle, usually blending cultural and social causes with political ends.

## Protecting the System: Counterinsurgency and Counterterrorism in Theory and Practice

The difficulties facing governments besieged by insurgents or terrorists may seem insurmountable at first glance, but numerous works have been written to explain how to quell them. This literature ranges from general theories and practical suggestions, based on hard-won experience, to complicated empirical models purporting to predict outcomes or test practical advice. Commentators have reduced complicated political–military struggles against forceful usurpers to a number of principles or formulas for success (see Box 10.3). Brigadier General Samuel B. Griffith suggested in 1961 that antiguerrilla operations could be summed up in three words: location, isolation, and eradication (Mao Tse-Tung 1961: 32). Griffith's summary is a useful reference point for exploring how to apply the strengths of a state (or group of states) against an irregular threat.

**BOX** 10.3   Principles, Prerequisites, and Laws of Counterinsurgency and Counterterrorism

(Material quoted from specific texts in chronological order)

**Charles W Gwynn**: Principles from *Imperial Policing* (1934)

- Policy remains vested in civil government
- Minimum use of force
- Firm and timely action
- Cooperation between civil and military authorities.

**David Galula**: Laws of counterinsurgency from *Counter-Insurgency Warfare* (1964)

- Support of the population necessary
- Support gained through an active minority
- Support from population is conditional
- Intensity of efforts and vastness of means are essential.

**Robert Thompson**: Principles of counterinsurgency from *Defeating Communist Insurgency* (1966)

- Clear political aim
- The government must function in accordance with the law
- The government must have an overall plan
- The government must give priority to defeating the political subversion, not the guerrillas
- The government must secure its base areas first (in the guerrilla phase).

**Frank Kitson**: Framework for an effective counterinsurgency campaign from *Bunch of Five* (1977)

- Good coordinating machinery (between civil and military agencies)
- Establishing the sort of political atmosphere within which government measures can be introduced with the maximum likelihood of success
- Intelligence (right information = sensible policy)
- Law (upholding the rule of).

**British Army:** Principles of counterinsurgency from British Army Field Manual Volume 1, Part 10: *Countering Insurgency* (2010)

- Primacy of political purpose
- Unity of effort
- Understand the human terrain
- Secure the population
- Neutralise the insurgent
- Gain and maintain popular support
- Operate in accordance with the law
- Integrate intelligence
- Prepare for the long term
- Learn and adapt.

**BOX** 10.3 *(continued)*

**US Army/Marine Corps**: Principles of counterinsurgency from FM 3-24/MCWP 3-33.5, *Insurgencies and Countering Insurgencies* (2014)

- Legitimacy is the main objective
- Counterinsurgents must understand the environment
- Intelligence drives operations
- Security under the rule of law is essential
- Counterinsurgents should prepare for a long-term commitment
- Manage information and expectations
- Use the appropriate level of force
- Learn and adapt
- Empower the lowest levels
- Support the host nation.

## Location

The most important phase of any counterinsurgency or counterterrorism campaign is recognizing that the threat exists. Counterinsurgency expert Robert Thompson believed it necessary to tackle an insurgency during its subversion and organization phase or at the first signs of a sustained campaign of violence (Thompson 1966: 50). In other words, he believed it necessary to defeat insurgents in both physical space *and* time. The problem for counterinsurgents and counterterrorists is distinguishing between lawful or unlawful forms of discontent. Restricting guaranteed rights and freedoms every time a bomb is detonated will undermine the credibility and intentions of the government. Waiting too long to uphold the rule of law, however, will give the insurgents or terrorists the necessary time to build a robust organizational infrastructure that only the most dedicated efforts might hope to defeat.

Terrorism and insurgency can be staved off with enough early warning, but this implies that an effective intelligence-gathering and assessment organization is operating. Few states possess such resources or foresight. Those willing and able to destroy the system need to be identified and tracked: this requires the assistance of a supportive populace. The question in pluralist systems is whether or not *potentially* seditious individuals can be monitored or arrested without violating civil liberties and undermining the rule of law. Muslim leaders in a number of Western countries, such as Sweden and Great Britain, have suggested that profiling of their community should be halted.

Upholding the rule of law is crucial if states are to preserve the legitimacy of their cause and maintain the moral high ground over insurgents or terrorists. Methods to counter terrorism, for example, must be effective yet stay within the boundary of the rule of law. This applies to both domestic and international measures. Citizens of democratic states are loath to given up rights and freedoms to combat threats especially if they intrude upon personal privacy. Managing how and when (and in what measure) to begin counterinsurgency and antiterrorism efforts, such as imposing curfews and controlling media access while upholding the rule of law, is the primary challenge to any government under siege. In most democratic societies, however, steps to counter terrorists rarely are preventative and almost always are taken *after* horrific acts of violence have been committed, as the Indian reaction to the Mumbai attacks of November 2008 suggest. Democracies run into greater trouble when international actions appear to contravene their domestic laws and international norms. For example, the 2014 publication of the Senate Select Intelligence Committee report on torture and 'enhanced interrogation methods', although contentious for reasons of domestic politics, is an important step in restoring the moral credibility of the United States internationally.

Once an irregular threat has been identified, various civil and military agencies must localize the threat while coordinating their response. They must identify safe houses, group members, and sources of supply. Gathering such information about the terrorists can be daunting, given the desire of most subversives to keep the organization small, stealthy, and secret. For a state providing direct counterinsurgency or counterterrorism support into a geographically and culturally unfamiliar country, as the United States did in South Vietnam, obtaining even basic information on subversives takes time. This problem is compounded when a state either does not have an effective and efficient security apparatus (Afghanistan) or the existing one evaporates and must be painstakingly reconstructed (Iraq). The time gained is used by insurgents to retain the initiative and develop their organizational base further.

## Isolation

Isolating insurgents and terrorists from their bases of support is probably the most important element of successful campaigns against them. Isolation can take the form of physical separation or political alienation. Physical separation can be achieved by moving villagers into more easily defended compounds, known in Malaya and Vietnam as 'strategic hamlets'. Preventative measures such as curfews, prohibited ('no-go') areas, food rationing, aggressive patrolling, and overt presence also can physically isolate insurgents. As with any form of deterrence, the threat posed by patrolling and presence must be a credible one and must not consist simply of half-hearted 'cordon and search' operations. Isolation also means limiting the mobility and range of the insurgents or terrorists, in effect taking away their space and their time. Insurgents and terrorists also can be cut off from their external sources of support by a combination of diplomatic pressure and military measures. Experts suggested the insurgencies in Iraq and Afghanistan could not be dealt with effectively until supply routes from neighbouring countries were cut off.

Segregating insurgents and terrorists from the population involves more than just physically separating them. To impose meaningful isolation, the state must defuse the irregular's most powerful asset: its political message. Widely held grievances that foster a potent source of recruitment and support must be mitigated by the government. Obviously, some messages are more influential than others: self-determination is difficult to counter by an eternal or occupying power, whereas demands for land reform or increased political representation can be more easily satisfied. The words of the government must be accompanied by effective deeds to show that the state can and will respond to what amounts to political extortion. The terrorist or insurgent's 'propaganda of the deed' must be diffused by government displays of a firm, yet lawful response. The displays can range from enforcing a 'no negotiations with terrorists' policy to simple measures like providing basic necessities and local security. The onus is on the representatives of the state to prove that they are *morally superior* to the guerrillas and terrorists and will provide for the needs of their citizens, including responding to the sources of disgruntlement that led to armed insurrection in the first place. Likewise, the terrorist or insurgent cause must be discredited. Leniency also should be extended to those insurgents and terrorists who give up the armed struggle. Above all, citizens must be convinced that the state's fight is their fight: they have an individual and collective interest in the state's success. Maintaining the link between citizens and state is crucial to ensure long-term security; the success of so-called 'awakening' of the Sunni tribal leaders in Anbar province was squandered by rampant corruption and blatant favouritism and nepotism in Iraq and made the area fertile ground in which ISIS could recruit. With little internal or external sustenance flowing to the rebels and a population willing to support the government, it is only a matter of time before the state's forces destroy the irregular threat.

## Eradication

Eradication involves the physical destruction of the insurgents or terrorists, although few would go so far as to follow Robert Taber's rhetorical advice: 'There is only one means of defeating an insurgent people who will not surrender, and that is extermination. There is only one way to control a territory that harbours resistance, and that is to turn it into a desert' (Taber 1972: 11). The state has numerous advantages over its opponents given its control over social, fiscal, and military resources. The most important question in democratic states is whether or not the leaders of the state can apply their resources effectively to extinguish the insurgent flame without alienating popular support for their own authority. Cultural context matters when determining a response. For example, the leaders of some European countries were hesitant to cast actions against al-Qaeda after September 2001 as a 'war' for cultural and political reasons based on their historical experience. Indeed, many continued to see the phenomenon of violent extremist terrorism exclusively as a domestic law enforcement issue within their sovereign borders, requiring civilian police or paramilitary forces, not as a *global* problem that might require the use of military forces.

Regardless of the forces used, theory and doctrine are rife with plans that discuss the destruction of guerrillas. These plans range from French Marshal Lyautey's innocuous-sounding 'oil patch' method applied in Morocco in the first quarter of the twentieth century to the more sinister-sounding Nazi German 'spider's web' and 'partridge drive' tactics. All theorists agree that eliminating the insurgents' safe havens must be a priority. Numbers also make a difference. US counterinsurgency doctrine suggests that 20–25 personnel are required for every 1,000 inhabitants (FM 3-24: 23). Most theorists also assert that 'special forces' are also needed to defeat the irregulars at their own game. Some advocate the use of technologies not available to the insurgents, such as helicopters and remote sensors, to enhance the force-to-space balance between government and irregular forces and to achieve superior mobility. Others suggest that a 'degrade and disruption' strategy, using a mixture of special forces and airpower in a relentless campaign to remove key leaders, managers, and facilitators—as is occurring in Iraq and Syria—will eventually erode terrorist groups into irrelevance.

**Critical Thinking**    Controversy surrounds the use of remotely piloted aircraft (RPA), more commonly known as 'drones', to strike terrorist leaders. Should drones be used?

### For

- *Jus in bello.* Killing identified terrorists, whose violence negates legal protection, is justified regardless of how it's done. There's no difference between using a precision guided weapon and sniper shot.

- *Selective violence.* States target on the basis of rigorously-enforced criteria to minimize collateral damage—after weeks or months of highly specialized intelligence collection. Such collection methods and processes cannot be divulged due to the damage caused to national security as a result. RPA strikes are less costly in lives lost than other options available.

- *Relative efficiency.* RPAs are much less costly in terms of the operating costs and in terms of domestic public opinion compared to other options. RPA strikes are used because no other reasonable option exists to capture terrorists, given where the latter are located. Other options are far too risky and time windows to act are extremely short.

### Against

- *Jus in bello.* National laws do not apply; drone strikes are extrajudicial killing (EJK) and illegal internationally by denying terrorists 'right to life' and 'right to due process'. Such strikes are tantamount to state-sanctioned murder.

- *Indiscriminate violence.* Far from being 'targeted', the so-called 'collateral damage' is much higher than reported, especially during repeat strikes (so-called 'double-taps'). This means far too many innocent civilians are killed in the process. Such violence only creates more terrorists than it actually kills.

- *Transparency.* Power to determine life and death must be under sufficient oversight. By keeping the processes and information secret, power can and will be abused. How sufficient is the information used to determine guilt—the results of which determine life or death? Who actually is watching the watchers? The public and the international community have a right to know.

There also are passive ways in which the state can subvert an insurgency and thereby diminish the number of guerrillas or terrorists. One such method combines psychological warfare techniques, promises of amnesty (e.g. the *Chieu Hoi,* or 'Open Arms' programme used in South Vietnam), cash incentives, or land to convince insurgents and terrorists that their struggle is in vain. Other methods, such as those tried with mixed success in Yemen and Saudi Arabia (the so-called 'Koranic Courts'), attempt to rehabilitate terrorists and reintegrate them into society. Other passive measures include engaging in political dialogue with, and offering support for, moderates within an irregular organization, convincing them of the need to start talking and stop fighting and causing groups to fracture, splinter, and perhaps turn on themselves.

Political will must underlie efforts to counter terrorism and insurgency. The eradication of an irregular movement is a gradual process of attrition that requires a significant and consistent investment in time and resources. Rarely have national leaders been able to sustain the political will necessary to defeat insurgents or terrorists, particularly when those leaders are intervening in irregular conflicts in other states. Equally daunting is the fact that the underlying causes of discontent often resurface and the embers of insurgency are rekindled in a different form.

The effects of terrorism can be limited through a combination of offensive and defensive measures, but ultimately bringing terrorists to justice, especially for crimes beyond state borders, can be accomplished by a combination of the political will to sustain the struggle, maintaining core societal valves and upholding norms, and making the best use of state capabilities. Bringing individuals to trial for actions below the threshold of 'an act of war' takes even greater reserves of time, patience, resolve, negotiation, and treasure. It took the United States 12 years and considerable third-party support, for example, to bring those allegedly responsible for the Lockerbie bombing to trial. In the end, the side that will prevail will be the one most willing to continue the struggle and make the least damaging choices throughout its course.

 **Key Points**

- Methods used by the state in response to local threats are aimed crucially at maintaining a lawful, hence political/moral, legitimacy.
- The strategy of state success is based on isolating the insurgents both physically and politically.
- The eradication of insurgents is often a slow process and will take different forms in different political and cultural contexts.

## Irregular Warfare Now and in the Future

The supposition that terrorism and irregular warfare involve the use of force strictly for political ends has been recently challenged. As stated in the introduction, some suggest that the irregular conflict is no longer about politics. In other words, wars of national liberation, ideological terrorism, and revolution have joined colonial small wars in the museum of 'conflict past'. Instead, some suggest that contemporary and future irregular threats are driven by a mixture of culture, religious fanaticism, and technology.

### Culture

Samuel Huntington famously argued in 1996 that future conflict on the macro level will result from differences in culture between incompatible civilizations. Others believe that on a micro level, sub-state warrior cultures will become the predominant irregular threat. Westerners fight wars according to established norms and modalities, whereas warriors will utilize their social and culture advantages to offset the technological advantages of Western soldiers (Hammes 2004). According to this argument, soldiers are no match for warriors. Proponents of this view suggest that the availability of modern small arms and disdain for Western rules of warfare give cultural warriors their military superiority. Political aims matter not to Somali clansmen, high on *khat*, driving around Mogadishu in heavily armed civilian vehicles. Warrior culture dictates goals—honour, plunder, or manhood—instead of politics.

Other observers argue that in the future violence will be ethnic or identity based. The political basis for war, Clausewitz's trinity of the people, the state, and the armed forces, is irrelevant. Where states cannot effectively govern, they cannot represent the will of the people. Without a state to sustain the armed forces, the only surviving element of Clausewitz's trinity is the people—which splinter in competing cultural and ethnic communities. The moral resolve of such cultural and social networks is superior precisely because they exist to fight. The conventional armed forces of developed nations will be increasingly irrelevant in the face of such superior will and approaches to warfare that offset technological advantages. The net effect is chaos and mayhem among sub-state groups within 'state' borders as the new norm for war.

## Religious Fanaticism

Religious beliefs often shape terrorists' and insurgents' causes and are used to obtain support among a community of the faithful. Throughout history, religion has been a powerful stimulus for political violence by Muslims, Christians, Jews, Sikhs, and other faiths as well. In exchange for personal sacrifice, earthly representatives of some faiths promise terrorist martyrs a glorious afterlife for conducting attacks, suicide or otherwise, that kill non-believers. Religion provides insurgent and terrorist leaders with a number of advantages for their cause. First, leaders such as Osama bin Laden used religion to provide a competing value structure and ideology to rally the deprived and disillusioned behind their cause. What bin Laden and his followers offer is an alternative to Western, materialist culture and an attempt to recapture previous glories of the mythic past. What has surprised Western analysts is the resonance that this vision has across cultural and ethnic lines—the degree of popular support this message continues to have more than a decade after 11 September 2001. Second, religion offers a rationale for action. Much like Che Guevara, Osama bin Laden's followers see themselves as social reformers. Terrorist attacks serve to raise the consciousness of the global Islamic community (the *ummah*) to the existing struggle as well to demonstrate to others that there is an alternative to their current situation. Religion can also blind the faithful to certain realities as well. Religious-inspired terrorist movements often overestimate the appeal of their message. As with political ideologues, including Mao Zedong, religious ideologues convince themselves that the future is predetermined based on the righteousness of their cause. Particularly heinous or indiscriminate actions over time may lead even the staunchest supporters, much less allies of convenience, to question the legitimacy and viability of religiously sanctioned terrorism. For example, some affiliated insurgent groups and external supporters of the Taliban and ISIS are distancing themselves from attacks that target or have killed large numbers of fellow Muslims as opposed to their notional enemies.

## Technology

The congruence of religion and WMD—including biological, chemical, radiological, and even nuclear weapons—portends a frightful and very real 'apocalypse now'. Modern religious fanatics do not have the political restraint of their terrorist predecessors and may simply be interested in killing as many non-believers as possible. Experts point to the ease with which chemical and biological agents, or 'poor man's atom bombs', can be manufactured or acquired; the decreasing frequency but increasing lethality of terrorist acts; and the breaking of a so-called WMD taboo by Aum Shinrikyo in Tokyo in 1995 and the US Congress anthrax spores mailing in October 2001. Those who track terrorist attempts to acquire WMD suggest that the question is not 'if' such attacks will occur but rather 'when'—and whether Western democracies will be able to manage the consequences.

## Information Technology

The Internet transcends borders, and therefore some observers believe that future irregular wars will be fought in cyberspace. Given the vulnerability of websites and servers to hackers, terrorists inevitably will become cyberterrorists through the World Wide Web. The alleged hacking by North Korea of Sony Corporation servers, as well as the 'defacing' of al-Qaeda affiliated websites by groups such as TeAmZ USA, are examples interpreted by some as evidence that cyberwar is a reality. Hacking and defacing provide glimpses into what ambitious cyberterrorists and activists can accomplish. Policymakers fear that cyberterrorists and 'infosurgents' will conduct electronic raids on vital national systems controlled by computers (e.g., financial services, transportation networks, and power grids). Particularly daunting is the prospect that terrorists or other insurgents will harness the Stuxnet code to sabotage critical infrastructure such as banking networks, power plants, or other key control systems. Fear is no longer based on the prospect of violence: information and the ability to control it has become the new form of power.

Whether or not terrorist and insurgent campaigns will be entirely 'virtual' is a matter of speculation. A technological reality is that access to the Web, satellite communications, and portable computers greatly enhance the capability of aspiring terrorists and insurgents. According to media reports, the group which rampaged through and besieged part of Mumbai in November 2008 made use of readily available cellular and satellite phones, as well as publicly available satellite maps and Global Positioning Satellite data, to coordinate their attack. Such technology and information was once the exclusive purview of major powers. Today, websites, portals, and weblogs allow the quick dissemination of propaganda, training materials, and 'best practices', while basic equipment such as a laptop, software, and a CD burner allow materials to be produced professionally and disseminated clandestinely. With a computer and connection to the Internet, an individual can do more damage than armed terrorist cells or small insurgent movements, as the example of American-born Anwar al-Awlaki suggests. His various electronically produced and distributed products, including the online *Inspire* magazine, have encouraged individuals around the globe to take up arms. More importantly, some senior al-Qaeda leaders view the future of the movement as a 'leaderless resistance' of compartmented, geographically dispersed cells. The net effect, observed in the Philippines, Iraq, and elsewhere, is that individuals or small insurgent cells can obtain training and mission planning materials, share information, and coordinate their activities with little fear of being caught by security forces.

**Key Points**

- Religion is useful as a rallying point and enabler for terrorism but cannot provide a strategy to achieve the desired objectives.
- Culturally inspired insurgents might change the nature of uprisings from traditional 'trinitarian' wars to chaotic ethnic conflict.
- Information technologies and the World Wide Web have provided terrorists with new capabilities to reach across time and space, creating vulnerability in a state-based system where control of information equals power.

 **Conclusion**

States will be plagued by terrorism and irregular warfare as long as individuals are willing to use violence for political purposes. The shocking cultural details of irregular conflicts, such as the Taliban, al-Qaeda's and ISIS's recorded beheadings of captives and the use of starvation as a weapon in Sudan and Somalia, can obscure the political purpose behind the fighting. Terrorism and irregular warfare have long been used to change political systems and acquire power; more recently, cultural schisms have led to a rise in terrorism carried out for religious and personal reasons.

Current re-evaluations of irregular warfare and terrorism often lack context. Religion, culture, ethnicity, and technology remain important elements of irregular warfare. They define how and why individuals take up arms against perceived injustices. But the *ultima ratio* for the use of irregular methods of war is to achieve *political* results. Shoko Asahara, the spiritual leader of the Aum Shinrikyo cult, only attempted to use chemical and biological agents *after* his political ambitions were thwarted in 1990. Revenge for his humiliation at the polls was perhaps the most significant reason for launching chemical and biological attacks. Likewise the stream of veiled threats of WMD use by al-Qaeda leaders should draw attention to the fact that the movement has failed since 2001 to achieve its stated objective of creating a theocracy to undertake social reform.

Warrior cultures may appear to espouse violence for its own sake, but at the root of their struggle is the quest for political autonomy, control, or power. The protracted guerrilla war fought by the Chechens against the Russians is little different from the one conducted in 1856: the Chechens' desire is to gain political autonomy from Moscow. Native Americans fought against the US Army in the nineteenth century to maintain autonomy and protect their traditional hunting grounds. Even ancient irregulars, classified as *barbarii* by the Romans, were resisting attempts to have *Pax Romana* imposed upon them.

So is the trinity of Clausewitz no longer relevant? To suggest so misrepresents its foundation and misconstrues the reasons why irregulars fight in the first place. After all, primordial violence (the people) serves no purpose unless it is subordinated ultimately to policy (the government). Violence undertaken for personal gain, be it financial or to enhance one's reputation, is nothing more than a criminal act in civil society and should be treated as such.

 **Questions**

1. What is the difference between terrorism and insurgency and why is it important to distinguish between them?

2. Does the nature or character of irregular warfare change—or do both?

3. Can terrorists and insurgents sacrifice the element of time to achieve political change and if so, under what conditions?

4. Why is the element of space easy to discuss in theory but difficult to incorporate in practice?

5. Why are irregular warfare theorists divided on the use of terror as a method of compelling support?

6. Is irregular warfare governed by the principles of war or does it have its own principles?

7. Why is locating terrorists and insurgents so difficult?

8. How is the balance struck between force and the rule of law on both sides of an irregular campaign?

9. How can those countering insurgents and terrorists win?

10. Has religion, culture, and technology changed the nature of terrorism?

 ## Further Reading

A. K. Cronin, *How Terrorism Ends* (Princeton, NJ: Princeton University Press, 2009) is a clearly written, analytically concise study of the different pathways to terrorist success or failure.

R. Debray, *Revolution in the Revolution? Armed Struggle and Political Struggle in Latin America* (London: Pelican, 1968) is written by a French philosopher and develops Che Guevara's concept of the *foco* more fully.

B. B. Fall, 'The Theory and Practice of Insurgency and Counter-Insurgency', *Naval War College Review*, 15(1) (1999): 46–57 offers a basic introduction to the core concepts of and relationship between insurgency and counterinsurgency.

C. Guevara, *Guerrilla Warfare*, 3rd edn (Wilmington, DE: Scholarly Resources, 1997) is an updated version of Che Guevara's manual on guerrilla warfare based on his Cuban experience.

J. Jansen, *The Dual Nature of Islamic Fundamentalism* (Ithaca, NY: Cornell University Press, 1997) offers numerous insights into the evolution of fundamentalist Islamic thought and its practice by the Muslim Brotherhood in Egypt.

T. E. Lawrence, 'The Evolution of a Revolt', *The Army Quarterly*, 1(1) (1920): 55–69 gives a distilled account of the strategy used during the Arab Revolt that was embellished considerably when published as *Seven Pillars of Wisdom: A Triumph* (London: Jonathan Cape, 1935), pp. 188–96.

C. Malkasian, *War Comes to Garmser* (Oxford: Oxford University Press, 2013) is one of the most important depictions of the internal state power dynamics, many with long histories, that confront external counterinsurgents.

M. Tse-Tung, *Selected Military Writings of Mao Tse-Tung* (Peking: Foreign Languages Press, 1966) presents a collection of Mao's most important tracts and provides insights into the evolution of his military thought on irregular warfare.

E. Simpson, *War from the Ground Up* (New York: Columbia University Press, 2012) is a thoughtful, provocative attempt to explain contemporary violence and update the ideas developed by Clausewitz.

 ## Web Links

Combating Terrorism Center (CTC) **http://www.ctc.usma.edu** was founded in 2001 and provides access to a range of outstanding reports and products, based on declassified documents and other primary source research that are available for download.

*Small Wars Journal* **http://smallwarsjournal.com** offers access to the blog, journal, and professional reading lists posted by a range of practitioners, academicians, and subject-matter experts.

Marx to Mao Website **http://www.marx2mao.com** provides the full text of most of Mao's writings on guerrilla warfare as well as those of V. I. Lenin.

U.S. Army Special Operations Command's Assessing Revolutionary and Insurgent Strategies (ARIS) website **http://www.soc.mil/ARIS/ARIS.html** features several useful studies and reports, a number of which have been updated, such as its 'Casebook on Insurgency and Revolutionary Warfare', 'Human Factors Considerations of Underground in Insurgencies', as well as an irregular warfare bibliography.

# 11

# The Second Nuclear Age: Nuclear Weapons in the Twenty-first Century

C. DALE WALTON

## Chapter Contents

 Reader's Guide

This chapter sets out to consider the role that nuclear weapons have played in international politics, both during and after the cold war. In particular, a distinction is drawn between the spread of nuclear weapons to more states, which is creating an increasing threat to international security, and the decline in the absolute number of nuclear weapons due to the reductions in the nuclear arsenals of the United States and Russia. Some attention is also given to other contemporary issues such as ballistic missile defences, the cultural dimensions of nuclear weapons acquisition, and the possibility of terrorists using nuclear weapons in the future.[1]

## Introduction

Since their invention, nuclear weapons have played an important role in the international system, even though they have not been used in wartime since 1945. During the cold war, both the United States and the Soviet Union built large and diverse nuclear arsenals, which included a mix of weapons and delivery vehicles. During this era, academics and policymakers struggled with many difficult issues related to these weapons, but in the United States and other North Atlantic Treaty Organization (NATO) countries special attention was paid to deterrence, particularly the use of nuclear weapons to deter the Soviet Union from launching an invasion of western and central European NATO countries. Thus, one might say that the main 'theme' of Western nuclear debate during the cold war was the use of nuclear weapons to prevent superpower war, either nuclear or conventional.

This First Nuclear Age—which lasted approximately from 1945 to the 1991 fall of the Soviet Union—was dominated by the American and Soviet superpowers, which first tested nuclear weapons in 1945 and 1949, respectively. Three other countries also became declared nuclear powers during the First Nuclear Age (Great Britain, France, and China), while at least three other states (South Africa, Israel, and India) became undeclared nuclear states, but the arsenals of all of these countries combined were dwarfed by those of either of the two superpowers. As a result, serious thinking about nuclear issues tended to focus on the United States and Soviet Union—the cold war era was a bipolar one, and that fact was reflected in the superpower nuclear arsenals (see Table 11.1).

Today, Moscow and Washington still possess the world's largest nuclear arsenals, but international political circumstances have changed dramatically in the post-Soviet period. While the Russo-American relationship has been chilly in recent years, the likelihood of a nuclear conflict between the two states nonetheless appears tiny. However, in other respects, the international environment is more dangerous than it was during the cold war era. The world has transitioned into a Second Nuclear Age, in which these weapons will proliferate horizontally to more states, including very dangerous and unstable regimes. Therefore, it is quite likely that the odds of a nuclear war occurring in any given year are much greater now than was the case in the First Nuclear Age.

The objective of this chapter is to explore the strategic role that nuclear weapons play in international politics and study how it has changed over time. The transition from the First to the Second Nuclear Age receives particular attention, and the chapter demonstrates how horizontal nuclear proliferation, the spread of nuclear weapons to more states or other international actors, is creating new threats to the international security environment even as the fears associated with the bipolar cold war stand-off are decreasing. (Vertical nuclear proliferation, by contrast, is an increase in the number of nuclear weapons. Therefore, a country that has five nuclear weapons has proliferated vertically if it produces a sixth one. Today, however, the total number of nuclear weapons world-wide is decreasing because of the shrinking Russian and American nuclear arsenals.)

**Table 11.1** Growth in the Number of Nuclear Powers

| Nuclear Weapon States | Date of First Test (Confirmed or Presumed) | Still Possesses Nuclear Weapons? |
| --- | --- | --- |
| United States | 16 July 1945 | Yes |
| USSR/Russia | 29 August 1949 | Yes |
| United Kingdom | 3 October 1952 | Yes |
| France | 3 December 1960 | Yes |
| China | 16 October 1964 | Yes |
| Israel | Uncertain | Yes |
| India | 18 May 1974 | Yes |
| South Africa | 22 September 1979 | No |
| Belarus | N/A | No |
| Kazakhstan | N/A | No |
| Ukraine | N/A | No |
| Pakistan | 28 May 1998 | Yes |
| North Korea | 9 October 2006 | Presumed Yes |

*Note:* Some countries possessed nuclear weapons for several years before conducting their first nuclear test. Belarus, Kazakhstan, and Ukraine inherited nuclear arsenals with the break-up of the USSR.

## The First Nuclear Age

The first nuclear test occurred on 16 July 1945 in New Mexico; less than one month later, on 6 and 9 August, nuclear weapons were used against two Japanese cities, Hiroshima and Nagasaki. These devices—nicknamed 'Little Boy' and 'Fat Man'—differed in their designs, but both were fission nuclear weapons. These weapons were the fruit of the Manhattan Project, a massive 'crash programme' to which the American government—worried that Nazi Germany might be the first country to obtain nuclear weapons—devoted billions of dollars and thousands of scientists, technicians, and other personnel.

For a time the United States was the only power capable of building nuclear devices, and thus enjoyed an atomic monopoly. This monopoly was, however, short-lived, partly because Soviet spies were providing data from the American nuclear programme to Moscow even as the (supposedly secret) Manhattan Project was ongoing. In 1949, the Soviet Union conducted its first nuclear test explosion.

By the mid-1950s both Washington and Moscow had tested fission-fusion nuclear weapons (more commonly referred to as thermonuclear weapons), which were even more powerful than their fission predecessors. Thermonuclear weapons use fissile material more efficiently than fission devices do, making larger yields—in essence, bigger explosions—possible. Nuclear yields are measured in kilotons, thousands of tons of TNT (dynamite) equivalent, and megatons, millions of tons of TNT equivalent. A five-kiloton weapon, for example, yields an explosion equivalent to 5,000 tons of TNT, while a two-megaton warhead's explosion equals 2,000,000 tons of TNT (see Box 11.1).

Almost immediately after the bombing of Hiroshima, a great debate began over the meaning of nuclear weapons for the future of international relations and, indeed, humanity itself. The first major text examining the impact of nuclear weapons on world politics, edited by Bernard Brodie, was titled *The Absolute Weapon*. The book's title is indicative of Brodie's views regarding the importance of these devices—like many other observers, he believed that nuclear arms were something other than 'normal' weapons and that their existence, in turn, would have a radical impact on the future course of international politics. Over the next several decades, a huge body of literature developed which addressed a myriad of issues related to the existence of nuclear weapons. For the purposes at hand, however, the most important writings addressed nuclear deterrence. In essence, nuclear deterrence examined how nuclear weapons could be used to prevent an opponent from undertaking an undesirable action.

---

 **BOX** 11.1   Fissile Material

For the building of nuclear weapons, the most important fissile materials are uranium 235 (U235) and plutonium 239 (P239). These radioactive isotopes are difficult to acquire. A given quantity of mined uranium contains very little U235; the latter must be separated from non-fissile uranium. Plutonium is not found in nature in any significant quantity—it is a by-product of nuclear processes guided by humans. The control of fissile materials is very important in preventing nuclear proliferation, but the generation of nuclear power requires fissile material. The International Atomic Energy Agency (IAEA) is tasked with ensuring that non-nuclear weapons countries which have nuclear power plants do not divert fissile material and use it to build nuclear weapons.

In the context of the cold war, perhaps the most critical deterrence issue from the Western perspective was preventing the Soviet Union from invading NATO's European members. Throughout the cold war, the Soviet Union enjoyed an enormous advantage over NATO in conventional military forces (all forces except for weapons of mass destruction, a category which includes nuclear, chemical, biological, and radiological weapons, are considered conventional). Strategists struggled with how to ensure that Moscow would not attempt to conquer vulnerable NATO countries, and their answers almost invariably relied on nuclear deterrence.

It generally was believed that Soviet leaders would not attack NATO countries if they were convinced that the United States would retaliate by initiating a nuclear attack against the Soviet Union. This is known as a countervalue threat—something that Soviet leaders valued, in this case the Soviet homeland itself, was held hostage to their good behaviour. Another sort of deterrence threat is against counterforce targets, the 'sinews' of state power: military forces, leadership targets, targets relevant to military command and control, and so forth. In general, one can say that the United States relied on a mix of countervalue and counterforce threats to deter the Soviet Union during the cold war (see Box 11.2).

During the First Nuclear Age, the two superpowers each built enormous arsenals of tactical nuclear weapons (TNWs) and strategic nuclear weapons. The distinction between the two types of weapons is somewhat artificial, but as a rule of thumb, TNWs are delivered by means such as tactical aircraft, artillery, or short-range ballistic or cruise missiles. TNWs are generally intended for use in battle, against troop concentrations, ships, or similar targets. (The superpowers even developed nuclear depth charges for use against enemy submarines.) Strategic nuclear weapons, by contrast, are usually delivered at very long ranges by intercontinental ballistic missiles (ICBMs), submarine-launched ballistic missiles (SLBMs) of intercontinental range, or long-range heavy bombers. These weapons can strike deep into enemy territory, thousands of miles from the point at which they were launched (see Box 11.3).

---

 **BOX** 11.2  Credibility

Credibility is central to the success of any deterrence threat. If a threat is not credible—in short, if the actor being threatened does not believe that its foe will carry out the threat—it is likely to ignore deterrence warnings and do what it wishes. Capability is also central to credibility—a would-be deterrer inherently is more credible if it clearly possesses the means necessary to make good its threat.

One can compare this nuclear deterrence credibility to prevention of crime: if a would-be thief believes that attempting a given robbery will lead to arrest, that individual likely will conclude that undertaking the act is not in his or her self-interest. This is surety of punishment. A related concept is severity of punishment: the thief who expects that the punishment for a particular crime will be heavy is more likely to be deterred than one who assumes that it will be light. Generally speaking, a deterrence threat that is both credible and severe is far more likely to deter an opponent than one that falls short in either, much less both, of these dimensions.

Every deterrence relationship is unique, and a would-be deterrer must try to understand what their counterpart values and how difficult it will be to dissuade the deterree from undertaking specific actions. Some activities may be easy to deter, while it might be very difficult or even impossible to prevent other ones. If deterrence does fail, a state then must decide whether to carry out its previous threats—and if it does not do so, its credibility will suffer. There is no simple deterrence formula that applies to all potential opponents; it is always important to understand the motivations and desires of those whom one is attempting to deter.

The United States and Soviet Union built tens of thousands of strategic and tactical warheads with an enormous variety of yields that ranged from less than one kiloton to tens of megatons. In many cases, several warheads were placed on a single delivery vehicle—the American MX ICBM, for example, was designed to carry up to ten Multiple Independently Targetable Reentry Vehicles (MIRVs). MIRVed warheads were first deployed in the 1970s. Before this time, there had been missiles with several warheads, but they were not independently targetable, which means they could not strike different targets.

 **Key Points**

- Nuclear weapons have not been used in conflict since atomic bombs were dropped on Hiroshima and Nagasaki, Japan in 1945.

- Nuclear warheads are categorized, along with chemical, biological, and radiological devices, as weapons of mass destruction.

- Competition in the building of nuclear arms was very closely tied to the cold war between the United States and the Soviet Union, and the theoretical models relating to deterrence that were built during that time reflect the bipolar competition between the two superpowers.

- Nuclear warheads are divided into a variety of categories, depending on their design, means of delivery, and other factors. Two of the most important distinctions are between fission and thermonuclear weapons and between tactical and strategic ones.

# Risks in the Second Nuclear Age

It would be excessive to claim that nuclear deterrence is either easy or always impossible in the twenty-first century. Deterrence concepts developed during the cold war continue to be useful when discussing today's challenges, but it perhaps is naive to assume that twenty-first-century actors—particularly, but not only, 'rogue' states such as Iran and North Korea—will act in a manner consistent with the assumptions of cold war deterrence theory. The assumptions regarding behaviour that underpin the body of deterrence theory are not universally applicable; every political culture is unique (indeed, every leader is unique), and it should not be expected that states will always act in a manner consistent with deterrence theory. Deterrence is not a panacea—threats, whether presently emerging or as yet unforeseen, cannot all be addressed successfully by consulting 'the cold war Deterrence Manual'.

Far too often, observers of international politics simply assume that leaders will not undertake particular actions because it would not be in their best interest to do so—with 'best interest' being defined by the observer. Thus, it is widely assumed that North Korea or Iran would, for example, never provide nuclear devices to terrorists or pre-emptively attack South Korea or Israel with such weapons. In both of these extreme examples, this assumption is likely to be correct—certainly, Pyongyang and Tehran are aware that such actions would be extraordinarily risky. However, even a very high probability that an event will not occur is not the same as a certainty that it will not occur.

There are still a great many controversies concerning the reliability of deterrence during the cold war. To claim that deterrence theory was proven to have worked well because there was no US–Soviet military conflict, much less a nuclear war, is to assume a causal relationship that may or may not exist. Certainly, the United States attempted to deter Soviet military aggression, but whether American deterrence actually prevented war between the two powers is unknown and, ultimately, unknowable. History, unlike a laboratory experiment, cannot be repeated, and we have no 'control cold war' to compare to the real cold war.

If American strategists had not developed a sophisticated body of deterrence theory, perhaps a nuclear conflict would have occurred—*or perhaps not*. Similarly, perhaps a US–Soviet nuclear conflict would have occurred despite American deterrence if not for historical happenstance. If we are unable to say with certainty that deterrence prevented the cold war from turning hot, we should be all the more cautious when attempting to predict the future behaviour of opponents whose decision-making is opaque and whose values are foreign to those prevailing in the West. To say that 'State X' will not commit a particular act because it would not be in its best interest to do so requires a judgement regarding the interests of that state. However, it is rare for all of a state's key leaders to hold essentially indistinguishable views on their country's wellbeing; for an outsider to simply assume that his or her own perspective will inevitably be reflected in that country's policy is perilous indeed.

Prudent leaders must factor in the risk of an unlikely event when making decisions; the mere fact that the use of nuclear weapons in a given situation may be imprudent, or even outright foolish, is no guarantee that such weapons will remain unused. This is not good news for the reliability of deterrence, and especially troubling when one considers that the two states mentioned earlier are not the only unpredictable countries that either currently have, or in the future may come to possess, nuclear weapons.

The simple answer to these uncertainties is to deny nuclear arsenals to rogue, or potentially rogue, states. However, there is every reason to believe that it will be impossible to do

---

 **BOX** 11.3  Terminology

- *Ballistic missile*. A missile with rocket motors that flies on a ballistic trajectory. Ballistic missiles carry a payload of conventional or WMD warheads, also known as reentry vehicles. Early ballistic missiles were inaccurate and could only carry relatively small payloads for short distances, but advanced missiles can be of intercontinental range and carry independently targetable warheads.

- *Cruise missile*. A missile with an air-breathing motor; in essence, a small, pilotless aircraft. Bombers can be equipped to carry nuclear-tipped cruise missiles.

- *Decapitation strike*. An attack intended to destroy the leadership and command, control, and communications (C3) network of an enemy nation.

- *Disarming strike*. An attack that attempts to destroy an enemy's nuclear forces. If a disarming strike is successful, the enemy state will not be utterly destroyed, but will be militarily helpless and compelled to negotiate a peace on the disarmer's terms.

- *Fallout*. Radioactive debris resulting from a nuclear explosion; also known as *residual radiation*. Heavier particles tend to settle in the area of the explosion, while lighter ones often travel great distances. Fallout contamination can result in serious, even fatal, health effects.

- *Nuclear effects*. A nuclear explosion creates blast, heat, and ionizing radiation, with fallout remaining after the explosion itself.

- *Triad*. The combination of SLBMs, ICBMs, and nuclear-armed long-range bombers that together comprise the strategic nuclear forces of the United States and Russia.

so consistently. Rather, we should expect the number of nuclear states to increase over time. This is not to say that there will be no non-proliferation victories. Some states seeking nuclear weapons will be dissuaded from acquiring them (as Libya was by the United States), and on rare occasions a nuclear state may even denuclearize (as South Africa did).

It is, however, very unlikely that this means that the spread of nuclear weapons can be reversed overall. Knowledge about any technology will be dispersed over time and nuclear weapons are an old invention—they were first built about seven decades ago. Unsurprisingly, there are increasing numbers of individuals from (currently) non-nuclear countries who are knowledgeable about nuclear weapons technology. The growing number of states with nuclear energy programmes makes it all the more difficult to eradicate proliferation.

The A. Q. Khan network provides an example of how challenging it may be to prevent nuclear proliferation in the Second Nuclear Age. Khan was the 'father' of Pakistan's nuclear weapons programme, and still is regarded by many Pakistanis as a national hero. Yet over time it became increasingly clear that he was at the centre of an international network trading in nuclear technology; in 2004, he publicly admitted to such activities, stating that his operation was not undertaken with the knowledge of Pakistan's government. However, he later renounced this confession, contending that it had been made under pressure, and that he was a 'scapegoat' whose activities were actually endorsed by his government.

The degree to which Khan acted with official approval remains disputed, but it is clear that his operation was an extensive one that provided proliferation-related information to a number of states. The Khan apparatus appears to have provided important assistance to the Iranian and North Korean nuclear programmes, but, beyond this, it demonstrated the increasing difficulty of controlling the spread of nuclear knowledge and materials, especially when informal criminal networks make it difficult to prove a state intended to help others proliferate. Events in recent years have also highlighted the difficulty of even ascertaining accurately whether a country is attempting to proliferate. In 2007, for example, the Israeli government struck an alleged Syrian reactor facility at which, apparently, a number of North Koreans were working—an event that shocked many observers, as Syria was not widely suspected to have a serious nuclear weapons programme, much less one closely coordinated with Pyongyang.

Although well-designed counterproliferation efforts can slow the spread of nuclear weapons, further proliferation should be regarded as being extremely likely. This, in turn, means that there will be more powers that possess the physical means to initiate nuclear war and, consequently, an increasingly complicated deterrence environment world-wide. The 'Second Nuclear Age' is distinct from the first in a number of key respects, one of the most important of which is the increasing unreliability of deterrence. As nuclear weapons proliferate horizontally, the risk of nuclear war occurring *somewhere* on earth can be expected to increase—especially as many of the proliferating states are not models of good international citizenship. Indeed, if a truly undeterrable leader ever comes to possess nuclear weapons and is determined to use them, deterrence would be impossible. Leaders ultimately *choose* to be deterred, which is to say that they decide not to accept the consequences that would flow from taking a particular action—basically, they are frightened away from doing something. If, however, they are willing to accept the consequences of their preferred action, they may do as they like.

While it is often assumed, based on the experience of the cold war, that nuclear weapons make countries more cautious and therefore less likely to go to war, there is reason to doubt that this will be true in all cases. We know very little indeed about nuclear decision-making in several countries currently armed with these weapons. Moreover, it is impossible to know how a country such as Iran, which apparently does not yet have nuclear weapons, but soon may obtain them, will act once it possesses a nuclear arsenal. There are also many questions about how willing a country such as China might be to risk nuclear war during a future crisis.

In all likelihood, the countries that are most reliably predictable in regard to nuclear strategic decision-making are stable democracies with a relatively long track record of nuclear possession; states such as Great Britain, France, and the United States would fit into this category. It is far more difficult to anticipate how countries such as North Korea, Iran, Russia, China, or Pakistan will act in the future (see Box 11.4).

In the case of most of these countries, we have little trustworthy information about their nuclear doctrine. Doctrine guides countries in their use of military power, and in the case of nuclear weapons it helps lay out a 'road map' as to the circumstances in which these devices might be used. While the cold war superpowers proved reluctant to use nuclear weapons in combat, there is no guarantee that all states will be similarly reticent. Indeed, governments which possess relatively weak conventional forces may see nuclear weapons as offering an inexpensive trump card that they may use against better-armed enemies. Over time, we will have a clearer notion of how various nuclear states will use their arsenals in negotiations and conflict. In any case, however, it is clear that in this Second Nuclear Age deterrence must be carefully tailored to the cultural, political, military, and other characteristics of the state that one is endeavouring to deter. Not all leaders are similar to the individuals who led the USSR; even if deterrence truly 'worked' during the cold war, it should be assumed that deterrence theory as it developed during that period is not infallible and that deterrence failure is entirely possible.

The role of ballistic missile defences (BMD) is another key distinction between the two nuclear ages. During the First Nuclear Age, the deployment of BMD was a matter of heated debate. BMD opponents warned that such defences would destabilize the nuclear balance between the superpowers and, therefore, encourage both countries to build more warheads so as to overwhelm the other side's BMD. This arms race and the general sense of instability might, it was feared, in turn increase the likelihood of a US–Soviet war. Regardless of whether the claims of BMD foes were accurate, the closing of the First Nuclear Age profoundly altered

---

 **BOX** 11.4   Unstable Nuclear States: The Pakistani Case

In the Second Nuclear Age, certain unstable states possess or are attempting to acquire nuclear weapons, and it should be remembered how quickly, and profoundly, the governments of troubled countries can be transformed. Pakistan provides one example. While Pakistan currently has an elected civilian government, it is widely feared that an internal coup, civil war, or other event could lead to regime change; a radical, perhaps even Taliban-led, regime could take power and/or the country might splinter, much as the Soviet Union did in 1991. The security situation has worsened in recent years, with political dysfunction and Islamist extremism feeding on each other and undermining that country's internal stability.

Today, India and Pakistan appear to have a reasonably stable deterrence relationship. One could argue that mutual deterrence is working tolerably well in South Asia, and even that a common fear of nuclear usage has prevented large-scale conventional war between the two countries. However, if Pakistan undergoes regime change or disintegrates, deterrence stability could vanish. This highlights one of the dangers of horizontal proliferation to unstable countries—even if the government that obtains nuclear arms is reasonably cautious, its successors may not be.

the international security environment. It was not unreasonable to believe that a superpower that already possessed thousands of nuclear weapons might build many thousands more. However, many of the small states constructing nuclear arsenals would be financially and technically incapable of building great numbers of missiles and warheads. In such cases, the fact that other states deploy BMD is unlikely to drive large-scale vertical nuclear proliferation. While some missile defence opponents worry that American construction of ballistic missile defences will convince countries with small nuclear arsenals to build many more warheads, in most cases they simply lack the resources to do so.

In 1971, the United States and Soviet Union agreed to the Anti-Ballistic Missile (ABM) Treaty. This agreement barred both countries from constructing comprehensive national missile defences (however, it did not absolutely ban all missile defences, as it allowed each power to maintain a very strictly limited BMD capability). The Treaty was representative of a specific vision of deterrence based on mutual assured destruction (MAD), which assumed that neither the United States and the Soviet Union would not use nuclear weapons if both believed that, no matter how successful a first strike might be, it would be impossible to eliminate the enemy's ability to launch a devastating retaliatory strike. MAD, in short, envisioned deterrence stability as requiring that any nuclear war be utterly devastating to both sides. At present, however, only the United States and Russia have nuclear arsenals sufficient to allow them to practice MAD reliably. Moreover, MAD is largely irrelevant to the current Moscow–Washington relationship; while there is tension between the two countries over Russian actions in Ukraine and other issues, nonetheless the contemporary international system differs radically from the cold war environment. Therefore, countries such as the United States can now look beyond MAD and ask how they can best address the potential threats posed by smaller nuclear powers, while the latter countries (as well as potential nuclear proliferators) have to take account of the possibility that the arsenal that they build may be defeated by a foe's missile defence.

The United States renounced the ABM Treaty in 2002, leaving it free to build missile defences, and that country now possesses a basic homeland missile defence. However, it is not the only state contemplating BMD defence of its territory. A variety of countries, including both nuclear and non-nuclear powers, have indicated interest in deployment of BMD. It is likely that, as the Second Nuclear Age matures, an increasing number of states will deploy these defences, which in turn will complicate the targeting strategy of nuclear powers, particularly ones with modest arsenals.

 **Key Points**

- With the end of the cold war, the world has entered a Second Nuclear Age in which the number of actors possessing nuclear weapons is progressively increasing even as the absolute number of such weapons is falling.

- Deterrence may prove unreliable in the future. Deterrence theories that were developed in the context of the struggle between the United States and the Soviet Union may prove to be inapplicable to powers such as North Korea and Iran.

- Strategic culture influences how a country uses its nuclear arsenal for deterrence and/or warfighting.

- Ballistic missile defences will be an important factor in nuclear decision-making in the future, and the existence of BMD may discourage some countries from attempting to acquire nuclear weapons.

## Adapting to the Second Nuclear Age

In many respects, humanity as a whole is far safer today than it was during the cold war. A US–Soviet nuclear war could well have spelt the end of modern civilization, at least in the northern hemisphere. Today, there appears to be little immediate danger of a civilization-shattering nuclear conflict. It is far more likely that the next nuclear war will involve, at most, a few dozen warheads rather than the tens of thousands that might have been used in a US–Soviet apocalypse. It may be cold comfort when one contemplates the horrors that even a 'small' nuclear war would entail, but the reality that there appears to be little danger of the modern world being wiped out in an afternoon is important nonetheless.

In this Second Nuclear Age, several presumptions, common in the cold war era, may prove to be problematic: that nuclear-armed powers will always be 'reasonable'; that BMD undermines deterrence; and that arms control and disarmament treaties are the best means to further counterproliferation efforts. The potential problems with the first two assumptions have already been addressed, and we shall now turn to the third one.

Non-proliferation and counterproliferation both relate to efforts to prevent the horizontal proliferation of nuclear weapons. While it is sometimes difficult to distinguish between the two activities, as a general rule the term 'non-proliferation' is used in reference to international legal arrangements such as the Nuclear Non-Proliferation Treaty (NPT). Counterproliferation, a term that has become popular in recent years, is more often used to refer to the *enforcement* of the NPT and other international agreements. Counterproliferation can involve a variety of measures, including military force.

The NPT, which was opened for signature in 1968 and went into force in 1970, is an international agreement that recognizes only five states—China, Great Britain, France, the Soviet Union/Russia, and the United States—as legitimate nuclear powers. All other states that signed the treaty agreed to refrain from obtaining nuclear weapons. India, Israel, and Pakistan never signed the NPT, while North Korea was formerly a signatory but withdrew from the treaty in 2003.

The overall success of the NPT is debatable. While the number of nuclear powers has not exploded in the years since the agreement first came into effect, it should be noted that the great majority of countries signing the NPT surely would not, in any case, have obtained nuclear weapons—most states are too small and/or too poor to afford nuclear arsenals, and many of those which could afford to maintain a nuclear force are inhibited by domestic pressures from obtaining one or simply feel that they do not need such weapons to ensure their security. Most leaders in countries such as Japan and South Korea, for example, are reasonably confident in the American 'nuclear umbrella' and therefore believe that, at present, the diplomatic and other costs of national proliferation outweigh its potential advantages.

A major vulnerability of the NPT and similar universal disarmament agreements is that compliance is essentially voluntary; such treaties have very weak provisions regarding inspection of suspect sites and no mechanism for seriously punishing bad actors. (The reason for this, in turn, is that, in order to maximize the number of signatories, such treaties basically accept the 'lowest common denominator'—the provisions must be acceptable to as many states as possible, including would-be bad actors which otherwise would refuse to accede to the agreement—see Box 11.5.)

**BOX** 11.5   Arms Control Treaties and the International Environment

History seems to indicate that arms control treaties, by themselves, do little or nothing to reduce the danger level in the international environment. If they did, there would never have been a Second World War, because the period after the First World War was a 'golden age' of arms control, with war itself essentially being banned by the 1928 Kellogg–Briand Pact. The fact that the number of warheads possessed by Russia and the United States decreased radically after the end of the cold war is instructive. One could argue that the successful negotiation of the bilateral Strategic Arms Reduction Talks (START) I, START II, Strategic Offensive Reduction Treaty (SORT), and New START agreements did not fundamentally alter the overall geostrategic environment, and that these treaties merely reflected the fact that the Russo–American relationship itself had changed radically. (See Chapter 12 for further detail on arms control.)

The case of Iraq before its occupation by the United States illustrates some of the short-comings of the NPT and other universal arms control agreements. As a militarily defeated state (in the 1991 Persian Gulf War), Iraq submitted to far more intrusive International Atomic Energy Agency (IAEA) inspections than are the norm. It was generally assumed even before the war that Iraq had a nuclear weapons programme, but the fact that Baghdad was quite close to actually building such devices shocked most knowledgeable observers. Despite this, the Iraqi government managed to avoid full disclosure of its WMD programmes and capabili-ties—and, of course, it is now clear that most of the world's intelligence agencies grossly over-estimated the progress of the Iraqi WMD programmes in the years between 1991 and 2003. If Iraq could mislead outsiders under such conditions, one can readily imagine how easy it would be for other states to do so.

The refusal of Iraq's Ba'ath Party to cooperate fully with IAEA inspections ultimately led to its downfall, but this was the result of Washington's initiative, not that of the IAEA or the United Nations. As the case of North Korea illustrates, apparent non-compliance with agreements such as the NPT does not always result in a prohibitive penalty. Indeed, North Korea at times has profited financially from its NPT non-compliance, thanks to the largesse of countries such as Japan, South Korea, and the United States, which agreed to provide that country with fuel oil, food, and other goods in exchange for ending its nuclear weapons programme. North Korea took the pay-off and built nuclear weapons nonetheless.

Counterproliferation measures, such as the Proliferation Security Initiative (PSI)—a US-led programme that allows states to cooperate in various ways to prevent the transfer of WMD materials and knowledge—attempt to plug the 'holes' in the NPT. While one cannot expect arms control and disarmament agreements to solve all proliferation problems, they *can* pro-vide useful leverage for countries that are dedicated to stopping WMD proliferation and are willing to actively enforce counterproliferation (see Box 11.6).

Together, non-proliferation and counterproliferation efforts may succeed in slowing con-siderably the horizontal proliferation of nuclear weapons, although one should not expect that they can stop it altogether.

Having considered the history of nuclear weapons and their continuing horizontal prolif-eration, it is useful to consider briefly how the political and military roles of these devices will

**BOX** 11.6   The Difficulties of Assertive Disarmament

Assertive disarmament is the use of military force to destroy a successful proliferator's actual nuclear arsenal or a would-be proliferator's capability to build nuclear weapons. However, assertive disarmament is very difficult and controversial, and for those reasons it rarely has been undertaken. The difficulties associated with the invasion and occupation of Iraq, a military undertaking largely motivated by WMD proliferation concerns, illustrate how costly assertive disarmament can be in both financial and human terms for the would-be disarmer. The United States has expressed deep concern over the North Korean and Iranian nuclear programmes for years and in both cases, at times, has hinted that it might assertively disarm these states. However, it has never actually attempted to do so, for a variety of reasons.

Even if the United States possessed highly detailed and specific intelligence on the location and character of all the sites relevant to the North Korean and presumed Iranian nuclear programmes (and it is unlikely that it does in fact have such near-perfect intelligence), it is quite possible that Washington would not choose to strike these facilities. In regard to North Korea, Washington fears that this would result in a full-scale war on the Korean Peninsula. Given that North Korea possesses great numbers of conventional artillery tubes and likely would inflict massive conventional damage on Seoul—killing tens of thousands of civilians—just in the early hours of a conflict, the risks of escalation strongly discourage a disarming strike.

The Iranian case is not quite so dire, but it is generally believed that Iranian facilities are widely dispersed and that destroying them would result in a large number of civilian casualties. Moreover, American policymakers fear that such a move would set back reform in Iran and turn the Iranian public against the United States. It is also possible that Iran would retaliate by undertaking terrorist attacks against US targets. Some observers expect that Israel eventually will strike Iran's facilities, but this would require Israeli leaders to accept the difficulties and dangers that would accompany such an action. It is far from certain that the latter are any more willing than their American counterparts to accept these consequences. The July 2015 diplomatic agreement between Iran and a number of other international actors, including the United States, may both avert Iranian proliferation and eliminate any perceived need for assertive disarmament.  However, at this time it is impossible to say with certainty whether the agreement will accomplish these twin goals.

North Korea and Iran present proliferation challenges that are unlikely to be resolved through the use of military force. Thus, responsible policymakers and military planners must work under the assumption that these powers either do possess nuclear weapons and will continue to do so (North Korea) or, depending on the ongoing diplomatic process and Iran's own willingness to abide by restrictions on its nuclear programme, may have such arms in the future.

develop as the Second Nuclear Age matures. Will norms against nuclear use grow stronger, with nuclear weapons eventually being banned outright world-wide? Will technological developments render these devices obsolete? Or will nuclear weapons continue to play a role in international politics?

There appears to be little likelihood that nuclear weapons will cease to be an international political tool, either being eliminated altogether or placed in the hands of an international authority such as the IAEA. Indeed, there has been no compelling evidence that progress has been made towards universal nuclear disarmament in recent years. While the absolute number of nuclear weapons in the world is decreasing, this is quite different from complete disarmament. None of the declared nuclear states have surrendered their nuclear arsenals or indicated a willingness to do so at any time in the foreseeable future, though they have all agreed publicly that universal disarmament is a laudable goal. At the same time, horizontal proliferation continues (see Critical Thinking).

**Critical Thinking**    Debating … Many observers contend that there is a taboo against the use of nuclear (as well as chemical and biological) weapons. However, its existence remains disputed. Does a nuclear taboo exist?

## For

- *The international price of nuclear use.* A broad international consensus exists that use of these devices is deeply disreputable and immoral under most, if not all, circumstances. A state that used such weapons likely would face international sanctions and/or other punishment, and other states might ally together for protection against the 'roguish' nuclear user. If the state was judged to be an ongoing danger to the international security environment, it might face severe pressure over a long time period or even attempted regime change by military means.

- *The personal price of nuclear use.* Regardless of the precise circumstances for nuclear use, those leaders who made the decision to use nuclear weapons would be condemned by at least part of the international community, and various non-governmental organisations (NGOs) and other actors would attempt, perhaps successfully, to ensure their trial and conviction for crimes against humanity.

## Against

- *Not all violations of norms are violations of taboos.* A deep reluctance to employ nuclear arms in warfare is a marked characteristic of recent history. However, 'taboo' is a powerful word, implying a deep-rooted and long-standing repugnance shared by almost all members of a particular society (most cultures, for example, have a taboo against cannibalism). While there clearly is broad distaste for the use of nuclear weapons, under certain extreme circumstances it might be accepted by most of the international community.

- *No true 'hard cases'.* The norm against the use of nuclear weapons has not faced a single severe 'stress test' in which non-use clearly would have led to disaster for a nuclear-armed country. For example, no nuclear-armed country has chosen to allow itself to be destroyed rather than use these weapons. Perhaps the closest that any country has come to using nuclear weapons was Israel early in the 1973 Yom Kippur War, when it was in danger of being overrun and conquered by an Egypt- and Syria-led coalition. Israel apparently prepared for possible use of its arsenal, but the invasion soon was turned back by conventional means.

The question of whether nuclear weapons will become outdated is a rather more complex one. While a few elegantly simple weapons have remained on the battlefield for millennia, it is usual for a weapon to have a fairly straightforward life cycle, offering great advantages to its possessors when first introduced and then, progressively, growing more outmoded as new weapons are invented until, eventually, it disappears entirely from military use. In due course, this perhaps will be the fate of nuclear weapons, but this life cycle process may require many decades, if not centuries. It is possible that the nuclear weapon will be dethroned from its position as 'the absolute weapon' by an even more devastating new weapon of mass destruction (there has been speculation, for example, on the feasibility of an 'antimatter bomb' that would be enormously powerful), and, certainly, militaries on the technological cutting-edge will continue to deploy ever more potent conventional weapons. However, for the foreseeable future, nuclear weapons will remain the most powerful destructive devices possessed by human beings.

Given this reality, it is clear that nuclear weapons will continue to have an international political role. While it is not possible to predict precisely how many states will come to possess these devices over the next few decades, it is very likely indeed that the number of nuclear-armed states will increase, perhaps dramatically. As more states acquire nuclear weapons—and as the nuclear club becomes more diverse ideologically and culturally—we will learn more about how robust deterrence is under a variety of conditions involving different actors. Perhaps we will find that there actually is a strong nuclear taboo which prevents leaders world-wide from 'pushing the button'. It is, however, all too plausible that we instead will see the breaking of the long nuclear truce.

 **Key Points**

- Non-proliferation and counterproliferation measures are used to control, and ideally prevent, the horizontal proliferation of nuclear weapons.

- The NPT acknowledges only five nuclear weapons states (China, France, Great Britain, the Soviet Union/Russia, and the United States) and forbids all other signatories from obtaining nuclear weapons. Most of the world's states are signatories, although some (including nuclear-armed countries such as India, Israel, and Pakistan) are not.

- Effective enforcement of universal disarmament agreements such as the NPT has proven difficult, especially as such agreements generally only have very weak inspection provisions.

- It is very unlikely that nuclear weapons will become obsolescent in the next several decades, or that the world's nuclear powers will all agree to dismantle their arsenals.

 ## Conclusion: Looking Towards the Third Nuclear Age?

Since 1945, nuclear weapons have played a central role in international relations, but over time that role has changed subtly; as the world has transitioned to the Second Nuclear Age, the 'nuclear club' has progressively become less exclusive. While non-proliferation and counterproliferation efforts may slow the spread of nuclear weapons, it should be expected that the number of nuclear-armed countries will continue to grow. There are several reasons for this, but the military utility and consequent usefulness of these devices for deterrence and coercion, as well as the prestige associated with possessing a nuclear arsenal, are the most important.

Nuclear arms are particularly valuable to states that, in conventional terms, are militarily weak relative to their foes. For example, in a conventional conflict, most states would find the military power of the United States overwhelming, but even a small nuclear arsenal would greatly complicate US war planning and raise the possibility of horrific American and allied casualties. In some cases, it might even be possible to prevent the United States from undertaking any military action, making it feasible for a country such as North Korea or Iran to prevail in a crisis. Nuclear possession is also associated with high status in the international community, since most very powerful states have these weapons. Although owning nuclear warheads does not, in isolation, make a country a great power, there is a unique status associated with nuclear possession, and this surely is one of the reasons why some lesser powers have gone to such extraordinary (and expensive) efforts to circumvent international non-proliferation regimes.

While deterrence theories developed during the cold war continue to provide useful guidance, as the group of nuclear-armed states has diversified the continued validity of these theories has become questionable. As we have seen, every country has a unique strategic culture, and cultural factors can have a significant influence on decisions related to nuclear acquisition, deterrence, and use. We should not expect that the very diverse group of leaders who will wield nuclear weapons in this century will all act as their Soviet and American counterparts did during the cold war.

The simple 'MAD worldview', which assumes that any nuclear war would involve thousands, or even tens of thousands, of nuclear warheads, and be utterly devastating both to the participants and other countries (which would experience the environmental side-effects of the massive nuclear exchange), is obsolete. In the cold war, the greatest fear of both superpowers was that the other would be able to disarm it almost entirely in a well-planned first strike. There was relatively little concern over whether surviving nuclear weapons, especially those mounted on SLBMs and ICBMs, might hit the enemy; so long as the command and control system and a modest percentage of a superpower's arsenal remained intact, it could execute a devastating counterstrike. Certainly, some warheads would fail to strike their targets for any number of reasons—including mechanical failure, simple inaccuracy, and other issues—but the superpower nuclear arsenals were so large that such problems would not undermine the ability to deliver a fatal blow.

In contrast, most of today's nuclear powers possess rather modest arsenals, and missile defences can complicate nuclear war planning exponentially. When a state with a small nuclear arsenal considers attacking a foe with a missile defence, the attacker cannot be certain how many, if any, of its warheads will break though the defence and strike their targets. It is likely that the proliferation of missile defences in this century will provide many states with a 'shield' that they can use to defend against the nuclear sword wielded by their enemies. Moreover, some states no doubt will, like the United States, seek to have both a nuclear sword and a BMD shield. Thus the argument, commonly made in the West during the cold war, that building defences against nuclear weapons is a waste of effort because many warheads would 'leak through' any defence is irrelevant with regard to most of the countries that are, or will be, nuclear-armed in this century. When a state only has a small number of nuclear weapons, it is conceivable that they could all be intercepted by a well-designed missile defence.

In the two decades of the Second Nuclear Age, we have seen clear patterns develop, such as continuing horizontal proliferation and an ongoing decrease in the size of the Russian and American nuclear arsenals. Most recently, the latter trend was reinforced by the New START treaty, which limits the two countries to 1,550 deployed warheads each. However, other countries, such as China, India, and Pakistan are increasing the size of their nuclear arsenals. This, combined with the spread of missile defences over time, has resulted in a complicated environment with many potential nuclear deterrence relationships.

There are still many uncertainties regarding how nuclear weapons will be used politically in the current nuclear age. Thus far, fortunately, most of the 'emerging' nuclear powers have been relatively cautious in regard to issuing nuclear threats. There are, however, many potential flashpoints—for example, India and Pakistan have a perpetually uneasy relationship, and if the North Korean government suffered a succession crisis or began to collapse internally, it is impossible to be certain how it might try to leverage its nuclear arsenal. Moreover, although we have not yet seen a cascade of nuclear proliferation where many states simultaneously sought nuclear weapons, it is possible that one will occur in the future. The Middle East may be a particularly fertile environment for a nuclear cascade, given Iran's possible nuclear proliferation efforts and the current political instability of most Arab countries. What sort of governments will continue to emerge from the 'Arab Spring' and the events following it is unknowable, but it is entirely possible that some of them will prove to be less reticent concerning nuclear proliferation than were their predecessors.

The great theme of the Second Nuclear Age is unpredictability—there is a lack of surety concerning how many nuclear-armed states there will be in coming years and how those states will use their arsenals for political gain. Perhaps even more worryingly, it is possible that one or more terrorist groups or other violent non-state actors will obtain nuclear weapons. There are many good reasons to celebrate the end of the First Nuclear Age and the consequent greatly diminished probability of a massive nuclear exchange, but it is, regrettably, all too possible that, sooner or later, nuclear weapons will be used *somewhere* in the world. If that were to occur, it might mark the beginning of a Third Nuclear Age—and that epoch could be one of both unbridled horizontal proliferation and repeated use of nuclear weapons.

**Questions**

1. What were the key characteristics of the First and Second Nuclear Ages? In what main respects do the two nuclear ages differ?

2. Why might the cold war model of nuclear deterrence be less relevant in the Second Nuclear Age? In what respects might it still be relevant?

3. Does the horizontal proliferation of nuclear weapons make nuclear war more likely? If so, why?

4. If many countries acquire ballistic missile defences, how might this affect vertical and horizontal proliferation world-wide?

5. How does the history of the A. Q. Khan network demonstrate the difficulties of controlling horizontal proliferation in the Second Nuclear Age?

6. Is it possible to halt the continuing horizontal proliferation of nuclear weapons? If so, how?

7. If it is not possible to stop the spread of nuclear weapons, is it at least possible to significantly slow the proliferation of these devices? If so, how?

8. How important were the US and Soviet nuclear arsenals in preventing the cold war from becoming a third world war?

9. Is a complete global abolition of nuclear weapons a plausible goal? If so, how might it be achieved?

10. Is it ever appropriate for a state to use military force to prevent a would-be proliferator from obtaining nuclear weapons? If so, under what conditions might it be correct to do so?

 **Further Reading**

F. Barnaby, *How to Build a Nuclear Bomb: And Other Weapons of Mass Destruction* (New York: Nation Books, 2004) explains, using accessible language, how a state or non-state actor might go about building weapons of mass destruction.

P. B. Bracken, *The Second Nuclear Age: Strategy, Danger, and the New Power Politics* (New York: Times Books, 2012) explores the concept of the Second Nuclear Age.

L. Freedman, *The Evolution of Nuclear Strategy*, 3rd edn (New York: Palgrave MacMillan, 2003) prsents a detailed discussion of the historical development of nuclear strategy in a variety of states.

L. Freedman, *Deterrence* (Cambridge: Polity Press, 2004) is a short work that introduces key deterrence concepts and explores how deterrence theory has evolved over time.

W. Langewiesche, *The Atomic Bazaar: The Rise of the Nuclear Poor* (New York: Farrar, Straus and Giroux, 2007) explores a number of issues related to horizontal proliferation, including the A. Q. Khan network and the danger of nuclear terrorism.

D. Miller, *The Cold War: A Military History* (New York: St Martin's Press, 1998) provides a general discussion of how the US and Soviet nuclear arsenals developed during the cold war.

K. B. Payne, *The Great American Gamble: Deterrence Theory and Practice from the Cold War to the Twenty-first Century* (Fairfax, VA: National Institute Press, 2008) explores the development of deterrence theory and how it may be applied today and in the future.

S. D. Sagan and K. N. Waltz, *The Spread of Nuclear Weapons: A Debate Renewed*, 2nd edn (New York: W. W. Norton, 2002) presents a debate between two international relations scholars about how horizontal nuclear proliferation impacts the global security environment.

## Web Links

Alsos Digital Library for Nuclear Issues **http://alsos.wlu.edu** is hosted by Washington and Lee University and is an excellent resource containing annotated descriptions of books, articles, and other materials. It is affiliated with the Nuclear Pathways project.

Federation of American Scientists **http://www.fas.org/nuke** the website of this anti-nuclear group contains regularly updated information about the nuclear arsenals of various countries.

Nuclear Age Peace Foundation **http://www.nuclearfiles.org** is another anti-nuclear group; it maintains the Nuclear Files site. The site contains considerable material concerning nuclear weapons and deterrence.

Nuclear Matters Handbook Expanded Edition **http://www.acq.osd.mil/ncbdp/nm/nm_book_5_11/index.htm** is an online volume maintained by the US Department of Defense as a resource for US government employees working on issues related to nuclear weapons and nuclear power generation.

Nuclear Pathways **http://www.nuclearpathways.org** a project that is part of the US National Science Digital Library, gathers together a variety of information on historical and current nuclear weapons issues.

# The Control of Weapons of Mass Destruction

JOHN BAYLIS

## Chapter Contents

 Reader's Guide

One of the most important questions facing humanity during the nuclear age has been how to control weapons regarded as uniquely abhorrent or particularly destructive. During the cold war, this had an added urgency because the numbers and destructive capacity of such weapons meant that they possessed the unique capability to destroy civilization as we know it. With renewed tensions between the US and Russia and the rise of China, arms control is once again an important topic of international security debates. Is the best way to try to negotiate the elimination of nuclear weapons and other weapons of mass destruction completely? Is a better approach to try, through diplomatic means, to manage these weapons to create as much stability in the international system as possible? Or, should more forceful means be used to prevent the proliferation of these weapons, especially to those 'rogue states' or terrorist organizations, who might be tempted to use them to upset the status quo? These questions and the changing international approach to dealing with weapons of mass destruction are the subject of this chapter.

## Introduction

Establishing controls over weapons or delivery systems is a difficult and painstaking process. Despite this, efforts to eliminate weapons through disarmament have a long history, and at least one writer has traced a lineage back to ancient times (Croft 1996). As an academic subject, however, arms control—the mutually agreed management of military relations—is a more recent arrival. A decade or so after the onset of the cold war in 1947, academic analysis and international policy began to converge, as the prospect of using arms control to stabilize the superpower relationship began to find favour. The hair-raising experience of the Cuban Missile Crisis only served to drive home that the relationship could be dangerously unstable and could not be relied upon to run itself. In a wider context, the lesson of the twentieth century seemed to be that warfare would almost always escalate upwards to the most destructive level, and increasingly it was not only the superpowers that possessed the most destructive technology. The spread of weapons of mass destruction (WMD), a term coined and defined by the United Nations in 1948, therefore became a key concern.

This chapter charts the shift that took place during the cold war from disarmament to arms control, and the shift in relative importance that occurred in the early post-cold war period from arms control to more forcible means to tackle proliferation. The chapter shows how concerns emerged in the 1980s and 1990s about the continuing utility of arms control as an effective means of dealing with weapons of mass destruction and how new ideas began to take shape, first in the Clinton administration, and then in the Bush administration, about more militarily driven approaches, associated with counterproliferation. The chapter ends with a discussion of 'the return to arms control' by the Obama administration and the challenges presented by new geopolitical tensions.

## Arms Control during the Cold War

Following the arms races and the slide to war in the late 1930s, disillusionment with disarmament, as a way to achieve peace and security, characterized official attitudes in the immediate aftermath of the Second World War. The limited attempts at arms control or disarmament that were made by the two emerging superpowers in the new cold war that developed only helped to reinforce the sceptical judgement of the day. Neither side was prepared to take risks with their own security (as they perceived it), especially when it came to weapons which could be a decisive influence in a future conflict. Far from easing the growing tension between the two superpowers in the late 1940s, the modest international control negotiations that were undertaken only exacerbated mistrust and heightened hostility.

By the mid-1950s, the lack of success in disarmament negotiations and growing awareness of the dangers of nuclear war produced a change in approach to arms control. Efforts to negotiate a general and comprehensive disarmament treaty were abandoned in favour of what were known as 'partial measures', such as the 1955 'Open Skies' agreement and negotiations designed to try to ban nuclear testing. Arms control was increasingly viewed as a way to deal with specific problems created by the cold war arms race.

This move towards greater flexibility at the policy level led to what has been described as 'new thinking' within the defence community. Although the ideas that emerged were not as original as the proponents sometimes claimed, a new literature began to appear in the late 1950s developing the theory of arms control (see Box 12.1). These new arms control theorists intended to work within the prevailing system of nuclear deterrence rather than to try to abolish it. Arms control was designed to 'strengthen the operation of the balance of military power against the disruptive effects of the arms dynamic, especially arms competition, arms racing and technological developments that tend to make nuclear and non-nuclear

**BOX** 12.1   Definitions of Arms Control

While the terms 'arms control' and 'disarmament' are sometimes used interchangeably, they reflect very different views about international politics. Hedley Bull, in his book *Control of the Arms Race*, defines disarmament as 'the reduction or abolition of armaments. It may be unilateral or multilateral; general or local; comprehensive or partial; controlled or uncontrolled.' Arms control, on the other hand, according to Bull, involves 'restraint internationally exercised upon armaments policy, whether in respect of the level of armaments, their character, deployment, or use' (Bull 1961:1).

John Spanier and Joseph Nogee in their study of *The Politics of Disarmament* provide a similar, although more specific definition of the differences between arms control and disarmament. In their formulation 'while disarmament refers to the complete abolition or partial reduction of the human and material resources of war, arms control deals with the restraints to be imposed upon the use of nuclear weapons' (Spanier and Nogee 1962: 15).

deterrence more difficult' (Buzan and Herring 1998: 212). Its essential aim was to reduce the likelihood and costs of war and to reduce expenditures on both nuclear and conventional arsenals.

As the superpowers edged back from the nuclear abyss after the Cuban Missile Crisis in October 1962, both realized, more than ever before, that they had a mutual interest in effective crisis management. The crisis highlighted the dangers of inadvertent escalation and miscalculation during periods of military confrontation and intense political instability. In June 1963, the United States and the Soviet Union signed a 'hotline' agreement to provide a secure, official, and dependable channel of communication between Moscow and Washington. The intensity of the crisis also highlighted the issue of nuclear testing. Reflecting the less ambitious agenda of the new arms control school, the United States, Britain, and the Soviet Union agreed on a Partial Test Ban Treaty in August 1963. The treaty prohibited all nuclear tests in the atmosphere, but allowed tests to continue underground. Significantly, neither French nor Chinese officials (who tested nuclear weapons in 1960 and 1964 respectively) were prepared to accede to the treaty because they believed it benefited more advanced nuclear states (see Box 12.2).

Limited as the treaty was, it encouraged further arms control initiatives. Between 1963 and 1968, the superpowers focused on their mutual interest in trying to negotiate a wider agreement to prohibit further nuclear proliferation. This culminated in the Non-Proliferation Treaty (NPT), which was signed in July 1968. Once again, initially, China and France refused to sign, and a number of other states rejected the treaty on the grounds that it froze the nuclear status quo and incorporated only a limited commitment by the nuclear powers to give up their own weapons. This latter criticism became perennial and was to bedevil the NPT process in later years.

The nuclear explosion by India in 1974, ostensibly for peaceful purposes, highlighted the weaknesses of the treaty. Despite this, the treaty provided some limited, but not unimportant benefits. It became the central plank of the nascent non-proliferation regime, which helped restrain the pace of further nuclear proliferation. It also emphasized the opportunities for cooperation between the superpowers during rocky times in their relationship.

By the mid-1970s, the superpowers also recognized their mutual interest in trying to control the use of pathogens and toxins as weapons of mass destruction. The Biological Weapons Convention (BWC), which entered into force in 1975, banned the development, production,

**Box** 12.2   What Are Weapons of Mass Destruction?

In the run-up to the 2003 war in Iraq, the term 'weapons of mass destruction' (WMD) took on a public profile that it had hitherto lacked, and a term that had previously been used largely by specialists (scientists, analysts, government officials, and activists) was now part of political rhetoric. Buzan and Herring define WMD as 'weapons of which small numbers can destroy life and/or inanimate objects on a vast scale very quickly', but note that this could conceivably be applied to weapons (such as fuel-air explosives) that are normally regarded as 'conventional' weapons (Buzan and Herring 1998: 53).

The term does in fact have an internationally accepted definition, one formulated by the United Nations Commission for Conventional Armaments in 1948. This defined WMD as: 'Atomic explosive weapons, radioactive material weapons, lethal chemical and biological weapons, and any weapons developed in the future which have characteristics comparable in destructive effect to those of the atomic bomb or other weapons mentioned above'.

This definition formed the basis for subsequent international agreements on controlling WMD. Nonetheless, the term should be used with more care than is usually the case in political rhetoric, since by its nature it conflates very different forms of weapon. Today, it can be regarded as a blanket term for nuclear and radiological, chemical and biological weapons.

*Nuclear weapons* work by nuclear fission using plutonium or uranium (fission or atom bombs) or by nuclear fusion (thermonuclear or hydrogen bombs). There are seven known nuclear-armed states in the world (Britain, China, France, India, Pakistan, Russia, and the United States). Israel neither acknowledges nor denies it has nuclear weapons but is widely believed to have them. North Korea is believed to possess a small and rudimentary capability, and concern existed in recent years that Iran was developing a nuclear weapons programme.

*Radiological weapons* are sometimes referred to as 'dirty bombs', and would work by surrounding conventional explosive with radioactive material. They do not involve any nuclear explosion, but rather the large-scale dispersal of radioactive toxic materials, thereby inflicting doses of radiation on nearby victims of the explosion. These weapons are widely associated with terrorists and other non-state actors.

*Biological weapons* are bacteria, viruses, or biological toxins that are intentionally disseminated in order to infect or poison individuals, such as troops or civilians. Examples of biological substances used in weapons include anthrax, smallpox, and ricin. Similarly, *chemical weapons* use the toxic effects of chemical substances to cause death, permanent harm, or incapacity to human beings. Examples include phosgene, mustard gas, and VX (nerve agent).

and stockpiling of biological and toxin weapons. It also required states to destroy 'the agents, toxins and weapons equipment and means of delivery in the possession of the parties' to the treaty. The main problem with the Convention, however, was that there was no provision for verification of compliance.

Between 1969 and 1972, the superpowers focused for the first time on the difficult task of limiting strategic armaments. In May 1972, the Strategic Arms Limitation Treaty (SALT) I was signed and covered a number of different areas, including limitations on ballistic missile defence. The aim of SALT I was to 'cap' missile and anti-ballistic missile (ABM) deployments at specific levels to prevent a future unrestricted arms race, which would lead to greater international instability. Despite the unprecedented nature of the agreement it quickly became the subject of criticism, both within the United States and in the arms control community itself. According to domestic critics, it froze the numerical superiority of the Soviet Union while at the same time allowing the Soviet Union to compete in those qualitative areas where the United States was in the lead. This failure to address the all-important qualitative issues (including missile accuracy and the placement of multiple warheads on ballistic missiles) was particularly disappointing even for many arms control supporters, who were concerned that the arms race had simply been moved from a quantitative to a qualitative arena.

Given the shortcomings of SALT I, it was not long before new negotiations began in Geneva. Progress, however, proved to be slow. The SALT II Agreement eventually reached in 1979 followed closely guidelines reached at Vladivostok five years earlier. The ceiling for strategic delivery vehicles was set at 2,400, with sublimits on ballistic missiles armed with Multiple Independently Targetable Re-entry Vehicles (MIRVs) and strategic bombers.

Almost immediately, however, the arms control process was derailed by the Soviet invasion of Afghanistan and in January 1980 President Carter asked the Senate to delay the ratification of the treaty. Although SALT II remained unratified, both the United States and the Soviet Union continued to abide by the limits of the treaty. Despite this tacit agreement, however, the following three years were characterized by frequent accusations by the Reagan administration that the Soviet Union was in breach of the Agreement.

By the end of the cold war, despite the 1987 Intermediate Nuclear Force (INF) Agreement (banning missiles with ranges between 500 and 5,000 kilometres), there was a growing disappointment in many quarters with the overall benefits of arms control. There had been periods of détente when arms control appeared to have played a part in helping to enhance confidence between the adversaries, especially by providing a forum for discussion of strategic thinking, the purposes behind force deployments, and concerns about the opponent's force structure and operations. This happened in the aftermath of the Cuban Missile Crisis and in the early 1970s. However, these periods were short-lived and more hostile relations followed. The effects of arms control were clearly limited and temporary. The critics of arms control felt that there was very little evidence that arms control had helped to improve superpower relations during periods of intense hostility. Indeed, they felt that the evidence seemed to support the view that differences over arms control more often than not exacerbated the problems which existed.

 **Key Points**

- The late 1950s brought 'new thinking' and the development of the theory of arms control.
- The aim of arms control was to make the prevailing system work more effectively.
- The Cuban Missile Crisis ushered in a new 'golden age' of arms control agreements.
- By the late 1970s, however, arms control as an approach to peace and security faced increasing problems.
- There were continuing difficulties in the 1980s, which meant that despite the INF Agreement in 1987 there was a growing feeling that the disadvantages of arms control outweighed the benefits.

## The Residual Role of Arms Control in the Post-Cold War Era

The ending of the cold war brought a flurry of arms control activity and some remarkably far-reaching progress which rebutted some of the criticisms that had been levied against the arms control concept. Following a number of years of detailed negotiation in 1991, a Strategic Arms Reduction Treaty (START I) was finally signed. Instead of merely imposing limits on increases in weapons, START reduced the number of strategic delivery vehicles and warheads in a verified process of drawdown.

With the disintegration of the Soviet Union, President Boris Yeltsin of Russia and President Bill Clinton continued the momentum of the early post-cold war years by signing a START II Treaty in 1993 reducing the number of warheads held by both sides even further. As a result of a Protocol to the START I Treaty signed in May 1992, it had been agreed, however, that START II would only enter into force once START I had been ratified by the United States and Russia and entered into force. This proved difficult due to several factors: increasing Russian concerns about the treaty's costs and strategic effects; the need to resolve a new debate over the ABM treaty before agreeing START II limits; and growing hostility towards North Atlantic Treaty Organization (NATO) expansion plans.

These bilateral difficulties were also evident in a number of other fields. Despite the notable achievement of securing the indefinite extension of the NPT in 1995, significant disagreements continued between the nuclear and non-nuclear states over the pace of nuclear disarmament (enshrined in Article 6 of the Treaty). At the same time, the nuclear tests carried out by India and Pakistan in May 1998 demonstrated the fragility of the non-proliferation norm outside the treaty in certain parts of the world. Similarly, an apparent breakthrough achieved with the Comprehensive Test Ban Treaty (CTBT) in 1996 ground to a halt in late 1999 when the US Senate refused to ratify the treaty (see Box 12.3).

Attempts to control other weapons of mass destruction also ran into difficulties at about the same time. The Chemical Weapons Convention (CWC), signed in 1993, and which entered into force in April 1997, also suffered from a number of serious weaknesses. The Convention was designed to ban the use of chemical weapons, as well as their development, production, transfer, and stockpiling. Stockpiles and production facilities were to be destroyed. Although there was some provision for verification through the OPCW based in The Hague, the wide-spread industrial and commercial production of chemicals made the Convention virtually impossible to police effectively. By 2002, 145 states had ratified both the Biological and Toxins and the Chemical Conventions, but in both cases, there were concerns that a significant number of states were developing weapons covertly.

There were also increasing concerns about the proliferation of nuclear weapons as the new century dawned. Despite the Strategic Offensive Reductions Treaty (SORT) of May 2002 (the Moscow Treaty), further reducing the number of US and Russian warheads to around 2,000 each over the following decade, there appeared to be an increasing incentive for some states and terrorist groups to acquire nuclear weapons and other weapons of mass destruction. With the cold war over, and the United States now the dominant power in the world, those who feared US hegemony or intervention in their internal affairs (like North Korea and possibly Iran) had an interest in developing their own 'ultimate' weapon. After 9/11 there were also concerns that terrorist groups, like al-Qaeda, with nothing to lose, have an interest in acquiring such weapons to further their regional and in some cases global ambitions. As such, the new geostrategic realities of the post-cold war era meant that attempts to control weapons of mass destruction faced new challenges.

By the close of the twentieth century, the picture was therefore a mixed one. Nuclear non-proliferation appeared to have successfully prevented the Kennedy-era fears that the number of nuclear-armed states might exceed 20 by the year 2000, the destruction of chemical weapons was proceeding globally if haltingly, and biological weapons remained,

**BOX** 12.3   International Regimes on WMD

The three key categories of WMD (nuclear, biological, chemical), plus the missile delivery systems usually associated with them, each have an international regime devoted to their control. They are in various stages of development (some might add disarray) and they have not advanced or progressed at an even pace.

The Treaty on the Non-Proliferation of Nuclear Weapons (NPT) entered into force on 5 March 1970 and currently has 189 member states. Only India, Israel, North Korea, and Pakistan remain outside it. The NPT's signatory states are divided into two categories: nuclear weapon states (NWS) and non-nuclear weapon states (NNWS). Under the terms of the treaty the latter agree to forgo nuclear weapons entirely, while the former (the five states, Britain, China, France, Russia, and the United States, that possessed nuclear weapons at the signing of the treaty) are committed to 'pursue negotiations in good faith' on nuclear disarmament. This stipulation, set out in Article 6 of the treaty, has proved recurrently controversial, since none of the five NWS has ever looked likely to move seriously towards such an end.

The other 'devil's bargain' in the NPT is drawn from Article 4, which notes the 'inalienable right' of the NNWS to develop civil nuclear power with the 'fullest possible exchange' of information with the NWS. This exchange of information is subject to various safeguards and inspections conducted by the International Atomic Energy Agency (IAEA—see http://www.iaea.org).

The Chemical Weapons Convention (CWC) is a multilateral treaty banning chemical weapons. It entered into force on 29 April 1997, currently has 164 states parties, and is implemented by the Organization for the Prohibition of Chemical Weapons (OPCW—see http://www.opcw.org). The Convention bans development, acquisition, or possession of chemical weapons by signatories; their use or preparation for use; the transfer of chemical weapons or any encouragement of chemical weapons in other states; and the destruction of chemical weapon stockpiles by signatories. The latter is significant: unlike the NPT, the CWC *compels* states parties possessing the banned weapons to dismantle their stocks, and it sets out clear timetables and deadlines for this work. In cases of non-compliance, the OPCW can recommend that the states parties take punitive action, and in extreme cases can refer the case to the UN Security Council.

The Biological Weapons Convention (BWC) entered into force on 26 March 1975 and currently has 150 states parties. It bans development, stockpiling, acquisition, retention, and production of biological agents and toxins, and all weapons designed to use them. Unlike the CWC, it does not ban the use of such weapons, which is affirmed in the 1925 Geneva Protocol.

for the great majority of states, beyond the pale of normal military arsenals. Nonetheless, the new century's advent was haunted by a growing feeling that as weapons of mass destruction proliferated to weak states and non-state actors, it would be increasingly difficult to bring traditional arms control techniques and principles to bear to address the new emerging threats.

 **Key Points**

- The post-cold war period saw a flurry of arms control agreements.
- Despite the lessening of hostility between the United States and Russia, however, progress was slow and intermittent.
- Increasingly the utility of arms control was perceived to have declined in the changed international environment which emerged after 9/11.

# From Arms Control to Counterproliferation

The United Nations and International Atomic Energy Agency inspectors of Iraqi WMD, after the 1991 Gulf War, found that Iraq had made considerably more progress on developing a nuclear capability than intelligence assessments had supposed. This suggested that proliferation might be moving more quickly than was apparent. The implications of this were far-reaching. Prior to 1990, US intelligence estimated that 20 states in the world possessed chemical weapons and ten were working on biological ones; it now appeared that either this number might be an underestimate, or that those states might be considerably more advanced than anyone had previously suspected. Concerns about hidden horizontal and vertical proliferation were therefore strengthened by the experience with Iraq, which in turn led to louder calls for more tools to tackle this problem.

Thus it appeared that the end of the cold war had spawned a new set of threats that might be smaller in scale, but more numerous and potentially more acute. In such conflicts, nuclear weapons were regarded as being likely to be deployed to deter, but chemical and biological weapons were potentially more likely to be deployed in order to be *used* (Lavoy, Sagan, and Wirtz 2000). The CIA Director James Woolsey put this succinctly when he said: 'it was as if we were struggling with a large dragon for 45 years, killed it, and then found ourselves in a jungle full of poisonous snakes' (Woolsey 1998).

The seriousness with which the threat was taken was due to an uncomfortable awareness that WMD might erode the ability of the United States to project military power around the world. Richard Betts alluded to this when he argued that WMD, particularly nuclear weapons, were now 'weapons of the weak—states or groups that are at best second class' (Betts 1998: 27). General Sundarji of the Indian Army similarly argued that '[o]ne principal lesson of the Gulf War is that, if a state intends to fight the United States, it should avoid doing so until and unless it possesses nuclear weapons'.[1]

Betts and Sundarji were both suggesting that, if Iraq had possessed a nuclear capability in 1991, Operation Desert Storm might never have been possible: the United States and its allies might have been deterred from intervening in Kuwait. Washington's confidence in its ability to resist the deterrent strategies of small hostile states might therefore be significantly eroded once these small states possess nuclear weapons. This may also be true for other NATO members who participated in the coalition, such as Britain, or for important regional allies such as Turkey.

Moreover, this problem was exacerbated by a perception (not one universally shared) that some states, or at least their leaders, are simply not deterrable. This is often raised in the context of the so-called 'rogue states'. Officials and analysts in the United States frequently claim that these states are not susceptible to deterrent-based strategies because their leaders are fanatical (i.e. too wedded to ideological or religious fervour), morally bankrupt (i.e. unlikely to recoil from mass casualties on their own soil), or simply crazy or irrational.

These concerns, centring on the possibility that WMD proliferation might either make it difficult for the United States to win a Gulf War-type conflict at acceptable cost, or deter it from acting at all, were at the heart of the Clinton administration's decision, announced in the Bottom Up Review of 1993, that WMD represented the most direct threat to US security. In December of the same year, US Secretary of Defense Les Aspin unveiled the Defense Counterproliferation Initiative (CPI) in a speech to the National Academy of Sciences.[2]

Aspin noted that the United States and NATO had used nuclear weapons as 'the equalizer' to compensate for Soviet conventional superiority. 'Today,' he continued, 'it is the United States that has unmatched conventional military power, and it is our potential adversaries who may attain nuclear weapons. We're the ones who could wind up being the equalizee.' In Aspin's view, potential US opponents were all at least capable of producing biological and chemical agents so that US commanders now had to assume that US forces were threatened by potential battlefield use of WMD.

The goals of the CPI were subsequently defined as:

1. to deter the acquisition of WMD;

2. to 'reverse WMD programmes diplomatically where proliferation has occurred';

3. to ensure that the US had 'the equipment, intelligence capability, and strategy to deter the threat or use of WMD'; and

4. to defeat an enemy armed with WMD. (Davis 1994: 9)

The goals of 'counterproliferation', however, were considerably better defined than the concept itself, and indeed the term ought to be used carefully, since it is used to mean different things by different people. Harald Müller and Mitchell Reiss noted in 1995 that there were at least four different definitions of exactly what constituted counterproliferation (Müller and Reiss 1995). See Box 12.4 for an explanation of the term and its usage.

---

 **BOX** 12.4   What's in a Name? The Emergence of Counterproliferation

Counterproliferation is defined by Butcher as 'the military component of non-proliferation, in the same way that military strategy is a component of foreign policy' (Butcher 2003: 17). This sounds relatively straightforward, but the term is in fact rather slippery and caution should be exercised when using it.

The term was popularized by Les Aspin's Counterproliferation Initiative (CPI). Several months after his 1993 speech, a National Security Council memo set out a possible definition of counterproliferation:

> [T]he activities of the Department of Defense across the full range of US efforts to combat proliferation, including diplomacy, arms control, export controls, and intelligence collection and analysis, with particular responsibility for assuring US forces and interests can be protected should they confront an adversary armed with WMD or missiles.
>
> Davis (1994: 8)

The Bush administration set out its WMD strategy in a companion document published in December 2002 (White House 2002). The term counterproliferation was given a rather clearer definition than it had hitherto possessed, and for the first time it appeared to be privileged over non-proliferation, of which it had hitherto been viewed as a subset. Counterproliferation was defined as having three key elements: interdiction of WMD transfers to 'hostile states and terrorist organizations'; deterrence of use; and defence. Significantly, the document explicitly states that 'US military forces and appropriate civilian agencies must have the capacity to defend against WMD-armed adversaries, including in appropriate cases through pre-emptive measures'.

The Bush administration's National Security Strategy 2002 appeared to herald a genuine change in this policy. As the administration was attempting to make a case for a pre-emptive/preventive attack on Iraq, its National Security Strategy appeared to generalize from this to make such attacks a part of a wider strategy against proliferation. Within a very short time after publication of the National

**BOX** 12.4  *(continued)*

Security Strategy, the United States had embarked upon the most far-reaching anti-WMD operation ever undertaken. This came with the war against Saddam Hussein's Iraq, undertaken in the face of widespread global suspicion and opposition.

   The following year, the US Joint Chiefs of Staff published a statement of its doctrine on countering WMD (Joint Chiefs of Staff 2004). This defined non-proliferation as actions to 'prevent the proliferation of WMD by dissuading or impeding access to, or distribution of, sensitive technologies' (2004: II.1), and specifically cited arms control and international treaties (especially the regimes and treaties on WMD) in the range of relevant activities. Counterproliferation was defined as military activities taken to defeat the threat or use of WMD, with its objective being to deter, interdict, attack, and defend against the range of WMD acquisition, development and employment situations. The inclusion of acquisition and development as counterproliferation (that is, military) targets is significant.

 **Key Points**

- Strategic responses against WMD proliferation are those involving military means. This is sometimes referred to as 'counterproliferation'.

- Post-cold war interest in such responses is driven by a combination of the emergence of smaller but potentially more immediate threats, and a sense that arms control may be of limited use.

- Concern about proliferation of WMD, particularly nuclear weapons, is significantly driven by a concern that they may be used to deter US-led intervention.

- The 1993 Counterproliferation Initiative was an attempt to develop a coherent strategy to allay those concerns.

- The most far-reaching counterproliferation came in 2003 with the war against Saddam Hussein.

## The Challenges of Counterproliferation

There are several problems and dilemmas associated with military responses to proliferation. The foremost difficulty, as we have seen in Box 12.4, is one of definition: the term 'counterproliferation' can refer to everything from protective clothing for troops to air strikes on nuclear facilities or even regime change. In the latter cases, it requires the surrounding 'political logic' to be more fully developed than is currently the case. Recent documents issued from Washington may suggest an increasing clarity of definitions.

   One possible place to develop this logic is the international regimes on WMD and the UN. The great unanswered question of these global WMD regimes has always been: what happens in cases of non-compliance? Counterproliferation can be seen as a response to this question that grew from the initial response of 'defend yourself from WMD attack' to more robust ways to use military force. In specific cases (e.g. the Israeli attack on Osirak in 1981) it has proven controversial, and has yet to make the transition in 'political logic' from its origins in national military strategy to an accepted international context. In general cases, such as the Proliferation Security Initiative (PSI), it is undeveloped but potentially more consensual.

Another, more difficult problem is the issue of operations in the face of an 'imminent threat'. This would perhaps get around the difficulties of generating institutional agreement in the UN for military operations, but still faces the prospect of assessing exactly what constitutes an 'imminent' threat (officials on both sides of the Atlantic have, since the invasion of Iraq, gone to extraordinary lengths to deny that they ever presented Iraq as an imminent threat).[3] As the authors of a 2005 report noted, the United States (and any state, for that matter) has 'the inherent right and a moral obligation' to take pre-emptive military action in the face of imminent threats, but needs clarification of the standards for 'imminence' (Perkovich et al. 2005: 38).

 **Key Points**

- Finding a 'political' logic into which preventive or pre-emptive action can be fitted has not always been easy.

- Pre-emptive operations tend to find their rationale and legitimacy in the context of an ongoing war, such as the 1991 Gulf War operations.

- Preventive operations find their justifying logic in the international norms surrounding WMD, such as the Proliferation Security Initiative, or in an existing strategic doctrine such as Israel's attack on Osirak in 1981.

## The Diplomatic Option: Military Responses Withheld?

North Korea and Iran in recent years have represented the foremost nuclear proliferation issues. North Korea was an NPT member state that withdrew membership, suspended withdrawal, and subsequently followed through with formal withdrawal. North Korea is commonly believed to possess a small number (6–8 is the largest estimate) of atomic weapons, and in recent years it has been engaged in a number of missile tests. Iran remains an NPT member, but the ongoing crisis over its plans for its nuclear power programme resulted in diplomatic attempts to persuade Tehran to give up what the West believe is an attempt to develop nuclear weapons by stealth.

In the case of North Korea, an operation against the Yongbyon facility was, apparently, seriously considered by the Clinton administration (Sokolski 2001: 96). The plans were not taken up, although one member of the Clinton administration wrote in 2003 that 'Washington still believed it has the option' of attacking Yongbyon, and that 'even if US forces struck after the plant goes hot, radioactive contamination would likely remain local' (Samore 2003: 18). No such plans were reported in the Iranian case, although the Bush administration's mantra was always that this option is emphatically 'not ruled out'. The Obama administration pledged a policy of engagement and 'tough but direct diplomacy', indicating a growing international sense that time was running short to head off a serious Iranian breakout capability.

In these cases, the 'red line', noted by Müller, against attacking facilities that contain nuclear fuel, combined with the political consequences of preventive operations, appears to have kept military action off the agenda. Samore goes on to point out that although the United States could launch a unilateral attack on North Korean nuclear facilities in theory, 'the reaction in Seoul and Tokyo could splinter the alliance' (Samore 2003: 19).

After years of confrontation over Iran's nuclear programme, involving economic sanctions and threats of military action to prevent the development of a nuclear weapons capability (as well as cyber attacks on Iran's nuclear facilities), political changes in Tehran with the election of President Hassan Rouhani led to renewed attempts to find a diplomatic solution. Talks from 2013 between the new Iranian government and the six-country group known as P5+1 (China, France, Russia, the UK, the US, and Germany) led to an agreement in 2015. This involved a promise to ease international sanctions in exchange for Iran drastically scaling back its enrichment of nuclear materials. The limitations were to be verified by the International Atomic Energy Agency (IAEA). For some the agreement was a major success. For others it was 'an historic mistake'. Whether the agreement turns out to be a long lasting example of military responses withheld remains to be seen.

 **Key Points**

- Preventive strategies are directed at the process of proliferation, and aim to snuff out development or acquisition of WMD.

- Pre-emptive strategies are directed at the deployed weapons and/or facilities, and aim to prevent their use in war.

- The dilemma over North Korea and Iran in recent years has been whether to continue with diplomatic initiatives or whether to pursue a preventive or pre-emptive strategy.

## The Return of Arms Control?

Cold war lessons suggest that arms control agreements have had some role to play in contributing to international security. The cold war experience also suggests that arms control is rarely of decisive importance and it is not wise to see them as a way of fundamentally resolving the world's problems. There are 'good' and 'bad' arms control agreements. Arms control, however, has rarely been seen as decisively important or a solution in its own right. On the contrary, it has traditionally been a fundamentally conservative policy, aimed solely at introducing some measure of predictability into an adversarial relationship. It cannot *by itself* create stability, much less peace, and to hope otherwise is to saddle it with unreasonable expectations that are bound to go unfulfilled.

Viewed in that more sober and cautious light, arms control as a means to control weapons of mass destruction should be viewed as a means to an end, never as an end in itself. It relies on the assumption that two or more states that are hostile to one another can also see a mutual interest in avoiding outright conflict. The relative decline in interest in arms control for a number of years after the cold war ended was a function of the fact that the confrontation between the United States and the Soviet Union was over, and the role of arms control was no longer needed to inject some stability or predictability into the conflict itself, but to assist in eliminating what was now surplus military capability. By 2001, it was believed that consolidation of ageing cold war arsenals no longer required formal, verified treaties.

**BOX** 12.5   The Destruction of Syrian Chemical Weapons

Since 2011 Syria has been in a state of civil war. In August 2013 a chemical attack took place in the Damascus suburb of Ghouta which Western governments attributed to the regime of the Syrian President Bashar al-Assad. Following threats by the Obama government of punitive military strikes against Syria, John Kerry, the US Secretary of State, and Sergey Lavrov, the Russian Foreign Minister (a close ally of the Syrian President), negotiated a deal whereby Syria agreed to join the Chemical Weapons Convention (CWC) and destroy its arsenal of chemical weapons. This plan was subsequently endorsed by the OPCW Executive Council and the UN Security Council.

In August 2014, despite some Western concerns that Syria had been 'dragging its feet' on implementing the agreement, President Obama announced that the most dangerous of Syria's chemical weapons had been eliminated aboard the US ship MV Cape Ray. Of the 1,300 metric tons of chemical weapons declared by Syria, 600 metric tons were neutralized aboard MV Cape Ray: 20 metric tons were weapons-usable sulphur mustard and the rest a sarin precursor known as DF. In addition, 130 metric tons of isopropanol had already been destroyed in Syria. Also shortly before the August 2014 announcement, the OPCW came to an agreement with Syria to destroy its 12 remaining chemical weapons facilities.

These agreements represented an important milestone in the destruction of Syria's chemical weapons. In late 2015 it was still too early, however, to conclude that Syria's chemical weapons capability as a whole had been destroyed. There remained doubts in the West that Syria had declared all of its chemical weapons and the OPCW continued to investigate ongoing allegations of further use of chemical weapons by the Syrian government in the civil war.

Although forceful counterproliferation seems likely to remain part of some states' strategy to deal with the proliferation of weapons of mass destruction, criticisms following the war in Iraq led to a renewed interest in the United States and elsewhere in the continuation and updating of arms control arrangements. What emerged was a broader strategy than in the past for controlling weapons of mass destruction. This framework or architecture consisted of attempts to shore up the non-proliferation regime, renewed interest in traditional bilateral and multilateral arms control measures, counterproliferation arrangements, together with what has been described as a 'network of partnership' activities designed to act as 'a web of denial' or a 'toolkit' that can be used against those states and non-state actors intent on pro-liferating weapons of mass destruction (Bernstein 2008). These latter activities included: the Proliferation Security Initiative (PSI); UN Resolutions 1540 and 1887; the Global Initiative to Combat Nuclear Terrorism; the Global Nuclear Energy Partnership; the Cooperative Threat Reduction Programme; and the April 2010 Nuclear Security Summit.

There was also a rise of what some have called 'the New Abolitionists'. In the *Wall Street Journal* in January 2008, George Shultz, William Perry, Henry Kissinger, and Sam Nunn called for new urgent action to reverse the continuing reliance on nuclear weapons globally in order to prevent their further proliferation 'into potentially dangerous hands'. The world, they said, was on 'the precipice of a new and dangerous nuclear era'. In particular, Shultz and his col-leagues urged action on bringing into force the Comprehensive Test Ban Treaty, a Fissile Material Cut-off Treaty, as well as further cuts in the offensive strategic capabilities of both the United States and Russia. These measures were needed, they argued, to shore up the Non-Proliferation Treaty which was in 'a precarious position'. These views were supported by

**BOX** 12.6   A World Without Nuclear Weapons

Today, the cold war has disappeared but thousands of those weapons have not. In a strange turn of history, the threat of global nuclear war has gone down, but the risk of a nuclear attack has gone up. More nations have acquired these weapons. Testing has continued. Some argue that the spread of these weapons cannot be checked—that we are destined to live in a world where more nations and more people possess the ultimate tools of destruction. This fatalism is a deadly adversary. For if we believe that the spread of nuclear weapons is inevitable, then we are admitting to ourselves that the use of nuclear weapons is inevitable. So today, I state clearly and with conviction America's commitment to seek the peace and security of the world without nuclear weapons. This goal will not be reached quickly—perhaps not in my lifetime. It will take patience and persistence. But now we, too, must ignore the voices who tell us that the world cannot change.

President Obama (Prague Castle, 5 April 2009)

four former British foreign and defence secretaries (Rifkind, Owen, Robertson, and Hurd) in an article in *The Times* on 30 June 2008 (Hurd et al. 2008). They argued for a new initiative to achieve progress on multilateral arms control and disarmament. In their view 'the ultimate aspiration should be to have a world free of nuclear weapons'. Even though this would take time, they argued that, with the necessary 'political will and improvements in monitoring the goal is achievable'. For such hard-headed individuals on both sides of the Atlantic to be supporting a new phase of arms reductions, leading possibly to complete nuclear disarmament, is of some significance. Even more significant, in a speech in Prague in April 2009, President Obama also indicated his support for a 'zero option' (see Box 12.6). The achievement of a nuclear-free world, as President Obama indicated, would be likely to take a long time, and remained very problematical. It would certainly require much more far-reaching arms control efforts but also more effective measures to achieve conflict resolution than presently existed.

Whether traditional arms control can re-emerge as a significant and sustained approach to international security and play an important role in the control of weapons of mass destruction in the future remains unclear at the time of writing. There are some reasons for optimism but also some important challenges (see Box 12.5). The NEW START Treaty in April 2010 between the US and Russia agreed to a limit of 700 missiles, 1,550 strategic warheads, and 800 launchers on either side by 2018. This represented a 30 per cent reduction from the levels agreed in the 2002 Moscow Treaty. Both sides also agreed to continue negotiations to deal with stored and non-strategic weapons. The 2010 US Nuclear Posture Review also argued for the reduction in the role of nuclear weapons in US security policy. The 2015 Agreement with Iran, if it holds, also represents an important success for the arms control agenda.

This attempt to reduce the saliency of nuclear weapons and to breathe new life into the arms control process, however, faces major contemporary challenges. Most important was the deterioration in the relationship between the United States (and Western countries) and Russia in 2014 over the Ukraine and latter's annexation of the Crimea. This resulted in Western sanctions and new NATO deployments in Eastern Europe. It was also claimed that through its actions Russia had violated the security assurances contained in the 1994 Budapest Memorandum (and thereby undermined non-proliferation efforts) and also that it was in breach of the 1987 INF Treaty which helped to bring the cold war to an end. These charges were denied by the Russian government. Both governments began a process of significant improvements in their nuclear capabilities and in late 2014 there were reports that Russia was scaling back its cooperation with the US in securing nuclear materials on Russian territory (*The Times*, 15 November 2014). The seriousness of the crisis raised doubts about the whole basis of future arms control arrangements between the two countries.

Apart from difficulties in the US–Russia strategic relationship, there are also ongoing problems with other arms control arrangements. The North Korean pursuit of nuclear weapons continues and at the time of writing no lasting agreement has been reached between the P5 + 1 and Iran. The CTBT Treaty remains some way from ratification and little progress has been made in recent years in negotiating the Fissile Materials Cut-off Treaty (FMCT). At the same time, there are continuing concerns about the need to bring India, Pakistan, and Israel into the Non-Proliferation regime, as well as the need to secure regional arms control arrangements in conflict-ridden areas like the Middle East. Dual use and new technologies, especially nanotechnologies, also continue to pose particularly hard problems for non-proliferation arrangements.

 **Key Points**

- Arms control should be seen as a means to an end, not an end in itself, and it depends upon mutual interests.

- Criticisms of counterproliferation following the Iraq war led to renewed interest in arms control, more broadly defined.

- Recent years have seen a rise of what have been called the 'New Abolitionists', who argue for new arms control initiatives as a result of new proliferation dangers and terrorist threats.

- The new Obama administration attempted to reduce the importance of nuclear weapons through supporting a 'return to arms control', leading to new nuclear arms control agreements. This initiative, however, was threatened by a deterioration in US–Russian relations over events in the Ukraine.

 **Critical Thinking**    'Does arms control contribute significantly to increased international security?'

**For**

- *Arms control helped prevent conflict in the cold war.* The fact that the cold war did not turn 'hot' provides evidence that arms control agreements reached, especially after the Cuban Missile Crisis, helped prevent the outbreak of war between the superpowers. The Hot Line Agreement, the Partial Test Ban Treaty, the Non-Proliferation Treaty, and the SALT I and SALT II Treaties all contributed to a recognition that the superpowers had vital mutual interests in avoiding nuclear war.

- *Arms agreements contributed to ending the cold war.* Agreements such as the Stockholm Accords of 1986 and the Intermediate Nuclear Force (INF) Agreement of 1987 played an essential part in building confidence between East and West, creating the necessary trust to reduce hostility.

- *Arms control can mitigate arms races.* Constant rapid technological changes and mutual suspicions inherent in a system of international anarchy help to encourage arms competition, which in turn poses dangers to international security. By addressing the instabilities of the military balance of power, arms control significantly contributes to the absence of great power conflict.

**Critical Thinking** *(continued)*

- *Grounds for optimism exist despite contemporary tensions.* Despite contemporary tensions between the US and Russia, Rose Gottemoeller, Acting Secretary of Arms Control and International Security in the US, declared in February 2014: 'Over the past few years, we have achieved significant results in cooperation with the Russians. This includes Russian support of Security Council resolutions that created the toughest sanctions ever on North Korea and Iran, our work together on eliminating Syria's chemical weapons, our continuing successful implementation of the New Start Treaty, and the completion of the 1993 US-Russian Federation Highly Enriched Uranium (HEU) Purchase Agreement' (US Department of State, 2014). Such statements reflect continuing mutual interests despite the differences between the two countries.

## Against

- *Few real restraints existed in the cold war.* Arms control had little or no impact on the prevention of war between 1945 and 1990. Nuclear testing continued, despite the partial Test Ban Treaty; proliferation was not prevented by the Non-proliferation Treaty; quantitative and qualitative improvements in strategic armaments continued in spite of the SALT I and II Treaties; and the MBFR Treaty failed to achieve conventional arms limitation.

- *Arms control did little to help end the cold war.* The end of the cold war was largely the result of political changes, especially in the Soviet Union, where Gorbachev recognised the crippling economic costs of the continuing arms competition with the United States.

- *Cosmetic arms control.* Where agreements were reached in the cold war, the states concerned merely agreed not to do those things they did not wish to do anyway.

- *Contemporary tensions.* Russian action in the Ukraine, especially its annexation of the Crimea, and Western responses, have had a detrimental impact on existing arms control arrangements. It remains the case that 'arms control is possible when it is unnecessary, and impossible when it is needed' (Gray 1992).

 **Conclusion**

Overall, there appears to be no single approach, whether it be disarmament, arms control, or counterproliferation, which provides an easy and sustainable solution to the problem of controlling weapons of mass destruction. The vision of a world free of such weapons should not be dismissed and nor should forceful counterproliferation be discounted in certain extreme situations. Both, however, raise serious problems. Arms control, both traditional treaties and new partnership arrangements, is not a panacea. The new initiatives introduced by the Obama administration in 2009 and 2010 aimed to re-invigorate the arms control process and were welcomed by many observers as an important contribution to global security. There was, at the time, a growing consensus that, despite their imperfections, arms control arrangements, more widely and consistently applied and more dependably verified and policed, could yield important benefits. Specifically, they could help to provide preventive barriers, greater assurance, and trust between states, which is essential in dealing with the critical political issues that cause states to arm themselves, as well as the contemporary dangers of terrorist groups using weapons of mass destruction. The 2015 Agreement with Iran would appear to support this view. Major geopolitical changes in recent years and the contemporary tensions in US–Russian relationship, however, seem to challenge this optimism. It remains to be seen whether the 'return to arms control' can be sustained in a new era of great power suspicion and rivalry.

 ## Questions

1. What are the differences between disarmament and arms control?
2. Which was the most important arms control agreement in the cold war?
3. What were the key criticisms of arms control by the end of the cold war?
4. How useful has arms control been in helping to preserve peace and security in the post-cold war period?
5. Is arms control compatible with counterproliferation?
6. Account for the growing interest in strategic military responses to proliferation.
7. Is traditional arms control coming back?
8. Is it possible to talk about a 'New Arms Control' and, if so, what does this mean?
9. What are the contemporary difficulties facing arms control?
10. What issues arise for strategists with low numbers of nuclear weapons?

 ## Further Reading

I. Anthony and A. D. Rotfeld (eds), *A Future Arms Control Agenda* (Oxford: Oxford University Press, 2001) provides an analysis of post-cold war thinking on arms control.

H. Bull, *The Control of the Arms Race* (London: Weidenfeld and Nicolson, 1961) is a classic study that developed the first modern concept of arms control.

I. Daalder and T. Terry (eds), *Rethinking the Unthinkable: New Directions in Nuclear Arms Control* (London: Frank Cass, 1993) is a useful volume on thinking about arms control shortly after the cold war ended.

S. Feldman, 'The Bombing of Osiraq—Revisited', *International Security* 7(2) (Autumn 1982): 114–42 is a useful source on the Israeli attack on Osiraq in 1981.

C. S. Gray, *House of Cards: Why Arms Control Must Fail* (Ithaca, NJ: Cornell University Press, 1992) provides an interesting and controversial critique of the utility of arms control.

E. Herring (ed.), *Preventing the Use of Weapons of Mass Destruction* (London: Frank Cass, 2000). This study explores the options for preventing use, rather than simply spread, of WMD.

J. A. Larsen and J. J. Wirtz (ed.), *Arms Control and Cooperative Security* (London: Lynne Rienner, 2009) contains some interesting articles on the relationship between arms control and its contribution to cooperative security.

H. Müller, D. Fisher, and W. Kötter, *Nuclear Non-Proliferation and Global Order* (New York: Oxford University Press, 1994) examines the relationship between non-proliferation and issues relating to international order.

T. Schelling and M. Halperin, *Strategy and Arms Control* (Washington, DC: Pergamon-Brassey's, 1985) is a classical study that helped to develop the concept of arms control.

William Walker, *A Perpetual Menace: Nuclear Weapons and International Order* (London: Routledge, 2011) provides an excellent analysis of the history of nuclear weapons and how they have affected international order.

## Web Links

The Acronym Institute for Disarmament Diplomacy **http://www.acronym.org.uk** provides a useful, and often critical, view of Western arms control policies.

The Defense Threat Reduction Agency **http://www.dtra.mil** covers the various approaches adopted by the US to reduce the threats to its national security.

Arms Control Association **http://www.armscontrol.org** gives information on a wide range of issues relating to arms control.

Center for Nonproliferation Studies, Monterey **http://cns.miis.edu** provides information on the activities and research undertaken by the Center.

# 13 Conventional Power and Contemporary Warfare

JOHN FERRIS

## Chapter Contents

 Reader's Guide

This chapter assesses conventional power today. It analyses how, and how far, conventional forces shape the contemporary world, whether by fighting wars or by backing policy in peace. This chapter examines how they function in areas ranging from distant strike to urban warfare, and compares their role to that of other forms of force, like weapons of mass destruction (WMDs) and terrorism. It ends by discussing the conventional strength of states in the world, and trends in its development and distribution.

## Introduction: Power and War—A History

In romance, war is like this. States fight, therefore armies enter *decisive battle*. One wins, the other loses, the victor gains, immediately, and both return to their seats. Sometimes war is like a waltz, but mostly not. Often, it is long and destructive, costing both sides more than they gain. Even victors suffer unintended damage. Battles are inconclusive, or victories have no value. Enemies refuse to surrender, or recover from defeat and force you to fight again. They reject your rules, evade your strengths, attack your weaknesses, and impose their will on you. Intentions and effects become confused. Paradox rules. Politicians imagine armies are military scalpels for political surgery, but in war, one operates with a battleaxe and without a medical licence on a patient who is trying to amputate your arm, in the dark.

This chapter examines the present and emerging state of conventional military power, including its distribution, what it can and cannot do, what is changing and what is not. One cannot understand these trends only by considering the record of conventional war. Nor can one look just at the states that most often fight them, or have the best weapons. Third-rate powers shape conventional war as much as advanced ones. All do so by their weaknesses as well as their strengths.

Refined power yields armed forces, which are usually small in size and costly to maintain. In the past, states have regularly fielded hundreds of thousands of soldiers (for example, in China between 453 and 221 BCE or Europe between 1660 and 1870 ACE)—and millions in the twentieth century. Yet these periods are unusual, because armies erode the wealth of nations and the power of states. In classical Greece, armies were usually fewer than 15,000 men, rarely 50,000; so too European empires of the nineteenth century. Since 1989, armies have again slipped in size. The greatest power on earth can barely send 100,000 soldiers on one expedition beyond its borders. Navies have been even smaller, because they are a rich state's weapon, dependent on industry and wealth. Expensive to build and maintain, fleets vanish without a regular programme of shipbuilding. Navies usually die in the dockyard, not battle. Few states maintain large navies for long; and those that do command the seas as armies rarely do the land. Sea power is the child of wealth and resolve; so too, air power. Military power has social roots, many forms, and a competitive nature—your system compared to the enemy's in specific circumstances. The edge of the razor is comparative advantage, your strengths, and ability to force them on the enemy. Numbers and technology matter, but not enough to win every time. A belligerent able to take heavy losses without surrendering beats one with high technology and low willpower. Able armies with no material edge whip larger enemies. Politics and willpower defeat firepower and technology, or vice versa. Small elite forces crush half-trained hosts, or not. It depends on the circumstances (see Box 13.1).

 **BOX** 13.1 The Intricacies of Power

Power is an alloy, formed from the interaction of material factors (geography, demography, and economy) and the administrative capacity and political structure of a state—its ability to command a people and tap these resources. The first group defines the potential power of a state, the second how much can be tapped. Their relationship converts material power from crude to finished form—from resources to forces. Overwhelming strength in one element may not a great power make, nor weakness in one destroy it. A poor country may remain a great power because its forces are large, its geopolitical position favourable, its institutions stable, and its statesmen able; thus, Prussia, 1740–1866. A rich country may not convert its wealth to power, and so will matter less in world affairs than is possible, viz., Japan and most European states since 1960. Rich states rarely tap their resources systematically for strategic purpose. That bolsters the position of anyone willing to do so, rich or not. In power, resolve outweighs wealth. Power is a concrete quality; the resources a state taps for strategic purposes, as against those it might, but does not. It takes different forms in diplomacy, a short campaign between two countries, or a prolonged and total war of attrition involving a state system. Usually, institutions are the main factor in power, because they turn raw into refined strength—a hard task, dominated by marginal superiority. For most of history, a state able to jump from tapping 1 per cent of its potential power to 2 per cent might so double its military capacity. The edge provided by institutions dulled from 1870 because, ironically, they became more effective, numerous, and common. Advanced states adopted many systems (conscript armies, General Staffs, central banks) which better turned wealth into power. Brute demographic and industrial strength was the key predictor of power in the First and Second World Wars. The value of institutional superiority rose again after 1945, at least for developing states. Israel's battlefield success stems from the fact that it possesses techniques like conscription and a quickly mobilized reserve while its neighbours do not.

Until 1945, the greatest form of military power was conventional force. It was the weapon of choice for the strong, particularly useful against the weak, common between neighbours. It could inflict more precise and powerful damage than irregular forces and keep battle from one's home, yet it had limits. Sometimes conventional war is unavoidable or an effective way to achieve ends. Merely to avoid defeat is good. More is possible if one is strong and smart, or the enemy weak and foolish—preferably both at once. Yet, as in any competition, the use of conventional force has unpredictable outcomes. Decisive battles are like strikes of lightning—they happen rarely. The greatest of world powers emerged through long runs of decisive victories over many enemies—Romans, Arabs, Mongols, British. These circumstances are significant, but not common. The classic example of a decisive battle is Cannae in 216 BCE—yet its victor lost that war. The average outcome of war is attrition, slow and costly to both sides. Conventional war is like gambling. All that is sure is an entry cost, and some combination of risk and gain. Some people love the risk, forget the odds, and think the pay-off certain; others fear to play; skill matters, and the strength of your hand; so does chance.

## New World Orders: 1945, 1989, 2001

Between 1815 and 1945, Western military systems beat all others at once. Europeans conquered the earth, and then destroyed each other. From the wreck emerged a new *world order*, defined by decolonization, the cold war, and nuclear weapons. The industrialized states were divided between two alliances, unequal in economics but balanced in destructive capability. They waged the greatest arms races ever known, with conventional and nuclear, chemical, and bacteriological WMDs. A war between them carried the risk of suicide. This made conventional strength just one part of power, imposed an upper limit on *the rationality of force*, and reshaped world politics. The industrialized states possessed more power than in 1939, but their influence declined. Decolonization was the primary political force; the cold war was a local phenomenon of the industrialized world. The European empires shattered, breaking the world into bits. Power had to be gained in each region. Success in one did not determine events in another. The USSR and the United States dominated the industrialized world, but neither picked up the pieces of imperialism. They simply established ties with regional successor states, some of which became stronger than most advanced countries.

Since 1945, the major industrialized states have not fought each other nor, excepting the guerrilla wars which accompanied decolonization and interventions against Islamic insurgents or for liberal humanitarianism after 1990, many other countries at all. War has rarely been fought by the strong nor practised at the state of the art. The core of world power was not the centre of world war. That was Asia and Africa, where most states lacked the economic or administrative abilities to fight total wars or to win quick and cheap victories. Most of these conflicts stemmed from the end of imperialism, whether wars of national liberation to overthrow it or of succession between new states, striving to determine strength, status, and frontiers. They ended by 1975. Wars in Africa were prolonged, indecisive, and destructive, because neither side could tap its resources well for military purposes. In Asia, some conventional wars were long and costly, but usually both sides halted long before their resources were exhausted. Asian regimes pursued limited aims with limited means. Conventional war was an important, but uncommon, aspect of international affairs. In these Third World wars, many states had modern weapons but few used them well. There was no dominant style of war because no one set of military conditions ruled. The relationship between victory on the battlefield and at the peace table was complex. Rarely did force achieve great aims, or precise ones.

In 1989, with the collapse of the Soviet bloc and Russian capabilities, the distribution of power in the world altered again, as did its nature. Western states, overwhelmingly superior in military technology, cut their forces and spending by 25 per cent, and assumed they could master the new world order. They were misinformed. The end of the cold war prompted the collapse of several states and another wave of wars of succession. In most of Asia, strong non-Western states became more powerful, continuing to dominate their regions and acquire WMDs. Arab powers slipped in status, because they no could longer gain free weapons from superpowers. In the Middle East, the United States used force for *realpolitik*, crippling Iraq and checking Iran. Otherwise, power became decoupled from policy. When Western states used their power, they did so in an odd way. Their peoples, reluctant to fight except for vital interests, sometimes wished one foreign party would cease to bully another and deployed token forces to achieve that end. They pursued international acts of charity through multilateral military means, driven not by reasons of state but public opinion, aiming not to defeat a foe but to do good and no bad. Such ends were hard to achieve or to pursue. Outrage did not make bullies mend their ways. The West found it hard to help the weak, or to prevent ethnic cleansing and mass murder in Rwanda or Bosnia.

Then, on 11 September 2001, al-Qaeda launched an act of 'propaganda by the deed', to rally Muslims against the United States. This attack tied together every level of force, from terrorism to WMDs, and plugged power back into politics. Rich states, fearing for their security, took hard actions. The United States ceased to swing between isolationism and internationalism. It bolstered its conventional power, declared policies of unilateralism and pre-emptive attack against anything it deemed a threat, and occupied Afghanistan and Iraq. The lonely hyperpower, pillar of the world order, was wounded. It pursued absolute security, which many states saw as a threat to themselves. It used all types of power to reshape all forms of politics everywhere in the world, at once. This affected the distribution of power, and its use.

 **Key Points**

- Several forms of a unified world political system have existed since 1800. Conventional force played a different role in each one.
- Conventional power was used frequently between 1815 and 1945. Military superiority underwrote European imperialism.
- After 1945, major states rarely used conventional force against each other, but did so more often against weaker states, which fought each other frequently.
- Since 1945, the power of conventional force has been limited by WMDs, and guerrilla warfare.

## Power and Hyperpower

If riches made strength, Europe would be the greatest power on earth, the United States second, and Japan and China tied for third, all close together; but the issue is the marriage of will and wealth. One may divide conventional military powers into four groups: *the United States, advanced states* (industrialized, capitalist, mostly liberal-democratic, ranging in size from Singapore to Germany), *developing powers* (with small-to-large industrial bases, and mostly authoritarian governments, like China, India, Russia, and Turkey) and *weak states* (most of those in Africa, and some in Asia). Weak states have little offensive power; their strength is the difficulty of occupation. Any rich country can speedily increase its conventional forces, and so change the distribution of strength in the world or its regions, but their ratio of will to power varies. Most European states have little power to project, and less will. Characteristic-ally, between 2001 and 2012, those with forces in Afghanistan usually forbade them to fight. They are unlikely to be attacked by conventional force or to fight each other, though Russia is a threat. With out-of-area capabilities small, they are most likely to use force against the weakest states, in humanitarian interventions. Britain and France can launch expeditionary forces, barely. Advanced states in Asia, like Singapore and Japan, maintain powerful defen-sive capabilities. Conventional power matters more to Israel than any other nation on earth, except North Korea. Many developing states tap far more of their resources for forces, and are far stronger in their own regions, than any rich country except Israel, South Korea, and the United States. Russia and China remain the world's second-strongest conventional powers, while others have large forces and some offensive capability. Russia's economy is fragile, how-ever, whereas China combines dynamic military and industrial strength. All these states stand well behind the state of the art, and are cautious about using such forces. Russia's experiences against Georgia in 2009 and Ukraine in 2014–2015, and those of Britain and France against Libya during 2011, show that even major powers cannot easily defeat fourth-rate foes.

Americans have a taste for, and the infrastructure to exercise, power across the world. Their post-9/11 expansion in military spending has stalled, but at far higher levels than in 2000. No other state has had the absolute and relative conventional power the United States possessed in 2015. Overwhelming strength at sea and in air, strike, and space dissuades any head-on challenges in these key areas. The United States has more aircraft carriers than the rest of the world combined, able to launch ten times as many aircraft. The American air force, the only one with the most advanced equipment, like stealth technology, matches the power of every other one on earth put together. This capacity underwrites Pax Americana just as sea power did Pax Britannica. It augments nuclear power as a means to deter attack and sustains the United States' loose leadership over all advanced countries, the structure through which Washington exerts political influence. This creates a key phenomenon in contemporary poli-tics, that rich states will not fight each other and often will cooperate. Yet these edges are of limited value in land combat—indeed, the cost needed to develop them weakens American power in that sphere. Its relative advantage lies in distant strike, compellence, deterrence, and dissuasion, and its weakness in close-quarter combat and occupation. The United States could smash the air and naval power of almost any developing country, but can occupy few of them. Threats of force serve Washington more than its use. These are just some of the para-doxes of conventional power in the contemporary world.

**Key Points**

- Overwhelming conventional power, along with nuclear weapons, make the United States the world leader. This strength supports dissuasion better than war.
- Many rich states have powerful conventional forces at home. Few have expeditionary capabilities.
- Some developing powers have powerful conventional forces at home. None can project it far from their borders.
- Most states have weak conventional forces.

## Military Affairs: Revolution and Counter-Revolution

Between 1989 and 2006, American military policy was driven by efforts to ride a Revolution in Military Affairs (RMA). Armed forces would act without friction on near-perfect knowledge, through the fusion of precision guided munitions (PGMs), information technology, and command, control, communications, computers, intelligence, surveillance, and reconnaissance (C4ISR). Conventional force would have more power as a tool of state and the leading powers greater superiority in it, than ever since Omdurman, the heyday of European imperialism.

These ideas were tested in recent conflicts, in Kosovo during 1999, and in Afghanistan, Gaza, and Iraq between 2001–2014. In these cases, the conversion of military to political success proved hard, but Western forces coordinated command and intelligence with unprecedented skill. This multiplied the strength of all forms of centralized firepower and rapid, precise, and long-distance weapons. These leaps in quality, and in the quantity of aircraft and PGMs, enabled strike forces to matter far more than ever before, equalling armies in land warfare.

Yet victory did not flow straight, or simply, from the RMA. Classic problems of information overload and friction between headquarters and inexperienced personnel swamped commands. Command and intelligence were no better than in 1944–1945, but the enemy was worse. Distant strike succeeded only when the machine performed without friction. Any friction yielded failure; no system is always perfect. Close-quarter battle shaped land war as much as distant strike, and mattered far more against guerrillas. These campaigns showed that Western powers cannot easily defeat any enemy with competent leadership, a decent army, and fair public consent. Nor are Americans the only people who can learn lessons.

These tests show the limits to ideas about *transformed forces*. They posit a world without strategy, a one-dimensional and one-sided struggle. The United States always plays to its strengths, and need never defend its weaknesses. High-technology forces assault weak enemies, without initiative. They play to your strengths. A fine-tuned, high-performance machine works perfectly, without any effort being made to hamper its effect. It is convenient when an enemy chooses to be foolish and weak, but that is its choice, not yours.

A smart but weak foe refuses any game where you can apply your strengths, and makes you play another. A tough and able foe turns the characteristics of your game into a strength of its own, by attacking any precondition for your machine to work and imposing its rules on you. By doing what suits them, they change their strengths and weaknesses—and yours.

The idea of an RMA was oversold, but has some value. In assessing power for air and sea, C4ISR matters as much as hardware. An air force with better C4ISR matches one with far more aircraft. The RMA did many things, but not everything. It has *multiplied American strengths, but not reduced its weaknesses*. The RMA increased the value of high technology and firepower in conventional war, but little else; where these things matter, they do more than ever; where they do not, nothing has changed. Its advocates assume that conventional power has grown steadily more powerful, and everything else weaker, that the RMA has universal force across all arms, instead of strength in some and weakness in others. Their arguments look at only one development, instead of the reciprocal relationship between several of them. The revolution is advancing; so is the counter-revolution.

Thus, strike weapons enable a new version of gunboat diplomacy, letting one destroy targets from a distance, so as to make a political point. They enable conventional forces to hit harder, further and more accurately than ever before; they reshape operations at sea and in the air, and what one can do with them; but that is not all of war, nor is it new. Technology enables transformation; that it has transformed the power of aircraft more than that of armies is suggestive. In land warfare, command and intelligence have never worked as they do at sea or in the air.

Perhaps conventional forces are midway through a decades-long transition from one set of forms—armies, navies, and air forces—to another, close-quarters land forces, navies, strike weapons, and space power. If so, some services may not survive as they are. If no aircraft have pilots, air forces and artillery might merge, and dominate blue water, where no large surface warships can survive the hostility of the United States. However, this transition is far from over and it will affect armies least—perhaps not much at all. No recent piece of technology except the atom bomb or nerve gas has changed land warfare so greatly as did bayonets, machine guns, tanks, or aircraft. Land warfare will continue to involve an equal and overlapping combination of close quarters and distant firepower, as it has done since 1940—or 1916.

At one and the same time, the strike capacity of advanced states has risen as has the power of terrorists against them, while nothing has changed in close-quarter combat or guerrilla warfare. Nor can any one master all these domains at once.

 **Key Points**

- Conventional forces take many forms. Their strength is hard to compare.
- High-technology forces can strike blows of unprecedented precision and weight, which has transformed sea power, air power, and all forms of distant strike.
- The power of armies has not been transformed for close-quarter combat, or against guerrillas.

# Arts of War

Armies cannot evade economics. To buy one thing is not to buy another. One maintains large standing forces only by reducing the procurement of new equipment, and vice versa. The entry cost for the RMA is high; to pay it incurs opportunity costs. This situation forces choices on all states, with a mixture of costs and benefits. The United States will lead in transformed forces, at cost in other areas, because it cares about them while no one else can keep up. Even its military budget, equal to almost every other state on earth, has limits. So to make anyone else think twice about competition, the United States will keep the entry cost to the RMA high. This will hamper its friends as well as its enemies. Nor is the new American way of war a model for everyone. In transformed power, the United States is a giant and everyone else a dwarf. Transformation gives no one else quite the same bang for a buck. It will be less cost-efficient for weak than for strong states. Its pressure on defence budgets reinforces the tendencies toward demilitarization in Europe, while complicating life for all other advanced powers. The RMA will give them the edge over enemies which cannot adopt such innovations, but not revolutionary ones. Israel does not need transformation to master Arab armies. It will not silence North Korean artillery in range of Seoul.

Comparative advantage takes many forms. The United States owns sea power, air power, and strike, with everything that that promises. Even forcing enemies to asymmetry has advantages, as unconventional means often solve problems worse than conventional ones. Between 1914 and 1945, surface fleets let one use the sea, while submarines merely limited one's power to do so. Of course asymmetry can be more successful. Air defence systems cheaply cripple the power of aircraft. Asymmetric means are unlikely to wreck (as compared to degrade) American strengths in the air or blue water, but the story is different on land. American choices for transformation will leave its enemies strong cards to play. Between 1870 and 1989, the standard form of armies was large conscript forces, able to deliver and absorb heavy punishment. Given their costs in money and skilled personnel, transformed armies will be smaller services, with unprecedented reliance on firepower and technology. Like eggshells armed with hammers, they can inflict damage, but not take it; closer to the model of artillery than infantry. When they are good they will be very good. They will be better than ever at anything dominated by firepower, but worse at anything else. They cannot take losses; they cannot easily deploy their strengths or shield their weaknesses in close-quarters combat. Once, an army able to defeat an enemy was big enough to occupy it—now, one can easily be powerful enough to crush a foe but too small to hold its territory. Western regular forces in Iraq and Afghanistan relied heavily on their reserves and mercenaries to function. Nor do Special Forces change this equation. These units are useful, but not new, essentially equalling the light infantry or cavalry maintained by states over past centuries, their mobility multiplied by air power.

Again, until 1945, nothing limited the upper edge of force except one's ability to get there. If one could annihilate an enemy, one did. No longer is that true, because of the mixture of images, ethics, and opinion aroused by modern media. A desire to minimize the deaths of enemy civilians, even of soldiers, complicates the use of power by Western states, as one tries to avoid overstepping the upper level of permissible force. Legal advisors serve on military staffs, to ensure that international law shapes the selection of targets to strike. Because they are the safest means to navigate near the tolerated limits on force, precision and control are the fundamental gains from transformation, while the most obvious use of PGMs is to assassinate individuals in irregular warfare. These gloves would come off if any people thought its vital interests were at stake—then conventional weapons could wreak mass destruction, to the surprise of the unwary instigator. Russia and China might do so from the start. Terrorists drive their devastation into levels once occupied by conventional forces, because images of ruthlessness and power play to their home demographic.

Developing states will maintain large forces for close-quarter combat. One lesson from recent wars is the difference a decent army and second-rate kit make. This is not a new lesson. Over the past century, developing states like Turkey, Vietnam, and Japan have created armies able to inflict heavy punishment while absorbing even more, making willpower a decisive factor and often beating richer but less resolute enemies. In ground war, defenders will be most strong and attackers least so, home field advantage will matter, and Western armies must handle cities. Urban combat divides the value of training, technology, and firepower and multiplies that of morale and the ability to take losses. Civilian casualties and relief efforts shape victory as much as tactics. Western forces will not enter urban warfare unless every other option is exhausted. Urban warfare and the price of occupation are the functional equivalents of WMDs for weak states. They will deter attack.

Developing countries will also aim to negate high-technology forces through asymmetric strategies. Any able enemy at war with the United States will jam any communications on the electromagnetic spectrum. This would damage American power far more than their own, and perhaps stall its entire war machinery. The final *asymmetric* response of enemies to American conventional power will be to pick up its pieces and go home—to WMDs or terrorism.

 **Key Points**

- The RMA will help the United States more than any other country.
- Transformed fighting services have weaknesses and strengths.
- When they can play to their strengths, they will succeed.
- Rational foes play to their strengths and their enemies' weaknesses. Developing countries may trump the RMA through asymmetric strategies, WMDs, urban warfare, guerrilla warfare, terrorism, or good forces with low technology.

## Military Balances

Sometimes, conventional power is easy to calculate. Each side fights the same way and has so many archers or tanks; you multiply the quantity by some coefficient representing quality, and Bob's your uncle. Today, simply to gauge conventional power is problematic, because its forms vary and are changing (see Box 13.2). Perhaps one can measure power in PGMs for all states, simply by multiplying their quality and quantity by some coefficient representing

C4ISR. So too with blue water navies, as they are rare and commentators agree on what makes power for them (that story ends at the green water mark). Such measurements are harder with armies. Those of developing powers have a strong but short punch, great on their borders but not beyond; best measured by the number of combat soldiers they could deploy on their frontier. North Korea or China could throw millions of soldiers to their frontiers, India or Turkey likely 400,000. Rich states have armies with longer range but less weight. Their strength is best measured by the combat troops ready for expeditionary service: Germany, Canada, and Australia might deploy 2,000 each, France and Britain, 10,000, and the United States, 140,000. World conventional power rests on a combination of a blue water fleet and an expeditionary capability, in which the United States stands alone in its class, with Britain and France the only bantams. To compare these forms of force is like gauging apples and oranges; the point is where the struggle occurs. In Fujian, the Chinese army would reign supreme; 50 miles off shore, it would drown.

The balance of power is changing most in Asia. India's competition with Pakistan is unlikely to end, but is one-sided. Pakistan strains its resources to play. It can exploit India's greatest weakness, the political fractures of a multinational state, but Pakistan could endanger its rival only with help from China or the United States. Indian cooperation with Washington trumps that ace. Indian leaders distort the danger of Pakistan, because a weak enemy suits them. India, however, does not seek to conquer its neighbours, however much it wishes them subordinate—few things could be more disastrous for India than conquering Pakistan and having to rule its people. Meanwhile, India can already project force far from its shores. It aims to be one of two dominant powers in the Indian Ocean, alongside the United States. Its landbased aviation and fleet, based around two old aircraft carriers and 25 decent destroyers and frigates, are good. That power will rise after 2015, as it junks old kit and acquires new, in particular by building an Indian aircraft carrier and other warships and weapons. If it acts on its declared policies, India will keep a decent fleet of the second rank. It cannot sail against American opposition, but then, no one can. If India continues its drift towards alignment with the West, and its moderate but sustained investment in new forces, it will be a major but regional sea power. That will strengthen its influence throughout the Indian Ocean littoral, but to what effect remains uncertain. Since 1949, India has found power and strategy hard to handle. It uses power merely as one means to demonstrate status, rather than as a tool to pursue interests. India, the least of the great powers, punches below its weight. It has more power than it uses.

In contrast, China has less power than it needs. It has great ambitions, and moderate strength. It aims to absorb Taiwan and remove the American containment of its coasts; easier said than done, on terrain where the United States is strong and China weak in both sea and air power. Since 1949, China has pursued the area-denial maritime strategy of a continental power—to keep rivals far away through land-based force and a brown water navy. China hopes to push that perimeter toward Japan and Taiwan, but is painfully slow in gathering the means, such as cruise missiles, better aircraft, and bigger ships. Over the past generation it has junked much old kit and built a medium-sized modern navy, which shows signs of striking for blue water. However, its efforts are unlikely to bear fruit for decades. American sea and air power can easily pin China on its coast, if they wish. Only if and when Taiwan and China are reunified will it break that barrier and reach blue water and so become a world naval power.

**BOX** 13.2  Arms and Power

Over the past century, many developing countries built good armament industries, resting on effective links between businesses and bureaucrats, and decent kit. They entered the state of the art, learning to copy and then innovate, by forming liaisons with arms producers in many states; buying much material and acquiring more via espionage; making weapons under licence and reverse engineering; and training labour to build munitions and designers to make them. While a score of states entered such arrangements, two cases transformed world power. In 1921 all Japanese warships and naval aircraft were versions of British equipment, gained through purchase or joint ventures. Over the next 20 years, it developed advanced naval and aeronautical industries through hard work and copies of all the kit it could buy. So too, Soviet tanks of 1941 derived from refinement of Western technology purchased a decade earlier. Its aircraft industry of 1951 relied heavily on Western designs acquired by aid, accident, and espionage.

Since 2000, arms sales have been driven by the hunger of firms for profits, and the desire of their states to strengthen those industries while acquiring political influence through their product. The United States makes massive arms sales to its allies, especially in the Persian Gulf, needing means to keep Iran in check. So too have France and Britain. Russia leads in the transfer of advanced military technology, so as to salvage its military-industrial base, the only area where its firms can compete on world terms. This provided its only success in industrial exports, but enabled China to strip Russian technology, and become a strategic and industrial competitor. India has licences to build or has entered into joint ventures with Russia on much modern equipment, like the Sukhoi-30 MKI aircraft and the T-90 tank. China purchased leading Russian aircraft, missiles, destroyers, and submarines, and also stole from it the technology for radar and data link systems, and fighters.

 **Key Points**

- Conventional power is hard to calculate. It depends on circumstances.
- Conventional forces take many forms, to handle different problems.
- They succeed by developing and exploiting comparative advantages over competitors.
- Only years of sustained effort enables any state to challenge an established air or sea power.

## World on the Scales

In 2015, the world confronts the biggest changes in power since 1989. China's rise alarms its neighbours, though it is decades away from being a global power. Europe, rich and weak, slides to strategic irrelevance as actor, though not object. The United States, a chastened superpower, must slash capabilities, especially in land forces. Just because a power declines while others rise, however, need not mean that it will fall, immediately. Its position may hold steady for decades, or tip suddenly at any time. In power, tipping points matter as much as trends. Unfortunately, they are harder to foresee.

The United States has reconsidered its strategies of 1989 and 2001. It will maintain far and away the largest military expenditure on earth, but cut it well below the level of inflation, forcing bitter budgetary battles, and killing some programmes. The United States will remain an unmatched power for decades to come, but its power is declining, and hyperpolarity vanishing, for reasons beyond its control. Other states, especially India, China, and Russia, are exercising their weight. Meanwhile, the first rise since 1989 in the size and quality of armed forces is occurring, as all major states pursue great programmes of rearmament to counter the rust-out of kit. Only some will succeed. Talk is cheap, weapons are not. They rise in price as they become more sophisticated, driving down orders, which increases unit costs. So to maintain national arms industries, states rarely buy equipment off the shelf from others, but prefer indigenous firms, usually more costly and of lesser quality than the best on earth. Without constant orders, arms firms wither. These factors drive supply and demand for the arms trade.

After 2000, military budgets jumped, but then stalled and now are falling. Western states almost doubled their military spending between 2000 and 2008, while that of China trebled, but most of that increase was lost to inflation. Governments are shocked to find how so much can buy so little. All navies and air forces are in crisis, as numbers of personnel and kit plummet to allow recapitalization. Western ones must explain why they need new equipment, when they already have the world's best, and threats are so weak and far away. The US Navy, a vaunted 600-ship navy in 1989, has 300 in 2015. Since 2001, the US Air Force has slashed its ranks to produce tiny numbers of its next two generation of fighters, the F-22 and F-35—183 F-22s eliminated 20,000 personnel, almost 10 per cent of the total. These pressures drove Western states to develop aircraft by international consortia, including the F-35. Washington's refusal to do so with the F-22, to maintain the secrecy of stealth technology, shaped its astronomical unit cost, of US$339,000,000 per aircraft. In order to buy new kit, between 1990–2009 Russia cut its army by 70 per cent, to 500,000 men, as China did its army by 20 per cent and its air force by 50 per cent. Moscow and Beijing have linked their status as powers to massive new arms programmes, like the Indo-Russian project for the fifth-generation Sukhoi/HAL fighter aircraft, intended to compete where American power is strongest. If these aims fail, so will their policies.

Cost barriers and economic recession cripple the ability of states to keep their place, and to develop dominant weapons systems, especially aircraft and warships. By 2015, after many problems, the F-35 programme finally jelled. This enabled Western countries to acquire advanced fighters, if they were willing to pay the price—not easy, since their defence budgets slipped by 10 per cent between 2010 and 2015. Russian and Chinese fighter programmes were less successful. While British and Japanese naval construction surged, other secondary fleets confronted a choice between rust or boom. In these spheres, no state faced greater trouble than Russia. Between 2000 and 2008, its defence expenditures quintupled after a decade-long collapse, which barely saved its conventional forces from becoming obsolete. Even so, its navy became a floating museum. Financial crises tripped Russian plans to construct or rebuild 54 warships between 2014 and 2020, and to commission 1,000 fixed wing aircraft and helicopters. Unless Russia makes military investments at the scale which bankrupted the USSR, Russian conventional power will fade: yet only these forces and its nuclear capability support its claims to be a great military power. How Russian leaders will harmonize this dissonance remains one of the great unknowns in power politics.

In the decade after 2015, the countries least affected by economic malaise may develop the capabilities to meet their declared policies. South Korea, China, India, and Japan are almost bound to become militarily more powerful, though the effect may be largely just to check each other. Most countries, however, will not match words with deeds, however much they hide decline through bluster, as squid flee behind ink.

A struggle will occur between the economic power and political will of major states, embodied in military procurement; the outcome will be measured in the quantity and quality of conventional forces. The only safe bets are that the United States will remain the greatest of powers and China its greatest competitor, that any country which fails in rearmament will fall in power, and that many will do so. Their efforts to achieve these ends, and their success compared to their rivals, will add uncertainty to the base of a new world order. Nothing drives a state towards desperation more than the fear that it is declining while a rival is rising (see Box 13.3).

 **BOX** 13.3   The Future of Power Relations

Power, in Asia and elsewhere, turns on the military application of industry. China and India have large sectors in those areas, inefficient and corrupt. Defence industries and governments have tangled relations. Firms in Chinese provinces, caught in political fiefdoms, rarely cooperate with those elsewhere, preventing economies of scale, or rationalization. In India, attempts to let private arms firms compete with state ones face paralysing resistance from industrial, labour, and political lobbies. Indigenous production of aircraft and the acquisition of foreign ones are delayed for decades as firms and the state tinker with contracts, especially over arrangements for technology transfer, though this happens in rich nations too. The developing states with the best military industrial bases are China, Russia, and Brazil, which produces large numbers of good indigenously designed aircraft and aggressively pursues technology transfer agreements with advanced powers—on a continent where conventional power matters little.

China and India depend on access to foreign technology; but each works with many partners, through which it builds advanced kit and tries to leapfrog time-consuming stages of technological development. Their civil economies have able elements in high technology, but weaknesses in innovation. China seeks to establish defence industries of the top rank by 2025, an ambitious, but achievable, aim. Since 1995, China has performed consistently at the upper bound of expectations; no other power has risen so fast and far. During those years, its air force leapt from weak and outdated in 1970 to just below the best secondary powers by 1995. Its rise exploited every relationship and technique, combining joint licences, reverse engineering and espionage, to strip Western technology in the 1980s, and Russian technology since then. India depends more on its suppliers and performs worse in programmes, though aided by foreign powers' greater willingness to exchange technology with Delhi than with Beijing. In 20 years, China and India will probably have established good military industries, and closed the gap with leading economies, even in defence electronics and information technology. Though the edge will remain with the rich, they may then be the world's second and third strongest economies and conventional powers, and growing fast.

 **Key Points**

- The distribution of conventional power is changing.
- Western countries are in decline.
- New world powers are emerging, especially China and India.
- The impact of these changes will vary with the desire of states to tap economic power for strategic purposes, and with the skill of their policies.

# War, What is It Good For?

Wars occur from combinations of intention and error. They are unusually likely when the nature and distribution of power change rapidly, as strong states misconstrue their strength while declining ones strive to hold what they have and growing ones seek to take more. These circumstances exist today. The American drawdown from Iraq and Afghanistan opens uncertainty across the Middle East, where ethnic and religious divisions rip states apart. Classic confrontations loom between rising and declining powers. Mexican stand-offs rule Asia: between India and Pakistan; North Korea vs South Korea, Japan and the United States; and Beijing vs most of its neighbours and Washington. Chinese power waxes steadily, but is not yet significant in WMDs or at sea. Since 1949, China has aimed to maximize its regional power, and has often provoked high-risk incidents, believing that teaching lessons to neighbours is a good thing and it can control the worst cases—characteristics shared, to lesser degrees, by the United States. Both countries believe they are on the defensive over Taiwan, and respond to perceived aggression in a tough and self-righteous manner. Meanwhile, just as the Soviet collapse reshaped power in Asia, so would any resurgence of Russia—or Japan.

The Middle East is governed not by stalemate but vacuum. Several Arab states, particularly Syria and Egypt, match Israel numerically in land and air forces, while Saudi Arabia and the Gulf States make large purchases of advanced weaponry. Outside Jordan and Hizbullah, these forces are poor in quality, while Israeli ones are excellent. The failure of its 2006 war with Lebanon shocked Israel into improving its army, which performed better the next times, in Gaza during 2008–2009, and 2013–2014. Israel, the military master of the Arab world, can overawe its neighbours and wreck any threat, yet it cannot directly translate that strength into political power, as demonstrated by its irrelevance during the greatest political change in the Middle East for generations, the Arab Spring of 2011. Turkey, militarily the next most powerful of regional states, does not handle this translation much better. The states best poised to manipulate these circumstances—Saudi Arabia, the Gulf States, and Iran—are militarily weak. Israel and America cannot use conventional force to block big dangers, such as the rise of jihadist regimes in Egypt or Saudi Arabia; though that could aid them in containment, as the United States did with Iraq and Iran between 1991 and 2003, and Islamic insurgency in Syria and Iraq during 2013–2015. Nor, short of occupying Lebanon or Gaza, can Israel destroy the ability of Hamas and Hizbullah to bombard its territory with missiles. The military weakness of Arab states and the turmoil within them make that region even less stable than usual.

In these cases, conventional force is part of power, but not the whole. It does not primarily define the balance between Israel, the United States, and Iran. A tough neighbourhood may drive Japan to increase its conventional power, but Tokyo has more to gain from nuclear weapons. Conventional power lets Western countries intervene in weak states, but not conquer them. It enables China and Russia to use subversion, coercion, and irregular force to bully weak neighbours, but not strong ones. NATO used conventional forces as a tripwire to check Russian actions in Eastern Europe during 2013–2015, but it really countered them through economic sanctions. China can strengthen its hand against the United States through conventional force to match American strengths, asymmetric force to degrade them, politics, or WMDs. The latter options are its best chances for success. For most developing states, WMDs offer the simplest military solution to strategic problems. For China in Taiwan, and Iran in Iraq and Afghanistan, political influence is a better instrument than armies, just as terrorism is a tool of policy by other means.

Bigger questions loom behind these matters, like the use of WMDs in conventional war. When only one side has chemical weapons, it routinely uses them, but not nuclear weapons. How far can states equipped with WMDs use conventional force against each other? They have often done so, but the rules for these games remain obscure. All major belligerents in Europe during 1939–1945 were equipped for gas warfare, but did not use it; so too in the Gulf War of 1991. Nuclear powers have fought each other, most notably India and Pakistan in the isolated region of Kargil during 2000; and Soviet pilots shot down many American air intruders over their territory in the 1950s and in the Korean War, and fought Israeli ones in 1970. Again, the single greatest factor in world politics since 1989 has been the relationship between overwhelming American power and its erratic use. The United States' search for absolute security made all its rivals insecure, looking for ways to defend themselves or escape the firing line. Its power and threats frightened many hostile states into changing their ways, but also convinced any serious rival that it must neutralize that threat, by being able to endanger America. American success in conventional power will drive any rational enemy to abandon head-on competition, and to pursue asymmetry or WMDs. The latter are easier to build and have a more certain deterrent effect.

 **Key Points**

- Wars occur from accident and intention.
- Conventional power is part of the balance in every zone of conflict.
- The limits of conventional power matter no less than its strengths.

 **Conclusion**

Conventional power is a great but limited tool of state. Once it was a spear against the strong; now, it is most valuable as a weapon against the weak. It remains the main shield for most states, but the sword of choice for few. It is more useful as a negative than a positive tool: to stop others from moving, as against doing so oneself. It is a fundamental means to demonstrate resolve, or support any strategies of dissuasion, subversion, and compellence, though no more so than nuclear power or diplomatic influence. Any state threatened by conventional force must match it or die. Such forces can save oneself, aid one's friends, destroy one's enemies, and, occasionally, strike like lightning. Still, their utility has slipped steadily over the past century, as has the willingness of states to use them. Conventional force has failed to achieve specific results predictably or cheaply. The outcome of its use has been more uncertain than ever before. Often, it has caused complex collateral damage, or trapped its users in the mire of world war, or guerrilla conflict. In the future, conventional force will be more discussed than used. When deployed, it will face characteristic problems, or victory traps. If one uses cruise missiles for diplomacy, a few civilian deaths will tarnish the political message. No matter the cause—*raison d'état* or humanitarian intervention, whether single-handed or under UN control—Western states will use conventional power primarily where the entry cost seems low and chances for success high: against weak or failing states. This raises immediate questions. Can outsiders end a civil war? Does occupation cause resistance? Will Western publics tolerate the violence necessary for victory except for defence of vital interests? Nor can armies be used on any great issue without raising the issue of WMDs.

Conventional force affects the policies of single actors, and the system as a whole. Many consequences of conventional power lie outside that plane, in what it drives states to do elsewhere. Its impact is most critical in deterring people from using an obvious tool, and in driving them to develop others. In theory, levels of force are divided; in reality, they are intertwined. An American air strike on Iranian nuclear power stations might spark terrorism across the Middle East. The pure game of conventional power is played in a narrow field between two limits: WMDs, and terrorism and guerrilla warfare. To be too good in this game is not a simple blessing. Too much success drives one's rival off this field to play on others. A rational enemy plays to its own strengths, not yours. Conventional power remains a strong card, perhaps the king of trumps in a game where the ace is unplayable, but it cannot take every hand. Perhaps it can take only one out of 13. The trick will be learning how to play that card only when it can take the game; and to know when that game is worth the gamble.

 **Critical Thinking**    Debating … Will China master East Asia by 2035?

### For

- *Economic power.* The Chinese economy, the most dynamic among major states, has grown more than any other since 1980. In 2015, its GDP is second only to the United States, larger but expanding more slowly.

- *Rising defence spending.* Chinese defence spending has been growing faster than in any other country, by 50 per cent between 2008 and 2014. In 2015, it almost matched that of any two other countries except the United States, though barely reaching 20 per cent of the American level.

- *Growing military capabilities.* China is militarily the strongest state in East Asia. Its capabilities are hard to calculate, as it deceives foreign powers, but Chinese firms produce large quantities of advanced land and air equipment, including fighters which match any others deployed in 2015, except the F-22 and F-35—the real competition.

- *Rivals' weaknesses.* Of China's neighbours, only India, Japan, and Russia can withstand its power by themselves. The offshore balancer, the United States, faces world-wide commitments with limited resources. Problems in Eastern Europe and the Middle East cripple its attempt to focus more resources in East Asia, via the Pacific pivot. China can multiply these problems by cooperating to cause trouble with American enemies in Eurasia, especially Russia.

- *Leverage.* China can turn its conventional power to political purpose by subverting or coercing its neighbours, making them accept its regional hegemony one by one, each step aiding the whole. Such political successes sap the effect of American conventional capabilities.

### Against

- *Slowing economy.* As with all developing economies, the growth rate of the Chinese economy slows as it matures, exacerbating problems caused by a corrupt state and an ageing and poor population.

- *Military technological inferiority.* Chinese warships and aircraft are one to three generations behind Western countries. They cannot easily eliminate that weakness, or match American military spending and technology, nor can Beijing mistake this inferiority.

- *Making enemies needlessly.* Chinese coercion angers its neighbours. The weak ones look for allies. The strong ones rearm. No power is more affected by the rise of China than Japan. None could do more to counter it. Japan has a better navy and air force than China and intends to maintain that status. If Japan wished, it could easily become the world's second sea and air power. India and even Russia also fear Chinese expansion.

- *Rivals' power.* The United States, Japan, and other Western powers are so powerful at sea and in the air that they can easily deploy forces superior to those of China in Asia over the next generation, tailored to defeat its challenge.

- *Containment.* The conventional power of the United States and its allies prevents China from coercing its neighbours through war. Chinese belligerence drives its neighbours toward American arms. The competition will turn to diplomacy, with possible outcomes ranging from a continuation of the status quo, to a change of Chinese policy, to its successful co-option of one neighbour or another, or war.

## Questions

1.  Did the United States win, or did Iraq lose, the Gulf War of 2003?
2.  How does sea power matter today, why, and to whom?
3.  What use are air power and PGMs to the United States, compared to nuclear power?
4.  What is a decisive battle? How many of them have happened since 1945?
5.  How will the economic decline of Western Europe, and the rise of China, affect their military power by 2025?
6.  Compare and contrast the conventional military power of Israel, Iran, and India. What good does it do them? What are the limits to its value?
7.  How far can states equipped with WMDs engage in conventional war?
8.  Is attrition the normal state of conventional war? Is indecisiveness its normal outcome?
9.  How, and how easily, can conventional forces defeat terrorists or guerrillas?
10. How will Russia and Japan respond to the rise of China?

 ## Further Reading

C. Archer, J. Ferris, H. Herwig, and T. Travers, *A World History of Warfare* (Lincoln, NE: University of Nebraska Press, 2002) offers a good modern account of the history of war.

International Institute for Strategic Studies, *The Military Balance* (London: IISS and Routledge) gives an authoritative, comprehensive, and annual assessment of conventional forces and weapons.

Jane's Information Group (various publications) is a credible source for information on conventional forces and weapons.

J. Lynn, *Battle, A History of Combat and Culture* (Boulder, CO: Westview Press, 2003) also offers a useful analysis of the history of war.

R. Weigley, *The Age of Battles: The Quest for Decisive Warfare* (Bloomington, IN: Indiana University Press, 1991) provides another perspective on the history of conventional war.

 ## Web Links

The Air War College Portal to the Internet **http://www.au.af.mil/au/awc/awcgate/awcgate.htm** is an excellent source for studies of current military topics, with links to official, semi-official, and unclassified websites.

The Center for Strategic and International Studies **http://www.csis.org** gives analyses of international strategic issues, particularly useful for conflicts as they occur.

The RAND Corporation **http://www.rand.org** presents excellent and wide-ranging studies of contemporary strategic policy and military forces, often surprisingly detailed.

Carnegie Endowment for International Peace **http://www.carnegieendowment.org** provides writings on international strategic issues and conflicts, from a liberal perspective.

International Crisis Group **http://www.crisisgroup.org** provides analyses of international strategic issues and conflicts, particularly their internal political dimensions.

# 14 Theory and Practice of Continental Warfare

STEPHEN BIDDLE

## Chapter Contents

 Reader's Guide

This chapter considers the relationship between ideas on conventional land warfare and actual experience since 1900. How well or badly have theorists anticipated the demands of such wars, and why did their ideas succeed or fail? The chapter presents technological change as the central challenge facing modern theorists, and identifies tactical and doctrinal responses that emerged very quickly in reaction to modern weapons' radical lethality. These responses emphasized cover, concealment, tight integration of suppressive fire and movement, depth, and reliance on withheld reserves at the cost of lighter forward deployments. These concepts subsequently formed the foundation for most modern systems of tactics and doctrine. Though theorists have periodically expected new weapons to invalidate this canon and demand radical new methods, such expectations have often been frustrated by subsequent experience; the most successful post-1900 doctrinal systems have often been the most conservative. The chapter traces this theory–practice relationship via four case studies: the European theatre in the two World Wars and the Mideast conflicts of 1973 and 1991. The chapter ends by considering the prospects for change looking forward, and concludes that powerful elements of continuity, as well as change, lie ahead.

## World War I: The Emergence of Modern Warfare

The First World War followed a series of dramatic technological changes. The industrial revolution had brought mass production, the substitution of machine for animal power, and dramatic improvements in metallurgy, agriculture, administration, and public health. Together these led to enormous increases in armies' size and firepower by 1914 (see Box 14.1).

**BOX** 14.1   Technological Change and Twentieth-century Armies

Technological change brought radical increases in the size and lethality of twentieth-century armies:

| 1812 | 1912 |
| --- | --- |
| Napoleon's Grande Armée numbers 600,000 and is most powerful in Europe | French Army numbers 1.6 million yet is only third largest in Europe |
| Muzzle-loading brass cannon can fire one 12-pound ball to a distance of 1,000 yards every 30 seconds | Steel breachloading field guns can fire one 18-pound shell to a distance of more than 12,000 yards every 10 seconds |
| Infantry battalion of 1,000 men with smoothbore flintlock muskets can project 2,000 musket balls to an effective range of 100 yards every minute | Infantry battalion of 900 men with magazine rifles and 4 machine guns can project over 21,000 rounds to an effective range of over 1,000 yards every minute |
| 2: Musket balls fired at each attacking soldier by a defending infantry unit of comparable size before attackers can close to bayonet range | 200: Bullets fired at each attacking soldier by a defending infantry unit of comparable size before attackers can close to bayonet range |

These changes posed major challenges. In Napoleon's day, attackers had room to manoeuvre and often sought to outflank defenders or feint them into exposed positions before risking an assault; by 1914, the massive new armies created continuous fronts over entire national frontiers, choking off manoeuvre room and eliminating assailable flanks. Napoleonic bayonet charges could reasonably hope to overrun weakened defences; by 1914, massed frontal assaults over open ground had become suicidal. The new firepower—what Ernst Junger called the '*storm of steel*'—posed radical new challenges in an era of continuous fronts. How could armies survive this storm of steel long enough to accomplish meaningful military missions?

Early experience of the new lethality in the 1899–1902 Boer War and 1904–1905 Russo-Japanese War triggered extensive debates in all European militaries over how to respond. Two broad approaches emerged almost immediately. The first used *cover and concealment* to reduce attackers' exposure while advancing; the second used *suppressive fire* to keep defenders' heads down while the attackers were exposed. Even before the Boer War ended, for

 **BOX** 14.2   The Tank in World War I

[In 1918] the dominant fact about the tank was that it was not durable. At Cambrai, 324 fighting tanks were committed. . . . At the end of the first day 65 had received direct hits, 71 had broken down, 43 were ditched and many others needed minor repairs. The casualties on 8 August 1918 were higher still and reflected improving German anti-tank artillery. Four hundred and fourteen started, but only 145 were runners on the second day, 85 on the third, 38 on the fourth and 6 remained on the fifth. The crews were exhausted by temperatures of well over 100 degrees Fahrenheit and the fumes and noise from engines and guns. A night on the march before a battle and another spent returning to harbour for maintenance usually meant thirty-six hours without sleep amid the strain of battle. Neither men nor machines were of much use on a second day of fighting. (Bidwell and Graham 1985: 137–8)

example, British tactics had shifted from massed attacks in line to 'open order' advances by short rushes, using terrain to conceal dispersed attackers prior to brief dashes in the open from one covered position to the next. During periods of exposure, artillery and rifle fire would suppress defensive positions to keep them from firing.

Two problems emerged, however. First, the required movement proved hard to control. Dispersion put more distance between leaders and led, making it hard for the former to keep their troops moving. Units could find cover but tended to remain there too long; attacks then lost momentum, degenerating into desultory small arms exchanges at extended range as troops went to ground and resorted to fire rather than movement. This gave defensive artillery time to extinguish stalled attacks.

Second, it proved hard to control the needed suppressive fires without leaving the shooters too exposed to survive counterfire. The key issue here was artillery support, which alone could provide the needed firepower. Artillery can fire directly over 'open sights' (i.e., with a flat trajectory at targets the gunners can see), or it can fire *indirectly* (shooting over intervening obstacles with an arced trajectory at targets the gunners cannot see). *Direct fire* is easier to control, since the gunners can see both the targets and their own infantry, making it much simpler to maintain suppressive fire until the infantry has almost overrun the target, then lifting fire at the last minute to avoid fratricide. Direct fire, however, required the guns to move well forward and thus exposed them to counterfire. *Indirect fire*, by contrast, allowed the guns to move rearward to safer positions, but complicated fire control as gunners could no longer see the battle they supported. Indirect fire required forward observers who could see the targets to communicate firing instructions back to blind gunners in the rear; this in turn made it much harder to maintain accurate suppressive fire over the target until the last minute, since delayed, garbled, imprecise, or interrupted messages could yield either a fatal gap in suppressive coverage (if the fire lifted too soon or fell long) or fratricide (if the fire lifted too late or fell short).

When the First World War began in August 1914, these difficulties led to slaughter. Suppressive fire was either inaccurate or unavailable; without it, attackers were either massacred in the open or pinned down behind cover to be decimated by hostile artillery. Germany's attempt to evade French defences by marching through Belgium thus bogged down at the Marne; France's attempt to break through German defences in the Battle of the Frontiers yielded trivial gains for horrifying casualties. By Christmas the front had ossified into a continuous line of trenches from the North Sea to the Swiss border.

This failure induced rapid tactical adaptation. Prewar thought emphasized infantry as the primary arm of decision, with artillery as a secondary supporting weapon. By March 1915, this was completely reversed. Artillery would now destroy entrenched defences outright via massive preparatory barrages, with infantry advancing afterwards merely to mop up the dazed survivors. As the French put it, '*l'artillerie conquiert, l'infantry occupiert*': the artillery conquers, the infantry occupies. This was meant to overcome the problems of fire control and manoeuvre control by decoupling fire from manoeuvre and de-emphasizing the latter: if artillery could not be controlled precisely enough to suppress defenders while attackers manoeuvred, then perhaps it could annihilate defenders by itself from safe positions in the rear while friendly infantry simply stayed out of harm's way.

The new tactics proved little better. Preparatory barrages reached extraordinary intensity: the ten-day Allied bombardment before Messines in July 1917 dropped about 1,200 tons of explosives—more explosive power than the US W48 tactical nuclear warhead—per mile of German frontage. Contrary to popular impression, such barrages were not utterly futile. One would assume that nuclear-scale firepower could batter down defences, and indeed it could. By 1917, such offensives routinely took defenders' forward trenches in the initial assault. But this was not sufficient. Ground could be *taken*—the problem was *holding* it afterward. The same inability to coordinate artillery fire and infantry manoeuvre that had doomed 1914's tactics now crippled their successors in 1915–1917: the infantry that had advanced into the defender's trenches following the preparatory barrage was now on its own without effective supporting fire. Defenders who knew the time and place of attack from the weeks-long offensive barrages used the time to mass reserves and defensive artillery behind their forward trenches; these reserves then struck the unsupported, overextended attackers with an artillery barrage of their own, ejecting them from their gains with a subsequent counterattack by fresh infantry. Either side could advance as far as a pre-planned artillery programme could carry it, but neither could go further, and neither could hold its gains against counterattack. The result resembled a form of *war on a tether*: the battle was actually quite fluid, but movement was limited to the reach of the preparatory artillery barrages on either side. Massive midwar offensives at the Somme, Verdun, Passchendaele, and the Chemin des Dames thus yielded no meaningful change in either side's positions.

Gradually, however, new tactics emerged which replaced the prewar emphasis on infantry and midwar emphasis on artillery with a *combined arms* approach in which infantry and artillery cooperated as co-equals. In the new approach, surprise was restored by restricting the preparatory artillery programme to a brief but intense 'hurricane barrage' designed not to destroy but merely to suppress defences. This temporary suppressive effect was exploited by independently manoeuvring infantry teams armed with hand grenades and portable light machine guns; these were trained to exploit covering terrain to find their own way forward via the path of least resistance. These independently manoeuvring assault teams were better able to sustain their advance through the depths of a defence; as the brief barrage denied the defender advance warning, defenders found it harder to amass sufficient reserves in time to repel the attack before it broke through.

In fact, the new system was not really new: it represented a return to prewar ideas on combining suppression and manoeuvre to enable an advance in the face of the new firepower. But whereas prewar armies were unable to master the technical challenges of fire and manoeuvre control, by 1918 the intricacies of controlling indirect fires and coordinating them with small-unit movement had finally been worked out. Over the long stalemate, hard trial and error gradually hammered out the systems of *'scientific' gunnery*, improved *small-unit leadership*, and *training* needed to make prewar ideas work.

The new techniques were first combined into a single system by the Germans; unveiled at Caporetto on the Italian front in November 1917, these methods subsequently produced a series of Western Front breakthroughs in the German Spring Offensives of March–June 1918. The British and French armies pieced the new system together more slowly, but eventually mastered important elements of it and employed these in the subsequent Allied offensives that prised the Germans out of the Hindenberg Line and forced them into full retreat over open ground on a more than 200-mile front by November 1918. The trench stalemate was thus broken by early 1918, and the last seven months of the war saw the return of movement to the Western Front—albeit movement at the speed of a walking infantryman.

**Key Points**

- Prewar theorists anticipated many of the problems posed by new firepower and mass armies.
- Their proposed solution of cover and concealment with suppressive fire-and-movement failed in practice because 1914's armies lacked the necessary skills to implement such demanding methods.
- Over the course of the long stalemate, these skills were gradually developed; by March 1918 the stalemate had been broken and movement restored to the Western Front.

## World War II: Responses to Mechanization

The years between the world wars saw another wave of technological change—or, more properly, the maturation of several new technologies that appeared during the latter years of the First World War. Collectively these are sometimes referred to as 'mechanization', or the re-equipment of armies with tanks, trucks, airplanes, and radio communications to allow these faster-moving, longer-range vehicles to coordinate their movements. All debuted in the First World War, and the tank in particular is sometimes described as central to the great stalemate's breakdown in 1918. Yet none played decisive roles in the First World War. The tank, for example, was far too vulnerable and mechanically unreliable to play more than a supporting role in the final offensives (see Box 14.2). Aircraft were important, but payload limitations restricted them largely to reconnaissance and counter-reconnaissance throughout the war; while bombing missions were attempted, these were at best secondary functions. Radio was available, but First World War wireless sets were too bulky and short-range to help much in mobile battlefield operations. The interwar period, however, saw great improvements in tanks' range and reliability, aircraft payload and performance, and the portability of long-range radios.

The interwar theoretical debate turned largely on these developments' consequences. Some, such as the British military intellectuals J. F. C. Fuller and Basil Liddell Hart, saw self-contained mobile formations waging a form of naval warfare on land: after heavy tanks breached the enemy's forward defences, massed squadrons of light tanks supported by aircraft would roam at large behind enemy lines, rapidly overrunning essential command and logistical infrastructure. The French theorist Charles de Gaulle called for autonomous tank formations not tied to the infantry's pace and capable of rapid, wide-ranging manoeuvre. Soviet Marshall M. N. Tukhachevsky advocated a 'deep battle' doctrine of air strikes and parachute infantry drops throughout the theatre of war, coupled with rapid advances over great distances by mobile ground forces to paralyse hostile command and disrupt enemy reserve movements.

In many ways, German theorists were among the least radical. The Germans studied their First World War experience carefully, retained most of their 1917–1918 doctrine as valid, updated it where necessary to accommodate new equipment, and subjected the results to extensive, rigorous field testing. The resulting *Panzer Division* was a combined arms formation wherein tanks, infantry, artillery, and engineers were to cooperate closely, exploiting local terrain to enable all-arms assault teams to overcome defences by combining movement with suppressive fires.

By contrast, France and Britain ultimately adopted much more tank-heavy armoured division organizations and used their tanks much more independently, expecting them to manoeuvre *en masse* with limited infantry support. Worse, they allowed much of the expertise in combined arms operations gained at such cost in 1915–1918 to atrophy. In France, civil–military tension produced a short-service conscript army unable to master the complex demands of late-war tactics. In Britain, a class-conscious officer corps ostracized the upstart technicians they had been forced to rely upon in wartime, placing birth and breeding above skill and eventually losing much of their collective expertise. In the USSR, a series of political purges killed or cashiered their most talented officers, stripping the military of the expertise it needed to cope with the complexities of modern warfare.

When war broke out in 1939, the result was a series of stunning German victories as the Panzer divisions spearheaded breakthroughs of ill-disposed, poorly conducted Allied defences. First World War defenders had learned the hard way to thin their forward positions, extend their defences into great depth, and withhold much of their total strength in reserve. Though this yielded ground initially, it provided the time and wherewithal needed to counter-concentrate before the attacker could break through, and forced attackers to fight the decisive battle in the depths of the defence, where an opposed advance of thousands of metres would have frayed even the best attackers' combined arms coordination. Yet French defences in the crucial Sedan sector in 1940, for example, were less than one-fifth the depth of typical 1917 German positions, with less than half the 1917 norm for reserves. Such shallow, forward defences were easier to control and less demanding of technical skill but dangerously brittle. When struck by German combined arms they shattered, enabling German armour to pour through the resulting gap and sprint to the English Channel in just weeks. The French theatre defence subsequently collapsed, knocking France out of the war and giving Germany in less than two months a victory that had eluded them for four years in World War I. Soviet defences in 1941 were similarly ill-disposed: the 'Stalin Line' defending Russia's prewar border was even shallower than French defences at Sedan. The Germans quickly broke through, encircling and killing or capturing in the process hundreds of thousands of Soviet troops.

Unlike France, however, the USSR's sheer size prevented Germany from destroying the Red Army in a single campaign. Halted as much by their own logistical limitations as by Soviet opposition, the Germans were turned back short of Moscow in the winter of 1941–1942. Coupled with Germany's defeat in the Battle of Britain, the resulting breathing space enabled a major redirection of Allied military doctrine as the Allies gradually relearned the hard lessons of 1917–1918. They deepened their defences, withheld larger reserves, and increasingly used those reserves in counterattacks to recapture lost ground rather than rigidly defending every inch from the outset. And they slowly, painfully, retaught themselves the importance of combined arms and tight integration of suppressive fire with movement. The tank-heavy early-war armoured divisions were replaced by better-balanced formations with a higher proportion of infantry, artillery, and engineers. Methods of cooperation between ground forces and supporting aircraft were hammered out. The complexities of infantry–artillery integration were rediscovered and overcome—and the new problem of infantry–armour coordination that the Germans had mastered by extending their First World War principles was gradually surmounted.

The result was the end of the rapid 'blitzkrieg' offensive successes of 1939–1941 as the Allies, too, adopted the crucial combination of *deep elastic defences*, *integrated fire-and-movement*, and *combined arms*. With both sides using such methods, quick, cheap break-throughs became impossible for either side, and the war settled into a long, hard process of the Allies methodically grinding down a numerically inferior Axis military.

Contrary to prewar armour theorists' expectations, the tank thus did not revolutionize warfare or create a form of naval conflict on land. Instead, it expanded the possibilities of traditional combined arms by providing a source of protected firepower with the mobility to exploit break-throughs where these occurred. Tanks carry heavier weapons, heavier armour, and more ammunition than infantry, but they are loud, harder to conceal, and have great difficulty seeing concealed targets when buttoned up. Operating alone, these shortcomings make tanks extreme-ly vulnerable to dug-in infantry which they cannot see, but which can strike tanks' less-protected flank and rear armour with short-range portable antitank weapons. Dug-in antitank guns pose even greater threats: properly concealed they are practically impossible for tank crews to see, yet their higher-velocity weapons can pierce even the heavy frontal armour of most tanks. Tanks thus cannot afford to operate exposed in the open: even with armour protection, they are still too vulnerable to survive an unsupported frontal assault against a well-prepared position. By contrast, when teamed with infantry and artillery the tank is a much more formidable weapon. Infantry can act as the tanks' eyes and ears, using their superior sensory acuity to find concealed defenders and pinpoint their locations for the tanks' superior firepower, while the tanks' heavier weaponry suppresses defensive fire to keep it from pinning down the thinner-skinned foot sol-diers. Artillery in turn provides the high-volume suppressive fire needed to cover more extended periods of exposure, enabling the tanks and infantry to conserve their (more limited) ammuni-tion supply for use at shorter ranges where fratricide risks limit the effectiveness of distant artillery firing indirectly. Then—if shallow, forward defensive dispositions permit—tanks' mobility permits them to come into their own in exploiting breakthrough. Without dug-in, concealed defences to overcome, tanks in exploitation can operate more independently, using their speed to conduct the kind of deep raiding operations that theorists like Fuller or Liddell Hart expected. In practice, however, these opportunities became fewer and fewer as the war progressed and defenders learned to deny tanks the conditions they needed for independent success. Hence the war that transpired was very different from the one radical theorists expected.

By 1943–1944, in fact, some of the war's most tank-heavy battles had become some of its costliest defensive stalemates. The war's single biggest tank action, the Battle of Kursk in July 1943, was a crushing offensive failure: the German attackers lost up to 2,900 tanks in just 18 days, a loss from which they never fully recovered. The war's greatest density of tanks per kilo-metre of frontage was the 1944 British offensive in Operation Goodwood; the attack gained less than 10 kilometres, costing the attackers more than a third of all the British armour on the continent in the process. By 1945, World War II had thus come to resemble the methodical offensives of 1918 more closely than the blitzkriegs of 1939–1941.

 **Key Points**

- Some interwar theorists expected mechanization to revolutionize warfare, with armoured vehicles taking over most combat roles and waging a free-flowing form of naval warfare on land.

- The war's early battles seemed to support this expectation, as German Panzer divisions spearheaded breakthroughs and deep exploitations of Allied defences.

- Germany's early successes, however, were enabled by flawed Allied defensive dispositions; as the Allies slowly relearned the lessons of 1917–1918, quick offensive success became impossible even for tanks.

- Once both sides had adopted cover and concealment, combined arms, tightly-coordinated suppressive fire-and-movement, defensive depth, and large reserve withholds, the war settled into a pattern of methodical advances by numerically superior attackers, with few decisive offensive breakthroughs possible for either side.

# The 1973 Arab–Israeli War: Relearning the Importance of Combined Arms

The 1973 Arab–Israeli War offers similar lessons. By 1973 the Israelis had fought a series of wars against Arab opponents, winning each despite sometimes prohibitive numerical odds. In the process, the Israelis had become convinced that the key to modern desert warfare lay in high-mobility operations by tank-aircraft task forces without significant reliance on artillery or dismounted infantry. Speed, daring, and deep penetrations without regard to flank security were increasingly emphasized; fire support was to be provided by aircraft in order to maintain the pace of the advance.

These theories stemmed from a particular interpretation of their experiences in the 1948, 1956, and 1967 wars. Israeli forces in the 1948 War of Independence were an improvised patchwork consisting mostly of infantry with little support from armour or artillery. Israel prevailed, but only after hard fighting against poorly organized opposition. By 1956 the Israeli army was better organized and trained, but still largely an infantry force. In the Suez War, this army defeated Egyptian defences in the Sinai in a nine-day campaign timed to coincide with British and French seizure of the Suez canal; though only a portion of Israel's forces had been fully mechanized, this armoured element produced results disproportionate to its strength. The Israeli senior leadership saw this as proof of the tank's potential in desert warfare and made great efforts to mechanize its forces afterwards. By 1967 they had amassed some 1,100 tanks, backed up with 260 combat aircraft. The ensuing Six Day War yielded one of the century's most one-sided offensive victories, as Israeli armour-aircraft task forces charged deep into the Sinai, cutting off much of the Egyptian army and destroying Egypt's theatre defences in just four days. Subsequent operations in the West Bank and Golan Heights defeated Jordanian and Syrian forces, producing a dramatic success against far more numerous Arab opponents.

In these conflicts, fast-moving tank columns had performed great feats; the more armour-intensive the operation, the more impressive the results had been. Israeli doctrine responded with a growing neglect of infantry or artillery support for the tanks that had accomplished such marvels. In modern mechanized warfare, it was thought, dismounted infantry would needlessly delay the mobile units on which success depended; infantry came to be seen as a specialty unit for independent use in built-up areas or other unusual terrain in which tanks and aircraft could not operate effectively.

In fact, however, Israel's success with such tank-heavy forces depended critically on their enemies' poor performance in the 1956 and especially 1967 wars. Ill-trained and ill-led, Arab infantry lacked the skills and motivation to exploit the weaknesses of unsupported Israeli armour. Disposed in shallow defences with inadequate reserves, Arab armies were unable to respond once Israeli tank charges overran their forward positions, giving tank-heavy Israeli exploitation forces maximum scope for decisive results.

Following the 1967 debacle, however, Egypt took steps to improve its performance. In particular, it focused great effort on training its infantry to stand fast against tanks, conceal their positions properly, and hit their targets. These initiatives fell far short of a complete reform of national military practice: Egyptian forces remained incapable of close combined arms cooperation or flexible manoeuvre, and their dispositions still tended to be too shallow and static. Nevertheless, they did accomplish one key goal: their infantry learned to carry out a tightly scripted advance, dig in properly at their new positions, and defend those positions tenaciously when attacked.

The result was a near disaster for Israel in the 1973 October War. Catching Israel by surprise, the Egyptians quickly crossed the Suez Canal, overwhelmed the unprepared garrison of the 'Bar Lev Line,' and advanced some four kilometres into the Sinai. There they dug in and awaited Israeli counterattack. Recovering from their initial unpreparedness, the Israelis quickly obliged. A series of 1967-style unsupported tank charges then impaled themselves on the Egyptian infantry positions, suffering enormous losses. Israeli tankers accustomed to overrunning poorly prepared Arab defensive positions now found themselves unable to locate well-concealed Egyptian infantry who stubbornly stuck to their positions and found easy targets for themselves in the Israelis' exposed tanks. Israeli pilots in turn suffered heavy losses as they tried to support the tank attacks while flying into an Egyptian air defence umbrella that likewise stood its ground and fought hard from prepared positions. In all, the Egyptian infantry shattered almost three full brigades of Israeli armour before the Israelis shifted tactics.

Faced with the failure of their prewar methods, the Israelis improvised. Without much infantry of their own, they adopted an *ad hoc*, all-mounted version of traditional suppressive fire-and-movement methods. Instead of storming the defences directly, a few tanks would move forward cautiously to draw fire, while others in stationary overwatch positions searched for the sources of the fire and returned it. The primary Egyptian antitank weapon was a slow-flying, wire-guided missile which required its operator to keep cross-hairs on the target until impact; Israeli overwatch tanks that observed the puff of smoke from the missile's launch and then hosed down the area with machine gun or cannon fire could thus readily distract (or sometimes kill) the operator, causing the launched missiles to lose guidance in midflight. Meanwhile the exposed lead tanks manoeuvred evasively and sought cover in more advanced positions. In this way the Israelis gradually worked their way forward by bounds.

These tactics were costly even so, but they enabled the Israelis to take ground. Eventually, they fought their way through Egyptian lines in a bitter action at the Battle of the Chinese Farm. Once through the Egyptians' forward defences, the Israelis could accelerate dramatically, as the Egyptians' lack of depth and reserves left them with little means of containing the breach. Israeli tank columns crossed the Suez Canal, turning north and south to overrun the command, logistical, and air defence infrastructure on which the remainder of the Egyptian defences depended, and cutting off the Egyptian Third Army on the Israeli side of the canal.

The Syrians, meanwhile, had attempted a clumsy massed tank attack in the open against Israeli defences in the Golan Heights. Poorly supported by either infantry or artillery, the Syrian armour suffered huge losses against a tiny Israeli defensive force, failing to dislodge the screening positions the Israelis relied upon to shield their mobilization. Once Israeli reinforcements arrived, these proved sufficient to retake all lost ground before an internationally brokered ceasefire ended the war on 24 October.

The Israelis thus prevailed, but the war had been both a close-run affair and an extremely costly victory. Israeli casualties in 1973 were three times those of 1967, and more than ten times higher than in 1956. The Arab offensives had come perilously close to breakthrough in their early stages, and for a country with as little strategic depth as Israel, breakthrough could have been fatal.

The war also provoked an international debate on the implications of new precision-guided munition (*PGM*) technology for war. The Israelis' heavy losses to Egyptian PGMs convinced many that the tank was now obsolete. Commentators widely predicted that the tank would now go the way of the battleship and the horse cavalry, and that the new technology of precision guidance would make battlefield manoeuvre impossible, choking off attacks and causing defence to dominate warfare once more.

In fact, this debate overestimated both the PGMs' actual effectiveness and the reasons for the effectiveness they did enjoy. The great majority of Israeli tank casualties were actually caused by unguided short-range antitank weapons wielded by Egyptian infantry and by conventional fire from Arab tank guns. And the reasons for the losses the Israelis did suffer to Egyptian PGMs lay less in the alleged superiority of PGM technology and more in the poor tactics the Israelis had fallen into following their victories in 1956 and 1967. Unsupported tank charges could succeed only against poorly trained infantry—against better-prepared troops such methods were suicidal whether the infantry had PGMs or not. Early in the war, before the Israelis developed appropriate countermeasures, the instrument by which Egyptian infantry took their toll was chiefly the wire-guided PGM, but its effectiveness was short-lived. Once the Israelis had learned to provide rudimentary suppressive fire, the PGMs became much less a factor, but the Israelis' continuing lack of adequate infantry and artillery support exposed them to continuing losses from less sophisticated weapons in the hands of well-concealed defenders. Neither the tank nor the PGM had obviated the need for combined arms, cover and concealment, tightly integrated fire and manoeuvre, or defensive depth and reserves. On the contrary, as the Israelis had demonstrated, these technological advances had actually *increased* their importance: the potential lethality and speed of the new weapons made the consequences of failing to adopt such measures increasingly painful.

---

 **Key Points**

- Prior to 1973, Israeli armoured successes against poorly trained Arab armies led Israel to neglect combined arms, cover, concealment, and suppressive fire-and-movement in favour of rapid advances by tank-heavy forces.

- When Egypt retrained its infantry after 1967, however, these tank-heavy Israeli methods became untenable: Egyptian infantry took a terrible toll on unsupported Israeli tank attacks in the early days of the 1973 October War Sinai campaign.

- Israel then adapted, but the results were still costly; even in modern desert warfare, the methods pioneered on the Western Front in 1917–1918 remained essential.

---

## The 1991 Gulf War: Revolution or Continuity?

The 1991 Persian Gulf War had a sweeping effect on Western military thought. Between 17 January and 28 February 1991, a US-led Coalition destroyed a defending Iraqi army of hundreds of thousands of soldiers, thousands of armoured vehicles, and tens of thousands of artillery pieces, for the loss of only 240 attackers. The Coalition loss rate of fewer than one fatality per 3,000 soldiers was less than one-tenth of the Israelis' in the 1967 war, less than one-twentieth of the Germans' in their blitzkriegs against Poland or France in 1939–1940, and nearly one-one-thousandth of the US Marines' in the invasion of Tarawa in 1943. Much heavier losses had been expected. The closest prewar casualty estimate was three times the actual figure; most were off by more than an order of magnitude, while some official projections were reportedly high by more than a factor of 200. This outcome was so surprising that it convinced many that a threshold has been passed and that the very nature of war itself has changed—that the world confronted a *revolution in military affairs* (RMA).

This revolution was said to stem from the effects of new information gathering, precision guidance, and air defence suppression technologies. The Coalition had deployed each of these—either for the first time or in newly mature form—whereas the Iraqi defenders had not. The conjunction of this new technology and an unprecedented outcome convinced many that these new tools rendered traditional military methods obsolete.

In many ways, however, this interpretation echoed the initial reaction of military thinkers to the 1973 Mideast war. New technology is a major feature of modern warfare; at first glance it is easy to attribute surprising outcomes to new weapons. But just as a closer examination of the 1973 experience showed that faulty tactics had been more important than technology in explaining Israel's heavy losses, so technology's role in the 1991 conflict has been exaggerated relative to the effects of tactics and doctrine. Neither tactics nor technology is irrelevant— both must be taken into account to explain the radical results of 1991. But without the flawed Iraqi methods of 1991, the same technology would probably have had much less radical effects—and the Iraqis' flaws were mostly the same ones that had bedevilled unsuccessful armies throughout the twentieth century: poor combined arms coordination, inability to integrate manoeuvre and suppressive fire, and poor exploitation of cover and concealment. These familiar mistakes, coupled with the increased lethality of new weapons, yielded a radically one-sided outcome in 1991, but this neither obviates the importance of orthodox tactics nor implies that wars of the future will necessarily resemble 1991.

The Gulf War was a response to Iraq's invasion of neighbouring Kuwait in August 1990. Halting at the border of Saudi Arabia, the Iraqis prepared a belt of defensive positions (the 'Saddam Line'), reinforced their garrisons, and sought to deter the West from responding. The US-led Coalition instead spent the next five months building up air, ground, and naval forces in Saudi Arabia, Turkey, and the Persian Gulf while seeking to persuade the Iraqis to withdraw. When neither side backed down, the Coalition launched a massive six-week air campaign beginning on 17 January 1991. This quickly crippled the Iraqi air defence system and destroyed key elements of the Iraqi command and control network, permitting more than a month of effectively uncontested, round-the-clock pounding of ground targets across Iraq and over the entire depth of the Kuwait Theatre of Operations. As the air war unfolded, the Coalition secretly positioned two corps of ground forces on the Iraqis' extreme right flank. Following an initial assault by two US Marine divisions against the Iraqi centre and left, these two corps launched a 'left hook' around the Iraqis' exposed inland flank. Progress was rapid everywhere as Iraqi conscript infantry at the border collapsed without much of a fight. The Iraqis' elite Republican Guard and a handful of army tank and mechanized divisions, however, stood their ground and attempted to fight back. Roughly five divisions of these forces occupied a prepared blocking position designed to protect the Iraqis' retreat route from Kuwait; this blocking force was destroyed in a series of battles beginning on 26 February. Kuwait City was liberated on 27 February. With the Iraqi blocking force destroyed and the Iraqi military in full flight, the war was halted at 8 a.m. local time on 28 February.

Much postwar commentary attributed the one-sidedness of the result to the high-tech air campaign, holding that it destroyed either the Iraqis' will or ability to resist before the ground invasion began on 24 February. This was not the case. Between 1,200 and 4,100 Iraqi armoured fighting vehicles evaded destruction by Coalition air forces in 1991. At least 1,200 of these were dug in astride the left hook's axis of advance and are known to have fought back when Coalition ground forces struck them beginning on 26 February. This was a lot of armour by historical standards. The Iraqi blocking force alone deployed more active armoured vehicles than the entire Israeli army did in 1967, and more than twice as many as the German army deployed in Normandy in July 1944. The Iraqi upper bound figure had about as many tanks as the entire Egyptian army in 1973. If these surviving Iraqis had merely inflicted as many casualties per capita as the Arabs did in 1967, the result would still have been a Coalition loss rate more than ten times higher than that of 1991. The Iraqi failure to do so cannot be attributed to the air campaign alone.

Others see the war's one-sidedness as the result of superior Coalition ground force technology: the thermal sights, stabilized 120 mm gun, depleted uranium (DU) ammunition, and new compound armour of the US M1A1 tank, it is argued, gave it an insurmountable advantage over the Iraqis' Soviet-built T-72s and T-55s. Here, too, the facts are hard to square with the argument. The US Marine Corps, for example, was equipped mainly with 1960s-era M60A1 tanks, yet they fought their way through hundreds of actively resisting Iraqi armoured vehicles with no greater losses than the better-equipped Army. In fact, some of the Marines' heaviest fighting was conducted not even by M60s but by wheeled, thin-skinned, light armoured vehicles. Alternatively, the Army itself deployed thousands of lightly armoured M2 and M3 Bradleys, which engaged in extensive close combat yet suffered very few casualties. If superior guns, superior armour, and thermal sights were responsible for the Coalition's low losses, then we would expect units fighting without these advantages to suffer heavily. Yet they did not.

Instead, the war's one-sidedness was the result of a powerful interaction between Iraqi tactical errors and new Coalition technology. The Iraqi army in 1991 displayed very poor professional military skills. Iraqi conscript infantry was neither skilled nor motivated, but even the elite Republican Guard—though motivated—was remarkably unskilled. Fighting positions for Republican Guard tanks and troops were haphazardly prepared; counterattacks were launched by armoured vehicles advancing in the open without accompanying fire support; marksmanship was remarkably bad; equipment was poorly maintained. Of course, the Iraqis were not the first to make such mistakes. The technical demands of modern tactics are exacting, and many armies have failed to master them completely. Such failures had cost lives throughout the twentieth century. As technology has become more sophisticated, however, the consequences of such errors have progressively risen.

For example, against the 1918 combination of attackers on foot with light machine guns of under 100 metres effective range and artillery with limited ability to adjust fire quickly, such defensive errors were harmful but not necessarily catastrophic. Poor British defensive methods in March 1918 yielded a German breakthrough and 40-mile exploitation, but the Allies were able to reestablish a front, continue the war, and ultimately prevail. By contrast, against mid-century armoured attackers with effective weapon ranges of 500–1,000 metres and supported by aircraft dropping unguided bombs, the cost was higher: poor French tactics in 1940 enabled the Germans to knock France out of the war in a matter of weeks, though German casualties were still in the tens of thousands. By 1991, however, Coalition attackers had all-weather, day/night thermal tank sights; stabilized 120 mm guns effective on the first shot at 3,000 metres; aircraft armed with PGMs and complete command of the sky; and attack helicopters with 5,000-metre-range missiles. Against such weapons, tactical slip-ups became very lethal very quickly to a very large number of defenders—and the cost of such mistakes rose to rapid annihilation with almost no ability to harm the opponent. In 1991, the Iraqis' mistakes were many and varied, and the Coalition's technology was sophisticated and diverse. This combination of manifold Iraqi errors and advanced Coalition technology provided many ways for defensive error and offensive technology to combine; this enabled a heterogeneous attack force, some of it sophisticated and some not, to find ways to prevail with very limited costs to any part of the offensive array.

By contrast, armies that properly exploit the potential of cover, concealment, suppressive fire, and combined arms are radically less vulnerable to even post-1991 firepower. For example, the Iraqis' poor position preparation left many armoured vehicles perched on the desert surface behind loose sand berms which offered neither concealment (they were the only prominent features in an otherwise flat desert landscape) nor cover (piled sand cannot stop 120 mm DU rounds); US tank crews, by contrast, dig fighting positions as ramps which conceal the entire vehicle below ground until the weapon is to be fired. Tanks dug into the ground properly can neither be seen by thermal sights nor killed by even 120 mm DU fire: with the vehicle hidden below grade there is nothing for even the most advanced sensor to see; a vehicle protected by solid earth cannot be destroyed even by today's most advanced antitank projectiles. Whereas the Iraqis' poor preparations left them radically vulnerable to new weapons, against properly prepared positions the same weapons would have been far less effective.

The result was thus an unprecedented outcome, but one with powerful elements of continuity with the military experience preceding it. New technology was important in the Gulf War, but its effects were shaped by the same tactical and doctrinal principles that have moulded land warfare since 1900. In an important sense, what the Gulf War shows is less a revolutionary change in warfare, and more an extension of central trends that have been visible throughout the military history of the twentieth century.

 **Key Points**

- The Coalition's radically one-sided victory in the Gulf War has convinced many theorists that new technology has revolutionized war.

- Technology, however, is not a sufficient explanation for the scale of the Coalition victory, which required a synergistic interaction between new Coalition technology and Iraqi tactical error.

- The key Iraqi errors were the same ones that many unsuccessful armies had made in twentieth-century warfare: poor combined arms coordination, inability to integrate manoeuvre and suppressive fire, and poor exploitation of cover and concealment.

- These familiar mistakes, coupled with the increased lethality of new weapons, yielded a radically one-sided outcome in 1991, but this neither obviates the importance of orthodox tactics nor implies that wars of the future will necessarily resemble 1991.

**Critical Thinking**   Debating … Has warfare been revolutionized?

Many believe that new technology has transformed land warfare, making traditional strategy and tactics obsolete.

## For

- *Information technology has transformed society*. Warfare is a reflection of the societies that wage it. The digital revolution has changed everyday life and civil production profoundly; surely war must follow suit.

- *Recent wars show high-tech domination*. In the 1991 Gulf War, the 2001–2002 toppling of the Taliban in Afghanistan, and the 2003 invasion of Iraq, a high-tech US military destroyed large but less advanced enemies with exceptionally low US casualties; this vast difference from mid-twentieth-century experience demonstrates that something fundamental has changed.

- *Military history shows waves of revolutionary innovation; we are due for another*. This is not the first time that we have seen such revolutionary change in war, many argue. Gunpowder, Napoleonic warfare, the machine gun, the tank, and the atom bomb show that the nature of war can change dramatically. It should not be surprising that a new wave of change would do the same now.

- *Externally-imposed disruption is necessary for military innovation*. Battleship admirals and cavalry generals are often the last ones to see new realities in war. Those who wait for the military to innovate on its own will be overtaken by rivals who insist on faster change.

## Against

- *Modern high-tech only dominates against weak enemies*. Low-casualty US victories in 1991, 2001–2002, and 2003 all came against weak foes whose mistakes enabled new technology to perform at proving-ground effectiveness. The same technology would accomplish far less against better-skilled enemies.

- *Analysts often over-predict technological revolution*. Each new wave of twentieth-century firepower improvement convinced some that technological revolution was at hand, yet each time strategy and tactics soon returned to traditional 'modern system' norms.

- *Adaptation to misperceived 'revolution' leaves states ill-prepared*. Advocates of artillery firepower in the First World War or tank-heavy mobility in 1973 left their armies poorly prepared for the combined arms methods needed for success. Modern advocates of small, highly mobile, high-tech ground forces would create armies ill-suited to warfare against skilled state opponents that can exploit cover and concealment. And small, high-tech forces would lack the troop strength needed for other kinds of conflict such as counterinsurgency or stability operations.

- *Motivated enemies will fight on, even against superior technology*. If a resolute enemy sees existential stakes in war, many argue, they will refuse to surrender but will instead disperse, seek cover, and intermingle with civilians while continuing resistance. Technology is thus not a substitute for the ability to close with and destroy committed foes.

 ## Conclusion

In the twenty-first century, many believe we are in a period of unique technological change. But in fact, rapid technical progress has been the normal condition of modern military experience. Since 1900 there has been continuous, rapid growth in the reach, lethality, speed, and

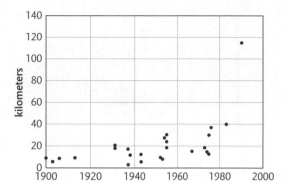

**Figure 14.1**  Growth in Artillery Range

information-gathering potential of armies (see Figures 14.1, 14.2, and 14.3)—and the question of how to respond to this rapid change has been a central focus of military thought throughout the period.

This response to technical change has displayed some important continuities. Again and again, armies have returned to a body of tactical and doctrinal principles that arose almost with the dawn of the era of modern firepower at the turn of the twentieth century. In an extended process of trial by fire, the concepts of combined arms, tight integration of movement and suppressive fire, aggressive use of cover and concealment, and defensive depth and reserves have repeatedly proven necessary for effective operations on a radically lethal modern battlefield. With each new wave of technology there has been a temptation to assume that war has now changed so dramatically that radical new methods will be needed to cope, yet repeatedly armies that strayed too far from these fundamentals have been driven back to them by painful experience.

From 1915 to 1917, European armies experimented with a doctrine of radical firepower in which artillery alone was to dominate the battlefield with crushing barrages of literally atomic magnitude; the resulting stalemate forced soldiers to develop the technical skills needed to implement close coordination between infantry manoeuvre and suppressive artillery. In the interwar period, Fuller and Liddell Hart called for massed tank formations to manoeuvre freely like ships at sea; the hard experience of the Second World War forced armies to bring balance to their armoured units and exploit cover and suppressive fire at the expense of a slower-paced, more methodical style of fighting.

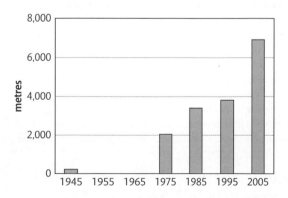

**Figure 14.2**  Growth in Antitank Lethality: Mean Penetration Range of US Heavy Antitank Weapons
(Mean lethal range for armour-penetrating weapons in a US armoured division when fired against the tanks in a representative opposing division, weighted by prevalence of each shooter and target type.)

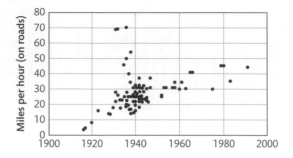

**Figure 14.3**  Growth in Tank Speeds

The 1973 October War spurred many to suppose that PGMs had doomed traditional weapons like tanks and that conventional tactics would yield to a firepower-dominated war of defensive position; the actual fighting, however, saw Israeli attackers striving to recreate orthodox tactics and subsequently finding that these took much of the sting out of the new PGMs.

With the 1991 Gulf War, many again believe that technology has revolutionized war and that the future will require a radical departure from traditional methods. The war itself, however, provides much less support for this view than typically supposed: the Iraqis were neither annihilated by precision attack from the air nor simply overmatched by superior ground force technology. Instead, Iraqi failure to master the complex demands of combined arms, cover, and concealment left them exposed to the latest in a longstanding series of increases in the lethality and reach of modern weapons—with catastrophic results for Iraqi ambitions in Kuwait.

More broadly, experience suggests a different model of military change. Rather than new technology creating periodic revolutionary breaks with the past, what technology actually did over the last century of warfare was to punish mistakes with increasing severity. The more lethal the weapons and the more effective the information-gathering systems for locating their targets, the more painful has been the failure to adopt cover, concealment, combined arms, and suppressive fire. The faster and longer-range the combat vehicles, the more damaging has been the failure to adopt depth and withhold sufficient forces in reserve. Armies that have failed to master these methods have thus suffered increasingly one-sided defeats since 1900. Armies that have implemented such methods, however, have been able to insulate themselves from the worst effects of the increasing speed and lethality of their opponents' weapons. As time has passed, technological change has thus increased, not decreased, the importance of this 'modern system' of tactics and doctrine. Militaries that implement it have seen their vulnerability rise only slowly as the nominal lethality of the battlefield has grown; militaries that fail to do so have been fully exposed to the effects of ever more powerful weapons, with ever bloodier consequences. Technological change in land warfare can thus be thought of as a wedge, driving apart the real military capability of armies that can, and those that cannot, implement the complex canon of orthodox modern tactics and doctrine—but with much less effect on the outcomes of wars between tactically astute combatants.

Inevitably the jury is still out on the effects of ongoing technological change. Perhaps the future will be radically different from the past; only time will tell. We would not be the first, however, to suppose so in peacetime only to discover otherwise in the hard school of wartime experience.

 **Questions**

1. How did European soldiers plan to cope with the new lethality of modern weapons prior to the First World War, and why did these plans fail in 1914?

2. What finally broke the trench stalemate in 1918?

3.  Which of the interwar theorists best anticipated the nature of the mid-century battlefield, and what made their ideas more successful?

4.  The 1956 and 1967 Mideast wars convinced many that tanks would dominate future desert warfare; the 1973 October War, conversely, convinced many that the tank was doomed. Were either of these views correct, and why or why not?

5.  Tanks are faster than infantry, enjoy superior armour protection, and carry heavier armament. They are better protected than artillery, and typically do not require remote observers to find targets for them as most artillery units do. Why, then, do all armies continue to field large numbers of infantry and artillery?

6.  What is the RMA thesis, and why does it matter?

7.  Many believe that the 1991 Gulf War signalled a revolution in military affairs. Did it? Why or why not?

8.  Military organizations are often criticized for trying to refight the last war, and for failing to innovate radically enough in the face of changing technology. Is this charge borne out by the experience of twentieth-century land warfare?

9.  Has changing technology increased or decreased the importance of combined arms, cover and concealment, tight integration of manoeuvre and suppressive fire, defensive depth, and large reserve withholds? Taken together, such methods comprise a very demanding style of warfare; some armies have proven able to master it, others not. How has changing technology affected the consequences of failure to master such techniques?

10. All historical processes display both change and continuity, in varying proportion. In what ways has the nature of land warfare changed since 1900, and what elements of continuity can be discerned? How have the major military events of the period been affected by each of these elements?

##  Further Reading

S. Biddle, *Military Power: Explaining Victory and Defeat in Modern Battle* (Princeton: Princeton University Press, 2004) presents the argument here in greater depth.

S. Bidwell and D. Graham, *Firepower: British Army Weapons and Theories of War, 1904–1945* (London: Allen and Unwin, 1985) details how one great power military, Britain's, responded to the incentives of changing technology, emphasizing social and organizational constraints on peacetime adaptation.

M. Doubler, *Closing with the Enemy: How the G.I.s Fought the War in Europe, 1944–1945* (Lawrence: University Press of Kansas, 1994) examines wartime adaptation in the US Army's 1944–1945 north-west European campaign.

D. Glantz and J. House, *When Titans Clashed: How the Red Army Stopped Hitler* (Lawrence: University Press of Kansas, 1995) analyses Soviet army adaptation, overturning a received view of the Soviets as clumsy and unable to change.

M. Gordon and B. Trainor, *Cobra II: The Inside Story of the Invasion and Occupation of Iraq* (New York: Vintage, 2007) considers the most recent example of twenty-first-century major combat, the US-led 2003 invasion of Iraq.

J. M. House, *Combined Arms Warfare in the Twentieth Century* (Lawrence: University Press of Kansas, 2001) provides a valuable overview of critical military developments across nations and eras.

H. Strachan, *European Armies and the Conduct of War* (London: Allen and Unwin, 1983) offers an account of European military development.

**Web Links**

Global Security **http://globalsecurity.org** offers background information on weapon systems, defence policy, and national military capabilities.

Strategic Studies Institute **http://www.strategicstudiesinstitute.army.mil** presents Army War College research findings.

Air Force Research Institute **http://www.au.af.mil/au/afri** provides Air University research findings.

# 15 Humanitarian Intervention and Peace Operations

SHEENA CHESTNUT GREITENS

## Chapter Contents

 Reader's Guide

Since the early 1990s, the number of humanitarian interventions and peace operations has increased, and their scope has expanded. This chapter begins by considering the transition from traditional peacekeeping to more ambitious post-cold war peace operations; it discusses some of the difficulties of principle and practice that emerged in that transition. The next section examines the politics of intervention and the constraints imposed by international and domestic politics. It then explores the applicability of the main principles of war to peace operations, and how these principles interact with political imperatives. Finally, the chapter concludes by outlining future challenges for peacekeeping and by examining the effects of peacekeeping and the perspectives of the individuals and communities targeted by intervention and peacekeeping efforts.[1]

## Introduction

Humanitarian intervention is directed towards two purposes: protecting fundamental human rights and providing emergency assistance. It can take non-military forms, such as emergency aid (money, medicine, food, and expertise) in the aftermath of a natural disaster or human rights promotion using diplomacy and sanctions. When reporters and policymakers speak of humanitarian intervention, however, they usually mean 'forcible military intervention in humanitarian crises'. In countries where ongoing conflict threatens aid operations, or regimes engage in massive human right abuses, intervening forces can undertake operations aimed at suppressing conflict and creating security.

Humanitarian interventions were relatively uncommon during the cold war, but have increased in both size and frequency since the early 1990s. As these interventions have grown in scope and complexity, they have also increased in importance. Until recently, however, strategic studies traditionally devoted relatively little attention to low-intensity conflict, focusing instead on war between major powers. Now, as the study of civil conflict gains increased prominence, students and scholars—like soldiers and statesmen—must understand the dynamics of humanitarian intervention and peace operations.

## The Changing Face of Peacekeeping

During the cold war, humanitarian intervention was rare for three reasons. First, the great powers focused their efforts on building up massive forces to deter the outbreak of World War III. They did intervene in Third World conflicts, but for the purpose of supporting their own (or undermining the other side's) client states. These interventions funded and armed clients engaged in human rights violations, and fuelled proxy wars rather than stopped them. Secondly, public audiences viewed these conflicts as elements of a larger cold war battle in which national security was a higher priority than human rights, so there was less public pressure on governments to respond to humanitarian crises by intervening. Thirdly, cold war politics paralysed the United Nations Security Council (UNSC) and prevented international collaboration on intervention. To be legal under international law, intervention must be authorized by a Security Council resolution, but that resolution can be vetoed by any of the permanent five members (P5) of the Security Council. With the P5 split—Britain, France, and the United States versus the Soviet Union and later communist China—the sides traded 279 vetoes during the cold war.

Despite these impediments, the UNSC authorized a few limited 'traditional peacekeeping' missions during the cold war. These missions lay somewhere between the United Nations' Chapter VI (on 'pacific settlement of disputes') and Chapter VII, which provides for the use of force to uphold international peace and security. Only once did the United Nations (UN) authorize a Chapter VII peace enforcement mission—in 1950 in Korea—and on one other occasion (in the Congo in 1960-1964), it allowed a peacekeeping mission to turn into peace enforcement. Thirteen traditional peacekeeping missions were established between 1948 and 1978, and none between 1978 and the end of the cold war. These missions typically occurred only after a conflict had ended and if the UN obtained the consent of belligerent parties. Their contingents were small, lightly armed, and supplied by neutral or non-aligned states. They relied on impartiality and goodwill to fulfil their mandates, which were typically to monitor ceasefires and supervise truces.

The end of the cold war created demand, opportunities, and incentives for intervention, and led to an unprecedented increase in the number and scale of military interventions by UN forces. A series of regional peace agreements (in Afghanistan, Angola, Namibia, Central America, and Cambodia) demanded peacekeeping forces to supervise ceasefires, demobilizations, and elections. At the same time, great power cooperation in the UN became possible, a new surplus of military power could be redeployed towards humanitarian ends, public pressure to respond to large-scale civilian suffering increased, and an ideological shift that emphasized democracy, liberal government, and human rights placed a new emphasis on preventing human suffering. Between 1988 and 1993, 20 new peacekeeping missions were established. The annual UN peacekeeping budget increased from US$230 million in 1988 to between US$800 million and US$1.6 billion in the 1990s and over US$7 billion today.

As a result, today's humanitarian interventions have become larger, more complex affairs. They involve a wider range of tasks, including protecting territory, people, and aid operations, disarming belligerents, monitoring demobilization, policing demilitarized sites, monitoring and running elections, and helping to reconstruct governments, police forces, and armies. It is probably more accurate to call these operations 'peace enforcement' than peacekeeping, because the forces involved in these operations are commonly intervening in situations where peace has not already been made. Today's operations are therefore based on a different understanding of the relationship between consent, impartiality, and force. Peacekeepers are often intervening without full consent of local parties to a conflict; strict impartiality against warring parties is unlikely or impossible in cases of genocide or when spoilers seek to use violence to undermine peace (Stedman 1997: 5). To accomplish the tasks assigned under these broadened mandates, peacekeepers have used more force, and used it more often, than had been expected previously.

## Peacekeeping after the Cold War

Three major operations in the 1990s affected the discourse and thinking on peacekeeping: Somalia, Bosnia, and Rwanda. These interventions illustrated the difficulties of adapting to a more expansive international peacekeeping mandate. They also illustrated the differences of opinion between intervention optimists, who argued that the international community can and should intervene forcibly to rebuild failed states and reform murderous ones, and intervention pessimists, who were generally sceptical about or opposed to international intervention into humanitarian crises and conflicts. (Many people fall somewhere between these two positions.)

In Somalia, optimism led the UN to expand a relatively successful limited mission focused on securing aid operations into an ambitious and ultimately failed operation that sought to disarm warring factions and reconstruct the Somali state. Failure in Somalia contributed to reluctance on the part of both the United Nations and the Clinton administration to intervene in Bosnia and Rwanda. In Bosnia, reluctance to call in air strikes when land forces were insufficient meant that peacekeepers did not prevent ethnic cleansing until after the failure to protect designated safe areas led to the slaughter of their male civilian inhabitants (Box 15.1).

While much of the world's attention focused on fighting in the Balkans, an estimated 800,000 people were massacred in approximately 100 days between April and July 1994 in Rwanda. When Hutu extremists began a campaign of mass slaughter against the Tutsi and moderate Hutus, the UN peacekeeping force assigned to monitor Rwanda's peace and power-sharing agreement found itself under-staffed, under-resourced, and unauthorized to use force to prevent genocide. The mission was not expanded in size and authorized to protect the population until May 1994, and even after that, UN member states declined to contribute forces. The genocide eventually ran out of steam as the Rwandan Patriotic Front swept down from Uganda to push back Hutu extremists, who fled to Zaire. Although sceptics claimed that

**BOX** 15.1   The UN's Failure to Stop Serb Spoilers in Bosnia

With the benefit of hindsight, one can see that many of the errors the United Nations made [in Bosnia] flowed from a single and no doubt well-intentioned effort: we tried to keep the peace and apply the rules of peacekeeping when there was no peace to keep . . . None of the conditions for the deployment of peacekeepers had been met: there was no peace agreement—not even a functioning ceasefire—there was no clear will to peace and there was no clear consent by the belligerents . . . Nor was the provision of humanitarian aid a sufficient response to 'ethnic cleansing' and to an attempted genocide.

Kofi Annan

the speed of the genocide was so fast that even the United States could not have intervened effectively (Juperman 2000), most observers concluded that the UN had enough warning of the genocide to have bolstered the mission and perhaps prevented the genocide, or at least slowed its pace. Ultimately, an independent inquiry charged the UN with 'overriding failure', and concluded that 'the Security Council bears responsibility for its lack of political will to do more to stop the killing'. The spillover of conflict from Rwanda into eastern Congo contributed to ongoing conflict in that country that was once referred to as 'Africa's World War'—involving eight countries, a myriad of armed groups, an estimated 5 million deaths, and the largest peacekeeping mission mounted by the UN at that time.

### Peacekeeping Since 2000

The notable failures of the mid-1990s led to a temporary lull in peacekeeping operations (Tharoor 1995–96). Despite some lower-profile successes, only one major UN mission was launched between 1993 and 1998, in Eastern Slavonia (Fortna and Howard 2008: 287–8). Gradually, however, several developments combined to rejuvenate peacekeeping and open space for more permissive norms around humanitarian intervention.

First, new institutions like the International Criminal Court and post-conflict tribunals in Rwanda, the former Yugoslavia, and elsewhere began to hold leaders accountable for breaches of humanitarian law. Secondly, the United Nations itself sought to reform peacekeeping operations. The Brahimi Report (2000) articulated a strategic perspective on peacekeeping, expanded the UN's Department of Peacekeeping Operations, and reformed the practices and processes of peace operations. Thirdly, internal conflict and mass atrocity were redefined as potential threats to 'international peace and security' (invoking Chapter VII). These efforts began in the early 1990s, but gained momentum towards the end of the decade.

Finally, the United Nations began increasingly to emphasize the importance of the protection of civilians (Wills 2009). The Security Council issued the first mandate including the protection of civilians in Sierra Leone in 1999, and the following year, the International Commission on Intervention and State Sovereignty (ICISS) convened for the first time. The ICISS would eventually issue a document titled 'Responsibility to Protect', which the UN and others have increasingly accepted (though not uniformly) as a global norm. This emphasis, combined with other developments, elevated civilian protection and placed significant limits on the previous norm of state sovereignty. In 2011, UN Resolution 1973 on Libya marked the first time that the UN had authorized the use of force to protect civilians against the wishes of a functional state (Bellamy and Williams 2011), and in 2013, after the failure to protect civilian populations in Sri Lanka in 2009, UN Secretary-General Ban Ki-Moon released a policy called 'Rights Up Front', in which the need to protect people from human rights violations occupies the centre of the UN's work.

Today, there are more peacekeepers deployed globally than at any point in the past: over 122,000 personnel from 122 countries in 16 operations on multiple continents as of September 2014—a ninefold increase since 1999 (UN Peacekeeping 2014). According to US Ambassador to the UN Samantha Power, two-thirds of them are now operating in active conflict areas (Power 2014). This expansion in scope, coupled with a continued expansion in the mandates given to peacekeeping forces, has led to operations that today are 'unparalleled in their organizational complexity and the scope of their ambition'. At the same time, their complexity and scale have created serious concern about overstraining the institutions responsible for peacekeeping activity (Paddon 2011).

Awareness of the limitations of UN capacity has resulted in the regionalization of peace operations in some cases, and a diversification of actors or division of labour between various organizations in others. African states, in particular, have been encouraged to develop a regional capacity for peace operations on the continent—an area with high demand for peace forces which the US and others are less keen to fill. The African Union operation in Sudan, which deployed in 2004, is an example of this shift towards regionalization. NATO, which deployed massive forces in Bosnia and Kosovo in the 1990s, has more recently conducted operations in Afghanistan and Libya. Regional organizations have also acted as gatekeepers in authorizing the use of force and shaping the mandates of interventions, as the League of Arab States and Gulf Cooperation Council both did with respect to Libya in 2011 (Bellamy and Williams 2011).

Often a single state or regional organization has led an intervention, either with the authorization of a UN resolution, and/or with a less coercive UN peacekeeping force following behind (Fortna and Howard 2008: 291–2). These regional coalitions were initially thought to enjoy several advantages over UN operations: greater force cohesion, better local knowledge, greater commitment to the mission, and more suitable force structure. Experience, however, has revealed unexpected problems with regionalization. When the Economic Community of West African States Ceasefire Monitoring Group attempted to restore order to the failed Liberian state in 1990–1996, it was divided by subregional rivalries between Francophone and Anglophone West African contributing states. The intervening forces also exhibited poor understanding of Liberia's political dynamics, relied on local surrogate forces who had an interest in continuing the conflict, and lacked the equipment, training, and logistical support for effective counterinsurgency operations. In more recent operations, such as those in Mali and the Central African Republic, troop shortfalls remain a serious problem, and regional organizations have not been able to take effective action without significant support from Western powers. In Darfur, the African Union operation was eventually replaced by a hybrid UN-AU mission (UNAMID) when the AU force failed to damp down violence. Serious questions about regionalization, therefore, remain unresolved today.

Thus, as the context of peacekeeping has changed and developed, the principles that have traditionally guided peacekeeping—impartiality, consent, and restraint on the use of force—have also been subject to continuous debate and renegotiation. Impartiality has been redefined as a lack of favouritism or prejudice rather than as neutrality, and UN guidelines emphasize that impartiality is not an excuse for inaction where mandates call for civilian protection. Because peacekeepers are more often intervening in situations where conflict is ongoing, their actions are often seen as taking one party's side over others. The UN Mission in South Sudan (UNMISS), for example, has been criticized by both the government and by anti-government forces for not being sufficiently impartial.

How we think about consent and restraint in using force in peacekeeping has also evolved. Consent, while still revered at the strategic level, is acknowledged to break down in tactical situations where forceful action is sometimes needed to execute the mandate. And the non-use of force has been abrogated when necessary for self-defence of the mission's forces or when essential to defend the mandate—which often now includes the protection of civilians. As each new situation poses different challenges to these principles, debate will undoubtedly continue.

 **Key Points**

- Limited traditional peacekeeping operations have given way in the post-cold war era to larger, more complex, and more ambitious peace operations.

- The debate between intervention optimists and pessimists played out in UN interventions in Bosnia, Somalia, and Rwanda. Critics charge that intervening forces tried to do too much in Somalia, failed to stop spoilers in Bosnia, and did not do enough in Rwanda.

- Peacekeeping operations have become more regionalized since 2000, but questions about how effective regional organizations can be remain.

- The shift towards peace operations has prompted a rethinking of the relationship between impartiality, consent, and the use of force.

# The Politics of Humanitarian Intervention

Political considerations focus international attention selectively on humanitarian crises, prompting a stronger response at some times and places than others and shaping the speed and scale of humanitarian intervention (Roberts and Zaum 2008; Hehir 2013). Serbia's repression in Kosovo triggered Western humanitarian intervention, but Russia's repression in Chechnya did not. Iraqi attacks on Kurds in 1991 resulted in the creation of a Kurdish 'safe haven' in Iraq, guarded by thousands of troops and Allied airpower, though even deadlier Iraqi attacks on Kurds several years earlier had led to no response. Political constraints and incentives define crises and shape responses at several different levels: at the level of domestic politics in both the state targeted for intervention and the states that are considering intervening, and at the level of international geopolitics—most commonly via the UN Security Council.

## Security Council Politics

The 15 members of the UN Security Council are responsible for authorizing forcible humanitarian interventions. Authorization requires a majority of nine UNSC members, but real power resides with the P5, who each have the right of veto. Conflict between the P5 during the cold war made the Security Council a moribund instrument for managing international security. Although cooperation between the P5 has improved since then, four political problems still dog UNSC sponsorship of humanitarian intervention.

First, the P5 are all states with great power interests and aspirations. Great power differences can produce a 'veto problem' if one P5 member simply refuses to contemplate a UN intervention that it considers threatening to its interests. Russia, for example, was prepared to veto UN intervention in Kosovo in the late 1990s, a problem that was resolved by NATO acting on humanitarian grounds without a Security Council resolution. More recently, Russia has opposed the use of force to intervene on humanitarian grounds in Syria, but has used the language of civilian protection to justify its interventions in Georgia and Ukraine. It is clear today that some members of the Security Council, including some of the P5, are reluctant to cede the principle of state sovereignty to a new norm of civilian protection, unless doing so suits their more traditionally defined national interests. Great power interests also shape the selectivity of interventions; France's history in Africa inclines it to intervene more often in this region, while China—a country that is traditionally sceptical of peacekeeping—recently provided a large contingent of peacekeepers to South Sudan where it has sizeable investments in the oil industry and a number of Chinese citizens working.

Second, there may be a 'logrolling problem'. If a particular crisis is associated with a certain P5 member (or members), others may withhold support or threaten to veto unless, in exchange, they are promised support for their interests. In the mid-1990s, for example, Russia and later China obstructed UNSC resolutions on peace operations in Haiti because Russia wanted UN endorsement of its own intervention in Georgia, while China wanted a public apology from Haiti for inviting Taiwan's Vice-President to Haiti's 1996 presidential inauguration.

Thirdly, even if the P5 agree to authorize a UN peace operations force, they must still overcome a 'posturing problem', which is a tendency to 'talk the talk but not walk the walk'. The great powers sometimes pass grand-sounding Security Council resolutions that are not backed by adequate political engagement and commitment of the necessary resources to implement the resolution. The creation of 'safe areas' in Bosnia is a classic example of this type of posturing problem. These areas were not actually safe because the Security Council was not prepared to deploy additional forces to protect them (see Box 15.1). Several UNSC members and the UN Secretariat warned at the time that 'without the provision of any credible military threat' these safe areas would be meaningless, but the great powers went ahead anyway. In today's missions, troop shortfalls remain common. The UN's Department of Peacekeeping Operations 'New Horizon' agenda, promulgated in 2009, has sought to expand partnerships as a means of overcoming resource and manpower shortages and providing more effective and timely responses, but building the capacity to effectively implement peacekeeping mandates is likely to remain a fundamental challenge (Welsh 2014).

Fourthly, even if the P5 are prepared to walk the walk, they can disagree on which direction to take. Great powers may disagree on the nature of the humanitarian crisis, or on the most effective response. This 'coordination problem' was evident in Bosnia, where the United States and its European allies had different perceptions of the conflict and because of that, disagreed on the appropriate response. The European powers saw an ethnic conflict to be solved by partition. The United States saw it as a war started by Serbia, and opposed partition because it would reward Serbian aggression. Only in 1995, when the United States accepted that partition was a necessary evil, was the international community able to solve the coordination problem and take effective action. Even when the UNSC appears to have achieved consensus, problems can arise with implementation. Members of the P5 may interpret mandates differently, or may in their own actions be combining intervention for humanitarian purposes with intervention that is aimed at other goals.

---

 **Critical Thinking**    Debating … Should the international community intervene in Syria?

In March 2011, protests in Syria were violently repressed by the government of President Bashar al-Assad. Opposition groups responded with armed resistance, and fighting escalated into civil war. The UN estimated that as of April 2014, over 191,000 people had been killed in the conflict, and that over 6.5 million people had been displaced within the country with another 3 million refugees fleeing outside Syria's borders. Debate over whether and how to intervene has occurred since the beginning of the conflict, and was particularly acute following reports of the regime's use of chemical weapons against civilians in 2013.

### For

- *A humanitarian crisis.* The escalating conflict in Syria has exacted increasing human costs and led to large-scale violations of human rights. Failing to intervene will deepen the current humanitarian crisis.

- *Risking instability and radicalization.* Failing to intervene will stall the country and the region in a state of chaos and instability. It could also create a power vacuum that could contribute to the radicalization of armed groups in ways that are detrimental to Western interests.

- *Credibility at stake.* Intervention is necessary to preserve Western credibility, especially after US President Barack Obama identified the use of chemical weapons as a 'red line'.

- *Success is possible.* Limited military action on the part of the West may be capable of accomplishing coalition goals and protecting Syrian civilians.

### Against

- *Too costly and too risky.* Mounting an effective intervention in the conflict in Syria would require a lot of resources. It would be very costly and too risky to Western forces.

- *Unlikely to succeed.* A limited, lower-risk intervention, on the other hand, would not accomplish the objectives of stability and civilian protection.

- *Inappropriate objectives.* Intervening would mean taking the side of the rebel forces against Assad, and regime change is not an appropriate objective for intervention. The lack of progress in Libya after NATO helped to remove Gaddafi illustrates why this is a bad idea.

- *Harmful to other important geopolitical relationships*. Intervening in Syria would place the West at increased risk of costly conflict with Russia and Iran, both of whom have provided support to the Syrian regime.

- *Likely to worsen instability and radicalization*. Providing support to the anti-Assad opposition in Syria also means supporting radical Islamists, including some of the very groups that coalition forces are fighting elsewhere. Because of this, intervention is not likely to make a positive contribution to regional stability.

## Public Opinion and Domestic Politics

Policymakers and commentators alike believe that Western public opinion can make or break humanitarian interventions. Two factors are thought to be particularly important in shaping public opinion: media coverage and casualties.

Media and technology shape the way that global events are reported and therefore shape the politics of humanitarian intervention. In the 1990s, policymakers and scholars referred to a 'CNN effect' after extensive television coverage of the 1990–1991 Gulf War seemed to change the way conflicts were reported. Media attention to Somalia and Bosnia, and the public outcry that followed, are thought to have prompted intervention in these places (Holbrooke 1999: 20; von Hippel 2000: 59). Media coverage and access to technology also, however, shape the selective nature of humanitarian intervention, helping to draw attention to some conflicts and not others. Diplomats and pundits have suggested that extensive coverage of the conflict in Syria, with videos uploaded every day onto YouTube, has helped prompt calls for intervention there, while areas such as South Sudan receive far less attention because their lack of technology and connectivity makes the costs of those conflicts less visible to a global audience.

Policymakers and pundits also assume that public support for humanitarian intervention depends on minimal peacekeeper casualties. The argument suggests that the public will be particularly sensitive to casualties in humanitarian interventions because these military actions are freely entered into by governments: they are 'wars of choice' as opposed to 'wars of necessity' fought to defend national security. Policymakers worry that media coverage of peacekeeping deaths will collapse public support for these operations, as happened in Somalia after the deaths of 18 American soldiers in the early 1990s.

Critics suggest that both claims are overstated. Arguments about the impact of media coverage underestimate the extent to which governments can frame the debate to choose the place and time of intervention. Leaders are most likely to be able to shape media coverage this way when they already know their desired course of action. Disunity and divided government, therefore, are thought to increase public responsiveness to media coverage and reduce leaders' ability to drive the media agenda. In Somalia, the Bush administration's uncertainty and a pro-intervention lobby in US aid agencies and Congress pushed the United States towards intervention, while the Clinton administration resisted calls for ground intervention in Kosovo because it was sure that it opposed intervention, and because that stance had support in Congress. Internal debate within the Obama administration about what the strategy should be has heightened the effect of public pressure to 'do something' in Syria as the costs of that conflict have mounted.

The effect of the media can also be overstated because media attention is often short-lived, and humanitarian crises often outlast the coverage of them in the news. Technology can also encourage oversimplification of complex problems and validate 'slacktivism', in which people make symbolic gestures of support, such as posting on social media, that do not have meaningful impact (Gladwell 2010; Lewis, Gray, and Meierhenrich 2014). Both the Save Darfur campaign of the mid-2000s and the 'Kony 2012' video have been criticized on these grounds (see Box 15.2).

Claims about casualties can be similarly misleading. Empirical evidence suggests that peacekeeper casualties do not necessarily result in public calls for immediate withdrawal

**BOX** 15.2   'Kony 2012' and #StopKony

In March 2012, California-based non-profit organization Invisible Children released an advocacy video called 'Kony 2012', which detailed the crimes of Ugandan warlord Joseph Kony and called for his immediate arrest. The video was viewed over 100 million times in a week and retweeted by prominent celebrities using the hashtag #StopKony. The social media campaign led to a US Senate resolution and public outcry over Kony's past atrocities in Uganda. Several weeks later, the African Union announced a decision to mobilize 5,000 troops to find and capture Kony, which had reportedly been planned prior to the launch of the video. The video itself quickly became the subject of controversy and criticism, both for its oversimplified presentation of the conflict and for its promotion of 'slacktivism'. As of mid-2015, Joseph Kony remains at large.

(Gelpi, Feaver, and Reifler 2009). Indeed, casualties can sometimes lead to a rallying of public support. In the case of Somalia, most Americans actually favoured increased US military involvement immediately following the killing of US soldiers, especially if ordinary Somalis wanted an American presence. Similarly, the execution of Western journalists in the Middle East in 2014 helped to harden popular and political opinion against the Islamic State.

 **Key Points**

- Humanitarian intervention is affected by domestic politics, politics in the Security Council, and the politics of the target country and region. All of these levels operate together to define the crisis and shape international responses.

- UN Security Council cooperation on humanitarian intervention can be hindered by one or more of the P5 seeking to advance their own national interests, either through logrolling or vetoing behaviour.

- Even when the P5 agree to act, effective intervention can be hampered by posturing, where tough talk is not matched by action, or lack of coordination, where states disagree on the best course of action.

- Technology and media coverage of conflict can help shape public demand for humanitarian intervention, but political elites can, under certain circumstances, still shape public debate to affect the place, time, and type of intervention.

- Although policymakers fear that casualties can collapse public support for intervention, this is not always the case.

## The Military Character of Peace Operations

To protect civilians or stop conflict, peace forces must be prepared to engage in combat. Most often, these military forces have been designed, equipped, and trained according to fundamental principles of war. These principles, however, do not always apply straightforwardly to peace operations. In fact, four main principles of war—clear identification of the objective, unity of effort, massing of forces, and surprise—are problematic when it comes to peace operations.

## Principles and Practicalities

The principle that military operations should be conducted towards clearly defined, decisive, and attainable objectives is difficult to achieve in peace operations, where objectives are often poorly defined. In a UN intervention, for instance, objectives are established by Security Council mandate, sometimes in consultation with the host government. In non-UN interventions, objectives are set by contributing national governments. As noted in the previous section, however, a number of political factors can prevent the construction of a mandate with a clear objective. Mandates may be deliberately vague to overcome coordination problems among great powers. They may be imprecise, non-credible, or simply unattainable when Security Council members want to threaten or coerce but are reluctant to commit to tough action or provide the necessary resources.

Mandates may also be unclear because peace operations themselves have become increasingly complex, and now include tasks aimed at longer-term goals like political stability and economic development. These tasks are not military in nature, but will impact the long-term success of military actions. Commanders who are given a complex mandate will attempt to translate it into more limited mission objectives that are both clear and attainable. Simpler and more limited objectives, however, will often be less decisive in the long-term. The UN mission in Somalia sought to create a secure environment for aid operations by keeping armed bandits at bay rather than disarming them, and in Bosnia, UN forces protected humanitarian aid by escorting convoys rather than securing routes because the latter would have involved using force to clear roadblocks. These objectives were attainable in the short-term, but a secure environment did not outlast the presence of peacekeepers.

The second principle, unity of effort, is achieved in war through unity of command: by placing all forces under a single commander. The coalition forces that liberated France in 1944 were led by one general (Dwight Eisenhower), as were those that liberated Kuwait in 1991 (Norman Schwarzkopf). Forces in peace operations, however, are often drawn from a wider variety of troop-contributing countries (TCCs) than forces in normal coalition warfare. Differences in military culture, lack of prior joint operational experience, and potential political rivalries between TCCs all inhibit the creation and operation of an effective command structure. Sometimes differences are so great that they render the chain of command inoperative, as in the bitter 2000 dispute between an Indian commander and the Nigerian and Zambian contingents in the UN force in Sierra Leone. The governments of TCCs also limit what the UN can do with their troops, placing restrictions on the rules of engagement, or bypassing the mission command structure and issuing instructions directly to their forces in the field, thereby creating two chains of command rather than one. Additionally, Western powers have sometimes supported UN missions with forces that were not actually under UN command. The Anglo–French Rapid Reaction Force in Bosnia, the US Quick Reaction Force in Somalia, and British military forces in Sierra Leone, for example, all remained under national political and military command.

Even if unity of command is achieved, commanders of peace operations must also coordinate with civilian agencies—often a multitude of UN, non-government, and local aid actors—to achieve unity of effort. This is especially challenging now that UN missions are 'integrated missions' involving more complex tasks and a wider range of actors (Metcalfe, Giffen, and Elhawary 2011). Here differences in military and civilian organizational cultures are even more pronounced, and can pose high barriers to effective, timely coordination. In Somalia, civil–military cooperation broke down when the military way of doing things—controlling movement and information—infuriated civilian aid agencies.

Thirdly, commanders seek to mass force by concentrating troops and deploying combat power at places and times that have greatest impact on the enemy. When it comes to peace operations, however, forces are commonly dispersed rather than concentrated, to maintain high visibility and provide security on the ground. Force dispersal means that fewer elements of combat power are available for decisive action, and limits the ability to mass force for maximal impact. The problems of under-resourced missions and disunity of command also greatly reduce possibilities for massing force.

The fourth principle, surprise, highlights the importance of striking the enemy when and where they least expect it. The critical ingredients for surprise are speed, secrecy, and deception. Lack of unity of command makes it difficult for peace forces to achieve speed in their area of operations. Secrecy is often compromised by the imperative for unity of effort, which requires peace forces to share operational information with civilian agencies, many of which in turn hire and share information with local staff. In Somalia, for instance, warlord leader Mohamed Farrah Aideed had excellent intelligence about peacekeeping operations partly because he used local aid workers as spies. Deception is also problematic in urban environments, because the local population can act as eyes and ears for belligerent parties.

Good intelligence is also critical to achieving surprise. Peacekeeping forces, however, often struggle to obtain good intelligence because their ability to monitor, communicate, and respond to developments is hampered by a lack of technology (and sometimes by their mission and command structure). In 2013, the Security Council authorized the first use of drones in peacekeeping, for surveillance and monitoring in the Democratic Republic of Congo. While there is broad agreement that drones can do much to improve the situational awareness of peacekeeping forces, their deployment may also put peacekeeping forces in a difficult position by making them aware of situations to which peacekeeping forces are obligated to respond—for example, to protect civilians—when they lack the physical and organizational capacity to do so. The authorization of drones for monitoring and surveillance also opens the question, currently unresolved, of whether armed drones should be employed for civilian protection if peacekeeping forces are insufficient or unable to reach a crisis location in time (Dorn 2011; Karlsrud and Rosen 2013).

## Public Opinion and Operational Pathologies

The political imperatives that shape peace operations pull them even further away from the traditional principles of war. Political sensitivity to casualties results in a focus on managing public opinion to maintain support for intervention. In Kosovo, NATO launched an elaborate public relations campaign to counter Serbia's portrayal of itself as a victim of NATO aggression. And during NATO's 2011 intervention into Libya, the Obama administration tried to focus public attention on human rights violations, though this was never the sole aim articulated (see Box 15.3).

Concerns with public opinion produce three specific pathologies in interventions and peace operations. First is the strategic compression of the battlefield. In conventional war,

**BOX** 15.3 NATO's 2011 Intervention in Libya

In March 2011, UNSC Resolution 1973 authorized a no-fly zone over Libya, demanding a ceasefire and an end to attacks on civilians. The resolution imposed tighter sanctions on the Libyan government and forbade any 'foreign occupation force' on Libyan soil. It passed unanimously, with ten votes in support and five abstentions (Brazil, China, Germany, India, and Russia). The resolution's aim was 'to protect civilians and civilian areas targeted by Colonel Muammar Al-Qadhafi, his allied forces, and mercenaries'. Members of the Obama administration, however, advanced at least five additional reasons for intervention: promoting regime change; sending a message to other dictators; supporting Libya's rebel movement; repaying European support in Afghanistan; and the belief that achieving the desired end-state would be easy. These actions, intended to increase public support for the intervention, made it harder to maintain a clear mission focus. As Micah Zenko noted:

> When presidents authorize military action, they must have a clear objective in mind. Without a singular, defined goal, policymakers cannot appropriately match means and ends, which increases the likelihood of failure . . . In the case of Libya, there was only one overarching rationale provided—the protection of civilians— yet the initial intervention and now the 97-day bombing campaign has been about so much more.

Zenko 2011; UNSC 2011

strategic outcomes are shaped by military action at the operational level: the success or fail- ure of entire campaigns. By contrast, in interventions or peace operations, tactical actions may have heightened strategic consequences. (The bombing of the Chinese embassy in Kosovo, for example, disrupted NATO strategy in 1999.) As a result, commanders make decisions with more awareness of the domestic political consequences of their actions, either through direct communication with those at home or through pressure from civilian authorities.

The second operational pathology is a heightened focus on full force protection so that intervening forces are not vulnerable to attack. Making full force protection an operational imperative can hinder effective execution of a mission. It concentrates force in situations when the dispersal of forces would be more effective, and often requires ground personnel to wear body armour and travel at high speeds, visibly demonstrating distrust towards local populations in situations when a more relaxed force posture would make it easier to build relations with local communities. Senior officers closer to political pressures are often more intent on force protection, while junior officers sometimes view the force protection require- ments as an impediment to success.

The third issue is an over-reliance on airpower and unrealistic expectations of what it can accomplish (see Box 15.4). As the 1990–1991 campaign in Iraq and more recent campaigns in Libya and Syria have shown, airpower is most effective when employed in synergy with land power to destroy military infrastructure and soften defences for land forces. Casualty aver- sion, however, makes Western powers deeply reluctant to put 'boots on the ground'. They seek to achieve force protection by making sure that the only forces deployed are in fast jets thousands of metres above the conflict.

Western airpower can sometimes be combined successfully with local land forces. NATO bombing of Bosnian Serb bases in 1995, combined with a successful Bosniak-Croat land offensive against Serb territory in Eastern Bosnia, forced Bosnian Serbs to sue for peace. NATO

**BOX** 15.4   Fatal Attraction: America and Airpower

Airpower can help sustain domestic support or coalition unity, but it cannot eliminate underlying political constraints. In Eliot Cohen's words, 'Airpower is an unusually seductive form of military strength, in part because, like modern courtship, it appears to offer gratification without commitment.' This view poses a challenge for airpower. Because policymakers often see airpower strikes as a low-risk, low-commitment measure, airpower will be called on when US public or allied commitment is weak—a situation that will make successful coercion far harder when casualties do occur or when air strikes fail to break adversary resistance. Airpower, like other military instruments, cannot overcome a complete lack of political will.

Byman and Waxman (2000: 38)

air operations in Libya in 2011 provided critical support to rebel forces seeking to advance and overthrow Muammar Gaddafi. At other times, however, rejection of ground intervention has had negative consequences. In Kosovo in 1999, NATO's restriction of its campaign to airpower alone gave Serb forces room to terrorize the Albanian population and drive them out of the province. The Kosovo Liberation Army (unlike the Croatian Army in Bosnia) could not generate enough combat power to be an effective surrogate ground force for NATO. As a result, Serb forces held out against NATO bombing for 78 days before capitulating—which they did only under threat of a ground invasion, and after the province had essentially been 'cleansed' of Albanians.

Many of these operational pathologies have been visible in coalition military operations in Afghanistan and Iraq as well as in the operations that followed. The US-led invasions of Afghanistan in 2001 and Iraq in 2003 are not examples of humanitarian interventions, because they were primarily about protecting the national security of the United States and its coalition partners from terrorism and weapons of mass destruction. Nevertheless, policymakers predicted that humanitarian outcomes and democracy promotion would be by-products of these operations. The post-conflict stabilization operations led by the United States in Iraq and NATO in Afghanistan have, however, been similar to peace operations. Force protection concerns affected US counterinsurgency strategy, informing the initial decision to concentrate rather than disperse forces in Iraq. Casualty aversion was also an issue. Although several thousand fatalities (nearly 7,000 as of late 2014) resulted in a marked decline in US public support for the operations and mounting political pressure for withdrawal, the United States 'surged' troops to both countries before eventually withdrawing. Finally, although these campaigns did not rely excessively on airpower, American experiences in Iraq and Afghanistan were critical to informing the Obama administration's decision to rely almost exclusively on airpower for NATO's intervention in Libya in early 2011 and have contributed significantly to the reluctance to send ground troops back to the Middle East as the conflict with the Islamic State unfolded in 2014. Precedents from the United States' global counterterrorism efforts have also shaped the 2011 'armed humanitarian intervention' in central Africa, where American special forces have been tasked to help regional militaries capture Joseph Kony and counter his Lord's Resistance Army, while engaging in combat only in self-defence. Thus despite the fact that they were not undertaken primarily for humanitarian purposes, operations in Iraq and Afghanistan will continue to influence future humanitarian interventions and peace operations.

**Key Points**

- In practice, peace operations often contravene one or more of the four main principles of war—clear identification of the objective, unity of effort, massing of forces, and surprise. Obtaining good intelligence in peace operations can also be difficult.

- Political imperatives, such as the need to manage public support, can create a number of operational pathologies during humanitarian interventions and peace operations.

- The operational pathologies imposed by political considerations include compression of the battlefield such that tactical incidents have disproportional strategic and political consequences, prioritizing force protection at the expense of mission requirements, and an over-reliance on airpower.

- Non-humanitarian military interventions and operations, such as the US-led coalition operations in Iraq and Afghanistan, are likely to affect the calculus about whether to intervene on humanitarian grounds in future scenarios, and are likely to shape the nature of any intervention.

 ## Conclusion: Problems and Prospects

This chapter has explored issues and debates surrounding humanitarian intervention and peace operations. In order to intervene, the international community must not only find the political will to intervene, but must manage both international and domestic politics and match the will to act with appropriate capacity and resource commitments. Peacekeeping forces must then balance consent, impartiality, and the need to use force to defend their mandates; inability to strike the correct balance can lead to a variety of failures. Additionally, domestic and international political pressures and incentives influence peace operations in ways that divert them from the principles of war. Each of these issues poses challenges for peacekeeping.

Nevertheless, intervention and peacekeeping are here to stay. Despite debate about the most effective form and organization of peacekeeping, there is broad consensus that it works. Studies that examine peace operations in the context of inter-state war as well as in cases of civil conflict suggest that the presence of peacekeepers makes re-emergence of civil war much less likely, even after peacekeepers go home (Fortna 2003, 2008; for a partially contrasting view, see Greig and Diehl 2005). And theoretical debates aside, there are more peacekeepers deployed now than ever before: 122,000 as of September 2014.

Future debates are likely to centre on what relationship peacekeeping should have with transitional administration and attempts at state building. Under transitional administrations, the UN not only takes on the tasks of multidimensional peace operations, but assumes executive authority over the state's administration and government. The process has only been attempted a handful of times—for example, during UN efforts in Namibia, Cambodia, Croatia, Kosovo, and East Timor. As more and more missions are integrated missions that involve numerous actors and a range of complex tasks, these questions will become increasingly important. Optimists emphasize the possibility that intervening actors—the United States, the United Nations, or any third party—can successfully build a state or democracy if they have the right strategy, resources, and political will. Others are sceptical, arguing that the success of intervention depends more on local capacity and local political dynamics than on anything foreigners do. The international community might be good at building telecommunications networks, the argument goes, but it is far worse at transforming local political culture to meet Western standards in areas like the rule of law (Stewart 2011). This emphasis on local actors parallels a call among scholars of peacekeeping for more attention to the 'perspectives of the peacekept' to assess how they respond to intervention and peacekeeping efforts—a topic that so far has received relatively little attention (Clapham 1998; Pouligny 2006; Autesserre 2014). Normatively, these developments also raise new questions about impartiality and under what circumstances building or supporting a state is the most important priority, particularly in cases where the government itself has been one of the chief violators of the emerging norm of civilian protection.

Humanitarian intervention and peace operations remain a fixture on the landscape of global politics. Given their importance, the questions and debates that surround these operations are likely to influence international practices—and the field of strategic studies—for years to come.

 ## Questions

1. Why was humanitarian intervention rare during the cold war?
2. How did peacekeeping change in the 1990s? Why? How did it change in the 2000s?
3. Is regionalization of peace operations a good idea?
4. Is impartiality possible during peacekeeping? Why or why not?
5. Are you an intervention optimist or pessimist? Why?
6. To what extent can public opinion 'make and break' humanitarian interventions? Why? What operational pathologies can public opinion create?
7. What four problems associated with the UN Security Council hinder effective action in response to humanitarian crises?
8. How well do the principles of war apply to peace operations?
9. Does peacekeeping work?
10. How much has technology changed the nature of peacekeeping? What exactly has changed and why?

 ## Further Reading

A. J. Bellamy, P. Williams, and S. Griffin, *Understanding Peacekeeping*, 2nd edn (Cambridge: Polity, 2010) is an excellent, up-to-date introductory text.

V. P. Fortna and L. M. Howard, 'Pitfalls and Prospects in the Peacekeeping Literature,' *Annual Review of Political Science* 11 (2008): 283–301 gives a concise, thorough review of contemporary debates and questions. Books written by each of these authors individually are also worth a careful read.

H. Langholtz, B. Kondoch, and A. Wells (eds), *International Peacekeeping: Yearbook of International Peace Operations* (Leiden: Brill, ongoing) is essential reading for scholars and students of peace operations, published annually.

L. Minear and T. G. Weiss, *Mercy Under Fire: War and the Global Humanitarian Community* (Boulder, CO: Westview Press, 1995) is a classic text on application of humanitarian principles to intervention in complex emergencies.

R. Paris, *At War's End: Building Peace After Civil Conflict* (Cambridge: Cambridge University Press, 2004) presents a critique of the democratisation and marketization agenda inherent in peace operations.

W. Shawcross, *Deliver Us From Evil: Warlords and Peacekeepers in a World of Endless Conflict* (London: Bloomsbury, 2000) gives a readable (and damning) account of UN operations in Cambodia, Somalia, Rwanda, Bosnia, and Kosovo.

R. Stewart, 'What Can Afghanistan and Bosnia Teach Us About Libya?' *The Guardian*, 7 October 2011, available at http://www.guardian.co.uk/world/2011/oct/08/libya-intervention-rory-stewart offers a sceptical view of intervention that argues for the importance of local capacity.

**United Nations Blue Book Series (New York: United Nations)** includes volumes on previous interventions, each with primary source materials and lengthy commentary by the Secretary General.

J. Welsh (ed.), *Humanitarian Intervention and International Relations* **(Oxford: Oxford University Press, 2004)** gives an examination of issues and cases through the lens of international relations theory.

N. J. Wheeler, *Saving Strangers: Humanitarian Intervention in International Society* **(Oxford: Oxford University Press, 2000)** considers the ethical case for intervention, and analyses cases during and after the cold war.

 ## Web Links

UN Department of Peacekeeping Operations **http://www.un.org/en/peacekeeping** contains a brief history of peacekeeping, discussion of principles and processes, overviews of current operations, and reports on past ones. The subsection on DPKO's 'Force For the Future Initiative' outlines UN efforts to modernize peacekeeping operations, including through innovation and technology.

United States Institute of Peace Library **http://www.usip.org/publications/peacekeeping-web-links** gives a fairly comprehensive list of web links on peacekeeping.

Website of the International Coalition for the Responsibility to Protect **http://www.responsibilitytoprotect.org** provides access to helpful resources on humanitarian intervention, including the International Commission on Intervention and State Sovereignty report, which offers a comprehensive analysis of its ethical, political, and military implications and case studies on past interventions.

Stimson Center Program on the Future of Peace Operations **http://www.stimson.org/programs/future-of-peace-operations/program-related-news** offers research and news commentary on current issues related to intervention and peace operations.

Security Council Report **http://www.securitycouncilreport.org** provides reports on the United Nations Security Council, including intervention and peacekeeping activities.

International Peace Institute **http://www.ipinst.org** focuses on conflict prevention and settlement and has provided training to UN peacekeepers. Links to Global Observatory, which provides interviews, maps, and other resources on conflicts world-wide.

New York University Center for International Cooperation **http://www.cic.nyu.edu** offers helpful events and publications on global peace operations, humanitarian intervention, and peacebuilding.

# 16

# The Rise of Cyberpower

JOHN B. SHELDON

## Chapter Contents

 ### Reader's Guide

Recent years have seen the rapid spread of information-communication technologies around the world, creating a globally connected domain called cyberspace. Every aspect of modern society, from how we communicate to how we wage war, can now be said to be cyberdependent. Nearly every function of modern society is enabled by cyberspace. This is both an advantage and a serious vulnerability. A variety of actors—ranging from individuals and small groups to non-state actors and governments—are developing cyber-attack capabilities that can disrupt and even destroy core elements of modern society. Defence against these threats is challenging because, in cyberspace, the offence is the dominant form of warfare. Yet, despite this advantage, cyber-attack entails risks. The pervasiveness of cyberspace, and the growing importance of cyberpower, is having a tangible impact on international politics and the use of military force in the twenty-first century. What are the implications of these trends, and why should strategists care about them?

## Introduction

The first electronic computer, the Electronic Numerical Integrator and Computer, had to be housed in a large building. It was developed in 1946 for the US Army to plot scores of artillery targets rapidly. Since then, computers have shrunk in size, become much more powerful, and now pervade every aspect of modern life. These developments—and the rapid and inexorable rise of the World Wide Web and the Internet—have produced startling and indelible changes in modern societies, the global economy, and in the conduct of politics and warfare. Indeed, these changes have occurred in such a relatively small space of time and with such scope that analysts and scholars have still to discern all of the implications of the rise of cyberpower.

The implications for strategy are similarly challenging to identify, though broad trends and issues are sufficiently well known that strategists are now able to analyse trends. Because cyberpower is having a broad and meaningful impact on the conduct of war, it is producing significant challenges for strategic studies. These broad and meaningful impacts, along with their attendant challenges and opportunities, may also be driving a change in the character of war. This chapter outlines these trends and issues and explains what it all means for the future of strategy and conflict.

## Terms and Definitions

Strategic studies, not unlike other disciplines, place a premium on definitions even though they are contextually and culturally situated. For example, an American definition of airpower may not necessarily resonate with, say, a Ugandan definition, given the vast differences in historical and operational experiences, as well as differences in capability and how the instrument of airpower is wielded to achieve political objectives set out by the respective polities. Ultimately, however, definitional debates about airpower, as well as land and sea power, tend to revolve around a handful of competing definitions.

Not so with cyberspace, and its consequential product, cyberpower. There is a plethora of competing definitions of cyberspace (see Box 16.1) and a number of competing definitions of cyberpower (see Box 16.3). Much of this definitional fruit salad can be explained away by

 **Box** 16.1   Selection of Competing Definitions of Cyberspace

Cyberspace is that intangible place between computers where information momentarily exists on its route from one end of the global network to the other.

Winn Schwartau, *Information Warfare*, 2nd edition (1996: 71)

'Cyberspace' is the information space consisting of the sum total of all computer networks.

Dorothy Denning, *Information Warfare and Security* (1999: 22)

Cyberspace consists of electronically powered hardware, networks, operating systems, and transmission standards.

Gregory J. Rattray, *Strategic Warfare in Cyberspace* (2001: 65)

Cyberspace: Domain characterized by the use of electronics and the electromagnetic spectrum to store, modify, and exchange data via networked systems and associated physical infrastructures.

General James E. Cartwright, Vice-Chairman of the Joint Chiefs of Staff, *Memorandum on Joint Terminology for Cyberspace Operations* (No Date: 7)

A global domain within the information environment consisting of the interdependent network of information technology infrastructures, including the Internet, telecommunications networks, computer systems, and embedded processors and controllers.

The Hon. Gordon England, Deputy Secretary of Defense (2008; quoted from Kuehl 2009: 27)

I think that a more accurate analogy can be found in the realm of science fiction's parallel universes—mysterious, invisible realms existing in parallel to the physical world, but able to influence it in countless ways. Although that's more metaphor than reality, we need to change the habit of thinking about cyberspace as if it's the same thing as physical space.

Jeffrey Carr, *Inside Cyber Warfare* (2010: xiii)

the fact that as strategic phenomena, both cyberspace and cyberpower are relatively new when compared to land, sea, air, and space power. Of equal plausibility, however, is that many strategists are confronted with the uncomfortable notion that cyberspace is an intangible, fluid, and counterintuitive phenomenon (or if one prefers, a domain, which is discussed later) that defies the neat categorizations of the other strategic domains. In contrast, the strategic effects that can be produced from cyberspace—cyberpower—are somewhat easier to grasp.

## Cyberspace

The term cyberspace was first coined in a 1982 short story titled 'Burning Chrome', by Canadian science fiction writer William Gibson, and later popularized in his famous 1984 novel *Neuromancer*. Gibson defined cyberspace as a 'consensual hallucination' (Gibson 1984: 51) that takes place when humans interact with networked computers. The term has morphed and evolved ever since.

For the strategist, definitions attempt to lend cyberspace a certain tangibility and uniformity similar to the definitions of land, sea, air, and space power. Given the plethora of definitions circulating today, each emphasizing one or more aspects of cyberspace over others, rendering a commonly held definition that all can refer to is most unlikely in the near future. Many definitions fail to emphasize the physical manifestations of cyberspace—such as computers and networks and other infrastructure—and the code that makes the machines and networks function. Other definitions depict cyberspace as an informational and virtual place that exists within an infrastructure that is implied. Such definitions emphasize the cognitive element where the human being interacts directly with information created, stored, and transmitted within cyberspace. Very few definitions combine the physical and cognitive elements of cyberspace, though cyberpower theorist Martin C. Libicki offers a characterization of cyberspace that includes the physical infrastructure, the code that provides the logic for computers to operate, and the human–computer interface that involves cognition (see Box 16.2).

All of the definitions in circulation today vary in terms of what constitutes cyberspace. As a result, some definitions include certain features that may be found in cyberspace, and others omit the same features. Definitional wars by nature can be tedious to those not directly

---

 **BOX** 16.2   Libicki's Three Layers of Cyberspace

Libicki divides cyberspace into three layers:

*Physical* comprising hardware, cables, satellites, routers, and other components of the physical infrastructure.

*Syntactic* comprising the code (software) that formats, instructs, and controls information.

*Semantic* comprising the cyberspace–human interface where information is meaningful to human beings.

Control of any one layer of cyberspace does not confer control of the other two remaining layers.

Martin C. Libicki, *Conquest in Cyberspace: National Security and Information Warfare* (2007: 8–9)

involved, but, in the case of cyberspace, what is and what is not included in any definition may have serious implications for its strategic application:

> The issue of defining cyberspace is not trivial. What we decide to include or exclude from cyberspace has significant implications for the operations of power, as it determines the purview of cyberspace strategies and the operations of cyberpower.
>
> Betz and Stevens (2012: 36)

An example of this issue can be found among cyberspace definitions that include the naturally occurring electromagnetic spectrum (EMS) and those that do not. The point being that inclusion or exclusion of the EMS in definitions can determine how, and by whom, cyberspace operations are conducted.

For the purposes of this essay, cyberspace is defined as:

> . . . a global domain within the information environment whose distinctive and unique character is framed by the use of electronics and the electromagnetic spectrum to create, store, modify, exchange, and exploit information via interdependent and interconnected networks using information-communication technologies.
>
> Kuehl (2009: 28)

## Cyberpower

If cyberspace is the domain where information can be created, stored, transmitted, and generally manipulated, then cyberpower is the process of converting information into strategic effect. This strategic effect ultimately manifests itself in the cognitive processes of human beings, but can also indirectly manifest itself in the strategic domains of land, sea, air, and space, as well as cyberspace itself.

Compared to cyberspace, there are relatively fewer definitions of cyberpower. Cyberpower definitions emphasize how cyberspace can be used to fulfil the ends of strategy. One category of definition emphasizes the instrumentality of cyberpower without discussing the dialectic process of exercising that power in the face of an adversary. The other category of definition acknowledges that cyberpower is used against a wilful and intelligent adversary that will probably also attempt to use cyberpower for their own ends. This chapter defines cyberpower as: the ability in peace, crisis, and war to exert prompt and sustained influence in and from cyberspace.

## Cyberwar?

In early 2010, former US Director of National Intelligence Vice-Admiral Mike McConnell, US Navy (retired), asserted: 'The United States is fighting a cyberwar today, and we are losing. It's that simple' (McConnell 2010). McConnell is among numerous commentators and authors who use the term cyberwar (or cyber warfare or cyber conflict) to describe the range of nefarious activities that take place in cyberspace every day. The vast majority of these activities range from young hackers showing off their skills and online political protest and dissent called hacktivism, to criminal activity and espionage; very few can actually be described as actual cyber-attacks that might cause serious harm to the national security of a state. This is

**BOX** 16.3   Competing Definitions of Cyberpower

The ability to use cyberspace to create advantages and influence events in all the operational environments and across the instruments of power.

Daniel T. Kuehl, *From Cyberspace to Cyberpower: Defining the Problem* (2009: 38)

Cyberpower can be defined in terms of a set of resources that relate to the creation, control, and communication of electronic and computer-based information-infrastructure, networks, software, human skills. This includes not only the Internet of networked computers, but also Intranets, cellular technologies, and space-based communications. Defined behaviorally, cyberpower is the ability to obtain preferred outcomes through use of the electronically interconnected information resources of the cyberdomain.

Joseph S. Nye, Jr., *The Future of Power* (2011)

Cyberpower is the national ability to disrupt [the] obscured bad actor somewhere in the digitized globe, whether nonstate or state, in proportion to its motivations/capabilities to attack with violent effects and yet be resilient against imposed or enhanced nasty surprises across all critical nationally sustaining systems.

Chris C. Demchak, *Wars of Disruption and Resilience: Cybered Conflict, Power, and National Security* (2011: ix)

. . . cyber-power can be understood as the variety of powers that circulate in cyberspace and which shape the experiences of those who act in and through cyberspace . . . [C]yber-power is therefore the manifestation of power in cyberspace rather than a new or different form of power.

David J. Betz and Tim Stevens, *Cyberspace and the State: Towards a Strategy for Cyberpower* (2012: 44)

not to deny that hacker pranks and hacktivism are bothersome, even serious, or that crime and espionage carried out by cyber means are not significant issues in need of coherent policy responses. There is a question, however, as to whether these activities together constitute a cyberwar and therefore merit the type of response that a war might warrant.

Some authors argue, however, that the rise of cyberspace has changed the character of war significantly, making any malign cyber incident conducted against a state or its society or economy a new form of conflict. Actors who hold some form of animus toward their target and create a cyber incident to coerce that target to acquiesce to their political objective are often seen as engaging in cyberwar. Chris Demchak describes this emerging situation as a change in the very nature of conflict:

> The nature of 'war' moves from societally threatening one-off clashes of violence between close neighbors to a global version of long-term, episodically and catastrophically dangerous, chronic insecurities that involve the whole society.

Demchak (2011: 4)

There are few examples of cyberpower being used in actual combat and the veracity of accounts of these isolated examples is subject to debate. For military planners, it is this use of cyberspace that is of significant interest. Since cyberpower in this context is used to achieve definable objectives as part of an overall strategy, it is perhaps more accurate to speak of 'cyberpower in war, or war by cyber means', rather than the more misleading term cyberwar (Sheldon 2011). Thomas Rid, however, argues that to speak of cyberpower even in this way does not reflect what he perceives is its true character. For Rid, cyberpower's limitations as an instrument of power are significant and therefore its contribution to the future of war-fare is likely to be constrained. Instead, Rid argues that cyberpower possesses the nonviolent potential to counter and even replace traditionally violent means to achieve political objec-tives. This can be achieved through espionage, sabotage, and subversion by cyber means and without resorting to physical violence (Rid 2013). As appealing as this argument is, it errone-ously assumes that the victims of such nonviolent cyber acts would be content for the issue to remain nonviolent.

Definitions of both cyberspace and cyberpower are at a conceptually embryonic stage, leaving strategists to sort out what is true, what is false, and what is eminently arguable. This state of affairs might lead some to argue that cyberspace as a strategic sphere is not only immature, but is perhaps unworthy of consideration within the mainstream of strategic stud-ies. Both assumptions would be a mistake. As a strategic sphere, cyberspace has been active in a variety of ways for many years now. Given the pervasiveness of cyberspace in every aspect of modern life, its workings and dynamics are of the greatest concern to strategic studies and to any practising strategist. After all, humans had been fighting on the land and at sea for many centuries before strategic theorists came along to define those activities and render them meaningful to political discourse. Why should cyberspace be any different?

 **Key Points**

- Definitions matter, but because cyberspace is a relatively new phenomenon within strategic studies it is likely that the definitional winnowing-out process will take at least several decades to complete.

- The popular term 'cyberwar' to some is a reflection of the changed character of war, but is also contested.

- Despite the plethora of definitions, cyberpower has been used for several decades. Practice drives theory, not the other way around.

## Cyberspace, Cyberpower, and the Infosphere

One can identify multiple known characteristics and attributes of cyberspace and cyberpower. These characteristics and attributes are based on empirical observations of how cyberspace works and how cyberpower is wielded. It is too soon to tell how many of the characteris-tics and attributes are permanent features of cyberspace and cyberpower, or whether they may change along with changes in cyber technologies or the motivations of actors that use cyberspace.

### The Infosphere

The infosphere, also known as the information environment or domain, is a realm without which cyberspace is meaningless and cyberpower does not exist. The infosphere is best thought of as a place in space and time where information exists and flows (Lonsdale 2004: 181). The currency of cyberspace is information found in the infosphere, and the use of the information to achieve political objectives is cyberpower. Information—how it is created, stored, communicated, and manipulated—is a product of the infosphere, yet cyberspace far from composes the sum of all infosphere activities. Cyberspace is merely a subset of the infosphere, albeit an increasingly significant one. The infosphere consists of everything from direct human interactions where information is exchanged, and mediated communication through such technologies as the telephone, and printed matter. Cyberspace, however, is rapidly filling the various functions of the infosphere. It seems, for example, that many people today actually would rather 'text' and 'chat' online than talk to each other.

## Cyberspace Characteristics

With its subordination to the infosphere noted, certain characteristics of cyberspace can be deduced and identified.

*Low cost of entry.* The resources and expertise required to enter, exist in, and exploit cyberspace are extremely modest compared to the resources and expertise required for exploiting the land, sea, air, and space domains. Anyone with access to networked information-communication technologies can use it.

*Multiple actors.* The low cost of entry into cyberspace means that the number and types of actors able to operate in the domain and potentially generate strategic effect is virtually unlimited when compared to the land, sea, air, and space domains. Individuals, groups, organizations, corporations, non-state actors, as well as states all participate in cyberspace.

*Cyberspace relies on the electromagnetic spectrum.* Cyberspace cannot exist without being able to exploit the naturally existing electromagnetic spectrum. Without the electromagnetic spectrum, not only would millions of information and communications technologies be unable to communicate with each other, but these technologies themselves would be unable to function.

*Cyberspace requires man-made objects to exist.* This makes cyberspace unique when compared to the land, sea, air, and space domains. Without integrated circuit boards, semiconductors and microchips, fibre optics, and other information and communications technologies, there would be no cyberspace.

*Cyberspace can be constantly replicated.* There can be as many cyberspaces at any one time as one can possibly generate. With cyberspace, there can be many existing simultaneously—some contested, some not. For the most part, nothing is final in cyberspace. With airpower, enemy aircraft can be destroyed, and there the matter ends. In cyberspace, a Salafist jihadi website, for example, can be purposefully shut down, only for the same group to start a new website within hours on a different server using a different domain name. Similarly, networks can be quickly repaired and reconstituted, thanks to relatively inexpensive and readily available hardware.

*Cyberspace is near instantaneous.* Information traverses cyberspace at what is called net-speed—the speed at which any part of the network at any one time is able to move information. In many cases net-speed is nearly the speed of light; in other cases it is not quite that fast. For a human user, however, modern networks can seem to move information almost instantaneously. While this characteristic is becoming commonplace about cyberspace, it can mask another reality that is perhaps more mundane. Information has to be sent and emerge into a form comprehensible and useful to human beings. The near-instantaneous speed of cyberspace can seemingly collapse time and space, yet the cognitive processes so crucial to cyberpower—creativity, or the response to strategic effect—still take place at a very human pace.

## Cyberpower Attributes

Similarly, certain characteristics of cyberpower can be deduced and identified.

*Cyberpower is pervasive.* Land, sea, air, and space power are able to generate strategic effect on each of the other domains, but nothing generates strategic effect in all domains so absolutely and simultaneously as cyberpower. Cyber dependencies are a matter of fact in the military, economy, and society of a growing number of countries, and they critically enable land, sea, air, and space power—as well as other instruments of power, such as diplomacy, media, and commerce.

*Cyberpower is complementary.* Unlike land, sea, and airpower, but in many ways like space power, cyberpower is largely a complementary instrument. It is indirect because the coercive ability of cyberpower is limited and is likely to remain limited. Shutting down a power grid via cyberpower, for example, would undoubtedly have catastrophic consequences, but rather than coercing its victim to concede to an attacker's demands, it may in fact only invite an even more catastrophic response.

*Cyberpower can be stealthy.* One of cyberpower's attractions for many users is the ability to wield it surreptitiously on a global scale without it being attributed to the perpetrator. Malicious software can be planted in enemy networks without knowledge until the cyber weapon is activated and causes its intended damage. Databases can be raided for classified or proprietary information, and the owners of that information may not be any the wiser as terabits of data are stolen. Similarly, private citizens can go about their day-to-day lives only to discover that cyber criminals have used their credit cards or ruined their credit rating by stealing their identity. This ability to use cyberpower stealthily, aided by the inherent difficulties of attributing the identity and motivation of most attackers, makes it a very attractive instrument for those who want to undertake clandestine nefarious activities.

## A Global Commons or 'Globally Connected Domain'

Cyberspace is often described as, and assumed to be, a global commons—an internationally recognized legal status granted to the international high seas, Antarctica, and outer space. This is an understandable assumption to make given the near ubiquity of cyberspace and its low cost of entry. Seemingly anyone and everyone can access cyberspace for free. The reality is somewhat more prosaic. Figures vary somewhat, but it is estimated that up to 90 per cent of the infrastructure that comprises cyberspace is privately owned, with the remaining 10 per cent or so owned by governments. Private and government ownership of an entity like cyberspace immediately calls into question the assumption that it is a global commons. Furthermore, to interact with cyberspace, one has to somehow gain access to a computer and a network. Although users only have to pay marginal costs for gaining access to cyberspace, sometimes these costs can be substantial, especially if high capacity systems are required to achieve major objectives.

Some authors recognize these facts but still proclaim cyberspace to be a global commons, citing the ubiquity of cyberspace and the ever-increasing hundreds of millions of people around the world who are interacting with it on a daily basis, perhaps giving cyberspace the *appearance* of being a global commons. Yet, such claims are problematic as more and more states—democracies and authoritarian regimes alike—are increasingly asserting sovereignty in cyberspace, leading to what some have identified as the growing territorializing of cyberspace. In response to claims that cyberspace is a global commons, others, such as the US government, recognize the unique elements of cyberspace—its global ubiquity, nearly three billion users, and massive international information flows—and have instead labelled it a 'globally connected domain' (US Joint Chiefs of Staff 2011: 3). This description is far from perfect, but is perhaps a more accurate reflection of the status of cyberspace in domestic and international politics.

 **Key Points**

- Cyberspace exists within the long-established information environment, or infosphere.
- Cyberspace has numerous characteristics that make it unique compared to the strategic domains of land, sea, air, and space power.
- Cyberpower possesses several attributes that make it an increasingly important strategic instrument.
- Cyberspace is often described as a global commons, but is perhaps best described as a globally connected domain.

## A New Dimension for Conflict

With nearly three billion users combined with the growing ubiquity of cyberspace in societies, it is not surprising that cyberspace has become a place of constant conflict, resulting in disruption, deception, and theft. While conflict is an ever-present feature of cyberspace, not all conflicts there equate to what many would regard as war in the Clausewitzian sense. Disputes involve personal vendettas, organizational rivalries, and private citizens motivated by nationalist sentiment. Attacks often involve the cyber networks of states, commercial enterprises, and individuals. States have also attacked cyber targets in other states, as is alleged to have happened in the Stuxnet malware attack against the nuclear facility at Natanz, Iran, in 2009 (see Box 16.4), as well as non-state organizations, as the alleged North Korean attack against Sony Pictures in November 2014 demonstrates.

Since cyberspace is offence-dominant for now, the advantage in cyber conflict can be said to favour the attacker. As a result, it might seem that cyberspace is a target-rich environment for any would-be attacker, though it should be noted that cyber-attack is not without its problems and challenges. Some scholars believe that the ease of cyber-attack against targets vital to the everyday functioning of modern societies heralds an age of perpetual disruption, the worst effects of which can only be mitigated by an emphasis on resilience in the networking of critical infrastructures and the storage and transmission of sensitive information.

### The Problem of Cyber Security

In cyberspace the offence enjoys an advantage over the defence, and so the challenge for those charged with cyber security is to be successful in maintaining defences all of the time, an impossible expectation to meet indefinitely. For any would-be cyber-attacker, the challenge is significantly easier in many respects: they only have to be successful once to attack a target system or network.

**BOX** 16.4  Stuxnet

Stuxnet is an unusual type of malicious software (malware) that targets computers and networks that meet very specific configurations. Where other types of malware harm every computer in infected networks, Stuxnet only harmed a specific set of computers in one location, namely a nuclear enrichment plant at Natanz in Iran. Discovered and made public in the summer of 2010, Stuxnet is said to have first appeared in June 2009, with follow-on variants detected in March and April 2010.

It is now widely believed that Stuxnet was developed by a state (recent revelations in the media suggest it was the United States and Israel, but neither government has officially admitted responsibility) to target centrifuges used to enrich uranium at a nuclear facility at Natanz, Iran. It is believed that of the approximately 4,700 centrifuges in operation at Natanz, about 1,000 were destroyed from late 2009 to early 2010. It is believed that Stuxnet destroyed the centrifuges by infecting their operational control system. According to reports, operators of the control system were unaware of anything untoward happening, apparently due to a feature of Stuxnet that deceived operators into believing that centrifuge operations were normal. In reality, Stuxnet compromised control of the centrifuges and spun approximately 10 per cent of them so fast that they were destroyed.

Stuxnet is believed to have set back the Iranian nuclear programme by several months, though at one point Israeli intelligence believed that the programme had been delayed by several years. Since then, the Iranians have redoubled their efforts in their nuclear programme, and it seems that while Stuxnet successfully struck its target its effect was temporary.

Despite this, Stuxnet is now widely regarded as a major turning point in the evolution of offensive cyber capabilities and cyber warfare in general. Stuxnet proves that an offensive cyber capability can more or less precisely target a remote system, compromise it, and cause physical destruction.

Effective cyber security cannot hope to prevent every cyber-attack from occurring. It can, however, mitigate the worst effects of any cyber-attack by reducing the prospects of any catastrophic consequence of an attack or by taking steps to reduce the extent or duration of any disruption caused by the initial attack. These mitigation measures involve technical solutions, inculcating a culture of cyber security, and implementing measures to ensure resilience.

Technical solutions to cyber-attack include up-to-date cyber security software, capabilities, and methods applied to information and communication technologies and networks, such as firewalls, anti-virus software, and thoroughly trained system administrators who maintain networks. Inculcating a culture of cyber security includes educating workforces who must use cyberspace in best cyber security practices and how to spot potential threats and problems, as well as enforcing laws and regulations against anyone who knowingly or negligently endangers cyber security. Resilience measures include better protection of sensitive information, perhaps by excluding it from accessible networks, as well as removing the interface between critical infrastructure and accessible networks to prevent remote, unauthorized access to services and systems that are important to societies.

Cyber security is also plagued by the problem of attribution. Cyber-attacks can be masked, routed through various countries, and even designed to give the appearance of originating from somewhere other than their true point of origin. For any victim of a cyber-attack, this makes it difficult to attribute a cyber-attack to its true perpetrator, limiting opportunities to apportion blame or formulate a response that might include a retaliatory cyber-attack or even the use of military force. Apportioning blame and formulating an appropriate response to cyber-attack is problematic because attribution can be extremely difficult.

Attribution is more than just locating the geographical origins of a cyber-attack. It is also about attributing the identity of the attacker and their motivations for the attack. Just because a cyber-attack may be attributed to have originated from a certain country, it does not necessarily mean that those who carried out the attack did so with the knowledge and authorization of the government of that country, or that the attack in question was indeed intended to be an act of war. Attribution of attacker identity and motivations is extremely hard to ascertain reliably and again stymies the attribution of responsibility for a cyber-attack, as well as the formulation of an appropriate response. For example, a cyber-attack might be attributed to have originated from a certain country, but cyber forensic tools and methods are unable to ascertain reliably whether the attack in question was carried out by a gang for criminal purposes or by agents of that country's government for the purposes of espionage.

Given the significant challenges involved with cyber security, coupled with the offensive advantage enjoyed by cyber-attack, a number of scholars have promoted the idea of cyber deterrence as a means of preventing catastrophic cyber-attacks. Conceptually, there is no such thing as cyber deterrence, there is only deterrence. Yet, still the notion that cyber-attacks might be deterred has some merit, depending on the deterrence strategy employed. A large portion of the literature concerned with cyberspace and deterrence focuses on deterrence by punishment strategies, whereby a cyber-attack is punished by a retaliatory cyber-attack or some other military, diplomatic, or economic response. The problem with the deterrence by punishment strategy is that it presumes not only that the victim of the cyber-attack will be able to attribute the location of where the attack originated, but also the identities and motivations of the attackers. Given that attribution is still a significant challenge, a deterrence by punishment strategy in cyberspace is both unreliable and carries a high degree of risk of not only overreaction to any attack, but even complete miscalculation that results in the punishment of innocent third parties. Furthermore, knowing that attribution is a challenge, any would-be cyber-attacker would find the deterrence by punishment strategy lacking in credibility, making it potentially worse than useless.

Deterrence by denial strategies, on the other hand, places the onus of miscalculation on the would-be cyber-attacker. Greater investment in cyber defences, creating a culture of cyber security, and resilience measures can raise the risks and reduce the benefits of mounting cyber-attacks. Handfuls of cyber-attacks might get through here and there, but the effort placed into the attack may prove to be too costly if successes are too few and far between.

The problem with deterrence by denial strategies in cyberspace is that they are costly to implement because they create operational inefficiencies and lead to a never-ending requirement for state of the art equipment and services. Creating a meaningful culture of cyber security among users of cyberspace to foster deterrence by denial forces users to comply with stringent security requirements that may not always be followed by users. Resilience measures are also very costly to implement because they require stand-alone platforms and back-up systems that are run in parallel to systems used on a day-to-day basis.

## The Challenges and Unknowns of Cyber-Attack

While cyber security is beset by challenges, it might seem that cyber-attack enjoys free rein in cyberspace. In reality, while the offence is dominant in cyberspace, cyber-attack is not only not without its own challenges, but is also beset with a number of unknowns.

The alleged US and Israeli Stuxnet operation against the Iranian nuclear programme provides a useful example. A cyber operation of this scale has many moving parts and is therefore subject to the friction that will inevitably arise out of such complexity. Advanced technical expertise, meticulous intelligence preparation, sophisticated logistics and tens, if not hundreds, of millions of dollars are required to pull off cyber-attacks on the scale of Stuxnet. All of these activities have also to be undertaken under the cover of the strictest secrecy to prevent the target from taking defensive measures that would eliminate operational or technical weaknesses before they can be exploited. Cyber-attacks involve extensive planning and preparation, and may fail long before they can be implemented.

Cyber-attacks are burdensome and time-consuming because their success depends on extensive intelligence collection and surveillance of targets. Intelligence collection and surveillance of targets in cyberspace requires penetrating adversary computers and networks, running the risk of discovery. Furthermore, though cyber-attacks might be successful, they will entail unforeseen and unintended consequences, including the risk of blowback. For example, malicious software (malware) might take down an intended target in cyberspace, but may then propagate throughout the network attacking unintended targets (hence the term 'blowback'), including cyber assets belonging to the attacker. An example of unintended consequences would be a cyber-attack against the critical infrastructure of a state that results in civilian casualties because hospitals were affected in the aftermath of power and telecommunication outages.

The offence-defence cycle and sustaining the offence in cyberspace are also challenges. The offence-defence cycle between cyber-attack capabilities and defences means that the effectiveness of offensive cyber weapons will be short lived. Once a belligerent tips their cyber-attack hand it does not take long for a defender to come up with a defence to a new offensive capability. This means that the employment of cyber-attack weapons will ideally be for a large strategic payoff, rather than a short-term tactical advantage. It also means that after a short time, the ability of an attacker to sustain the offence in cyberspace becomes increasingly challenging as the initiative starts to shift towards the defence.

 **Key Points**

- Cyber security—or cyber defence—is exceptionally challenging due to the offensive advantage enjoyed by cyber-attackers.

- Attribution of attacker identity and motivation is particularly challenging and can stymie an effective response.

- In cyberspace, deterrence by denial strategies is more effective than deterrence by punishment.

- While it is easier to attack rather than defend in cyberspace, cyber-attack is not without its risks and challenges.

## A Twenty-first-century Revolution in Military Affairs?

Individuals, organizations, non-state actors, and states are using cyberspace, and wielding cyberpower, every day in new and innovative ways for the purposes of achieving political objectives. Cyberspace and cyberpower enable existing human activities and types of military power, but they do not render them obsolete. Cyberpower also changes the character of human activity. For instance, cyberspace has radically changed how corporations organize themselves. Cyberspace has also created the opportunity for super-empowered individuals to emerge in the realm of economic activity. In the realm of strategy, cyberpower is recasting the context in which all strategic activity takes place, namely international politics. Cyberpower also blurs the distinction between war and peace, undermines the privileged role of the state in war, and might possibly have long-term implications for how military forces are organized.

## Cyberpower Recasts International Politics

The pervasiveness of cyberspace, and the ubiquity of cyberpower, has an impact on international relations and the privileged role of the state in international politics.

The rise of cyberpower has helped developing states accelerate their economic development, while enabling their military, diplomatic, and cultural instruments of national power. Cyberpower has allowed a number of developing states to enjoy significant economic growth and a commensurate increase in the potency of their instruments of national power, thus enabling them to catch up with developed states. This phenomenon, best demonstrated by the rise of India and China, has recast the distribution of power within international politics resulting in net gains for rising powers, and relative losses for established, developed powers.

The rise of cyberpower has also empowered individuals, organizations, and non-state actors, allowing them to have a global reach, a form of global influence, that hitherto was unavailable to them because it was too expensive or beyond their technical capabilities. The mass leaking of classified information by US Army service member Bradley Manning and then by US National Security Agency (NSA) contractor Edward Snowden are both examples of this disproportionate influence and reach. They also highlight the potential damage that can be caused by a disaffected insider to any organization where access to vast quantities of information is unrestricted. Cyberspace can also enable individuals and groups with belligerent intentions to use cyber capabilities offensively against targets across the world, as demonstrated by hackers from the terrorist group Islamic State when they breached and temporarily hijacked the social media capabilities of US Central Command in January 2015. This empowering of individuals and groups has led to a redistribution of power within international politics that further undermines the monopoly of power traditionally enjoyed by states. Nevertheless, this empowerment through cyberpower only goes so far. States still enjoy capabilities and capacities for the employment and projection of power that are beyond the reach of individuals and groups. Although many scholars believe that cyberpower significantly undermines state power by weakening state sovereignty, states are also finding various ways of asserting their sovereignty in cyberspace.

Claims that cyberpower has recast international politics for individuals and groups at the expense of states has greater plausibility than the assertion that cyberpower renders state sovereignty irrelevant. The state will continue to be the primary actor in international politics, despite the irritation felt in capitals across the globe about certain activities undertaken by individuals and groups in cyberspace.

**Critical Thinking**    Debating … Is cyberwar possible?

### For

- *Developed states are vulnerable.* Modern societies are highly networked by computers, especially in terms of their critical national infrastructures, making anonymous cyber-attacks very attractive to enemies.
- *Disruptive cyber-attacks have already occurred.* Cyber warfare's potential has already been demonstrated by the joint US/Israeli attack on Iran's Natanz nuclear facility in 2010 and Israel's attack on a suspected nuclear facility in Syria in 2007 which disabled Syrian radar installations prior to the attack.
- *War includes non-physical effects.* War includes social, political, and cultural effects, as well as 'kinetic' (i.e. physical) effects. Cyber-attacks may be non-violent, but they can be used to steal secrets and distort decision-making in ways that can win wars. Cyber-attacks can therefore be an important part of warlike operations, in terms of sabotage and espionage, as well as intelligence activities.

### Against

- *Cyberwar is unlikely in a globalized world.* It can be argued that the interconnected nature of the Internet and of global information-communication technologies decreases, rather than increases, the likelihood of cyberwar in terms of direct state to state attacks. Mutual vulnerability creates a form of deterrence.
- *War is by nature violent.* War, as defined by Clausewitz, requires violence to be perpetrated. Digital attacks are non-violent. According to Thomas Rid, 'Never has a human being been injured or hurt as an immediate consequence of a computer attack.'
- *No country has gone to war in cyber space.* Digital attacks can be a part of sabotage or espionage, but these activities are not new. As such digital weapons may be part of future military conflict, but this does not deserve the label 'cyber-warfare'.

## A Coming Change in the Character of War?

Cyberpower is a useful strategic instrument since it can be wielded globally with a certain degree of anonymity in peace, crisis, and war. Cyberpower enables global reach, creating the ability to attack critical systems such as national infrastructure remotely, duping individuals into divulging sensitive information, and disrupting services. Such attacks, deception operations, and disruptions by cyberpower potentially blur the distinction between peace and war. Terrorism, and the use of terrorists as proxies by states, already blurs this distinction but cyberpower adds to what might potentially be a dangerous ambiguity between peace and war. States subject to countless cyber-attacks that lead to significant societal disruption, or suffer the loss of sensitive information related to national defence, may perceive that they are the victims of actions that are a prelude to war or merit a military response. Misperception and miscalculation are major risks in such circumstances. If these kinds of attacks, disruptions, and deception operations become the norm in international politics, they might come to be perceived as a kind of background noise to the everyday dynamics of international relations. For some observers, these trends indicate that we are entering an age of perpetual disruption.

Cyberpower creates great efficiencies in how people organize activities. Cyberpower also magnifies the ability of individuals to control operations and transmit virtually unlimited amounts of data across the planet at virtually no cost, creating opportunities that were unimaginable only a few decades ago. Cyberpower has already demonstrated these opportunities and benefits in the economic sphere, with corporations increasing both productivity and profit margins while using fewer people and leaner, flatter, and more responsive organizational structures. Modern militaries are also subject to these greater efficiencies and magnified effects thanks to cyberpower, creating leaner force structures and more automated capabilities, which place a premium on recruiting more highly skilled personnel. Military hierarchies are likely to shrink in size, as will numbers of personnel required to staff them. There is already a growing reliance on automated capabilities and systems, such as remotely piloted vehicles, and the cost of training even the lowest-ranking serviceperson is increasing due to the complex technical skills required in modern militaries. The implications of these cyberpower trends within militaries are debatable, and cannot be divorced from the context of how, when, and for what purpose military force will be used in the twenty-first century. Nevertheless, it is plausible to suggest that as military organization and structure changes due to the pervasiveness of cyberpower, when and how military force will be used might also change. These changes might culminate in a twenty-first-century revolution in military affairs (RMA) if they lead to new military doctrines, force structures, and changes in the conduct of war.

 **Key Points**

- Cyberpower has contributed to the redistribution of power taking place in international politics today.
- Cyberpower has empowered individuals, organizations, and non-state actors, allowing them greater participation and influence in international politics.
- Cyberpower has not rendered the state irrelevant. It has made sovereignty more porous, but states are increasingly asserting sovereignty in cyberspace.
- Cyberpower is impacting not only the structure of military force, but also how it is used and in what circumstances. It might produce a revolution in military affairs in the twenty-first century.
- Some believe that the rise of cyberpower heralds the arrival of an age of perpetual disruption.

 **Conclusion**

Cyberspace continues to pervade ever more deeply into every function of modern societies around the world. The dependencies and complex interactions that emerge in cyberspace benefit societies because of the low-cost communication it facilitates and because of the efficiencies and automation of tedious functions it creates and enables. These dependencies and complex interactions also create a host of vulnerabilities throughout modern society. These vulnerabilities can be exploited by those intent on launching cyber-attacks.

As more and more state functions, including military capabilities and command and control, become increasingly dependent on cyberspace, strategists should concern themselves with the vulnerabilities and opportunities created by cyberspace. The challenge is finding the right balance between absolute cyber security that will invariably constrain the use of cyberspace and unconstrained cyber-attack that ricochets throughout networks with unintended consequences, creating a real risk of blowback.

Nearly every facet of strategy in the contemporary world is affected, influenced, and shaped by cyberpower. The implications of this have yet to play out fully, and it is for these reasons that cyberspace and cyberpower are of vital interest and importance to the strategist and strategic studies.

 Questions

1. Why are there so many definitions of cyberspace and cyberpower? Are definitions important, or is it more important that various actors are using cyberspace?

2. What is the difference between cyberspace and cyberpower?

3. Is there such a thing as cyberwar?

4. What is the relationship between the infosphere and cyberspace? What is the difference between the two?

5. What makes cyberspace unique compared to the other strategic domains?

6. What attributes might cyberpower possess other than those discussed in this chapter?

7. Why is cyber security so challenging? What is your opinion of the cyber security solutions offered in this chapter? What would you do differently?

8. What makes cyber-attack so dangerous, despite the fact that it is easier to do when compared to cyber security?

9. Is the rise of cyberpower a potential revolution in military affairs? If your answer is yes, why? If your answer is no, why not?

10. Relate cyberpower to other strategic issues covered in this book—what possible connections are you able to discern?

 Further Reading

J. Arquilla and D. Ronfeldt (eds), *In Athena's Camp: Preparing for Conflict in the Information Age* (Santa Monica, CA: RAND, 1997). A groundbreaking collection of essays that helped define the field, including Arquilla and Ronfeldt's classic essay, 'Cyberwar is Coming!'

S. W. Brenner, *Cyberthreats: The Emerging Fault Lines of the Nation State* (New York: Oxford University Press, 2009). A comprehensive analysis of cyber threats and the problem of attributing them.

R. A. Clarke and R. K. Knake, *Cyber War: The Next Threat to National Security and What to Do About It* (New York: Ecco, 2010). Provides some thought-provoking solutions to the cyber security problem, as well as other policy issues pertaining to cyberspace, from a US perspective. Regarded by many to be alarmist in its assessment of cyber threats.

F. D. Kramer, S. H. Starr, and L. K. Wentz (eds), *Cyberpower and National Security* (Washington, DC: Potomac Books, 2009). An excellent collection of essays covering all the major cyberspace policy issues of concern to any modern state.

M. C. Libicki, *Conquest in Cyberspace: National Security and Information Warfare* (Cambridge: Cambridge University Press, 2007). One of the major theoretical works on cyberspace and cyberpower in recent years.

D. J. Lonsdale, *The Nature of War in the Information Age: Clausewitzian Future* (London: Frank Cass, 2004). A landmark work that applies Clausewitzian strategic logic to cyberpower and demolishes the arguments of cyber true-believers.

J. S. Nye, Jr, *The Future of Power* (New York: Public Affairs, 2011). Provides an interesting analysis of how cyberpower is significantly impacting international politics.

W. A. Owens, K. W. Dam, and H. S. Lin (eds), *Technology, Policy, Law, and Ethics Regarding US Acquisition and Use of Cyberattack Capabilities* (Washington, DC: The National Academies Press, 2009). A US National Research Council report that provides an exhaustive and detailed survey of the implications of acquiring and using cyber-attack capabilities.

T. Rid, *Cyber War Will Not Take Place* (New York: Oxford University Press, 2013). A refreshingly contrarian yet rigorous counter to the cyberwar narrative.

P. W. Singer and A. Friedman, *Cybersecurity and Cyberwar: What Everyone Needs to Know* (New York: Oxford University Press, 2014). By far the most comprehensive primer on cyber security and warfare issues.

 ## Web Links

Atlantic Council's *Cyber Statecraft Initiative* **http://www.acus.org/tags/cyber-statecraft-initiative** provides excellent analysis of cyberpower issues and their impact on national security, statecraft, and international politics.

The Citizen Lab **http://citizenlab.org** is hosted by the Munk School of Global Affairs at the University of Toronto and is an innovative outfit standing at the intersection of digital media, global security, and human rights. The Citizen Lab has helped produce a series of reports that have, among other things, uncovered an alleged Chinese cyber espionage ring and exposed the sale of Internet filtering technologies by Western corporations to authoritarian regimes.

Cyberwarzone **http://cyberwarzone.com** is a useful site for news and analysis on nation-state cyber-attacks and criminal and terrorist uses of cyberspace.

Army Cyber Institute **http://www.westpoint.edu/acc/SitePages/Home.aspx** is a useful resource for the latest military thinking on cyber issues and war.

Krypt3ia **http://krypt3ia.wordpress.com** is a thoughtful and detailed blog on cyber security and warfare.

# Geopolitics and Grand Strategy

STEFANIE ORTMANN AND NICK WHITTAKER

## Chapter Contents

 ### Reader's Guide

Geopolitics and grand strategy are modern concepts of statecraft associated with the rise and decline of Great Powers. This chapter looks at the concept of geopolitics and its significance for grand strategy. It does so by tracing the development of the concepts and showing how the meaning of the concepts evolved in response to changing world historical contexts. It explains why geopolitics and grand strategy are associated with the politics of Great Powers and why these concepts are currently making a comeback. The chapter then goes on to discuss the pitfalls and problems associated with formulating a grand strategy, and why geopolitics is as much about interpretation as it is about objective geographical factors.

## Introduction

The idea that world politics is ultimately driven by competition between a small number of Great Powers has recently been making a comeback. For more than a decade after the end of the cold war, it had been possible to believe that the rivalry between Great Powers was being replaced with the benign hegemony of the United States, the guarantor of a new liberal world order. As US President Clinton proclaimed in 1992, 'In a world where freedom, not tyranny, is on the march, the cynical calculus of power politics does not compute. It is ill-suited to a new era' (Clinton 1992). However, this picture no longer captures the dynamics of international politics. As Russia is at loggerheads with the West over Ukraine and China shows increasing assertiveness in the South China Sea, geopolitical rivalries are once again returning to the centre stage of world affairs. Nor is this just about military sabre-rattling in a few regions of the world. Partly as a result of increased economic interdependence since the end of the cold war, some non-Western states, first and foremost China, have gone through a sustained period of accelerated economic growth. In the meantime, the US and other major Western economies have suffered relative economic decline, a development accelerated by the effects of the global economic crisis of 2008.

In response, there have been calls for a new grand strategy to preserve the power of the United States in the face of this emerging challenge to its global dominance, with a renewed focus on geopolitics to counter the rise of China and other regional powers in the non-Western world. In the broadest sense, geopolitics is about the political implications of geographical space, the way that geography may contribute to conflict or convey strategic advantages. In association with grand strategy, it is a concept that is intimately connected to the idea of Great Powers as central actors in world affairs.

Grand strategy is an evolution of strategy away from a narrow focus on victory in war towards a much broader, more long-term vision that is essentially political in nature (see Box 17.1). The strategist and historian Paul Kennedy sees the essence of grand strategy in

---

 **BOX** 17.1   Evolving Definitions of Grand Strategy and Geopolitics

### Grand Strategy

Grand strategy should both calculate and develop the economic resources and manpower of nations in order to sustain the fighting services. [...] it should not only combine the various instruments, but so regulate their use as to avoid damage to the future state of peace—for its security and prosperity.

Sir Basil Liddell Hart (1935)

Strategy is the art of controlling and utilizing the resources of a nation [...] including its armed forces to the end that its vital interest shall be effectively promoted and secured against enemies, actual, potential or merely presumed. The highest type of strategy—sometimes called grand strategy—is that which so integrates the policies and armaments of the nation that the resort to war is either rendered unnecessary or is undertaken with the maximum chance of victory.

Edward Mead Earle (1943)

The crux of grand strategy lies therefore in policy, that is, the capacity of the nation's leaders to bring together all of the elements, both military and non-military, for the preservation and enhancement of the nation's long-term (that is, in wartime and peacetime) best interests.

Paul Kennedy (1991)

In a world where great states confront overstretch, they must make hard choices. Thus, in the end, grand strategy is more often than not about the ability to adjust to the reality that resources, will, and interests inevitably find themselves out of balance in some areas.

Williamson Murray (2011)

As far as a world power like America is concerned, a grand strategy involves first imagining some future world order within which the nation's standing, prosperity and security are significantly enhanced, and then plotting and maintaining a course to that desired end while employing—to the fullest extent possible—all elements of our nation's power toward generating those conditions. Naturally, such grand goals typically take decades to achieve.

Thomas P. Barnett (2011)

**BOX** 17.1 *(continued)*

Strategy is oriented towards the future. It is a declaration of intent and an indication of the possible means required to fulfil that intent. But once strategy moves beyond the near term, it struggles to define exactly what it intends to do. [...] The operational plans of military strategy look to the near term and work with specific situations. Grand strategy, on the other hand, can entertain ambitions and goals that are more visionary and aspirational than pragmatic and immediate.

Hew Strachan (2011)

## Geopolitics

For the first time we can perceive something of the real proportion of features and events on the stage of the whole world, and may seek a formula which shall express certain aspects [...] of geographical causation in universal history.

Halford Mackinder (1904)

Not by accident is the word 'Politik' preceded by that little prefix 'geo.' This prefix ... relates politics to the soil. It rids politics of arid theories and senseless phrases which might trap our political leaders into hopeless utopias. It puts them back on solid ground. Geopolitik demonstrates the dependence of all political developments on the permanent reality of the soil.

Karl Haushofer (1942)

Geography is the most fundamental factor in the foreign policy of states, because it is the most permanent.

Nicholas Spykman (1942)

1. All politics is geopolitics. 2. All strategy is geostrategy. 3. Geography is 'out there' objectively as environment or 'terrain.' 4. Geography also is 'within us,' in here, as imagined spatial relationships.

Colin Gray (1999a)

The geopolitical imagination [...] has never exercised absolute power over the course of world politics, in the sense of transcending the effects of technological, economic and other material determinants [...] the modern geopolitical imagination has, however, provided meaning and rationalization to practice by political élites the world over. It has defined the 'ideological space,' to use Immanuel Wallerstein's phrase, from which the geographic categories upon which the world is organized and works are derived

John Agnew (2003)

deliberating the proper balance of priorities of a state by coordinating ends and means (Kennedy 1991). Although security remains central, grand strategy is not limited to military strategy. Security in the context of grand strategy may be understood as securing and enhancing the state's interests, and securing it against external threats and possible opponents. Grand strategy draws on all the military, diplomatic, cultural, and economic means and instruments at the state's disposal. In the most basic terms, it refers to a long-term, multi-dimensional plan for securing and enhancing a state's power and prosperity. It is associated with states that have a wide range of global interests and a number of resources that can be mobilized, including the use of force. As the historian and strategist Williamson Murray put it, 'grand strategy is a matter involving great states and great states alone' (Murray 2011: 1). However,

**BOX** 17.2   The Persistence of Identity Narratives: Britain as an Island

The idea of being an island has shaped British foreign policy for centuries. In the past, Britain's island status and its focus on sea power was central to the maintenance of the British Empire. It also meant that Britain was perceived to be separate from the rest of Europe. This might seem obvious: after all, Britain is physically separated from the continent by the English Channel. But while this separateness is reflected in identity narratives, British and continental European histories have always been intertwined through trade, invasions, and shared culture.

Britain's island identity has remained significant in British politics to this day, even though technological change, not least the channel tunnel, has vastly diminished physical distance. During debates about whether Britain should join the European Communities (now the European Union) in the 1960s, British politicians wondered whether Britain was really a part of Europe, and if joining would mean separation from the rest of the world. In the late 1980s Prime Minister Margaret Thatcher frequently depicted Britain as an island separate from Europe, with more in common with other English-speaking places like the US, Canada, and Australia. The government which came to office in 2010 has pursued similar themes. Prime Minister David Cameron has argued that Britain's island geography is important and Foreign Secretary William Hague announced that Britain needed to be at the centre of a world-wide diplomatic network to ensure global influence. This idea resembles the imperial 'lines of communication' in which Britain, as an island and a Sea Power, had to maintain control of strategic points around the world, thereby linking it to places like India, Singapore, and Australia.

it also implies a situation where resources are limited and where the leader of a powerful state has to make strategic, long-term choices about how to selectively invest resources and project its power.

In all of this, geography matters. Trade and communication routes are strategically important for large, economically powerful states, as is the location of natural resources. Any projection of power will have a geographical focus, since no state has the resources to be equally engaged everywhere at the same time. There is an important cultural component to this geographical factor—the outlooks of British and continental policymakers differ dramatically, partly because of Britain's position as an island at the margin of the continent. Technological changes have significantly altered the significance of this geographic factor over the last century, but the image of Britain as an island remains powerful and is influential in Britain's relations with Europe today (see Box 17.2).

## Imperial Competition and the Invention of Geopolitics

Geopolitics and grand strategy are practical political concepts rather than academic theories. They do however share a focus on the politics of Great Powers and an emphasis on statecraft with classical Realism (see introductory chapter by Baylis and Wirtz). They also share the assumption that there are timeless patterns of state behaviour that can be uncovered and used as guidance for policymakers' decisions—patterns that are at least in part determined by geography. In line with this anchoring in classical Realist thought, grand strategy is often depicted as a way of thinking that applies across all times and all places. This is not the case. Grand strategy and geopolitics are distinctly modern and European concepts of statecraft, emerging as approaches to international politics only at a time when European and later US power acquired global reach. As the British geographer Halford Mackinder put it in 1904, by the turn of the twentieth century international politics for the first time had become a 'closed political system [...] of world-wide scope' (Mackinder 1904: 27). The development of geopolitics and grand strategy occurred in this context.

Mackinder's observation described a genuinely new development that reflected the imperial expansion of the European powers. By the beginning of the twentieth century, Britain, France, the Russian empire, and a number of latecomers to the imperial game were mapping and reclaiming most parts of the globe, often in competition with each other. By this point, the development of the European system of states had produced a small number of particularly powerful states, the Great Powers, which claimed special responsibility for managing international affairs. The colonial expansion of European Great Powers ushered in a new global competition, as unmapped and unclaimed parts of the globe became increasingly scarce. The 'scramble for Africa' between Britain, France, and other European powers and the colonial 'Great Game' in Central Asia between the British and the Russian empire heightened international tensions.

Imperial expansion highlighted the importance of geographical factors. Increasingly far-flung supply and trade routes by land and sea needed to be secured to enable economic growth at home. Overseas territories rich in natural resources were seen as strategic necessities for enhancing the prosperity and power of colonial states. Colonial expansion fuelled capitalist development and enabled the British Empire to become a global hegemonic power. But by the last decades of the nineteenth century, both the newly unified German state and the United States were rapidly industrializing and began to challenge Britain's economic dominance. Germany in particular was becoming a disruptive force in international political dynamics still dominated by the European powers. As a latecomer to the circle of European Great Powers, the German Reich had missed out on much of the colonial expansion, but its leaders set out to change that by aggressive global politics. This included investing heavily in naval rearmament—potentially challenging British naval power at the same time as Britain acquired ever more far-flung possessions in Africa, Asia, and the Pacific.

The increasingly tense international situation at the turn of the twentieth century was reflected in attempts by various European and American thinkers to systematically explain international affairs by reference to geography. The American naval strategist Alfred Thayer Mahan argued that sea power was of crucial strategic importance and advocated that the US join the imperial scramble. Partly due to his influence, the US entered the naval arms race and became engaged in Cuba, Puerto Rico, and the Philippines. In contrast, Mackinder, a geographer and politician, was worried about Britain's long-term decline. He believed that new technologies such as the railways were increasing the strategic significance of land over sea, increasing the power of Germany and the Russian empire and threatening the global dominance of Britain, which largely relied on sea power. He declared one area in particular to be central to global dominance: the Eurasian Heartland, comprising large parts of Russia and Central Asia (see Figure 17.1).

Mackinder condensed his theory into a famous, and still influential, quote: 'Who rules East Europe commands the Heartland: Who rules the Heartland commands the World Island: Who rules the World Island commands the World' (Mackinder 1919). The size of countries and the importance of population growth was the main concern of German geographers, most notoriously Friedrich Ratzel, who developed the concept of *Lebensraum* ('living space') which later became central in Hitler's geopolitical thinking. Ratzel posited a historical difference between the settled Aryan races populating German territory and the marauding tribes

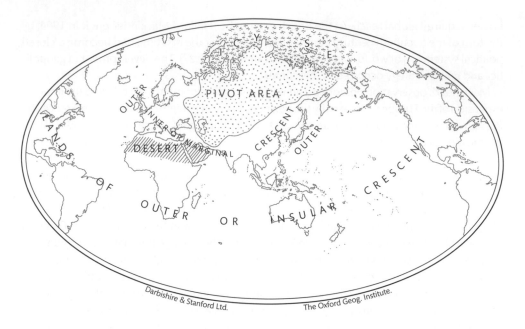

**Figure 17.1** Mackinder's View of the Heartland

*Source:* H.J. Mackinder, 'The Geographical Pivot of History', *The Geographical Journal*, vol. 24, no. 4, 1904, p. 435.

to the east that threatened them. He proposed that modern Germany should secure additional land and resources to counter an ever-present threat from Russia. Rudolph Kiellen, the Swedish geographer who first coined the term *Geopolitik* (geopolitics) combined elements of these theories in his claim that states have to face two strategic imperatives to survive and thrive: demography, or the management of people (*ethnopolitik*), and the management of territorial expansion (*geopolitik*).

These classical geopolitical theories reflected prevalent ideas of their time. They grew out of a belief that everything, including international politics, could be understood scientifically by uncovering the causal factors that drive the behaviour of human beings and states. Geography was seen as such an objective factor in world politics. By virtue of natural resources, climate, location, and size, strategic advantages were bestowed on some states, while others were trapped in unfavourable conditions. However, this was also a time of rapid technological change fuelled by scientific discovery, and this was reflected in the concern of Mackinder and others with technology and its interaction with geography. Importantly, these thinkers saw competition as the essence of world politics, pitting states against each other in a race for global dominance. What was at stake was survival—the idea that only the strongest, most resourceful states would continue to exist. This vision was influenced by a popular pseudo-scientific theory of the time, Social Darwinism. It revolved around the idea that there is a process of natural selection, a fight for the survival of the fittest and strongest, not just among species but also between peoples and states. Germany and the United States in particular were cast as vigorous and rapidly growing, while established powers such as Britain and France were exhausted and in decline.

**Key Points**

- The emergence of geopolitics reflected a new sense that the world was now a unified political space at the end of the nineteenth century, which emerged as a result of the imperial competition of European Great Powers.

- It also reflected a shifting constellation of power, with British economic strength in decline and Germany and the United States rising as new powerful actors in world politics.

- Classical geopolitical thought links territory to power and sees world politics as a competition between the most powerful states. It proposes that geographical and other environmental factors explain why some states thrive while others decline.

## World War II, the Cold War, and the Development of Grand Strategy

From the start, geopolitical thought was about strategy—geographic factors were thought to determine the behaviour of states over long periods of time and could therefore be drawn on for the formulation of a strategy over decades. In the interwar years, this expansion of the strategic horizon was reflected in the new concept of grand strategy (see Box 17.1). Basil Liddell Hart, the British military historian who first coined the phrase, referred to grand strategy as the 'higher level' of wartime strategy, coordinating all the resources at a state's disposal towards the political ends of a war. After the outbreak of World War II, the term was adopted by American strategists, in particular Edward Mead Earle, whose thoughts on grand strategy remained influential for decades to come. Another wartime advocate of a US grand strategy, Nicholas Spykman, adopted Mackinder's theory of the heartland to respond to the looming conflict with the Soviet Union at the end of the war. Arguing that control over the 'rimland', Central Europe, would decide the fate of world politics, he urged US policymakers to remain engaged in Europe to counter possible Soviet dominance of the continent.

Both Mead Earle and Spykman responded to the growing threat of a large-scale confrontation with the Soviet Union, which became a reality as World War II drew to an end. Spykman's admonition did become US policy, and as the cold war unfolded, a grand strategy inspired by a geopolitical view of the world remained one of its guiding principles. From the start, the cold war was a global struggle with specific regional geopolitical dynamics. Stalin installed communist leaders in the newly liberated states of Eastern Europe and integrated these states into a Soviet-led alliance system that was motivated by geopolitics as much as ideology. This was mirrored in the development of the US strategic doctrine of containment, which similarly applied a geopolitical rationale to the ideological focus of the cold war, and remained in place until the demise of the Soviet Union (see Box 17.3).

Given the global scope of the cold war and its long-term strategic horizon, it may seem surprising that the actual concepts of geopolitics and grand strategy were by no means central tenets of strategic thinking during the cold war and fell out of use for decades, to be revived only in the 1970s and 1980s. In part, this reflected the way that geopolitical ideas had become thoroughly de-legitimized by their association with Nazi Germany. Another factor was the start of the nuclear arms race between the Soviet Union and the United States, which seemed

**BOX** 17.3  Containment

Containment was first developed at the onset of the cold war by George F. Kennan, a diplomat who had studied the Soviet Union closely. He proposed a strategy which relied on countering Soviet influence 'by the adroit and vigilant application of counterforce at a series of constantly shifting geographical and political points' (Kennan 1947). By the 1950s, the competition for spheres of influence between the United States and the Soviet Union acquired a global dimension, partly as a result of decolonization in Africa and Asia. Containment was reformulated and expanded into what became known as 'domino theory'—the idea that Soviet influence had to be countered everywhere, since one state turning communist could easily spread communism to neighbouring states until an entire world region would fall. Containment was a form of geopolitics, but one which encompassed ideological competition as well as competition for resources. It required the US to engage across all areas of the globe to stop the spread of communism, whether or not the countries concerned were strategically important. In Vietnam in particular, hundreds of thousands of US soldiers were sent to help fight communist guerrillas in a costly, drawn-out, and ultimately unsuccessful war. Overall, containment was a consistent, if not always consistently implemented, grand strategic framework that was remarkably long-lived. Since the Soviet Union remained the much weaker economy, containment was an effective long-term strategy that helped to drain Soviet resources, though it was by no means the only factor in the collapse of the Soviet Union.

to obliterate the geographical factor in world politics. As both sides developed inter-continental ballistic missile systems capable of destroying each other's cities in a matter of hours, a grand strategy based on geopolitical considerations—such as the difference between land power and sea power—seemed obsolete. In fact, deterrence, the foundation of US military strategy during the cold war, had no connection to geopolitical reasoning; it was purely based on out-arming and out-spending the Soviet Union, expanding nuclear and conventional capabilities to deter the Soviet Union from using its own nuclear weapons.

By the 1970s, as the economic burden of the nuclear arms race began to be felt in the US, and it seemed for a while that the Soviet Union would become the dominant military power, geopolitics began to be re-evaluated in US policy circles. This revival was associated in particular with two influential figures, Henry Kissinger and Zbigniew Brzezinski. Kissinger, as national security advisor to President Nixon, was the architect of warmer relations with communist China, a policy that was later expanded by Brzezinski. Kissinger's understanding of geopolitics as Great Power politics was influenced by a deep knowledge of European history and the varying ways in which the balance of power between the European Great Powers had played out over centuries. He believed in the continuing relevance of power balancing as a principle of international politics. Brzezinski's understanding of geopolitics drew more explicitly on Mackinder's heartland theory. Like Mackinder, he saw control over the Eurasian landmass as central to world domination and eventual victory in the cold war. Both Kissinger and Brzezinski advocated a move away from the bipolar stalemate between the United States and the Soviet Union towards a more dynamic multipolar order by engaging with communist China, which a decade earlier had fallen out with the Soviet Union over questions of communist doctrine. A US–Chinese rapprochement was aimed at weakening the grip of the Soviet Union over the Eurasian landmass, and above all at preventing a mending of relations between the two communist countries which would have led to absolute Soviet dominance of the Eurasian continent.

**Key Points**

- The concept of Grand Strategy was first developed in the context of World War II and was an extension of the long-term strategic view inherent in geopolitical thought.

- Both the Soviet Union and the United States acted geopolitically during the cold war. Containment was a grand strategy informed by geopolitical reasoning, but driven by ideological concerns rather than resource competition.

- The revival of geopolitics in the 1970s occurred at a time when the US was seen to be in relative decline, and means other than the nuclear arms race were sought to secure its position.

## Geopolitics and Grand Strategy Today

Geopolitics and grand strategy as concepts of statecraft first emerged at a specific historical constellation: the long-term decline of a hegemonic power and the rise of new challengers. There are parallels between the situation of the British empire at the turn of the twentieth century and the global position of the United States today. The period of global primacy that the US enjoyed after the cold war may not be over, but global shifts are unfolding that make it appear less durable and absolute than a decade ago. As in the case of imperial Britain, this is driven by relative economic decline. The inexorable economic rise of China, now the world's second largest economy, was accelerated by the global economic crisis of 2008, which many emerging economies weathered much better than Europe and the United States. Nor is this just an issue of Chinese economic growth. Over the last two decades, the combined GDP of the Group of Seven industrialized nations as a percentage of the world's total has decreased from over 70 per cent to 50 per cent (Zongze 2014). This redistribution of global wealth away from the US and Western Europe towards the major developing economies in the global South is unprecedented in the modern era.

Consequences of this shift are beginning to affect international politics. As the US academic Jon Alterman put it, China's demands are now 'too large not to affect the global environment, and its external vulnerabilities are too large to rely on others to defend them' (Alterman 2013: 2). Familiar geopolitical themes, such as the need to secure resources, are driving China's new global engagement. China is poor in energy resources and aims to secure supplies for its expanding economy. It is now the world's second largest consumer of oil and its demand for gas is rapidly increasing (US Energy Information Administration Report 2014). The presence of China in regions such as the Middle East and its growing energy relationship with Russia has broader geopolitical implications. It gives new leverage to regional players the US has been trying to isolate, such as Syria and Iran, and provides the backdrop for Russia's assertiveness over Ukraine. China's current reliance on energy supplied via sea routes controlled by the United States has been driving regional tensions over Chinese territorial claims in the South China Sea (see Box 17.4).

Unlike Germany in the 1890s, neither China nor Russia is directly challenging the US in military terms, and would not be in a position to do so. US defence spending is in decline, but the United States remains the world's largest military power by far, accounting for more than a third of total global military expenditure in 2013 (International Institute for Strategic

**BOX** 17.4   Obama's 'Pivot to Asia'

Obama's 'Pivot to Asia', a major strategic shift to a renewed engagement in East Asia, was partly motivated by a wish to curb increasing Chinese assertiveness in the region. China has been staking out territorial claims over islands in the South China Sea, to secure maritime shipping routes as well as potential energy resources in the maritime shelf belonging to these islands. It has increased its naval presence and started to invest heavily in building up a blue water navy. This has led to tensions with some of its neighbours, in particular Vietnam, the Philippines, and Japan—the latter being two key US military allies in the region. The military dimension of the pivot may be contributing to a 'spiral of insecurity' in which the other side reacts to a perceived threat by building up its own military capacities. Partly in response to the pivot, China has accelerated and expanded its naval armament. Japan, China's traditional adversary in the region, has been encouraged by the renewed US engagement to escalate its own simmering tensions with China and is pushing for re-militarization. While the pivot may have reassured America's partners and thwarted Chinese ambitions in the short term, the result has been a negative transformation of the overall security dynamics of the region.

Studies, *The Military Balance*, 2013). Yet, both China and Russia are rearming. Russia is currently embarking on an ambitious programme of military modernization, while China is increasing its defence spending by double digits each year. And as Russia's stand-off with the West over Ukraine and China's stance in the South China Sea demonstrate, both are increasingly willing to challenge regional security orders sustained by the United States. In addition, as the territorial order imposed by Western colonial powers is breaking down in the Middle East, Iran is seizing its chance to extend its regional influence and challenge the dominance of US allies such as Saudi Arabia. In all these regions, new security issues are becoming intertwined with more traditional geopolitical challenges to US primacy.

 **BOX** 17.5   Russia, Ukraine, and the West

The recent stand-off between Russia and the West over influence in Ukraine seems to confirm Brzezinski's dictum that Ukraine is a 'pivot state' because of its sensitive geopolitical location (Brzezinski 1997). While Ukraine's strategic location is important to Russia, and it is the main transit country for Russia's pipelines to the European Union (EU), Russia's meddling in Eastern Ukraine is not explained by a focus on resources and geostrategic location alone. Ukraine is central for Russian identity narratives as the location of the first Russian state. After the collapse of the Soviet Union, many Russians found it hard to accept Ukrainian independence. Putin's project of a Eurasian customs and economic union was partly designed to bind Ukraine to Russia and stop its move towards closer association with the EU. The immediate context that triggered the Ukrainian crisis was plans by then president Victor Yanukovich to sign an association (trade) agreement with the EU. This was not a geopolitical zero-sum game—the trade agreement and the Eurasian customs union were not mutually exclusive. Relations between Russia and the EU have deteriorated over the past decade, partly as a result of EU support for the democratic 'colour revolutions' in Georgia and Ukraine and the erosion of Russian democracy under Putin. There is now a clear rejection by the Kremlin of a liberal, European identity for Russia. In terms of broader geopolitics of identity, the EU, just like the US, has become Russia's external 'Other' against which Russian identity is defined. The association agreement was perceived in Moscow in terms of these geopolitics of identity, as a move to join a liberal Western 'Other'. Ukraine is pivotal because of the meaning attached to it by Russian policymakers, which in turn links to broader perceptions of the relationship between Russia and the West.

In this complex strategic environment, a number of American commentators have argued that the United States suffers from 'imperial overstretch', a term coined by Paul Kennedy for a situation where excessive defence budgets undermine the prosperity of a country and weaken it internationally as a result (Kennedy 1988). While the proportion of US defence spending in relation to GDP is still less than that of many smaller states, stagnant economic growth since the global economic crisis means that bloated defence budgets are becoming a problem. At the same time, the diverging nature of the actual and potential threats presented by transnational terrorism and the revival of geopolitical competition mean that there are increasingly hard choices to be made about how to invest limited resources.

The emphasis on peacetime development reflects shifting understandings of Great Power competition and Great Power war since 1945. Before World War I, wars between Great Powers were frequent and limited in scale, and often used to effect power transitions. However, World War I and World War II showed that military technology had developed to a point where war between major industrialized states involved exorbitant social and economic costs. This was exacerbated by the arrival of atomic weapons at the onset of the cold war. A highly interdependent global economy has further diminished the returns and increased the costs of Great Power war. Partly as a result of these developments, there has been no direct war between major powers since 1945. It is therefore not surprising that the current discourse on rising powers has foregrounded relative economic development over simple rankings of military capabilities. The broader aim of securing the prosperity and power of the polity may or may not mean a major role for defence and the armed forces—it depends on the nature of the strategic environment, which determines how these aims can be achieved.

 **Key Points**

- The rise of China and the relative economic decline of the US are driving the current revival of interest in geopolitics and grand strategy.

- China's economic expansion and its need for energy supplies are already having an effect on political dynamics in various regions of the world.

- The US remains militarily dominant. Russia, China and some other states are rearming, but at present this is not a direct challenge.

- It has been argued that the US suffers from 'imperial overstretch', spending so much on its defence budget that it is weakened overall.

- The emphasis of grand strategy has shifted to peacetime development, partly because war between Great Powers now seems improbable.

## Grand Strategy in a Complex World

It is not difficult to find declarations of long-term strategic ambitions in the public statements of policymakers, especially those representing major powers. However, a proliferation of strategic documents and the declaration of lofty aims are not necessarily an indication that a grand strategy exists and is being implemented. The historical record is patchy. As Williamson Murray remarked, 'those who have developed successful grand strategies in the past have been very much the exception … a strategic framework, much less a grand strategy has rarely guided those responsible for the long-term survival of the state' (Murray 2011: 3). There are many obstacles to the successful formulation of a grand strategy, let alone its implementation, in an uncertain and complex international environment. A grand strategy is by its very nature comprehensive, encompassing in the words of one author 'a clear understanding of the nature of the international environment, a country's highest goals and interests within that environment, the primary threats to those goals and interests, and the way that finite resources can be used to deal with competing challenges and opportunities' (Brands 2014: 13). A grand strategist must understand and assess an exceptionally broad range of factors, individually and in relation to each other. As Lawrence Freedman has pointed out, this is a problematic assumption (Freedman 2013). There are limitations related to the imperfect functioning of the machinery of the state within which the grand strategist must operate. The information reaching the decision maker from the lower levels of bureaucracy may be incomplete or biased, and the gap between formulation and implementation of policies is exponentially increased in a strategy aimed at guiding policy over a long period of time in diverse and evolving circumstances. Even assuming a perfectly operational decision-making environment, the level of complexity involved in formulating a grand strategy poses questions about its feasibility. The holistic assessment of such a broad range of factors may simply surpass the limits of human intelligence. It certainly raises questions about contingency and predictability in a system as complex as the international environment.

A grand strategy is a guiding framework that allows policymakers to steer through the uncertainties of a complex international environment. Finding such a framework becomes more difficult the more uncertain this environment is and the more it presents different and sometimes mutually incompatible strategic challenges. It is not a coincidence that conceptions of grand strategy first emerged at a time when the range of actors posing a potential threat to Britain and the United States was limited and the threat was clear. The idea of a grand strategy bears the imprint of its time, in particular in implicit assumptions about just how clear and consensual the interests and goals of a state really are. The current revival of thinking about grand strategy faces a very different scenario from that of the cold war—in fact, calls for a new grand strategy for the United States have arisen precisely because of this new complexity. Moreover, the ends of a grand strategy, in the most general sense of defining the national interest, have also become more difficult to formulate in the absence of a single overarching threat. While there is a connection between primacy and prosperity, the precise balance is ultimately a political decision and open to political contestation, especially where competing demands are made on finite resources.

Even where ends are reasonably clear, the long-term nature of grand strategy and the complexity of the global environment make it difficult to employ adequate means and formulate concrete policies. In a complex system, there will be contingencies and unpredictable events with multiple interdependent causes, sometimes the future unintended consequences of strategic decisions taken today. These contingencies may escalate into 'black swan' events: improbable, large-scale events that have transformative effects and are largely unpredictable to a given set of observers (Taleeb and Blythe 2011). In fact, contingent events are commonplace in international history and are often the cause of major upheavals. The collapse of the Soviet Union and 9/11 both fall into this category; informed observers failed to predict them, and their consequences changed the dynamics of international politics. By definition, there can be no planning for the surprising and unexpected, though grand strategies should provide guiding principles for making sense of and responding to these kinds of large-scale events. However, there is a real danger that the interpretative 'lenses' provided by a grand strategy may blind the decision-maker to the transformative consequences of a contingent event and thus prevent rather than enable an adequate reaction. The line between a clear guiding principle and rigidity is thin, and it can have far-reaching consequences when crossed. A grand strategy that fails to grasp the way that a contingent event changes the dynamics of international interaction, or that has identified trends in world politics wrongly from the outset, may trigger the very kind of development it set out to avoid. Strategic decisions are applied in context, in a highly dynamic international environment populated by other actors that inevitably react to policy moves directed at them (see Box 17.4).

Policymakers are well aware of the uncertainties of their decision-making environment. Since the end of the cold war, strategic documents make habitual reference to the complexity of the international environment and stress the need for adaptability and flexibility in strategic planning. Given its extended time horizon, grand strategy must be flexible and able to adapt to changing contexts in a complex and always evolving international system. However, if flexibility and adaptability are key, is the formulation of long-term holistic frameworks a useful endeavour? Critics of the idea of grand strategy have pointed out that it is too general and the international environment too complex for it to be of much use in concrete situations facing the decision-maker (Strachan 2011; Krasner 2010). And yet, while the difficulties inherent in grand strategic thinking are immense, in a modern state the lack of an overall strategic direction can be even more detrimental. This remains true above all for Great Powers, which will by definition have a wide variety of divergent and sometimes contradictory interests in far-flung locations, but rarely enough resources to cover all of them.

In the absence of a grand strategic framework, strategic decisions will still be made, but the risk that they will be based on short-term pressures or on unexamined bias increases. Frequently, the result may be non-decisions, 'muddling through' as a result of bureaucratic inertia, or policies formulated on the basis of past approaches wholly inadequate for a changing strategic context (Lindblom 1959). This kind of non-decision can have far-reaching consequences. The failure to formulate a new European security architecture that could bind in a newly democratic Russia after the fall of the Soviet Union is a case in point. Instead, NATO, the cold war institution that had been created explicitly to defend Western Europe against the Soviet Union, reformulated its mission statement and was enlarged eastwards. The unintended consequence of NATO enlargement and further NATO actions in Europe, especially the bombardment of Serbia over Kosovo in 1999, was a strengthening of nationalist and anti-Western forces in Russia and an increasingly fraught relationship with the West. William Clinton, the US president endorsing these decisions, did not believe in the idea of grand strategy (Brands 2014). The initial decision to enlarge seems to have been driven mainly by persistent lobbying by the smaller East European states and a vague sense that this would help consolidate a liberal community of values in Europe (Schimmelpfennig 2000). Somewhat ironically given what has been said about the pitfalls of grand strategy, its long-term horizon and holistic approach may be necessary to recognize the dangerous implications of short-term decisions responding to past contexts.

---

 **Key Points**

- In a complex and fluid world, it has become much more difficult to formulate grand strategies.
- Rigid grand strategies, or those based on the wrong assumptions, can have negative consequences, since they blind decision-makers to unpredictable changes in the strategic environment.
- For a large powerful state, grand strategic planning may be necessary, since the effects of simply 'muddling through' may be worse.

---

## Rethinking Geopolitics

The grand strategist must be flexible and adaptable, but also look out for persistent structures that allow him or her to specify strategic aims. The original association between geopolitics and grand strategy derives exactly from this conundrum. Constants such as a state's size, location, climate, and resources were seen as objective constraining and enabling factors that allowed predictions of a state's power and influence. Even though the scientific credentials of this kind of geographical determinism have long since been called into question, geography remains inextricably intertwined with the making of grand strategy. For one, grand strategy has to be geographically specific in the sense of being located in and directed at a specific context. Factors of physical geography, like the size of states, their location and their neighbours, remain fundamentally important in this regard. The isolated geographical position of the United States, without major competitors or threats in close proximity, provides security but also makes it logistically difficult to project power. On the other hand, Russia's open and porous borders, its proximity to major competitors, and its harsh climate are all potential vulnerabilities. A state's access to resources also remains central, and hydrocarbon resources in particular are as important now as they were when classical geopolitical thinkers first constructed their theories. Nevertheless, resource bases, just as other aspects of physical geography, are not a fixed and unchanging factor of world politics. Currently, a major strategic shift is under way as a result of new technologies for the exploitation of non-conventional energy resources. If implemented, it will make the United States less dependent on oil from the Middle East, and may result in it becoming a net energy exporter (Sergie 2014). As this example illustrates, seemingly permanent geographic factors such as the location of resources can be altered by the development of new technologies. The interaction between geography and technological change is a central feature of geopolitics.

Nevertheless, an emphasis on the relationship between geography and technology fails to capture a central way in which geography becomes relevant to world politics. As the strategist Colin Gray put it, 'although there is a brute force existentiality to physical geography, as a generalization it is geography in the mind, of the imagination, that matters most. [. . .] The geography is as unarguable as its perceived political meaning is contestable' (Gray 2013: 118). The geographical context within which policymaking necessarily orients itself not only refers to factors of physical geography. Brute geographical facts acquire their significance in particular cultural and social contexts. This starts with the fact that cultures and civilizations are located in particular geographical spaces, a central factor that underpins cultural distinctiveness. On a different scale, human beings attach meaning to places, meaning that can become politically and strategically significant. Often, especially where particular sites and territories are part of narratives of collective identity, these interpretations can become powerful mobilizing factors. This has been true for the many ethnic conflicts of the post-cold war world. But identity and territory are also linked in the nation-state, and interpretations of geography can be and often are a powerful influence on foreign policymaking. Often, these identity narratives are about dynamics of 'Othering', the inclusion in or exclusion from an imagined geopolitical space. The relationship between Russia and the 'West' (in itself such an imagined space, comprising countries and institutions supporting a US-dominated liberal order) is a case in point and underpins the current conflict in Ukraine (see Box 17.5).

The role played by interpretation and identity complicates the uses of geography for the making of grand strategy. Yet, the effects of geography are inescapable in international politics, whether they are the 'brute force' of geographical constraints in a given strategic context, or the role played by interpretations of geography. There clearly is value in reflecting on the way that decision-makers' interpretations of geography may affect their formulation of strategy, as well as in understanding the meaning particular geographic factors have for an adversary. As the persistent identity of Britain as an island nation illustrates, specific interpretations of geography in a narrative of collective identity are remarkably long-lived (see Box 17.2). However, this comes with a caveat—it is all too easy to assume that interpretations of geography in identity narratives are fixed, leading to the kind of rigidity that undermines the aims of a grand strategy. Instead, collective meanings and identities are changeable and often politically contested, and are always re-interpreted in particular contexts. Classical geopolitics conceptualized the geographic factor as timeless and universal. However, the basic meaning of geopolitics, the political uses of geography, draws attention to context, which is always situated and specific. Interpretations of geographical factors, just as objective geographic constraints, may be long-lived, but it is the task of the grand strategist to assess how they play out in any given situation.

 **Key Points**

- Geography is not a fixed and immutable factor in world affairs.
- Technological change affects the way that geographical factors play out in international politics.
- Geographical factors matter both as external constraints and because they are interpreted and politically contested, and often part of identity narratives.
- This duality complicates the uses of geopolitics for grand strategy, but also adds a new, important dimension that makers of grand strategy need to take into account.

**Critical Thinking**    Debating … Should the US pull back?

The US has not substantially reduced its military spending from cold war levels and continues to pursue active, global foreign policies. With financial pressures and recent, unpopular wars in Afghanistan and Iraq, should the US pull back from the world?

## For

● *Favourable geopolitics.* With two weak and friendly neighbours—Canada and Mexico—and surrounded by open seas, there is no genuine threat to US territory. Its huge nuclear arsenal also acts as a powerful deterrent.

● *Creating more enemies.* By aggressively pursuing the 'war on terror', the US is already creating more enemies amongst Muslims. An active foreign policy might encourage rivals such as China and Russia into an alliance which could dominate Eurasia.

● *Free-riding allies.* America's allies can 'free-ride' on US power. NATO members are able to reduce military spending, knowing that they are protected by the US nuclear umbrella; Israel and Taiwan can embark upon risky policies guaranteed by Washington.

## Against

● *No danger from rival coalitions.* US military preponderance means it need not worry about coalitions of other powers forming against it. Moreover, China and Russia have a long history of mutual suspicion.

● *Defence technology leverage.* By maintaining a large defence budget, the US has leverage over other countries which need American technology. Britain, for example, can only purchase certain components of its nuclear deterrent from the US.

● *Strong, prosperous relationships.* Alliances such as NATO lessen the likelihood of being dragged into unnecessary wars by creating a network of strong relationships and trust. These alliances and active American engagement in the world guarantee global trade and prosperity.

 **Conclusion**

Formulating and implementing a grand strategy in today's complex international environment is an exceedingly difficult task, and not helped by the fact that geography is not the kind of scientific long-term grounding for grand strategy that the classical geopoliticians imagined. However, this complexity may be the very reason a grand strategy should be attempted. In an evolving international environment, it is dangerous to continue implementing policies and approaches that no longer fit the times. It is equally dangerous to attempt a grand strategy directed at the wrong target, and with an erroneous understanding of what is needed to achieve desired ends—US President George W. Bush's strategy in the war on terror may serve as an example. Nevertheless, the multiple challenges that affect the world today are so diverse that a concerted attempt to balance ends and means seems more necessary than ever. In democratic states this means that the welfare and prosperity of the nation, in line with the values of the polity, are the ultimate end. Grand strategy is about the right balance between means and ends, not about hedging against all possible threats and winning wars at all costs. In all of this, thinking geopolitically is central, in the most basic sense that geography is central to politics and foreign policy must be geographically focused. However, geographic factors are not an objective and unchanging determinant of world politics. Their political implications may lay precisely in the meanings they carry for particular actors. Perceptions of geographical factors, especially where they involve identity narratives, can be long-lasting, but they are not fixed and the way they become politicized in any particular situation is highly context-dependent. Even though this complicates the relationship between geopolitics and grand strategy, it remains a fundamental factor that the grand strategist has to grapple with in a challenging and fluid international environment.

## Questions

1. What are the aims of grand strategy?

2. Why is there renewed interest in geopolitics and grand strategy at this particular historical juncture?

3. What explains the emergence of geopolitical thought at the turn of the twentieth century?

4. Compare and contrast evolving definitions of grand strategy and geopolitics. How and why have these definitions changed?

5. To what extent was the grand strategy of containment during the cold war motivated by geopolitical reasoning?

6. What are the problems inherent in formulating grand strategies? Can they be overcome?

7. Why is grand strategy associated with the statecraft of Great Powers?

8. How has geopolitics traditionally been associated with grand strategy? What are the problems of this association?

9. If geopolitics is both about the 'out there' and the 'in here', as Colin Gray has written (Box 17.1), what is its use for the formulation of grand strategy?

10. Is the rise of China a challenge to US primacy?

## Further Reading

J. Agnew, *Geopolitics: Re-visioning World Politics*, 2nd edn (London: Routledge, 2003) critically investigates the way that modern world politics is underpinned by a European geopolitical imagination associated with the rise of the great powers.

H. Brands, *What Good Is Grand Strategy? Power and Purpose in American Statecraft from Harry S. Truman to George W. Bush* (Ithaca, NY: Cornell University Press, 2014) is a spirited recent defence of the idea that grand strategy is both useful and doable, with in-depth case studies of successes and failures in US grand strategy.

Z. Brzezinski, *The Grand Chessboard: American Primacy and Its Geostrategic Imperatives* (New York: Basic Books, 1997) reformulates Mackinder's heartland theory for the post-cold war world. A classic read by one of the architects of the geopolitical revival in the US.

C. S. Gray and G. Sloan (eds), *Geopolitics, Geography, and Strategy* (London: Routledge, 1999) is an edited volume covering a wide range of topics and approaches, from treatments of military strategy to critical reflections on geography and culture.

J. J. Grygiel, *Great Powers and Geopolitical Change* (Johns Hopkins University Press, 2006) emphasizes the interplay between technological change and geography and analyses in historical case studies how Great Powers have responded to such dramatic geopolitical changes as the discovery of new trade routes and continents.

P. Kennedy, *The Rise And Fall Of The Great Powers: Economic Change And Military Conflict* (London: Unwin Hyman, 1988) offers a magisterial account of relative economic decline and its effects on world politics that remains essential reading.

J. J. Mearsheimer, *The Tragedy of Great Power Politics*, 2nd updated edn (New York: Norton, 2014) stresses the pursuit of primacy as a central driving force in world politics. Consistently insightful, with a new chapter on the role of China in world affairs.

W. Murray, R. H. Sinnreich, and J. Lacey (eds), *The Shaping of Grand Strategy: Policy, Diplomacy, and War* (Cambridge: Cambridge University Press, 2011) is an exploration of grand strategy in history by a group of leading historians, with insightful general discussions of the meaning of grand strategy and the many failures in its implementation.

##  Web Links

International Security Network, University of Zurich **http://www.isn.ethz.ch** contains a wealth of relevant information, including articles on geopolitics and grand strategy.

Exploring Geopolitics **http://www.exploringgeopolitics.org/I_About.html** though not currently updated as of 2014, this remains a rich resource on classical and contemporary geopolitics.

*Foreign Policy* magazine **http://foreignpolicy.com** analyses US foreign policy, often with an eye for geopolitical questions and discussions of US grand strategy.

# Part III

The Future of
Strategy

# Strategic Studies and its Critics

COLUMBA PEOPLES

## Chapter Contents

 **Reader's Guide**

This chapter introduces readers to the criticism levelled at strategic studies from the 'Golden Age' of nuclear strategy through to contemporary critiques. It begins by reviewing prominent critical appraisals of deterrence theory in the 1960s, a time when several fundamental criticisms of strategic studies were made. The chapter then outlines how these critiques were subsequently addressed by strategic theorists. As strategic studies has evolved and changed, however, so too have the arguments made against it. Critical approaches to the study of security have, largely in opposition to strategic studies, developed multifaceted critiques that encompass issues ranging from the use of gendered terminology to an alleged Western-centric bias. The chapter assesses the current status of the relationship between strategic studies and its critics, and the important role that critical engagement might play in the future development of strategic studies.

## Introduction

For as long as the activity of theorizing conflict has existed, there have been those who have endeavoured to render its purpose irrelevant. Just as modern strategic studies can be said to have its pre-history in the broader study of how to fight and win wars, encompassing thinkers such as Sun Tzu, Machiavelli, and Clausewitz, there is an oppositional history of thinkers such as Immanuel Kant and the Abbé de Saint Pierre that have endeavoured to theorize the conditions in which war might itself become outdated and obsolete as an activity (see Waltz 1962: 331; Dunn 1991: 59). This latter tradition of attempting to identify the possibilities for 'perpetual peace' (as Kant would have it) was at odds with the basic assumption made by classical strategists: that war is an inevitable occurrence, which in turn necessitates sustained reflection on its purpose and effective conduct. These parallel traditions of 'thinking war' on the one hand and 'thinking peace' on the other remained largely independent, albeit related, intellectual activities.

Modern strategic studies has been marked by a more direct engagement between proponents of strategic theory and those who criticize its purpose and existence. The dawn of the 'nuclear age' and the exponential rise of strategic studies as a subdiscipline of international relations during the cold war gave rise to extensive criticism of strategic studies. With the advent of nuclear weapons and, by the 1960s, the condition of 'Mutual Assured Destruction' (MAD), many began to criticize strategic studies as contributing to (rather than diminishing) the prospect of nuclear conflict. The study of nuclear strategy was variously decried by critics as unethical, unscholarly, and uncritical of the status quo in world politics. As Hedley Bull noted in his seminal 1968 article 'Strategic Studies and its Critics', 'civilian strategic analysts . . . have from the first been subject to criticism that has called into question the validity of their methods, their utility to society, and even their integrity of purpose' (Bull 1968: 593).

Yet the relationship between strategic studies and its critics is more complex than is presented by a picture of nuclear strategists under siege from their opponents. Proponents of strategic studies have, in response to criticism, often articulated trenchant defences of the study of strategy, and strategic studies has also been subjected to internal critiques that have fostered its development. In addition, although some of the original criticism of nuclear strategy identified by Bull persists, the nature and range of critical assessments of strategic studies have diversified beyond many of these initial concerns.

This chapter draws together key themes in critiques of the study of strategy to heighten awareness of how strategic studies has developed into its current form. Even if certain disputes between proponents and critics of strategic studies remain seemingly irresolvable, reviewing this debate provides a more holistic picture of the state of strategic studies and the prospects for its future development.

## Strategy and its Critics in the 'Golden Age'

The period running from the aftermath of World War II through to the end of the 1960s is often referred to as the 'Golden Age' of strategic studies (Gray 1982a; Wæver and Buzan 2010: 467–70). During this period, a new breed of strategic thinker rose to prominence: the so-called 'civilian strategist' (Jervis 1979; Williams 1993: 104). Whereas previously issues of strategy had largely been the preserve of military practitioners, a 'second wave' of non-military academics such as Bernard Brodie, Herman Kahn, Thomas Schelling, and Albert Wohlstetter became the dominant voices of strategy in the new, nuclear age (Freedman 1986). The academic study of strategy also grew exponentially as did its prominence and influence on policy through academic think tanks such as the RAND corporation (Kaplan 1983).

The role of these civilian strategists was, as the title of Herman Kahn's (1962) work famously put it, *Thinking about the Unthinkable*; the world had, mercifully, only witnessed the use of nuclear weapons in conflict on two occasions, Hiroshima and Nagasaki. However, limited experience with these revolutionary weapons meant that military practitioners had only marginally greater claim to expertise on the question of nuclear warfare than non-military experts. Additionally, the vast destructive power of atomic weapons convinced many in government that strategy *really was* too important a matter to be left to the generals. Given the paucity of battlefield experience, Kahn and other civilian strategists consequently argued that 'scientific' methods such as game theory and systems analysis were necessary additions to the strategist's intellectual armoury. They looked to theoretical innovations drawn from fields such as economics and mathematics to better think through possible paths to nuclear conflict and the means by which to prevent it. Mathematical demonstrations of the vulnerability of American missile silos to a Soviet nuclear strike, for instance, were argued to provide meaningful constructions of the 'unthinkable' scenario of nuclear conflict (Barkawi 1998: 172). As Wæver and Buzan note, the US government actively fostered the growth of deterrence theory in this phase as the theories produced and promised 'ever new and ever more complex' frameworks for attempting to understand the nuclear dimension of the cold war, and 'all this seemed highly useful because the theories actually produced their own reality of abstractions, the world of "secure second strike capability," "extended deterrence," and "escalation dominance"' (2010: 468).

The magnitude of the task taken on by the civilian strategists ensured that these 'Wizards of Armageddon' (Kaplan 1983) had a high political—and public—profile. For example, well-informed viewers of Stanley Kubrick's (1964) film *Dr. Strangelove: Or how I learned to stop worrying and love the Bomb* could easily recognize the parody of Herman Kahn in the figure of the film's eponymous central character, Dr Strangelove, and his blasé proposals on how a select band of elites might survive a nuclear conflict and its aftermath in facilities deep underground. Elements of Strangelove's dialogue were virtually paraphrased from Kahn's *On Thermonuclear War* (Kaplan 1983: 231). The Strangelove character—and indeed the film's central narrative plot, in which the United States accidentally begins an all-out nuclear war—though fictional, provides a window into a particular view of nuclear strategy that began to emerge in the 1960s: that the new 'science' of theorizing nuclear conflict was an incomprehensible activity that was at best morally questionable and at worst bordered on the absurd.

## Strategy and Conscience: The Moral Foundation of Criticism of Strategic Studies

This critical view of nuclear strategy was most notably articulated in the work of Anatol Rapoport (1964) and Philip Green (1966). Green himself noted that his own critique of nuclear strategy was inspired by 'a feeling of strangeness induced by a lengthy study of the literature of nuclear deterrence' (Green 1966: 5), and both Rapoport and Green found it difficult to fathom the idea that otherwise well-educated scholars could countenance the idea of building theories about the possibility of nuclear war. At issue for these critics of the civilian strategists was a perceived evasion of a fundamental moral and ethical question: namely, whether it was ethical to encourage the planning and study of nuclear warfare.

The most prominent text in this line of criticism was Rapoport's *Strategy and Conscience*, which, as described in its preface by Karl Deutsch, was 'written as a protest against a glib and shallow fashion of contemporary thought [nuclear strategy] that embodies and enhances man's inhumanity to man' (Rapoport 1964: vii). Rapoport argued that scholarly proponents of nuclear deterrence had overlooked basic questions of conscience. While Kahn and others speculated about the possibilities of surviving and prevailing in nuclear conflict, Rapoport wondered how those engaged in such thinking could live with themselves in the first place.

Rapoport and Green both argued that the study of nuclear strategy, and its pretensions to scholarly and scientific rigour, essentially neglected key moral questions. For Green, euphemisms associated with deterrence theory such as 'delicate balance of terror', 'rational' responses to a nuclear strike, and 'making the unthinkable thinkable' obfuscated the moral reality of nuclear war and the unavoidable fact that whole populations could be wiped out in a nuclear holocaust (Green 1966: xi). Green argued that nuclear strategy, rather than operating in a moral vacuum, actually contained 'a hidden ethical stance' (1966: 226). The civilian strategists had erroneously convinced themselves, Green believed, that questions of nuclear deterrence were scientific rather than moral issues: 'The real error in all theorising of this type,' Green asserted, 'lies in the attempt to somehow separate the "analytical" components of a policy problem from the political and moral ones' (1966: 239). Green believed that strategists could never remove themselves entirely from their own values and attitudes in spite of their pretensions to 'scientific' objectivity. These calculations, construed in abstract terms, could eventually produce consequences that would make Hiroshima and Nagasaki seem like minor events.

## The Dangerous Games of Strategy

The critics of the civilian strategists did not, however, limit themselves to statements of moral outrage. The protests of anti-war and anti-nuclear protestors had long fallen on deaf ears within the strategic studies community of the postwar era. The civilian strategists perceived themselves to be involved in the business of protecting the United States and its Western allies from an obdurate, nuclear-armed opponent, and calls for nuclear disarmament were consequently dismissed as a dangerous form of idealism. Hence, Rapoport and Green both took the view that a more sustained critique of deterrence theory's claims to scientific rigour was required. Rapoport, for example, was motivated by a genuine abhorrence of what he perceived to be the callousness of strategic thought when it came to discussing nuclear conflict. Because he believed that moral critiques of strategy tended to be dismissed, Rapoport argued that the moral force of criticism needed to be supplemented by a critique of the civilian strategists' pride in the 'rationality' of nuclear deterrence. Rapoport made a plea to 'come to grips with these issues instead of playing games of strategy for enormous and unrecoverable stakes' (1964: xxiii).

Rapoport noted the tendency of the civilian strategist to portray himself as a 'master of a new science, whose principles are spelt out in abstract, often mathematical, terms' (1964: xviii). *Strategy and Conscience* thus attempted to engage strategic studies on its own terrain: that of systems analysis and, in particular, game theory as employed in the work of Kahn, Thomas Schelling, and Glenn Snyder. Rapoport, himself eminently qualified in the fields of mathematical theories of social interaction and game theory, argued that the adoption of game theoretic models (such as prisoner's dilemma and the chicken game—see Web Links for a brief introduction) into nuclear strategy encouraged oversimplification of the realities of the cold war stand-off. Rapoport questioned the assumption of rational actors—with similar interests—that operated at the heart of game theory. In his view, this assumption lacked any relation to reality. His critique of the nuclear strategists described the actual differences between American and Soviet ideologies in practice as a means of countering the argument that 'players' in game scenarios could be regarded as holding equivalent interests. Green was likewise critical of systems analysis, ideas for civil defence, and game theory. He argued:

> All that a reference to game theory can possibly do is provide an algebraical illustration of a verbal argument that one has already made. The illustration can be no better than the verbal argument; in most of the cases . . . it is actually worse.
>
> Green (1966: 125)

Ultimately, Green argued of deterrence theorists, 'their air of authority was and is completely spurious' (Green 1966: xi).

 **Key Points**

- The 'Golden Age' of strategic studies between the mid-1950s and mid-1960s saw the rise of a new breed of 'second wave' civilian strategists that favoured the incorporation of game theory and systems analysis into the study of nuclear strategy and deterrence.

- The rise of deterrence theory generated strident moral critiques that questioned the ethical foundations of the activity of theorizing nuclear war.

- These moral critiques were accompanied by attacks on deterrence theorists' pretensions to scientific objectivity and on the application of abstract mathematical and economic models as the basis for thinking about nuclear war and formulating US nuclear policy.

## Strategic Studies Strikes Back

The most prominent response to Rapoport and Green's critiques came in Hedley Bull's 1968 article 'Strategic studies and its critics', which provides not only a comprehensive overview of these critics' arguments but also a staunch rebuttal of most of their criticism. Bull was sympathetic to some elements of Rapoport and Greene's critiques, agreeing that strategic studies had become prone to abstract and technical analysis. Nevertheless, Bull largely refuted the charges levelled at strategic studies and argued that the suggestion that strategists were either immoral or amoral was misguided. Strategists did operate according to a moral calculus in his view: that of protecting the national interest (Bull 1968: 596). The purpose of deterrence, Bull also noted, was primarily to *prevent* the outbreak of nuclear war, an ultimately moral goal. Bull believed that strategic studies was a largely positive force in the postwar era. Strategists, he argued (and this would become a common refrain of later defences of strategic studies), dealt with the realities of world politics, the threat of nuclear war included. They 'take for granted the existence of military force', he argued, as a means of establishing greater knowledge about its dynamics and how it might be controlled (Bull 1968: 600). Strategic studies was thus more realistic than proposals for the abolition of either nuclear weapons or the use of military force in its entirety. Moreover, Bull argued that proposals for disarmament were in themselves based on a particular form of strategic reasoning because they make a claim about the relationship between military force and the possible ends of policy and in this sense are 'not a statement about [strategic studies] from outside' (Bull 1968: 606).

Defenders of strategic studies attempted a series of responses to Rapoport, arguing, for example, that Rapoport overstated the influence of game theory within American strategic thought of the 1960s. Many within strategic studies, however, were also beginning to recognize the ill effects of game theory and pretensions to scientific objectivity. Bull, for example, though ultimately a defender of strategic studies, lamented the general absence of analysis of historical context and reference to concrete cases from strategic studies in the 1960s. Similarly Bernard Brodie, who had initially encouraged the incorporation of economic theories into strategic studies in the late 1940s, also came to regret the level of abstraction encouraged by the use of various types of formal analysis by nuclear strategists (see Betts 1997: 16).

As strategic studies evolved and attempted to redress these perceived failings, Rapoport's critique increasingly appeared to be tied to the Golden Age of strategic thinking. His critique of strategy as a 'mode of thought', as Rapoport himself acknowledged, centred on the issue of 'rationality' as understood and prized by second wave strategists such as Kahn, Snyder, and Schelling—those whom Rapoport referred to as 'abstractionists' (Rapoport 1964: 177). Yet, as a new generation of strategic thinkers—described as 'neo-traditionalists' by Rapoport—began to question these same issues, the substantive part of Rapoport's critique became somewhat anachronistic (Rapoport 1964: 180).

By the 1980s a 'third wave' of strategists had emerged (Jervis 1979; Williams 1993: 293–324). These strategic thinkers saw themselves as engaged in a *reconstructive* critique of strategy: that is, a form of critique intended to rectify perceived flaws of the 'second wave' thinking that was so heavily criticized by Rapoport and Green. This third wave differed markedly from Rapoport and Green, however, because most of the thinkers associated with it distanced themselves from these radical moral critiques of strategic studies. Instead, critique was now seen as a means of revitalizing, rather than vilifying, strategic studies. As Colin S. Gray, one of the foremost thinkers in the third wave, argued: 'An important distinction should be drawn between friendly, as opposed to unfriendly, critics of strategic studies' (see Box 18.1) (Gray 1982b: 44).

'Friendly' critics included Bull as well as Gray himself. Building on the analysis offered by Bull, Gray dismissed the kind of radical opposition to strategic studies offered by Rapoport and Green. Gray argued that the failings of 'abstractionist' second wave strategic thinking should not be construed as a failure of strategic studies per se; it was, he argued, 'more sensible to criticize what may be termed the vulgarization of strategic thinking in the second half of the 1960s, and the near cessation of innovative strategic thinking in that period and later' (Gray 1982b: 19). The advent of game theory and systems analysis was indeed, in Gray's view, a retrograde step with regard to nuclear strategy. Nevertheless, Gray saw 'little merit in many of the criticisms voiced from the left of the political spectrum' (Gray 1982b: 5). In common with Bull, Gray argued that proponents of disarmament and alternative world orders had as yet failed to illustrate the validity of such options (Gray 1982b: 41–2) and that strategic studies remained a necessity of the nuclear age.

Yet Gray himself admitted to being 'far from uncritical of contemporary strategic studies' (Gray 1982b: 5). Those associated with the third wave—including, most prominently, Gray and

**BOX** 18.1 Strategists Respond to the Critics

To be blunt, deterrence theory justifies the indiscriminate killing of innocent persons under certain circumstances.

Green (1966: 225)

Pseudo-science such as that of deterrence theorists . . . constitutes a disservice not only to the scholarly community, but ultimately to the democratic political process as well.

Green (1966: 276)

Strategic thinking has produced thus far at best something like 'The Intelligent Robot's Guide to International Politics'.

Karl Deutsch (in the preface to Rapoport 1964: xiv–xv)

Strategists as a class, it seems to me, are neither any less nor any more sensitive to moral considerations than are other intelligent and educated persons in the West . . . What critics take to be the strategists' insensitivity to moral considerations is in most cases the strategists' greater sense of the moral stature of the American and Western political objectives for which war and the risk of war must be undertaken.

Bull (1968: 596–7)

The strategic approach to international relations is rooted in [the] consciousness of the vulnerability of the cultural and political base from which the political scientist operates. He may need the soldier and the policeman to create a favourable environment in which he can discover how to dispense with their services.

Howard (1976b: 69)

Strategists are just as attracted to conditions of permanent peace as others, but they insist upon proper identification of the problems of political transition. They resent quite vehemently the charge, or intimation, that *they* themselves comprise an important part of the problem.

Gray (1982b: 8–9)

Robert Jervis—challenged prior assumptions of deterrence theory, especially the concept of rational deterrence itself. In opposition to the abstract nature of game theory and systems analysis, the third wave of theorizing 'stressed the need for inductive methodologies and called for concrete historical evidence to counter and correct the misconceptions which, it argued, had resulted from the abstract rationalism and deductive reasoning of second wave strategy' (Williams 1993: 105).

One strand that emerged from this reassessment of strategic studies replaced prior abstract rationalism with a focus on political and strategic culture as a factor in particular 'national styles' (Gray 1986) of different states with regard to nuclear strategy. Ken Booth had previously charged strategic studies with 'ethnocentrism': that is the phenomenon by which 'societies look at the world with their own group as the centre, and they perceive and interpret other societies within their own frames of reference' (Booth 1979: 13). Booth noted that the deterrence theorists of the Golden Age failed to anticipate that there might be other ways of thinking about strategy. They assumed their own standards of rationality to be universally applicable and consequently believed that strategic thinking that deviated from it must be inferior. This assumption of a universal rationality created a serious risk of misperception, in particular misperception of Soviet strategic thinking and intentions by US strategic planners (Snyder 1977). This was a theme also picked up by Robert Jervis' (1976) *Perception and Misperception in International Relations*, in which Jervis sought to investigate the psychological dimension of deterrence, which was largely absent from second wave thinking.

The more controversial aspect to emerge from this third wave critique, however, was Gray's claim that 'American strategic studies is remarkably thin at the level of operational analysis . . . civilian scholars have almost totally neglected the question of how we fight a nuclear war and for what objectives—if deterrence fails' (Gray 1982b: 12). The advent of the Ronald Reagan era in the United States—and with it the onset of the so-called 'second cold war'—saw this question gain a new degree of prominence and notoriety. Gray and Keith Payne considered possible scenarios in which deterrence mechanisms might be inadequate (Gray and Payne 1980). They also countenanced the possibility of fighting and prevailing in a nuclear conflict with the Soviet Union should deterrence fail. Gray and Payne argued that this position was morally preferable to sole reliance on a theory in which both the US and the USSR risked mutual annihilation. The Reagan administration was seen to be sympathetic to this view, with Reagan himself commenting widely on his dissatisfaction with the continuing possibility of mutual assured destruction. Yet the idea of nuclear conflict remained to many unnerving, and theories for 'victory' in nuclear conflict represented 'a new and dangerous mythology about nuclear weapons' (Lawrence 1988: 4) that risked reversing the 'taboo' (Tannenwald 1999) on the use of nuclear weapons. As a result, the attempt to revitalize strategic studies associated with the third wave of strategic studies generated a new round of criticism from outside the strategic community.

---

 **Key Points**

- Proponents of strategic studies in the 1970s defended its moral virtues on the grounds that the study of nuclear strategy and the prevention of nuclear war were more realistic than the idea of nuclear disarmament.

- Though they did not accept prior moral critiques of strategic studies, theorists associated with the 'third wave' of strategic studies acknowledged the level of abstraction associated with 'second wave' deterrence theory as problematic.

- Deterrence theorists such as Colin S. Gray and Robert Jervis also questioned deterrence theory's reliance on a monolithic notion of 'rationality'.

- Thinkers associated with the third wave attempted to redirect strategic studies back towards a focus on cultural particularity, history, and 'national styles' in the making of nuclear strategy.

---

## Critical Approaches to Strategic Studies

Since the early 1980s, a subtle but distinct shift in the criticism levelled at strategic studies has emerged. The moral dimension of the critique still remained a feature. Indeed, the literature on the ethics of nuclear war and the ethics of strategic studies became more sophisticated (Nye 1988; Lee 1996). In reaction to the conditions of the 'second cold war', however, the type of moral outrage found in earlier critiques came to be associated more with a populist rather than a scholarly critique of strategic studies. Examples of the latter could still be found (Lawrence 1988); but moral objections to strategic studies increasingly came to be enveloped within a broader opposition to nuclear weapons in general (Schell 1982, 1984). As Lawrence noted, 'Paradoxically . . . the new security of the Reagan era made individuals feel less secure and put defence issues into the centre of political debate' (1988: x). At a public level, this shift was manifest in the growth in popular anti-nuclear movements such as the Campaign for Nuclear Disarmament (CND) in Western Europe and the Nuclear Freeze movement in the United States.

With the cold war's end, strategic studies came under increasing scrutiny. As Ken Booth and Eric Herring note, the importance of the military dimension of world politics is not in question in the post-cold war era; but:

> What is in question is the appropriate intellectual status of strategic studies in relation to the study of international politics as a whole, its relationship with other subfields (such as 'security studies'), the utility of the military factor in the contemporary world, and what an appropriate strategic studies syllabus looks like now that its forty-year politico-military context has disappeared.
>
> Booth and Herring (1994: 110)

As part of a broader 'critical' turn within the discipline of International Relations (see Smith, Booth, and Zalewski 1996), several scholars began to question not only the dominance of strategic studies as a mode of approaching world politics, but also the impact of its once privileged place within the discipline. What were the implications, critical scholars now wondered, of viewing the world through the lenses of strategic studies?

The attempts to address this question are grouped here under the heading of 'Critical Approaches to Strategic Studies'. The phrase is used as shorthand to denote understandings of strategic studies that are not necessarily overtly polemical (even though they may sometimes be so), but draw on 'critical' theories (such as poststructuralism, feminism, and variants of Marxian theory) to question the place and effects of strategic studies (see Peoples 2007; Peoples and Vaughan-Williams 2014). The development of these types of critiques can be linked to the so-called post-positivist turn in international relations theory (Smith, Booth, and Zalewski 1996) and the emergence of 'critical security studies' (see Krause and Williams 1997; Booth 2005). The latter development, critical security studies, is predicated on a critique of 'traditional' security studies (effectively a synonym for strategic studies), so it is unsurprising that we find a range of critiques of strategic studies here.

## The World According to Strategic Studies

Typical of this critical move against strategic studies is Bradley S. Klein's *Strategic Studies and World Order: The Global Politics of Deterrence.* Klein argues:

> Questions of war and peace are too important to leave to students of Strategic Studies. Or to put it another way, insights from social and political theory can help us enhance our appreciation of such social constructs as 'the balance of power', 'alliances', 'security' and 'deterrence'. Each of these is, after all, a social practice, not a primordial given.
>
> Klein (1994: 3)

Klein's argument, and its emphasis on 'social construction', identifies a fundamental difference between strategic studies and those critical approaches that seek to question it. Defenders of strategic studies such as Bull and Gray claimed that study of strategy took conflict and violence to be a given feature of world politics on a pragmatic basis. In other words, strategic theorists defended their position on the basis that they were simply attempting to theorize practices in the world 'out there', where military force is frequently and invariably used to achieve political ends.

Klein, like many others who adopt a critical approach to strategic studies, attempts to unsettle this logic. 'The ability of strategic violence to reconcile itself with liberal discourse and modern civil society is possible,' Klein argues, 'only because that violence draws upon a variety of discursive resources that are themselves constructed as rational, plausible, and acceptable' (Klein 1994: 5). Strategic studies does not simply acknowledge the existence of violence in world politics; it also prescribes and precludes the use of violence in certain ways and for certain purposes. Similarly Ken Booth, extending the logic of his earlier reflections on ethnocentrism, declares:

> What gradually dawned was that what purported to be rational and objective strategic theory was often a rationalization of national prejudice, and that strategic practice was best understood as applied ethics—a continuation of (moral) philosophy with an admixture of firepower. Strategic theory helped to constitute the strategic world, and then strategic studies helped to explain it—self-reverentially and tautologically.
>
> Booth (1997: 96)

From this point of view, strategic studies is not simply an objective attempt taking place at a scholarly distance to understand the use of force. Instead, it is part of the broader legitimation of strategic violence for the purposes of maintaining a particular vision of world order, and this vision reflects the geographical–political context in which the disciplinary study of strategy evolved in the twentieth century (that is, primarily in Britain and the United States). Strategic studies has, Klein argues, provided a map of the world in which Western society has always ended up on the 'good' side (Klein 1994: 5) and has thus been a complicit and pivotal part in the making of the 'modern west' (Klein 1994: 16). In a similar vein, Barkawi and Laffey (2006: 335–8) argue that strategic studies is indelibly marked by its Anglo-American origins and, they contend, a persistent tendency towards 'Orientalism' in which non-Western states and subjects are rendered as passive objects. Western states and values are those that have most often been implicitly and explicitly defended and operative within strategic studies according to Klein: thus 'Strategic studies today . . . is an essential component in the articulation of the world order in terms that create and perpetuate a global political vision in which Western values, institutions, and political economies are valorized' (1994: 41).

This Western-centric view, Klein argues, applies not only to deterrence theory's focus on the survival and maintenance of the Western alliance during the cold war, but also to concerns over the spread of nuclear weapons to non-Western states (see also Mutimer 2000). Additionally, Klein points to the work of pre-nuclear strategists such as Alfred Thayer Mahan as indicative of a broader but largely unacknowledged linkage between geopolitics and geoeconomics in Western strategic studies (for a related argument, see O'Tuathail 1996). During the cold war, deterrence did not only fend off major power conflict; it was also, Klein argues, 'a part of the ongoing making and remaking of a post-war order in which sovereign states have been integrated, at times forcefully, within a global market system' (Klein, 1994: 80). Strategic studies, for Klein, played a pivotal part in justifying institutional integration and alliances (such as the North Atlantic Treaty Organization) during the cold war, but equally obscured the economic and cultural dimensions of such integration. By concentrating attention on the military stand-off between non-communist West and communist East, strategic studies during the cold war helped draw focus away from Western economic and military intervention in the global 'South', a legacy that it has yet to shake off entirely. For Klein, 'Strategic Studies represents a rei-fication of the politics of Western culture, enshrined in a geopolitical, statist representation of the sovereign spaces within which that culture may legitimately pursue its projects' (1994: 125).

## The Ends of Strategy and the Role of Defence Intellectuals

If strategic studies as a discipline stands charged with constructing a particular vision of world order that historically privileges a Western set of values and geopolitical vision, then its pro-ponents are, from a critical perspective, equally culpable. Cold war strategists 'found their vocation,' Tarak Barkawi argues, 'in meaningful constructions of the conflict, of the nature of the Western "self" to be secured and the Communist "other" it was to be secured from' (Barkawi 1998: 161; see also Barkawi and Laffey 2006). In doing so, strategists and defence intellectuals, critics argue, contributed to a political project—the construction and mainte-nance of Western superiority—even when they conceived themselves simply to be adding to an objective field of study (Garnett 1987: 22-3), or benignly contributing to the defence of liberal democratic values (Howard 1976b: 75).

Many strategic theorists have long been aware of this critique. Indeed, some have seen it as a virtue of the profession. Hedley Bull argued that postwar strategists were motivated by a 'greater sense of the moral stature of the American and Western political objectives for which war and the risk of war must be undertaken' (Bull 1968: 597). Likewise, Michael Howard candidly declared:

> I myself am one of those fortunate people for whom the existing order is tolerable, and I want to maintain it . . . If the existing framework of international order is to be preserved, a deter-rent capacity must be maintained against those, whatever their ideological persuasion, whose resentment at its injustices tempts them to use armed force to overthrow and remould it.
>
> Cited in Klein (1994: 99)

This debate about scholarly support to Western foreign and defence policy raises the issue of the role of the 'defence intellectual', and the relationship between strategic theory and policy. Although contemporary strategists may not have the same access to government circles enjoyed by the civilian strategists of the 1960s, strategic studies still aspires to the status of a 'policy sci-ence' (Barkawi 1998: 160) and aims to be relevant to policymakers—even if practitioners are not always convinced that the academic world can produce ideas that are of practical relevance (see Chapter 21 in this edition by Lawrence Freedman: 'Does Strategic Studies Have a Future?').

From a critical perspective, this aspiration to provide direct advice to government officials is problematic for several reasons. First, there is the unresolved issue of identifying the proper relationship between academics and practitioners. This is not an issue that is exclusive to strategic studies, nor is it an entirely novel question, although it is often depicted as ethically problematic given the perceived relationship between 'strategy and slaughter' (Gray 1982a; Wallace 1996; Shaw 2003: 269).

Second, Marxist and other critically oriented scholars have also often charged Anglo-American strategic studies as being complicit in the perpetuation of the 'military–industrial complex' (Wright 1956; Sarkesian 1972), whereby strategic studies is seen as the legitimating academic arm of the 'war industry' (Wæver and Buzan 2010: 468).

Third, critics argue that the aspiration towards the status of policy-science has encouraged strategists to concentrate on the means rather than the ends of military force (Barkawi 1998: 160; Wyn Jones 1999: 131). Since strategists tend to assume that the 'national interest' is there to be served, they consequently focus on identifying the best means available to achieve those ends. This focus on the means, not the ends of strategy, critics argue, is why proponents of strategic studies had such an overt preoccupation with missile numbers and weapons' characteristics during the cold war, and hence their continuing emphasis on the study of technological innovation and the effects of the so-called 'revolution in military affairs' today. Richard Wyn Jones, for instance, asserts that '[s]trategy has tended to be the preserve of the bean counters and those whose parameters extend little further than a detailed knowledge of the latest weapons system' (Wyn Jones 1999: 131). Against the self-image of the subdiscipline, Wyn Jones charges that strategic studies is consequently much less Clausewitzian—in taking account of the *relationship* between means and ends—than its exponents often claim. This tendency towards 'means-fetishism', as Wyn Jones terms it, leads him to suggest that strategic studies is not necessarily immoral but rather amoral. Concentration on the means and techniques by which the practice of strategy is to be pursued leads to what he (drawing on the critical theory of the Frankfurt School) identifies as a form of 'instrumental rationality' within strategic studies, a form of study that is more concerned with the instruments of violence than the ends they are used to achieve (Wyn Jones 1999; Booth 2005: 267–8) and the ethical and political consequences associated with those ends.

## Sex, Death, and the Language of Strategic Studies

Critics often focus on the language and terminology employed within strategic studies, in particular the use of euphemisms, metaphors, and technical jargon to describe the instruments and activity of war. This critique has antecedents in the criticism levelled at US cold war strategic planners and deterrence theorists. The activity of 'thinking about the unthinkable', as Herman Kahn had called it, led theorists of nuclear war to imagine scenarios of nuclear conflict and develop terminology to articulate these scenarios. Hence deterrence theory came to be suffused with terms such as 'MIRVing', 'throw-weights', and 'penetration aids' as well as the copious use of acronyms (Green 1986). Critics argued that this not only rendered the study of nuclear strategy arcane and inaccessible to non-specialists, but that the tendency towards euphemism and metaphor, by introducing a level of technical abstraction into the language of strategy, helped distance strategic theorists and planners from the human consequences of nuclear conflict. Philip Green wrote in 1966:

> More than any other aspect of the thought of deterrence theorists, perhaps this reliance on euphemism reveals the deep problem of ethical justification which is central to their writings . . . Perhaps they are unwilling to face those questions directly.
>
> Green (1966: 223)

This idea that strategists shirk from accurately describing their subject of study has more recently been restated by several critical approaches to strategy. These approaches place crucial emphasis on the role of social construction. That is, whereas most strategists have tended to assume that we can make objective claims about the world and the place of conflict in it, critical approaches to strategy assume that the ways in which we interpret and discursively construct the world through language in itself has major significance. According to Carol Cohn, strategic studies has a 'specialized language', which she terms as 'technostrategic' in order to denote the 'intertwined, inextricable nature of technological and nuclear thinking' (Cohn 1987: 690). Cohn, upon attending a workshop on nuclear weapons taught by defence academics in the mid-1980s, was struck by the fact that 'there seems to be no graphic reality behind the words, as they speak of 'first strikes', "counterforce exchanges", and "limited nuclear war", or as they debate the comparative values of a "minimum deterrent posture" versus a "nuclear war-fighting capability" '. She comes to the conclusion that 'language both reflects and shapes the nature of the American nuclear strategic project, that it plays a central role in allowing defence intellectuals to think and act as they do' (Cohn 1987: 690).

Beginning from a feminist perspective, Cohn was struck by the gendered and sexual connotations of much of the terminology used within the male-dominated field of strategic studies:

> Lectures were filled with discussion of vertical erector launchers, thrust-to-weight ratios, soft lay downs, deep penetration, and the comparative advantages of protracted spasm attacks . . . Sanitized sexual abstraction and sexual and patriarchal imagery, even if disturbing, seemed to fit easily into the masculinist world of nuclear war planning.
>
> Cohn (1987: 692, 687; 1993)

Yet Cohn warns that we should avoid the 'uncomfortably reductionist' temptation to conflate the motivations behind strategic planning too easily with notions of male sexual desire or underlying psychological dynamics (see Caldicott 1986). What is most conspicuous about the language of strategy, Cohn argues, is its 'domesticated' nature: that is, the extent to which modern strategic terminology denotes means and methods of destruction with familiar domestic images (the 'Christmas tree farm' cited by Cohn in Box 18.2 is a prime example). As a result, the terms used to describe nuclear conflict are:

> racy, sexy, snappy. You can throw them around in rapid-fire succession. They are quick, clean, light; they trip off the tongue. You can reel off dozens of them in seconds, forgetting about how one might just interfere with the next, not to mention with the lives beneath them.
>
> Cohn (1987: 704)

---

 **BOX** 18.2   Sex and Death in the World of Nuclear Strategy

On a Trident submarine, which carries twenty-four multiple warhead nuclear missiles, crew members call the part of the submarine where the missiles are lined up in their silos ready for launching 'the Christmas tree farm'. What could be more bucolic—farms, silos, Christmas trees? In the ever-friendly, ever-romantic world of nuclear weaponry, enemies 'exchange' warheads; one missile 'takes out' another; 'coupling' is sometimes used to refer to the wiring between mechanisms of warning and response, or to the psychopolitical links between strategic (intercontinental) and theatre (European-based) weapons. The patterns in which a MIRVed missile's nuclear warheads land is known as a 'footprint'. These nuclear explosives are not dropped; a 'bus' 'delivers' them. In addition, nuclear bombs are not referred to as bombs or even warheads; they are referred to as 'reentry vehicles', a term far more bland and benign, which is then shortened to 'RVs,' a term not only totally abstract and removed from the reality of a bomb but also resonant with the image of recreational vehicles of the ideal family vacation.

Cohn (1987: 698)

Cohn argues that theorists and practitioners can think and act as they do by articulating the 'unthinkable' via familiar words and imagery. Even though Cohn's critical assessment of strategic studies derives from the cold war context, its analysis remains highly relevant, given that contemporary warfare increasingly relies on complex technology. With conflict mediated via technological means, and nuclear and conventional simulations of conflict scenarios now the norm when it comes to the formulation of military strategy (for advanced Western militaries at least), the prevalence of technostrategic language within strategic studies is even more apparent. 'Information warfare', 'network-centric warfare', 'smart bombs' are just a few examples of techno-speak common within the language of contemporary strategic studies. In addition, the rising use of armed unmanned drones as a feature of early twenty-first century warfare—particularly by, though not limited to, the US military in contexts including Afghanistan, Pakistan, and Iraq—attests to the continuing trend of 'remote warfare' in which 'kinetic force' (another euphemism) is authorized and enacted at a distance from the use and effects of such weapons. What Cohn, Klein, and Wyn Jones seek to alert us to is the risk that the familiar and 'snappy' nature of strategic language can create a corresponding conceptual distance between the process of theorizing strategic violence and its actual effects. The potential problem in Cohn's eyes is not that the language of strategy is inaccessible, but that, once learned, it is all *too* accessible, making it too easy to reduce human conflict to a series of sanitized euphemisms and abstractions.

 **Key Points**

- Recent critical approaches to strategic studies have focused on its role in constructing a particular West-centric vision of world order, the relationship between strategic theory and policymaking, and the language of strategic studies.

- Strategic studies has been accused of promoting a vision of world order that has legitimated and justified Western dominance, particularly during the cold war when strategic studies' concern with the superpower rivalry obscured increased Western intervention in the non-Western world.

- Critical approaches to strategic studies have questioned strategists' aspirations to the status of a 'policy science', arguing that an unquestioning focus on serving the national interest has led to an overly technical and instrumental approach.

- The role of social construction and the language of strategic studies have also come under scrutiny. Feminist scholars have argued that strategic studies has tended to employ gendered terminology, and uses words and images that lead to a sanitized, domesticated, and ultimately more permissive view of military force.

## A Continuing Debate?

There has been little recent direct engagement between contemporary proponents and critics of strategic studies. In part, this is due to a growing degree of incommensurability between the two camps: that is, because proponents and critics of strategic studies tend to begin from increasingly divergent assumptions, dialogue and substantive engagement between the two has been relatively sparse. Additionally, most scholars operating from critical perspectives are not seeking to create a 'better' form of strategic studies, but alternatives to this enterprise. Rather than seeking to regenerate strategic studies, critical approaches to strategic studies have contributed to a more expansive conception of security studies that encompasses multiple non-military issues, such as economics, the environment, health, and migration. These new approaches tend to depict strategic studies as their more traditional and restricted alter ego.

This process has been accelerated by the alleged inadequacy of strategic studies for dealing with post-cold war issues. Indeed, those operating from critical approaches have been prominent in questioning the relevance of strategic studies in the contemporary world. Although some proponents of strategic studies continue to espouse its 'timeless' principles, critics argue that strategic studies is outdated and anachronistic (see Box 18.3 and Critical Thinking).

One of the strongest criticisms mounted against strategic studies in the post-cold war era is that it no longer offers appropriate tools to study major issues, even conflict, in world politics. Whereas strategic studies tended in the past to focus on state and superpower rivalries, the 'new wars' of the post-cold war era have mainly tended to be intra-state conflicts (Kaldor 1999). Because military threats, particularly those related to global terrorism, are non-state in character some critics have predicted the 'gradual supercession' of strategic studies (Shaw 2003).

It is this issue of relevance that has produced the greatest reaction among proponents of strategic studies (see Critical Thinking). They have generally recognized the need for further evolution from the types of studies that preoccupied them during the cold war. Many have acknowledged that strategic studies may have been 'too dominant' (Betts 1997: 32; Baylis 2001: 1) within the study of world politics during the cold war and that during that period 'the political framework ha[d] been taken too much for granted and strategic studies ha[d] become infatuated with the microscopic analysis of military technology and the acquisition of equipment by the forces of both sides' (Freedman cited in Barkawi 1998: 181; see also Chapter 21 by Freedman in this volume, 'Does Strategic Studies Have a Future?'). Conversely, some have claimed that critical approaches to the study of security, in assuming 'traditional' strategic studies as their intellectual 'Other', have been too pre-occupied with 'widening' their scope of vision to include non-military issues. Since war remains an endemic feature of modern politics, what is instead required—scholars such as Tarak Barkawi (2011) have argued—is a hybrid form of 'critical war studies' that retains a central focus on organized violence as a social phenomenon but employs a wider range of critical theoretical resources than traditional strategic studies.

---

 **BOX** 18.3   The Continuing Relevance of Strategic Studies?

Whether humans navigate by the stars or via the satellites of the US Global Positioning System (GPS), and whether they communicate by smoke signals or via space vehicles, matters not at all for the permanent nature of strategy.

Gray (1999b: 182)

In the historical military sense preferred by Gray, [strategy] faces not rapid redundancy but gradual supercession . . . The demand for justice in war has, of course, facilitated a limited rehabilitation of military power . . . However . . . it hardly provides sufficient scope for a general rehabilitation of strategic thinking about force.

Shaw (2003: 276–7)

**Critical Thinking   Debating ... Do virtues exist in a 'strategic approach' to the study of war?**

## For

- *Identification of timeless principles.* Strategic studies seeks to classify, characterize, and better understand aspects of international relations—particularly those related to armed conflict—that remain constant over time.

- *Armed conflict is an endemic feature of political life.* Though regrettable, war is a recurrent feature of political life and requires a dedicated body of knowledge to prevent and mitigate its worst effects.

- *Protection from the threat of war.* In the contemporary era, war has become so potentially destructive that we need a strategic approach to ensure its avoidance.

- *Providing a guide for action.* Strategic studies can 'speak truth to power': it can advise policymakers on how best to avoid war where possible, and how to prevail in war when necessary.

## Against

- *A static and inflexible approach.* Scholars within strategic studies too often assume that political life is a realm of recurrence and repetition, dominated by states as key actors and legitimating the current status quo.

- *By assuming conflict, strategists accept it as inevitable.* Strategists claim to focus on how the world 'is' rather than how it 'ought to be', but in doing so they tend to shift the focus away from how conflicts might be resolved or overcome.

- *Preparations for war create further insecurities.* The Latin adage of 'If you want peace, prepare for war' is outdated in the age of contemporary warfare and especially in the context of the potential for nuclear conflict, which would render the political ends of strategy self-defeating.

- *Uncritical acceptance of existing power relations.* Strategists too often assume the virtues of serving power-holders as a kind of vocation, whereas a more critical outlook would question the extent to which existing power relations create and are based on forms of inequality.

 ## Conclusion

Viewed from the perspective of its critics, strategic studies is ripe for an overhaul in the twenty-first century and, as many of the contributions to this volume attest, it has already begun to address a much wider range of issues relevant to the contemporary world. Contemporary strategic studies is clearly more than simply the study of nuclear war and nuclear weapons, even as this remains a central concern. There will always be those who view strategic studies, pejoratively, as nothing more than the 'conjectural art of butchering one's neighbour' (Danchev 1999: 313), and strategy simply as an accomplice of 'slaughter' (Shaw 2003). Yet those who oppose the purpose and existence of strategic studies need to mount sustained and viable critiques of a field of study that is attempting to evolve away from its cold war incarnation. The extent to which strategic studies can do so, and its ability to address the critiques reviewed here, should be the source of critical analysis in the future. Critique, friendly or even unfriendly, can still play a major role in this regard by questioning the assumptions of contemporary strategic studies and by holding a critical mirror up to its development.

Questions

1. Why did strategists seek to apply game theory to the study of nuclear deterrence, and what are the main criticisms of this application?

2. How convincing are moral critiques of strategic studies? Are strategy and ethics compatible?

3. Is it possible to achieve scientific objectivity in the study of strategy?

4. What are the main differences between 'second wave' and 'third wave' strategic thinking?

5. Why do critical approaches to strategic studies emphasize the role of social construction?

6. Does strategic studies have an inherent Western bias?

7. Why is the relationship between strategic studies and policymaking potentially problematic according to critics?

8. What are the main foundations of feminist critiques of strategic studies?

9. Do critical approaches to the study of strategy have anything to contribute to the development of strategic studies?

10. Is strategic studies still relevant to the study of contemporary conflict?

 Further Reading

R. K. Betts, 'Should Strategic Studies Survive?' *World Politics* 50(1) (October 1997): 7–33 gives a qualified but robust defence of the relevance of strategic studies in the post-cold war era.

H. Bull, 'Strategic Studies and its Critics', *World Politics* 20(4) (July 1968): 593–605 is the seminal riposte to the criticisms levelled at strategic studies and the 'civilian strategists' during the 1960s.

C. Cohn, 'Sex and Death in the Rational World of Defense Intellectuals', *Signs* 12(4) (Summer 1987): 687–718 offers a feminist critique of strategic studies and deterrence theory.

C. S. Gray, *Strategic Studies: A Critical Assessment* (London: Aldwych Press, 1982) is a spirited if 'friendly' critique of the study of strategy as it developed in the postwar era.

P. Green, *Deadly Logic: The Theory of Nuclear Deterrence* (Ohio, OH: Ohio State University Press, 1966) is somewhat dated but identifies several issues, such as the use of euphemism and metaphor in the language of strategic studies, that remain pertinent objects of criticism today.

B. S. Klein, *Strategic Studies and World Order: The Global Politics of Deterrence* (Cambridge: Cambridge University Press, 1994) gives a broadly post-structuralist assessment of the role of strategic studies in constructing the modern West.

P. Lawrence, *Preparing for Armageddon: A Critique of Western Strategy* (Brighton: Wheatsheaf, 1988) continued the moral critique of strategic studies in the context of the 'second cold war'.

A. Rapoport, *Strategy and Conscience* (New York: Harper and Row, 1964) identifies, like Philip Green, several strands of moral criticism of strategic studies that still resonate today, even if the object of his critique has evolved substantially since the time of writing.

M. Shaw, 'Strategy and Slaughter', *Review of International Studies*, 29(2) (2003): 269–77 offers an ardent critique of Colin S. Gray's argument for the timeless wisdom of strategy.

R. Wyn Jones, *Security, Strategy and Critical Theory* (Boulder, CO: Lynne Rienner, 1999) draws on the critical theory of the Frankfurt School and Antonio Gramsci to critique the foundational assumptions of 'traditional' strategic studies and outline a 'critical' alternative.

 **Web Links**

*The Concise Encyclopaedia of Economics* **http://www.econlib.org/library/Enc/GameTheory.html** offers for the uninitiated a brief introduction to game theory, as employed during the 'Golden Age' of strategic studies.

The Campaign for Nuclear Disarmament (CND) **http://www.cnduk.org** maintains the moral arguments for nuclear disarmament that continue to counter the focus on the strategic use of nuclear weapons within strategic studies.

The Nuclear Age Peace Foundation **http://www.wagingpeace.org** also maintains a staunch critique against the possession of nuclear weapons.

Robert S. McNamara 'Apocalypse Soon' **http://foreignpolicy.com/2009/10/21/apocalypse-soon/** the former US Secretary of Defense, who oversaw the US nuclear arsenal between 1961 and 1968, argued in 2005 that US reliance on nuclear weapons is immoral.

The Nuclear Security Project **http://www.nuclearsecurityproject.org** was founded by a group of four former US 'cold warriors'—former Secretary of State George P. Schultz, former Secretary of Defense William J. Perry, former Secretary of State Henry A. Kissinger, and former Senator Sam Nunn—and argues that nuclear weapons are a source of strategic instability in the post-cold war context.

# A New Agenda for Security and Strategy?

JAMES J. WIRTZ

## Chapter Contents

 **Reader's Guide**

This chapter explores a series of issues that have not been included traditionally on national security agendas or considered to be within the purview of strategy. Unlike most assessments of non-traditional security issues, it does not define a specific problem as a threat to national security simply because it creates the possibility of casualties, damage to personal property, or threatens economic prosperity. Rather, it develops a utilitarian assessment of environmental, resource, and population issues to discover if strategy, military force, or existing strategic literature can address these issues and problems in a useful way. If strategy, strategists, or military force can address a specific problem, or if it can be determined that they are a cause of a particular problem, or if they can be forced to change in response to some transnational trend, then the issue should be a subject for strategy and strategists. The chapter also suggests that non-traditional security issues are beginning to influence core national security considerations in ways that were not fully anticipated by proponents of a new agenda for security and strategy.

## Introduction

During the cold war, high politics dominated national security agendas. Issues of war and peace, nuclear deterrence and crisis management, summit diplomacy, arms control, and alliance politics preoccupied those people with a professional or personal interest in world politics or military strategy. By contrast, low politics—the environment, the management of scarce resources, or efforts to constrain population growth—were often perceived as a source of trouble, but rarely as a threat to national security. Occasionally, issues of low politics managed to reach national security agendas. Fallout from nuclear testing in the atmosphere prompted a growing awareness of the environmental consequences of the nuclear arms race, leading to the Partial Test Ban Treaty (1963). The oil shocks of the 1970s made Americans aware of their dependence on foreign oil and the important role conservation could play in preserving US economic prosperity and diplomatic leverage. However, for the most part, high and low politics were treated as separate issues by policymakers and scholars alike.

Starting in the late 1980s, some scholars came to believe that the hierarchy between high and low politics had been reversed. They suggested that non-traditional issues should be placed at the top of national security agendas. Several theories of international relations can explain the rise to prominence, so to speak, of low politics. Realists, for example, might suggest that, as the overarching preoccupation with the cold war evaporated, issues once considered 'lesser included threats' could be expected to appear more important. They would also note that with the collapse of the cold war divide, management of these global issues might become increasingly possible, especially if the United States, the lone superpower, used its diplomatic, economic, and military leverage to good effect. Neo-institutionalists would probably add that new forms of transnational management are increasingly important in world affairs. They might point to the prominent role played by international governmental organizations (IGOs, e.g. the United Nations), international non-governmental organizations (INGOs, e.g. the Carnegie Endowment for International Peace or Greenpeace), or even a plethora of grass-roots movements in tackling tough issues that transcend international boundaries. These local organizations and movements not only push global issues—women's rights, ozone depletion, the acquired immune deficiency syndrome (AIDS) epidemic—onto national agendas, they also help initiate and coordinate international responses to transnational problems. Scholars who focus on the way the communications revolution is changing human interaction often highlight the fact that groups of people scattered across the globe can now orchestrate political or informational campaigns using the Internet. Grass-roots organizations now monitor deforestation in the Amazon or search for unauthorized development along the California Coast. Individuals, educated and empowered by new communication technologies, are increasingly aware of the suffering of others in distant lands. There is a growing awareness, especially among people in the developed world, that international boundaries are a weak barrier to the problems that afflict the poorest parts of the planet.

At the dawn of the new century, however, perspectives about the relative importance of low and high politics again changed when the darkest side of the information revolution became apparent. Al-Qaeda and its supporters have exploited modern communication and transportation systems to launch terrorist attacks against innocent civilians in New York, London, Madrid, Bali, and Paris. The debate about the relative importance of high and low politics seemed to come full circle. The low politics of the information revolution, globalization, and demographics are now the stuff of high politics, influencing national security and homeland defence agendas around the world.

## The Need for a Conceptual Framework

To say that low politics are perceived as more important in the aftermath of the cold war is beyond dispute. Major research projects had already been undertaken in the 1990s by Thomas Homer-Dixon and his colleagues at the University of Toronto and by the International Peace Research Institute, Oslo (PRIO), to demonstrate a link between resource scarcity and the outbreak of war or other forms of violence (Homer-Dixon 1991). Other researchers have noted that damage to the environment should be considered as a threat to national security because it can cause casualties or even kill. Marc Levy, for instance, has suggested that damage to the earth's ozone layer should be considered to be a security threat because it causes cancer, blindness, and even death (Levy 1995). However, to say that environmental damage or resource scarcity should now be considered as national security issues raises a host of problems, especially for those who are concerned with the development of military strategy. It is not exactly clear, for instance, how military forces can help reduce the build-up of greenhouse gases in the atmosphere to prevent global warming. Similarly, it is not clear how military action could help stop the Ebola epidemic that swept through the West African countries of Liberia, Sierra Leone, and Guinea in 2014. Non-traditional threats to national security clearly exist, but it is difficult to discern how military formations, strategy, or strategists can respond constructively to these matters. Further complicating the issue is the fact that low and high politics are interacting in complex ways; issues of low politics are not completely divorced from grand strategy. For example, the possibility that Tehran might acquire nuclear weapons does not pose an immediate threat to Middle East energy reserves, but it produces a global economic impact by causing the price of oil to rise in already tight energy markets. Low politics, while not posing direct security threats themselves, are shaping and are in turn being shaped by traditional strategic concerns.

Those who suggest that environmental or global issues are a national security threat often resort to Malthusian scenarios to justify their judgements (Orme 1997). Resource scarcity or the disorder produced by overpopulation or rapid depopulation, for instance, are identified as causes of war, but these Malthusian scenarios are not entirely plausible, and recent studies have found only an extremely modest impact of resource scarcity on the outbreak of violence (Goldstone 2002). Malthusian scenarios seem to suggest that the military should prepare to contain the symptoms of nagging transnational problems before they burst into some sort of cataclysmic fury. One might also hope that educational, technical, or social action could be taken before environmental, resource, or population pressures produce wars that literally involve battles for human survival. No one would disagree that these environmental or global issues are important, it just seems unlikely that negative trends will continue indefinitely into the future and produce raging resource wars (see Box 19.1).

Already, there are positive signs on the horizon. Population growth rates, which reached a peak of 2 per cent per year in the 1960s, are declining and will continue to do so just as long as people grow healthier, wealthier, and better educated.

Defining some transnational issues as national security threats can create a new set of problems. Often military forces are the only units available that possess the logistical capabilities or able-bodied and disciplined workforce needed to cope with the aftermath of natural or political disasters. As the effort to provide disaster relief to victims of the 2004 tsunami

**BOX** 19.1   Thomas Robert Malthus

Malthus was born on 13 February 1766. He graduated from Jesus College, Cambridge in 1788, worked for a time as a minister, and returned to Cambridge as a fellow in 1793, the year Louis XVI was guillotined by revolutionaries. Malthus took a dim view of utopian philosophies advanced by William Godwin and M. Condorcet. In response, in 1798 he published *An Essay on the Principle of Population as It Affects the Future Improvement of Society*. Using data supplied by none other than Benjamin Franklin on the population growth rates of American villages, Malthus offered a startling observation: populations grow in a geometric fashion while food supplies only increase by an arithmetic ratio. In other words, if current trends continued, the human race would inevitably outpace the food supply, leading to cataclysmic social collapse. Two factors might hold off this day of reckoning: efforts to reduce birth rates, which Malthus termed 'preventive measures'; and war, disease, and starvation, developments described by the misnomer 'positive measures'. Luckily, Malthus's predictions proved incorrect. He failed to account for the fact that trends rarely continue indefinitely into the future. In fact, the amount of raw materials used per unit of economic output has actually been decreasing over the last century, while available resources have been increasing. Once adjusted for inflation, *The Economist's* index of prices of industrial raw materials has dropped 80 per cent since 1845.

demonstrated, military and naval forces drawn from 19 countries and non-governmental organizations worked together to provide food, shelter, and medical supplies, especially to people left isolated by the effects of the tidal wave. Regardless of circumstances or initial intentions, however, the introduction of military forces risks making things worse by turning a public health crisis or police problem into an armed conflict. The UN intervention in Somalia, for instance, quickly deteriorated from an effort to prevent mass starvation into a particularly nasty form of warfare: urban combat. Launching a *war* on drugs inevitably leads to casualties among innocent bystanders, disruption of peasant life, increased rural poverty, and armed resistance. Soldiers also complain that humanitarian operations, peacekeeping duties, or conducting border patrols divert resources and training away from their primary responsibility: preparing to engage in conventional combat and win the nation's wars. Although military forces will continue to play a critical role in responding to natural disasters, simply defining environmental, resource, or population problems as security issues is not without costs or risks.

Instead of becoming mired in the debate about the gravity of today's environmental problems or what constitutes an appropriate mission for military units, it would be better to assess this new security agenda to determine if and how strategy can respond to these issues. This utilitarian assessment would unfold along three dimensions. First, if military units can take some action that addresses a particular problem or issue in a useful way, then the subject is of importance to strategy and strategists. However, if the threat of force, the use of force, or even the logistical or technical assistance that can be supplied by military units does little to respond to a given problem, it is probably best not to treat the specific issue as a security threat. Secondly, if military action somehow produces environmental, resource, or demographic consequences, then these issues are of interest to strategists. The time has arrived to measure the cost of conflict by using more than just the immediate losses of blood and treasure. A global perspective requires strategists to consider the long-term environmental consequences of war and preparations for war. Thirdly, low politics are of strategic interest when they create effects that are likely to shape the way force is used in the future. In other words, will low politics create changes in the international security environment that will force a significant transformation of strategy, military force structure, or doctrine? This utilitarian assessment stands in contrast to typical discussions of environmental or resource issues, because it defines security threats in terms of what constitutes an appropriate response (i.e. use of force), rather than the potential of an issue to threaten a nation's or an individual's wellbeing (i.e. scarcity of potable water).

Is there a new agenda for security and strategy? The answer might in fact be yes: especially if strategy, strategists, or military force can address a specific problem, can be the cause of a specific problem, or can be forced to change in response to some transnational trend. What follows is a brief survey of the relationship of strategy to several transnational issues that are said to make up a new agenda for security and strategy.

---

 **Key Points**

- Scholars debate whether to include non-traditional issues—pollution, threats to biodiversity, disease—on national security agendas.

- Malthusian scenarios remain popular as a justification for treating environmental issues as security problems.

- Defining social or environmental issues as national security problems is not without costs and risks.

- A utilitarian assessment may be useful to determine if there is a new agenda for security and strategy.

---

## Population: The Demographics of Global Politics

Nearly every problem identified in this chapter is rooted in the population explosion that occurred in the twentieth century. Since the mid-century, the number of people living on the planet has grown by 3.5 billion; over 6 billion people were alive at the start of the twenty-first century. With luck, total population should stabilize somewhere between 9 and 10 billion people by 2050. Fertility rates are decreasing not just in developed countries, but also in urban areas in the developing world, as women gain more access to education, health care, and job opportunities. Estimates seem to agree that the rate of global population has been slowing for several decades; global population will actually *start declining sometime between 2050 and 2100* (United Nations 2011).

Although the news about the world's population problem is not all bad, three caveats are often raised about these positive trends that paint a somewhat darker picture of both our immediate and medium-term future. First, most of the population growth in the years ahead will occur in the poorest countries that are already strained to the limit when it comes to feeding, housing, and educating their existing populations. By contrast, in the developed world, population growth rates in many cases have dipped below 'replacement levels', creating a different sort of crisis. Too few people of working age will be available to contribute to pay-as-you-go pension systems, creating the possibility of a systemic social crisis. Secondly, most of the population growth is taking place in urban areas. In 2015, the world had 27 megacities with populations exceeding 10 million and by 2030, 60 per cent of the world's people will probably live in urban areas, up from 50 per cent in 2015 (National Intelligence Council

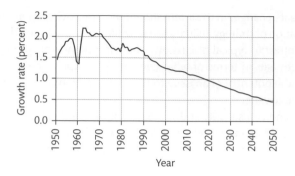

**Figure 19.1**  World Population Growth Rates: 1950–2050

*Source:* U.S. Census Bureau, International Data Base, December 2013 Update.

2012). Urban planners, government officials, and military officers are concerned that megacities will tax social and basic services well beyond their limits, leaving millions of people to live in urban squalor and chaos. Megacities in the developing world can also erupt into spontaneous violence following some local insult or even a sporting event. Even cities in the developed world can burst into violence: thousands of armed gang members can plunge sections of Los Angeles into chaos and looting for days before police and national guard units are able to restore order. Thirdly, most of this additional population will be very young, leading observers to note that, in parts of the developing world, it will be some time before population growth rates peak (see Figure 19.1).

Although strategists find little to dispute in the observation that over-population creates enormous social, resource, and environmental strains, they are most interested in exploring the divergent demographic trends at the heart of the population problem. In other words, what are the strategic implications of an ageing and shrinking Western population on the one hand, and an explosion in the number of young people in the developing world on the other? For the developing world, the concern is that the inability to provide employment and basic services to this surging population will produce poverty, chaos, and hopelessness. Some observers believe that young people, concentrated by the millions in megacities, will fall under the sway of a virulent nationalism, messianic leaders, or millenarian movements, leading to waves of local violence or international terrorism. Most major revolutions have been accompanied by a so-called 'youth bulge', while scholars have also noted that youth bulges are associated with the outbreak of small conflicts (Goldstone 2002). Young men with little prospect of a traditional home, family, or occupation might find an outlet for their ambitions in war. By contrast, the slow or even negative population growth in the West will make it increasingly difficult to fill the ranks of the armed forces, forcing militaries to rely on technology to compensate for an absence of volunteers. The demands for health care and the high pension costs created by an ageing population will also make it difficult for industrialized nations to afford large defence budgets.

These population demographics constitute a strategic issue because they will force changes in future defence policies and strategy. Differences in population growth create trends that influence military strategy and defence policy. Exactly how will demographics transform this strategic setting? Martin van Creveld (1991) and Stephen Cimbala (1997) offer a pessimistic view of these trends. They believe that nation-states are losing their monopoly on the use of force as urban mobs and transnational movements take matters into their own hands. Violence is becoming less politically organized; the world is descending into chaos and war-lordism. By contrast, some observers would predict that these population demographics are already producing different attitudes towards the death and destruction of war. In the West, a rising aversion to casualties is already shaping national strategies. In some countries in the developing world, warrior cultures glorify war, swelling the ranks of millenarian, fundamentalist, or anarchist movements with thousands of untrained and lightly armed volunteers. It is probably not a coincidence that most of the terrorists who participate in al-Qaeda suicide attacks are unmarried males. It is probably wrong, however, to suggest that warrior culture offers a superior approach to the conventional battlefield than the combined arms attack that can be unleashed by military professionals. No amount of élan will save units caught in the open by a well-timed artillery barrage or an air strike using fuel-air explosives, although basic infantry tactics, such as the use of cover, can help mitigate the lethality of modern weaponry (Biddle 2003a). On a more positive note, some observers have suggested that as birth rates decline, people everywhere will be less willing to see what may be their only child sacrificed in some dubious military adventure, and if democracy continues to spread, they would have the means of making these feelings known to their elected officials.

 **Key Points**

- Although population growth rates are slowing, total world population will continue to increase for the next 30 years.

- Future population increases will be centred in the developing world, leading to a concentration of young people in megacities.

- Because they influence the context of diplomatic and military policy, divergent demographic trends will shape strategy and strategic thinking.

 **Critical Thinking**   Debating ... Will demographic change bring peace?

Youthful countries—those with populations with a median age of 25 years or less—have accounted for nearly 80 per cent of armed civil and ethnic conflicts since the 1970s. Except for Sub-Saharan Africa, however, the median age of societies is increasing. Countries, especially in the West, are ageing rapidly. Will the end result be a more peaceful world?

For

- **Reprioritization of resources.** As nations struggle to meet the demands of an ageing, and less productive, population, they will be forced to devote increasing resources to social services and fewer resources to military endeavours and foreign escapades. Interest in using force to achieve national objectives will decline.

*(continued...)*

**Critical Thinking**    *(continued)*

- *Lack of human capital.* Because of their productivity and relative scarcity, young people will be seen as too valuable to be engaged in 'non-productive' activities, such as war. Militaries will shrink, and the use of force will decline, simply due to the lack of available participants.

- *Pensioners are risk averse*. Ambitious, energetic, and romantic, youthful populations are easily excited and misled by ideologues and revolutionaries who promise various forms of wealth, glory, and power but in the end only deliver chaos, anarchy, and war. Older populations are wiser and more pacific—they will choose peace over war.

## Against

- *Other trends spell trouble.* Global warming, resource scarcity, or food and water shortages will create new sources of conflict as states attempt to secure supplies for their ageing populations. Regardless of how old they are, people like to eat.

- *Demographic asymmetries will create domestic instability.* To compensate for ageing populations, developed countries will increasingly rely on youthful immigrant populations as a work force, leading to ethnic or religious turmoil as newcomers clash with established societies. Domestic instability can spill over into international conflict.

- *The strategist's view.* The future will be determined by the way ageing and rich countries *interact* with more youthful and poorer developing states. Just because one party in a potential conflict prefers peace, the status quo does not guarantee that the outcome will be peaceful. A looming faceoff between old rich nations and young poor nations is not exactly a recipe for peace.

## Commons Issues

Issues that transcend international boundaries are often referred to as commons problems. Although some countries can contribute more or less to a specific commons problem, efforts to stop the tragedy of the commons, to borrow Garrett Hardin's famous phrase, require some form of collective action on the part of most members of the international community. Most low politics problems could be classified as commons issues, but environmental and resource issues generally come to mind when policymakers and scholars think about transnational issues.

Air pollution, especially the release of carbon dioxide from motor vehicles and coal-fired electric plants, destruction of the ozone layer through the release of chlorofluorocarbons, and global warming produced by greenhouse gases are all quintessential commons problems.

In other words, it would be impossible for a single state or a group of states to slow the destruction of the ozone layer, for example by banning the manufacture of chlorofluoro-carbons, if other states continued to release these substances into the atmosphere. Water pollution, depletion of underground aquifers, and the protection of migratory species (e.g. fish) are often depicted as commons problems, although their effects are generally confined to specific regions. Depletion of aquifers and fish stocks, however, can create local economic catastrophes when farmers lose the water needed to irrigate their crops and fishers are forced to abandon traditional means of earning a living.

Threats to biodiversity, especially deforestation of tropical rainforests, occur on specific national territories, but they are slowly destroying the 'common heritage of humankind'. Deforestation destroys habitats needed by the planet's non-human inhabitants: tropical rain-forests are home to half of the world's known species. Deforestation can also have region-al climatic effects because trees are a key link in the evapotranspiration cycle between soil and the atmosphere. Trees also help to protect delicate topsoil by providing erosion control against landslides and flooding. Forests help to slow global warming because trees act as a major sink of carbon dioxide in the atmosphere. Global or regional environmental problems can sometimes have acute local consequences (see Box 19.2).

By contrast, local environmental damage can produce global environmental consequenc-es. Sometimes commons problems are created when the effects of localized insults to the environment have a global impact, and sometimes they are created when millions of small and relatively innocuous events have a cumulative effect that produces global consequences or local disasters. The distinguishing characteristic of all of these issues, however, is the fact that either their causes or their effects are beyond the reach of any one state.

Although commons issues pose an existential threat to all humanity, at times they do shape decisions about war and peace. Concerns about access to oil supplies (one natural resource that remains key to modern industrial economies) was a clear motivation behind the formation of a US-led international coalition to oust Iraq from Kuwait in the early 1990s. By contrast, con-cern about disrupting tight oil markets has slowed the international response to an apparent Iranian effort to create a nuclear weapons industry. Shots have also been exchanged in fishing disputes as boats and crews are seized for poaching in waters claimed by a specific state. Water wars are possible in the future, especially as rivers and aquifers are drained to make deserts in

 **BOX** 19.2  The Tragedy of the Commons

Imagine you lived near the west coast of the United States and every spring you had the opportunity to go salmon fishing. The fish were plentiful and it was easy for you to catch a couple of dozen fish in a single morning. In any event, there are plenty of fish in the sea, and no matter how full you loaded up your boat, you could never make much of a dent in the salmon population. There would always be fish willing to take your bait. Now imagine if thousands of your neighbours up and down the coast went fishing too and proceeded to fill their boats with fish. Even though no one wanted it to happen and no one individual would be responsible, it would not be long before salmon became extremely scarce, producing a tragedy of the commons.

The tragedy of the commons is an example of the tyranny of small decisions, a situation in which unintended and negative consequences are produced by individuals following their reasonable, albeit narrow, self-interest. Each fisher, rationally acting to fulfil his or her self-interest, gains the extra benefit of a large catch, while the entire community bears the cost of depleting the fishery. Even if individuals refrain from filling their boats, it would only make it safe for others to 'free-ride' on their self-restraint. In other words, collective action is needed to capture the externalities involved in exploiting the fishery (i.e. getting fishers to pay the full cost of their catch) and to prevent free-riding. When a commons problem occurs within national boundaries, it is easy for the state to capture these externalities and to corral free-riders. When fisheries are open, for example, the State of California limits salmon catches to two fish per day by licensed fishers. Fish have to be longer than 24 inches and it is illegal to take protected salmon species (e.g. Coho salmon). However, when the commons crosses international borders, capturing externalities and corralling free-riders requires international collaboration.

one state bloom at the expense of fields in neighbouring countries. Therefore, as a proximate cause of war, commons issues should be a concern to strategists; but, so far at least, with the exception of the Gulf War, shots have been exchanged only in a limited way.

By contrast, most commons problems are probably beyond the reach of strategy. It is difficult to imagine how military action might resolve many transnational problems. For instance, the existence of strategists, strategy, and military infrastructure did little to deplete aquifers; it is difficult to see how they can help conserve or replenish these underground water supplies. Moreover, because war is a state activity undertaken to achieve political objectives, there is little political motivation to undertake military action in response to commons issues. In other words, few would suggest that wars should be launched to stop individuals in other states from killing tigers, from practising slash and burn agriculture, or from constructing electric power plants that use coal as an energy source. Even if it were possible to use military force to solve a commons problem, it would be highly unlikely that any single state would launch this type of military endeavour. By definition, the benefits gained from using military force to resolve commons problems are outweighed by the costs of action. Everyone would benefit, but the state taking action would bear all of the costs. This is the very dilemma that lies at the heart of the tragedy of the commons. Collective action is needed to capture the externalities (the unpaid costs that are inevitably involved in all human activity) that lie at the heart of most commons problems. Strategists might contribute to the effort to devise a collective response to commons issues, but it would probably be better if this response were based on enlightened self-interest, not point of the gun environmentalism. Although commons issues might some day force military action or shape military strategies (e.g. military action to protect oil supplies), it is probably best not to treat commons issues as military problems.

 **Key Points**

- The tragedy of the commons is generally produced by an international failure to undertake collective protection of the environment or to conserve resources.
- The resolution of commons issues probably lies beyond the realm of strategy.

## Direct Environmental Damage

Military action or the manufacturing of military weapons can result in significant environmental damage, although these insults to the environment probably fall short of constituting a commons problem. Sometimes the impact of military activity is limited or unknown. For example, military aircraft often jettison fuel in an emergency, but it is unclear if much environmental damage occurs in peacetime from this practice. As British MP Archie Hamilton noted in 1992:

> RN (Royal Navy) and RAF (Royal Air Force) pilots are instructed to jettison fuel under carefully controlled conditions which ensure that the great majority of fuel evaporates before it reaches the ground. There is, therefore, minimal environmental impact at ground or sea level. The evaporated fuel is widely dispersed. Most of it is biodegradable and that which remains has no known effects on the atmosphere. There are no products in military aviation jet fuel known to cause greenhouse effects, damage to the ozone layer, or air pollution in the lower atmosphere.

Hamilton is probably correct that dumping jet fuel in the atmosphere does not pose much of a problem in peacetime: British flyers were only forced to jettison fuel on average about twice a month in the 1980s. However, in wartime, mission requirements might cause enormous amounts of fuel to be jettisoned. If this happened over a relatively small area, would it have an environmental impact?

An issue that often bedevils assessments of the environmental impact of military activity is the effort to use 'green' arguments to derail programmes for political purposes. A case in point is the alleged negative environmental and long-term health consequences produced by the use of depleted uranium (DU) in heavy tank armour, antitank munitions, and even as counterweights in commercial aircraft. DU is used primarily as a kinetic-kill projectile because it is very heavy and dense: no nuclear reaction occurs when a DU projectile strikes a tank, for example. Depending upon the type of impact, small amounts of DU may be released in the form of tiny, relatively insoluble particles of uranium oxide or even as larger pieces of metallic uranium. There is little scientific data on the health effects of DU, although studies exist about the health effects of uranium, a similar material. Based on studies undertaken on uranium workers, no negative health effects have been established following exposure to radiation through ingestion and inhalation of DU particles or through wounds contaminated by DU. Nevertheless, many media reports and Internet campaigns decry the environmental and health impact of the use of DU on the battlefield.

Some military weapons can potentially produce catastrophic damage to the environment and extremely significant health risks, even if they are not used in battle. The cost of dismantling and destroying these weapons is staggering and involves scientific and engineering capabilities that are far more advanced than the original efforts to make the weapons themselves. However, successful programmes are possible. For example, in November 2000, after nearly 10 years of operation, the Johnston Atoll Chemical Agent Disposal System (JACADS) finally eliminated the remnants of the US chemical weapons stockpile (see Table 19.1). JACADS was the world's first full-scale facility built to destroy chemical weapons. Johnston Atoll, located 717 nautical miles southwest of Oahu, is one of the most isolated atolls in the world. Remaining off-limits for the indefinite future, Johnston Atoll will soon serve as a wildlife refuge.

Other facilities, especially those involved in nuclear weapons programmes, are neither as isolated nor as easily cleaned up. In the mid-1990s, the US Department of Energy estimated that it would cost at least 160 billion dollars to clean up facilities once involved in the manufacture of nuclear materials at Hanford Reservation, Savannah River, Oak Ridge, Idaho National Engineering and Environmental Laboratory, and Rocky Flats. The Department of Defense also identified 26,500 other locations at existing or former military bases that have been contaminated by nuclear or industrial pollutants. Only 1,700 of these sites had been cleaned up by 1996.

The environmental problems facing Russia are also severe. Scores of old nuclear-powered submarines lie rusting at their berths throughout the Russian north and far east, and Russian spent fuel storage facilities are nearly full. A lack of resources makes it nearly impossible for the Russians to undertake a complicated clean-up process. The submarine must be retired from active status; its missiles must be removed. Spent nuclear fuel must be extracted, making it safe to disconnect its reactor and reactor circuits. Spent fuel can then be transported for reprocessing and low- and high-level waste collected for storage. The reactor compartment can then be cut away from the rest of the hull so that it can be sealed for long-term storage.

**Table 19.1** US Stockpile Destroyed by JACADS

| Agent | Item | Quantity | Pounds |
| --- | --- | --- | --- |
| HD-blister | 155mm projectiles | 5,670 | 66,339.0 |
| HD-blister | 105mm projectiles | 46 | 136.6 |
| HD-blister | M60 projectiles | 45,108 | 133,970.7 |
| HD-blister | 4.2 mortars | 43,600 | 261,600.0 |
| HD-blister | Ton containers | 68 | 116,294.0 |
| GB-nerve | M55 rockets | 58,353 | 624,377.1 |
| GB-nerve | 155mm projectiles | 107,197 | 696,780.5 |
| GB-nerve | 105mm projectiles | 49,360 | 80,456.8 |
| GB-nerve | 8in. projectiles | 13,020 | 188,790.0 |
| GB-nerve | MC-1 bombs | 3,047 | 670,340.0 |
| GB-nerve | MK 94 bombs | 2,570 | 277,560.0 |
| GB-nerve | Ton containers | 66 | 101,158.0 |
| VX-nerve | M55 rockets | 13,889 | 141,769.8 |
| VX-nerve | 155mm projectiles | 42,682 | 256,092.0 |
| VX-nerve | 8in. projectiles | 14,519 | 210,525.5 |
| VX-nerve | Land mines | 13,302 | 139,671.0 |
| VX-nerve | Ton containers | 66 | 97,360.0 |

Although the costs of cleaning up after the cold war are only now being assessed, clearly strategists and policymakers need to take into account the environmental impact of yesterday's and today's defence policies. Of course, at the time, these costs paled in significance when compared to the perceived military threats posed by the cold war, but today strategists and policymakers must consider the lasting legacy of nuclear, chemical, and biological weapons manufacturing and disposal. Full disclosure of these 'hidden' costs might cause those who seek to develop a robust nuclear arsenal—here Indian, Pakistani, or Chinese leaders come to mind—to think about the potential consequences of their defence industrial policy.

 **Key Points**

- Military action can result in direct environmental damage.
- Surplus or lost munitions as well as industrial processes related to military activity can create serious environmental hazards.
- Military operations often entail 'hidden' costs that sometimes only become apparent many years after weapons have been produced or hostilities cease.

## Disease

Although disease has been a scourge throughout human existence, public health initiatives (providing people with clean water and proper sanitation), vaccination, quarantine, and the discovery of antibiotic drugs in the mid-twentieth century helped to reduce the outbreak of

**Table 19.2** Pathogenic Microbes Identified since 1973 and the Diseases they Cause

| Year | Microbe | Type | Disease |
|------|---------|------|---------|
| 1973 | Rotavirus | Virus | Infantile diarrhoea |
| 1977 | Ebola virus | Virus | Acute haemorrhagic fever |
| 1977 | *Legionella pneumophila* | Bacterium | Legionnaires' disease |
| 1980 | Human T-lymphotrophic virus | Virus | T-cell lymphoma |
| 1981 | *Staphylococcus aureus* | Bacterium | Toxic shock syndrome |
| 1982 | *Escherichia coli* 0157:H7 | Bacterium | Haemorrhagic colitis |
| 1982 | *Borrelia burgdorferi* | Bacterium | Lyme disease |
| 1983 | Human immune deficiency virus | Virus | Acquired immune deficiency syndrome (AIDS) |
| 1983 | *Helicobacter pylori* | Bacterium | Peptic ulcer disease |
| 1989 | Hepatitis C | Virus | Parentally transmitted non-A, non-B liver infection |
| 1992 | *Vibrio cholerae 0139* | Bacterium | New strain/epidemic cholera |
| 1993 | Hantavirus | Virus | Adult respiratory distress syndrome |
| 1994 | Cryptosporidium | Protozoa | Enteric disease |
| 1995 | Ehrlichiosis | Bacterium | Severe arthritis |
| 1996 | NvCJD | Prion | New variant Creutzfeldt–Jakob disease |
| 1997 | HVN1 | Virus | Influenza |
| 1999 | Nipah | Virus | Severe encephalitis |

communicable disease, at least in the industrial world. Today, public health officials in the West focus on modifying people's lifestyles to reduce the incidence of cancer (caused by smoking) and cardiovascular disease (accelerated by modern diets and a lack of exercise). The human genome project also holds out the prospect of new treatments for all types of illnesses, especially those linked to genetic disorders. Life expectancies have increased steadily over the last century. More people survived infancy because of prenatal care, public health, and vaccination against childhood diseases, and treatments emerged to arrest, if not completely cure, disorders (cardiovascular disease, cancers) that killed previous generations by the time they reached their seventieth birthday. Progress was even achieved on a global scale: ask your parents (grandparents?) to show you their smallpox vaccination (see Table 19.2).

If one takes a global perspective, however, the news is not so encouraging. Public health officials are bracing themselves for a long-overdue outbreak of a deadly strain of influenza. They fear the outbreak of new diseases that are resistant to existing treatments and drugs. They worry that unknown bacteria or viruses that have lain dormant deep within tropical rainforests will soon be disturbed by encroaching humans, producing new epidemics of dangerous diseases.

World Health Organization officials also warn that the seven infectious diseases that caused the highest number of deaths at the turn of the century will remain serious threats for decades to come.

### Human Immune Deficiency Virus/Acquired Immune Deficiency Syndrome (HIV/AIDS)

At the turn of the century, about 40 million people across the globe were living with HIV/AIDS. Infection and death rates have slowed in the West in response to preventive measures and expensive multi-drug treatments. The pandemic continues to spread throughout the developing world and is making inroads in India, Russia, and China. Sub-Saharan Africa is the centre of the AIDS epidemic: already 10–20 per cent of the adults in the region are infected with the disease. The social and economic costs of the disease are staggering. African economies are experiencing a steady decline in gross domestic product (GDP) due to the AIDS epidemic, and entire generations of children will become AIDS orphans.

### Tuberculosis (TB)

Once thought to be controlled in the developing world by public health efforts and drug treatments, TB is increasing in Russia, India, South East Asia, sub-Saharan Africa, and parts of Latin America. Particularly disturbing is the emergence of a drug-resistant form of TB. Up to 50 per cent of the people infected with drug-resistant TB will die despite treatment. Many TB infections occur in conjunction with HIV/AIDS. By 2020, TB will probably rank second behind HIV/AIDS as a leading cause of death by infectious disease.

### Malaria

Once thought to be coming under control by public health measures and prophylaxis treatments, malaria is a tropical disease that is on the rise. In sub-Saharan Africa, infection rates have jumped 40 per cent over the last 30 years and new drug-resistant strains of the disease are emerging. One potential consequence of climatic change could be an increase in malaria's geographic range.

### Hepatitis B and C

World-wide, 350 million people are chronic carriers of these viruses. Up to 25 per cent of the people infected with the virus will develop cirrhosis of the liver or liver cancer. There is no vaccine against hepatitis C.

### Influenza and Respiratory Infections

Airborne viruses pose an increasing threat in an age of air travel. Coronaviruses that can be spread by person-to-person contact (e.g. coughing or sneezing) are difficult to contain. In February 2003, an outbreak of severe acute respiratory syndrome (SARS) in Asia quickly spread to more than 24 countries around the world. Over 8,000 people became infected and about 700 of those infected died. Fears have also emerged about avian influenza, especially the strain H5N1. In humans, the disease has generally been contracted by individuals who have come into close contact with infected birds, but transmission from person to person has been recorded. The virus has not completely jumped the species barrier, but because viruses can change quickly, scientists fear that H5N1 could someday easily infect humans, a species with little natural immunity to this virus. H5N1 might be capable of producing a lethality rate in excess of 50 per cent in humans.

## Diarrhoeal Diseases

Infection with *Escherichia coli* is the most common cause of this disease, but dysentery and rotaviral diarrhoea occur throughout the developing world and are now beginning to affect parts of the former Soviet Union. Contaminated food and water spread the disease. In 1996, for the first time in a century, there was also a major outbreak of cholera in Latin America. Most of the victims of diarrhoeal diseases are children under the age of 5 in the developing world.

## Measles

Because of the relatively low vaccination rates in sub-Saharan Africa, measles kills just under 1 million people a year and infects about 4 million children every year. Measles is also the leading cause of death among refugees and displaced persons, especially during recent humanitarian operations.

Several developments are responsible for the increasing threat of infectious diseases. First, refugee movements caused by political and natural disasters subject millions of refugees to primitive living conditions that breed and spread disease. Ethnic conflict, civil wars, and famine spread disease quickly as refugees move across borders. Secondly, unprotected sex with multiple partners and intravenous drug use are largely responsible for the spread of AIDS. Thirdly, modern technology and production practices are not foolproof. Imported food produced by non-hygienic practices can spread pathogens and bacteria (*Cyclospora ssp, Escherichia coli*, and *Salmonella*) quickly across national borders. Modern food production practices have also created problems in the food supply. Bovine spongiform encephalopathy (mad cow disease), for example, was spread by the practice of including mammalian tissues in animal feed intended for cows and other ruminants. Fourthly, land use practices, even efforts to restore natural habitats, can breed and spread disease. For example, reforestation in the United States and Europe is responsible for an increase in Lyme disease as deer ticks have more opportunities to find human hosts. Encroachment on rain forests also brings people into close contact with animals carrying malaria, yellow fever, leishmaniasis, or even heretofore unknown and potentially dangerous diseases. Fifthly, international travel and commerce can spread viruses, pathogens, and bacteria faster than the incubation period of the diseases they cause. Today's cross-border movement of over 2 million people per day guarantees that disease outbreaks will be difficult to contain. Sixthly, the widespread use of antibiotics in livestock production and the overuse and misuse of antibiotics by people have accelerated the evolution of a variety of strains of drug-resistant microbes. An expanding number of strains of TB, malaria, and influenza are virtually impossible to treat and HIV also displays a high rate of adaptation to drug treatments.

War and civil strife can lead to disease outbreaks by creating refugee disasters and a breakdown in public health care. Throughout history, war has often been accompanied by disease. Soldiers have spread disease in the field and have brought it back with them when they returned home. Today, for instance, the so-called 'Gulf War Syndrome'—a strange mix of debilitating symptoms—is said to occur among US soldiers who returned otherwise unhurt from the 1991 Coalition victory against Iraq. Military forces can be enlisted to help fight the spread of disease through efforts to quarantine affected populations, to move supplies into regions stricken by epidemics, or to use field medical facilities to treat local populations. From a strategic perspective, infectious diseases continue to shape military strategy because disease can create casualties just as easily as enemy fire. In fact, throughout most of history, disease killed far more soldiers than enemy action. Although military forces are at best a third- or fourth-order defence against the spread of disease (and are just as likely to help spread disease as to contain it), infectious disease shapes the security environment and should be included on the new security agenda.

 **Key Points**

- A variety of factors are causing the spread of infectious diseases, especially in the developing world.
- New strains of drug-resistant diseases are emerging.
- The HIV/AIDS pandemic is likely to worsen in India, Russia, and China.

## Sensitivities and Vulnerabilities

Although talk of increasing globalization and interdependence is clichéd, non-traditional security issues have begun to influence strategy and defence priorities in ways that were not fully anticipated by advocates of the new agenda for security in the early 1990s. Malthusian scenarios have not materialized, but low politics are having an impact on real-world conflicts and are shaping national security strategies. Some countries are increasingly sensitive or even vulnerable to developments in the realm of low politics.

Sensitivity and vulnerability are terms drawn from Robert Keohane and Joseph Nye's work on complex interdependence (Keohane and Nye 2001). Sensitivity refers to the ability of developments outside national boundaries to influence domestic events in other countries. The 2014 Ebola outbreak, for example, led officials in the United States to alert domestic public health officials to monitor hospital admissions for patients who might be exhibiting signs of the disease. Such a precautionary measure entailed some costs and produced political controversy, but it did not pose a fundamental disruption to life in the United States. By contrast, vulnerabilities can cause significant disruption to domestic economic, social, or political activity. The emergence and spread of SARS in 2003, for example, crossed the line from sensitivity to vulnerability because it significantly affected international travel and Asian economies.

Sensitivities and vulnerabilities now seem endemic across a whole range of issue areas, produced by complex global systems and relationships that are not well understood. The 2008 economic crisis rocked global credit and equity markets as policymakers and investors alike learned too late about the 'risks' that were buried deeply inside their portfolios. National economies were highly coupled in unexpected ways, producing a global economic downturn. The world economy is also dependent on a global energy market to move petroleum and natural gas from producers to consumers, but scholars worry that that market might collapse in the face of 'peak oil': a situation where oil demand outstrips production. They worry that a market mechanism might be slow to create alternative energy sources and might not build needed production capacity in slow economic times, which would lead to wild and politically destabilizing swings in price during an economic upturn. They also worry about the potential for the militarization of energy security, especially if some governments lose faith in the market mechanism to supply the energy they need. The stability of the energy market itself, not necessarily the price or location of energy resources, thus becomes an issue of national strategic interest and subject of concern to strategists.

 **Key Points**

- Although they have not risen to the top of national security agendas, issues of low politics are beginning to interact with local political and military events to produce global consequences.

- Countries are beginning to exhibit sensitivities and vulnerabilities to issues of low politics.

- Complex social, political, and economic relationships are emerging that can threaten regional and global stability, often in unanticipated ways.

 ## Conclusion

Those who advocate including resource, environmental, or population issues on national security agendas might suggest that this chapter ignores a critical point: many of these global developments threaten the health and welfare of both individuals and states and therefore should be considered as threats to security. They might suggest that the fact that military forces or strategists are ill-equipped to deal with emerging problems demonstrates that traditional ways of thinking about security are simply not up to the challenge of dealing with emerging twenty-first-century security issues. A decision not to treat the emergence of a drug-resistant strain of TB as a threat to national security, for example, would thus be viewed as an effort to minimize the importance of the issue, but the fact that something is a threat to health and welfare does not make it a security problem in the sense that strategy or military force can minimize it. Hundreds of thousands of people every year are killed in road accidents, but no one would suggest that military force should somehow be used to improve highway safety.

By contrast, the purpose of this chapter was not to dismiss these global trends and transnational issues as threats to national or individual security or to minimize the gravity of the challenges created by environmental damage, disease, or population growth in the developing world. Instead, it offered a mixed assessment of the ability of strategy or military force to respond to global issues. On balance, there was a significant and growing interaction between strategy and many of the items on the new agenda for national security. While not a security issue per se, demographics or resource issues (tight energy markets) are interacting with other trends to shape the global security environment and influence strategy. The complexity of these energy and financial markets can also act as a wild card, making it hard for strategists to gauge the impact of events on distant shores and across disparate issue areas. The spread of infectious disease might also play a greater part in the making of strategy and defence policy in the years ahead. Environmental damage caused by the manufacture, maintenance, and disposal of weaponry is also an issue of concern to strategists. Indeed, the issues that appear to be beyond the reach of strategy are the environmental, resource, and commons problems that generated interest in a new concept of security in the first place. Those who see these issues as important should be relieved by the assessment presented in this chapter. Defining these issues as engineering, public health, or educational problems is far more constructive than somehow trying to resolve them by the threat or use of force. In an increasingly globalized and complex world, issues of low politics appear to be capable not of creating conflict, but of exacerbating the effects of political and military disputes.

 Questions

1. Why are low politics now given priority by policymakers and scholars?
2. Why would globalization help to slow population growth rates in the developing world?
3. Although energy resources are vital, why is it that states have only fought recently over oil?
4. Can you think of a way to threaten or use force to resolve commons issues?
5. What would be the social or political consequences of attempting to use military units to enforce a disease quarantine?
6. Do you think it is realistic to expect that countries currently building a nuclear infrastructure would want to do so in a way that protects the environment?
7. What are the emerging points of interaction between low and high politics today?
8. Will people pay attention to environmental issues if they are not defined as threats to national security?
9. Is the process of globalization increasing the relevance of low politics on national security agendas?
10. Do you think that demographic trends will inevitably lead to decades of violence and instability?

 Further Reading

P. F. Diehl and N. P. Gleditsch, *Environmental Conflict: An Anthology* (Boulder, CO: Westview, 2000) presents an overview of research on the relationship between the environment and security.

N. P. Gleditsch, 'Whither the Weather? Climate Change and Conflict' *Journal of Peace Research* (2012) 49(1): 3–9 is a selection from a special issue of the *Journal of Peace Research* that finds only a modest relationship between climate change and the occurrence of conflict.

R. O. Keohane and J. S. Nye, *Power and Interdependence* (Reading, MA: Addison-Wesley, 1989) addresses the theoretical implications of the differences between high and low politics.

R. A. Matthew, J. Barnett, B. McDonald, and K. L. O'Brien (eds), *Global Environmental Change and Human Security* (Cambridge, Massachusetts: MIT Press, 2010) assesses the impact of environmental change on human security.

D. Moran and J. A. Russell (eds), *Energy Security and Global Politics: The Militarization of Resource Management* (New York: Routledge, 2009) discusses energy markets and the prospects that the search for energy supplies could produce conflict.

S. I. Schwartz, *Atomic Audit: The Costs and Consequences of US Nuclear Weapons since 1940* (Washington, DC: Brookings Institution, 1998) is an effort to assess overall costs of the US nuclear programme.

 Web Links

National Intelligence Council **http://www.dni.gov/index.php/about/organization/global-trends-2030** provides information about global trends and what they portend for the future.

Overpopulation **http://www.overpopulation.org** provides data and analysis about negative consequences of demographic change.

US Center for Disease Control **http://www.cdc.gov** provides information about disease outbreaks; US Food and Drug Administration **http://www.fda.gov/default.htm** provides public health information.

US Census Bureau **http://www.census.gov/main/www/popclock.html** provides data and analysis of US and international demographics.

Woodrow Wilson Center **http://www.wilsoncenter.org** runs the Environmental Change and Security Project (ECSP), which publishes an annual report that contains articles, reviews, conference reports, and contact information for a host of issues and projects related to the new national security agenda; ECSP can be contacted by email at **ecspwwic@wwic.si.edu**

# 20 The Practice of Strategy

COLIN S. GRAY AND JEANNIE L. JOHNSON

## Chapter Contents

 **Reader's Guide**

This chapter defines the requirements of good strategy-making. It begins by explaining why good strategists are hard to find and then critically examines the deficits of contemporary strategic education: insufficient attention to strategic classics and strategic history, and a pronounced bias towards American-centric topics and perspectives. A lack of universal theory is identified as critical. A remedy is offered: The General Theory of Strategy. The chapter closes with a call for the regular reassessment of strategic plans and engagements, and with a strong reminder that strategy is a practical subject and knowledge from its study must be communicated to those who need it.

## Introduction: Strategic Expertise

Strategic geniuses are born rather than made. It is exceedingly difficult to 'do' strategy competently. Happily, however, one need not be a strategic genius to succeed, just better than the enemy's strategist. A strategist needs to be, simply, 'good enough'. That said, modern strategic studies has not performed well as an educator of strategic minds. The evidence in support of this harsh judgement lies both in what is absent from the literature and in the quality of official performance. This chapter outlines the qualities a good strategist needs to be effective and the obstacles to competent strategic performance.

Strategic expertise is rare for at least three reasons: the position of strategist is ill-defined; the education currently on offer for would-be strategists suffers chronic, debilitating gaps and biases; and the profession has yet to come to terms with a general theory of strategy which binds together the discipline and provides structure for action.

There are professional politicians, policymakers, and professional soldiers, but there are no truly professional strategists. Strategists have to be a mixture of theorist, planner, leader, and commander, and these in the right balance for any particular time and place. One might suggest that general staffs do strategy as operational plans, but their mandates do not typically extend across the strategy bridge to the political realm—the realm which establishes the 'so what' behind military planning.

## Improving a Strategic Education

Even the most promising students of strategy remain hampered by a faulty education: one which slights the classics of strategy and strategic history, and remains unbalanced in favour of American tasks and priorities. In our opinion, the understudied classics are located in the works of nine authors written over the course of 2,500 years: Sun Tzu, Thucydides, Niccolò Machiavelli, Carl von Clausewitz, Baron Antoine-Henri de Jomini, Basil H. Liddell Hart, J. C. Wylie, Edward N. Luttwak, and Bernard Brodie.

There are three divisions in the canon of classic strategic theory. The first has three entries.

1. Carl von Clausewitz, *On War*. This is the most profound book on the theory of war and strategy ever written. It is long, philosophical, and something of a nightmare in organization. It was written between 1816 and 1831, and its argument reflects major shifts in the author's understanding, sometimes imperfectly transcribed into the text. Nonetheless, *On War* is the richest mine of strategic wisdom available.

2. Sun Tzu, *The Art of War*. As cryptic, indeed axiomatic, in style as Clausewitz is philosophical and wordy, Sun Tzu's is a brilliant terse treatise. It could be an ancient Chinese PowerPoint briefing. Unlike Clausewitz, Sun Tzu offers direct advice to help his reader be victorious in war. Also unlike Clausewitz, Sun Tzu writes not just narrowly about war, but rather about broad relationships among war, strategy, and statecraft.

3. Thucydides, *The Peloponnesian War*. It is best studied in the version Thucydides, *The Landmark Thucydides: A Comprehensive Guide to 'The Peloponnesian War'*. Thucydides did not set out to write a general theory of strategy. *The Peloponnesian War*, however, contains some of the finest literary examples of grand strategic reasoning ever committed to paper, as well as richly detailed cases of military strategy. The reader receives a general strategic education from the superb description and analysis in historical context.

The second division of classical strategists has five members.

4. Niccolò Machiavelli, *The Prince*. This classic work explains tersely and with consummate honesty what war is all about and why states wage it—because of clashing political interests as the fuel for armed conflict. Politics, after all, is the womb in which war develops, as Clausewitz later insists.

5. Baron Antoine-Henri de Jomini, *The Art of War*. Jomini is undervalued today, so far has his mantle of authority slipped from his paramount position in the middle of the nineteenth century. He was probably the most perceptive interpreter of Napoleon's way of warfare. Although his *The Art of War* is flawed and certainly dated in much of its detailed advice, it is nonetheless populated with significant insights into war as a whole, warfare, strategy, operational art, tactics, technology, and logistics. It deserves to be read, albeit with care, by strategists today.

6. Basil H. Liddell Hart, *Strategy: The Indirect Approach*. This volume is a work of great breadth and depth, marred principally by the author's determination to sell the 'indirect approach' as the magical elixir that delivers success. Despite defying easy definition, the indirect approach is a valid and important idea. However, since it can have no meaning other than being whatever the enemy does not expect (i.e. the direct approach), it cannot serve as the all-context key to victory as its prophet claims; its logic is fatally circular.

7. Edward N. Luttwak, *Strategy: The Logic of War and Peace*. This book is very recent, but it has undeniable classic features. The author treats the several levels of war systematically, emphasizing the pervasiveness of paradox and irony as inherent features of strategy. Furthermore, Luttwak's insight that there is no natural harmony among policy, strategy, operations, and tactics, though hardly original, nonetheless is both profound and of huge practical significance.

8. J. C. Wylie, *Military Strategy: A General Theory of Power Control*. This is probably the most competent, and notwithstanding its wonderful brevity, the deepest work on The General Theory of Strategy written in the twentieth century. Following Clausewitz, Wylie wisely insists that the primary task of a strategist is to control the enemy; a vital idea that is often missed.

The third division has only one entry:

9. Bernard Brodie, *Strategy in the Missile Age* and *War and Politics*. These two books reveal that Brodie deserves inclusion as a member of the highly exclusive category of great theorists of strategy. Although nearly all of the Brodie canon was focused on American defence problems in the emerging nuclear and missile ages, his strategic theoretical range was extensive and his judgements were profound. We predict that he will merit reading a century from now, a judgement that confers at least candidate classic status among the great strategic thinkers.

A study of the strategic classics must be married to a study of strategic history. History, which begins today if one is looking backwards, is the only evidence we have; all else is speculation. The history-averse 'presentist' is likely to discover that his own life experience provides unduly thin pickings as an education for action. Napoleon said there are two sources of education for a general, his own experience and the experience of other generals (Chandler 1988: 81). Since we cannot know anything in detail about the future, and the present is inherently transient, we need to extract whatever is extractable from our all too rich strategic history. Contexts change their character, but our 'present' has a plethora of antecedents. The Romans knew about counterinsurgency operations and counterterrorism, and so did Alexander.

The dangers of an ahistorical mindset are worthy of emphasis. Ignorant of history, the strategist will see the ever-changing present as a succession of surprises even though strategic history is a truly grand narrative showing more continuities than discontinuities. It is poor history that leads people to invent allegedly great discontinuities: the nuclear age, the cold war, post 9/11, and now 'the return of geopolitics' or 'power politics' (as if there could be any other kind!). A mind without stores of historical past will fail to see patterns and will be tempted to treat current events as singular, or unprecedented, or to pin the cause of modern happenings on particular national traits.

History's 'ages', 'eras', 'turning points', 'tipping points', 'revolutions', 'strategic moments', and the like, are generally scholars' inventions, leaving a strategist who fails to earn his own studied interpretation of history easy prey for half-baked ideas and dodgy history (e.g.

'fourth-generation warfare', 'the Pentagon's new map', 'effects-based operations') (Hammes 2004; Barnett 2004; Anderson 2009: 78–81). The three leading thrust points of modern strategic studies—deterrence, limited war, and arms control—were all promoted, though not invented, in the mid-to-late 1950s by brilliant minds undisturbed by much grasp of history. Modern strategic theory was designed as a potent exercise in rational choice. Much of the contestably arrogant theory developed in the 1950s and 1960s was dangerously wrong, in substantial part because it could not accommodate the abundant evidence supplied by history concerning the role of contingency, especially human contingency.

Ideally, the good strategist must be a *shrewd* historian. Although history is the only strategic evidence we have, the merits and credibility of its recorders are eminently arguable. History cannot teach us anything, it is not an agent with a will. The challenge is to allow historical education to provide the perspective we need in order to make prudent policy now. Historical perspective is desirable, but it is not virus-free. Historical analogies can be misleading and hindsight tempts us to interpret events from our own perspective rather than a perspective which faithfully reflects the thinking of those who lived them. We in the twenty-first century now know that the cold war was a 'long peace', but in the 1950s and 1960s those of us who were there did not know that. Were the 1930s 'the path to war'? Well, obviously yes, but they did not seem that way to a lot of people at the time. The more historical evidence one acquires, the better one will become in drawing useful historical parallels and avoiding the pitfalls of oversimplification or retrospective mirror imaging.

Ahistoricism is made all the more dangerous when combined with national bias. Modern strategic studies have been largely Western, most especially American, in source, focus, and therefore outlook. The American character of these studies has been inevitable and unstoppable, even had anyone wanted to stop it. Strategic pondering needs problems to ponder and, unsurprisingly for a superpower, the United States has had more ponder-worthy strategic problems than have most polities. In addition, the openness of American society and the constitutionally mandated decentralization of the federal government have provided a wealth of opportunities for armchair strategists. US officialdom is willing to share its secrets with those scholars who show promise of being helpful. By contrast, Britain is more like the former USSR in this regard, as are nearly all polities.

There are fundamentally practical reasons for the continuing US domination of strategic studies. These include monetary and career incentives and the opportunity for influence. It is a minor paradox: you can only really 'do' strategic studies professionally in the United States, because only there can you float, career-wise, among academia, think tank, industry, and government while holding a security clearance—the ticket that allows access to the inner circles of government. However, to be a player you must address current US issues as defined by US officials which may well limit the integrity of your scholarship, including an overemphasis on some issues to the neglect of others. For instance, for most of the modern period, irregular warfare was not regarded by the profession's leaders, or their US government, as serious business. Nuclear proliferation, counterinsurgency, and counterterrorism were marginal concerns to the nuclear-focused folk who did the 'big important stuff'. Ironically, as history's revenge, in official estimation today it is nuclear matters (except the essentially hopeless quest for nuclear non-proliferation) that are marginal to the strategic studies profession. On a more macro scale, some matters of general theory continue to receive insufficient attention, including analyses of military doctrine, command, logistics, and civil–military relations.

**BOX** 20.1   Alternate Strategic Narratives

The Russian world view has been largely shaped by its 'geography, by a long history of "tribal" conflicts under the Mongols, [by] the expansion and rule of a multiethnic empire, and by a deep authoritarianism' (Ermarth 2009: 86–7). Fritz Ermarth argues that this helps explain Russians' comfort with martial values and their emphasis on mass in defence matters. Technological advances, he argues, are sought after as 'mass multipliers', rather than as a means of fighting well with fewer men.
   Sarah Chayes describes aspects of identity and warfare practised in Afghanistan:

> It is a state founded not on a set of thoughts held in common and articulated through texts and institutions, but rather a state founded on the strategic nature of its territory—the crux between empires. It is a state founded on a fluid and tenuous interaction between collective structures, structures of nation, of tribe, of family, and a highly developed sense of freedom, a violent aversion to submission.

(Chayes 2007: 101)

Chayes argues that Afghans grudgingly gather into a nation from time to time, but tribal ties never lose their pre-eminence. Therefore, when the national government comes under attack, Afghans are quick to dissolve it 'and run like water between the fingers of their would-be conquerors' (Chayes 2007: 68).
   Greg Giles outlines aspects of Iranian strategic perspective that would be alien to most Western observers:

> Shi'a attitudes toward war are less goal-oriented than western concepts. As evidenced by Khomeini's conduct of the 8-year war with Iraq, struggle and adversity are to be endured as a sign of commitment to the true faith. Defeat is not necessarily equated with failure. This emphasis on continuing the struggle against oppression and injustice rather than on achieving 'victory' is seen as producing a high tolerance of pain in Iran.

(Giles 2003: 147)

Perhaps more seriously, the US-coloured thread which weaves through the bulk of the strategic literature results in a distinct ethnocentrism. America is an amazingly open society and government structure, but its strategic studies are essentially impregnable to alien strategic world views. There is nothing wrong per se with a focus upon the leading global player, but the relentlessly American character of modern and contemporary strategic studies all but mandates that we do a poor job of understanding other cultures and traditions. Even if we only want to kill opponents, as opposed to bending their will by persuasion, a lack of understanding is apt to be a major handicap. Most polities in the world have strategic narratives of their own that are different from the American-centred view of the world (see Box 20.1). A strategic studies profession largely owned or rented by the United States cannot help but be poorly equipped to cope with events shaped in large part by the beliefs and choices of those socialized by profoundly un-American experiences.

 **Key Points**

- Competent professional strategists are hard to come by.
- The position of strategist is ill-defined and daunting.
- Modern strategic studies has done a poor job of educating those interested in the trade. Its deficits include insufficient attention to the classics and strategic history as well as a pronounced bias towards American issues and security concerns.

**Critical Thinking**   Debating … Can we train successful strategists?

## For

- *Strategic success is relative.* Although strategic genius tends to be possessed by '[o]nly the most mentally stable, physically robust, best broadly educated, technically sound, and naturally intuitively gifted people' (Gray 2010a: 64), a *successful* strategist does not need to be one of these, he needs only to be better in some political or economic contest than the adversary's strategist.

- *When without genius, educate.* All warring factions have only the human condition from which to select strategic thinkers. Genius is rare, which places premium on the best trained, best educated thinkers in the business.

- *Vicarious experience is valuable and available.* History offers a wealth of relevant lived experience. For those willing to invest in it, study of the strategic past offers specific insight into how military and political problems have been addressed across thousands of years of belligerent history. A historically shrewd strategist faces nothing new under the sun.

- *Institutionalization is key.* It is not strategic talent, but rather the institutionalization of strategic roles which is lacking. Those polities willing to formalize and reward the occupation of national strategist will inspire increased rigour in relevant educational structures and be positioned to attract the best and brightest to strategic professional ranks.

## Against

- *Strategic wisdom will be trumped by strategic palatability.* The best educated among strategists will sustain a position within policy circles only by exercising the level of self-restraint in logic and imagination required for their messages to be palatable to political masters. Strategic education cannot substitute for political will.

- *Strategic studies are irretrievably lost to American parochial concerns.* American interests, bound by geopolitical context, the limits of American cultural imagination, and American national politics, will continue to be the interests which drive the discipline of strategic studies so long as the US remains the primary national power offering funding, access, and career opportunities to strategic thinkers.

- *Strategists are hostage to their own contexts.* The lessons of vicarious experience may be learned by students of strategy but prove inadmissible to their time and place. No matter how talented, well educated, or steeped in history, strategists will remain hostage to their own domestic political, social, cultural, and economic contexts. These value-laden or material contextual constraints, along with chance and human contingency, may render irrelevant the best training and vicariously acquired historical experience.

- *Democracy gets in the way.* The split in civil–military relations necessary to modern democracies will ensure that a formalized post of strategist is never realized. An effective grand strategist must have significant influence over both military operations and, more importantly, the political ends which inspire them. Because these lie in separate military and civilian spheres of influence within democracies, a unitary position of strategist will not be trained toward and institutionalized.

## The General Theory of Strategy

Perhaps the most important gap in the current state of a strategic education and the most serious hindrance to achieving comprehensive strategic effect is the lack of a general theory of strategy. Because the human race has an eternal strategic history—a history shaped, or at the least influenced, by force—there always will be a demand for strategic study. A country or other security community may either decide not, or be unable, to 'do' strategy. Such a country, however, will perform strategically, regardless of its ability to do strategy purposefully. Often polities decide on policy, then decide on action, but neglect to tie the two realms together. The purpose of the strategist is to bridge this gap by being well armed with The General Theory of Strategy. Modern strategic studies must make a convincing case to would-be strategists that their plans and conduct as planners and commanders depend upon a general theory of strategy and that military doctrines about contemporary 'best practice' should derive from that theory.

A single general theory of strategy must pertain to all periods, types of warfare, technologies, and belligerents. The central assumption of a general theory of strategy is that the core components of strategy *writ large* remain constant. Each core component must be considered in the process of creating individual strategies adapted to the needs of a particular time and place. In sum: sound strategies will claim universal strategic theory as one parent, and the particular demands of the contemporary military and political context as the other. The core components of The General Theory of Strategy are outlined in Box 20.2 and then described in detail (Gray 1999b, 2010a).

---

 **BOX** 20.2   The General Theory of Strategy

### Understanding the nature and character of strategy:

- Defining strategic terms: grand strategy, military strategy, strategy bridge
- Strategy is a political instrument
- Strategy is adversarial
- Strategy is subject to the human condition
- Strategy may produce ironic effects

### Making strategies: seven contexts:

- Political
- Sociocultural
- Economic
- Technological
- Military
- Geographical
- Historical

### Executing strategies:

- Difficulties and friction
- Time
- Logistics
- Information and intelligence
- Military doctrine
- Strategists and the strategy bridge.

## Understanding the Nature and Character of Strategy

### Defining Strategic Terms

A conversation about strategic theory cannot begin without some agreement on the use of terms. As described earlier, strategy is here assumed to have a constant nature. Strategies, on the other hand, have been variously labelled as direct or indirect, sequential or cumulative, attritional or manoeuvrist-annihilating, persisting or raiding (expeditionary), coercive or brute force, offensive or defensive, symmetrical or asymmetrical, or a complex combination of other asserted labels (Gray 2010a: 65).

Other terms in frequent use include *grand strategy*: the orchestration and employment of any or all the assets of a security community (a wide, rather comprehensive list), including its military instrument, for political purposes. *Military strategy* comprises the direction and use made of force and the threat of force for political purposes. Implicit in the above two definitions is the assumption that someone, a professional strategist we advocate, must consciously and competently bind the coercive elements of the state to its contemporary political purposes. This engineer of strategy must build and maintain a *strategy bridge* that connects the realm of military power to that of political statecraft (Gray 2010a: 28–9). As we go on to describe, this bridge is trafficked by persons with institutional ties of distinctive variety and preferences. Being able to communicate effectively with each and march them to common cause presents the would-be strategist with a heroic challenge.

### Strategy is a Political Instrument

Military institutions fight, but political institutions declare war. Strategies function with, if not principally for, political consequences. Therefore, strategy should be made with an eye steadily fixed on political considerations. Today's wars are scrutinized through moral, cultural, and legal public lenses in ways absent prior to the mid-nineteenth century. The result is that even sound military strategies risk failure if not backed by strong domestic political support.

### Strategy is Adversarial

The immediate purpose of strategy is to constrict an enemy's choices and exploit these for political purposes. There is no point in constructing strategies without an extant adversary. Without an obvious foe, strategists must select from among plausible adversaries and treat these as sentient, wilful actors in a contest of domination. Too often imagined adversaries are treated as static entities, likely to respond along rational and predictable pathways. A strategist would do well to keep in mind paradoxical and ironic aspects of strategy: what works well today frequently does not work well tomorrow—and it does not work well tomorrow in good part because it worked well today. Nimble adversaries will make sure of this.

### Strategy is Subject to the Human Condition

Strategies are made and carried out by *people*. The well-educated strategist will consider both human nature—the instincts, spirit, and limitations of the mortal frame shared by humans as a species—as well as the individual idiosyncrasies of great men and women who may play pivotal roles in the shaping of history. Strategists have personalities that are the products of their biology and life experience. When adversarial actors are treated as rational choice automatons, the planner is also likely to underrate the role of contingency. Eccentric action is always possible.

## Strategy May Produce Ironic Effects

History provides us with a long legacy of strategies resulting in unintended consequences—explicit ironies of the political aims intended. Strategic annals are likely to recount that the US invading Iraq in the name of defeating terrorism may have had the opposite effect—inspiring and even enabling Islamist terrorism to reach new heights. There is good reason that prudence is regarded as the cardinal virtue in statecraft and strategy; it mandates concern for the consequences of decision.

## Making Strategies: Seven Contexts

The General Theory of Strategy makes clear that the particular details of each newly crafted strategy are *derived from* and must be attentively *executed within* each of seven contexts (Gray 2010a: 38–9). Humans, with all of their idiosyncrasies and foibles, add an extra dose of contingency into each contextual category.

### Political

'Politics' is a handy label for the often complex process of negotiation and dialogue between and among a strategy's stakeholders, both civilian and military, domestic and allied. Strategy is inescapably a negotiated product consistently revised by changing circumstances on the home front or developments on the battlefield. A political context stretches the breadth of the security-related decision-making process: the internal machinations of relevant bureaucracies, their negotiations with relevant policymakers, the input and influence of pressure groups and popular opinion, the political conditions of the adversary, and the myriad political pressures external to the state.

Keeping the strategy bridge in good repair requires that the strategist have a nuanced understanding of each key political player and be able to induce cooperative, complementary behaviour towards the nation's political ends. This coordination challenge on the home front is likely to prove more difficult than direct military defeat of an adversary. Without conscious strategic coordination, however, a politico/military quest may remain rudderless, riding waves of immediate institutional interest and short-term tactical advantage—a strategic style that has produced many of history's ironic, even disastrous, strategic effects.

### Sociocultural

Sociocultural dynamics influence the strategists who craft policy and the national populace to whom they must answer; it is an essential and vastly understudied component in the orchestration of war. Culture is admittedly complex and difficult to capture in theory and even more in practice. Polities as well as individuals may possess multiple cultures. That said, in order to function in a less than chaotic way, national or subnational groups must agree upon a base-line of acceptable and unacceptable activities (an ethical code), usually supported by a sense of group identity and a set of beliefs about how the world works.

Even the most talented strategists may not be able to change strategically unhelpful cultural inclinations at home, but an understanding of these vulnerabilities may allow the strategist to hedge against them and play to strengths. Conversely, understanding the culturally nuanced habits (customs) of an adversary does not guarantee predictive power over his next move, but may help the strategist narrow the field of most likely behaviours and help him anticipate strategic vulnerabilities born of cultural preference.

A serious study of culture and society has not typically been the forte of modern strategic studies. Recent counterinsurgency efforts have highlighted this deficit. Success in people-centric warfare requires a sound knowledge of social structure and culture. Advantage in any sort of conflict is aided by an understanding of the locus of social authority, how it is established and communicated, and what can be done to undermine the popular legitimacy of a society's war-making institutions (see Box 20.3).

Strategy is formed and executed in a social, value laden environment. Perhaps because ethics and values are so deeply internalized, this aspect of the sociocultural context is conspicuously missing from classic discussions of warfare. Only when group ethics are compromised, as in the Abu Ghraib scandal, do communities tend to verbalize, or perhaps even recognize, their ethical statutes. It is moral beings, however, who construct strategy and their respective value sets cannot be omitted from consideration. Evaluation of the effectiveness of strategies will be subjected to value-laden assessments of the conflict by participants, domestic and global observers, and the adversary. Exposure of ethical violations is near certain to reduce morale among troops and diminish support for the war effort at home.

## Economic

The genius of the strategist will always be bounded by the amount of resources at hand. Economics and logistics may be the tedium of warfare, but those who plan without a keen eye to either will pay a heavy price. Indeed, historian Sir Michael Howard offers the opinion that '[t]he strategy adopted is always more likely to be dictated more by the availability of means than by the nature of ends' (Howard 1991b: 32).

## Technological

The technology possessed by the belligerents involved may not directly determine the outcome, but neither can it be dismissed as an unimportant element for strategy. Technology may

---

 **BOX** 20.3

[W]hen security communities exercise strategic choice they do so not with a completely open, or blank, mind on strategic ideas, but rather with values, attitudes and preferences through which they filter new data, and in terms of which they judge among alternative courses of action.

Gray (1999: 29)

award one side strong logistical advantage. The human requirement is unarguably 'different for the warrior who must dispatch his enemy within arm's length, as extended by an edged or pointed weapon, and the "warrior" who "wields" a keyboard to dispatch an unmanned cruise missile to its target' (Gray 1999: 37). Technological advantage can prove decisive, but it may also backfire. A superpower sitting on technological superiority may underinvest in raw human cleverness. History has demonstrated that strategies devised by a technologically disadvantaged, but strategically cunning, foe can win the day. The morale of troops is more likely to prove decisive than is the quality of their weaponry, which is not to deny that the latter can harm the former.

## Military

Military administrations recruit, train, and arm forces: transforming society's resources into military instruments. Since the war for which you are best prepared tends to be the one you would prefer to fight, military administrations may press for particular warfare strategies, whether or not these are the right fit for the current threat environment. The clever strategist must be acutely aware of the embedded preferences of distinct service cultures and the impact these will have on the execution of security policy.

Political and military command can be devastating when incompetent, or the decisive factor in victory. Leadership in war has dominated the literature on military history. Our modern fascination with, and often overdeveloped confidence in, technology, however, threatens to diminish an emphasis on the skills of the leaders behind the weapons, as well as the willingness of troops to fight and risk death and injury.

## Geographical

The geography of war has expanded beyond the traditional domains of land and sea. Today's theatres include air and space and the ever-increasing reach of cyber connections. The role played by terrain, climate, and distance may be determined by the extent to which they can be trumped by technology. Military might, however, is never as fungible as its wielders would like. Long-range weapon systems that can traverse thousands of miles and strike with surgical accuracy may not, in fact, diminish the salience of geography. These long-range stand-off weapons may be irrelevant when conflicts are waged in urban settings, tribal lands, or any other setting in which nominally powerful weapons are either ethically or practically unfit for battle.

Any geography—land, space, cyberspace, sea, or air—that presents a vulnerability to the adversary is likely to be exploited. At the end of the day, however, the advantage gained there must answer to an essential element of ground truth: 'Every specific strategy, no matter how particular to armed forces, specialized for, say, air or space warfare, has to contribute to a total strategic effect upon the land, the only geography suitable for human habitation' (Gray 2010a: 40).

## Historical

Fate assigns a strategy's historical context in the stream of time. Battlefield wisdom derived from recent experience, combined with hindsight notions of the nation's proudest military moments, tends to produce what is believed to be the range of admissible strategic choices. A strategist cannot help but be influenced by the tenor of the time in which he resides, but can manage wider perspective and surer footing by acquiring a deeper foundation of strategic history than that possessed by his counterparts.

## Executing Strategies

### Difficulties and Friction

Key to strategy is a sound understanding that friction, chance, and uncertainty (Clausewitz 1976: 85–6) inevitably play a significant role. Untimely rainfall, plans falling into the hands of the enemy, or cultural missteps that inspire a local blood feud, may strip away the fortunes of an otherwise successful contender. All rational choice, planning, and training are subject to the dynamics of a battlespace rife with uncertainty. Once the enemy is engaged, the foresee-able future is discovered not to be so. The inevitability of friction, however, should not inhibit a strategist from careful and multivariate planning. Friction should be treated as an assumed variable, contingency plans put in place, and flexible response considered the norm.

### Time

Because humans tend to assume that time is even-handed to all parties, it is often ignored as a component of strategy; but time is not even-handed. Lengthy wars may advantage irregular forces and enervate professional militaries that are hostage to budget cycles and impatient domestic opinion. Western societies who define success through results-oriented metrics and deadlines are vulnerable to opponents who do not. Time, to reinforce the cliché, may cost advanced militaries inordinate amounts of money and nothing less than political defeat.

### Logistics

Scholars often forget that the process of applying elegant strategic ideas is unromantically bureaucratic. When theorists debate strategic concepts, they are prone to assume logistical feasibility. This may be a vast assumption. If a fighting force cannot be effectively supplied, and moved, it cannot fight. It cannot prevail. The organization of strategic initiatives includes staffing and coordinating, costing and reviewing, overseeing and providing feedback. This requires a military administration that aspires to, and attains, logistical excellence.

### Information and Intelligence

The value of information and intelligence is weighed largely by its contribution to achieving strategic surprise. It is a curious feature of strategic history that given the substantial effort applied to crafting deception strategies aimed at surprising the enemy, rather little attention is devoted to the subject of how, precisely, one *benefits* from surprise and wields it to full strategic advantage.

In this area as well as others the information and intelligence front has a spotty record. Recent Western engagement in irregular conflicts, where populations variously hide, abet, or oust militants from their midst, has inspired a rededication to refining intelligence gathered through human and technological means and improving what have traditionally been simplistic and ineffective information campaigns. Western militaries have not been very good at recording and building on lessons learned in the information aspect of warfare, and thus force themselves to learn from raw experience lessons their predecessors could supply from the past.

## Military Doctrine

Civilian and military scholars write strategic theory. These ideas are transformed by military administrations into doctrine, the purpose of which is to identify best current practice concerning 'what to think and how to do it'. When constructed top-down, in this fashion, doctrine may prove an unreliable guide for actual military behaviour, serving rather as an icon, an idealized version of how the organization aims to perform, or representing an administrative attempt to move an otherwise tradition-bound institution in a new direction.

In ideal form, strategic ideas and the attendant doctrine are objectively tied to security realities. In practice, military doctrine, often distinct to the particular services, is more often than not a detailed legitimization of a preferred way of fighting. Jointness (cross-service cooperation) often loses in this battle—with doctrine being crafted and pursued for the purposes and futures of individual services rather than as an attempt to operate in complementary strategic fashion.

Given these realities, it may be that the most important role played by a strategist in the formation of doctrine is not recommending the particulars of operational or tactical approach, but rather orchestrating and streamlining the *process* of strategic planning, ensuring that players are not engaging in cross-purposes and coordinating their efforts for comprehensive strategic effect. In an orderly, if fictional to this point, strategic universe, The General Theory of Strategy would educate the writers of doctrine and inspire the pens of disparate security institutions to scribe complementary means towards common ends. In the non-fictional universe it is as well to understand that the doctrine that is followed is the doctrine that is believed, not necessarily the one that is written and taught officially.

## Strategists and the Strategy Bridge

The last point of The General Theory of Strategy risks stating the obvious: strategy must be planned and coordinated by a competent strategist. At the risk of redundancy, we emphasize again: the task of a strategist is formidable in the extreme. Even a sound education may bring only partial success. Strategy is an art, not a science, requiring physical and moral fortitude, exceptionally good judgement, and more than one's share of luck: little of which is likely to be much enhanced by formal education. Training and command experience fare no better as preparatory ground. Each can prove a false friend when confidently misapplied to the next war. Given the awesome challenges to sound strategic conduct, it is not hard to see why few people can qualify as competent strategists. That said, it may be worth sounding a hopeful note: Box 20.4 highlights five strategists worthy of acclaim.

A strategist's maintenance of the strategy bridge requires a personality that can tolerate, if not connect to, lead players on both sides of the river. The character traits that make a successful politician may pose incompatible contrasts to those that define a soldier's soldier. The potential for friction is enormous. Not only must an adept strategist be able to manage a set

**BOX** 20.4 Five Good (Enough) Strategists

Strategic competence, even genius, reveals itself on a spectrum of better to worse, not simply in two categories, 'good' and 'bad'. Even superior strategists had days of poor performance; a highly gifted strategist can be defeated by a yet more highly gifted strategist in the enemy's camp. Circumstances and contexts contributed hugely to the ability of the strategist to demonstrate his gifts. A strategist as planner or commander needs only to be good enough, not perfect; and many a poor strategist has been rescued by the willingness of his troops to fight.

Given the heavy focus in this chapter upon the strategist as conceptualizer, it might be helpful to balance the account by citing five outstanding examples of planners and commanders—individuals who clearly were 'good enough' strategists.

*Alexander*, rightly termed the Great (356–323 BC), was probably the finest strategist of all time. He was obliged by culture and circumstance to play all strategic roles personally: head of state and policymaker, heroic leader/warrior (a role required of a Macedonian head of state), grand strategist, and military strategist. Alexander's vast empire was acquired and briefly secured not only on the battlefield, but also by prudent grand strategy, wise military choices, cunning diplomacy, and intensely personal leadership of all kinds. He was never defeated in the course of his short, bloody career (Lonsdale 2007).

*Ulysses S. Grant* (1822–1885) and *Robert E. Lee* (1807–1870), respectively by 1864 the commanders-in-chief of the Union and Confederate armies in America, were both outstanding strategists. The battlefield generalship of both has been controversial among scholars. Both have been criticized for their willingness to accept eye-wateringly heavy casualties, often suffered in frontal assaults against the recently improved small arms and somewhat modernized artillery of the day. As matters of sound strategic judgement, Grant and Lee had no superior option other than to seek decision by battle. Both waged an offensive style of warfare brilliantly: Lee to compensate for material and human shortages; Grant for the purpose of exploiting the Union's human and logistical advantages (Keegan 1987; Reid 2005; Glatthaar 2008).

In its war with the Irish Republican Army (IRA) from 1919–1921, Britain was both fortunate and unfortunate in the person of the leader of its enemy, *Michael Collins* (1890–1922). Collins, nominally only the IRA's Director of Intelligence, proved a formidable foe. A graduate of a British internment camp as a consequence of his participation in the strategically absurd, though spiritually uplifting, 1916 Dublin Rising, Collins decided that he would try to win a war for Irish independence, not simply make the traditional futile blood sacrifice (e.g. 1916). He largely taught himself by hard experience how to wage the only kind of warfare that the outnumbered and outgunned IRA could win, that of an irregular kind (guerrilla and terroristic). Collins proved a master strategist for irregular conflict. For most of the war he out-generalled the British by a wide margin, even though by mid-1921 he was in effect defeated militarily. He understood that above all else terrorism and guerrilla warfare were political theatre. Collins waged a struggle against British political will by challenging British values. When he judged that the gun had won all that it could win, he made peace with a British government that was seeking an exit from most of Ireland. The British were fortunate in having to deal with so pragmatic and far-sighted an Irish leader and military leader-commander as Collins. Many Irishmen were not as realistic as Collins in his willingness to accept a compromise settlement in 1921 (Townshend 1975; Foy 2006).

Field Marshal *Sir Alan Brooke* [usually Alanbrooke] (1883–1963) was Britain's Chief of the Imperial General Staff (CIGS) from December 1941 until 1946. His statue outside the British Ministry of Defence proclaims on its plinth, 'Master of Strategy'. Following a distinguished, if brief, record of senior battlefield command (most especially as commander of II Corps in the Dunkirk Campaign of 1940), Alanbrooke rose to head the Army and then to chair the British Chiefs of Staff Committee. Perhaps even more important than the high quality of most of his own strategic judgements on the conduct of the war, his primary duties were to hold a daily running dialogue—frequently animated—with his charismatic and forceful political master, Winston Churchill. He also managed grand strategic relations with Britain's US ally. Given that the British strategic, and therefore political, hand, became weaker and weaker vis-à-vis the US as well as the USSR from 1942 to 1945, Alanbrooke needed all his gifts and education as a master of strategy (Roberts 2008).

of strong and conflicting personalities, he must be able to carry communications effectively between them.

Frictions of personality may be compounded by deficits in strategic understanding. Strategic studies cannot hold itself hostage to official clients who may not 'get it', who may not really understand what it means to 'do strategy'. More often than not, policymakers will be insufficiently educated in The General Theory of Strategy to recognize good strategy from bad. The truth is, the pragmatic clients of strategic studies are not interested in the nature of war, they need to know what to do *now*. Scholarly students of strategy usually do work irrelevant to the immediate needs of the state, which means that their products have to be placed in a current context before they can contribute to security *now*. The now is always moving; the longer-term view of the scholar never arrives. Policymakers and soldiers live in the immediate context, and a professional strategic advisor or executive must learn how to deliver his advice in a way that answers the questions sitting in their inboxes. If strategic advice is not accessible and immediately relevant it cannot be useful.

These components, or dimensions, of a universal theory of strategy are not rank ordered in relative importance, nor are they meant to be mutually exclusive. They overlap and influence one another. Moreover, the significance of each must vary from historical context to context. The purposes of defining the essential components of strategy are to put defensible parameters around the strategist's field, and to identify a knowledge base convertible into practical advice for the problems of the day. General strategic theory hitches contemporary strategic issues to a common post, and supplies reins to the strategist who may otherwise ride from one conflict to the next without direction or basic understanding of the nature of war.

 **Key Points**

- Due to the inevitability of conflict between human societies, the need for strategy is permanent. Polities that fail to construct and follow a deliberate strategy will nonetheless act to strategic effect.

- Strategic studies must provide would-be strategists with a general theory of strategy. This construct defines the field of a strategist and identifies the inherent and enduring components of strategy regardless of type of conflict. A comprehensive understanding of The General Theory of Strategy illuminates the daunting nature of the challenge that the strategist strives to meet.

- The elements of strategic theory proffered here are not listed by priority or importance. Contemporary strategies should draw upon The General Theory of Strategy as one parent and the current socio/political, military context as the other. The aspect of strategy that requires the most attention and resource will be dictated by the specific contexts of the day.

- Strategic competence has been achieved as manifest by five sound strategists highlighted here.

- Policymakers are not often attuned to the theory or practice of strategy. It is the job of a professional strategist to explain the utility of the chosen strategy to those who must enact it.

## A Call for Consummate (Re)Assessing

Given the limits of human wisdom and the role of contingency, no contemporary strategy, no matter how tightly married to a sound understanding of general theory, will achieve a perfect score in strategic effect. A good strategist is obliged consistently to reassess her strategies, processes, strategic education, and traffic management on the strategy bridge in order to increase strategic prowess.

Assessment of any particular modern or historical strategy presents its own challenges. Every assessment is a judgement-set made by particularly encultured persons *today*. Despite inherent subjectivity, consistent reassessment of our own and others' strategies has value. There is a chance that it may improve self-awareness of bias, identify errors, allow suggestions for improvement, and educate the strategist with knowledge for its own sake. After all, the strategist is a scholar; one of his or her roles is to search for truth.

With that in mind we suggest that an educated strategist needs to be armed with nine fundamental questions:

1.  What is it all about? (i.e. what are the stakes at hand?)

2.  What strategic effect are we having?

3.  Is the strategy selected tailored to meet our political objectives?

4.  What are the probable limits of our power as a basket of complementary agencies of influence, and in our endeavour to control the enemy's will?

5.  How might the enemy strive to thwart us?

6.  What are our alternative courses of action or inaction? What are their prospective costs and benefits?

7.  How robust is our home front?

8.  Does the strategy we prefer today draw prudently and honestly upon the strategic education that history provides?

9.  What have we overlooked? (Crowl 1987: 39–48; Gray 2010a: 16–17)

The good strategist needs to be a sceptic, not a cynic, though the latter attitude would often be excusable. He has to be ready to question official arguments, demands, decisions, and performance. Above all else, he has to remember at all times the core of his duties. The good strategist is locked into an adversarial project in which the enemy always has a vote. This the strategist must counter by delivering the compound of consequences that we know as 'strategic effect' from the world of operations and tactics, and thereby secure some control over the will and ability of the enemy to resist. This, in the proverbial nutshell, is what strategy and the strategist's duty is all about.

---

 **Key Points**

- Strategic reassessment will always suffer from the cultural and time-driven bias of the reassessor, but must be conducted despite its flaws if we hope to identify errors and improve performance.

- The questions that drive a reassessment should examine the extent to which our strategy has enabled, and will continue to enable, achievement of political objectives. This assessment must include the likely moves of the adversary as well as the disposition of our domestic population.

- The essential role of the strategist is to deliver the sort of strategic effect that will collapse the enemy's will to resist.

## Conclusion

Even the most accomplished strategist is likely to perform in ways that are context-bound and rendered imperfect by bias as well as by ignorance. It does not follow, however, that strategic studies are harmful or unnecessary. Rather, they are essential, even though they can only be performed by flawed people working through somewhat dysfunctional institutions. This is who we are and how we have to work—period.

The only way forward is to continue to practise the virtues of good strategic studies, to take seriously the application of universal theory, and to require more rigour and breadth in the studies we produce. Our trade has timeless relevance, but statesmen can choose, and have, from time to time and place to place, chosen to ignore it. Should the position of professional strategist ever emerge within the polities of power, that rank will have been earned by virtue of a sound understanding of the belligerent past and the ability to make its lessons practicable to those crafting the future.

 ## Questions

1.  What factors inhibit the rise of professional strategists?

2.  Where is current strategic education most in need of improvement?

3.  What cautions ought to be kept in mind when reading strategic history? Are records of ancient conflicts relevant to military matters today?

4.  Why are 'modern strategic studies' and 'American strategic studies' nearly synonymous?

5.  What are the dangers posed by an overwhelmingly American perspective in strategic studies?

6.  What is the purpose of a universal theory of strategy? What issues must it address?

7.  What material, political, organizational, geographical, or even accidental factors may inhibit strategic genius? How does human contingency play a role?

8.  Why might the talents of some of the most gifted strategists in history be lost on the casual observer? What are the most pronounced achievements of Alexander? How does he compare with a modern strategist like Collins?

9.  Describe the bridge a strategist must build between the political and military worlds. What are the difficulties in doing so? What tasks must be performed? What skills are required?

10. What are the objectives of a rigorous reassessment of strategy? What factors must be considered?

 ## Further Reading

B. Brodie, *War and Politics* (New York: Macmillan, 1973) is a late career work (he died in 1978) that is all about the practice of strategy through the twentieth century. Because his career began before 1945, his writings had a personal historical depth that most of his professional peers lacked.

C. von Clausewitz, *On War*, translated by M. Howard and P. Paret (Princeton, NJ: Princeton University Press, 1976) is the foundation text for the conceptual education necessary if one is to understand, let alone practise, war and strategy.

C. S. Gray, *The Strategy Bridge* (Oxford: Oxford University Press, 2010) explains that the sole purpose and therefore value of strategic theory is to assist strategic practice. The 'good enough' practising strategist needs to be an educated strategist.

A. H. de Jomini, *The Art of War* (1838; London: Greenhill Books, 1992) is a valuable complement, and occasional corrective, to Clausewitz, particularly in his (Jomini's) detailed treatment of doing strategy and operations. The details are dated, of course, but most of the concerns generically are not.

B. H. Liddell Hart, *Strategy: The Indirect Approach* (1941; London: Faber and Faber, 1967) provides important insight into why and how strategy has been practised, set usefully in the context of historical experience, though admittedly an experience contestably interpreted.

E. N. Luttwak, *Strategy: The Logic of War and Peace*, **revised edn (Cambridge, MA: Harvard University Press, 2001)** offers insights on the nature of strategy that are quite original, if not always sound (e.g. he mistakes irony for paradox). His argument is powerful and obliges the reader to grapple with the practical implications of the nature and structure of strategy (with its different levels).

J. A. Olsen, and C. S. Gray (eds), *The Practice of Strategy: From Alexander the Great to the Present* (Oxford: Oxford University Press, 2011) show from historical experience how the theory and practice of strategy have always been interdependent.

Thucydides, *The Landmark Thucydides: A Comprehensive Guide to 'The Peloponnesian War'*, R. B. Strassler (ed.), **revised from translation by R. Crawley (*c*.400 BC) (New York: The Free Press, 1996)** tells the story of a very great war, but also, indirectly, his narrative offers a master-class on the practice of grand strategy.

S. Tzu, *The Art of War*, **edited and translated by R. D. Sawyer (*c*.490 BC) (Boulder CO, Westview Press, 1994)** offers direct advice for all time on the practice of statecraft and strategy, as well as on the qualities needed for competent generalship.

J. C. Wylie, *Military Strategy: A General Theory of Power Control* (1967; Annapolis, MD: Naval Institute Press, 1989) uses theory to make sense of the practice and malpractice of modern strategy. He is terse, clear, and anchored firmly in experience, some of it his own.

 ## Web Links

US Department of Defense **http://www.defense.gov** offers links to each of the US armed services, providing some insight into their distinctive roles and perceptions of the current threat environment.

The Clausewitz homepage **http://www.clausewitz.com/index.htm** introduces students to the writings of the Great Prussian himself and provides links to the most recent scholarly work on Clausewitzian topics.

Sun Tzu Art of War page **http://suntzusaid.com** provides students with a translation of Sun Tzu's work as well as a paragraph-by-paragraph commentary.

Muir S. Fairchild Research Information Center **http://www.au.af.mil/au/aul/bibs/great/great.htm** provides bibliographies on great warriors, thinkers, and leaders. Available on their list are resources for Clausewitz, Jomini, Sun Tzu, Liddell Hart, Brodie, Ulysses S. Grant, and Robert E. Lee.

# Does Strategic Studies Have a Future?

LAWRENCE FREEDMAN

## Chapter Contents

 ## Reader's Guide

This concluding chapter considers whether strategic studies has a future as an area of academic study. It charts the rise and fall of the subject in the universities and suggests reasons why it should be revived and how this might be achieved. The chapter starts by looking at the early development of strategic studies. Strategic studies was largely undertaken outside the universities and was initially influenced by the physical sciences and engineering. Even as traditional military patterns of thought appeared inadequate in the thermonuclear age, academics still found it difficult to impose a scholarly framework for the subject that could survive shifts in policy. By the end of the cold war, strategic studies was essentially a broad enquiry, drawing on a range of expertise. With the end of the cold war, the big issues that had animated the study of military strategy subsided and some questioned the continued relevance of the topic. There was a risk that strategic studies would be caught between the scholarly virtues and disciplinary organization required by the universities and the pressures and urgency of strategic practice, which is inherently interdisciplinary. Realism, the intellectual basis of strategic studies, has also been challenged for being simplistic, for making exaggerated claims for its objectivity, and for disregarding domestic and transnational factors. Furthermore, some view realism as being preoccupied with armed force to the exclusion of peaceful means of exerting influence and resolving disputes, to the point of legitimizing armed force as an acceptable instrument of policy.

A way forward is suggested based on the idea that the course of history can be altered by the choices made by individuals, groups, and governments. These decisions provide the subject matter for strategic studies. They do not need to be choices made only by states nor are they only about the use of armed force. Armed forces, however, provide the starkest choices that can be confronted and so provide a natural starting point for any attempt to create a general theory of strategy, while organized violence poses a series of challenges that deserves special study.

# Introduction: The Development of Strategic Studies

Initially strategic studies developed outside the universities. Before the cold war there were military theorists and commentators, such as John 'Boney' Fuller and Basil Liddell Hart in Britain, who often had substantial practical experience of the subject but who wrote largely for a popular and a professional audience rather than an academic one. Their subject matter was similar to that of later strategic studies, and those who survived into the nuclear age fitted in perfectly well with the new milieu. There was some pioneering activity in the universities after the First World War with the moves to establish the scientific study of international affairs as a contribution to the avoidance of future wars. Many of those in this field had an interest in military matters although few claimed expertise in how best to fight wars, and, as we will discuss, the bias in the discipline was to some extent antistrategic.

The special flavour of strategic studies after the Second World War came from those who had been working in the physical sciences and engineering rather than the social sciences and humanities, many with their consciences stung and their policy interest engaged through the Manhattan Project. Those who had worked on operational problems from convoy protection to choosing targets for air raids had firm views about how the conduct of war could no longer be left to what they often took to be the rather primitive, intuitive forms of reasoning of the professional military. The conviction that civilians had critical contributions to make to strategic policy grew as traditional military patterns of thought appeared to be quite inadequate in the thermonuclear age. The combination of the arms race and the cold war created the conditions for the growth of a substantial research-led policy community outside the universities—new government agencies, congressional committees, think tanks and 'beltway bandits'.

This created a market for professionally trained civilian strategists that university departments might attempt to fill. It also meant that academics were never able to impose a scholarly framework for the subject that could independently survive shifts in the policy framework. Few really tried to do so. From the start it was the salience of the policy issues rather than intellectual curiosity that led to the growth of the strategic studies community. The universities were certainly not hostile to policy-led research. The cold war coincided with the expansion of the universities throughout the Western world—not only in size but also in the range of their activities. They took in subjects that were often practical in nature and moved well beyond established disciplinary boundaries. If gender and the media could become appropriate subjects for university departments, then it would have been surprising if questions of armed force had escaped the net. More seriously, those making the case for higher education were pleased to have examples of contributions to national strength. When the universities went to the US Congress for more funds after the Soviet Union had apparently rushed ahead in the technological race in October 1957 with the launch of the world's first artificial satellite (Sputnik 1) their case was made in the name of national security. Many academics thrilled to a potential role in a wider public debate, even if this meant enduring snide remarks about abstract theorizing removed from real life, and certainty that their weightier tomes would be left unread while their short, snappy opinion pieces might reach presidents and prime ministers. Academic exponents of strategic studies might have had much more training in the use of evidence and sophisticated forms of analysis but they could still drift easily into advocacy, preferring popular and professional audiences to the dustier academic conferences.

Little attempt was made to use the cold war opportunities to establish strategic studies as an academic subject. No core curriculum was developed, and there was probably only a brief period in the early 1960s, the end of what was later described as the 'golden age', when there was a serious body of literature with which everyone in the field was reasonably familiar. There was not even a consensus on how academic work in this area should be described. The policy influence was always apparent. 'Military studies' appeared too technical and narrow, redolent of map-reading and staff exercises, and contradicted the factors that had shaped the civilian role in strategic policy: the prejudice against professional military thought; the democratic conviction that at any rate the military sphere should be subordinated to the civil: and the Clausewitzian presumption that if, as the master insisted, war is concerned with the pursuit of politics by other means, then military means could only be properly understood by reference to political purposes.

## In and Out of the Cold War

But what political purposes? As the ends of policy seemed somewhat fixed during the cold war, at least at the governmental level, the focus was very much on means. The contest between liberal capitalist and state socialist forms of government was inescapable and was not seriously up for debate in Western countries. The central problem of policy was about how, if at all, political benefit might be extracted from a nuclear arsenal without triggering a cataclysmic conflagration. Any benefit would have to be deterrent because once the weapons were used the consequences were bound to be catastrophic. But if use led to catastrophe, then how could nuclear threats be made to work for the sake of deterrence, and what options would be available should deterrence fail? How could credibility be injected into preposterous posturing? The conundrums and paradoxes of nuclear deterrence drew in academic interest. This could be done not only by exploring ways of reinforcing deterrence, thereby avoiding war, but also by evaluating the other policy instruments that might reduce dependence upon this high-risk approach. They became interested in particular in arms control as a form of cooperative management of the strategic relationship between the two superpowers. Over time this had an important consequence in that it encouraged a perspective that went beyond the purely national to the systemic. If rational Soviet policies were as important as rational American policies, then American policy should be designed to coax out of Moscow a more rational Soviet policy.

The changes in the character and tempo of the cold war naturally influenced strategic studies. After the Berlin and Cuban crises of the early 1960s, further development of the purer theories of deterrence seemed less important. Academics began to find a role in questioning official policy and warning of the limits to deterrence, the distorting effects of domestic and organizational politics on crisis management, and the perils of misperception. The second-order technical studies sought to offer ways out of practical difficulties experienced in arms control negotiations. A further development came as it was recognized that too much of the 'golden age' literature had taken the political context for granted, or had at least failed to appreciate the dynamic consequences of the upheavals in the Third World. After Vietnam these aspects of strategy were much harder to ignore. To understand the conditions in which armed forces might be used, or at least threatened, it was necessary to delve into a diverse range of regions. It seemed more important to draw attention to the complexities of the

Middle East or Central America than to think up fancy but safe ways to threaten Armageddon. Furthermore, as even official deterrence policies moved to reduce their nuclear bias and strengthen their conventional elements, professional military knowledge and experience appeared much more relevant. So, well before the end of the cold war, the field of strategic studies (now often known as security studies) had become much more diffuse. There was no recognized academic discipline, only a broad area of study coming under a variety of headings (peace, war, defence, security, strategy, arms control). The only unifying factor was that the interest lay beyond practical matters concerned with the actual employment of armed force to the political purposes for which it might be employed and the political measures that might be adopted either to prevent this employment or to bring it to an end.

In these circumstances it was inevitable that those working in the universities would have to follow the shifts in focus in the wider policy debate. Given the sort of upheavals associated with the end of the cold war and its aftermath, this was no small matter. When the policy issues of the day moved from such topics as great power confrontation and nuclear arms control to at first intra-state wars and humanitarian intervention and later on to terrorism and counterinsurgency, then quite different skills might be needed. To deal with the old agenda one might hope for scholars with a grasp of traditional statecraft, a knowledge of the political thinking at the highest levels of the world's key capitals, sensitivity to alliance relations, and a technical understanding of the properties of the critical weapons systems and how they might be employed. Add in such questions as the management of defence budgets and the intricacies of arms control negotiations and it can soon be seen that during the cold war years strategic studies had to draw on a great variety of types of expertise.

Then out goes the cold war and in comes ethnic conflict, carrying with it vast quantities of anthropological and sociological literature, combined with a necessity to follow political developments in small and weak states, whose leading lights are not themselves plugged in to the international policy circuit, dirty little militia wars and microscopic terrorist cells, problems of humanitarian intervention and social and economic reconstruction as ways of preventing, resolving, and recovering from conflicts, and large issues of forms of Islam and whether Western democracy can be exported. Some argued for an even more complete shift away from the traditional agenda, insisting that the staples of conflict and violence must give way to, or at least accommodate, the vital factors of environment and economics. A hypothetical university department set up to address strategic studies during the cold war would find that the original interdisciplinary requirements—polymathic enough—were suddenly expanded to absurd lengths.

Not surprisingly, academics often appeared to be as uncertain about the future of the international system and how to handle the new agenda as were the policymakers. It became even more difficult to give confident advice in the form of three crisp bullet points. Policymakers became impatient with those qualities that academics believe to be those most valuable: long-term thinking, stretching the bounds of the possible, and taking complexity as a challenge rather than an excuse for not going into too much detail. Academics in the strategic/security studies field could see their funding in decline and their best work crowded out by partisan clamour, parochial agency interest, and the more sensationalist fare on offer.

While the pull from the policy world was to go for the simple, the snappy, and the short-term, the push from the academic world was almost exactly in the opposite direction. The study of international relations, established to address the problem of war, sought to gain respectability by acquiring all the attributes of a proper discipline, including a preoccupation with theory and methodology. Academic advancement had come to depend on 'conspicuous scholarship'—publishing in the right journals, linking relatively innocuous case studies to great theoretical issues and, through extensive footnotes, demonstrating a capacity to reference (though not necessarily to read) all potentially relevant literature. To those for whom language itself had become an ideological battlefield, and all empiricism suspect, policy relevance signified the antithesis of sound scholarship and certainly not its highest aspiration.

As the empirical side of the business became much more challenging and the professional imperatives more theoretical, academic strategic studies lacked replenishment. Young academics were discouraged from entering into the increasingly time-consuming business of making sense of contemporary affairs—getting to know foreign countries, exploring their history, establishing networks of contacts, and following the intricate twists and turns of policy debates and military decisions. Often filling the gap were journalists, reflecting their professional inclination to seek out unique sources and interview the key players, and a lack of interest in theory. For example, journalists rather than academics wrote most of the memorable, and reliable, accounts of the Iraq and Afghanistan Wars. At the same time, those less interested in telling stories and more concerned to influence policy, possibly by becoming policymakers themselves, gravitated to the think tanks, where they could produce serious and often quite technical studies addressing critical issues. Think tanks, however, had their own problems, such as the need to satisfy funders through constant attention to the news agenda or else the promotion of a particular worldview. Without the continuity provided by teaching programmes, and the recruitment opportunities that come with doctoral students and post-doctoral fellows, critical mass could be hard to sustain.

The problem, therefore, notably but not uniquely in the United States, was that the challenge of making sense of contemporary international conflict and the determination to turn international relations into either a pseudo-science or a critical discourse led the universities to opt out of strategic studies. In their different ways journalists and think-tankers could fill some of the gaps, but their interests and contributions were likely to be more fleeting. Their roles overlapped with that of the universities but they were not the same. At their best, universities could offer durable departments with their own intellectual traditions, opportunities for independent research, a tolerance of the sort of eccentricity and playfulness that could lead to real innovation, a capacity to see the bigger picture, an ability to draw on wider theories, and the constant refreshment that came from encounters with fresh generations of students.

 **Key Points**

- Cold war strategy was relatively simple, focusing particularly on the requirements of deterrence.
- Even before 1991, the field of strategic studies became more diffuse as the political context of international relations changed.
- The opening of a new era of ethnic conflict in the 1990s and terrorism in the 2000s presented strategists with a more complex international environment that required a wide range of new expertise.
- In the post-cold war period, uncertainty predominated and policymakers became less interested in what academic strategists had to say, while many scholars turned their attention to what was regarded as the academically more respectable pursuit of the study of theory and methodology.

## Strategy and the Crisis in Social Science

The study of strategy posed a further and particular challenge to the social sciences. It tended to adopt the perspective of individual actors within the system, as they try to make sense of their environment and shape it to their needs as best they can. Much social science theorizing necessarily seeks to reduce the importance of human agency—by looking for patterns and regularities in areas which we might have thought in our naivety to be governed by choice. Deliberate political change is still inadequately studied in political theory except in a rather cynical way. There is no point in studying strategy unless one believes that the course of history can be altered by the choices made by individuals, even if not always in the ways they would wish. Those who believe that the analysis of politics and international relations requires attempts to identify long historical cycles, or universal laws of political life, or invariable patterns of behaviour, or structural determinants of actions that leave little scope for local decision are unlikely to find strategy particularly interesting or even relevant. Instead of finding anomalous behaviour intriguing, they may find it irritating because it undermines the predictive power of their models.

Strategy is important only if it is believed that individuals, groups, and governments face real choices and that the reasoning which informs these choices is worthy of careful examination. By focusing on actors within the system and their sense of their own interests and aspirations, strategic studies must be seditious. It encourages the analysis of those situations where order is absent or elsewhere; disorder is encouraged by those who believe that it will be to the advantage of those on whose behalf they are acting.

This appreciation—almost celebration—of choice is essential to the study of strategy. Strategy is undertaken in the conviction that it is possible to manipulate and shape one's environment rather than simply become the victim of forces beyond one's control. For this reason, students of strategy are naturally political voyeurs, observing the choices of others with a discerning eye, whether or not they have sympathy with their ultimate aims.

Therefore it might be argued that there is no reason in principle why strategic studies, defined as an intellectual approach to certain types of problems, rather than a field of study, could not become more prominent in academic life. Indeed we know this to be the case. There are now far more courses about strategy in management departments than in international relations departments, although unfortunately this development has encouraged the rather loose view of strategy as being concerned with more visionary planning or the management of large organizations in uncertain environments. Nonetheless, the classical military strategists—Sun Tzu more than Clausewitz—loom large in the management literature, far more so than the business strategists loom in the military literature. Furthermore, many of the more formal methodologies, of which the most famous remains game theory, developed in the late 1950s with nuclear deterrence in mind, have become even more influential in economics and management studies (see Box 21.1).

This has returned to political science departments as rational choice theory, although in a form that often appears to confirm the old jibe that political science is an area of study that in failing to achieve science avoids that dangerous subject, politics. It offers undoubted analytical rigour, a shared starting point for numerous lines of enquiry, and considerable theoretical promise. The problem is that the methodology can be off-putting and restrictive, readily and usefully applied to only a limited number of types of choices. It copes poorly with complexity, as well as requiring bold assumptions about what it means to be rational. This is especially disconcerting when

**BOX** 21.1   Similarities and Differences between the Ideas of Clausewitz and Sun Tzu

The extent of the cultural and historical gaps separating Sun Tzu's *The Art of War* and Clausewitz's *On War*, not to mention the apparently contradictory nature of their most well-known dicta, has encouraged the a priori assumption that Sun Tzu and Clausewitz espouse essentially antagonistic theories. However, closer scrutiny reveals that while a number of differences exist, so do many similarities and complementary ideas.

The main points on which Sun Tzu and Clausewitz disagree concern the value of intelligence, the utility of deception, the feasibility of surprise attack, and the possibility of reliably forecasting and controlling the course of events on the battlefield. On the qualities requisite for a military commander, though, they agree in principle but differ in emphasis: Sun Tzu relies chiefly on the master of war's skill in making calculated, rational choices, while Clausewitz considers the military genius's artistic intuition to be the critical factor. Finally they hold similar views on the primacy of politics in war; the need to preserve the professional autonomy of the military in action; the overall importance of numerical superiority; and the folly of not securing victory as rapidly and decisively as possible once war has become inevitable.

Handel (1996)

studying armed conflict, famed for its tendency to irrationality and the imperfection of available information (pushed by Clausewitz to the centre of his theory with his stress on friction and the fog of war). Game theory provided an important means of thinking through the alternative options that presented themselves to policymakers in the nuclear age, and in particular the need to recognize the incentives for cooperation in the midst of antagonism, but it could never capture the range of factors that would shape the critical decisions. Moreover, even in economics, where rational choice theory has a much more natural home, there has been a move, in behavioural economics, towards integrating the insights from psychology and accepting that rationality is always bounded and that individual actions can rarely be understood outside their social context.

 **Key Points**

- Strategic studies, with its focus on the importance of deliberate political choice, poses problems for the social sciences, which emphasize wider patterns of behaviour and the limited opportunities for achieving change.

- Strategists are 'voyeurs', scrutinizing the choices made by others concerned with difficult decisions about the role of armed force.

- Strategic studies can be seen as an intellectual approach to specific problems rather than a distinct field of study.

## The Academic and Policy Worlds

The challenge is therefore more than how to re-engage with the policy world. The relationship between academics and policymakers is bound to be fraught with ethical and practical difficulties. The need for access and the desire for influence must be balanced against the risk that critical faculties might be blunted and intellectual integrity corrupted in the search for preferment. The academic should be under no obligation to become a practitioner. In terms of defining a field of study, the vantage point of a student of strategy is quite different from that of a practitioner. When the former tries to second-guess the latter in an effort to display some superior wisdom, then they might well deserve to be treated with contempt. The most helpful role remains that which can be properly described as 'academic' (even though in the policy world this is all too often synonymous with irrelevant). Unless the academic has special and relevant expertise, for example in the politics of a particular region, then the main task may be to conceptualize and contextualize rather than provide specific guidance. If it is done well the practitioner should be able to recognize the relevance for whatever may be the problem at hand.

The stressed and busy practitioner might complain that, however subtle the analysis, academic work is unlikely to be addressing the current crisis or the next policy priority in the form in which it is being faced. Compared with academic specialists, the practitioner must range far and wide because of the nature of the judgements to be made, often in a hurry. It may be necessary to address the efficiency of various forms of coercion as well as inducements, and in so doing to draw on views about human nature under stress, problems of organization of large groups of people on the move, negotiating techniques, visions of a good society, and standards of ethical conduct. Consider a general entering into battle. He (and now possibly she) must consider:

- politics (how best to define the goal of the campaign, the importance of keeping allies close, what the people back home will stand);
- engineering (how well the weapons work, are likely to work in practice, possible modifications to suit local conditions, ensuring that they are properly maintained);
- sociology (the likely cohesion of forces under fire);
- psychology (how to motivate troops under fire);
- geography (the possible impact of terrain on particular tactics);
- history (what other generals got away with in similar circumstances);
- economics (the rate at which material can be expended in the light of the likely length of the conflict).

Note that all these considerations apply only to getting the best out of one's own side. Add the need to think about an enemy and even more types of issue have to be factored into the strategic deliberations.

Furthermore, practitioners expect to be judged by results. They will therefore tend to rely on what works for them. This may be intuition and hunch, or lessons drawn from searing experience or remembered bits of history. These may be relied upon in preference to excellent information sources and exemplary staff work. When matters are finely balanced but a decision still has to be taken, a feeling about the issue may be as good a guide as any. This may strike an academic as being wholly inappropriate or based on disgracefully exaggerated generalizations. Certainly the results from such approaches can be very poor, but whether a proper academic methodology would do any better is a moot point when there is no time for long projects and there can be little tolerance of too many caveats. Wise strategists may research their decisions as much as possible, but time often precludes further deliberation. When a general is wondering whether an enemy formation might break in the face of a sudden attack, he is not going to be impressed if he is told that more research is needed or that his working hypothesis is inherently untestable. Once a fateful decision has been taken, an open mind becomes a luxury because any reappraisal may result in confused orders and demoralization.

Strategic practice, as opposed to the theory, demands risk-taking on behalf of a wider constituency, normally with the lives of service personnel and possibly with whole societies, and this brings with it certain responsibilities. It involves mobilizing human and material resources according to a developed plan against anticipated opposition and in pursuit of stated objectives. If the objectives are misplaced, the plan misconceived, or the resources unavailable or poorly mobilized, then the strategy will fail and this will be the strategist's responsibility. It is this sense of being tested by practice and judged by results that gives strategic reasoning its edge. The unaccountable academic should properly feel a degree of humility when advising on such matters. To a far greater sense than academics might like to admit, the practice of strategy may depend more on character and political acumen than research.

This may help explain why the study of strategy is accommodated only with difficulty in academic life. As practice it provides opportunity for chance and irrationality to hold sway. The purist might be appalled at the arbitrary mixture of politics, sociology, economics, psychology, and history that regularly influence decisions in crisis and combat, never mind the great contributions made by intuition and hunch. Yet the fact that reality rarely shows respect for disciplinary boundaries might give the academic pause for thought, as might evidence of the extent to which carefully qualified propositions, excessively crafted formulations, and a reluctance to pronounce until all possible avenues of research have been exhausted can get in the way of clear thinking.

Effective policy outside academia draws on a range of considerations that within academia are each confined to their own disciplinary box. Within the universities, intellectual progress is assumed to depend on commonly accepted methodologies being rigorously applied within a known conceptual framework to produce results able to withstand peer review. The process is watched over sternly by professional associations and journal editors—the 'gatekeepers'. They ensure that standards are maintained so that progress can be measured. Without the disciplinary boxes it could well be that teaching and research would become unmanageable. Nonetheless, disciplinary boundaries are often artificial, and sustained through jargon that excludes the uninitiated. Indeed academics often develop particular strategies to sustain these disciplinary boundaries and to fight off intellectual intruders. Yet many of the most important academic cleavages cut across these boundaries. Fads and fashions—from rational actor theory to deconstructionism—migrate easily. Often the most innovative and influential figures are those who refuse to be confined by the established boundaries, but are happy to borrow from others. Imaginative academic administrators often ignore them. In universities as in other organizations the closer one gets to particular decisions the more complex and multifaceted they appear. Practical problems can rarely be encapsulated in the terms of a single discipline. Life is interdisciplinary.

**Key Points**

- Tensions inevitably exist between the academic and policy worlds with their different responsibilities.
- 'Practitioners' often complain about the irrelevance of academic studies to immediate problems they face.
- Strategic reality is wide ranging and interdisciplinary and does not fit neatly into the narrow focus of most university departments.

 **Critical Thinking**   Debating … Should academics advise governments on national security policy?

### For

- *Academics have a responsibility to share their knowledge.* Those who have the resources and time to study matters relevant to vital areas of policy have a duty to share their findings, even if they may not get much response and their findings may be rejected. While it can be difficult for academics to second-guess particular decisions, they can still enrich a policy debate.

- *Policymakers need critical friends.* There are risks in cosying up too close to the centres of power, but it is possible to retain academic independence and professional integrity so long as there is confidence in the underlying research and analysis. The best policymakers know that outside advice is not helpful if it just echoes established views. They can cope with challenge and unorthodox ideas.

- *Academics may be of greatest value contributing to a wider public debate.* Rather than speaking truth to power directly, academics might do better as commenters on policy and participants in a continuing conversation. With social networking sites, there are now few barriers to academics' expression. They can provide context by explaining the background to a regional crisis or the limits of policy instruments such as sanctions, while unpacking concepts such as 'hearts and minds', 'soft power', and 'pre-emption' to reveal the ideas that lie behind them and the problems they raise.

- *Engaging in such debates benefits academic research.* Dispensing with some of the theoretical packaging and methodological caveats requires academics to expose their underlying assumptions and core arguments to scrutiny. To the extent that they do get close to policymaking, they can develop a keener appreciation of the workings of government and the practical management of international affairs.

### Against

- *Academics have less to offer than they recognize.* Academics should take care when they present themselves as speaking 'truth' to power. They may be independent of government but they still have their own biases and agendas that affect how they view issues. Research prompted by a particular policy issue may take years to complete, by which time the debate has moved on. The methods of academic research and the language in which it is presented tend not to be appreciated in policy circles.

- *Just because advice is offered doesn't mean it will be accepted.* Policy will reflect many factors that have little to do with reason and analysis. Policymakers are fallible and subject to influence by multiple sources. They also have to worry about getting support elsewhere in government, winning votes in Parliament or Congress, presenting it to the public, and then perhaps gaining Alliance or Security Council support.

*(continued . . . )*

**Critical Thinking** *(continued)*

- *Academics have to compromise to gain a hearing.* Policymakers tend to ignore academics perceived to be outside the mainstream and known for eccentric, maverick, or ideologically suspect views. To gain access, therefore, they must present themselves as respectable and sound, even though that may mean playing down the real significance of their research and staying quiet on issues that matter to them. Dissenting views on the American role, the value of interventions, or nuclear deterrence may struggle to get a hearing.

- *Once academics become part of a policymaking process, they become invested in the policy.* There is always a risk of co-option. Becoming associated with a particular policy, perhaps by being cited by the government as a supporting expert, means that the academic will become invested, and strain to justify it, however controversial and however unfortunate its effects in practice.

## Realism: Old and New

A starting point for a revival of strategy might be to return to the realist tradition. Contemporary students of politics and international relations often criticize this tradition as being simplistic and obsolescent, bound up with the assumption that the only choices that matter are those that states make about military power. There are three aspects to the critique: an epistemological challenge to what is taken to be exaggerated claims for objectivity as if this is the only true reflection of 'reality'; the disregard of domestic and transnational factors; and the preoccupation with armed force to the exclusion of peaceful means of exerting influence and resolving disputes. This latter complaint can be taken further and developed into a charge that the realists legitimize armed force as an acceptable instrument of policy. This charge at the level of basic morality is directly related to the first, apparently more scholastic, complaint about objectivity. The realists might claim that they do no more than attempt to make sense of the world as they find it while their critics suggest that the very language and concepts they use encourage a very particular and dangerous view of the world. In recent years this critique has become more subdued as many leading realists have warned about the dangers of imprudent commitments in support of idealistic objectives to promote freedom and democracy while neglecting questions of order and stability. Realism tends to be conservative, not neo-conservative.

A defence of strategic studies does not require a defence of realism, however much the two have been linked in the past. There are, however, elements of the realist tradition that are worth preserving while other aspects need updating. An approach to political analysis that prided itself on coming to terms with the world as it was rather than as idealists would like it to be is now supposed to depend on a dubious claim that key international events can largely be explained by the structurally defined means by which states must safeguard their security. There is room for a non-dogmatic realism that would acknowledge the significance of non-state actors, the impact of social, economic, cultural, and local political factors on state behaviour, the importance of values and mental constructs, and can be sensitive to the epistemological issues raised by presumptions of objectivity. If practitioners of international politics now talk regularly about issues of identity, norms, and globalization, then they are part of international reality. To be powerful was often described within the realist tradition in terms of possessing substantial assets—so much wealth or military capabilities. Yet poor strategy can see these squandered or trivialized, while good strategy can extract substantial political effects from meagre resources. In this sense strategy is essentially an art, less about applying power and more about creating it in the first place. This requires a much more subtle view of power, as existing only within political relationships, manifest as actors are able to alter the behaviour of others according to their own preferences.

The constructivist position, which is now emerging as a safe haven for those troubled by structural realism while leery about following postmodernist theory into a deconstructed, relativist mire, stresses the importance of the interaction between the way we describe the world and how we act within it. This can represent a real advance on the tendency within the realist tradition to think of power as a measurable resource. This leads to a view of strategy as no more than a mechanical matter of expending these resources in the pursuit of clearly defined objectives. Put this way, it can appear as almost a science, opening up possibilities for prediction. The practical strategist is more likely, however, to be, perhaps unwittingly, something of a constructivist. Effective strategy requires a clear sense of the dynamic relationship between ends and means, knowing that how ends are defined in the first place is critical to whether available means will be adequate. The ability to emerge victorious out of a conflict may depend on sensitivity as to what opponents may think are their vulnerabilities or what your side can be persuaded is an area of comparative advantage. Vital judgements—such as finding the optimum balance among broadening a coalition to maximize the isolation of the opponent, the limited time available for coalition formation, the goals that will have to be dropped to bring in the most reluctant, the extra obligations that might have to be accepted, the otherwise neutral opinions that might be offended—turn on the way we understand the workings of our own and other political systems.

 **Key Points**

- Despite critiques of realism, there are elements of this school of thought that remain very useful in the study of strategy, while there are other elements that can be brought up to date.

- A case can be made for a non-dogmatic realism, which provides a more subtle approach to the role of power in international politics than the neo-realist approach, which emphasizes the structural constraints on state behaviour.

- Newer constructivist approaches also help to focus attention on the important dynamic relationship between ends and means, which is crucial in the outcome of any conflict.

## The Study of Armed Force

A new realism should therefore have no trouble looking beyond what makes states secure and more towards what makes individuals and particular groups secure. It must also admit that the business of states, once almost completely bound up with security, now takes in a wide range of economic, social, and environmental issues. From this it follows that the course and character of all conflicts, and the role to be played by armed force, must be reappraised. Strong rates of economic growth and forms of interdependence may well reduce tensions between states and create a stake in peaceful coexistence. Equally, financial crises can create intense forms of stress and reignite nationalist urges. Environmental disasters can undermine the credibility of the state apparatus so that it becomes vulnerable to other types of challenges. Changes in family structures and social mores may affect attitudes to violence, and so on. As has become painfully apparent over the past two decades, proposals to discard the traditional focus on organized violence turned out to be premature. When governments are determined to resort to force it is as well that they understand their chosen instrument.

Strategy is more ubiquitous than violence. It is present wherever there is politics, which is in all human institutions, evident in any move to mobilize support, sideline opponents, and so on. The study of strategy does not depend on the possibility of a violent aspect to human affairs. Nonetheless it can still be argued that this possibility can have an important impact on attempts to develop general theories of strategy, capable of addressing all manner of political situations. If strategy is about choice then armed force provides some of the most perplexing and starkest choices that can be confronted. At these points of choice can be observed clashes between conflicting interests and values, the rough impact of brute force, and the more subtle effects achieved by guile and wiles. It is the case that most political objectives can be met without the use or threatened use of violence. There are other sources of power. However, physical violence is the ultimate and, if available, can overwhelm all others. The threat posed is one that no individual or group or state can ignore because it challenges their whole existence. It is one that is only likely to be made when basic values are at stake. Situations involving the purposive use of violence are likely to stand out from the run of the mill activities at both the national and international levels. By their nature they concentrate minds on fundamentals. Ethically and politically they require exceptional justification. For all these reasons they provide a natural starting point for any attempt to build up a general theory of strategy.

This is not the same, however, as arguing that formulations developed with armed force in mind can serve a variety of purposes. For example politicians may dramatize the more troublesome social problems by calling for 'wars' against them (on drugs, cancer, etc.) and suggest that strong generalship is needed for them to be defeated. This is perhaps what happened with the 'war on terror', when a rhetorical device urging a determined effort to deal with an undoubted scourge was taken too literally. The unreflective application of the war analogy can hinder understanding by attempting to squeeze quite different types of issues into an inappropriate conceptual framework geared to military threats. In the case of drugs, for example, it may have some relevance to confrontations with Third World drug cartels but less so with attempts to make sense of patterns of consumption. Equally the notions of 'economic security' can encourage a confrontational approach to trade policy and 'environmental security', a search for explanations based on hostile actions rather than natural causes or everyday economic activity. Even more difficult is a term such as 'internal security' which might once have referred to the ability of states to deny armed groups, whether criminal or political, the ability to challenge their authority, but which now takes in anything to do with the control of borders, including economic migration or the smuggling of contraband. This has become particularly evident with the 'war on terror'. Treating it as a traditional war, against an implacable enemy determined to use every means at its disposal, has encouraged a 'whatever it takes' attitude, aimed at eliminating the enemy, and has discouraged more political approaches, designed to marginalize radicals.

A different approach would be to acknowledge that the characters and competencies of states have been subject to many changes while asserting that an enduring feature remains the aspiration to define and dominate the means of legitimate violence within territorial borders. The challenges can come from other states, or from within states in the form of secessionists or revolutionaries or elitist conspirators, or from non-state actors in the form of drug cartels and gangsters, religious sects, and minority political movements. This continues to provide a relatively sharp focus for strategic studies and provides some compensation for an unavoidably wide context.

There is no reason in principle why the strategic imagination should not be directed towards improving the human condition through finding ways to restrict and progressively reduce the role of armed force. Much strategic studies activity has been about the peaceful settlement of disputes, arms control, and generally supporting the work of the United Nations. Major international negotiations require as much of a strategic sensibility as do major wars. Yet, and this may only be a matter of temperament, there does tend to be a dark side to the strategic imagination that picks up intimations of disorder at times of stability, that senses the fragility of human institutions even while striving to reinforce them, that cannot stop thinking of war while promoting peace. This dark side may explain the accusations of allowing armed force far more prominence than it deserves. The defence is that constant consideration of the potential for instability and conflict can help prevent it from being realized. Moreover, if the strategic imagination fails to be able to generate scenarios for war, except by combining in an unlikely and tenuous fashion a series of gloomy hypotheses, then that itself is a positive sign.

 **Key Points**

- A new realism requires a broader focus than in the past to understand the nature of present-day conflicts, but care must be taken not to overlook the traditional role of armed force.

- Strategy is present wherever there is politics, and although political ends can be met without violence, force often remains the ultimate arbiter of political disputes.

- Despite attempts to apply the 'war' analogy ever more widely, strategic studies remains a subject that focuses on the role of armed force both in peacetime and in war.

 ## Conclusion: Does Strategic Studies Have a Future?

Karl Marx once observed that men make their own history but not in the circumstances of their own choosing. The study of strategy should help with the understanding of how individuals and groups go about history-making and in so doing reshape the circumstances that they face. These circumstances include many others, also engaged in their own history-making. I have argued that this activist view with its stress on choice and power is distinctive and cannot be confined within the boundaries of a specific academic discipline. It needs to be asserted against those who are more determinist in their outlook or transfixed by patterns and cycles in human behaviour or see the exercise of power as a failure of social institutions rather than part of their natural condition. I have further argued that the study of strategy can benefit from being pushed to extremes, by looking at those circumstances in which the prospect or actuality of organized violence looms large. There is a further benefit in that as we have not yet succeeded in banishing armed force from human affairs there are many extreme situations to be faced.

These extreme situations provide an agenda for policymakers that students of strategy may feel well placed to address. Upon this may depend the future of strategic studies in terms of academic organization. This will be testing in a number of respects. First, they will only be able to sustain any claim of relevance if they have kept in touch with the range of possible situations that might tend to extremes. This range has expanded, as it has taken in the many problems of weak states and the challenges posed by radical Islamist movements, but at the same time the most extreme situations, that is, major wars among the great powers, still appear unlikely. The conflicts of the 2000s have demonstrated the need for an approach that combines general understanding of strategic behaviour with the specifics of a set of conflicts which are individually complicated. Secondly, with an agenda that is becoming both more diffuse and in certain respects less pressing, there may be less coherence to strategic studies. Thirdly, there will remain a need for caution and humility. There is an enormous gulf between offering advice and taking responsibility for decisions with potentially severe consequences, normally taken in imperfect conditions in terms of what is known and the time for deliberation. Fourthly, for all these reasons it must never be forgotten that strategy is an art and not a science.

 ## Questions

1. What were the implications of the early development of strategic studies?
2. What role does realism play in strategic studies?
3. What is meant by the term 'the golden age of strategic studies'?
4. How did the cold war affect the development of the study of strategy?
5. To what extent did the end of the cold war alter the agenda of strategic studies?
6. Can the academic study of strategy help the 'practitioner' of strategy?
7. What challenges does strategic studies pose for the social sciences?
8. Does strategic studies have to be bound to the 'realist tradition' in the study of politics?
9. What is the future of strategic studies according to the author?
10. Do you agree with this view?

 ## Further Reading

L. Freedman, *The Evolution of Nuclear Strategy*, 3rd edn (New York: St Martin's Press, 2004) deals with the history of all aspects of nuclear strategy.

L. Freedman, *Strategy: A History* (Oxford: Oxford University Press, 2013) covers recent debates.

C. Gray, *Modern Strategy* (Oxford: Oxford University Press, 1999) offers a modern Clausewitzian approach.

M. I. Handel, *Masters of War: Classical Strategic Thought* (London: Frank Cass, 1996) covers Clausewitz and Sun Tzu.

B. Heuser, *The Evolution of Strategy: Thinking War from Antiquity to the Present* (New York: Cambridge University Press, 2010) is an impressive history of the development of strategic thought.

P. Paret (ed.), *Makers of Modern Strategy: From Machiavelli to the Nuclear Age* (Princeton, NJ: Princeton University Press, 1986) provides the best overall coverage of strategic studies.

# Web Links

International Institute for Strategic Studies **http://www.iiss.org** provides political-military strategic assessments through expert commentary, strategic dossiers, a database on Armed Conflict, and publications such as the journal *Survival* and *The Military Balance*, a comprehensive annual review of defence capabilities and developments.

Royal United Service Institute **http://www.rusi.org** is a London-based think tank offering defence and security-focused commentary and analysis.

United States Army War College, Strategic Studies Institute **http://www.strategicstudiesinstitute.army.mil** provides strategic research and analysis for the United States military, particularly the Army, and a broader community of strategic analysts.

Institute for Security Studies **http://www.iss.co.za** is a think tank working on security issues in Africa, with a particular focus on conflict and human security.

War on the Rocks, **http://www.warontherocks.com** is a platform for analysis, commentary, debate, and multimedia content on foreign policy and national security issues through a realist lens.

# Notes

**Chapter 7**

1. The conventional version of the JSF is expected to have a combat radius of less than 600 miles—a figure which requires some scrutiny, since real combat radii have been known to be less than those of stated number. Lockheed Martin Corp., 'F-35 Lightning II: The Future is Flying'. n.d. Accessed at http://www.lockheedmartin.com/data/assets/aeronautics/products/f35/A07-20536AF-35Broc.pdf

2. This problem became more difficult as the South Vietnamese—lacking American mass, fire control, and air power—took over the war. See David Ewing Ott, Field Artillery, 1954–1973, Vietnam Studies (Washington, DC: Department of the Army, 1975), p. 226. The Soviet M1954(M-46)130mm gun has a range of 27.5km; the M-114 155mm howitzer a range of 14.6km. Of course, many different artillery pieces were used by both sides. http://en.wikipedia.org/wiki/130_mm_towed_field_gun_M1954_(M-46) and http://en.wikipedia.org/wiki/M144_155_mm_howitzer

**Chapter 8**

1. All statements of facts or opinion are those of the author and do not reflect the official positions or views of the US government or any US government agency.

2. The work of Richards Heuer (1999) has significantly advanced analysts' understanding of their cognitive limitations; the development of structured analytic techniques has continued both in intelligence training courses as well as other research institutions.

**Chapter 11**

1. The author wishes to acknowledge the contribution of Professor Colin S. Gray to this work, which is based on a co-authored chapter that appeared in an earlier version of this textbook.

**Chapter 12**

1. Quoted in Robert G. Joseph and John F. Reichart, *Deterrence and Defense in a Nuclear, Biological, and Chemical Environment*, Occasional Paper of the Center for Counterproliferation Research (Washington, DC: National Defense University, 1995), 4.

2. The text of Aspin's speech can be accessed at http://www.fas.org/irp/offdocs/pdd18.htm

3. The British Foreign Secretary, Jack Straw, for example, told the House of Commons that 'we never, ever, said that there was an imminent threat', and claimed that instead he had merely said there was a 'clear and present danger'. See House of Commons *Official Report*, 22 October 2003, Column 677. In Washington, Defense Secretary, Donald Rumsfeld told an interviewer 'You and a few other critics are the only people I've heard use the phrase immediate threat. I didn't, the President didn't. And it's become kind of folklore that that's what happened.'

**Chapter 15**

1. The author wishes to acknowledge the contribution of Professor Theo Farrell, who co-authored earlier editions of this chapter, and to thank Emily Paddon for helpful feedback and Jason Kwon for excellent research assistance.

# Bibliography

Abadie, A. and J. Gardeazabal (2004) *Terrorism and the World Economy*. Cambridge, MA: Center for International Development.

Abrahms, M. (2004) 'Are Terrorists Really Rational? The Palestinian Example', *Orbis* 48(3): 533–49.

Abrahms, M. (2006) 'Why Terrorism Does Not Work', *International Security* 31(2) (Fall): 42–78.

Acharya, A. (2004) 'How Ideas Spread: Whose Norms Matter? Norm Localization and Institutional Change in Asian Regionalism', *International Organization* 58(2): 239–75.

Adamsky, D. (2010) *Culture of Military Innovation: The Impact of Cultural Factors on the Revolution in Military Affairs in Russia, the US, and Israel*. Palo Alto, CA: Stanford University Press.

Addington, L. H. (1994) *The Patterns of War since the Eighteenth Century*, 2nd edn. Bloomington, IN: Indiana University Press.

Adefuye, A. (1992) *Culture and Foreign Policy: The Nigerian Example*. Lagos: Nigerian Institute of International Affairs.

Agnew, J. (2003) *Geopolitics: Re-visioning World Politics*. London: Routledge.

al-Zawahiri, A. (2001) *Knights Under the Prophet's Banner*. Available at http://www.fas.org/irp/world/para/ayman_bk.html

al-Zawahiri, A. (2005) 'Letter from al-Zawahiri to Zarqawi', translated by the Foreign Broadcast Information Service, October.

Allison, G. (2004) *Nuclear Terrorism: The Ultimate Preventable Catastrophe*. New York: Times Books.

Almond, G. and S. Verba (1965) *The Civic Culture: Political Attitudes and Democracy in Five Nations*. Boston, MA: Little, Brown & Co.

Alterman, J. F. (2013) 'Statement for the U.S.-China Economic and Security Review Commission: China in the Middle East'. Washington, DC: Center for Strategic and International Studies.

American Society of International Law (1994) United States: *Administration Policy on Reforming Multilateral Peace Operations*. Washington, DC: American Society of International Law.

Anderson, W. F. (2009) 'Effects-based Operations: Combat Proven', *Joint Force Quarterly* 52 (1st quarter): 78–81.

Angell, N. (1914) *The Great Illusion*. London: Heinemann.

Annan, K. (1999) *Statement on receiving the report of the Independent Inquiry into the Actions of the United Nations during the 1994 Genocide in Rwanda*. 16 December. Available at http://www.un.org/News/ossg/sgsm_rwanda.htm

Anthony, I. and A. D. Rotfeld (eds) (2001) *A Future Arms Control Agenda*. Oxford: Oxford University Press.

Archer, C., J. Ferris, H. Herwig, and T. Travers (2002) *A World History of Warfare*. Lincoln, NE: University of Nebraska Press.

Ardrey, R. (1966) *The Territorial Imperative*. New York: Atheneum.

Arend, A. C. and R. J. Beck (1993) *International Law and the Use of Force: Beyond the Charter Paradigm*. London: Routledge.

Arkin, W. M. (1998) *The Internet and Strategic Studies*. Washington, DC: SAIS, Center for Strategic Education.

Aron, Raymond (1966) *Peace and War: A Theory of International Relations*. New York: Doubleday.

Arquilla, J. and D. Ronfeldt (eds) (1997) *In Athena's Camp: Preparing for Conflict in the Information Age*. Santa Monica, CA: RAND

Arquilla, J. and D. Ronfeldt (eds) (2001) *Networks and Netwars*. Santa Monica, CA: RAND. http://www.rand.org/publications/MR/MR1382/

Aussaresses, P. (2005) *The Battle of the Casbah: Terrorism and Counter-Terrorism in Algeria, 1955-1957*. New York: Enigma.

Autesserre, S. (2014) *Peaceland: Conflict Resolution and the Everyday Politics of International Intervention*. Cambridge: Cambridge University Press.

Bacevich, A. J. (1986) *The Pentomic Era: The US Army between Korea and Vietnam*. Washington, DC: National Defense University Press.

Ball, D. (ed.) (1993) *Strategic Culture in the Asia-Pacific Region (with Some Implications for Regional Security Cooperation)*. Canberra: Strategic and Defence Studies Centre, Australian National University.

Banchoff, T. (1999) *The German Problem Transformed: Institutions, Politics and Foreign Policy, 1945–1995*. Ann Arbor, MI: University of Michigan Press.

Banerjee, S. (1997) 'The Cultural Logic of National Identity Formation: Contending Discourses in Late Colonial India'. In V. M. Hudson (ed.) *Culture and Foreign Policy*. Boulder, CO: Lynne Rienner.

Barkawi, T. (1998) 'Strategy as a Vocation: Weber, Morgenthau and Modern Strategic Studies', *Review of International Studies* 24: 159–84.

Barkawi, T. and M. Laffey (2006) 'The Postcolonial Moment in Security Studies', *Review of International Studies* 32(4): 329–52.

Barkawi, T. and M. Laffey (2011) 'From War to Security: Security Studies, the Wider Agenda and the Fate of the Study of War', *Millennium: Journal of International Studies* 39(3): 701–6.

Barnaby, F. (2004) *How to Build a Nuclear Bomb: And Other Weapons of Mass Destruction.* New York: Nation Books.

Barnes, R. (2005) 'Of Vanishing Points and Paradoxes: Terrorism and International Humanitarian Law'. In R. Burchill, N. D. White, and J. Morris (eds) *International Conflict and Security Law: Essays in Memory of Hilaire McCoubery.* Cambridge: Cambridge University Press.

Barnett, T. P. M. (2004) *The Pentagon's New Map: War and Peace in the Twenty-first Century.* New York: Berkeley Books.

Barnett, T. P. M. (2009) *Great Powers: America and the World after Bush.* New York: G. P. Putnam's Sons.

Barnett, T.P.M. (2011) 'Globoglobalization glossary: Grand Strategy', available at http://thomaspmbarnett.com/glossary/ (accessed 12/12/2014).

Baylis, J. (2001) 'The Continuing Relevance of Strategic Studies in the Post-Cold War Era', *Defence Studies* 1(2): 1–14.

Baylis, J., S. Smith and P. Owens (2014) *The Globalization of World Politics: An Introduction to International Relations*, 6th edn. Oxford: Oxford University Press.

Baylis, J., K. Booth, J. Garnett, and P. Williams (1987) *Contemporary Strategy.* New York: Holmes & Meier.

BBC (2005) 'IAEA Urged to Refer Tehran to the UN', BBC news 19 September 2005. Available at http://www.bbc.news.co.ik/l.hi/world/middle_east/4259018.stm

BBC (2009) 'Stakes High for Obama on Iran', BBC news 15 January 2009. Available at http://www.bbc.news.co.ik/l.hi/world/middle_east/7829313.stm

Beam, L. (1992) *Leaderless Resistance.* Available at http://www.crusader.net/texts/bt/bt04.html

Beaufre, A. (1965a) *An Introduction to Strategy.* London: Faber & Faber.

Beaufre, A. (1965b) *Deterrence and Strategy.* London: Faber & Faber.

Beckett, I. F. W. (2001) *Modern Insurgencies and Counter-insurgencies: Guerrillas and their Opponents since 1750.* London: Routledge.

Belissa, M. & P. Leclerq (2001) 'The Revolutionary Period, 1789–1802'. In A. Hartmann and B. Heuser (eds), *War, Peace and World Orders from Antiquity until the 20th Century.* London: Routledge.

Bellamy, A. J., P. Williams, and S. Griffin (2010) *Understanding Peacekeeping.* 2nd edn. Cambridge: Polity.

Bellamy, A. J. and P.D. Williams (2011) 'The New Politics of Protection? Cote d'Ivoire, Libya, and the Responsibility to Protect', *International Affairs* 87(4): 825–50.

Benedict, R. (1946) *The Chrysanthemum and the Sword.* Boston, MA: Houghton Mifflin.

Benjamin, D. and S. Simon (2005) *The Next Attack.* New York: Times Books.

Benson, P. (2012) 'Intelligence Budget Continues to Drop', CNN Security Blog, 30 October, available at http:security.blogs.cnn.com/2012/10/30/intelligence-budget-drops-for-first-time-since-911/

Berdal, M. and M. Serrano (eds) (2002) *Transnational Organized Crime and International Security.* Boulder, CO: Lynne Rienner.

Bergen, J. D. (1986) *Military Communications: A Test for Technology.* Washington, DC: Center of Military History.

Berger, T. U. (1998) *Cultures of Antimilitarism: National Security in Germany and Japan.* Baltimore, MD: Johns Hopkins University Press.

Bernstein, P. (2008) 'International Partnerships to Combat Weapons of Mass Destruction', Occasional Papers 6. Washington DC: National Defense University Center for the Study of Weapons of Mass Destruction.

Berntsen, G. and R. Pezzullo (2006) *Jawbreaker: The Attack on Bin Laden and Al-Qaeda: A Personal Account by the CIA's Key Field Commander.* New York, NY: Crown Publishers.

Best, G. (1982) *War and Society in Revolutionary Europe, 1770-1870.* London: Fontana.

Betts, R. K. (1997) 'Should Strategic Studies Survive?', *World Politics* 50(1) (October): 7–33.

Betts, R. K. (1998). 'The New Threat of Mass Destruction', *Foreign Affairs* 77(1): 30–1.

Betts, R. K. (2007) *Enemies of Intelligence: Knowledge and Power in American National Security.* New York: Columbia University Press.

Betz, D. J. and T. C. Stevens (2012) *Cyberspace and the State: Towards a Strategy for Cyberpower.* Abingdon, Oxon: Routledge.

Beyerchen, A. (1996) 'From Radio to Radar: Interwar Military Adaptation to Technological Change in Germany, the United Kingdom and the United States'. In W. Murray and A. R. Millett (eds) *Military Innovation in the Interwar Period.* Cambridge: Cambridge University Press.

Biddle, S. (2002) *Afghanistan and the Future of Warfare: Implications for Army and Defense Policy.* Carlisle, PA: US Army War College Strategic Studies Institute.

Biddle, S. (2003a) 'Afghanistan and the Future of Warfare', *Foreign Affairs* 82(2): 31–46.

Biddle, S. (2003b) Operation Iraqi Freedom: Outside Perspectives. Testimony before the House Armed Services Committee, 21 October.

Biddle, S. (2004) *Military Power: Explaining Victory and Defeat in Modern Battle*. Princeton, NJ: Princeton University Press.

Biddle, S. (2005) *American Grand Strategy After 9/11: An Assessment*. Carlisle, PA: US Army War Studies Strategic Studies Institute. Available at http://www.strategicstudiesinstitute.army.mil/pubs/display.cfm?pubID = 603

Bidwell, S. D. Graham (1985) *Firepower: British Army Weapons and Theories of War, 1904-1945* London: Allen and Unwin.

Black, J. (2001) *War*. London: Continuum.

Black, J. (2002) *Warfare in the Western World, 1882–1975*. Chesham: Acumen.

Blair, D. (2009) *Remarks of Director of National Intelligence*, Commonwealth Club of San Francisco, 15 September available at http://www.dni.gov/speeches/20090915_speech.pdf

Blomberg, S., G. Hess and A. Orphanides (2004) 'The Macroeconomic Consequences of Terrorism', Working Paper No. 1151 Munich: CESIFO.

Booth, K. (1979) *Strategy and Ethnocentrism*. London: Croom Helm.

Booth, K. (1981) *Strategy and Ethnocentrism*. New York: Holmes and Meier.

Booth, K. (1997) 'Security and Self: Reflections of a Fallen Realist'. In K. Krause and M. C. Williams (eds) *Critical Security Studies: Concepts and Cases*. London: UCL Press.

Booth, K. (2005) 'Beyond Critical Security Studies'. In K. Booth (ed.) *Critical Security Studies and World Politics*. Boulder, CO: Lynne Rienner.

Booth, K. and E. Herring (1994) *Keyguide to Information Sources in Strategic Studies*. London: Mansell.

Booth, K. and R. Trood (eds) (1999) *Strategic Culture in the Asia-Pacific*. New York: Macmillan.

Boulding, K. (1956) *The Image*. Ann Arbor, MI: University of Michigan Press.

Boyes, R. (2014) 'Powerful Message to Putin', *The Times*, 15 November.

Bracken, P.B. (2012) *The Second Nuclear Age: Strategy, Danger, and the New Power Politics*. New York: Times Books.

Brands, H. (2014) *What Good Is Grand Strategy? Power and Purpose in American Statecraft from Harry S. Truman to George W. Bush*. Ithaca, NY: Cornell University Press.

Brenner, S. W. (2009) *Cyberthreats: The Emerging Fault Lines of the Nation State*. New York: Oxford University Press.

Brent, J. and V. P. Naumov (2003) *Stalin's Last Crime: The Plot Against the Jewish Doctors, 1948–1953*. New York: Perennial.

Breuning, M. (1997) 'Culture, History, Role: Belgian and Dutch Axioms and Foreign Assistance Policy'. In V. M. Hudson (ed.) *Culture and Foreign Policy*. Boulder, CO: Lynne Rienner Publishers.

Brodie, B. (1946) *The Absolute Weapon*. Harcourt, Brace & Co.

Brodie, B. (1959) *Strategy in the Missile Age*. Princeton, NJ: Princeton University Press.

Brodie, B. (1973) *War and Politics*. London: Cassell; New York: Macmillan.

Brownlie, I. (1963) *International Law and the Use of Force by States*. Oxford: Clarendon Press.

Brownlie, I. (1990) *Principles of Public International Law*. Oxford: Oxford University Press.

Brunt, P. A. (1965a) 'Spartan Policy and Strategy in the Archidamian War', *Phoenix* 19(4) (Winter): 255–80.

Brunt, P. A. (1965b) 'The Aims of Alexander' *Greece & Rome* 12: 205–15.

Brzezinski, Z. (1997) *The Grand Chessboard: American Primacy and Its Geostrategic Imperatives*. New York: Basic Books.

Bull, H. (1961) *The Control of the Arms Race*. London: Weidenfeld & Nicolson.

Bull, H. (1968) 'Strategic Studies and its Critics', *World Politics* 20(4): 593–605.

Bull, H. (1977) *The Anarchical Society: A Study of Order in World Politics*. London: Macmillan.

Bunn, E. (2007) 'Can Deterrence Be Tailored?', *Strategic Forum*. Paper No. 225. Institute for National Security Studies. Washington, DC: National Defense University.

Burchill, S., R. Devetak, A. Linklater, M. Patterson, C. Reus-Smit, and J. True (2005) *Theories of International Relations*, 3rd edn. London: Macmillan.

Burkard, S., D. Howlett, H. Müller and B. Tertrais (2005) 'Effective Non-Proliferation: The European Union and the 2005 NPT Review Conference'. Chaillot Paper No. 72. Paris: EU-ISS.

Busmiller, E. (2011) 'Videotapes From Bin Laden's Hide-out Released', *New York Times*, 7 May, available at www.nytimes.com/2011/05/08/world/asia/08intel.html

Butcher, M. (2003) *What Wrongs Our Arms May Do: The Role of Nuclear Weapons in Counterproliferation*. Washington, DC: Physicians for Social Responsibility. Available at http://www.psr.org/documents/psr_doc_0/program_4/PSRwhatwrong03.pdf

Butterfield, H. (1952) *History and Human Relations*. London: Collins.

Butterfield, H. and M. Wight (1966) *Diplomatic Investigations*. London: Allen & Unwin.

Buzan, B. and L. Hansen (2009) *The Evolution of International Security*. Cambridge: Cambridge University Press.

Buzan, B. and E. Herring (1998) *The Arms Dynamic in World Politics.* London: Lynne Rienner.

Byers, M. (2000) *The Role of Law in International Politics: Essays in International Relations and International Law.* Oxford: Oxford University Press.

Byers, M. (2004) 'Agreeing to Disagree: Security Council Resolution 1441 and International Ambiguity', *Global Governance* 10(2): 165–86.

Byman, D. A. and M. C. Waxman (2000) 'Kosovo and the Great Air Power Debate', *International Security* 24(4) (Spring): 14.

Caldicott, H. (1986) *Missile Envy: The Arms Race and Nuclear War.* Toronto: Bantam.

Callwell, C. E. (1899) *Small Wars: Their Principles and Practice.* London: Her Majesty's Stationery Office.

Calvert, J. (2004) 'The Mythic Foundations of Radical Islam', *Orbis* 48 (Winter): 29–41.

Carr, E. H. (1942) *Conditions of Peace.* London: Macmillan & Co.

Carr, E. H. (1946) *The Twenty Years' Crisis 1919–1939,* 2nd edn. London: Macmillan.

Carr, J. (2010) *Inside Cyber Warfare.* Sebastopol, CA: O'Reilly Media.

Carter, A. and L. C. Johnson (2001) 'Beyond the Counterproliferation Initiative'. In H. Sokolski and J. Ludes, *Twenty-First Century Weapons Proliferation.* London: Frank Cass.

Cartwright, Gen. J. E., USMC (n.d.) 'Memorandum for Chiefs of the Military Services, Commanders of the Combatant Commands, Directors of the Joint Staff Directorates. Subject: Joint Terminology for Cyberspace Operations.' Washington, DC: The Vice-Chairman of the Joint Chiefs of Staff.

Carvin, S. (2008) 'Linking Purpose and Tactics: America and the Reconsideration of the Laws of War During the 1990s', *International Studies Perspective* 9(2): 128–43.

Cashman, G. (1993) *What Causes War? An Introduction to Conflict.* New York: Lexington Books.

Castells, M. (1998) *The End of Millennium, iii. The Information Age, Economy, Society and Culture.* Oxford: Blackwell.

Cebrowski, A. and J. Garstka (1998) 'Network-Centric Warfare: Its Origin and Future', *U.S. Naval Institute Proceedings* 124(1): 29.

Cénat, Jean-Philippe (2010): *Le roi stratège: Louis XIV et la direction de la guerre, 1661–1715.* Rennes: Presses Universitaires.

Center for the Study of Intelligence (2004) *Intelligence and Policy: The Evolving Relationship, Roundtable Report,* 10 November. Washington, DC: Georgetown University.

Cerny, P. (1986) 'Globalization and the Disarticulation of Political Power: Towards a New Middle Ages', *Civil Wars* 1(1): 65–102.

Cha, V. D. (2000) 'Globalization and the Study of International Security', *Journal of Peace Research* 37(3): 391–403.

Chandler, D. G. (ed.) (1988) *The Military Maxims of Napoleon,* translated by G. C. D'Aguilar. New York: Macmillan.

Chayes, S. (2007) *The Punishment of Virtue.* London: Portobello Books.

Chivers, C. J. (2010) *The Gun.* New York: Simon & Schuster.

Churchill, W. (1926) *The World Crisis, 1911–1914.* New York: Charles Scribner's Sons.

Cimbala, S. J. (1997) *The Politics of Warfare: The Great Powers in the Twentieth Century.* University Park, PA: Pennsylvania State University Press.

Cirincione, J., J. B. Wolfsthal and M. Rajkumar (2005) *Deadly Arsenals: Nuclear, Biological and Chemical Threats,* 2nd edn. Washington, DC: Carnegie Endowment for International Peace.

Clapham, C. (1998) 'Being Peacekept'. In O. Furley and R. May (eds), *Peacekeeping in Africa.* Aldershot: Ashgate.

Clarke, A. C. (1970) 'Superiority'. In A. C. Clarke, *Expedition to Earth.* New York: Harcourt, Brace & World.

Clarke, R. A. and R. K. Knake (2010) *Cyber War: The Next Threat to National Security and What to Do About It.* New York: Ecco.

Claude, I. L. ([1832] 1962) *Power and International Relations.* New York: Random House.

Clausewitz, C. von (1976) *On War,* translated and edited by M. Howard and P. Paret. Princeton, NJ: Princeton University Press.

Clausewitz, C. von (1982) *On War.* Harmondsworth: Penguin.

Clausewitz, C. von (1989) *On War,* edited and translated by M. Howard and P. Paret. Princeton, NJ: Princeton University Press.

Clausewitz, C. von (1993) *On War,* edited and translated by M. Howard and P. Paret. London: Everyman's Library.

Cline, L. (2005) *Psuedo Operations and Counterinsurgency: Lessons from Other Countries.* Carlisle, PA: Strategic Studies Institute. Available at http://www.strategicstudies-institute.army.mil/pubs/display.cfm?PubID 607

Clinton, W. J. (1992) cited in: 'New York Times, the 1992 campaign, excerpts from speech by Clinton on US role', published 2 October 1992, available at http://www.nytimes.com/1992/10/02/us/the-1992-campaign-excerpts-from-speech-by-clinton-on-us-role.html (accessed 12/12/14).

Clutterbuck, R. (1990) *Terrorism and Guerrilla Warfare: Forecasts and Remedies*. London: Routledge.

Cohen, E. A. (1996) 'A Revolution in Warfare', *Foreign Affairs* 75(2) (March/April): 37–54.

Cohen, E. A. (2002) *Supreme Command: Soldiers, Statesmen, and Leadership in Wartime*. New York: Free Press.

Cohen, S. (2002) *India, Emerging Power*. Washington, DC: Brookings Institution Press.

Cohn, C. (1987) 'Sex and Death in the Rational World of Defense Intellectuals', *Signs: Journal of Women in Culture and Society* 12(4): 687–718.

Cohn, C. (1993) 'Wars, Wimps, and Women: Talking Gender and Thinking War'. In M. Cooke and A. Woollacott (eds) *Gendering War Talk*. Princeton NJ: Princeton University Press.

Collins, A. (1998) 'GRIT, Gorbachev and the End of the Cold War', *Review of International Studies*, 24(2) (April): 201–19.

Congressional Budget Office (2005) *Federal Funding for Homeland Security: An Update*. Available at http://www.cbo.gov/ftpdocs/65xx/doc6566/7-20-HomelandSecurity.pdf

Contamine, P. (1986) *La Guerre au Moyen Age*, 2nd revised edn. Paris: Presses Universitaires de France; Engl translation of the first edition (1984) *War in the Middle Ages* translated by M. Jones. Oxford: Blackwell.

Cordesman, A. H. (2002) *The Lessons of Afghanistan, Warfighting, Intelligence, Force Transformation,Coun terproliferation and Arms Control*. Washington, DC: Center for Strategic and International Studies.

Cordesman, A. H. (2003a) *The 'Instant Lessons' of the Iraq War, Main Report, Seventh Working Draft*. Washington, DC: Center for Strategic and International Studies.

Cordesman, A. H. (2003b) *The Iraq War: Strategy, Tactics and Military Lessons*. Washington, DC: Center for Strategic and International Studies.

Cordesman, A. H. (2004) *The War After the War: Strategic Lessons of Iraq and Afghanistan*. Washington, DC: Center for Strategic and International Studies.

Cornish, P. and G. Edwards (2001) 'Beyond the EU/NATO Dichotomy: The Beginnings of a European Strategic Culture', *International Affairs* 77(3): 587.

Cornish, P. and G. Edwards (2005) 'The Strategic Culture of the European Union: A Progress Report', *International Affairs* 81(4): 801–20.

Creveld, M. van (1989) *Technology and War from 2000 B.C. to the Present*. New York: Free Press.

Creveld, M. van (1991) *The Transformation of War*. New York: Free Press.

Croft, S. (1996) *Strategies of Arms Control: A History and Typology*. Manchester: Manchester University Press.

Cronin, A. K. (2002/3) 'Behind the Curve: Globalization and International Terrorism', *International Security* 27(3) (Winter): 30–58.

Cronin, A. K. (2011) *How Terrorism Ends: Understanding the Decline and Demise of Terrorist Campaigns*. Princeton, NJ: Princeton University Press.

Crowl, P. A. (1987) 'The Strategist's Short Catechism: Six Questions without Answers'. In G. E. Thibault (ed.) *Dimensions of Military Strategy*. Washington, DC: US Government Printing Office for National Defense University.

Cruz, C. (2000) 'Identity and Persuasion: How Nations Remember their Pasts and Make their Futures', *World Politics* 52(3): 275–312.

Daalder, I. and T. Terry (eds) (1993) *Rethinking the Unthinkable: New Directions in Nuclear Arms Control*. London: Frank Cass.

Danchev, A. (1999) 'Liddell Hart and the Direct Approach', *The Journal of Military History* 63(2): 313–37.

Daudet, L. (1918) *La guerre totale*. Paris: Nouvelle Librairie.

Davis, Z. S. (1994) *US Counterproliferation Policy: Issues for Congress. CRS Report for Congress*. Washington, DC: Congressional Research Service.

Dawkins, R. (1976) *The Selfish Gene*. Oxford: Oxford University Press.

De Castro, R. C. (2014) 'Philippine Strategic Culture: Continuity in the Face of Changing Regional Dynamics', *Contemporary Security Policy* 35(2): 249–69.

De Vol, R. and P. Wong (2005) *Economic Impacts of Katrina*. Santa Monica, CA: Milken Institute.

Debray, R. (1968) *Revolution in the Revolution: Armed Struggle and Political Struggle in Latin America*. London: Pelican.

Demchak, C. C. (2011) *Wars of Disruption and Resilience: Cybered Conflict, Power, and National Security*. Athens, GA: The University of Georgia Press.

Denning, D. (1999) *Information Warfare and Security*. New York: ACM Press.

Department of the Army (1994) *US Army Field Manual 100-23: Peace Operations*. Washington, DC.

Department of the Army (2007) *FM 3-24, Counterinsurgency Field Manual*. Chicago, IL: University of Chicago Press.

Department of Defense Directive 3000.07 (2008) *Irregular Warfare (IW)*.

Department of Homeland Security (2007a) *After Action Quick Look Report*. Available at http://www.fema.gov/pdf/media/2008/t4_after%20action_report.pdf

Department of Homeland Security (2007b) TOPOFF 4 Frequently Asked Questions. Available at http://www.dhs.gov/xprepresp/training/gc_1179422026237.shtm

Department of Justice (2004) *A Review of the FBI's Handling of Intelligence Information Related to the September 11 Attacks*. Washington, DC: Office of the Inspector General, November, redacted and unclassified: released publicly June 2005.

Deptula, D. A. (2001) *Effects-Based Operations: Change in the Nature of Warfare*. Arlington, VA: Aerospace Education Foundation.

Desch, M. C. (1998) 'Culture Clash: Assessing the Importance of Ideas in Security Studies', *International Security* 23(1) (Summer): 141–70.

Diehl, P. F. and N. P. Gleditsch (2000) *Environmental Conflict: An Anthology*. Boulder, CO: Westview.

Director of National Intelligence (2005) *The National Intelligence Strategy of the United States: Transformation Through Integration and Innovation*. Washington, DC: Director of National Intelligence.

Director of National Intelligence (2007) *The 100 Day Plan: Integration and Collaboration*. Washington, DC: Director of National Intelligence.

Director of National Intelligence (2009) *National Intelligence Strategy*, August, available at http://www.nytimes.com/2011/09/30/business/global/germany-parliament-votes-to-expand-euro-bailout-und.html?_r=1

Director of National Intelligence (2010) *News Release*. NR-21-10, 28 October.

Director of National Intelligence (2014) *The National Intelligence Strategy of the United States*, September, available at http://www.dni.gov/files/documents/2014_NIS_Publication.pdf

Dixon, C. A. and O. Heilbrunn (1962) *Communist Guerrilla Warfare*. New York: Praeger.

Dobbie, C. (1994) 'A Concept for Post-Cold War Peacekeeping', *Survival*, 36(3) (Autumn): 121–48.

Dorn, A. W. (2011) *Keeping Watch: Monitoring, Technology, and Innovation in UN Peace Operations*. Tokyo: UN University Press.

Doubler, M. (1994) *Closing with the Enemy: How the G.I.s Fought the War in Europe, 1944–1945*, Lawrence: University Press of Kansas.

Douhet, G. (1983) *The Command of the Air*, translated by D. Ferrari. Washington, DC: New York, Coward-McCann; previously published New York, 1942.

Doyle, M. W. (1983) 'Kant, Liberal Legacies and Foreign Affairs', *Philosophy and Public Affairs* 12: 205–35.

Doyle, M. W. (1986) 'Liberalism and World Politics', *American Political Science Review* 80: 1151–69.

Dueck, C. (2004) 'The Grand Strategy of the United States, 2000–2004', *Review of International Studies* 30(4) (October): 511–35.

Duffield, J. S. (1999a) *World Power Forsaken: Political Culture, International Institutions and German Security Policy after Unification*. Stanford, CA: Stanford University Press.

Duffield, J. S. (1999b) 'Political Culture and State Behavior', *International Organization* 53(4): 765–804.

Duffy, H. (2005) *The 'War on Terror' and the Framework of International Law*. Cambridge: Cambridge University Press.

Dunn, D. J. (1991) 'Peace Research Versus Strategic Studies'. In K. Booth (ed.) *New Thinking About Strategy and International Security*. London: Harper Collins.

Earle, E. (1943) *Makers of Modern Strategy: Military Thought from Machiavelli to Hitler*. Princeton, NJ: Princeton University Press.

Ebel, R. H., R. Taras, and J. D. Cochrane (1991) *Political Culture and Foreign Policy in Latin America: Case Studies from the Circum-Caribbean*. Albany, NY: State University of New York.

Eckstein, H. (1998) 'A Culturalist Theory of Political Change', *American Political Science Review* 82: 790–802.

Eden, L. (2004) *Whole World on Fire: Organizations, Knowledge, and Nuclear Weapons Devastation*. Ithaca, NY: Cornell University Press.

Ellis, J. (2003) 'The Best Defence: Counterproliferation and US National Security', *Washington Quarterly* 26(2): 115–33.

Enders, W. and T. Sandler (2004). 'What do We Know about the Substitution Effect in Transnational Terrorism?' In A. Silke and Gilardi (eds) *Terrorism Research*. London: Frank Cass.

Enthoven, A. C. and K. V. Smith (2005) *How Much is Enough? Shaping the Defense Program, 1961–1969*. Santa Monica, CA: RAND.

Ermarth, F. (2009) 'Russian Strategic Culture in Flux: Back to the Future?' In J. L. Johnson, K. M. Kartchner, and J. A. Larsen (eds) *Strategic Culture and Weapons of Mass Destruction: Culturally Based Insights into Comparative National Security Policymaking*. London: Palgrave Macmillan.

Esdaile, C. (2008) 'De-constructing the French Wars: Napoleon as anti-Strategist', *Journal of Strategic Studies* V 31(4): 512–52.

European Union (2003) *A Secure Europe in a Better World: European Security Strategy*. Available at http://ue.eu.int/uedocs/cmsUpload/78367.pdf

Fall, B. B. (1998) 'The Theory and Practice of Insurgency and Counterinsurgency', *Naval War College Review* 15(1): 46–57.

Farrell, T. (2001) 'Transnational Norms and Military Development: Constructing Ireland's Professional Army', *European Journal of International Relations* 7(1): 63–102.

Farrell, T. and T. Terriff (eds) (2001) *The Sources of Military Change: Culture, Politics, Technology*. Boulder, CO: Lynne Rienner.

Feinstein, L. and A-M. Slaughter (2004) 'A Duty to Prevent', *Foreign Affairs* 83(1): 136–50.

Feldman, S. (1982) 'The Bombing of Osiraq: Revisited', *International Security* 7(2) (Autumn): 114–42.

Feng, H. (2009) 'A Dragon on Defense: Explaining China's Strategic Culture'. In J. L. Johnson, K. M. Kartchner, and J. A. Larsen (eds) *Strategic Culture and Weapons of Mass Destruction: Culturally Based Insights into Comparative National Security Policymaking*. London: Palgrave Macmillan.

Ferris, J. (2004a) 'A New American Way of War? C4ISR, Intelligence and IO in Operation Iraqi Freedom, a Preliminary Assessment', *Intelligence and National Security* 14(1).

Ferris, J. (2004b) 'Netcentric Warfare and Information Operations: Revolution in the RMA?', *Intelligence and National Security* 14(3).

Findlay, T. (2002) *The Use of Force in UN Peace Operations*. Oxford: Oxford University Press.

Fingar, T. (2011) *Reducing Uncertainty: Intelligence and National Security* (Stanford, CA: Stanford University Press).

Fischer, D. H. (1970) *Historians' Fallacies: Toward a Logic of Historical Thought*. New York: Harper and Row.

Fleck, D. (ed.) (2008) *The Handbook of International Humanitarian Law*, 2nd edn. Oxford: Oxford University Press.

Florida International University (2010) *Comparative Strategic Cultures Project*. Applied Research Center. http://strategicculture.fiu.edu/Studies.aspx

Flynn, F. (2007) *America the Vulnerable and The Edge of Disaster: Rebuilding a Resilient Nation*. London: Random House.

Flynn, M., M. Pottinger, and P. Batchelor et al. (2010) *Fixing Intel: A Blueprint for Making Intelligence Relevant in Afghanistan*. Washington, DC: Center for New American Security, January, available at http://www.cnas.org/files/documents/publications/AfghanIntel_Flynn_Jan2010_code507_voices.pdf

Flynn, S. (2004) *America the Vulnerable: How Our Government is Failing to Protect us from Terrorism*. New York: Harper Collins.

Flynn, S. (2007) *The Edge of Disaster: Rebuilding a Resilient Nation*. New York: Random House.

Fontenot, G., E. J. Degen and D. Tohn (2004) *On Point: The United States Army in Operation Iraqi Freedom*. Fort Leavenworth, KS: US Army Training and Doctrine Command.

Forester, C. S. (1943) *The Ship*. Boston, MA: Little, Brown & Co.

Forsythe, D. (2008) 'The United States and International Humanitarian Law', *Journal of Human Rights* 7(1) (Spring): 25–33.

Fortna, V. P. (2003) 'Inside and Out: Peacekeeping and the Duration of Peace after Civil and Interstate Wars', *International Studies Review* 5(4): 97–114.

Fortna, V. P. (2008) *Does Peacekeeping Work? Shaping Belligerents' Choices After Civil War*. Princeton, NJ: Princeton University Press.

Fortna, V. P. and L. M. Howard (2008) 'Pitfalls and Prospects in the Peacekeeping Literature', *Annual Review of Political Science* 11: 283–301.

Foy, M. T. (2006) *Michael Collins' Intelligence War: The Struggle between the British and the IRA, 1919–1921*. Stroud, UK: Sutton Publishing.

Franck, T. M. (1990) *The Power of Legitimacy among Nations*. Oxford: Oxford University Press.

Franck, T. M. (2001) 'Terrorism and the Right to Self-Defense', *American Journal of International Law* 95(4): 839–43.

Franck, T. M. and N. S. Rodley (1973) 'After Bangladesh: The Law of Humanitarian Intervention by Force', *American Journal of International Law* 67(2): 275–305.

Freedman, L. (1986) 'The First Two Generations of Nuclear Strategists'. In P. Paret (ed.) *Makers of Modern Strategy: From Machiavelli to the Nuclear Age*. Oxford: Clarendon Press.

Freedman, L. (2003) 'Prevention, Not Preemption', *Washington Quarterly* 26(2): 105–14.

Freedman, L. (2004) *Deterrence*. Cambridge: Polity Press.

Freedman, L. (2004) *The Evolution of Nuclear Strategy*, 3rd edn. New York: St Martin's Press.

Freedman, L. (2006) *The Transformation of Strategic Affairs*, London: Routledge.

Freedman, L. (2013) *Strategy: A History*, Oxford: Oxford University Press.

Freud, S. (1932) 'Why War?'. In *The Standard Edition of the Complete Psychological Writings of Sigmund Freud*, *xxii, 197–215*. London: Hogarth Press.

Freud, S. (1968). 'Why War?'. In L. Bramson and G. W. Geothals, *War: Studies from Psychology, Sociology, Anthropology*. New York and London: Basic Books.

Friedman, N. (2000) *Seapower and Space: From the Dawn of the Missile Age to Net-Centric Warfare*. Annapolis, MD: Naval Institute Press.

Friedman, N. (2003) *Terrorism, Afghanistan and America's New Way of War*. Washington, DC: US Naval Institute Press.

Friedman, T. (2002) *Longitudes and Attitudes: Exploring the World After September 11*. New York: Farrar Straus & Giroux.

Fukuyama, Francis (1999) 'Second Thoughts', *The National Interest* 56 (Summer): 16–33.

Fuller, J. F. C. (1926) *The Foundations of the Science of War*. London: Hutchinson.

Fuller, J. F. C. (1932) *The Dragon's Teeth; A Study of War and Peace*. London: Constable.

Fuller, J. F. C. (1942) *Machine Warfare: An Enquiry into the Influences of Mechanics on the Art of War*. London: Hutchinson.

Fuller, J. F. C. (1945) *Armament and History; A Study of the Influence of Armament on History from the Dawn of Classical Warfare to the Second World War*. New York: Charles Scribner's Sons.

Gaddis, J. L. (1986) 'The Long Peace: Elements of Stability in the Postwar International System', *International Security* 10(4): 99–142.

Gaddis, J. L. (2002) *The Landscape of History: How Historians Map the Past*. Oxford: Oxford University Press.

Galula, D. (1964) *Counterinsurgency Warfare*. New York: Praeger.

Ganor, B. (2005) *The Counter-Terrorism Puzzle: A Guide for Decision Makers*. New Brunswick, NJ: Transaction.

Garcia Fitz, F. (1998) '¿Hube estrategia en la edad media? A propósito de las relaciones castellano-musulmanas durante la segunda mitad del siglo XIII', in *Revista da Faculdade de Lettras*, Series II 15(2): 837–54.

Garnett, J. C. (1987) 'Strategic Studies and its Assumptions'. In J. Baylis, K. Booth, J. Garnett, and P. Williams, *Contemporary Strategy: Theories and Policies*, 2nd edn. London: Croom Helm.

Gat, A. (1992) *The Development of Military Thought: The Nineteenth Century*. Oxford: Oxford University Press.

Gat, A. (1993) *Clausewitz and the Enlightenment: The Origins of Modern Military Thought*. Oxford: Oxford University Press.

Gates, D. (2003) *Sky Wars: A History of Military Aerospace Power*. London: Reaktion Books.

Geertz, C. (1973) *The Interpretation of Cultures*. New York: Basic Books.

Gelpi, C., P. Feaver, and J. Reifler (2009) *Paying the Human Costs of War: American Public Opinion and Casualties in Military Conflicts*. Princeton University Press.

George, A.L. (2003) 'The Need for Influence Theory and Actor-Specific Behavioral Models of Adversaries'. In B. R. Schneider and J. M. Post (eds) *Know Thy Enemy: Profiles of Adversary Leaders and Their Strategic Cultures*. Alabama, GA: US Air Force Counterproliferation Center.

George, R. Z. and J. Bruce (eds) (2008) *Analyzing Intelligence: Origins, Obstacles, and Innovations*. Washington, DC: Georgetown University Press.

Gibson, W. (1984) *Neuromancer*. New York: Ace Books.

Giles, G. F. (2003) 'The Crucible of Radical Islam: Iran's Leaders and Strategic Culture'. In B. R. Schneider and J. M. Post (eds) *Know Thy Enemy: Profiles of Adversary Leaders and Their Strategic Cultures*. Alabama, GA: US Air Force Counterproliferation Center.

Gillingham, J. (1992) 'War and Chivalry in the History of William the Marshal', reprinted in M. Strickland (ed.), *Anglo-Saxon Warfare: Studies in Late Anglo-Saxon and Anglo-Norman Military Organisation and Warfare*. Woodbridge: Boydell Press.

Gilpin, R. (1981) *War and Change in World Politics*. Cambridge: Cambridge University Press.

Gladwell, M. (2010) 'Small Change: Why the Revolution Will Not be Tweeted', *The New Yorker*, 4 October.

Glantz, D. and J. House (1995) *When Titans Clashed: How the Red Army Stopped Hitler*. Lawrence: University Press of Kansas.

Glatthaar, J. T. (2008) *General Lee's Army: From Victory to Collapse*. New York: The Free Press.

Gleditsch, N. P. (2012) 'Whither the Weather? Climate Change and Conflict', *Journal of Peace Research* 49(1): 3–9.

Glenn, J. (2009) 'Realism versus Strategic Culture: Competition and Collaboration?' *International Studies Review* 11: 523–51.

Glenn, J., D. Howlett, and S. Poore (eds) (2004) *Neorealism versus Strategic Culture*. London: Ashgate.

Goldman, E. O. (2003) 'Introduction: Security in the Information Age'. In E. O. Goldman (ed.) 'National Security in the Information Age', special issue, *Contemporary Security Policy* 24(1): 1.

Goldstone, J. A. (2002) 'Population and Security: How Demographic Change can Lead to Violent Conflict', *Journal of International Affairs* 56(1): 3–22.

Goldsworthy, A. (2001) *The Punic Wars*. London: Cassell.

Goodrich, L. M. and E. Hambro (1949) *Charter of the United Nations: Commentary and Documents*. Boston, MA: World Peace Foundation.

Gordon, M. (1990) 'Generals Favor "No Holds Barred" by U.S. if Iraq Attacks the Saudis', *The New York Times*, 25 August.

Gordon, M. and B. Trainor (2007) *Cobra II: The Inside Story of the Invasion and Occupation of Iraq*. New York: Vintage.

Gorman, S. (2011) 'Drones Evolve Into Weapon in Age of Terror: Intelligence Services Overcome Philosophical, Legal Misgivings Over Targeted Killings', *Wall Street Journal*, 8 September.

Gottman, J. (1948) 'Bugeaud, Gallieni, Lyautey: The Development of French Colonial Warfare'. In E. M. Earle (ed.) *Makers of Modern Strategy: Military Thought from Machiavelli to Hitler*. Princeton, NJ: Princeton University Press.

Government Accountability Office (2003) *Nuclear Security: NNSA Needs to Better Manage its Safeguards and Security Program*, GAO-03-471. Washington, DC: Government Accountability Office.

Government Accountability Office (2005) *Terrorist Financing: Better Strategic Planning Needed to Coordinate U.S. Efforts to Deliver Counter-Terrorism Financing Training and Technical Assistance Abroad*, GAO-06-19. Washington, DC: Government Accountability Office.

Gowans, A. L. (1914) *Selections from Treitschke's Lectures on Politics*. London and Glasgow: Gowans & Gray.

Graeger, N. and H. Leira (2005) 'Norwegian Strategic Culture after World War II: From a Local to a Global Perspective', *Cooperation and Conflict* 40(1): 45–66.

Grant, G. (2005) 'Network Centric: Blind Spot', *Defense News* 12 September: 1.

Gray, C. (2002) 'From Unity to Polarization: International Law and the Use of Force against Iraq', *European Journal of International Law* 13(1): 1–19.

Gray, C. (2008) *International Law and the Use of Force*, 3rd edn. Oxford: Oxford University Press.

Gray, C. S. (1981) 'National Style in Strategy: The American Example', *International Security* 6(2) (Fall): 35–7.

Gray, C. S. (1982a) *Strategic Studies and Public Policy: The American Experience*. Lexington, KY: The University Press of Kentucky.

Gray, C. S. (1982b) *Strategic Studies: A Critical Assessment*. London: Aldwych Press.

Gray, C. S. (1986) *Nuclear Strategy and National Style*. Lanham, MD: Hamilton Press.

Gray, C. S. (1992) *House of Cards: Why Arms Control Must Fail*. Ithaca, NY: Cornell University Press.

Gray, C. S. (1997) 'The American Revolution in Military Affairs: An Interim Assessment', *The Occasional*. Strategic and Combat Studies Institute, Wiltshire, UK.

Gray, C. S. (1999a) *Modern Strategy*. Oxford: Oxford University Press.

Gray, C. S. (1999b) *The Second Nuclear Age*. Boulder, CO: Lynne Rienner.

Gray, C. S. (2002) *Strategy for Chaos: Revolutions in Military Affairs and the Evidence of History*. London: Frank Cass.

Gray, C. S. (2010a) *The Strategy Bridge*. Oxford: Oxford University Press.

Gray, C. S. (2010b) 'Strategic Thoughts for Defence Planners', *Survival* 52(3): 159–78.

Gray, C. S. (2013) *Perspectives on Strategy*. Oxford: Oxford University Press.

Gray, C. S. (2014) *Strategy and Defence Planning: Meeting the Challenge of Uncertainty*. Oxford: Oxford University Press.

Gray, C. S. and K. B. Payne (1980) 'Victory is Possible', *Foreign Policy* 39: 14–27.

Gray, C. S. and G. Sloan (1999) *Geopolitics, Geography, and Strategy*. London: Routledge.

Green, J. (1986) *The A-Z of Nuclear Jargon*. New York: Routledge.

Green, M. J. and B. Gill, eds (2009) *Asia's New Multilateralism: Cooperation, Competition, and Search for Community*. New York: Columbia University Press.

Green, P. (1966) *Deadly Logic: The Theory of Nuclear Deterrence*. Columbus, OH: Ohio State University Press.

Greig, J. M. and P. F. Diehl (2005) 'The Peacekeeping-Peacemaking Dilemma', *International Studies Quarterly* 49(4): 621–45.

Griffith, S. (1961) *Mao Tse-Tung on Guerrilla Warfare*. New York: Praeger.

Groves, B. N. (2010) 'The Multiple Faces of Effective Grand Strategy', *Journal of Strategic Security* 3(2): 1–12.

Grygiel, J. J. (2006) *Great Powers and Geopolitical Change*. Baltimore, MD: Johns Hopkins University Press.

Grygiel, J. J. (2013) 'Educating for National Security', *Orbis*, 57(2): 201–16.

*Guardian, The* (2009) 'US fears that Iran has the Capability to build a nucler bomb', 2 March.

Guevara, C. (1997) *Guerrilla Warfare*, 3rd edn. Wilmington, DE: Scholarly Resources.

Guibert, C. (texts S of 1772 and 1790) in B. Heuser, translator and ed., *The Strategy Makers: Thoughts on War and Society from Machiavelli to Clausewitz*. Santa Barbara, CA: Praeger-ABC Clio.

Gwynn, C. W. (1934) *Imperial Policing*. London: Macmillan & Co.

Hagood, J. (2007) 'Towards a Policy of Nuclear Dissuasion: How Can Dissuasion Improve U.S. National Security?' In O. C. W. Price and J. Mackby (eds) *Debating 21st Century Nuclear Issues*. Washington, DC: Center for Strategic and International Studies.

Hamilton, A. (1992) *Parliamentary Debate*. Available at http://www.parliament.the-stationery-office.co.uk/pa/cmigg/2g3/cmhansrd/1992-06-29/writtens-6.html

Hammes, T. X. (2004) *The Sling and the Stone: On War in the 21st Century*. St Paul, MI: Zenith Press.

Handel, M. I. (1994) 'The Evolution of Israeli Strategy: The Psychology of Insecurity and the Quest for Absolute Security'. In W. Murray, M. Knox, and A. Bernstein (eds) *The Making of Strategy: Rulers, Wars and States*. Cambridge: Cambridge University Press.

Handel, M. I. (1996) *Masters of War: Classical Strategic Thought*. London: Frank Cass.

Handel, M. I. (2001) *Masters of War: Classical Strategic Thought*, 3rd edn. London: Frank Cass.

Hanson, V. D. (2001) *Carnage and Culture: Landmark Battles in the Rise of Western Power*. New York: Anchor Books.

Harris, B. F. (2014) 'United States Strategic Culture and Asia-Pacific Security', *Contemporary Security Policy* 35(2): 290–309.

Hartmann, A. and B. Heuser (eds) (2001) *War, Peace and World Orders from Antiquity until the* 20th *Century*. London: Routledge.

Haushofer K. (1942) 'Why Geopolitik?' In G. Ó Tuathail, S. Dalby, and P. Routledge (eds) (2006) *The Geopolitics Reader*. London: Routledge.

Haushofer K. (1988) 'Why Geopolitik?' In G. Ó Tuathail, S. Dalby, and P. Routledge (eds), *The Geopolitics Reader*. London: Routledge.

Hays, P. L., B. J. Vallance, and A. R. Van Tassell (eds) (2000) *Spacepower for a New Millennium: Space and US National Security*. New York: McGraw-Hill.

Hehir. A. (2013) 'The Permanence of Inconsistency: Libya, the Security Council, and the Responsibility to Protect', *International Security* 38(1): 137–59.

Heikka, H. (2005) 'Republican Realism: Finnish Strategic Culture in Historical Perspective', *Cooperation and Conflict* 40(1): 91–119.

Henkin, L. (1968) *How Nations Behave: Law and Foreign Policy*. New York: Columbia University Press.

Herring, E. (ed.) (2000) *Preventing the Use of Weapons of Mass Destruction*. London: Frank Cass.

Herzog, A. (1963) *The War-Peace Establishment*. London: Harper & Row.

Heuer, R. (1999) *Psychology of Intelligence Analysis*. Washington, DC: Center for the Study of Intelligence.

Heuser, B. (2010a) *The Evolution of Strategy: Thinking War from Antiquity to the Present*. Cambridge: Cambridge University Press.

Heuser, B. (2010b) *The Strategy-Makers: Thoughts on War and Society from Machiavelli to Clausewitz*. Santa Barbara, CA: ABC-Clio.

Heuser, B. (2012) 'A National Security Strategy for England: Matthew Sutcliffe, the Earl of Essex, and the Cadiz Expedition of 1596'. In O. R. Morales (ed.), *Redes y espacios de poder de la comunidad irlandesa en España y la América española, 1600–1825*. Valencia: Albatros Ediciones: 117–35.

Hoffer, E. (1952) *The True Believer: Thoughts on the Nature of Mass Movements*. London: Secker & Warburg.

Hoffman, B. (2006) *Inside Terrorism*. New York: Columbia University Press.

Holbrooke, R. (1999) 'No Media—No War', *Index on Censorship* 28(3): 20.

Holsti, O. (1976) 'Foreign Policy Formation Viewed Cognitively'. In R Axelrod (ed.) *Structure of Decision*. Princeton, NJ: Princeton University Press.

Homer-Dixon, T. F. (1991) 'On the Threshold: Environmental Changes as Causes of Acute Conflict', *International Security* 16(2) (Fall): 76–116.

Honig, J. W. (2001) 'Avoiding War, Inviting Defeat: The Srebrenica Crisis, July 1995 ', *Journal of Contingencies and Crisis Management* 9(4): 201.

Honig, J. W. (2012) 'Reappraising Late Medieval Strategy: The Example of the 1415 Agincourt', *War in History* 19(2): 123–51.

Horowitz, D. L. (1985) *Ethnic Groups in Conflict*. Berkeley, Los Angeles, London: University of California Press.

House, J. M. (2001) *Combined Arms Warfare in the Twentieth Century*. Lawrence: University Press of Kansas.

Howard, M. (1976a) *War in European History*. Oxford: Oxford University Press.

Howard, M. (1976b) 'The Strategic Approach to International Relations', *British Journal of International Studies* 2(1): 67–75.

Howard, M. (1983) *The Causes of Wars*. London: Counterpoint.

Howard, M. (1991a) *The Lessons of History*. New Haven, CT: Yale University Press.

Howard, M. (1991b) 'British Grand Strategy in World War 1'. In P. Kennedy (ed.), *Grand Strategies in War and Peace*. New Haven, CT: Yale University Press.

Howard, M. (1991c) 'Clausewitz, Man of the Year', *New York Times* 28 January, A17.

Howarth, D. (1974) *Sovereign of the Seas: The Story of British Sea Power*. London: Collins.

Howlett, D. and J. Glenn (2005) 'Epilogue: Nordic Strategic Culture', *Cooperation and Conflict* 40(1): 121–40.

HPSCI (House Permanent Select Committee on Intelligence) (2006) *IC21: The Intelligence Community in the 21st Century*, Staff Study.

Hudson, V. M. (ed.) (1997) *Culture and Foreign Policy*. Boulder, CO: Lynne Rienner.

Hughes, C. W. (2004) 'Japan's Re-emergence as a "Normal" Military Power', *Adelphi Paper* 368.

Hughes, T. P. (1998) *Rescuing Prometheus*. New York: Pantheon Books.

Hughes, W. (1986) *Fleet Tactics: Theory and Practice*. Annapolis, MD: Naval Institute Press.

Huntington, S. (1993a) 'The Clash of Civilizations', *Foreign Affairs* 72(3): 22–49.

Huntington, S. (1993b) 'Response: If Not Civilizations, What? Paradigms of the Post-Cold War World', *Foreign Affairs* 72(5): 186–94.

Huntington, S. (1996) *The Clash of Civilizations: Remaking of World Order*. New York: Simon & Schuster.

Hurd, D., M. Rifkind, D. Owen, and G. Robertson (2008) 'Stop Worrying and Learn to Ditch the Bomb', *The Times* 30 June. Available at http://www.timesonline.co.uk/tol/comment/columnists/guest_contributors/article4237387.ece

Hurd, I. (1999) 'Legitimacy and Authority in International Politics', *International Organization* 53(2): 379–408.

Hyde-Price, A. (2004) 'European Security, Strategic Culture and the Use of Force', *European Security* 13(1): 323–43.

Hymans, J. E. C. (2006) *The Psychology of Nuclear Proliferation: Identity, Emotions, and Foreign Policy.* Cambridge: Cambridge University Press.

IHS Jane's Defense & Security Intelligence & Analysis (various publications).

*Independent, The* (2000) 'UN must Rethink its Peace-keeping Role, says Annan', *Independent* 29 May. Available at http://www.independent.co.uk/news/world/africa/un-must-rethink-its-peacekeeping-role-says-annan-715960.html

International Institute for Strategic Studies (2012) *The Military Balance.* London: IISS and Routledge.

International Institute for Strategic Studies (2013) *The Military Balance.* London: IISS and Routledge.

International Institute for Strategic Studies (2014) *The Military Balance.* London: IISS and Routledge.

Iraqi WMD Commission (2005) *Commission on the Intelligence Capabilities of the United States Regarding Weapons of Mass Destruction, Report to the President,* 31 March.

Isaacson, W. (1999) 'Madeline's War', *Time* 17 May.

Jackson, R. H. (1993) *Quasi-States: Sovereignty, International Relations and the Third World.* Cambridge: Cambridge University Press.

Janda, L. (1995) Shutting the Gates of Mercy: The American Origins of Total War, 1860–1880', *Journal of Military History* 59(1): 15.

Jansen, J. (1997) *The Dual Nature of Islamic Fundamentalism.* Ithaca, NY: Cornell University Press.

Jenkins, B. M. (1987) 'Will Terrorists Go Nuclear?'. In W. Laqueur and Y. Alexander (eds) *The Terrorism Reader: A Historical Anthology.* New York: Meridian.

Jenkins, B. M. (2008) *Will Terrorists Go Nuclear?* New York: Prometheus.

Jervis, R. (1976) *Perception and Misperception in International Politics.* Princeton, NJ: Princeton University Press.

Jervis, R. (1979) 'Deterrence Theory Revisited', *World Politics* 31(2): 289–324.

Jervis, R. (2010) *Why Intelligence Fails: Lessons from the Iranian Revolution and the Iraq War.* Ithaca NY: Cornell University Press.

Joes, A. J. (1992) *Modern Guerrilla Insurgency.* Westport, CT: Praeger.

Johnson, J. L., K. M. Kartchner, and J. A. Larsen (eds) (2009) *Strategic Culture and Weapons of Mass Destruction: Culturally Based Insights into Comparative National Security Policymaking.* London: Palgrave Macmillan.

Johnson, L. and J. Wirtz (2008) *Intelligence and National Security: The Secret World of Spies: An Anthology.* Los Angeles, CA: Roxbury Publishing Company.

Johnson, R. A. (2014) 'Predicting Future War', *The US Army War College Quarterly, Parameters* 44(1): 65–76.

Johnston, A. I. (1995) *Cultural Realism: Strategic Culture and Grand Strategy in Chinese History.* Princeton, NJ: Princeton University Press.

Joint Staff (2012) *Decade of War Volume 1: Enduring Lessons from the Past Decade of Operations,* Joint and Coalition Operational Analysis, J-7, 15 June, available at http://blogs.defensenews.com/saxotech-access/pdfs/decade-of-war-lessons-learned.pdf

Jomini, de, A.-H ([1838] 1992) *The Art of War.* London: Greenhill Books.

Jones, A. (1987) *The Art of War in the Western World.* Chicago, IL: University of Illinois Press.

Joseph, R. G. and J. F. Reichart (1995) *Deterrence and Defence in a Nuclear, Biological, and Chemical Environment.* Occasional Paper of the Center for Counterproliferation Research. Washington, DC: National Defense University.

Juperman, A. J. (2000) 'Rwanda in Retrospect', *Foreign Affairs* 79(1) (January/February): 94–113.

Kagan, K. (2006) 'Redefining Roman Grand Strategy', *The Journal of Military History* 70(2): 333–62.

Kahn, H. (1960) *On Thermonuclear War.* Princeton, NJ: Princeton University Press.

Kahn, H. (1962) *Thinking About the Unthinkable.* New York: Horizon Press.

Kaldor, M. (1999) *New and Old Wars: Organized Violence in a Global Era.* Cambridge: Polity Press.

Kalyvas, S. (2006) *The Logic of Violence in Civil War.* Cambridge: Cambridge University Press.

Kaplan, D. E. (2005a) 'Hearts, Minds and Dollars', *US News and World Report* 25 April.

Kaplan, D. E. (2005b) 'The New Business of Terror', *US News and World Report* 5 December.

Kaplan, E. et al. (2005) 'What Happened to Suicide Bombings in Israel? Insights from a Terror Stock Model', *Studies in Conflict and Terrorism* 28: 225–35.

Kaplan, F. (1983) *The Wizards of Armageddon.* Stanford, CA: Stanford University Press.

Karatzogianni, A. (2004) 'The Politics of "Cyberconflict" ', *Journal of Politics* 24(1): 46–55.

Karlsrud, A. and F. Rosen (2013) 'In the Eye of the Beholder? The UN and the Use of Drones to Protect Civilians' Stability', *International Journal of Security & Development* 2: 1–10.

Karp, A. (2006) 'The New Indeterminacy of Deterrence and Missile Defence'. In I. Kenyon and J. Simpson (eds) *Deterrence in the New Global Security Environment*. London: Routledge.

Kartchner, K. M. (2009) 'Strategic Culture and WMD Decision Making'. In J. L. Johnson, K. M. Kartchner, and J. Larsen (eds) *Strategic Culture and Weapons of Mass Destruction: Culturally Based Insights into Comparative National Security Policymaking*. New York: Palgrave Macmillan.

Katzenbach, Jr., E. J. and G. Z. Hanrahan (1962) 'The Revolutionary Strategy of Mao Tse-Tung'. In F. M. Osanka (ed.) *Modern Guerrilla Warfare: Fighting Communist Guerrilla Movements, 1941–1961*. New York: Free Press.

Katzenstein, P. J. (ed.) (1996) *The Culture of National Security: Norms and Identity in World Politics*. New York: Columbia University Press.

Keegan, J. (1987) *The Mask of Command*. New York: Viking Penguin.

Keegan, J. (1993) *A History of Warfare*. New York: Knopf.

Keegan, J. (2004) *The Iraq War*. New York: Knopf.

Kegley, C. W. and E. R. Wittkopf (1997) *World Politics: Trends and Transformation*. New York: St Martins Press.

Kennan, G. F. (1947) 'The Sources of Soviet Conduct', *Foreign Affairs* 25: 576–82.

Kennedy, P. (1988) *The Rise And Fall Of The Great Powers: Economic Change And Military Conflict*. London: Unwin Hyman.

Kennedy, P. (ed.) (1991) *Grand Strategies in War and Peace*. New Haven: Yale University Press.

Kent, S. (1966) *Strategic Intelligence for an American World Policy*. Princeton, NJ: Princeton University Press.

Kenyon, I. and J. Simpson (eds) (2006) *Deterrence in the New Global Security Environment*. London: Routledge.

Keohane, R. O. (2001) *International Institutions and State Power: Essays in International Relations Theory*. San Francisco, CA: Westview Press.

Keohane, R. O. (2002) *Power and Governance in a Partially Globalizing World*. New York: Routledge.

Keohane, R. O. and J. S. Nye (2001) *Power and Interdependence*, 3rd edn. New York: Longman; originally Reading, MA 1989: Addison-Wesley.

Kerr, R. et al. (2005) 'Intelligence and Analysis on Iraq: Issues for the Intelligence Community', *Studies in Intelligence* 49(3): 152–61.

Kier, E. (1995) 'Culture and Military Doctrine: France between the Wars', *International Security* 19(14): 65–94.

Kievet, J. and S. Metz (1994) *The Revolution in Military Affairs and Conflict Short of War*. Carlisle, PA: US Army War College Strategic Studies Institute.

Kilcullen, D. (2009) *The Accidental Guerrilla: Fighting Small Wars in the Midst of a Big One*. Oxford: Oxford University Press.

Kipp, J., L. Grau, K. Prinslow, and Captain D. Smith (2006) 'The Human Terrain System: A CORDS for the 21st Century', *Military Review* (September/October): 8–15.

Kiras, J. D. (2005) 'Terrorism and Globalization'. In J. Baylis, S. Smith, and P. Owens (eds) *The Globalization of World Politics: An Introduction to International Relations*, 5th edn. Oxford: Oxford University Press.

Kissinger, H. A. (1957) *Nuclear Weapons and Foreign Policy*. New York: Harper & Row.

Kitson, F. (1977) *Bunch of Five*. London: Faber & Faber.

Klare, M. (2001) 'The New Geography of Conflict', *Foreign Affairs* 80(3): 49–61.

Klein, B. S. (1994) *Strategic Studies and World Order: The Global Politics of Deterrence*. Cambridge: Cambridge University Press.

Klein, Y. (1991) 'A Theory of Strategic Culture', *Comparative Strategy* 10(1): 3–23.

Klonis, N. I. (pseud.) (1972) *Guerrilla Warfare*. New York: Robert Speller & Sons.

Knopf, J. (2010) 'The Fourth Wave in Deterrence Research', *Contemporary Security Policy* 31(1): 1–33.

Konkel, F. (2014) 'The Intelligence Community's Big Data Problem', *FCW*, 13 March, available at www.fcw.com/articles/2013/06/17/big-data-savings.aspx

Kosal, M. (2005) *Terrorist Incidents Targeting Industrial Chemical Facilities: Strategic Motivations and International Repercussions*. Stanford, CA: Center for International Security and Cooperation, unpublished manuscript.

Kramer, F. D., S. H. Starr, and L. K. Wentz (eds) (2009) *Cyberpower and National Security*. Washington, DC: Potomac Books.

Krasner, S. (2010) 'An Orienting Principle for Foreign Policy: The Deficiencies of "Grand Strategy" ', *Policy Review* 163: 5.

Krause, K. and M. C. Williams (eds) (1997) *Critical Security Studies: Concepts and Cases*. London: UCL Press.

Krepinevich A. F. (1994) 'Cavalry to Computer: The Pattern of Military Revolution', *The National Interest* (Fall): 30–42.

Kritsiotis, D. (2004) 'Arguments of Mass Confusion', *European Journal of International Law* 15(2): 233–78.

Kuehl, D. T. (2009) 'From Cyberspace to Cyberpower: Defining the Problem'. In F. D. Kramer, S. H. Starr, and L. K. Wentz (eds) *Cyberpower and National Security*. Washington, DC: Potomac Books.

Kuhn, K. (1987) 'Responsibility for Military Conduct and Respect for International Humanitarian Law', Dissemination, ICRC.

Kupchan, C. (1994) *The Case for Collective Security*. Ann Arbor, MI: University of Michigan Press.

Kydd, A. H. and B. F. Walter (2006) 'The Strategies of Terrorism', *International Security* 31(1) (Summer): 46–80.

Ladis, N. (2003) 'Assessing Greek Strategic Thought and Practice: Insights from the Strategic Culture Approach'. Doctoral dissertation, University of Southampton.

Langewiesche, W. (2007) *The Atomic Bazaar: The Rise of the Nuclear Poor*. New York: Farrar, Straus and Giroux.

Lantis, J. S. (2002) *Strategic Dilemmas and the Evolution of German Foreign Policy since Unification*. Westport, CN: Praeger.

Lantis, J. S . (2005) 'American Strategic Culture and Transatlantic Security Ties'. In K. Longhurst and M. Zaborowski, *Controversies in Politics* 24(1): 46–55.

Lantis, J. S. (2009) 'Strategic Culture and Tailored Deterrence: Bridging the Gap Between Theory and Practice', *Contemporary Security Policy* 30(3): 467–85.

Lantis, J. S. (ed.) (2014) 'Strategic Cultures and Security Policies in the Asia-Pacific', Special Issue of *Contemporary Security Policy* 35(2): 166–86.

Laqueur, W. (1996). 'Postmodern Terrorism', *Foreign Affairs* 75(5): 24–37.

Laqueur, W. (1999) *The New Terrorism: Fanaticism and the Arms of Mass Destruction*. New York: Oxford University Press.

Larsen, J. A. (1997) 'NATO Counterproliferation Policy: A Case Study in Alliance Politics', INSS Occasional Paper 17. Denver, CO: USAF Institute for National Security Studies. Available at http://www.usafa.af.mil/df/inss/OCP/ocp17.pdf

Larsen, J. A. and J. J. Wirtz (eds) (2009) *Arms Control and Cooperative Security*. London: Lynne Rienner.

Lasswell, H. D. (1936) *Politics: Who Gets What, When, How*. New York: McGraw-Hill.

Lauterpacht, H. (1952) 'The Revision of the Law of War', *British Yearbook of International Law* 29: 360–82.

Lavoy, P., S. Sagan, and J. Wirtz (eds) (2000) *Planning the Unthinkable: How New Powers Will Use Nuclear, Biological, and Chemical Weapons*. Ithaca, NY: Cornell University Press.

Lawrence, P. (1988) *Preparing for Armageddon: A Critique of Western Strategy*. Brighton: Wheatsheaf.

Lawrence, T. E. (1920) 'The Evolution of a Revolt', *The Army Quarterly* 1(1): 55–69.

Lawrence, T. E. (1935) *Seven Pillars of Wisdom: A Triumph*. London: Jonathan Cape.

Le Bohec, Y. (2014) *La Guerre romaine*. Paris: Tallandier.

Le Bon, G. (1897) *The Crowd: A Study of the Popular Mind*, 2nd edn. London: Fisher Unwin.

Leavenworth, K. S. (2004) US Army Training and Doctrine Command.

Lee, S. P. (1996) *Morality, Prudence, and Nuclear Weapons*. Cambridge: Cambridge University Press.

Legro, J. W. (1996) 'Culture and Preferences in the International Cooperation Two-step', *American Political Science Review* 90(1): 118–37.

Leo VI (*c*.900) *Taktika*, trans & ed. by G. Dennis (2010) *The Taktika of Leo VI*. Washington, DC: Dumbarton Oaks.

Levy, M. (1995) 'Is the Environment a National Security Issue?', *International Security* 20(2): 35–62.

Levy, J. S. and W. R. Thompson (2010) *The Causes of War*. Chichester: Wiley-Blackwell.

Lewis, K., K. Gray, and J. Meierhenrich (2014) 'The Structure of Online Activism', *Sociological Science* 1: 1–9.

Lia, B. and T. S Hegghammer (2004) 'Jihadi Strategic Studies: The Alleged Al Qaida Policy Study Preceding the Madrid Bombings', *Studies in Conflict and Terrorism* 27: 355–75.

Libicki, M. C. (2007) *Conquest in Cyberspace: National Security and Information Warfare*. Cambridge: Cambridge University Press.

Liddell Hart, B. H. (1929) *The Decisive Wars of History: A Study in Strategy*. London: G. Bell.

Liddell Hart, B.H. (1935) *When Britain goes to War*. London: Faber & Faber.

Liddell Hart, B. H. ([1941] 1967) *Strategy: The Indirect Approach*. London: Faber & Faber.

Lind, J. M. (2004) 'Pacifism or Passing the Buck? Testing Theories of Japan's Security Policy', *International Security* 29(1) (Summer): 92–121.

Lindblom, C. E. (1959) 'The Science of "Muddling Through" ', *Public Administration Review* 19(2): 79–88

Lindley-French, J. (2002) 'In the Shade of Locarno? Why European Defence is Failing', *International Affairs* 78(4): 789–811.

Litwak, R. (2003) 'The New Calculus of Pre-emption', *Survival* 44(4): 53–79.

Lock, E. (2010) 'Refining Strategic Culture: Return of the Second Generation', *Review of International Studies* 36(1): 685–708.

Lockhart, C. (1999) 'Cultural Contributions to Explaining Institutional Form, Political Change and Rational Decisions', *Comparative Political Studies* 32(7): 862–93.

Long, J. M. (2009) 'Strategic Culture, Al-Qaeda, and Weapons of Mass Destruction'. In J. L. Johnson, K. M. Kartchner, and J. A. Larsen (eds) *Strategic Culture and Weapons of Mass Destruction: Culturally Based Insights into Comparative National Security Policymaking.* London: Palgrave Macmillan.

Longhurst, K. (2005) *Germany and the Use of Force: The Evolution of German Security Policy 1990–2003.* Manchester: Manchester University Press.

Longhurst, K. and Marcin Zaborowski (eds) (2005) *Old Europe, New Europe and the Transatlantic Security Agenda.* London: Routledge.

Lonsdale, D. J. (2004) *The Nature of War in the Information Age: Clausewitzian Future.* London: Frank Cass.

Lonsdale, D. J. (2007) *Alexander the Great: Lessons in Strategy.* Abingdon, UK: Routledge.

Looney, R. E. (2005) 'The Business of Insurgency: The Expansion of Iraq's Shadow Economy', *The National Interest* 81 (Fall): 117–21.

Lorenz, K. (1966) *On Aggression.* New York: Harcourt, Brace & World.

Lorenz, K. (1976) *On Aggression.* New York: Bantam.

Lowenthal, M. (2011) *Intelligence: From Secrets to Policy.* 5th edn. Washington, DC: CQ Press.

Ludendorff, E. (1935) *Der Totale Krieg.* Munich: Ludendorff Publishing; trs by A. S. Rapoport (1936) in *The Nation at War*, London: Hutchinson.

Luttwak, E. (1999) [1976] *The Grand Strategy of the Roman Empire: from the First Century A.D. to the Third.* London: Weidenfeld & Nicolson.

Luttwak, E. (2001) *Strategy: The Logic of War and Peace*, revised and enlarged edn, Cambridge, MA: Belknap Press.

Luttwak, E. (2009) *The Grand Strategy of the Byzantine Empire.* Cambridge, MA: Belknap Press.

Lynn, J. (1999) *The Wars of Louis XIV, 1667–1714.* Harlow: Pearson Education.

Lynn, J. (2003) *Battle: A History of Combat and Culture.* Boulder, CO: Westview Press.

McConnell, M. (2008) 'Remarks By Director Mike McConnell to the US Geospatial Intelligence Foundation (USGIF) GEOINT 2008 Symposium', 30 October.

McConnell, M. (2010) 'To win the cyber-war, look to the Cold War', *The Washington Post*, 28 February. Available at http://www.washingtonpost.com/wp-dyn/content/article/2010/02/25/AR2010022502493.html

McCoubrey, H. (1998) *International Humanitarian Law*, 2nd edn. Aldershot: Dartmouth.

McCuen, J. (1966) *The Art of Counter-Revolutionary Warfare.* Harrisburg, PA: Stackpole.

McGoldrick, D., Rowe, P., and Donnelly, E. (eds) (2004) *The Permanent International Court: Legal and Policy Issues.* Oxford: Hart Publishing.

MacKenzie, D. (1990) *Inventing Accuracy: An Historical Sociology of Nuclear Missile Guidance.* Cambridge, MA: MIT University Press.

Mackinder, H. J. (1904) 'The Geographical Pivot of History (Read at the Royal Geographical Society, 25 January 1904)', *The Geographical Journal* 23: 421–437.

Mackinder, H. J. (1919) *Democratic Ideals and Reality: A Study in the Politics of Reconstruction.* London: Henry Holt.

McMillan, J. (2005) 'Treating Terrorist Groups as Armed Bands: The Strategic Implications'. In J. S. Purcell and J. D. Weintraub (eds) *Topics in Terrorism: Toward a Transatlantic Consensus on the Nature of the Threat.* Washington, DC: Atlantic Council of the United States.

McNeil, W. H. (1982) *The Pursuit of Power.* Oxford: Basil Blackwell.

Mahan, A. (1890) *The Influence of Seapower on History, 1660–1783.* Boston, MA: Little, Brown & Co.

Mahnken, T. G. (2001) 'Counterproliferation: A Critical Appraisal'. In H. Sokolski and J. M. Ludes (eds) *Twenty-First Century Weapons Proliferation: Are we Ready?* London: Frank Cass.

Mahnken, T. G. (2009) 'US Strategic and Organizational Subcultures'. In J. L. Johnson, K. M. Kartchner, and J. A. Larsen (eds) *Strategic Culture and Weapons of Mass Destruction: Culturally Based Insights into Comparative National Security Policymaking.* London: Palgrave Macmillan.

Mahnken, T. G. (2011) 'Cyberwar and Cyber Warfare'. In K. M. Lord and T. Sharp (eds) *America's Cyber Future: Security and Prosperity in the Information Age.* Washington, DC: Center for a New American Security.

Mahnken, T. G. (2012) *Competitive Strategies for the 21st Century: Theory, History and Practice.* Palo Alto, CA: Stanford University Press.

Mahnken, T. G. and J. A. Maiolo (2008) *Strategic Studies: A Reader.* Abingdon: Routledge.

Malici, A. (2006) 'Germans as Venutians: The Culture of German Foreign Policy Behavior', *Foreign Policy Analysis* 2(1) (January): 37–62.

Malkasian, C. (2013) *War Comes to Garmser.* Oxford: Oxford University Press.

Marighella, C. (1969) *Minimanual of the Urban Guerrilla.* Available at http://www.baader-meinhof.com/index.htm

Masood, S. (2012) 'Pakistan Gives US a List of Demands, Including an End to CIA Drone Strikes', *New York Times*, 12 April, available at http://www.nytimes.com/2012/04/13/world/asia/pakistan-demands-an-end-to-cia-drone-strikes.html?_r=0

Mattern, J. B. (2005) *Ordering International Politics: Identity, Crisis, and Representational Force.* London: Routledge.

Matthew, R. A., J. Barnett, B. McDonald, and K. L. O'Brien (eds) (2010) *Global Environmental Change and Human Security*. Cambridge, Massachusetts: MIT Press.

Matthews, K. (1996) *The Gulf Conflict and International Relations*. London: Routledge.

Mazaar, M. (2010) 'The Open-source Century: Information, Knowledge, and Intelligence in the 21st Century', *World Politics Review*, 28 September, available at http://www.worldpoliticsreview.com/articles/6535/the-open-source-century-information-knowledge-and-intelligence-in-the-21st-century

Mazetti, M. (2013) 'New Terror Strategy Shifts CIA Focus Back to Spying', *New York Times*, 23 March, available at www.nytimes.com/2013/05/24/us/politics

Mead Earle, E. (ed.) (1943) *Makers of Modern Strategy: From Machiavelli to Hitler*. Princeton, NJ: Princeton University Press.

Mearsheimer, J. J. (2014) *The Tragedy of Great Power Politics*, 2nd edn. New York: Norton.

Medina, C. (2008) 'The New Analysis'. In R. George and J. Bruce, *Analyzing Intelligence: Origins, Obstacles, and Innovations*. Washington, DC: Georgetown University Press.

Meilinger, P. (2008) 'Clausewitz's Bad Advice', *Armed Forces Journal International*, August.

Meron, T. (2006) *The Humanization of International Law*. Leiden: Martinus Nijhoff.

Messenger, C. (1976) *The Art of Blitzkrieg*. London: Ian Allan Ltd.

Metcalfe, V., A. Giffen, and S. Elhawary (2011) *UN Integration and Humanitarian Space*. London: Overseas Development Institute.

Meyer, C. O. (2004) *Theorising European Strategic Culture: Between Convergence and the Persistence of National Diversity*. Centre for European Policy Studies, Working Document 204 (June) www.ceps.be

Milevski, L. (2014) 'Strategy Versus Statecraft in Crimea', *The US Army War College Quarterly, Parameters* 44(2): 23–33.

Miller, D. (1998) *The Cold War: A Military History*. New York: St Martin's Press.

Miller, G. (2014) 'Germany Orders CIA Station Chief to Leave Over Spying Allegations', *Washington Post*, 10 July 2014, at http://www.washingtonpost.com/world/europe/germany-expels-us-intelligence-station-chief-over-spying-allegations/2014/07/10/dc60b1f0-083c-11e4-8a6a-19355c7e870a_story.html

Milliken, J. (1999) 'The Study of Discourse in International Relations', *European Journal of International Relations* 5(2): 225–54.

Minear, L. and T. G. Weiss (1995) *Mercy under Fire: War and the Global Humanitarian Community*. Boulder, CO: Westview Press.

Miskimmon, A. (2004) 'Continuity in the Face of Upheaval—British Strategic Culture and the Impact of the Blair Government', *European Security* 13(3): 273–99.

Mitra, S. K. (2002) 'Emerging Major Powers and the International System (An Indian View)'. In A. Dally and R. Bourke (eds) *Conflict, the State and Aerospace Power*. Canberra: RAAF Aerospace Centre.

Moir, L. (2002) *The Law of Internal Armed Conflict*. Oxford: Oxford University Press.

Moran, D. (2006) *Wars of National Liberation*. Washington, DC: Smithsonian Books.

Moran, D. and J. A. Russell (eds) (2009) *Energy Security and Global Politics: The Militarization of Resource Management*. New York: Routledge.

Morgan, P. (2003) *Deterrence Now*. Cambridge: Cambridge University Press.

Morris, J. C. (2005) 'Normative Innovation and the Great Powers'. In A. Bellamy (ed.) *International Society and its Critics*. Oxford: Oxford University Press.

Morris, J. C. and N. J. Wheeler (2007) 'The Security Council's Crisis of Legitimacy and the Use of Force', *International Politics* 44(2/3): 214–32.

Morris, J. C. and N. J. Wheeler (2012) 'Human Welfare in a World of States: Reassessing the Balance of Responsibility'. In J. Connelly and J. Hayward (eds), *The Withering of the Welfare State: Regression*. London: Palgrave Macmillan.

Moskos, C. C., J. A. Williams, and D. R. Segal (eds) (2000) *The Postmodern Military: Armed Forces after the Cold War*. New York: Oxford University Press.

Müller, H. and M. Reiss (1995) 'Counterproliferation: Putting Old Wine in New Bottles', *Washington Quarterly* (Spring): 145–9.

Müller, H., D. Fisher, and W. Kötter (1994) *Nuclear Non-Proliferation and Global Order*. New York: Oxford University Press.

Munck, R. (2000) 'Deconstructing Terror: Insurgency, Repression and Peace'. In R. Munck and P. L. de Silva (eds) *Postmodern Insurgencies: Political Violence, Identity Formation and Peacemaking in Comparative Perspective*. New York: St. Martin's Press.

Munkler, H. (2005) *The New Wars*. Cambridge: Polity Press.

Murray, W. (1997) 'Thinking about Revolutions in Military Affairs', *Joint Force Quarterly* (Summer): 69–76.

Murray, W. (2011) *Military Adaptation in War: With Fear of Change*. Cambridge: Cambridge University Press.

Murray, W. and R. Scales (2003) *The Iraq War: A Military History*. Cambridge, MA: Harvard University Press.

Murray, W., M. Knox, and A. Bernstein (eds) (1994) *The Making of Strategy: Rulers, States, and War*. Cambridge: Cambridge University Press.

Murray, W., R. H. Sinnreich, and J. Lacey (eds) (2011) *The Shaping of Grand Strategy: Policy, Diplomacy, and War*. Cambridge: Cambridge University Press.

Mutimer, D. (2000) *The Weapons State: Proliferation and the Framing of Security*. Boulder, CO: Lynne Rienner.

Nadelmann, E. (1993) *Cops across Borders*. State College, PA: Penn State University Press.

Naim, M. (2005) *Illicit: How Smugglers, Traffickers and Copycats are Hijacking the Global Economy*. New York: Doubleday.

Nasution, A. H. (1965) *Fundamentals of Guerrilla Warfare*. New York: Praeger.

Nathan, A. J. and A. Scobell (2012) 'How China Sees America: The Sum of Beijing's Fears', *Foreign Affairs* 91(5): 32–47.

National Intelligence Council (2004) *Mapping the Global Future*. Washington, DC: Government Printing Office.

National Intelligence Council (2012) *Global Trends 2030: Alternative Worlds*. Washington, DC: Government Printing Office.

National Resources Defense Council, http://www.nrdc.org/nuclear/nudb/datab19.asp

*National Security Strategy of the United States* (2010) Office of the President of the United States, May, available at http://www.whitehouse.gov/sites/default/files/rss_viewer/national_security_strategy.pdf

Negroponte, J. (2006) 'The Science and Technology Challenge', Remarks of the Director of National Intelligence at the Woodrow Wilson International Center for Scholars, 25 September.

Nelson, K. L. and S. C. Olin, Jr. (1979) *Why War: Ideology, Theory, and History*. Berkeley and Los Angeles, CA: University of California Press.

Neustadt, R. E., and E. R. May (eds) (1986) *Thinking in Time: The Uses of History for Decision Makers*. New York: Free Press.

Newman, R. (1961) Review in *Scientific American* 204(3): 197.

Newmann, I. B. and H. Heikka (2005) 'Grand Strategy, Strategic Culture, Practice: The Social Roots of Nordic Defense', *Cooperation and Conflict* 40: 5–23.

Niebuhr, R. (1932) *Moral Man and Immoral Society: A Study in Ethics and Politics*. New York and London: Charles Scribner's Sons.

Nietzsche, E. (1966) *The Philosophy of Nietzsche*. New York: New American Library.

Nietzsche, F . (1996) *Beyond Good and Evil*, translated by W. Kaufmann . New York: Random House.

Nikephoros Phokas (mid-950s) *Peri Paradromes*, translated and edited by G. Dennis, *Three Byzantine Military Treatises* (Washington, DC: Dumbarton Oaks, 1985): 146–239.

Nofi, A. A. (1982) 'Clausewitz on War', *Strategy and Tactics* 91: 16.

Nye, Jr., J. S. (1986) *Nuclear Ethics*. London: Macmillan.

Nye, Jr., J. S. (1988) *Nuclear Ethics*. New York: Free Press.

Nye, Jr., J. S. (2011) *The Future of Power*. New York: Public Affairs.

O'Connell, M. E. (2002) 'The Myth of Preemptive Self-Defense', *American Society of International Law*. Available at http://www.asil.org/taskforce/oconnell.pdf

O'Connell, R. L. (1989) *Of Arms and Men: A History of War, Weapons and Aggression*. Oxford: Oxford University Press.

O'Hanlon, M. E. (2000) *Technological Change and the Future of Warfare*. Washington, DC: Brookings Institution Press.

O'Hanlon, M. E. (2009) *The Science of War Defense Budgeting, Military Technology, Logistics, and Combat Outcomes*. Princeton, NJ: Princeton University Press.

Olsen, J. A., and C. S Gray (eds) (2011) *The Practice of Strategy: From Alexander the Great to the Present*. Oxford: Oxford University Press.

Olson, W. C., D. S. McLellan, and F. A. Sondermann (1983) *The Theory and Practice of International Relations*, 6th edn. Englewood Cliffs, NJ: Prentice Hall.

O'Neill, B. (1990) *Insurgency and Terrorism: Inside Modern Revolutionary Warfare*. Washington, DC: Brassey's.

Oppel, R. (2007) 'Foreign Fighters in Iraq Are Tied to Allies of US', *New York Times*, 22 November.

Orme, J. (1997) 'The Utility of Force in a World of Scarcity', *International Security* 22(3): 136–67.

Oros, A. (2014) 'Japanese Strategic Culture and Security Identity in a Fourth Modern Incarnation?' *Contemporary Security Policy* 35(2): 227–248.

Osgood, R. E. (1962) *An Alternative to War and Surrender*. Chicago, IL: Chicago University Press.

Osgood, R. E. (1962) *NATO: The Entangling Alliance*. Chicago, IL: University of Chicago Press.

O'Tuathail, G. (1996) *Critical Geopolitics: The Politics of Writing Global Space*. London: Routledge.

Owens, W. A. (1995) *High Seas: The Naval Passage to an Uncharted World*. Annapolis, MD: Naval Institute Press.

Owens, W. A. and E. Offley (2000) *Lifting the Fog of War*. New York: Farrar, Straus, & Giroux.

Owens, W. A., K. W. Dam, and H. S. Lin (eds) (2009) *Technology, Policy, Law, and Ethics Regarding US Acquisition and Use of Cyberattack Capabilities*. Washington, DC, The National Academies Press.

Paddon, E. (2011) 'Partnering for Peace: Implications and Dilemmas', *International Peacekeeping* 18(5): 518–35.

Paget, J. (1967) *Counter-Insurgency Fighting*. London: Faber & Faber.

Pape, R. (2005) *Dying to Win: The Strategic Logic of Suicide Terrorism*. New York: Random House.

Paret, P. (ed.) (1986) *Makers of Modern Strategy: From Machiavelli to the Nuclear Age*. Princeton, NJ: Princeton University Press.

Paris, R. (2004) *At War's End: Building Peace After Civil Conflict*. Cambridge: Cambridge University Press.

Parker, G. (1996) *The Military Revolution: Military Innovation and the Rise of the West 1500–1800*. Cambridge: Cambridge University Press.

Parker, G. (1998) *The Grand Strategy of Philip II*. New Haven, CT: Yale University Press.

Parsons, T. (1951) *The Social System*. London: Routledge and Kegan Paul.

Payne, K. B. (1996) *Deterrence in the Second Nuclear Age*. Lexington, KY: University Press of Kentucky.

Payne, K. B. (2001) *The Fallacies of Cold War Deterrence and a New Direction*. Lexington, KY: University Press of Kentucky.

Payne, K. B. (2002) 'Deterrence: Theory and Practice'. In J. Baylis, E. Cohen, C. S. Gray, and J. W. Wirtz (eds) *Strategy in the Contemporary World: An Introduction to Strategic Studies*. Oxford: Oxford University Press.

Payne, K. B. (2007) 'Deterring Iran: The Values at Stake and the Acceptable Risks'. In P. Clawson and M. Eisenstadt (eds) *Deterring the Ayatollahs: Complications in Applying Cold War Strategy to Iran*. Policy Focus No. 72 Washington, DC: The Washington Institute for Near East Policy.

Payne, K. B. (2008) *The Great American Gamble: Deterrence Theory and Practice from the Cold War to the Twenty-first Century*. Fairfax, VA: National Institute Press.

Pelfrey, W. (2005) 'The Cycle of Preparedness: Establishing a Framework to Prepare for Terrorist Threats', *Journal of Homeland Security and Emergency Management* 2(1): 1–21.

Peoples, C. (2007) 'Technology and Politics in the Missile Defence Debate: Traditional, Radical, and Critical Approaches', *Global Change, Peace and Security* 19(3): 265–80.

Peoples, C. and N. Vaughan-Williams (2014) *Critical Security Studies: An Introduction*. Oxon: Routledge.

Perkovich, G. (2004) 'The Nuclear and Security Balance'. In F. R. Frankel and H. Harding (eds) *The India-China Relationship*. New York: Columbia University Press.

Perkovich, G., J. T. Matthews, J. Cirincione, R. Gottemoeller, and J. B. Wolfsthal (2005) *Universal Compliance: A Strategy for Nuclear Security*. Washington, DC: Carnegie Endowment for International Peace.

Perlez, J. and J. Cochrane. (2013) 'Obama's Absence Leaves China as Dominant Force at Asia-Pacific Meeting', *New York Times*, 8 October: A6.

Peters, R. (1994) 'The New Warrior Class', *Parameters* 24(2): 16–26.

Petroski, H. (1982) *To Engineer is Human: The Role of Failure in Successful Design*. New York: Random House.

Petroski, H. (1992) *The Evolution of Useful Things*. New York: Vintage Books.

Pictet, J. (1985) *Development and Principles of International Humanitarian Law*. The Hague: Martinus Nijhoff.

Pillar, P. (2006) 'Intelligence, Policy, and the War in Iraq', *Foreign Affairs* (March/April): 15–27.

Pillar, P. (2011) *Intelligence and US Foreign Policy: Iraq, 9/11 and Misguided Reform*. New York: Columbia University Press.

Pollack, K. M. (2002) *Arabs at War: Military Effectiveness, 1948–1991*. Lincoln, NE: University of Nebraska Press.

Poore, S . (2004) 'Strategic Culture'. In J. Glenn, D. Howlett, and S. Poore, *Neorealism versus Strategic Culture*. Aldershot: Ashgate.

Porch, D ([2000] 2001) *Wars of Empire*. London: Cassell.

Porter, P. (2009) *Military Orientalism: Eastern War Through Western Eyes*. London: Hurst.

Pouligny, B. (2006) *Peace Operations Seen From Below: UN Missions and Local People*. Bloomfield, CT: Kumarian.

Power, S. (2014) 'On Peacekeeping', Remarks, American Enterprise Institute, 7 November.

President's Review Group (2013) *Liberty and Security in a Changing World, Report and Recommendations of the President's Review Group on Intelligence and Communications Technologies*, 12 December, available at http://www.whitehouse.gov/sites/default/files/docs/2013-12-12_rg_final_report.pdf

Preston, R. A. and S. F. Wise (1970) *Men in Arms: A History of Warfare and its Interrelationship with Western Society*, 2nd edn. New York: Praeger, pp. 104–5.

Pye, L. (1985) *Asian Power and Politics: The Cultural Dimension of Authority*. Cambridge, MA. Harvard University Press.

Quester, G. (1977) *Offense and Defense in the International System*. New York: John Wiley and Sons.

Quester, G. (1984) 'War and Peace: Necessary and Sufficient Conditions'. In R. O. Matthews, A. G. Rubinoff, and J. G. Stein (eds) *International Conflict and Conflict Management*. Scarborough, Ontario: Prentice-Hall.

Qurashi, A. (2002) 'Al-Qa'ida and the Art of War', *Al-Ansar* www-text in Arabic, FBIS document ID GMP20020220001830[0].

Raine, L. P. and F. J. Cilluffo (eds) (1994) *Global Organized Crime: The New Empire of Evil*. Washington, DC: Center for Strategic and International Studies.

Ralph, J. (2007) *Defending the Society of States: Why America Opposes the International Criminal Court and its Vision of World Society*. Oxford: Oxford University Press.

Rapoport, A. (1964) *Strategy and Conscience*. New York: Schocken Books/Harper & Row.

Rapoport, A. (1965) 'The Sources of Anguish', *Bulletin of Atomic Scientists* 21(10) (December): 25–36.

Rassmussen, M. (2005) ' "What's the Use of it?," Danish Strategic Culture and the Utility of Armed Force', *Cooperation and Conflict* 40: 67–89.

Rattray, G. J. (2001) *Strategic Warfare in Cyberspace*. Cambridge, MA: MIT Press.

Rattray, G. J. (2002) 'The Cyberterrorism Threat'. In R. D. Howard and R. L. Sawyer (eds) *Terrorism and Counterterrorism: Understanding the New Security Environment*. Guildford, CT: McGraw-Hill.

Raudzens, G. (1990) 'War-Winning Weapons: The Measurement of Technological Determinism in Military History', *Journal of Military History* 54 (October): 403–33.

Rauschning, H. (1939) *Germany's Revolution of Destruction*, translated by E. W. Dickes. London: Heinemann.

Record, J. (2003) *Bounding the Global War on Terrorism*. Carlisle, PA: Army War College.

Record, J. (2004) *Dark Victory: America's Second War Against Iraq*. Washington, DC: US Naval Institute Press.

Reid, B. H. (2005) *Robert E. Lee, Icon for a Nation*. London: Weidenfeld and Nicolson.

Reus-Smit, C. (2004) *The Politics of International Law*. Cambridge: Cambridge University Press.

Reus-Smit, C. (2007) 'International Crises of Legitimacy', *International Politics* 44(2/3): 157–74.

Ricks, T. (2006) *Fiasco: The American Military Adventure in Iraq*. New York: Penguin.

Rid, T. (2013) *Cyber War Will Not Take Place*. New York: Oxford University Press.

Rink, M. (1999) *Vom 'Partheygänger' zum Partisanen: Die Konzeption des kleinen Krieges in Preußen, 1740–1813*. Frankfurt/Main: Peter Lang.

Roberts, A. (2008) *Masters and Commanders: How Roosevelt, Churchill, Marshall, and Alanbrooke Won the War in the West*. London: Allen Lane.

Roberts, A. and D. Zaum (2008) *Selective Security: War and the United Nations Security Council Since 1945*. London: International Institute for Strategic Studies.

Roberts, M. (1956) *The Military Revolution, 1560–1660*. Belfast: Marjory Boyd.

Robertson, S. (2001) 'Experimentation and Innovation in the Canadian Armed Forces', *Canadian Military Journal*, 64.

Robinson, L. (2008) *Tell Me How this Ends: General David Petraeus and the Search for a Way Out of Iraq*. New York: Public Affairs.

Robinson, P., N. de Lee, and D. Carrick (eds) (2008) *Ethics Education in the Military*. Aldershot: Ashgate.

Rodger, N.A.M. (2004) *The Safeguard of the Sea: A Naval History of Britain, 660–1649*. London: Penguin.

Rogers, C. J. (2000) *War Cruel and Sharp: English Strategy under Edward III, 1327–1360*. Woodbridge: Boydell Press.

Rogers, C. J. (2002) 'The Vegetian "Science of Warfare" in the Middle Ages', *Journal of Medieval Military History* 1: 1–19.

Rose, M. (1995) 'A Year in Bosnia: What has been Achieved', *RUSI* (140/3): 22–5.

Rosen, S. (1995) 'Military Effectiveness: Why Society Matters', *International Security* 19(14): 5–31.

Rosen, S. (1996) *Societies and Military Power*. Ithaca, NY: Cornell Studies in Security Affairs.

Rosen, S. (2005) *War and Human Nature*. Princeton, NJ: Princeton University Press.

Rosenau, J. N. (1990) *Turbulence in World Politics*. Princeton, NJ: Princeton University Press.

Rousseau, J. J [1754] 1993) 'A Discourse on the Origin of Inequality'. In G. D. H. Cole (ed.) *The Social Contract and Discourses*. London: J. M. Dent.

Ruan, Z. (2014) 'The Money has Gone East', *The World Today* 70(6).

Rumsfeld, D. (2003) *Memo on Global War on Terrorism*. Available at http://www.usatoday.com/news/washington/executive/rumsfeld-memo.htm

Rumsfeld, D. (2011) *Known and Unknown: A Memoir*. New York: Sentinel.

Russell, R. B. (1958) *A History of the United Nations Charter*. Washington DC: Brookings Institute.

Rynning, S. (2003) 'The European Union: Towards a Strategic Culture? ', *Security Dialogue* 34(4) (December): 479–96.

Sagan, S. (2005) 'Learning from Failure or Failure to Learn: Lessons from Past Nuclear Security Events'. Paper presented to the IAEA International Conference on Nuclear Security, 16 March.

Sagan, S. and K. N. Waltz (2002) *The Spread of Nuclear Weapons: A Debate Renewed*, 2nd edn. New York: W. W. Norton.

Sageman, M. (2004) *Understanding Terror Networks*. Philadelphia, PA: University of Pennsylvania Press.

Sageman, M. (2007) *Leaderless Jihad: Terror Networks in the Twenty-First Century*. Philadelphia, PA: University of Pennsylvania Press.

Samore, G. (2003) 'The Korean Nuclear Crisis', *Survival* 45(1): 8–9.

Sarkesian, S. C. (ed.) (1972) *The Military-Industrial Complex: A Reassessment*. Beverly Hills, CA: Sage.

Sassòli, M. (2004) 'The Status of Persons Held in Guantanamo under International Humanitarian Law', *Journal of International Criminal Justice* 2(1) (March): 96–106.

Schabas, W. A. (2004) *An Introduction to the International Criminal Court*, 2nd edn. Cambridge: Cambridge University Press.

Schell, J. (1982) *The Fate of the Earth*. London: Picador.

Schell, J. (1984) *The Abolition*. New York: Knopf.

Schelling, T. C. (1963) *Strategy of Conflict*. New York: Oxford University Press.

Schelling, T. C. and M. Halperin (1985) *Strategy and Arms Control*. Washington, DC: Pergamon-Brassey's.

Schimmelfennig, F. (2000) 'NATO's Enlargement to the East: An Analysis of Collective Decision-making' EAPC-NATO Individual Fellowship Report 1998–2000.

Schmid, A. P. and A. J. Jongman (1988) *Political Terrorism: A New Guide to Actors, Authors, Concepts, Data Bases, Theories and Literature*. New Brunswick, NJ: Transaction Books.

Schmidt, B. and B. S. Zyla (eds) (2013) *European Security Policy and Strategic Culture*. London: Routledge.

Schmidt, B., D. Howlett, J. Simpson, H. Müller, and B. Tertrais (2005) *Effective Non-proliferation: The European Union and the 2005 NTPT Review Conference*. Chaillot Paper 77. Brussels: EU Institute for Security Studies.

Schwartau, W. (1996) *Information Warfare*, 2nd edn. New York: Thunder's Mouth Press.

Schwartz, S. I. (1998) *Atomic Audit: The Costs and Consequences of US Nuclear Weapons since 1940*. Washington, DC: Brookings Institution.

Schwartz, S. I. (2003) *China's Use of Military Force: Beyond the Great Wall and the Long March*. Cambridge: Cambridge University Press.

Schwartzstein, S. J. D. (ed.) (1996) *The Information Revolution and National Security: Dimensions and Directions*. Washington, DC: Center for Strategic and International Studies.

Schwartzstein, S. J. D. (ed.) (1998) *Cybercrime, Cyberterrorism and Cyberwarfare: Averting an Electronic Waterloo*. Washington, DC: Center for Strategic and International Studies.

Schweller, M. and X. Pu (2011) 'After Polarity: Emerging Powers in the Age of Disorder', *Global Governance* 17(3): 285–97.

Scobell, A. (2002) *China and Strategic Culture*. Carlisle, PA: US Army War College, Strategic Studies Institute, May.

Scobell, A. (2014) 'China's Real Strategic Culture: a Great Wall of the Imagination', *Contemporary Security Policy* 35(2): 211–26.

Seffers, G. (2013) 'Big Data in Demand for Intelligence Community', *SIGNAL Magazine*, 4 January, available at www.afcea.org/content/?q=node/10510

Sepp, K., R. Kiper, J. Schroder, and C. Briscoe (2004) *Weapon of Choice: U.S. Army Special Operations in Afghanistan*. Fort Leavenworth, KS: US Army Command and General Staff College Press.

Sergie, M. A. (2014) 'U.S. Energy Exports', Council on Foreign Relations, available at http://www.cfr.org/energy-and-environment/us-energy-exports/p33532

Sextus Iulius Frontinus (between AD 84 and 96) *Stratagematon*, translated and edited by Charles E. Bennett, *Frontinus: The Stratagems and the Aqueducts of Rome*. London: William Heinemann for Loeb, 1925.

Shaw, M. (2003) 'Strategy and Slaughter', *Review of International Studies* 29(2): 269–77.

Shaw, R. P. and Y. Wong (1985) *Genetic Seeds of Warfare: Evolution, Nationalism and Patriotism*. London: Unwin Hyman.

Shawcross, W. (2000) *Deliver us from Evil: Warlords and Peacekeepers in a World of Endless Conflict*. London: Bloomsbury.

Shay, J. (1994) *Achilles in Vietnam: Combat Trauma and the Undoing of Character*. New York: Simon & Schuster.

Sheldon, J. B. (2011) 'Stuxnet and Cyberpower in War', *World Politics Review*. Available at http://www.worldpoliticsreview.com/articles/8570/stuxnet-and-cyberpower-in-war

Shultz, G., W. Perry, H. Kissinger, and S. Nunn (2008) 'Toward a Nuclear Weapon-free World', *Wall Street Journal*, 15 January A 15. Available at http://online.wsj.com/public/article_print/SB120036422673589947.html

Sims, J. and B. Gerber (eds) (2005) *Transforming US Intelligence*. Washington, DC: Georgetown University Press.

Simpson, E. (2012) *War from the Ground Up*. New York: Columbia University Press.

Singer, M. and A. Wildavsky (1993) *The Real World Order: Zones of Peace/Zones of Turmoil*. Chatham House, NJ: Chatham House Publishers.

Singer, P. W. (2009) *Wired for War: The Robotics Revolution and Conflict in the 21st Century*. New York: Penguin.

Singer, P. W. and A. Friedman (2014) *Cybersecurity and Cyberwar: What Everyone Needs to Know*. New York: Oxford University Press.

Sloan, E. (2002) *The Revolution in Military Affairs*. Montreal: McGill-Queen's Press.

Smith, D. G. (1990) *Combating Terrorism*. London: Routledge.

Smith, H. (2005) *On Clausewitz: A Study of Military and Political Ideas*. New York: Palgrave Macmillan.

Smith, Sir R. (2006) *The Utility of Force: The Art of War in the Modern World*. London: Penguin.

Smith, S., K. Booth, and M. Zalewski (eds) (1996) *International Theory: Positivism and Beyond*. Cambridge: Cambridge University Press.

Snyder, J. (1977) *The Soviet Strategic Culture: Implications for Nuclear Options*, R-2154-AF. Santa Monica, CA: Rand Corporation.

Snyder, J. (2002) 'Anarchy and Culture: Insights from the Anthropology of War', *International Organization* 56(1) (Winter): 7–45.

Sokolski, H. (2001) *Best of Intentions: America's Campaign Against Strategic Weapons Proliferation*. London: Praeger.

Sokolski, H. and J. Ludes (2001) *Twenty-First Century Weapons Proliferation*. London: Frank Cass.

Spanier, J. W. and J. L. Nogee (1962) *The Politics of Disarmament: A Study of Soviet-American Gamesmanship*. New York: Praeger.

Spykman N. ([1942] 1970) *America's Strategy in World Politics: The United States and the Balance of Power*. Hamden, CT: Archon.

Stedman, S. J. (1997) 'Spoiler Problems in Peace Processes', *International Security* 22(2) (Fall): 5–53.

Stewart R. (2011) 'What Can Afghanistan and Bosnia Teach Us About Libya?' *The Guardian*, 7 October. Available at http://www.guardian.co.uk/world/2011/oct/08/libya-intervention-rory-stewart

Stolfi, R. H. S. (1970) 'Equipment for Victory in France in 1940', *History* 55(183): 1–20.

Stone, P. (2003). 'Iraq-al-Qaeda Link Weak Say Former Bush Officials', *National Journal*, 8 August.

Stout, M., J. Huckabey, J. Schindler, and J. Lacey (2008) *The Terrorist Perspectives Project: Strategic and Operational Views of Al Qaida and Associated Movements*. Annapolis, MD: Naval Institute Press.

Strachan, H. (1988) *European Armies and the Conduct of War*. London: Routledge.

Strachan, H. (2005) 'The Lost Meaning of Strategy', *Survival* 47(3) (Autumn): 33–54.

Strachan, H. (2011) 'Strategy and Contingency', *International Affairs* 87(6): 1281–96.

Strong, J. (forthcoming) 'Why Parliament Now Decides on War: Tracing the Growth of the Parliamentary Prerogative through Syria, Libya and Iraq', *British Journal of Politics and International Relations*, published online on 14 June 2014 at http://onlinelibrary.wiley.com/doi/10.1111/1467-856X.12055/pdf

Suganami, H. (1996) *On the Causes of War*. Oxford: Clarendon Press.

Sun Tzu (1963) *The Art of War*, translated by S. B. Griffith. Oxford: Oxford University Press.

Sun Tzu (1993) *The Art of War*, translated by R. Ames. New York: Ballantine Books.

Sun Tzu (1994) *The Art of War*, edited and translated by R. D. Sawyer (*c*.490 BC) . Boulder CO, Westview Press.

Sutcliffe, M. (1593) *The Practice, Proceedings and Lawes of Armes*. London: Deputies of C. Barker.

Swidler, A. (1986) 'Culture in Action: Symbols and Strategies', *American Sociological Review* 51(2): 273–86.

Taber, R. (1970) *The War of the Flea: Guerrilla Warfare Theory and Practice*. London: Paladin.

Taleb, N. N. (2010) *The Black Swan: The Impact of the Highly Improbable*. New York: Random House.

Taleb, N. N. and, M. Blythe (2011) 'The Black Swan of Cairo: How Suppressing Volatility Makes the World Less Predictable and More Dangerous', *Foreign Affairs* 90(3): 33–47.

Tannenwald, N. (1999) 'The Nuclear Taboo: The United States and the Normative Basis of Nuclear Non-Use', *International Organization* 53(3): 83–114.

Tannenwald, N. (2005) 'Stigmatizing the Bomb: Origins of the Nuclear Taboo', *International Security* 29(4): 5–49.

*Technology Review* (2004) 'We Got Nothing until They Slammed into Us', 107(9) (November): 36–45.

Terriff, T., A. Karp, and R. Karp (eds) (2006) *The Right War? The Fourth Generation Warfare Debate*. London: Routledge.

Tharoor, S. (1995–6) 'Should United Nations Peacekeeping Go "Back to Basics" ', *Survival* 37(4) (Winter): 52–64.

Thompson, K. (1960) 'Moral Purpose in Foreign Policy: Realities and Illusions', *Social Research* 27(3): 261–76.

Thompson, M., R. Ellis, and A. Wildavsky (1990) *Cultural Theory*. Boulder, CO: Westview Press.

Thompson, R. (1966) *Defeating Communist Insurgency: Experiences from Malaya and Vietnam*. London: Chatto & Windus.

Thornton, E. P. (1981). 'A Letter to America', *The Nation*, 232, 24 January.

Thucydides ([c.400 BC] 1996) *The Landmark Thucydides: A Comprehensive Guide to 'The Peloponnesian War'.* R. B. Strassler (ed.), revised from translation by R. Crawley. New York: The Free Press.

Till, G. (2004) *Seapower: A Guide for the Twenty-first Century.* London: Frank Cass.

Tilly, C. (1975) *The Formation of National States in Western Europe.* Princeton, NJ: Princeton University Press.

Toffler, A. and H. Toffler (1993) *War and Antiwar: Survival at the Dawn of the 21st Century.* Boston, MA: Little, Brown & Co.

Townshend, C. (1975) *The British Campaign in Ireland, 1919–1921: The Development of Political and Military Policies.* Oxford: Oxford University Press.

Traina, G. (2014) 'La guerre mondiale des Romains', *L'Histoire,* No. 405 (November): 76–81.

*Transnational Organized Crime* (1998) 'Special Issue: The United States International Crime Control Strategy' 4(1).

Treverton, G. (2001) *Reshaping National Intelligence for an Age of Information.* Cambridge: Cambridge University Press.

Treverton, G. (2003a) 'Intelligence: The Achilles Heel of the Bush Doctrine', *Arms Control Today* 33(6) (July/August): 9.

Treverton, G. (2003b) *Reshaping National Intelligence for an Age of Information.* Cambridge: Cambridge University Press.

Trinquier, R. (1964) *Modern Warfare: A French View of Counterinsurgency.* New York: Praeger.

Tse-Tung, Mao (1961) *Mao Tse-Tung on Guerrilla Warfare.* New York: Praeger.

Tse-Tung, Mao (1966) *Selected Military Writings of Mao Tse-Tung.* Peking: Foreign Languages Press.

Tse-Tung, Mao (1967) *Selected Military Writings of Mao Tse-Tung,* 2nd edn. Peking: Foreign Languages Press.

United Nations (1945) *Charter of the United Nations.* New York: United Nations. Available at http://www.un.org/en/documents/charter

United Nations (1949) *The Geneva Convention.* New York: United Nations. Available at http://www.unhchr.ch/html/menu3/b/91.htm

United Nations (1992) *An Agenda for Peace. Preventive Diplomacy, Peacemaking and Peacekeeping. Report of the Secretary-General Pursuant to the Statement Adopted by the Summit Meeting of the Security Council on 31 January 1992.* New York: United Nations. Available at http://www.unh.org/Docs/SG/agpeace.html

United Nations (2000) Resolution 1296. Available at http://daccessdds.un.org/doc/UNDOC/GEN/Noo/399/03/PDF/Noo39903.pdf?OpenElement

United Nations (2011) Peacekeeping, 'Background Note: United Nations Peacekeeping'. Available at http://www.un.org/en/peacekeeping/documents/backgroundnote.pdf

United Nations (2011) 'World Population to reach 10 Billion by 2100 if Fertility in all Countries Converges to Replacement Level', May 3, United Nations Press Release http://esa.un.org/wpp/Other-Information/Press_Release_WPP2010.pdf

United Nations (2011) Security Council Department of Public Information 'Security Council Approves "No-Fly Zone" over Libya, Authorizing 'All Necessary Measures' to Protect Civilians, by Vote of 10 in Favour with 5 Abstentions', SC/10200, 17 March. Available at http://www.un.org/News/Press/docs/2011/sc10200.doc.htm

United Nations (2014) 'Fact Sheet: UN Peacekeeping Operations'.

United Nations, Blue Book Series. New York: United Nations.

UK Army Field Manual (1995) *Wider Peacekeeping.* London: HMSO.

US Army/Marine Corps (2007) Principles of Counterinsurgency from FM 3–24, *Counterinsurgency Field Manual.* Chicago: University of Chicago Press.

US Army Military History Institute (2002) *Operation Enduring Freedom, Strategic Studies Institute Research Collection,* Tape 032602a, CPT H. et al. Memorandum for the Record, CPT H. int., 2 July 2002.

US Army Military History Institute (2003) *Operation Enduring Freedom, Strategic Studies Institute Research Collection,* Tape 042403a2sb St Col al Saadi int.

US Department of Homeland Security (2003) *Characteristics and Common Vulnerabilities Report for Chemical Facilities,* version 1, revision1. Washington, DC: US Department of Homeland Security.

US Department of Justice (2005) Office of the Inspector General, *A Review of the FBI's Handling of Intelligence Information Related to the September 11 Attacks.* Washington. DC: Office of the Inspector General, November 2004; redacted and unclassified: released publicly June.

US Department of State (2014) Remarks by Rose Gottemoeller, Acting Under Secretary for Arms Control and International Security, 'Arms Control Priorities in 2014 and Beyond', 14 February.

US Energy Information Administration Report (2014), 'China', available from http://www.eia.gov/countries/cab.cfm?fips = ch

US Joint Chiefs of Staff (2004) *Joint Doctrine for Combating Weapons of Mass Destruction.* Washington, DC: Department of Defense.

US Joint Chiefs of Staff (2011) *The National Military Strategy of the United States of America: Redefining*

*America's Military Leadership*. Washington, DC: Joint Chiefs of Staff.

US Joint Forces Command (2001) *A Concept for Rapid Decisive Operations*. Norfolk, VA: Joint Forces Command J9 Joint Futures Lab.

US Joint Forces Command (2008) *The Joint Operating Environment: Challenges and Implications for the Future Force*. Suffolk, VA: US Joint Forces Command.

United States Strategic Command (2004) *Strategic Deterrence Joint Operating Concept*, Version 1.0. Offut Air Force Base, NE: U.S. Strategic Command.

United States White House (2002) *The National Security Strategy of the United States of America*. Available at http://www.white-house.gov/nsc/nss.pdf

Van Evera, S. (2009) *The Causes of War*. Ithaca, NY: Cornell University Press.

Vasconcelos, A. D. (2009) *What Ambitions for European Defence in 2020?* Paris: European Union Institute for Security Studies.

Vaughn, J. and T. Dunne (2015) 'Leading from the Front: America, Libya and the Localisation of R2P', *Cooperation and Conflict* 50(1): 29–49.

Vickers, M. (1996) *Warfare in 2020: A Primer*. Washington, DC: Center for Strategic and Budgetary Assessments.

Von Hippel, K. (2000) *Democracy by Force: US Intervention in the Post-Cold War World*. Cambridge: Cambridge University Press.

Wæver, O. and B. Buzan (2010) 'After the Return to Theory: The Past, Present, and Future of Security Studies'. In A. Collins (ed.) *Contemporary Security Studies*. Oxford: Oxford University Press, pp. 463–83.

Walker, W. (2011) *A Perpetual Menace: Nuclear Weapons and International Order*. London: Routledge.

Wallace, W. (1996) 'Truth and Power, Monks and Technocrats: Theory and Practice in International Relations', *Review of International Studies* 22(3): 301–21.

Walt, S. M. (1991) 'The Renaissance of Security Studies', *International Studies Quarterly* 35: 211–39.

Waltz, K. N. (1959) *Man, the State, and War*. New York: Columbia University Press.

Waltz, K. N. (1962) 'Kant, Liberalism and War', *American Political Science Review* 56(2): 331–40.

Waltzer, M. (1978) *Just and Unjust Wars*. London: Allen Lane.

Warner, M. (2002) 'Wanted: A Definition of Intelligence', *Studies in Intelligence* 46(3): 21.

Weigley, R. (1976) *The American Way of War: A History of United States Military Strategy and Policy*. New York: Macmillan.

Weigley, R. (1988) 'Political and Strategic Dimensions to Military Effectiveness'. In A. R. Millett and W. Murray

(eds) *Military Effectiveness*, vol. 3. *The Second World War*. Boston, MA: Allen & Unwin.

Weigley, R. (1991) *The Age of Battles: The Quest for Decisive Warfare*. Bloomington, IN: Indiana University Press.

Weinberger, S. (2008) 'The Pentagon's Culture Wars', *Nature* 455(2): 583–5.

Weiss, T. and C. Collins (2000) *Humanitarian Challenges and Intervention: World Politics and the Dilemmas of Help*. Boulder, CO: Westview Press.

Weller, M. (2000) 'The US, Iraq and the Use of Force in a Unipolar World', *Survival* 41(4): 81–100.

Weller, M. (2012) *Iraq and the Use of Force in International Law*. Oxford: Oxford University Press.

Welsh, J. (ed.) (2004) *Humanitarian Intervention and International Relations*. Oxford: Oxford University Press.

Welsh, J. (2014) 'Implementing the "Responsibility to Protect": Catalyzing Debate and Building Capacity'. In A. Betts and P. Orchard (eds), *Implementation in World Politics: How Norms Change Practice*. Oxford: Oxford University Press.

Weltman, J. J. (1995) *World Politics and the Evolution of War*. Baltimore, MD and London: Johns Hopkins University Press.

Wendt, A. (1992) 'Anarchy is what States Make of it: The Social Construction of Power Politics', *International Organization* 46(2): 391–426.

Wendt, A. (1995) 'Constructing International Politics', *International Security* 20(1): 73–4.

Wendt, A. (1999) *Social Theory of International Politics*. Cambridge: Cambridge University Press.

Wheeler, N. J. (1999) 'Humanitarian Intervention in World Politics'. In J. Baylis and S. Smith (eds) *The Globalization of World Politics*. Oxford: Oxford University Press.

Wheeler, N. J. (2000) *Saving Strangers: Humanitarian Intervention in International Society*. Oxford: Oxford University Press.

Wheeler, N. J. and A. Bellamy (2005). 'Humanitarian Intervention and World Politics'. In J. Baylis and S. Smith (eds) *The Globalization of World Politics*. Oxford: Oxford University Press.

Wheeler-Bennett, J. (1935) *The Pipe Dream of Peace: The Story of the Collapse of Disarmament*. New York: Morrow.

White, N. D. (1997) *Keeping the Peace*. Manchester: Manchester University Press.

White House (1993) *Gulf War Air Power Survey*. Washington, DC: Government Printing Office.

White House (2000) *A National Security Strategy for a Global Age*. Washington, DC: Government Printing Office.

White House (2002) *National Strategy to Combat Weapons of Mass Destruction*. Washington, DC: Government Printing Office.

White House (2003) *National Strategy for Combating Terrorism*. Washington, DC: Government Printing Office.

White House (2006) *National Strategy for Combating Terrorism*, 2nd edn. Washington, DC: Government Printing Office.

Wilkinson, P. (1986) *Terrorism and the Liberal State*. London: Macmillan.

Wilkinson, P. (2001) *Terrorism and Democracy: The Liberal State Response*. London: Frank Cass.

Williams, M. (1993) 'Neorealism and the Future of Strategy', *Review of International Studies* 19(2): 103–21.

Williams, M. (2007) *Military Organizational Cultures: Culture and Security: Symbolic Power and the Politics of International Security*. New York: Routledge.

Wills, S. (2009) *Protecting Civilians: The Obligations of Peacekeepers*. Oxford: Oxford University Press.

Wilson, E. O. (1978) *On Human Nature*. Cambridge, MA: Harvard University Press.

Wilson, H. W. (1928) *The War Guilt*. London: Sampson Low.

Wilson, R. W. (2000) 'The Many Voices of Political Culture: Assessing Different Approaches', *World Politics* 52(2): 246–73.

Wohlstetter, R. (1962) *Pearl Harbor: Warning and Decision*. Palo Alto, CA: Stanford University Press.

Woodbury, G. L. (2004) Recommendations for Homeland Security Organizational Approaches at the State Government Level. Monterey: Naval Postgraduate School, Master's thesis.

Woolsey, J. (1998) Testimony to the Committee on National Security, US House of Representatives, 12 February.

Wright, G. (1968) *The Ordeal of Total War 1939–1945*. New York: Harper & Row.

Wright, M. C. (1956) *The Power Elite*. London: Oxford University Press.

Wylie, J. (1989) *Military Strategy: A General Theory of Power Control*. Annapolis, MD: Naval Institute Press.

Wyn Jones, R. (1999) *Security, Strategy and Critical Theory*. Boulder, CO: Lynne Rienner.

Yarger, H. R. (2008) *Strategy and the National Security Professional: Strategic Thinking and Strategy Formulation in the 21st Century*. Westport, CT: Praeger Security International.

Yin, T. (2011) ' "Anything But Bush?": The Obama Administration and Guantanamo Bay', *Harvard Journal of Law and Public Policy* 34(2): 453–92.

Zaborowski, M. (2004) 'From America's Protégé to Constructive European: Polish Security Policy in the Twenty-first Century', Occasional Paper No. 56 Paris: European Union Institute for Security Studies.

Zenko M. (2011) 'Libya: "Justifications" for Involvement', website of the Council on Foreign Relations, posted 24 June. Available at http://blogs.cfr.org/zenko/2011/06/24/libya-justifications-for-intervention/

# Index

Note: in Arabic terms, 'al-' is ignored in filing order